THE BICENTENNIAL EDITION
OF THE
WORKS OF JOHN WESLEY

Editor-in-Chief FRANK BAKER

*The Directors of the Bicentennial Edition of
the Works of John Wesley
gratefully acknowledge the financial support
in the preparation of this volume of
the Reverend Lewis C. and Rita Ann Holland
of West Texas*

THE WORKS OF
JOHN WESLEY

VOLUME 3

SERMONS
III
71–114

EDITED BY

ALBERT C. OUTLER

ABINGDON PRESS

NASHVILLE

1986

The Works of John Wesley, Volume 3
SERMONS, III, 71–114

Library of Congress Cataloging in Publication
Data

Wesley, John, 1703-1791.
   The works of John Wesley.
   Includes indexes.
   Contents: v. 1. Sermons I, 1-33—v. 2. Sermons II,
34-70—v. 3. Sermons III, 71-114 / edited by Albert C.
Outler.
   1. Methodist Church—Collected works. 2. Theolo-
gy—Collected works—18th century. I. Outler, Albert
Cook, 1908- . II. Title.
BX8217.W5 1984   252'.07   83-22434

ISBN 0-687-46212-6 (v. 3)
ISBN 0-687-46211-8 (v. 2)
ISBN 0-687-46210-X (v. 1)

THE MONOGRAM USED ON THE CASE AND HALF-TITLE IS
ADAPTED BY RICHARD P. HEITZENRATER FROM ONE OF
JOHN WESLEY'S PERSONAL SEALS

MANUFACTURED BY THE PARTHENON PRESS AT
NASHVILLE, TENNESSEE, UNITED STATES OF AMERICA

THE BICENTENNIAL EDITION OF
THE WORKS OF JOHN WESLEY

THIS edition of the works of John Wesley reflects the quickened interest in the heritage of Christian thought that has characterized both ecumenical insurgency and dominant theological perspectives during the last half-century. A fully critical presentation of Wesley's writings had long been a desideratum in order to furnish documentary sources illustrating his contribution to both catholic and evangelical Christianity.

Several scholars, notably Professor Albert C. Outler, Professor Franz Hildebrandt, Dean Merrimon Cuninggim, and Dean Robert E. Cushman, discussed the possibility of such an edition. Under the leadership of Dean Cushman, a Board of Directors was formed in 1960 comprising the deans of four sponsoring theological schools of Methodist-related universities in the United States: Drew, Duke, Emory, and Southern Methodist. They appointed an Editorial Committee to formulate plans, and enlisted an international and interdenominational team of scholars for the Wesley Works Editorial Project.

The works were divided into units of cognate material, with a separate editor (or joint editors) responsible for each unit. Dr. Frank Baker was appointed textual editor for the whole project, with responsibility for supplying each unit editor with a collated critical text for his consideration and use. The text seeks to represent Wesley's thought in its fullest and most deliberate expression, in so far as this can be determined from the available evidence. Substantive variant readings in any British edition published during Wesley's lifetime are shown in appendices to the units, preceded by a summary of the problems faced and the solutions reached in the complex task of securing and presenting Wesley's text. The aim throughout is to enable Wesley to be read with maximum ease and understanding, and with minimal intrusion by the editors.

It was decided that the edition should include all Wesley's original or mainly original prose works, together with one volume devoted to his *Collection of Hymns for the use of the People called*

Methodists, and another to his extensive work as editor and publisher of extracts from the writings of others. An essential feature of the project is a Bibliography outlining the historical settings of over 450 items published by Wesley and his brother Charles, sometimes jointly, sometimes separately. The Bibliography also offers full analytical data for identifying each of the two thousand editions of these 450 items that were published during the lifetime of John Wesley, and notes the location of copies. An index is supplied for each unit, and a General Index for the whole edition.

The Delegates of the Oxford University Press agreed to undertake publication, but announced in June 1982 that because of severe economic problems they would regretfully be compelled to withdraw from the enterprise with the completion in 1983 of Vol. 7, the *Collection of Hymns.* The Abingdon Press offered its services, beginning with the publication of the first volume of the *Sermons* in 1984, the bicentennial year of the formation of American Methodism as an autonomous church. The new title now assumed, however, refers in general to the bicentennial of Wesley's total activities as author, editor, and publisher, from 1733 to 1791, especially as summarized in the first edition of his collected works in thirty-two volumes, 1771–1774.

Dean Robert E. Cushman of Duke University undertook general administration and promotion of the project until 1971, when he was succeeded by Dean Joseph D. Quillian, Jr., of Southern Methodist University, these two universities having furnished the major support and guidance for the enterprise. During the decade 1961–70 literary planning was undertaken by the Editorial Committee, chaired by Dean Quillian. International conferences were convened in 1966 and 1970, bringing together all available unit editors with the committee, who thus completed their task of achieving a common mind upon editorial principles and procedure. Throughout this decade Dr. Eric W. Baker of London, England, serving as a General Editor along with Dean William R. Cannon and Dean Cushman, assisted the Directors in British negotiations, as well as at the conferences. In 1969 the Directors appointed Dr. Frank Baker, early attached to the project as bibliographer, and later as textual editor, as their Editor-in-Chief also. In 1971 they appointed a new Editorial Board to assist him in coordinating the preparation of the various units for publication. Upon Dean Quillian's retirement in 1981 he was succeeded as President of the project by Dean James E. Kirby, Jr., also of Southern Methodist University.

Other sponsoring bodies were successively added to the original four: The United Methodist Board of Higher Education and Ministry, The Commission on Archives and History of The United Methodist Church, and Boston University School of Theology. For the continuing support of the sponsoring institutions the Directors express their profound thanks. They gratefully acknowledge also the encouragement and financial support that have come from the Historical Societies and Commissions on Archives and History of many Annual Conferences, as well as the donations of The World Methodist Council, The British Methodist Church, private individuals, and foundations.

On June 9, 1976, The Wesley Works Editorial Project was incorporated in the State of North Carolina, U.S.A., as a nonprofit corporation. In 1977 by-laws were approved governing the appointment and duties of the Directors, their Officers, and their Executive Committee.

THE BOARD OF DIRECTORS

President: James E. Kirby, Dean of Perkins School of Theology, Southern Methodist University, Dallas, Texas

Vice-President: Robert E. Cushman, The Divinity School, Duke University, Durham, North Carolina

Secretary: Donald H. Treese, Associate General Secretary of the Division of the Ordained Ministry, the United Methodist Board of Higher Education and Ministry, Nashville, Tennessee

Treasurer: Thomas A. Langford, The Divinity School, Duke University, Durham, North Carolina

Editor-in-Chief: Frank Baker, The Divinity School, Duke University, Durham, North Carolina

Associate Editor-in-Chief: Richard P. Heitzenrater, Perkins School of Theology, Southern Methodist University, Dallas, Texas

James M. Ault, Bishop of The United Methodist Church, Pittsburgh, Pennsylvania

CONTENTS

Signs, Special Usages, Abbreviations   xiii

SERMONS ON SEVERAL OCCASIONS, 71–114

71.	Of Good Angels	3
72.	Of Evil Angels	16
73.	Of Hell	30
74.	Of the Church	45
75.	On Schism	58
76.	On Perfection	70
77.	Spiritual Worship	88
78.	Spiritual Idolatry	103
79.	On Dissipation	115
80.	On Friendship with the World	126
81.	In What Sense we are to Leave the World	141
82.	On Temptation	156
83.	On Patience	169
84.	The Important Question	181
85.	On Working Out Our Own Salvation	199
86.	A Call to Backsliders	210
87.	The Danger of Riches	227
88.	On Dress	247
89.	The More Excellent Way	262
90.	An Israelite Indeed	278
91.	On Charity	290
92.	On Zeal	308
93.	On Redeeming the Time	322

94. On Family Religion   333
95. On the Education of Children   347
96. On Obedience to Parents   361
97. On Obedience to Pastors   373
98. On Visiting the Sick   384
99. The Reward of Righteousness   399
100. On Pleasing All Men   415
101. The Duty of Constant Communion   427
102. Of Former Times   440
103. What is Man? (Psalm 8:3-4)   454
104. On Attending the Church Service   464
105. On Conscience   479
106. On Faith (Heb. 11:6)   491
107. On God's Vineyard   502
108. On Riches   518

A Miscellany of Published Sermons

(Sermons not included in any of Wesley's collections
of *Sermons on Several Occasions*)

109. The Trouble and Rest of Good Men   531
110. Free Grace   542
111. National Sins and Miseries   564
112. On Laying the Foundation of the New Chapel   577
113. The Late Work of God in North America   594
114. On the Death of John Fletcher   610

APPENDICES

A. The Sermons as Ordered in This Edition   631
B. The Sermons in Chronological Sequence   639
C. The Sermons in Alphabetical Order   646

ILLUSTRATIONS

facing page

1. *Sermons on Several Occasions*   2
2. *The Important Question,* 1775   179
3. *A Sermon preached . . . before the Humane
   Society,* ['The Reward of Righteousness'], 1777   399
4. *A Sermon Preached at St. Mary's in Oxford* ['The
   Trouble and Rest of Good Men']   531
5. *The Late Work of God in North America,* 1778   592
6. *On the Death of John Fletcher,* 1785   608

SIGNS, SPECIAL USAGES, ABBREVIATIONS

[ ]	Indicate editorial insertions or substitutions in the original text, or (with a query) doubtful readings.
. . .	Indicate a passage omitted by the writer from the original and so noted by Wesley, usually by a dash.
[. . .]	Indicate a passage omitted from the original text to which the present editor is drawing attention. (N.B. The distinguishing editorial brackets are not used in the introductions and footnotes.)
[[ ]]	Entries within double brackets are supplied by the editor from shorthand or cipher, from an abstract or similar document in the third person, or reconstructed from secondary evidence.
a, b, c,	Small superscript letters indicate footnotes supplied by Wesley.
1, 2, 3,	Small superscript figures indicate footnotes supplied by the editor.
Cf.	'Cf.' before a scriptural or other citation indicates that Wesley was quoting with more than minimal inexactness, yet nevertheless displaying the passage as a quotation.
See	'See' before a citation indicates an undoubted allusion, or a quotation which was not displayed as such by Wesley, and which is more than minimally inexact.
π;	π; indicates a quotation which has not yet been traced to its source.

Wesley's publications. Where a work by Wesley was first published separately its title is italicized—except in the Contents, opening titles, and Appendices A and B—even where (as occasionally in the *Sermons*), the eventual title thus italicized is not that under which it was first published; where it first appeared within a different work such as a collected volume, the title is given within quotation marks. References such as *'Bibliog,* No. 3' are to the forthcoming Bibliography in this edition (Vols. 33–34), which has a different numbering system from Richard Green's *Wesley Bibliography,* although cross-references to Green's numbers are given in the new Bibliography.

Abbreviations. The following are used in addition to many common and obvious ones such as B[oo]k, ch[apter], *c[irca],* col[umn], com[ment], cont[inued], ed[itio]n, espec[ially], intro[duction, ductory], l[ine], MS[S], n[ote], orig[inal], p[age], para[graph] or ¶, P[ar]t, sect[ion] or §, st[anzas], ver[se/s], Vol[ume].

AM	Wesley, John, *Arminian Magazine* (1778–97), cont. as *Methodist Magazine* (1798–1821), and *Wesleyan Methodist Magazine* (1822–1913).
ANF	*Ante-Nicene Fathers* (New York, 1978–79).

AV   Authorized Version of the Bible, 1611 ('King James Version').

BCP   *The Book of Common Prayer as Revised and Settled at the Savoy Conference, Anno 1662*, London, William Pickering, 1844 (which adds marginal numbering for the successive liturgical units).

BL   The British Library, London (formerly British Museum).

Boston   Boston, Thomas, *Human Nature in its Fourfold State*, Edinburgh, 1720.

Bibliog   Bibliography of the publications of John and Charles Wesley, in preparation by Frank Baker to form Vols. 33–34 of this edn.

Christian Lib. Wesley, John, ed., *Christian Library*, 50 vols., Bristol, 1749–55.

Curnock   Curnock, Nehemiah (ed.), *The Journal of the Rev. John Wesley, A.M., . . . enlarged from Original Manuscripts*, 8 vols., London, 1909–16.

CWJ   Wesley, Charles, *Journal*, ed., Thomas Jackson, 2 vols., London, 1849.

DNB   *The Dictionary of National Biography*, ed. Sir Leslie Stephen and Sir Sidney Lee, 22 vols., Oxford, Oxford University Press, 1921–23.

General Rules   Wesley, John, *The Nature, Design, and General Rules of the United Societies* . . . , Newcastle, Gooding, 1743 (*Bibliog*, No. 73).

Homilies   *Certain Sermons or Homilies appointed to be read in Churches in the Time of the late Queen Elizabeth* (1623), Oxford, Oxford University Press, 1840.

Jackson   Jackson, Thomas, ed., *The Works of the Rev. John Wesley*, 3rd edn., 14 vols., London, Mason, 1829–31.

JWJ   Wesley, John, *Journal*, in preparation by W. Reginald Ward to form Vols. 18–24 of this edn.; cf. Curnock.

Kempis   *De Imitatione Christi*, published by John Wesley as *The Christian's Pattern*, London, Rivington, 1735 (*Bibliog*, No. 4).

LACT   Library of Anglo-Catholic Theology (Oxford, 1841–63).

Law,   Law, William, *A Serious Call to a Devout and Holy Life* (1729),
   Serious Call as reprinted in his *Works*, 9 vols., London, 1762, Vol. IV.

LCC   Library of Christian Classics (Philadelphia, 1953—).

LPT   Library of Protestant Thought (Oxford, 1964—).

Loeb   The Loeb Classical Library, London, Heinemann; Cambridge, Massachusetts, Harvard University Press.

MA   Methodist Archives, The John Rylands University Library of Manchester.

MM   *Methodist Magazine* (London, 1798–1821).

Migne, *PG, PL*   Migne, J. P., ed., *Patrologiae Cursus Completus, Series Graeca* (Paris, 1857–66), and *Series Latina* (Paris, 1878–90).

Moore   Moore, Henry, *Life of the Rev. John Wesley*, 2 vols., London, Kershaw, 1824-25.

NEB   New English Bible.

Notes   Wesley, John, *Explanatory Notes upon the New Testament*, London, Bowyer, 1755 (*Bibliog*, No. 209).

NPNF, I, II   *Nicene and Post-Nicene Fathers of the Christian Church*, First Series (New York, 1886-90), and Second Series (New York, 1890-1900).

OED   *The Oxford English Dictionary upon Historical Principles*, Oxford, Clarendon Press, 1933.

Poet. Wks.   Wesley, John and Charles, *The Poetical Works*, ed. G. Osborn, 13 vols., London, Wesleyan-Methodist Conference Office, 1868-72.

Seymour   [Seymour, A. C. H.], *The Life and Times of Selina, Countess of Huntingdon*, 2 vols., London, Painter, 1840.

SOSO   Wesley, John, *Sermons on Several Occasions*, 1746-60, 1771, 1787-88.

Southey   Southey, Robert, *The Life of Wesley*, ed. C. C. Southey (including *in full*, as does that of 1846, 'Remarks on the Life and Character of John Wesley', by Alexander Knox), 2 vols., London, Longman, etc., 1864.

Sugden   Sugden, E. H., ed., *Wesley's Standard Sermons*, 2 vols., London, Epworth Press, 1921.

Telford   Telford, John, ed., *The Letters of the Rev. John Wesley*, 8 vols., London, Epworth Press, 1931.

TR   *Textus Receptus* (the 'Received Text', which underlies the AV).

Tyerman *(JW)*   Tyerman, Luke, *The Life and Times of the Rev. John Wesley*, 3 vols., London, Hodder and Stoughton, 1870-71.

[Wesley,] *Works*   Wesley, John, *The Works of the Rev. John Wesley*, 32 vols., Bristol, Pine, 1771-74, (*Bibliog*, No. 334).

WHS   *The Proceedings of the Wesley Historical Society* (Burnley and Chester, 1898—).

WMM   *Wesleyan Methodist Magazine* (1822-1913).

SERMONS

O N

Several Occasions.

By J O H N   W E S L E Y, M. A.

Late Fellow of *Lincoln-College*, OXFORD.

V O L U M E S   V–VIII.

(CONTINUED FROM THEIR BEGINNING
IN VOLUME 2, PAGE 349)

OF GOOD ANGELS
OF EVIL ANGELS

AN INTRODUCTORY COMMENT

These twin essays in angelology were written as a single exercise in January 1783, and then published in four successive instalments with texts but no titles in the Arminian Magazine, *1783 (Vol. VI, January through April), under the rubric, 'Original Sermons by the Rev. John Wesley, M. A., Sermons XIII and XIV'. The paired sermons, with their present titles, were then published in* SOSO, *VI.103-45, and not published again in Wesley's lifetime.*

He must have thought that he needed to say something about the place and role of angels in 'the great chain of being' which, along with the Christian Platonists, he conceived of as the general structure of creation (see No. 56, 'God's Approbation of His Works', I.14 and n.). This would also help explain his placement of these sermons here, after his delineations of the limits of knowledge and reason. But angelology was not one of his prime interests; this is suggested by the fact that he had preached from Heb. 1:14 only three times before (in 1752, 1758, and 1782) and from Eph. 6:12 only once (in 1759); his other references to angels are few and scattered in his writings as a whole.

Wesley's ideas here, with a single puzzling exception (see No. 72, 'Of Evil Angels', I.3), are unsurprisingly conventional. One finds much the same viewpoints in Anglican theology in the seventeenth and eighteenth centuries, usually in connection with a doctrine of Providence or other comments on 'the ways of God to men'. However, there are two identifiable sources closer than others to Wesley's basic arguments here; only their practical applications are clearly different. One of these is Bishop George Bull, Some Important Points of Primitive Christianity, *especially Sermons 11 and 12. Note that Wesley has reversed Bull's order. This would follow his other main source, Thomas Crane's second chapter, 'Of Good and Bad Angels', in* Isagoge ad Dei Providentiam. *And, of course, the great cosmic vision of* Paradise Lost *stands in Wesley's further background here. It is interesting that Wesley could not have known Milton's chapter IX, 'Of the Special Government of Angels', in his posthumous* De Doctrina Christiana, *since that was not published until 1825. But there is nothing in this part*

3

of Milton's 'doctrine' from which Wesley would have dissented. And, on a crucial point, that it was a majority *of the angels who fell and enlisted under Satan's banner, Milton's scenario in* Paradise Lost *is clearly decisive here.*

Of Good Angels

Hebrews 1:14

Are they not all ministering spirits, sent forth to minister unto them that shall be heirs of salvation?

5   1. Many of the ancient heathens had (probably from tradition) some notion of good and evil angels. They had some conception of a superior order of beings between men and God, whom the Greeks generally termed demons ('knowing ones')[1] and the Romans, *genii.* Some of these they supposed to be kind and

10   benevolent, delighting in doing good; others to be malicious and cruel, delighting in doing evil. But their conceptions both of one and the other were crude, imperfect, and confused, being only fragments of truth, partly delivered down by their forefathers, and partly borrowed from the inspired writings.

15   2. Of the former, the benevolent kind, seems to have been the celebrated demon of Socrates, concerning which so many and so various conjectures have been made in succeeding ages. 'This gives me notice', said he, 'every morning, of any evil which will befall me that day.'[2] A late writer, indeed (I suppose one that

20   hardly believes the existence of either angel or spirit), has published a dissertation wherein he labours to prove that the

---

[1] A doubtful definition; cf. δαίμων in Liddell and Scott, and Arndt and Gingrich, *Greek-English Lexicons.*

[2] An echo of Plato's *Apology*, 31, 40.

demon of Socrates was only his reason.[3] But it was not the manner of Socrates to speak in such obscure and ambiguous terms. If he had meant his reason he would doubtless have said so. But this could not be his meaning. For it was impossible his reason should give him notice every morning of every evil which would befall him that day. It does not lie within the province of reason to give such notice of future contingencies. Neither does this odd interpretation in any wise agree with the inference which he himself draws from it. 'My demon', says he, 'did not give me notice this morning of any evil that was to befall me today. Therefore I cannot regard as any evil my being condemned to die.'[4] Undoubtedly it was some spiritual being, probably one of these ministering spirits.

3. An ancient poet, one who lived several ages before Socrates, speaks more determinately on this subject. Hesiod does not scruple to say:

> Millions of spiritual creatures walk the earth Unseen.[5]

Hence, it is probable, arose the numerous tales about the exploits of their demigods, *minorum gentium*.[6] Hence their satyrs, fauns, nymphs of every kind, wherewith they supposed both the sea and land to be filled. But how empty, childish, unsatisfactory, are all

---

[3] Cf. John Gilbert Cooper, *The Life of Socrates* (1750); his discussion of Socrates's 'familiar' is in III.81-96, but to a quite different point than Wesley's. Cooper is concerned to deny that Socrates had, or claimed to have, supernatural powers (p. 89). Instead, his 'familiar' was 'nothing more than that inward feeling inseparable from the hearts of all good and wise men which . . . gives [them] an almost prophetic sensation of what ought to be done, before the slower faculties of the mind can improve the moral rectitude of conduct'. Thus, it was much more a certain 'prescience' than *reason* in Wesley's sense, and Cooper goes on to speak of it thus. For other comments on Socrates's 'demon', see Adam Clarke, *Memoirs*, p. 144 n.: 'a tingling in the ears'; A. E. Taylor, *Socrates* (New York, Doubleday Anchor Books, 1953), p. 44 n.: 'supernatural sign'; Xenophon, *Memoirs* (*Works*, trans. by Sarah Fielding), pp. 511-12: 'an uncommon strength of judgment'. For other references to Socrates in the *Sermons*, cf. No. 70, 'The Case of Reason Impartially Considered', II.6 and n.

[4] Plato, *Apology*, 40.

[5] Actually, this is Milton's paraphrase of Hesiod; cf. No. 70, 'The Case of Reason Impartially Considered', II.1 and n.

[6] Cf. Hesiod, *Works and Days*, ll. 155-73: ἡμίθεοι (i.e., demigods). In his [*Tusculan*] *Disputations*, I.xiii.29, Cicero uses the phrase, *majorum gentium*, to denote 'the superior deities' (*dii consentes*). *Minorum gentium* would thus, by inference, denote 'lesser deities'. However, no such usage is recorded in Lewis and Short, *A Latin Dictionary*. The oft-cited instance in Cicero's *Epistolae ad Familiares* (*Letters to Friends*), IX.xxi.2, clearly does not apply.

the accounts they give of them—as, indeed, accounts that depend upon broken, uncertain tradition can hardly fail to be!

4. Revelation only is able to supply this defect; this only gives us a clear, rational, consistent account of those whom our eyes have
5 not seen, nor our ears heard:[7] of both good and evil angels. It is my design to speak at present only of the former, of whom we have a full, though brief, account in these words: 'Are they not all ministering spirits, sent forth to minister unto them that shall be heirs of salvation?'

10 I. 1. The question is, according to the manner of the Apostle, equivalent to a strong affirmation. And hence we learn, first, that with regard to their essence or nature they are all spirits: not material or corporeal beings; not clogged with flesh and blood[8] like us, but having bodies, if any, not gross and earthly like ours,
15 but of a finer substance, resembling fire or flame more than any other of these lower elements. And is not something like this intimated in those words of the Psalmist, 'Who maketh his angels spirits, and his ministers a flame of fire!'[a] As spirits he has endued them with understanding, will, or affections (which are indeed
20 the same thing, as the affections are only the will exerting itself various ways), and liberty. And are not these—understanding, will, and liberty—essential to, if not the essence of, a spirit?[9]

2. But who of the children of men can comprehend what is the *understanding* of an angel? Who can comprehend how far their
25 *sight* extends? Analogous to sight in men, though not the same—but thus we are constrained to speak through the poverty of human language! Probably not only over one hemisphere of the earth, yea, or

Tenfold the length of their terrene,[10]

30 or even of the solar system; but so far as to take in at one view the whole extent of the creation. And we cannot conceive any defect in their perception, neither any error in their understanding. But in what manner do they use their understanding? We must in no

---

[a] [Cf.] Ps. 104:4 [AV; Wesley uses 'spirits' here as does AV; BCP, 'winds'].

---

[7] See Isa. 64:4; 1 Cor. 2:9.
[8] Cf. No. 24, 'Sermon on the Mount, IV', III.5 and n.
[9] Cf. No. 60, 'The General Deliverance', I.4 and n.
[10] Milton, *Paradise Lost*, vi.78; see No. 54, 'On Eternity', §17 and n.

wise imagine that they creep from one truth to another by that
slow method which we call reasoning. Undoubtedly they see at
one glance whatever truth is presented to their understanding;[11]
and that with all the certainty and clearness that we mortals see
the most self-evident axiom. Who then can conceive the extent of 5
their *knowledge?* Not only of the nature, attributes, and works
of God (whether of creation or providence), but of the circumstances, actions, words, tempers, yea, and thoughts of men? For
although God only 'knows the hearts of all men';[12] unto whom
'known are all his works', together with the changes they undergo, 10
'from the beginning of the world';[13] yet we cannot doubt but his
angels know the hearts of those to whom they more immediately
minister. Much less can we doubt of their knowing the thoughts
that are in our hearts at any particular time. What should hinder
their seeing them as they arise? Not the thin veil of flesh and 15
blood! Can these intercept the view of a spirit? Nay,

> Walls within walls no more its passage bar,
> Than unopposing space of liquid air.[14]

Far more easily, then, and far more perfectly than we can read a
man's thoughts in his face, do these sagacious beings read our 20
thoughts, just as they rise in our hearts, inasmuch as they see their
kindred spirit more clearly than we see the body. If this seem
strange to any who had not adverted to it before, let him only
consider. Suppose my spirit was out of the body, could not an
angel see my thoughts? Even without my uttering any words (if 25
words are used in the world of spirits)? And cannot that
ministering spirit see them just as well now that I am in the body?
It seems therefore to be an unquestionable truth (although
perhaps not commonly observed) that angels know not only the
words and actions, but also the thoughts, of those to whom they 30
minister. And indeed without this knowledge they would be very
ill qualified to perform various parts of their ministry.

3. And what an inconceivable degree of *wisdom* must they have
acquired by the use of their amazing faculties, over and above that

[11] For Wesley's speculation that angelic knowledge is intuitive, cf. No. 10, 'The Witness of the Spirit, I', I.12 and n.
[12] Cf. Acts 1:24.
[13] Acts 15:18.
[14] Mark Le Pla, *A Paraphrase on the Song of the Three Children* (1724), st. 25, ll. 7-8, 'O ye Lightnings'; cf. Wesley, *A Collection of Moral and Sacred Poems* (1744), II.121.

with which they were originally endued, in the course of more
than six thousand years. (That they have existed so long we are
assured; for they 'sang together' 'when the foundations of the
earth were laid'.[15]) How immensely must their wisdom have
5 increased during so long a period, not only by surveying the hearts
and ways of men in their successive generations, but by observing
the works of God—his works of creation, his works of
providence, his works of grace! And above all by 'continually
beholding the face of their Father which is in heaven'![16]
10   4. What measures of *holiness*, as well as wisdom, have they
derived from this inexhaustible ocean!

> A boundless, fathomless abyss,
> Without a bottom or a shore![17]

Are they not hence, by way of eminence, styled 'the holy angels'?
15 What goodness, what philanthropy, what love to man, have they
drawn from those rivers that are at his right hand! Such as we
cannot conceive to be exceeded by any but that of God our
Saviour. And they are still drinking in more love from this
'fountain of living water'.[18]
20   5. Such is the knowledge and wisdom of the angels of God, as
we learn from his own oracles. Such are their holiness and
goodness! And how astonishing is their *strength!* Even a fallen
angel is styled by an inspired writer, 'the prince of the power of
the air'.[19] How terrible a proof did he give of this power in
25 suddenly raising the whirlwind which 'smote the four corners of
the house',[20] and destroyed all the children of Job at once! That
this was his work we may easily learn from the command to 'save
his life'.[21] But he gave a far more terrible proof of his strength (if
we suppose that 'messenger of the Lord' to have been an evil
30 angel, as is not at all improbable) when he smote with death a
hundred, fourscore and five thousand Assyrians in one night, nay,

---

[15] Cf. Job 38:6, 7. Wesley's comment that the foundations of the world were laid more
than six thousand years before would mean that he was using Archbishop Ussher's date of
4004 B.C., a figure already commonplace because of its use as a fixture as a marginal note in
many edns. of the AV; cf. Robert K. Merton, *On the Shoulders of Giants* (New York, A
Harbinger Book, Harcourt, Brace and World, Inc., 1965), p. 80 and n.

[16] Cf. Matt. 18:10 (*Notes*). The early Wesley makes the same point on the wisdom of
angels; see No. 135, 'On Guardian Angels', II.2.

[17] Probably Isaac Watts; cf. No. 54, 'On Eternity', §18 and n.

[18] Cf. Jer. 2:13; 17:13; cf. *Notes* on John 4:10, 14.

[19] Eph. 2:2.   [20] Job 1:19.   [21] Job 2:6.

possibly in one hour, if not one moment.[22] Yet a strength abundantly greater than this must have been exerted by that angel (whether he was an angel of light or of darkness, which is not determined by the text) who 'smote' in one hour 'all the first-born of Egypt, both of man and beast'.[23] For considering the extent of the land of Egypt, the immense populousness thereof, and the innumerable cattle fed in their houses and grazing in their fruitful fields, the men and beasts who were slain in that night must have amounted to several millions! And if this be supposed to have been an evil angel, must not a good angel be as strong, yea, stronger than him? For surely any good angel must have more power than even an 'archangel ruined'.[24] And what power must the 'four angels' in the Revelation have, who were appointed to 'keep the four winds of heaven'?[25] There seems therefore no extravagance in supposing that, if God were pleased to permit, any of the angels of light could heave the earth and all the planets out of their orbits; yea, that he 'could arm himself with all these elements',[26] and crush the whole frame of nature. Indeed we do not know how to set any bounds to the strength of these first-born children of God.

6. And although none but their great Creator is omnipresent; although none beside him can ask, 'Do not I fill heaven and earth?'[27]; yet undoubtedly he has given an immense sphere of action (though not unbounded) to created spirits. 'The prince of the kingdom of Persia' (mentioned Daniel 10:13), though probably an evil angel, seems to have had a sphere of action, both of knowledge and power, as extensive as that vast empire. And the same, if not greater, we may reasonably ascribe to the good angel whom he withstood for one and twenty days.[28]

7. The angels of God have great power, in particular over the human body; power either to cause or remove pain and diseases; either to kill or to heal. They perfectly well understand whereof we are made; they know all the springs of this curious machine;[29] and can doubtless, by God's permission, touch any of them so as

---

[22] 2 Kgs. 19:35; 'the angel of the Lord'—i.e., lit., 'the messenger of the Lord'.
[23] Cf. Exod. 12:12.
[24] Cf. Milton, *Paradise Lost*, i.593; and see No. 72, 'Of Evil Angels', I.3, where a longer passage is quoted.
[25] Cf. Rev. 7:1.   [26] A paraphrase from Milton, *Paradise Lost*, vi.220-23.
[27] Jer. 23:24.   [28] Dan. 10:13.
[29] Wesley's body-soul dualism, in the tradition of Descartes, regarded the human body as a 'curious machine', as also in No. 51, *The Good Steward*, I.4 and n.

either to stop or restore its motion. Of this power, even in an evil angle, we have a clear instance in the case of Job, whom he 'smote with sore boils' all over, 'from the crown' of the head 'to the sole of the foot'.[30] And in that instant undoubtedly he would have
5 killed him if God had not 'saved his life'.[31] And on the other hand, of the power of angels to heal we have a remarkable instance in the case of Daniel. 'There remained no strength in me (said the prophet), neither was there breath in me. Then one came and touched me, and said, Peace be unto thee: be strong, yea, be
10 strong. And when he had spoken unto me, I was strengthened.'[b] On the other hand, when they are commissioned from above, may they not put a period to human life? There is nothing improbable in what Dr. Parnell supposes the angel to say to the hermit concerning the death of the child:

15   To all but thee in fits he seemed to go:
                    And 'twas my ministry to deal the blow.[32]

From this great truth the heathen poets probably derived their imagination that Iris used to be sent down from heaven to discharge souls out of their bodies.[33] And perhaps the sudden
20 death of many of the children of God may be owing to the ministry of an angel.

II. So perfectly are the angels of God qualified for their high office. It remains to inquire how they discharge their office. How do they minister to the heirs of salvation?
25 1. I will not say that they do not minister at all to those who

---

[b] [Dan. 10:] ver. 17, etc. [espec. ver. 18].

---

[30] Cf. Job 2:7.

[31] Job 2:6.

[32] Thomas Parnell, 'The Hermit', 230-31. Wesley had included an extract of this in *A Collection of Moral and Sacred Poems* (1744), I.275-76. Other quotations from this same poem are in No. 80, 'On Friendship with the World', §28 and n. The idea of the inscrutable purposes of God in cases of untimely death appears in a letter to Mrs. Betty Bradburn, Feb. 28, 1782, and in JWJ, Sept. 25, 1789: '[Mr. Henderson] could not save the life of his only son, who was probably taken to bring his father to God.'

[33] Iris was the goddess of the rainbow, daughter of Light (Electra) and Wonder (Thaumas). In the *Iliad* she is mentioned frequently as a 'swift-footed messenger', especially from Zeus or Hera to the lesser gods and to men; she disappears from the *Odyssey* where her role and function are taken by Hermes. This allusion to her 'discharging souls out of their bodies' has no explicit textual warrant; it may be a curious inference from *Iliad*, xxiii.161-262 (the story of the funeral pyre of the Trojan heroes and of Iris's assistance in kindling the fire).

through their obstinate impenitence and unbelief disinherit
themselves of the kingdom. This world is a world of mercy,
wherein God pours down many mercies even on the evil and the
unthankful. And many of these, it is probable, are conveyed even
to them by the ministry of angels; especially so long as they have 5
any thought of God, or any fear of God before their eyes.[34] But it
is their favourite employ, their peculiar office, to minister to the
heirs of salvation; to those who are 'now saved by faith', or at least
seeking God in sincerity.

2. Is it not their first care to minister to our souls? But we must 10
not expect this will be done 'with observation'[35]—in such a
manner as that we may clearly distinguish their working from the
workings of our own minds. We have no more reason to look for
this than for their appearing in a visible shape. Without this they
can in a thousand ways apply to our understanding. They may 15
assist us in our search after truth, remove many doubts and
difficulties, throw light on what was before dark and obscure, and
confirm us in the truth that is after godliness.[36] They may warn us
of evil in disguise, and place what is good in a clear, strong light.
They may gently move our will to embrace what is good, and fly 20
from that which is evil.[37] They may many times quicken our dull
affections, increase our holy hope or filial fear, and assist us more
ardently to love *him* who has first loved *us*.[38] Yea, they may be sent
of God to answer that whole prayer put into our mouths by pious
Bishop Ken: 25

> O may thy angels while I sleep,
> Around my bed their vigils keep;
> Their love angelical instil;
> Stop every avenue of ill.

> May they celestial joys rehearse, 30
> And thought to thought with me converse![39]

[34] Rom. 3:18.
[35] Luke 17:20.
[36] Titus 1:1.
[37] See Rom. 12:9.
[38] See 1 John 4:19.
[39] Thomas Ken, 'An Evening Hymn', in *A Manual of Prayers* (1709), st. 10; repeated,
along with st. 11, in No. 132, 'On Faith, Heb. 11:1', §12. See also Wesley's letter to Hester
Ann Roe, Dec. 9, 1781. In 1684, Ken had been consecrated Bishop of Bath and Wells. In
1689 he was deposed as a Nonjuror but refused the offer of reinstatement after the death
of his replacement Benjamin Kidder in 1703. For another reference of Wesley's to Ken,
see No. 102, 'Of Former Times', §11.

Although the manner of this we shall not be able to explain while we dwell in the body.

3. May they not minister also to us with respect to our bodies, in a thousand ways which we do not now understand? They may
5 prevent our falling into many dangers which we are not sensible of; and may deliver us out of many others, though we know not whence our deliverance comes. How many times have we been strangely and unaccountably preserved in sudden and dangerous falls? And it is well if we did not impute that preservation to
10 chance,[40] or to our own wisdom or strength. Not so; it was God gave his angels charge over us, and in their hands they bore us up.[41] Indeed men of the world will always impute such deliverances to accident or to second causes. To these possibly some of them might have imputed Daniel's preservation in the
15 lion's den. But himself ascribes it to the true cause: 'My God has sent his angel, and shut the mouths of the lions.'[c]

4. When a violent disease, supposed to be incurable, is totally and suddenly removed, it is by no means improbable that this is effected by the ministry of an angel. And perhaps it is owing to the
20 same cause that a remedy is unaccountably suggested either to the sick person, or some attending upon him, by which he is entirely cured.[42]

5. It seems, what are usually called divine dreams may be frequently ascribed to angels.[43] We have a remarkable instance of
25 this kind related by one that will hardly be thought an enthusiast; for he was a heathen, a philosopher, and an emperor. I mean Marcus Antoninus. 'In his *Meditations* he solemnly thanks God for revealing to him, when he was at Cajeta, in a dream, what totally cured the bloody flux, which none of his physicians were
30 able to heal.'[44] And why may we not suppose that God gave him this notice by the ministry of an angel?

6. And how often does God deliver us from evil men by the

---

[c] Dan. 6:22.

[40] Cf. No. 69, 'The Imperfection of Human Knowledge', II.1 and n.

[41] See Ps. 91:11-12; Matt. 4:6.

[42] Cf. No. 135, 'On Guardian Angels', II.2.

[43] Cf. No. 125, 'Human Life a Dream', §4 and n.

[44] The quotation here has not been located. Its source, however, and one that Wesley had read, was the so-called 'Meditations' of Marcus Aurelius, i.17(8); the text is ὡς μὴ πτύειν αἷμα καὶ μὴ ἰλιγγιάν—i.e., spitting up blood and a spell of vertigo. 'Cajeta' would be the present-day Gaeta.

ministry of his angels, overturning whatever their rage, or malice, or subtlety had plotted against us! These are about their bed, and about their path, and privy to all their dark designs;[45] and many of them undoubtedly they bring to nought by means that we think not of. Sometimes they blast their favourite schemes in the beginning; sometimes when they are just ripe for execution. And this they can do by a thousand means that we are not aware of. They can check them in their mid-career, by bereaving them of courage or strength; by striking faintness through their loins, or turning their wisdom into foolishness. Sometimes they bring to light the hidden things of darkness,[46] and show us the traps that are laid for our feet. In these and various other ways they hew the snares of the ungodly in pieces.[47]

7. Another grand branch of their ministry is to counterwork evil angels; who are continually going about, not only as roaring lions, seeking whom they may devour;[48] but more dangerously still, as angels of light,[49] seeking whom they may deceive. And how great is the number of these! Are they not as the stars of heaven for multitude?[50] How great is their rage, envy, malice, revenge! Such as the wickedest men on earth never felt. How great is their subtlety! Matured by the experience of above six thousand years. How great is their strength! Only inferior to that of the angels of God. The strongest of the sons of men are but as grasshoppers before them.[51] And what an advantage have they over us by that single circumstance, that they are invisible! As we have not strength to repel their force, so we have not skill to decline it. But the merciful Lord hath not given us up to the will of our enemies. 'His eyes', that is his holy angels, 'run to and fro over all the earth.'[52] And if our eyes were opened we should see, 'they are more that are for us than they that are against us. We should see',[53]

A convoy attends,
A minist'ring host of invisible friends.[54]

[45] See. Ps. 139:2 (BCP).   [46] 1 Cor. 4:5.
[47] See Ps. 129:4 (BCP).   [48] See 1 Pet. 5:8.
[49] See 2 Cor. 11:14.
[50] Deut. 1:10; 10:22; 28:62.
[51] See Num. 13:33.
[52] Cf. 2 Chr. 16:9; Zech. 4:10.
[53] Cf. 2 Kgs. 6:16-17.
[54] Charles Wesley, *Funeral Hymns*, 1746 (*Bibliog*, No. 115), p. 23 (Hymn 15, st. 7 in *Poet. Wks.*, VI.211); see also No. 84, *The Important Question*, II.4.

And whenever those assault us in soul or in body, these are able, willing, ready to defend us; who are at least equally strong, equally wise, and equally vigilant. And who can hurt us while we have armies of angels and the God of angels on our side?

5   8. And we may make one general observation: whatever assistance God gives to men by men, the same—and frequently in a higher degree—he gives to them by angels.[55] Does he administer to us, by men, light when we are in darkness, joy when we are in heaviness, deliverance when we are in danger, ease and
10   health when we are sick or in pain? It cannot be doubted but he frequently conveys the same blessings by the ministry of angels; not so sensibly, indeed, but full as effectually, though the messengers are not seen. Does he frequently deliver us by means of men from the violence or subtlety of our enemies? Many times
15   he works the same deliverance by these invisible agents. These shut the mouths of the human lions, so that they have no power to hurt us. And frequently they join with our human friends (although neither they nor we are sensible of it) giving them wisdom, courage, or strength, without which all their labour for
20   us would be unsuccessful. Thus do they secretly minister in numberless instances to the heirs of salvation; while we hear only the voices of men, and see none but men round about us.

9. But does not the Scripture teach, 'The help which is done upon earth, God doth it himself'?[56] Most certainly he does. And
25   he is able to do it by his own immediate power; he has no need of using any instruments at all, either in heaven or earth. He wants not either angels or men to fulfil the whole counsel of his will. But it is not his pleasure so to work. He never did; and we may reasonably suppose he never will. He has always wrought by such
30   instruments as he pleases: but still it is God himself that doth the work. Whatever help therefore we have, either by angels or men, is as much the work of God as if he were to put forth his almighty arm and work without any means at all. But he has used them from the beginning of the world: in all ages he has used the
35   ministry both of men and angels. And hereby especially is seen 'the manifold wisdom of God in the Church'.[57] Meantime the same glory redounds to him as if he used no instruments at all.

---

[55] Cf. No. 135, 'On Guardian Angels', III.1.
[56] Cf. Ps. 74:13 (BCP; cf. AV here); see also No. 67, 'On Divine Providence' §29, for a comment on God's 'immediate power'.
[57] Cf. Eph. 3:10 (*Notes*).

10. The grand reason why God is pleased to assist men by men, rather than immediately by himself, is undoubtedly to endear us to each other by these mutual good offices, in order to increase our happiness both in time and eternity. And is it not for the same reason that God is pleased to give his angels charge over us? Namely, that he may endear us and them to each other; that, by the increase of our love and gratitude to them, we may find a proportionable increase of happiness when we meet in our Father's kingdom. In the meantime, though we may not worship them (worship is due only to our common Creator), yet we may 'esteem them very highly in love, for their works' sake'.[58] And we may imitate them in all holiness; suiting our lives to the prayer our Lord himself has taught us; labouring to do his will on earth as angels do it in heaven.

I cannot conclude this discourse better than in that admirable collect of our Church:

'O everlasting God, who hast ordained and constituted the services of angels and men in a wonderful manner; [mercifully] grant that as thy holy angels always do thee service in heaven, so by thy appointment they may succour and defend us on earth, through Jesus Christ our Lord.'[59]

---

[58] 1 Thess. 5:13.

[59] The Collect for the Feast of St. Michael and All Angels, Sept. 29; the Prayer Book text reads, 'wonderful order' rather than 'wonderful manner'. Bishop Bull concludes his Sermon 12 with 'The Preface and Sanctus' in the Order for Holy Communion in place of a conventional ascription. For Wesley's use of ascriptions, cf. No. 1, *Salvation by Faith*, III.9 and n.

Of Evil Angels

Ephesians 6:12

We wrestle not against flesh and blood, but against principalities, against powers, against the rulers of the darkness of this world, against wicked spirits[1] in heavenly places.

1. It has been frequently observed that there are no gaps or chasms in the creation of God, but that all the parts of it are admirably connected together, to make up one universal whole. Accordingly there is one chain of beings,[2] from the lowest to the highest point, from an unorganized particle of earth or water to Michael the archangel. And the scale of creatures does not advance *per saltum*,[3] by leaps, but by smooth and gentle degrees; although it is true, these are frequently imperceptible to our imperfect faculties. We cannot accurately trace many of the intermediate links of this amazing chain, which are abundantly too fine to be discerned either by our senses or understanding.

2. We can only observe, in a gross and general manner, rising one above another, first, inorganical earth, then minerals and vegetables in their several orders; afterwards insects, reptiles, fishes, birds, beasts, men, and angels. Of angels indeed we know nothing with any certainty but by revelation. The accounts which are left by the wisest of the ancients, or given by the modern heathens, being no better than silly, self-inconsistent fables, too gross to be imposed even upon children. But by divine revelation we are informed that they were all created holy and happy; yet they did not all continue as they were created—some kept, but some left, their first estate. The former of these are now good angels; the latter, evil angels. Of the former I have spoken in a

---

[1] Translated thus in Wesley's *Notes*.

[2] For other references to this favourite notion of Wesley's, cf. No. 56, 'God's Approbation of His Works', I.14 and n.

[3] The 'fixity of species' and their continuous gradation was a basic supposition of Aristotelian biology which Wesley still took for granted; cf. *Historia Animalium*, VIII.588*a-b*.

preceding discourse; I purpose now to speak of the latter. And
highly necessary it is that we should well understand what God
has revealed concerning them, that they may gain no advantage
over us by our ignorance, that we may know how to wrestle against
them effectually. For 'we wrestle not against flesh and blood, but 5
against principalities, against powers, against the rulers of the
darkness of this world, against wicked spirits in heavenly places.'

3. This single passage seems to contain the whole Scripture
doctrine concerning evil angels. I apprehend the plain meaning of
it, literally translated, is this: 'Our wrestling', the wrestling of real 10
Christians, 'is not' only, or chiefly, 'against flesh and blood'—
weak men or fleshly appetites and passions—'but against
principalities, against powers'—the mighty *princes* of all the
infernal legions,[4] with their combined forces: and great is their
power, as is also the power of the legions which they 15
command—'against the rulers of the world' (this is the literal
meaning of the word). Perhaps these principalities and powers
remain chiefly in the citadel of their kingdom. But there are other
evil spirits that range abroad, to whom the provinces of the world
are committed. 'Of the darkness'—chiefly the spiritual dark- 20
ness—'of this age'—which prevails during this present state of
things—'against wicked spirits'—eminently such, who mortally
hate and continually oppose holiness, and labour to infuse
unbelief, pride, evil desire, malice, anger, hatred, envy, or
revenge—'in heavenly places'—which were once their abode, 25
and which they still aspire after.

In prosecuting this important subject, I will endeavour to
explain, first, the nature and properties of evil angels; and,
secondly, their employment.

I. 1. With regard to the first, we cannot doubt but all the angels 30
of God were originally of the same *nature*. Unquestionably they
were the highest order of created beings. They were spirits, pure,
ethereal creatures, simple and incorruptible; if not wholly
immaterial, yet certainly not encumbered with gross, earthly flesh
and blood. As spirits they were endued with understanding, with 35
affections, and with liberty, or a power of self-determination; so

---

[4] Jackson emended the original 'legions' to 'regions', and may have had a textual
warrant, since he had before him Wesley's annotated copy of *Sermons*, Vol. VI, now
missing.

that it lay in themselves either to continue in their allegiance to
God or to rebel against him.

2. And their original *properties* were doubtless the same with
those of the holy angels. There is no absurdity in supposing
Satan, their chief, otherwise styled 'Lucifer, son of the morning',[5]
to have been at least 'one of the first, if not the first Archangel'.[6]
Like the other sons of the morning, they had a height and depth of
understanding quite incomprehensible to us. In consequence of
this they had such knowledge and wisdom that the wisest of the
children of men (had men then existed) would have been mere
idiots in comparison of them. Their strength was equal to their
knowledge, such as it cannot enter into our heart to conceive;
neither can we conceive to how wide a sphere of action either
their strength or their knowledge extended. Their number God
alone can tell: doubtless it was only less than infinite. And a third
part of these stars of heaven the arch-rebel drew after him.[7]

3. We do not exactly know (because it is not revealed in the
oracles of God) either what was the occasion of their apostasy, or
what effect it immediately produced upon them. Some have not
improbably supposed that when God 'published the decree'
(mentioned Psalm 2:6-7) concerning the kingdom of his
only-begotten Son to be over all creatures, these first-born of
creatures gave place to pride, comparing themselves to him
(possibly intimated by the very name of Satan, Lucifer, or
Michael, which means, 'Who is like God?').[8] It may be, Satan,
then first giving way to temptation, said in his heart, 'I too will
have my throne. "I will sit upon the sides of the north! I will be like
the Most High." '[9] But how did the mighty then fall![10] What an
amazing loss did they sustain! If we allow of them all, what our
poet supposes concerning their chief in particular:

---

[5] Isa. 14:12.   [6] Milton, *Paradise Lost*, v.659-60.
[7] See Rev. 12:4.

[8] *AM* (1783) reads 'Satan, Lucess, or Michael . . .', obviously a printer's error. In the
errata to *AM* and in his personal copy Wesley altered this to 'Satan, successor of Michael'.
For *SOSO* (1788) he altered it yet again to the reading here preferred. This preference
presupposes Wesley's agreement with traditional angelology, in which Satan and Lucifer
are allied, and Michael has no such successor—cf. Rev. 12:7-9 and Isa. 14:12-20 (AV);
see also J. B. Russell, *Satan, the Early Christian Tradition* (Cornell Univ. Press, 1981), pp.
67, 131, 194. The problem of Wesley's first alteration, however, still remains as an
unaccountable anomaly.

[9] Isa. 14:13-14.

[10] See 2 Sam. 1:19, 25, 27. Cf. Charles Wesley's hymn on Gen. 1:27, *Short Hymns on
Select Passages of the Holy Scriptures*: 'How are the mighty fallen!' (*Poet. Wks.*, IX.2).

His form had not yet lost
All its original brightness, nor appeared
Less than archangel ruined, and the excess
Of glory obscured;[11]

If we suppose their outward form was not entirely changed 5 (though it must have been in a great degree, because the evil disposition of the mind must dim the lustre of the visage), yet what an astonishing change was wrought within when angels became devils, when the holiest of all the creatures of God became the most unholy! 10

4. From the time that they shook off their allegiance to God they shook off all goodness, and contracted all those tempers which are most hateful to him, and most opposite to his nature. And ever since they are full of pride, arrogance, haughtiness, exalting themselves above measure; and although so deeply 15 depraved through their inmost frame, yet admiring their own perfections. They are full of envy, if not against God himself (and even that is not impossible, seeing they formerly aspired after his throne), yet against all their fellow-creatures; against the angels of God, who now enjoy the heaven from which they fell; and 20 much more against those worms of the earth who are now called to 'inherit the kingdom'.[12] They are full of cruelty, of rage, against all the children of men, whom they long to inspire with the same wickedness with themselves, and to involve in the same misery.

5. In the prosecution of this infernal design they are diligent in 25 the highest degree. To find out the most effectual means of putting it into execution, they apply to this end the whole force of their angelical understanding. And they second it with their whole strength, so far as God is pleased to permit. But it is well for mankind that God hath set them their bounds which they cannot 30 pass. He hath said to the fiercest and strongest of the apostate spirits, 'Hitherto shalt thou come, and no farther.'[13] Otherwise how easily and how quickly might one of them overturn the whole frame of nature! How soon would they involve all in one common ruin, or at least destroy man from the face of the earth![14] And they 35 are indefatigable in their bad work: they never are faint or weary. Indeed it seems no spirits are capable of weariness but those that inhabit flesh and blood.

[11] Cf. Milton, *Paradise Lost*, i.591-94; and see No. 71, 'Of Good Angels', I.5 and n.
[12] 1 Cor. 6:9, etc. [13] Job 38:11. [14] Gen. 6:7.

6. One circumstance more we may learn from the Scripture concerning the evil angels. They do not wander at large, but are all united under one common head. It is he that is styled by our blessed Lord, 'the prince of this world';[15] yea, the Apostle does
5 not scruple to call him 'the god of this world'.[16] He is frequently styled 'Satan', the adversary, being the great adversary both of God and man. He is termed, 'the devil'; by way of eminence, 'Apollyon',[17] or the destroyer; 'the old serpent',[18] from his beguiling Eve under that form; and 'the angel of the bottomless
10 pit'.[19] We have reason to believe that the other evil angels are under his command; that they are ranged by him according to their several orders, that they are appointed to their several stations, and have from time to time their several works and offices assigned them. And undoubtedly they are connected
15 (though we know not how; certainly not by love) both to him and to each other.

II. But what is the employment of evil angels? This is the second point to be considered.
20 1. They are (remember! so far as God permits) κοσμοκρά-τορες,[20] 'governors of the world'! So that there may be more ground than we are apt to imagine for that strange expression of Satan when he had 'showed' our Lord 'all the kingdoms of the world, and the glory of them': 'All these things will I give thee, if
25 thou wilt fall down and worship me.'[a] It is a little more particularly expressed in the fourth chapter of St. Luke. 'The devil showed unto him all the kingdoms of the world in a moment of time.'[21]

---

[a] Matt. 4:8-9.

---

[15] John 12:31; 14:30; 16:11.

[16] 2 Cor. 4:4.

[17] Rev. 9:11; see also Matthew Poole, *Annotations;* Matthew Henry, *Exposition;* and Wesley, *Notes,* on the meaning of the name (from ἀπολλύειν, to destroy). Wesley says: 'Both Abaddon and Apollyon signify a destroyer. By this he [Apollyon] is distinguished from the dragon, whose proper name is Satan.' But he would also have had in mind 'the foul fiend' in Bunyan's *Pilgrim's Progress* who assaults Christian on his way through the Valley of Humiliation.

[18] Rev. 12:9; 20:2.

[19] Rev. 9:11.

[20] Cf. Eph. 6:12, and the references in the intertestamental literature in Arndt and Gingrich, *Greek-English Lexicon.* For Wesley's satanocratic views, cf. No. 12, 'The Witness of Our Own Spirit', §10 and n.

[21] Luke 4:5.

(Such an astonishing measure of power is still left in the prince of darkness!) 'And the devil said, All this power will I give thee, and the glory of them: for that is delivered unto me; and to whomsoever I will, I give it.'[b] They are 'the rulers of the darkness of this age'[22] (so the words are literally translated), of the present state of things, during which 'the whole world lieth in the wicked one.'[23] He is the element of the children of men only, those who fear God being excepted. He and his angels, in connection with, and in subordination to him, dispose all the ignorance, all the error, all the folly, and particularly all the wickedness of men, in such a manner as may most hinder the kingdom of God, and most advance the kingdom of darkness.

2. 'But has every man a particular evil angel as well as a good one attending him?' This has been an exceeding ancient opinion both among the Christians and the Jews before them. But it is generally doubted whether it can be sufficiently proved from Scripture. Indeed it would not be improbable that there is a particular evil angel with every man, if we were assured there is a good one. But this cannot be inferred from those words of our Lord concerning little children, 'In heaven their angels do continually see the face of their Father which is in heaven.'[24] This only proves that there are angels who are appointed to take care of little children. It does not prove that a particular angel is allotted to every child. Neither is it proved by the words of Rhoda, who hearing the voice of Peter said, 'It is his angel.'[25] We cannot infer any more from this, even suppose 'his angel' means his guardian angel, than that Rhoda believed the doctrine of guardian angels, which was then common among the Jews. But still it will remain a disputable point (seeing revelation determines nothing concerning it) whether every man is attended either by a particular good or a particular evil angel.

3. But whether or no particular men are attended by particular evil spirits, we know that Satan and all his angels are continually warring against us, and watching over every child of man. They are ever watching to see whose outward or inward circumstances, whose prosperity or adversity, whose health or sickness, whose

---

[b] [Luke 4:] ver. 5, 6.

---

[22] Eph. 6:12 (*Notes*).   [23] 1 John 5:19 (*Notes*).
[24] Cf. Matt. 18:10.   [25] Acts 12:15.

friends or enemies, whose youth or age, whose knowledge or
ignorance, whose business or idleness, whose joy or sorrow, may
lay them open to temptation. And they are perpetually ready to
make the utmost advantage of every circumstance. These skilful
5 wrestlers espy the smallest slip we make, and avail themselves of it
immediately; as they also are 'about our bed, and about our path,
and spy out all our ways'.[26] Indeed each of them 'walketh about as
a roaring lion, seeking whom he may devour',[27] or whom he may
'beguile through his subtlety, as the serpent beguiled Eve'.[28] Yea,
10 and in order to do this the more effectually they transform
themselves into angels of light. Thus

> With rage that never ends
> Their hellish arts they try:
> Legions of dire, malicious fiends,
15 > And spirits enthroned on high.[29]

4. It is by these instruments chiefly that the 'foolish hearts' of
those that know not God 'are darkened';[30] yea, they frequently
darken in a measure the hearts of them that do know God. 'The
god of this world knows' how to 'blind our hearts,'[31] to spread a
20 cloud over our understanding, and to obscure the light of those
truths which at other times shine as bright as the noonday sun. By
this means he assaults our faith, our evidence of things unseen.[32]
He endeavours to weaken that hope full of immortality[33] to which
God had begotten us,[34] and thereby to lessen, if he cannot
25 destroy, our joy in God our Saviour. But above all he strives to
damp our love of God, as he knows this is the spring of all our
religion, and that as this rises or falls the work of God flourishes
or decays in the soul.

5. Next to the love of God there is nothing which Satan so
30 cordially abhors as the love of our neighbour. He uses therefore

---

[26] Cf. Ps. 139:2 (BCP).
[27] Cf. 1 Pet. 5:8.
[28] Cf. 2 Cor. 11:3.
[29] Charles Wesley, 'Hymns for the Watch-night', No. 8, st. 7, ll. 5-8, in *Hymns and Sacred Poems* (1749), II.130 (*Poet. Wks.*, V.272). See also, No. 83, 'On Patience', §2, where the first four lines of this stanza appear.
[30] Cf. Rom. 1:21.
[31] Cf. 2 Cor. 4:4.
[32] See Heb. 11:1.
[33] Wisd. 3:4. For Wesley's other uses of this text, cf. Nos. 74, 'Of the Church', §9; 87, 'The Danger of Riches', I.11, II.12; and 129, 'Heavenly Treasure in Earthen Vessels', I.3.
[34] See 1 Pet. 1:3.

every possible means to prevent or destroy this; to excite either private or public suspicions, animosities, resentment, quarrels; to destroy the peace of families or of nations, and to banish unity and concord from the earth. And this indeed is the triumph of his art; to embitter the poor, miserable children of men against each 5 other, and at length urge them to do his own work, to plunge one another into the pit of destruction.[35]

6. This enemy of all righteousness is equally diligent to hinder every good word and work. If he cannot prevail upon us to do evil he will, if possible, prevent our doing good. He is peculiarly 10 diligent to hinder the work of God from spreading in the hearts of men. What pains does he take to prevent or obstruct the general work of God! And how many are his devices to stop its progress in particular souls![36] To hinder their continuing or growing in grace, in the knowledge of our Lord Jesus Christ![37] To lessen, if not 15 destroy, that 'love, joy, peace'; that 'long-suffering, gentleness, goodness'; that 'fidelity, meekness, temperance',[38] which our Lord works by his loving Spirit in them that believe, and wherein the very essence of religion consists.

7. To effect these ends he is continually labouring with all his 20 skill and power to infuse evil thoughts of every kind into the hearts of men. And certainly it is as easy for a spirit to speak to our heart as for a man to speak to our ears. But sometimes it is exceeding difficult to distinguish these from our own thoughts, those which he injects so exactly resembling those which naturally arise in our 25 own minds. Sometimes indeed we may distinguish one from the other by this circumstance: the thoughts which naturally arise in our minds are generally, if not always, occasioned by, or at least connected with, some inward or outward circumstance that went before. But those that are preternaturally suggested have 30 frequently no relation to or connection (at least none that we are able to discern) with anything which preceded. On the contrary they shoot in as it were across, and thereby show that they are of a different growth.[39]

8. He likewise labours to awaken evil passions or tempers in 35 our souls. He endeavours to inspire those passions and tempers

[35] Ps. 55:23 (AV).
[36] Cf. No. 42, 'Satan's Devices', *passim*.
[37] See 2 Pet. 3:18.
[38] Gal. 5:22-23 (*Notes*).
[39] Cf. No. 41, *Wandering Thoughts, passim*.

which are directly opposite to 'the fruit of the Spirit'.[40] He strives
to instil unbelief, atheism, ill-will, bitterness, hatred, malice,
envy—opposite to faith and love; fear, sorrow, anxiety, worldly
care—opposite to peace and joy; impatience, ill nature, anger,
5 resentment—opposite to long-suffering, gentleness, meekness;
fraud, guile, dissimulation—contrary to fidelity; love of the world,
inordinate affection, foolish desires—opposite to the love of God.
One sort of evil desires he may probably raise or inflame by
touching the springs of this animal machine,[41] endeavouring thus
10 by means of the body to disturb or sully the soul.

9. And in general we may observe that as no good is done, or
spoken, or thought by any man without the assistance of God,
working together *in* and *with* those that believe in him; so there is
no evil done, or spoke[n], or thought, without the assistance of the
15 devil, 'who worketh with energy', with strong though secret
power, 'in the children of unbelief'.[42] Thus he 'entered into'[43]
Judas, and confirmed him in the design of betraying his Master.
Thus he 'put it into the heart' of Ananias and Sapphira 'to lie unto
the Holy Ghost'.[44] And in like manner he has a share in all the
20 actions and words and designs of evil men. As the children of God
'are workers together with God'[45] in every good thought, or word,
or action; so the children of the devil are workers together with
him in every evil thought, or word, or work. So that as all good
tempers, and remotely all good words and actions, are the fruit of
25 the good Spirit; in like manner all evil tempers, with all the words
and works which spring from them, are the fruit of the evil spirit;
insomuch that all the 'works of the flesh',[46] of our evil nature, are
likewise the 'works of the devil'.[47]

10. On this account, because he is continually inciting men to
30 evil, he is emphatically called, 'the tempter'.[48] Nor is it only with
regard to his own children that he is thus employed. He is
continually tempting the children of God also, and those that are
labouring so to be:

[40] Gal. 5:22; Eph. 5:9.
[41] Cf. No. 51, *The Good Steward*, I.4 and n.
[42] Cf. Eph. 2:2.
[43] Luke 22:3.
[44] Cf. Acts 5:3.
[45] Cf. 2 Cor. 6:1.
[46] Gal. 5:19.
[47] 1 John 3:8.
[48] Matt. 4:3; 1 Thess. 3:5.

> A constant watch he keeps;
> He eyes them night and day:
> He never slumbers, never sleeps,
> Lest he should lose his prey.[49]

Indeed the holiest of men, as long as they remain upon earth, are 5
not exempt from his temptations. They cannot expect it; seeing 'it
is enough for the disciple to be as his Master.'[50] And we know he
was tempted to evil till he said, 'Father, into thy hands I commend
my spirit.'[51]

11. For such is the malice of the wicked one that he will 10
torment whom he cannot destroy. If he cannot entice men to sin
he will (so far as he is permitted) put them to pain. There is no
doubt but he is the occasion, directly or indirectly, of many of the
pains of mankind; which those who can no otherwise account for
them lightly pass over as 'nervous'. And innumerable 'accidents', 15
as they are called, are undoubtedly owing to his agency, such as
the unaccountable fright or falling of horses, the overturning of
carriages, the breaking or dislocating of bones; the hurt done by
the falling or burning of houses, by storms of wind, snow, rain, or
hail, by lightning or earthquakes. But to all these, and a thousand 20
more, this subtle spirit can give the appearance of 'accidents', for
fear the sufferers, if they knew the real agent, should call for help
on one that is stronger than him.

12. There is little reason to doubt but many diseases likewise,
both of the acute and chronical kind, are either occasioned or 25
increased by diabolical agency; particularly those that begin in an
instant, without any discernible cause; as well as those that
continue, and perhaps gradually increase, in spite of all the power
of medicine. Here indeed 'vain men' that 'would be wise'[52] again
call in the nerves to their assistance. But is not this explaining 30
ignotum per ignotius—a thing unknown by what is more

---

[49] Cf. Charles Wesley, *Hymns and Sacred Poems* (1749), II.119, No. 2 of 'Hymns for the Watch-night' (*Poet. Wks.*, V.261):

> A constant watch he keeps,
> He eyes me night and day,
> And never slumbers, never sleeps,
> Lest he should lose his prey.

See also No. 132, 'On Faith, Heb. 11:1', §10, where Wesley again quotes this quatrain.
[50] Cf. Matt. 10:25.
[51] Luke 23:46.
[52] Job 11:12.

unknown?[53] For what do we know of the nerves themselves? Not even whether they are solid or hollow!

13. Many years ago I was asking an experienced physician, and one particularly eminent for curing lunacy, 'Sir, have you not seen reason to believe that some lunatics are really demoniacs?' He answered: 'Sir, I have been often inclined to think that most lunatics are demoniacs. Nor is there any weight in that objection that they are frequently cured by medicine. For so might any other disease occasioned by an evil spirit, if God did not suffer him to repeat the stroke by which that disease is occasioned.'[54]

14. This thought opens to us a wider scene. Who can tell how many of those diseases which we impute altogether to natural causes may be really preternatural? What disorder is there in the human frame which an evil angel may not inflict? Cannot he smite us, as he did Job, and that in a moment, with boils from the crown of the head to the sole of the foot?[55] Cannot he with equal ease inflict any other either external or internal malady? Could not he in a moment, by divine permission, cast the strongest man down to the ground, and make him 'wallow foaming',[56] with all the symptoms either of an epilepsy or apoplexy? In like manner, it is easy for him to smite any one man, or everyone in a city or nation, with a malignant fever, or with the plague itself, so that vain would be the help of man.

15. But that malice blinds the eyes of the wise,[57] one would imagine so intelligent a being would not stoop so low as it seems the devil sometimes does to torment the poor children of men! For to him we may reasonably impute many little inconveniences which we suffer. 'I believe' (said that excellent man, the Marquis de Renty, when the bench on which he sat snapped in sunder

---

[53] A Latin tag long since a commonplace; cf. Chaucer, 'The Canon's Yeoman's Tale', l. 904, *Canterbury Tales* (1687), p. 109. See Wesley's letter to William Law, Jan. 6, 1756: '*ignotum per aeque ignotum*'; and also *A Farther Appeal*, Pt. I, V.9 (11:147 in this edn.).

[54] Probably Thomas Deacon (1698–1753), a physician and schismatic non-juring bishop, much interested in demoniacal possession and exorcisms. In No. 132, 'On Faith, Heb. 11:1', §8, Wesley speaks of 'one of the most eminent physicians I ever knew, particularly in cases of insanity, Dr. Deacon'. He had known Deacon first at Oxford, and in his diary records a visit with Deacon in Manchester on May 17, 1733 (and occasional visits thereafter). See also *The Principles of a Methodist Farther Considered*, IV.7, and Wesley's letter to Thomas Stedman, Aug. 13, 1774. The same idea had already been suggested by Joseph Mede, Discourse VI, on John 10:20, *Works*, p. 29.

[55] Job 2:7.

[56] Mark 9:20.

[57] Deut. 16:19.

without any visible cause), 'that Satan had a hand in it, making me to fall untowardly.'[58] I know not whether he may not have a hand in that unaccountable horror with which many have been seized in the dead of night, even to such a degree that all their bones have shook. Perhaps he has a hand also in those terrifying dreams[59] which many have, even while they are in perfect health.

It may be observed in all these instances we usually say 'the devil', as if there was one only; because these spirits, innumerable as they are, do all act in concert, and because we know not whether one or more are concerned in this or that work of darkness.

[III.] It remains only to draw a few plain inferences from the doctrine which has been delivered.

1. And first, as a general preservative against all the rage, the power, and subtlety of your great adversary, 'put on the panoply', the whole armour, 'of God,'[60] universal holiness. See that 'the mind be in you which was also in Christ Jesus',[61] and that ye 'walk as Christ also walked';[62] that ye have a conscience void of offence toward God and toward men.[63] So shall ye 'be able to withstand'[64] all the force and all the stratagems of the enemy. So shall ye be able to 'withstand in the evil day',[65] in the day of sore temptation. And 'having done all, to stand'[66]—to remain in the posture of victory and triumph.

2. To his 'fiery darts', his evil suggestions of every kind, blasphemous or unclean, though numberless as the stars of heaven, oppose 'the shield of faith';[67] a consciousness of the love of Christ Jesus will effectually quench them all.

> Jesus hath died for *you*!
> What can your faith withstand?
> Believe, hold fast your shield! and who
> Shall pluck you from his hand?[68]

[58] Cf. Saint-Jure, *Life*, p. 96: 'He told her [the Prioress of the Carmelites of Dijon] that being led into his Chapel of Citry, and set down upon a bench, by reason of his sickness, the bench broke, without any appearance at all to him that such a thing could happen, and that he believed, the evil spirit had broken it, to move him to impatience, making him to fall untowardly: "But by the mercy of God, I was no more moved thereat", said he, "than you see me now, although the pains that surprised me were very sharp." ' Cf. also, Wesley, *An Extract of the Life of M. de Renty* (Bibliog, No. 43), London, 1741, p. 21 (iv. 4).

[59] Cf. No. 124, 'Human Life a Dream', §4 and n.   [60] Cf. Eph. 6:11.
[61] Cf. Phil. 2:5.   [62] Cf. 1 John 2:6.   [63] Acts 24:16.   [64] Eph. 6:13.
[65] *Ibid.*   [66] *Ibid.*   [67] Eph. 6:16.
[68] Cf. Charles Wesley, 'The Whole Armour of God', in *Hymns and Sacred Poems* (1749), I.237 (*Poet. Wks.*, V.42). Orig., second line reads, 'What can his love withstand?'

3. If he inject doubts whether you are a child of God, or fears lest you should not endure to the end, 'Take to you for a helmet the hope of salvation.'[69] Hold fast that glad word, 'Blessed be the God and Father of our Lord Jesus Christ, who according to his
5 abundant mercy hath begotten us again unto a living hope of an inheritance incorruptible, undefiled, and that fadeth not away.'[70] You will never be overthrown, you will never be staggered by your adversary, if you 'hold fast the beginning of this confidence steadfast unto the end.'[71]

10 4. Whenever the 'roaring lion, walking about and seeking whom he may devour',[72] assaults you with all his malice, and rage, and strength, 'resist' him, 'steadfast in the faith'.[73] Then is the time, having cried to the Strong for strength,[74] to 'stir up the gift of God that is in you;'[75] to summon all your faith, and hope, and love;
15 to turn the attack in the name of the Lord, and in the power of his might;[76] and 'he will' soon 'flee from you.'[77]

5. But 'there is no temptation', says one, 'greater than the being without temptation.'[78] When therefore this is the case, when Satan seems to be withdrawn, then beware lest he hurt you more
20 as a crooked serpent than he could do as a roaring lion. Then take care you are not lulled into a pleasing slumber, 'lest he should beguile you as he did Eve', even in innocence, and insensibly draw you 'from your simplicity toward Christ',[79] from seeking all your happiness in him.

25 6. Lastly, if he 'transform himself into an angel of light',[80] then are you in the greatest danger of all. Then have you need to beware, lest you also fall where many mightier have been slain: then have you the greatest need to 'watch and pray, that ye enter not into temptation.'[81] And if you continue so to do, the God
30 whom you love and serve will deliver you. 'The anointing of the

---

[69] Cf. 1 Thess. 5:8.
[70] Cf. 1 Pet. 1:3-4.
[71] Cf. Heb. 3:14.
[72] Cf. 1 Pet. 5:8.
[73] 1 Pet. 5:9.
[74] See No. 48, 'Self-denial', III.4 and n.
[75] Cf. 2 Tim. 1:6.
[76] Eph. 6:10.
[77] Jas. 4:7.
[78] Miguel de Molinos, *The Spiritual Guide Which Disentangles the Soul* (1688), I.63. Wesley extracted this for the *Christian Lib.*, XXXVIII.262: 'Finally thou art to know, that the greatest temptation is to be without temptation.'
[79] Cf. 2 Cor. 11:3.   [80] Cf. 2 Cor. 11:14.   [81] Matt. 26:41.

Holy One shall abide with you, and teach you of all things.'[82] Your eye will pierce through snares:[83] you shall know what that 'holy, and acceptable, and perfect will of God is',[84] and shall hold on your way till you 'grow up in all things into him that is our head, even Christ Jesus.'[85]

5

January 7, 1783[86]

---

[82] Cf. 1 John 2:20, 27 (*Notes*).
[83] See Job 40:24.
[84] Cf. Rom. 12:1, 2.
[85] Cf. Eph. 4:15.
[86] Date as added in *AM*.

SERMON 73

OF HELL

AN INTRODUCTORY COMMENT

This is a sermon on yet another topic about which Wesley had previously written very little and which, apparently, had not bulked large in his oral preaching save as it mirrored the conventional eschatological ideas of the day. As early as 1731, in Oxford, he had preached from Mark 9:48; he had used the same text again in 1770. Still later, in 1788, he would produce another sermon on hell and heaven (see No. 115, 'Dives and Lazarus'). In all of these his views of hell and perdition were wholly conventional; already he had, as a matter of course, included the phrase, 'descended into hell' in the text of the Apostles' Creed in his revision of the Order of Morning Prayer in The Sunday Service *(1784), and he would never have approved its omission by the American Methodists (1786 and thereafter). When Wesley's references to hell (here and elsewhere) are compared to a classical Puritan statement like Jonathan Edwards's famous 'Sinners in the Hands of an Angry God' (first preached in 1741 and then published as Sermon XV in* Sermons on Various Subjects, *1765), Wesley's emphases seem low-keyed. But when compared to a more direct source (viz., Isaac Watts, Discourses XII and XIII on Mark 9:46, in* The World to Come . . . *[1745], in* Works, *I.705-52), the resemblances are striking. If anything, Wesley's tone is more severe than Watts's.*

'Of Hell' was finished on October 10, 1788, at Newport on the Isle of Wight; it was, therefore, written on the road during a regular preaching mission (cf. JWJ, October 7-11). One may guess that it was written expressly for inclusion in the Arminian Magazine *since it promptly appeared there, without a title but numbered as 'Sermon XII' in the ensuing issues (Vol. V, 1782, November and December, pp. 565-69, 623-32)—i.e., before the twin sermons on angels. In* SOSO, *VI, he reversed this order and placed 'Of Hell' after the other two (i.e., pp. 147-69). It was reprinted separately in 1789 and 1790, with a different title, 'The Eternity of Hell Torments'. What is more distinctive than the doctrines in this sermon are Wesley's applications of them, and his obvious efforts to update them with illustrations both from the traditional sources and contemporary ones as well.*

30

Wesley had already included an eschatological discourse on 2 Pet. 3:10-13, by James Knight, in his own collected Works (1773), XX. 290-321; cf. Knight, A Discourse on the Conflagration and Renovation of the World (1736). A copy of Wesley's extract is still extant—in the Methodist Archives in the John Rylands Library, Manchester—in a hand closely resembling Wesley's own (but probably by John Jones). It had the following quaint superscript that would date from somewhere toward the end of the nineteenth century:

> The celebrated John Wesley gave this to a Mr. Whitney who gave it to Ann Livingston of Deptford, who, after giving it to Mrs. Eleanor Smith, she in her turn, gave it to John Overton of Rose Cottage, King's Road, Chelsea.

Of Hell

Mark 9:48

Where their worm dieth not, and the fire is not quenched.

1. Every truth which is revealed in the oracles of God is undoubtedly of great importance. Yet it may be allowed that some of those which are revealed therein are of greater importance than others, as being more immediately conducive to the grand end of all, the eternal salvation of men. And we may judge of their importance even from this circumstance, that they are not mentioned once only in the sacred writings, but are repeated over and over. A remarkable instance of this we have with regard to the awful truth which is now before us. Our blessed Lord, who uses no superfluous words, who makes no 'vain repetitions',[1] repeats it over and over in the same chapter, and as it were in the same breath. So verse 43, 44: 'If thy hand offend thee', if a thing or person as useful as a hand be an occasion of sin, and there is no other way to shun that sin, 'cut it off. It is better for thee to enter into life maimed, than having two hands to go into hell; into

---

[1] Matt. 6:7.

unquenchable fire, where their worm dieth not, and the fire is not
quenched.' So again, verse 45, 46: 'If thy foot offend thee, cut it
off. It is better for thee to enter halt into life, than having two feet
to be cast into hell; into unquenchable fire, where their worm
5 dieth not, and the fire is not quenched.' And yet again, verse 47,
48: 'If thine eye', a person or thing as dear as thine eye, 'offend
thee', hinder thy running the race which is set before thee,[2] 'pluck
it out: it is better for thee to enter into the kingdom of God with
one eye, than having two eyes to be cast into hell-fire; where their
10 worm dieth not, and the fire is not quenched.'

2. And let it not be thought that the consideration of these
terrible truths is proper only for enormous sinners. How is this
supposition consistent with what our Lord speaks to those who
were then doubtless the holiest men upon earth? 'When
15 innumerable multitudes were gathered together, he said to his
disciples' (the apostles) 'first of all, I say unto you, my friends,
Fear not them that can kill the body, and after that have no more
that they can do. But I say unto you, Fear him who after he hath
killed hath power to cast into hell; yea, I say unto you, Fear him!'[a]
20 Yea, fear him under this very notion, of having power to cast into
hell; that is, in effect, fear lest he should cast you into the place of
torment.'[3] And this very fear, even in the children of God, is one
excellent means of preserving them from it.

3. It behoves therefore not only the outcasts of men but even
25 'you, his friends', you that fear and love God, deeply to consider
what is revealed in the oracles of God concerning the future state
of punishment. How widely distant is this from the most elaborate
accounts which are given by the heathen authors! Their accounts
are (in many particulars at least) childish, fanciful, and
30 self-inconsistent. So that it is no wonder they did not believe
themselves, but only related the tales of the vulgar. So Virgil
strongly intimates, when, after the laboured account he had given
of the shades beneath, he sends him that had related it out at the
ivory gate, through which (as he tells us) only *dreams* pass; thereby
35 giving us to know that all the preceding account is no more than a

---

[a] Luke 12:1, 4-5.

---

[2] See Heb. 12:1.
[3] Luke 16:28.

dream.[4] This he only insinuates; but his brother poet, Juvenal, speaks out flat and plain:

> *Esse aliquos manes, et subterranea regna, . . .*
> *Nec pueri credunt, nisi qui nondum aere lavantur*[5]—

'Even our children do not believe a word of the tales concerning 5 another world.'

4. Here, on the contrary, all is worthy of God the Creator, the Governor of mankind. All is awful and solemn, suitable to his wisdom and justice by whom 'Tophet was ordained of old';[6] although originally 'prepared', not for the children of men, but 10 'for the devil and his angels'.[7]

The punishment of those who in spite of all the warnings of God resolve to have their portion with the devil and his angels[8] will, according to the ancient and not improper division, be either *poena damni*, what they lose, or *poena sensus*, what they feel.[9] After 15

---

[4] Cf. Virgil, *Aeneid*, vi.893-98:

> Sunt geminae Somni portae; quarum altera, fertur
> Cornea, qua veris facilis datur exitus umbris,
> Altera candenti perfecta nitens elephanto,
> Sed falsa ad caelum mittunt insomnia Manes.
> His ubi tum natum Anchises unaque Sibyllam
> Prosequitur dictis portaque emittit eburna.

Dryden's translation (which Wesley had in mind) stresses the image of 'the ivory gate':

> Two gates the silent house of Sleep adorn;
> Of polish'd iv'ry this, that of transparent horn:
> True visions thro' transparent horn arise;
> Thro' polish'd iv'ry pass deluding lies,
> Of various things discoursing as he pass'd,
> Anchises hither bends his steps at last.
> Then, thro' the gate of iv'ry, he dismiss'd
> His valiant offspring and divining guest.

Virgil's source was Homer, *Odyssey*, xix.562-67; cf. also No. 132, 'On Faith, Heb. 11:1', §16.

[5] Juvenal, *Satires*, ii.149, 152: 'There are [stories about] the Manes [ghosts and infernal deities] and the underworld . . . that children do not believe except those too young to be allowed in the public baths.' The Latin quotation, with a slightly different translation, is repeated in No. 132, 'On Faith, Heb. 11:1', §17. Hesiod also speaks of 'spiritual creatures' which Milton then versifies; see No. 70, 'The Case of Reason Impartially Considered', II.1 and n.

[6] Cf. Isa. 30:33.   [7] Matt. 25:41.   [8] *Ibid.*

[9] Cf. one of Wesley's favourite essays, Thomas Boston, *Human Nature in Its Fourfold State* (1720), State IV, Head VI, pp. 424 ff. The idea, however, comes from a familiar scholastic distinction between the punishment of bereavement and deprivation (*poena damni*), i.e., of what had been valued in this life, and the active punishment of the bodily

considering these separately I shall touch on a few additional circumstances, and conclude with two or three inferences.

    I. 1. And, first, let us consider the *poena damni*, the punishment of loss. This commences in that very moment wherein the soul is
5 separated from the body; in that instant the soul loses all those pleasures, the enjoyment of which depends on the outward senses. The smell, the taste, the touch delight no more; the organs that ministered to them are spoiled, and the objects that used to gratify them are removed far away. In the dreary regions
10 of the dead all these things are forgotten; or, if remembered, are only remembered with pain, seeing they are gone for ever. All the pleasures of the imagination are at an end.[10] There is no grandeur in the infernal region; there is nothing beautiful in those dark abodes, no light but that of livid flames. And nothing new, but one
15 unvaried scene of horror upon horror. There is no music but that of groans and shrieks, of weeping, wailing, and gnashing of teeth;[11] of curses and blasphemies against God, or cutting reproaches of one another. Nor is there anything to gratify the sense of honour: no, they are the heirs of shame and everlasting contempt.[12]
20   2. Thus are they totally separated from all the *things* they were fond of in the present world. At the same instant will commence another loss—that of all the *persons* whom they loved. They are torn away from their nearest and dearest relations, their wives, husbands, parents, children, and (what to some will be worse than
25 all this) the friend which was as their own soul.[13] All the pleasure they ever enjoyed in these is lost, gone, vanished away. For there is no friendship in hell.[14] Even the poet who affirms (though I know not on what authority),

Devil with devil damned
Firm concord holds;[15]

30

---

senses *(poena afflictiva seu sensus)*. Cf. Thomas, *Summa Theologia*, Appendix I, Q. 2, Art. 1 [Respondeo], and cf. R. J. Deferrari (ed), *A Lexicon of St. Thomas* (1948), 844, for definitions and citations from Thomas. The idea, of course, runs back to patristic eschatology; cf. the article on 'Hölle', in *Lexikon für Theologie und Kirche*.

[10] For more instances of this phrase, 'pleasures of the imagination', see No. 44, *Original Sin*, II.10 and n.

[11] See Matt. 8:12; 13:42.   [12] Dan. 12:2.

[13] See 1 Sam. 18:1, 3; 20:17; and No. 47, 'Heaviness through Manifold Temptations', III.4.

[14] The thesis of J.-P. Sartre, *Huis Clos* (Paris, Gallimard, 1947); translated by Stuart Gilbert as *No Exit* (New York, Knopf, 1948).

[15] Milton, *Paradise Lost*, ii.496-97.

does not affirm that there is any concord among the human fiends that inhabit the great abyss.

3. But they will then be sensible of a greater loss than that of all they enjoyed on earth. They have lost their place in Abraham's bosom,[16] in the paradise of God.[17] Hitherto indeed it hath not entered into their hearts to conceive what holy souls enjoy in the garden of God,[18] in the society of angels, and of the wisest and best men that have lived from the beginning of the world (not to mention the immense increase of knowledge which they will then undoubtedly receive). But they will then fully understand the value of what they have vilely cast away.

4. But as happy as the souls in paradise are, they are preparing for far greater happiness. For paradise is only the porch of heaven; and it is there the spirits of just men are made perfect.[19] It is in heaven only that there is the fullness of joy, the pleasures that are at God's right hand for evermore.[20] The loss of this by those unhappy spirits will be the completion of their misery. They will then know and feel that God alone is the centre of all created spirits; and consequently that a spirit made for God can have no rest out of him.[21] It seems that the Apostle had this in his view when he spoke of those 'who shall be punished with everlasting destruction from the presence of the Lord'.[22] Banishment from the presence of the Lord is the very essence of destruction to a spirit that was made for God. And if that banishment lasts for ever, it is 'everlasting destruction'.

Such is the loss sustained by those miserable creatures on whom that awful sentence will be pronounced, 'Depart from me, ye cursed!'[23] What an unspeakable curse, if there were no other! But alas! This is far from being the whole; for to the punishment of *loss* will be added the punishment of *sense*. What they lose implies unspeakable misery, which yet is inferior to what they feel. This it is which our Lord expresses in those emphatical words, 'where their worm dieth not, and the fire is not quenched'.

---

[16] Luke 16:22.   [17] Rev. 2:7.
[18] Ezek. 28:13; 31:8, 9.
[19] See Heb. 12:23. In Wesley's eschatology, paradise was regarded as only 'the ante-chamber of heaven' (cf. Nos. 84, *The Important Question*, II.4; and 115, 'Dives and Lazarus', I.3 and n.); he sharply distinguished this from what he understood of the Roman Catholic doctrine of purgatory.
[20] See Ps. 16:11 (AV).
[21] Augustine, *Confessions*, I.i; cf. No. 3, '*Awake, Thou That Sleepest*', II.5 and n.
[22] 2 Thess. 1:9.   [23] Matt. 25:41.

II. 1. From the time that sentence was pronounced upon man, 'Dust thou art, and unto dust thou shalt return,'[24] it was the custom of all nations, so far as we can learn, to commit dust to dust: it seemed natural to restore the bodies of the dead to the general mother earth. But in process of time another method obtained, chiefly among the rich and great, of burning the bodies of their relations, and frequently in a grand magnificent manner. For which purpose they erected huge funeral piles, with immense labour and expense. By either of these methods the body of man was soon restored to its parent dust. Either the worm or the fire soon consumed the well-wrought frame; after which the worm itself quickly died, and the fire was entirely quenched. But there is likewise a worm that belongs to the future state; and that is a worm that never dieth. And there is a fire hotter than that of the funeral pile; and it is a fire that will never be quenched.

2. The first thing intended by the worm that never dieth seems to be a guilty conscience, including self-condemnation, sorrow, shame, remorse, and a sense of the wrath of God. May not we have some conception of this by what is sometimes felt even in the present world? Is it not of this chiefly that Solomon speaks when he says, 'The spirit of a man may bear his infirmities', his infirmities or griefs of any other kind, 'but a wounded spirit who can bear?'[25] Who can bear the anguish of an awakened conscience, penetrated with a sense of guilt, and the arrows of the Almighty sticking in the soul, and drinking up the spirit![26] How many of the stout-hearted have sunk under it, and chose strangling rather than life![27] And yet what are these wounds, what is all this anguish of a soul while in this present world, in comparison of those they must suffer when their souls are wholly awakened to feel the wrath of an offended God! Add to these all unholy passions, fear, horror, rage; evil desires, desires that can never be satisfied. Add all unholy tempers, envy, jealousy, malice, and revenge; all of which will incessantly gnaw the soul, as the vulture was supposed to do the liver of Tityus.[28] To these if we

[24] Cf. Gen. 3:19.   [25] Cf. Prov. 18:14.   [26] See Job 6:4.   [27] See Job 7:15.

[28] Cf. Homer, *Odyssey*, xi.576-81. Tityus was 'a son of Earth' whose body covered 'nine acres' and who was punished for his assault upon Leto by having two vultures to tear away at his liver. This is to be distinguished from the more familiar Promethean myth in Hesiod's *Theogony* where, for stealing fire from heaven and giving it to man, Prometheus is punished by being chained to a rock where an eagle gnawed away at his liver even as it was also continually renewed. Cf. *Theogony*, 559-86 for the story of the 'crime' and 521-25 for the 'punishment'; cf. also No. 84, *The Important Question*, III.10. In No. 15, *The Great*

add hatred of God and all his creatures—all these united together may serve to give us some little, imperfect idea of the worm that never dieth.

3. We may observe a remarkable difference in the manner wherein our Lord speaks concerning the two parts of the future punishment. He says, 'Where *their* worm dieth not' of the one; 'where *the* fire is not quenched' of the other. This cannot be by chance. What then is the reason for this variation of the expression?

Does it not seem to be this? 'The fire' will be the same, essentially the same, to all that are tormented therein—only perhaps more intense to some than others, according to their degree of guilt. But 'their worm' will not, cannot be the same. It will be infinitely varied according to the various kinds as well as degrees of wickedness. This variety will arise partly from the just judgment of God, 'rewarding every man according to his works'.[29] For we cannot doubt but this rule will take place no less in hell than in heaven. As in heaven 'every man will receive his own reward', incommunicably his own, according to 'his own labours',[30] incommunicably his, that is, the whole tenor of his tempers, thoughts, words, and actions;[31] so undoubtedly every man in fact will receive his own bad reward, according to his own bad labour. And this likewise will be incommunicably *his own*, even as his labour was. Variety of punishment will likewise arise from the very nature of the thing. As they that bring most holiness to heaven will find most happiness there, so on the other hand it is not only true that the more wickedness a man brings to hell the more misery he will find there; but that this misery will be infinitely varied according to the various kinds of his wickedness. It was therefore proper to say 'the fire' in general, but 'their worm' in particular.

4. But it has been questioned by some whether there be any fire in hell—that is, any material fire. Nay, if there be any fire it is unquestionably material. For what is immaterial fire? The same as immaterial water or earth! Both the one and the other is absolute nonsense, a contradiction in terms. Either therefore we must affirm it to be material, or we deny its existence. But if we

---

Assize, III.2, Wesley defines pride, malice, revenge, rage, horror, despair as the 'dogs of hell'.
[29] Cf. Matt. 16:27.   [30] 1 Cor. 3:8.
[31] The phrase, 'incommunicably his own, according to "his own labours" ', is omitted in *SOSO* (1788) and subsequent edns.

granted them there is no fire at all there, what would they gain
thereby? Seeing this is allowed on all hands, that it is either fire
or something worse. And consider this: does not our Lord speak
as if it were real fire? No one can deny or doubt of this. Is it
5 possible then to suppose that the God of truth would speak in this
manner if it were not so? Does he design to fright his poor
creatures? What, with scarecrows? With vain shadows of things
that have no being? O let not anyone think so! Impute not such
folly to the Most High!

10   5. But others aver: 'It is not possible that fire should burn
always. For by the immutable law of nature it consumes whatever
is thrown into it. And by the same law, as soon as it has consumed
its fuel, it is itself consumed; it goes out.'

It is most true that in the present constitution of things, during
15 the present laws of nature, the element of fire does dissolve and
consume whatever is thrown into it. But here is the mistake: the
present laws of nature are not immutable.[32] When the heavens
and the earth shall flee away,[33] the present scene will be totally
changed; and with the present constitution of things, the present
20 laws of nature will cease. After this great change nothing will be
dissolved, nothing will be consumed any more. Therefore if it
were true that fire consumes all things now, it would not follow
that it would do the same after the whole frame of nature has
undergone that vast, universal change.

25   6. I say, 'If it were true that fire consumes *all things* now.' But
indeed it is not true. Has it not pleased God to give us already
some proof of what will be hereafter? Is not the *linum asbestum*, the
incombustible flax, known in most parts of Europe?[34] If you take a
towel or handkerchief made of this (one of which may now be
30 seen in the British Museum[35]) you may throw it into the hottest

[32] An echo of Malebranche's 'occasionalism', which Wesley found more congenial for
apologetic purposes than the Newtonian world-view of '[physical] laws'. Cf. Wesley's
letter to 'John Smith', June 25, 1746, §7; see also Malebranche's *Treatise Concerning the
Search After Truth* (1964), VI.ii.3.

[33] See Matt. 24:35, etc.

[34] Chambers's *Cyclopaedia* has a two-column article on asbestos and Wesley has more
than two pages on it in the *Survey* (1777), II.319-21. See also Peter Sterry, *Free Grace
Exalted* (1670), p. 12: 'They say of the Romans of old that they had a sort of linen that
would not be burnt in the fire, and after they had burned their dead as was their custom,
they took up the bones and wrapt them in that linen and therein burnt them to ashes
unmixed from the common ashes.' See also No. 54, 'On Eternity', §7 and n.

[35] In the *Survey, ibid.*, an experiment with the attempted burning of 'a handkerchief of
[asbestos]' is reported. The reference to the British Museum applies to the Sir Hans

fire, and when it is taken out again it will be observed, upon the nicest experiment, not to have lost one grain of its weight. Here therefore is a substance before our eyes, which even in the present constitution of things (as if it were an emblem of things to come) may remain in fire without being consumed. 5

7. Many writers have spoken of other bodily torments added to the being cast into the lake of fire. One of these, even pious Kempis, supposes that misers, for instance, have melted gold poured down their throats; and he supposes many other particular torments to be suited to men's particular sins.[36] Nay, 10 our great poet himself supposes the inhabitants of hell to undergo variety of tortures; not to continue always in the lake of fire, but to be frequently 'by harpy-footed furies haled'[37] into regions of ice, and then back again through 'extremes by change more fierce'.[38] But I find no word, no tittle of this, not the least hint of it, in all the 15 Bible. And surely this is too awful a subject to admit of such play of imagination. Let us keep to the written Word. It is torment enough to dwell with everlasting burnings.[39]

8. This is strongly illustrated by a fabulous story, taken from one of the eastern writers, concerning a Turkish king who, after 20 he had been guilty of all manner of wickedness, once did a good thing; for seeing a poor man falling into a pit, wherein he must have inevitably perished, and kicking him from it, he saved his life. The story adds that when for his enormous wickedness he was cast into hell, that foot wherewith he had saved the man's life 25 was permitted to lie out of the flames.[40] But allowing this to be a real case, what a poor comfort would it be! What if both feet were permitted to lie out of the flames, yea, and both hands, how little would it avail! Nay, if all the body were taken out, and placed where no fire touched it, and only one hand or one foot kept in a 30 burning fiery furnace, would the man meantime be much at ease? Nay, quite the contrary. Is it not common to say to a child, 'Put

Sloane Collection which, in Wesley's time, was in the great buildings on Great Russell Street. In 1826 this collection (with the 'towel or handkerchief' to which Wesley refers) was transferred to the new Museum of Natural History on West Cromwell Road.

[36] A puzzle; no such reference appears in Kempis, although there is a passage where it would have been relevant; cf. *Imitation*, i.24 (see Wesley's translation, *The Christian's Pattern*, 1735, pp. 56-61). Nor has any other likely source been located. For other references to Kempis, see No. 55, *On the Trinity*, §1 and n.

[37] Milton, *Paradise Lost*, ii.596.

[38] *Ibid.*, 599. [39] Isa. 33:14.

[40] π; source not identified.

your finger into that candle: can you bear it even for one minute? How then will you bear hell-fire!' Surely it would be torment enough to have the flesh burnt off from only one finger. What then will it be to have the whole body plunged into a lake of fire 5 burning with brimstone!⁴¹

III. It remains now only to consider two or three circumstances attending the never-dying worm and the unquenchable fire.

1. And first consider the company wherewith everyone is surrounded in that place of torment. It is not uncommon to hear 10 even condemned criminals in our public prisons say, 'O! I wish I was hanged out of the way, rather than to be plagued with these wretches that are round about me.' But what are the most abandoned wretches upon earth, compared to the inhabitants of hell? None of these are as yet perfectly wicked, emptied of every 15 spark of good; certainly not till this life is at an end; probably not till the day of judgment. Nor can any of these exert without control their whole wickedness on their fellow-creatures. Sometimes they are restrained by good men; sometimes even by bad. So even the torturers in the Roman Inquisition are 20 restrained by those that employ them when they suppose the sufferer cannot endure any more. They then order the executioners to forbear; because it is contrary to the rules of the house that a man should die upon the rack.⁴² And very frequently, when there is no human help, they are restrained by God, who 25 hath set them their bounds which they cannot pass, and saith, 'Hitherto shall ye come, and no farther.'⁴³ Yea, so mercifully hath God ordained that the very extremity of pain causes a suspension of it. The sufferer faints away, and so (for a time at least) sinks into insensibility. But the inhabitants of hell are perfectly wicked, 30 having no spark of goodness remaining. And they are restrained by none from exerting to the uttermost their total wickedness. Not by men; none will be restrained from evil by his companions in damnation. And not by God; for he hath forgotten them, hath

⁴¹ Rev. 19:20.

⁴² Wesley's knowledge of the Inquisition, apart from the common store of anti-Roman lore from which this detail probably comes, was largely based on Michael Geddes, *A View of the Inquisition of Portugal; with a list of the Prisoners which came out of the Inquisitions of Lisbon, in an Act of Faith* (1682), in *Miscellaneous Tracts* (1730), I.385-443; and Samuel Chandler, *The History of Persecution* (1736). See also Nos. 82, 'On Temptation', II.2; and 91, 'On Charity', III.10.

⁴³ Cf. Job 38.11.

delivered them over to the tormentors.[44] And the devils need not
fear, like their instruments upon earth, lest they should expire
under the torture. They can die no more: they are strong to
sustain whatever the united malice, skill, and strength of angels
can inflict upon them. And their angelic tormentors have time 5
sufficient to vary their torments a thousand ways. How infinitely
may they vary one single torment—horrible appearances!
Whereby, there is no doubt, an evil spirit, if permitted, could
terrify the stoutest man upon earth to death.

2. Consider, secondly, that all these torments of body and soul 10
are without intermission. They have no respite from pain; but 'the
smoke of their torment ascendeth up day and night.'[45] Day and
night! That is speaking according to the constitution of the
present world, wherein God has wisely and graciously ordained
that day and night should succeed each other, so that in every four 15
and twenty hours there comes a

> Daily sabbath, made to rest
> Toiling man and weary beast.[46]

Hence we seldom undergo much labour, or suffer much pain,
before 20

> Tired nature's kind restorer, balmy sleep,[47]

steals upon us by insensible degrees, and brings an interval of
ease. But although the damned have uninterrupted night, it
brings no interruption of their pain. No sleep accompanies that
darkness: whatever either ancient or modern poets, either Homer 25
or Milton, dream, there is no sleep either in hell or heaven.[48] And
be their suffering ever so extreme, be their pain ever so intense,
there is no possibility of their fainting away—no, not for a
moment.

Again. The inhabitants of earth are frequently diverted from 30
attending to what is afflictive by the cheerful light of the sun, the
vicissitudes of the seasons, 'the busy hum of men',[49] and a

---

[44] See Matt. 18:34.   [45] Cf. Rev. 14:11.

[46] Mark Le Pla, *A Paraphrase on the Song of the Three Children*, st. 21, ll. 7-8 (cf. Wesley,
A Collection of Moral and Sacred Poems [1744], II.119).

[47] Cf. Edward Young, *Night Thoughts*, i.1 (Wesley, *A Collection of Moral and Sacred
Poems* [1744], II.229); 'Tired Nature's sweet restorer, balmy sleep!'

[48] See No. 51, *The Good Steward*, II.10 and n.

[49] Milton, *L'Allegro*, l. 118. Cf. Wesley's Preface to *Sermons* (1746), §5, where he speaks
of 'the busy ways of men'.

thousand objects that roll around them with endless variety. But the inhabitants of hell have nothing to divert them from their torments even for a moment:

> Total eclipse: no sun, no moon![50]—

5 no change of seasons or of companions.[51] There is no business, but one uninterrupted scene of horror, to which they must be all attention. They have no interval of inattention or stupidity: they are all eye, all ear, all sense. Every instant of their duration it may be said of their whole frame that they are

10
> . . . tremblingly alive all o'er,
> And smart and agonize at every pore.[52]

3. And of this duration *there is no end!* What a thought is this! Nothing but eternity is the term of their torment! And who can count the drops of rain, or the sands of the sea, or the days of 15 eternity? Every suffering is softened if there is any hope, though distant, of deliverance from it. But here,

> Hope never comes, that comes to all[53]

the inhabitants of the upper world! What, sufferings never do end!

20
> Never! Where sinks the soul at that dread sound!
> Into a gulf how dark, and how profound![54]

Suppose millions of days, of years, of ages elapsed; still we are only on the threshold of eternity! Neither the pain of body nor of soul is any nearer at an end than it was millions of ages ago. When 25 they are once cast into τὸ πῦρ τὸ ἄσβεστον[55] (how emphatical!),[56] 'the fire, the unquenchable', all is concluded: 'their worm dieth not, and the fire is not quenched!'[57]

---

[50] George Frederick Handel, *Samson, An Oratorio* (1742):

> Total eclipse: No sun, no moon,
> All dark amidst the blaze of noon!

Cf. Milton, *Samson Agonistes*, ll. 80-81.

[51] See above, I.2: 'no friendship in hell'.   [52] Pope, *Essay on Man*, i.197-98.

[53] Milton, *Paradise Lost*, i.66-67; see also No. 84, *The Important Question*, II.7.

[54] Cf. *The Last Day*, iii.156-57; see No. 54, 'On Eternity', §15 and n.

[55] Mark 9:43.   [56] Cf. No. 72, 'Of Evil Angels', II.10.

[57] Mark 9:44, 46, 48. Cf. No. 15, *The Great Assize*, III.1, where endless torment is also affirmed.

Such is the account which the Judge of all[58] gives of the punishment which he has ordained for impenitent sinners. And what a counterbalance may the consideration of this be to the violence of any temptation! In particular to the fear of man, the very use to which it is applied by our Lord himself. 'Be not afraid of them that kill the body, and after that have no more that they can do: but fear him who after he hath killed hath power to cast into hell.'[b]

What a guard may these considerations be against any temptation from pleasure! Will you lose, for any of these poor, earthly pleasures which perish in the using (to say nothing of the present substantial pleasures of religion), the pleasures of paradise, such 'as eye hath not seen, nor ear heard, neither hath it entered into our hearts to conceive'?[59] Yea, the pleasures of heaven, the society of angels, and of the spirits of just men made perfect,[60] the conversing face to face with God your Father, your Saviour, your Sanctifier, and the drinking of those rivers of pleasure[61] that are at God's right hand for evermore?[62]

Are you tempted by pain either of body or mind? O compare present things with future. What is the pain of body which you do or may endure, to that of lying in a lake of fire burning with brimstone?[63] What is any pain of mind, any fear, anguish, sorrow, compared to 'the worm that never dieth'? *That never dieth!* This is the sting of all! As for our pains on earth, blessed be God, they are not eternal. There are some intervals to relieve, and there is some period to finish them. When we ask a friend that is sick how he does, 'I am in pain now,' says he, 'but I hope to be easy soon.' This is a sweet mitigation of the present uneasiness. But how dreadful would his case be if he should answer: 'I am all over pain, and I shall never be eased of it. I lie under exquisite torment of body and horror of soul; and I shall feel it for ever.' Such is the case of the damned sinners in hell. Suffer any pain, then, rather than come into that place of torment.[64]

I conclude with one more reflection, taken from Dr. Watts:

---

[b] Luke 12:4-5.

---

[58] Heb. 12:23.
[59] Cf. 1 Cor. 2:9.
[60] Heb. 12:23.
[61] See Ps. 36:8.
[63] Rev. 19:20.

[62] See Ps. 16:11 (AV).
[64] See Luke 16:28.

It demands our highest gratitude that we who have long ago deserved this misery are not yet plunged into it, while there are thousands who have been adjudged to this place of punishment before they had continued so long in sin as many of us have done. What an instance is it of divine goodness that we are not under this
5 fiery vengeance! Have we not seen many sinners, on our right and left, cut off in their sins? And what but the tender mercy of God hath spared us week after week, month after month, and given us space for repentance? What shall we render unto the Lord for all his patience and long-suffering, even to this day? How often have we incurred the sentence of condemnation by our repeated
10 rebellion against God? And yet we are still alive in his presence, and are hearing the words of hope and salvation. O let us look back and shudder at the thoughts of that dreadful precipice, on the edge of which we have so long wandered! Let us fly for refuge to the hope that is set before us, and give a thousand thanks to the divine mercy that we are not plunged into this perdition.[65]

15 Newport, Isle of Wight, Oct. 10, 1782[66]

---

[65] An abridgement and paraphrase of Watts's longer and more graceful 'Reflection V', in his Discourse XII, 'The Nature of the Punishments in Hell' (on Mark 9:46), in *The World to Come* . . . ; see *Works*, I.724.
[66] Place and date as in *AM*.

OF THE CHURCH

AN INTRODUCTORY COMMENT

Wesley spent the month of September 1785 in and around Bristol. This was the year after the Deed of Declaration and after Wesley's 'ordinations' of Coke, Whatcoat, and Vasey for their ministries in America. The Deed and the ordinations had been widely taken, not without reason, as portents of separation from the Church of England,[1] despite Wesley's oft-repeated disavowals of all such intentions. Indeed, the Journal entry for Sunday, September 4, tells us of his reaction to this continuing suspicion: 'Finding a report had been spread abroad that I was going to leave the Church, to satisfy those that were grieved concerning it, I openly declared in the evening that I had now no more thought of separating from the Church than I had forty years ago.'[2] He went beyond the 'open declaration'; he began to write this sermon, 'Of the Church,' the first written summary of his ecclesiology. It was finished on September 28, and published in the Arminian Magazine *for the following January and February (1786), IX.8-15, 71-75, without a title but numbered as 'Sermon XXXI.' Tyerman omits it from his list of Wesley's 'original sermons [for the year 1785] which are well worth reading' (*Life *of Wesley, III.470). Wesley's reasons for its particular placement in* SOSO, *VI.171-90, can only be conjectured. It was not reprinted in his lifetime.*

One is bound to be impressed by Wesley's wholly unselfconscious assumption that, even after all he had done that would inevitably lead to separation, he was, and always had been, a devoted and loyal Anglican. He speaks quite naturally of 'our [Anglican] liturgy', as when he cites the eucharistic prayer 'for the whole state of Christ's church militant here on earth' (§5). His personal definition of church (§14) is, or so he claims, 'exactly agreeable to the nineteenth article of our church' (§16), although he feels free to interpret this article more comprehensively than its authors had ever intended.[3] However, his final conclusions are

---

[1] Cf. Frank Baker, *John Wesley and the Church of England*, chs. 13–16.

[2] JWJ, Sept. 4-30, 1785.

[3] So as, e.g., §§17–19, to include in 'the church' all true believers among the Dissenting churches, and even those in the Church of Rome.

neither Anglican, Lutheran, nor Calvinist. The essence of the church, for Wesley, need not be sought in its visible institutions, not even some invisible numerus electorum. *The church as Body of Christ is the company of all true believers, 'holy' because its members are themselves holy (§28). This is, therefore, an unstable blend of Anglican and Anabaptist ecclesiologies; it is also one of Wesley's more daring syntheses. Its outworkings in the subsequent histories of Methodist and Anglican ecclesiology have yet to be probed as deeply as they deserve, which is also to say that its ecumenical significance has yet to be fully appreciated.*

Of the Church

Ephesians 4:1-6

I beseech you that ye walk worthy of the vocation wherewith ye are called, with all lowliness and meekness, with long-suffering, forbearing one another in love; endeavouring to keep the unity of the Spirit in the bond of peace. There is one body, and one Spirit, even as ye are called in one hope of your calling; one Lord, one faith, one baptism; one God and Father of all, who is above all, and through all, and in you all.

1. How much do we almost continually hear about the Church! With many it is matter of daily conversation. And yet how few understand what they talk of! How few know what the term means! A more ambiguous word than this, the 'church', is scarce to be found in the English language. It is sometimes taken for a building set apart for public worship, sometimes for a congregation or body of people united together in the service of God. It is only in the latter sense that it is taken in the ensuing discourse.

2. It may be taken indifferently for any number of people, how small or great soever. As 'where two or three are met together in his name',[1] there is Christ; so (to speak with St. Cyprian) 'where two or three believers are met together, there is a church.'[2] Thus

---

[1] Cf. Matt. 18:20.

[2] Cyprian, *On the Unity of the Church*, xii (*Fathers of the Church*, New York, 1947, XXXVI.107; cf. also *Ancient Christian Writers*, London, 1957, 25:54-55).

it is that St. Paul, writing to Philemon, mentions 'the church which is in his house';[3] plainly signifying that even a Christian family may be termed a church.

3. Several of those whom God had 'called out' of the world (so the original word properly signifies),[4] united together in one congregation, formed a larger church: as the church at Jerusalem, that is, all those in Jerusalem whom God had so called. But considering how swiftly these were multiplied after the day of Pentecost, it cannot be supposed that they could continue to assemble in one place; especially as they had not then any large place, neither would they have been permitted to build one. In consequence they must have divided themselves, even at Jerusalem, into several distinct congregations. In like manner, when St. Paul several years after wrote to the church in Rome (directing his letter 'to all that are in Rome, called to be saints')[5] it cannot be supposed that they had any one building capable of containing them all; but they were divided into several congregations, assembling in several parts of the city.

4. The first time that the Apostle uses the word 'church' is in his preface to the former Epistle to the Corinthians: 'Paul, called to be an apostle of Jesus Christ, unto the church of God which is at Corinth'; the meaning of which expression is fixed by the following words, 'to them that are sanctified in Christ Jesus, with all that in every place' (not Corinth only; so it was a kind of circular letter) 'call upon the name of Jesus Christ our Lord, both yours and ours'.[6] In the inscription of his second letter to the Corinthians he speaks still more explicitly: 'Unto the church of God which is at Corinth, with all the saints that are in all Achaia'.[7] Here he plainly includes all the churches or Christian congregations which were in the whole province.

5. He frequently uses the word in the plural number. So Gal. 1:2: 'Paul, an apostle, . . . unto the churches of Galatia'—that is, the Christian congregations dispersed throughout that country. In all these places (and abundantly more might be cited) the word church or churches means, not the buildings where the

---

[3] Philem. 2; cf. Col. 4:15.

[4] Wesley here assumes the lexical kinship of κλήσεως ἐκλήθητε (Eph. 4:1) and ἐκκλησία with their common verbal root, καλέω. But see K. L. Schmidt, 'ἐκκλησία' in Gerhard Kittel, ed., *Theological Dictionary of the New Testament*; cf. 'καλέω', ibid.

[5] Rom. 1:7. [6] Cf. 1 Cor. 1:1-2.

[7] 2 Cor. 1:1.

Christians assembled (as it frequently does in the English tongue) but the people that used to assemble there—one or more Christian congregations. But sometimes the word 'church' is taken in Scripture in a still more extensive meaning, as including all the Christian congregations that are upon the face of the earth. And in this sense we understand it in our liturgy[8] when we say, 'Let us pray for the whole state of Christ's church militant here on earth.'[9] In this sense it is unquestionably taken by St. Paul in his exhortation to the elders of Ephesus, 'Take heed to the church of God, which he hath purchased with his own blood.'[a] The 'church' here undoubtedly means the catholic or universal church, that is, all the Christians under heaven.

6. Who those are that are properly 'the church of God' the Apostle shows at large, and that in the clearest and most decisive manner, in the passage above cited; wherein he likewise instructs all the members of the church how to 'walk worthy of the vocation wherewith they are called'.[10]

[I.][11] 7. Let us consider, first, who are properly 'the church of God'? What is the true meaning of that term? 'The church at Ephesus', as the Apostle himself explains it, means, 'the saints', the holy persons, 'that are in Ephesus',[12] and there assemble themselves together to worship God the Father and his Son Jesus Christ—whether they did this in one, or (as we may probably suppose) in several places. But it is the church in general, the catholic or universal church, which the Apostle here considers as 'one body'; comprehending not only the Christians 'in the house of Philemon',[13] or any one family; not only the Christians of one congregation, of one city, of one province or nation; but all the persons upon the face of the earth who answer the character here given. The several particulars contained therein we may now more distinctly consider.

8. 'There is one Spirit' who animates all these, all the living

---

[a] Acts 20:28.

---

[8] Note this unselfconscious citation of the BCP as 'our'.

[9] 'The Prayer for the Church' in the BCP, Communion.

[10] Cf. Eph. 4:1.

[11] Wesley's basic division of this sermon is by consecutively numbered sections, but he apparently intended to introduce a parallel numbering of three major divisions, prefixing 'II' to §20, which would imply an omitted 'I' at this point and 'III' at §27.

[12] Eph. 1:1.   [13] Cf. Philem 2.

members of the church of God. Some understand hereby the Holy Spirit himself, the fountain of all spiritual life. And it is certain, 'If any man have not the Spirit of Christ, he is none of his.'[14] Others understand it of those spiritual gifts and holy dispositions which are afterward mentioned.

9. 'There is', in all those that have received this Spirit, 'one hope', a hope full of immortality.[15] They know, to die is not to be lost: their prospect extends beyond the grave. They can cheerfully say, 'Blessed be the God and Father of our Lord Jesus Christ, who, according to his abundant mercy, hath begotten us again unto a lively hope by the resurrection of Jesus Christ from the dead, to an inheritance incorruptible, and undefiled, and that fadeth not away.'[16]

10. 'There is one Lord' who has now dominion over them, who has set up his kingdom in their hearts, and reigns over all those that are partakers of this hope. To obey him, to run the way of his commandments, is their glory and joy. And while they are doing this with a willing mind they, as it were, 'sit in heavenly places with Christ Jesus'.[17]

11. 'There is one faith,' which is the free gift of God, and is the ground of their hope. This is not barely the faith of a heathen;[18] namely, a belief that 'there is a God', and that he is gracious and just, and consequently 'a rewarder of them that diligently seek him'.[19] Neither is it barely the faith of a devil; though this goes much farther than the former. For the devil believes, and cannot but believe, all that is written both in the Old and New Testament to be true. But it is the faith of St. Thomas, teaching him to say with holy boldness, 'My Lord and my God.'[20] It is the faith which enables every true Christian believer to testify with St. Paul, 'The life which I now live I live by faith in the Son of God, who loved me and gave himself for me.'[21]

12. 'There is one baptism,' which is the outward sign our one Lord has been pleased to appoint of all that inward and spiritual grace which he is continually bestowing upon his church. It is likewise a precious means whereby this faith and hope are given to those that diligently seek him. Some indeed have been inclined

---

[14] Rom. 8:9.
[15] Wisd. 3:4; cf. No. 72, 'Of Evil Angels', II.4 and n. Also note the echoes here of the older debates between the Quakers and the Anglicans.
[16] 1 Pet. 1:3-4.   [17] Cf. Eph. 2:6.
[18] For Wesley's categories of faith, see No. 1, *Salvation by Faith*, I.2 and n.
[19] Heb. 11:6.   [20] John 20:28.   [21] Cf. Gal. 2:20.

to interpret this in a figurative sense, as if it referred to that baptism of the Holy Ghost which the apostles received at the day of Pentecost, and which in a lower degree is given to all believers.[22] But it is a stated rule in interpreting Scripture never to
5 depart from the plain, literal sense, unless it implies an absurdity.[23] And beside, if we thus understood it, it would be a needless repetition, as being included in, 'There is one spirit.'

13. 'There is one God and Father of all' that have the Spirit of adoption, which 'crieth in their hearts, Abba, Father';[24] which
10 'witnesseth' continually 'with their spirits'[25] that they are the children of God; 'who is above all'—the Most High, the Creator, the Sustainer, the Governor of the whole universe. 'And through all'—pervading all space, filling heaven and earth:

Totam
15 *Mens agitans molem, et magno se corpore miscens.*[26]

'And in you all'—in a peculiar manner living in you that are one body by one spirit:

Making your souls his loved abode,
The temples of indwelling God.[27]

20 14. Here then is a clear unexceptionable answer to that question, What is the church? The catholic or universal church is all the persons in the universe whom God hath so called out of the world as to entitle them to the preceding character; as to be 'one body', united by 'one spirit'; having 'one faith, one hope, one
25 baptism; one God and Father of all, who is above all, and through all, and in them all.'

---

[22] An allusion to the views of Quakers and pentecostalists who had either rejected sacramental baptism or had claimed that 'the baptism of the Spirit' superseded it.

[23] For an earlier version of this basic hermeneutical principle, see No. 21, 'Sermon on the Mount, I', §6 and n.

[24] Cf. Gal. 4:6.   [25] Cf. Rom. 8:16.

[26] Cf. Virgil, *Aeneid*, vi. 726-27:

Totamque infusa per artus
Mens agitat molem et magno se corpore miscet.

The all-informing soul,
That fills, pervades, and actuates the whole.

Cf. also Nos. 77, 'Spiritual Worship', I.6; 118, 'On the Omnipresence of God', II.1; *An Earnest Appeal*, §19 (11:51 in this edn.); and *The Doctrine of Original Sin*, Pt. I, I.13.

[27] Cf. Charles Wesley, 'Groaning for the Spirit of Adoption', in John and Charles Wesley, *Hymns and Sacred Poems* (1740), p. 132 (*Poet. Wks.*, I.308).

15. That part of this great body, of the universal church, which inhabits any one kingdom or nation, we may properly term a 'national' church, as the Church of France, the Church of England, the Church of Scotland. A smaller part of the universal church are the Christians that inhabit one city or town, as the church of Ephesus, and the rest of the seven churches mentioned in the Revelation. Two or three Christian believers united together are a church in the narrowest sense of the word. Such was the church in the house of Philemon, and that in the house of Nymphas, mentioned Col. 4:15. A particular church may therefore consist of any number of members, whether two or three, or two or three millions. But still, whether it be larger or smaller, the same idea is to be preserved. They are one body, and have one Spirit, one Lord, one hope, one faith, one baptism, one God and Father of all.

16. This account is exactly agreeable to the nineteenth Article of our Church, the Church of England—only the Article includes a little more than the Apostle has expressed.

Of the Church

The visible church of Christ is a congregation of faithful men, in which the pure word of God is preached, and the sacraments be duly administered.[28]

It may be observed that at the same time our Thirty-nine Articles were compiled and published a Latin translation of them was published by the same authority. In this the words were *coetus credentium*,[29] 'a congregation of believers', plainly showing that by 'faithful men'[30] the compilers meant men endued with 'living faith'.[31] This brings the Article to a still nearer agreement to the account given by the Apostle.

But it may be doubted whether the Article speaks of a

[28] The first half of the first sentence of Art. XIX which, in turn, had been borrowed from Art. VIII of the *Augsburg Confession* (1530).

[29] An interesting conflation here. The Latin text of the Article (1517) reads *coetus fidelium*; but in Art. VIII of the *Augsburg Confession* the church is defined as a *congregatio sanctorum et vere credentium*. For evidence that Wesley preferred his conflated phrase, see *An Earnest Appeal*, §76 (11:77 in this edn.); see also his letter to his brother Charles, Aug. 19, 1785. For the official texts of the Confession and of the Articles, see Philip Schaff, *Creeds*, III.3-73, 486-516.

[30] This is English for *fidelium*. Thus, it would seem that Wesley had both the Anglican Article and the Lutheran Confession somehow conflated in his mind.

[31] The official texts (as in Arts. XII and XXIX) read 'lively' for 'living', as does 'A Catechism' in the BCP. 'The Prayer for the Church' in the Order of Holy Communion refers to God's 'true and lively Word'.

particular church or of the church universal. The title, 'Of the Church', seems to have reference to the catholic church. But the second clause of the Article mentions the particular churches of Jerusalem, Antioch, Alexandria, and Rome. Perhaps it was in-
5　tended to take in both—so to define the universal church as to keep in view the several particular churches of which it is composed.

17. These things being considered, it is easy to answer that question, What is 'the Church of England'? It is that part, those members, of the universal church, who are inhabitants of
10　England. The Church of England is that 'body' of men in England in whom 'there is one Spirit, one hope, one Lord, one faith', which have 'one baptism', and 'one God and Father of all'. This and this alone is the Church of England, according to the doctrine of the Apostle.

15　18. But the definition of a church laid down in the Article includes not only this but much more, by that remarkable addition, 'in which the pure Word of God is preached, and the sacraments be duly administered'. According to this definition those congregations in which the pure Word of God (a strong
20　expression) is not preached are no parts either of the Church of England or the church catholic. As neither are those in which the sacraments are not duly administered.

19. I will not undertake to defend the accuracy of this definition. I dare not exclude from the church catholic all those
25　congregations in which any unscriptural doctrines which cannot be affirmed to be 'the pure Word of God' are sometimes, yea, frequently preached. Neither all those congregations in which the sacraments are not 'duly administered'. Certainly if these things are so the Church of Rome is not so much as a part of the catholic
30　church; seeing therein neither is 'the pure Word of God' preached nor the sacraments 'duly administered'. Whoever they are that have 'one Spirit, one hope, one Lord, one faith, one God and Father of all', I can easily bear with their holding wrong opinions, yea, and superstitious modes of worship. Nor would I
35　on these accounts scruple still to include them within the pale of the catholic church. Neither would I have any objection to receive them, if they desired it, as members of the Church of England.[32]

---

[32] An echo of the same point about theological opinions already made in No. 39, 'Catholic Spirit', *passim*. For Wesley's pluralism and vision of 'comprehension' cf. No. 7, 'The Way to the Kingdom', I.6 and n.

II.[33] 20. We proceed now to the second point. What is it to 'walk worthy of the vocation wherewith we are called'?

It should always be remembered that the word 'walk' in the language of the Apostle is of a very extensive signification. It includes all our inward and outward motions, all our thoughts, and words, and actions. It takes in not only everything we do, but everything we either speak or think. It is therefore no small thing to walk, in this sense of the word, 'worthy of the vocation wherewith we are called'—to think, speak, and act, in every instance in a manner worthy of our Christian calling.

21. We are called to walk, first, 'with all lowliness'; to have that mind in us which was also in Christ Jesus,[34] not to think of ourselves more highly than we ought to think,[35] to be little, and poor, and mean, and vile in our own eyes; to know ourselves as also we are known[36] by him to whom all hearts are open;[37] to be deeply sensible of our own unworthiness, of the universal depravity of our nature (in which dwelleth no good thing[38]), prone to all evil, averse to all good, insomuch that we are not only sick but dead in trespasses and sins,[39] till God breathes upon the dry bones,[40] and creates life by the fruit of his lips.[41] And suppose this is done, suppose he has now quickened us, infusing life into our dead souls; yet how much of the carnal mind remains! How prone is our heart still to depart from the living God! What a tendency to sin remains in our heart, although we know our past sins are forgiven![42] And how much sin, in spite of all our endeavours, cleaves both to our words and actions! Who can be duly sensible how much remains in him of his natural enmity to God? Or how far he is still alienated from God by the ignorance that is in him?[43]

22. Yea, suppose God has now thoroughly cleansed our heart, and scattered the last remains of sin; yet how can we be sensible enough of our own helplessness, our utter inability to all good, unless we are every hour, yea, every moment, endued with power from on high? Who is able to think one good thought, or to form one good desire, unless by that Almighty power which worketh in

[33] See §7 above n. 11, p. 48.
[34] See Phil. 2:5.
[35] See Rom. 12:3.
[36] See 1 Cor. 13:12.
[37] BCP, Communion, Collect for Purity.
[38] Rom. 7:18.
[39] Eph. 2:1.
[40] See Ezek. 37:1-10.
[41] See Isa. 57:19.
[42] An echo of the problem of the residue of sin in believers; cf. No. 13, *On Sin in Believers*, intro., I.6, III.1-9, and n.
[43] See Eph. 4:18.

us both to will and to do of his good pleasure?[44] We have need
even in this state of grace to be thoroughly and continually
penetrated with a sense of this. Otherwise we shall be in a
perpetual danger of robbing God of his honour, by glorying in
5 something we have received as though we had not received it.

23. When our inmost soul is thoroughly tinctured therewith, it
remains that we be 'clothed with humility'.[45] The word used by St.
Peter seems to imply that we be covered with it as with a surtout;[46]
that we be all humility, both within and without, tincturing all we
10 think, speak, and do. Let all our actions spring from this fountain;
let all our words breathe this spirit; that all men may know we have
been with Jesus, and have learned of him to be lowly in heart.

24. And being taught of him who was meek as well as lowly in
heart,[47] we shall then be enabled to 'walk with all meekness', being
15 taught of him who teacheth as never man taught,[48] to be meek as
well as lowly in heart. This implies not only a power over anger,
but over all violent and turbulent passions. It implies the having
all our passions in due proportion; none of them either too strong
or too weak, but all duly balanced with each other, all subordinate
20 to reason; and reason directed by the Spirit of God. Let this
equanimity govern your whole souls, that your thoughts may all
flow in an even stream, and the uniform tenor of your words and
actions be suitable thereto. In this patience you will then 'possess
your souls',[49] which are not our own while we are tossed by unruly
25 passions. And by this all men may know that we are indeed
followers of the meek and lowly Jesus.

25. Walk with all long-suffering. This is nearly related to
meekness, but implies something more. It carries on the victory
already gained over all your turbulent passions, notwithstanding
30 all the powers of darkness, all the assaults of evil men or evil
spirits. It is patiently triumphant over all opposition, and
unmoved though all the waves and storms thereof go over you.
Though provoked ever so often, it is still the same, quiet and
unshaken; never being 'overcome of evil, but overcoming evil
35 with good'.[50]

---

[44] See Phil. 2:13.
[45] 1 Pet. 5:5.
[46] A French loanword already defined by Johnson, *Dictionary*, as 'a large coat worn over all the rest'—which is to say, a mantle, as here.
[47] See Matt. 11:29.   [48] See John 7:46.
[49] Cf. Luke 21:19.   [50] Cf. Rom. 12:21.

26. The 'forbearing one another in love' seems to mean not only the not resenting anything, and the not avenging yourselves; not only the not injuring, hurting, or grieving each other, either by word or deed; but also the bearing one another's burdens;[51] yea, and lessening them by every means in our power. It implies the sympathizing with them in their sorrows, afflictions, and infirmities; the bearing them up when without our help they would be liable to sink under their burdens; the endeavouring to lift their sinking heads, and to strengthen their feeble knees.[52]

[III.][53] 27. Lastly: the true members of the church of Christ 'endeavour', with all possible diligence, with all care and pains, with unwearied patience (and all will be little enough), 'to keep the unity of the Spirit in the bond of peace'; to preserve inviolate the same spirit of lowliness and meekness, of long-suffering, mutual forbearance and love; and all these cemented and knit together by that sacred tie, the peace of God filling the heart. Thus only can we be and continue living members of that church which is the body of Christ.

28. Does it not clearly appear from this whole account why, in the ancient Creed commonly called the Apostles', we term the universal or catholic church, 'the holy catholic church'? How many wonderful reasons have been found out for giving it this appellation! One learned man informs us, 'The church is called holy because Christ the head of it is holy.' Another eminent author affirms, 'It is so called because all its ordinances are designed to promote holiness;' and yet another, 'Because our Lord *intended* that all the members of the church should be holy.'[54] Nay, the shortest and the plainest reason that can be given, and the only true one, is: the church is called 'holy' because it is holy; because every member thereof is holy, though in different

---

[51] See Gal. 6:2.
[52] See Job 4:4.
[53] See §7, above.
[54] A drastic oversimplification of a complex question about the holiness of the church that runs back at least to Novatian and Cyprian, to the Donatists and Augustine, and which had become focused in the debate about 'the *marks* of the church': i.e., 'one, *holy*, catholic, and apostolic'. Cf. Heinrich Schmid, *Doctrinal Theology of the Evangelical Lutheran Church*, p. 588; and Heinrich Heppe, *Reformed Dogmatics*, pp. 662-63. From his own time and tradition, Wesley is echoing the discussion of 'The Holy Catholick Church' in John Pearson's magisterial *An Exposition of the Creed* (1659), Art. IX, 343-45. Wesley's own conclusion is closer to the Donatists and Anabaptists than to most of his fellow Anglicans; cf. Edmund Gibson, *Codex Juris Ecclesiastici Anglicani* (1713), Title I, chs. i, vi.

degrees, as he that called them is holy.[55] How clear is this! If the church, as to the very essence of it, is a body of believers, no man that is not a Christian believer can be a member of it. If this whole body be animated by one spirit, and endued with one faith and 5 one hope of their calling; then he who has not that spirit, and faith, and hope, is no member of this body. It follows that not only no common swearer, no sabbath-breaker, no drunkard, no whoremonger, no thief, no liar, none that lives in any outward sin; but none that is under the power of anger or pride, no lover of the 10 world—in a word, none that is dead to God—can be a member of his church.

29. Can anything then be more absurd than for men to cry out, 'the Church! the Church!'[56] and to pretend to be very zealous for it, and violent defenders of it; while they themselves have neither 15 part nor lot therein,[57] nor indeed know what the church is? And yet the hand of God is in this very thing! Even in this his wonderful wisdom appears, directing their mistake to his own glory, and causing 'the earth to help the woman'.[58] Imagining that they are members of it themselves, the men of the world 20 frequently defend the church. Otherwise the wolves that surround the little flock on every side would in a short time tear them in pieces. And for this very reason it is not wise to provoke them more than is unavoidable. Even on this ground let us, if it be possible, as much as lieth in us, live peaceably with all men.[59] 25 Especially as we know not how soon God may call them too out of the kingdom of Satan into the kingdom of his dear Son.[60]

30. In the meantime let all those who are real members of the church see that they walk holy and unblameable in all things. 'Ye are the light of the world!' Ye are 'a city set upon a hill, and cannot

[55] See 1 Pet. 1:15.

[56] Cf. Wesley's *Notes* on Matt. 22:14: 'Many hear [the Gospel], few believe. Yea, many are members of the visible but few of *the invisible church*.' In CWJ, Oct. 27, 1739, there is a complaint against 'our modern Pharisees' who keep only to a minimum of outward observances. 'And yet these men cry out, "The Church! The Church!" when they themselves will not hear the church. . . .' This phrase ('The Church! The Church!') had been a popular mob outcry, as in the Sacheverell riots of 1709; cf. Thomas Hearne, *Reliquiae Hernianae*, I.187-88 (Mar. 4, 1710), and in the Lord Gordon riots of 1780. Addison mentions the cry in *The Spectator*, No. 567, July 14, 1714: 'These people may cry, "Church, Church", as long as they please, . . . but the proof of the pudding is in the eating.'

[57] See Acts 8:21.   [58] Cf. Rev. 12:16.
[59] See Rom. 12:18.
[60] Col. 1:13.

be hid. O let your light shine before men!"[61] Show them your faith by your works.[62] Let them see by the whole tenor of your conversation that your hope is all laid up above! Let all your words and actions evidence the spirit whereby you are animated! Above all things, let your love abound.[63] Let it extend to every child of 5 man; let it overflow to every child of God. By this let all men know whose disciples ye are, because you love one another.[64]

Bristol, Sept. 28, 1785[65]

---

[61] Cf. Matt. 5:14, 16.
[62] See Jas. 2:18.
[63] See Phil. 1:9.
[64] See John 13:35.
[65] Place and date as in *AM*.

ON SCHISM

AN INTRODUCTORY COMMENT

Talk of separation of the Methodists from the Church of England would not down either amongst certain Anglicans who feared it or many Methodists who would be content with nothing less. In both groups, the terms 'separation' and 'schism' were understood as synonymous. Wesley continued strenuously to deny any intention of separation, and effectively to block the designs of his own separatists. His own ideas about schism were, however, both interesting and unconventional and, finally, it seemed imperative that he expound them, first to his own people as an antidote to internal strife, and then to any others who might welcome yet another profession of his own Anglican loyalties. This must have been a recent project in his mind, since we have no record of his using 1 Cor. 12:25 as a sermon text before or after.

This is yet another sermon written on the run; its postscript places and dates it at 'Newcastle-under-Lyme, March 30, 1786'. The Journal *also places him at Newcastle on that date, and the diary records that afternoon's sequence as 'dinner, sermon, letters'. Clearly, however, this sermon was not much more than an extra chore within the larger programme of an eighty-two-year-old evangelist. It was promptly published in the May and June issues of the* Arminian Magazine *for 1786 (IX.238-44, 293-98), without a title but numbered as 'Sermon XXXIII' (and as a sequel to the sermon 'On Divine Providence'; see No. 67). The title, 'On Schism', was added when it was reprinted in* SOSO, *VI. 191-210, and its placement as a sequel to 'Of the Church' is logical and clear. It was not reprinted in Wesley's lifetime.*

On Schism

1 Corinthians 12:25

That there might be no schism in the body.

1. If there be any word in the English tongue as ambiguous and indeterminate in its meaning as the word 'church', it is one that is nearly allied to it, the word 'schism'. It has been the subject of innumerable disputes for several hundred years; and almost innumerable books have been written concerning it in every part of the Christian world. A very large share of these have been published in our country; particularly during the last century, and the beginning of the present. And persons of the strongest understanding and the most consummate learning have exhausted all their strength upon the question, both in conversation and writing. This has appeared to be more necessary than ever since the grand separation of the reformed from the Romish Church. This is a charge which the members of that Church never fail to bring against all that separate from her; and which consequently has employed the thoughts and pens of the most able disputants on both sides. And those of each side have generally, when they entered into the field, been secure of victory; supposing the strength of their arguments was so great that it was impossible for reasonable men to resist them.

2. But it is observable that exceeding little good has been done by all these controversies. Very few of the warmest and ablest disputants have been able to convince their opponents. After all that could be said, the Papists are Papists and the Protestants are Protestants still. And the same success has attended those who have so vehemently disputed about separation from the Church of England. Those who separated from her were eagerly charged with schism: they as eagerly denied the charge. And scarce any were able to convince their opponents, either on one side or the other.[1]

---

[1] Richard Baxter had emphatically denied, as in 'Catholic Unity' (1657), *Works*, IV. 652-53, the charge of schism leveled against those who differed from and defied bishops and kings who had themselves, in his view, led the church astray. From the other side, however, Robert South, 'the scourge of fanatics', fiercely attacked all Puritans and, later,

3. One great reason why this controversy has been so unprofitable, why so few of either side have been convinced, is this: they seldom agreed as to the meaning of the word concerning which they disputed. And if they did not fix the
5 meaning of this, if they did not define the term before they began disputing about it, they might continue the dispute to their lives' end without getting one step forward; without coming a jot nearer to each other than when they first set out.

4. Yet it must be a point of considerable importance, or St. Paul
10 would not have spoken so seriously of it. It is therefore highly needful that we should consider,

　　　　First, the nature, and
　　　　Secondly, the evil of it.

I.1. It is the more needful to do this because among the
15 numberless books that have been written upon the subject, both by the Romanists and Protestants, it is difficult to find any that define it in a scriptural manner. The whole body of Roman Catholics define schism, 'a separation from the Church of Rome'; and almost all our own writers define it, 'a separation
20 from the Church of England'. Thus both the one and the other set out wrong, and stumble at the very threshold. This will easily appear to any that calmly consider the several texts wherein the word 'schism' occurs, from the whole tenor of which it is manifest that it is not a separation *from* any church (whether general or
25 particular, whether the catholic or any national church) but a separation *in* a church.

2. Let us begin with the first verse wherein St. Paul makes use of the word. It is the tenth verse of the first chapter of his First Epistle to the Corinthians. The words are, 'I beseech you,
30 brethren, by the name of the Lord Jesus, that ye all speak the same thing, and that there be no schisms (the original word is σχίσματα) among you.'[2] Can anything be more plain than that

Nonconformists as schismatics; cf. *Sermons* (1844), Vol. I (Nos. IV, XXI), Vol. II (Nos. XVII, XVIII), Vol. III ('Posthumous Sermons', No. IV), and Vol. IV (Nos. XXIV, XXXIII). See also Irène Simon, *Three Restoration Divines*, ch. IV, sect., 'Robert South', pp. 238-43. Wesley would have known the article on 'Schism' in Chambers's *Cyclopaedia*, which lists the twenty-four schisms that the Roman Catholics reckon as having occurred, including 'the English schism'. Chambers himself lists as schismatics all 'nonconformists, *viz.*, the presbyterians, independents, anabaptists, who contend for a further reformation'.

　[2] In the *Notes* for 1 Cor. 1:10, Wesley defines 'schism' as 'alienation of affection' within a congregation and asks, 'Is this word ever taken in any other sense in Scripture?' Evidence

the 'schisms' here spoken of were not separations *from* but divisions *in* the church of Corinth? Accordingly it follows, 'But that ye be perfectly united together in the same mind and in the same judgment.' You see here that an union in mind and judgment was the direct opposite to the Corinthian schism. This 5 consequently was not a separation from the church or Christian society at Corinth, but a separation in the church—a disunion in mind and judgment (perhaps also in affection) among those who, notwithstanding this, continued outwardly united as before.

3. Of what nature this schism at Corinth was is still more clearly 10 determined (if anything can be more clear) by the words that immediately follow. 'Now this I say'—this is the schism of which I speak: you are divided into separate parties, some of you speaking in favour of one, some of another preacher—'Every one of you saith, I am of Paul, and I of Apollos, and I of Cephas' (or Peter).[a] 15 Who then does not see that the schism for which the Apostle here reproves the Corinthians is neither more nor less than the splitting into several parties, as they gave the preference to one or another preacher? And this species of schism there will be occasion to guard against in every religious community. 20

4. The second place where the Apostle uses this word is in the eighteenth verse of the eleventh chapter of this Epistle. 'When ye come together in the church', the Christian congregation, 'I hear that there are divisions' (the original word here also is $\sigma\chi\acute{\iota}\sigma\mu\alpha\tau\alpha$, 'schisms') 'among you.' But what were these 'schisms'? The 25 Apostle immediately tells you: 'When you come together', professing your design is 'to eat of the Lord's Supper, everyone taketh before another his own supper,'[b] as if it were a common meal. What then was the schism? It seems in doing this they divided into little *parties*, which cherished anger and resentment 30 one against another, even at that solemn season.

5. May it not be observed (to make a little digression here for the sake of those who are troubled with needless scruples on this head) that the sin which the Apostle charges on the communicants at Corinth in this chapter is usually quite misunderstood. It 35 was precisely this and nothing else, 'the taking one before another

[a] Ver. 12.   [b] Ver. 20[-21].

---

of Wesley's preoccupations with tasks other than proofreading may be seen in the fact that in the texts of both *AM* and *SOSO*, VI.196-97, his printers had printed $\chi\iota\sigma\mu\alpha\tau\alpha$ instead of $\sigma\chi\acute{\iota}\sigma\mu\alpha\tau\alpha$, and Wesley had left both instances uncorrected.

his own supper'; and in such a shocking manner that while 'one
was hungry, another was drunken'. By doing this, he says, 'ye eat
and drink' (not 'damnation'—a vile mistranslation of the
word[3]—but) 'judgment', temporal judgment, 'to yourselves:'
5 which sometimes shortened their lives. 'For this cause'—for
sinning in this vile manner—'many are sick and weak among
you.'[4] Observe here two things: first, what was the sin of the
Corinthians. Mark it well and remember it. It was 'taking one
before another his own supper', so that while 'one was hungry,
10 another was drunken'. Secondly, what was the punishment? It
was bodily weakness and sickness, which, without repentance,
might end in death. But what is this to *you*? You cannot commit
their sin; therefore you cannot incur their punishment.

    6. But to return. It deserves to be seriously remarked that in
15 this chapter the Apostle uses the word 'heresies' as exactly
equivalent with the word 'schisms'. 'I hear', says he, 'that there
are schisms among you, and I partly believe it.'[c] He then adds,
'For there must be heresies' (another word for the same thing)
'among you, that they which are approved among you may be
20 made manifest.'[d] As if he had said, 'The wisdom of God permits it
so to be for this end, for the clearer manifestation of those whose
heart is right with him.' This word, therefore, 'heresy'—which
has been so strangely distorted for many centuries, as if it meant
erroneous opinions, opinions contrary to the faith delivered to the
25 saints, which has been made a pretence for destroying cities,
depopulating countries, and shedding seas of innocent blood—
has not the least reference to opinions, whether right or wrong. It
simply means, wherever it occurs in Scripture, *divisions* or *parties*
in a religious community.

30   7. The third, and the only remaining place in this Epistle
wherein the Apostle uses this word, is the twenty-fifth verse of the
twelfth chapter; where speaking of the church (he seems to mean
the church universal, the whole body of Christ) he observes, 'God
hath tempered the body together, having given more abundant
35 honour to that part which lacked, that there might be no schism in

---

[c] Ver. 18.   [d] Ver. 19.

[3] I.e., κρίμα, a forensic term meaning 'judgment' or at worst 'condemnation'. In the
Vulgate, Jerome had translated it as *'iudicium'*. In his own translation for the *Notes* Wesley
had already 'corrected' the AV's reading, 'damnation', to 'judgment'.
[4] 1 Cor. 11:29-30.

the body.'ᵉ He immediately fixes the meaning of his own words: 'But that the members might have the same care one for another: and whether one member suffer, all the members suffer with it; or one member be honoured, all the members rejoice with it.'⁵ We may easily observe that the word 'schism' here means the want of this tender care for each other. It undoubtedly means an alienation of affection in any of them toward their brethren, a division of heart, and parties springing therefrom, though they were still outwardly united together, though they still continued members of the same external society.

8. But there seems to be one considerable objection against the supposing 'heresy' and 'schism' to mean the same thing. It is said, St. Peter, in the second chapter of his Second Epistle, takes the word 'heresies' in a quite different sense. His words are: 'There shall be among you false teachers who will bring in damnable (or destructive) heresies, denying the Lord that bought them.'ᶠ But it does by no means appear that St. Peter here takes the word 'heresies' in any other sense than St. Paul does. Even in this passage it does not appear to have any reference to opinions, good or bad. Rather it means they will 'bring in', or occasion, 'destructive parties' or 'sects' (so it is rendered in the common French translation)⁶ who 'deny the Lord that bought them'— such sects now swarm throughout the Christian world.

9. I shall be thankful to anyone who will point to me any other place in the inspired writings where this word 'schism' is to be found. I remember only these three.⁷ And it is apparent to every impartial reader that it does not in any of these mean a separation from any church or body of Christians, whether with or without cause. So that the immense pains which have been taken both by

ᵉ Ver. 24-25.   ᶠ Ver. 1.

---

⁵ 1 Cor. 12:25-26.
⁶ I.e., *'faux docteurs, qui introduiront des sectes pernicieuses . . .'* (the Geneva version, 1560).
⁷ Wesley is relying, of course, on memory, not a concordance. Three other uses of the Greek σχίσμα occur in John (7:43; 9:16; 10:19), each translated 'division' (thus supporting his case); there are also two other instances referring to a 'rent' in a garment (Matt. 9:16; Mark 2:21). There were at least seventeen New Testament concordances available in Wesley's time (of varying degrees of completeness) from John Marbeck (1550) to Matthew Pilkington (1749). The most popular of these were John Downame's (1630, with its latest edn. in 1773) and Alexander Cruden's (1738). But Wesley's grasp of Scripture amounted to his being something of a concordance, viva voce—and this at age eighty-two!

Papists and Protestants in writing whole volumes against schism as a separation, whether from the Church of Rome or from the Church of England, exerting all their strength, and bringing all their learning, have been employed to mighty little purpose. They
5 have been fighting with shadows of their own raising; violently combating a sin which had no existence but in their own imagination, which is not once forbidden, no, nor once mentioned either in the Old or New Testament.

[II.] 10.[8] 'But is there no sin resembling what so many learned and
10 pious writers have termed "schism"? And against which all the members of religious communities have need to be carefully guarded?' I do not doubt but there is; and I cannot tell whether this too may not in a remote sense be called 'schism'. I mean, 'a causeless separation from a body of living Christians'. There is no
15 absurdity in taking the word in this sense (though it be not strictly scriptural). And it is certain all the members of Christian communities should be carefully guarded against it. For how little a thing soever it may seem, and how innocent soever it may be accounted, schism, even in this sense, is both evil in itself, and
20 productive of evil consequences.

11. It is evil in itself. To separate ourselves from a body of living Christians with whom we were before united is a grievous breach of the law of love. It is the nature of love to unite us together, and the greater the love the stricter the union. And while this
25 continues in its strength nothing can divide those whom love has united. It is only when our love grows cold that we can think of separating from our brethren. And this is certainly the case with any who willingly separate from their Christian brethren. The pretences for separation may be innumerable, but want of love is
30 always the real cause; otherwise they would still hold the unity of the spirit in the bond of peace.[9] It is therefore contrary to all those commands of God wherein brotherly love is enjoined: to that of St. Paul, 'Let brotherly love continue;'[10] that of St. John, 'My beloved children, love one another;'[11] and especially to that of our
35 blessed Master, 'This is my commandment, that ye love one

---

[8] An omission here (by Wesley or his printers) in the order of subdivisions. In Preface, §4, two main heads are announced and I.1-9 has dealt with the nature of schism. Here he turns to his second main head 'the evil of [schism]' without a proper indication.
[9] Eph. 4:3.   [10] Heb. 13:1.
[11] Cf. 1 John 4:7.

another, as I have loved you.'[12] Yea, 'By this', saith he, 'shall men know that ye are my disciples, if ye love one another.'[13]

12. And as such a separation is evil in itself, being a breach of brotherly love, so it brings forth evil fruit; it is naturally productive of the most mischievous consequences. It opens a door to all unkind tempers, both in ourselves and others. It leads directly to a whole train of evil surmisings, to severe and uncharitable judging of each other. It gives occasion to offence, to anger, and resentment, perhaps in ourselves as well as in our brethren; which, if not presently stopped, may issue in bitterness, malice, and settled hatred; creating a present hell wherever they are found, as a prelude to hell eternal.

13. But the ill consequences of even this species of schism do not terminate in the heart. Evil tempers cannot long remain within before they are productive of outward fruit. Out of the abundance of the heart the mouth speaketh.[14] As he whose heart is full of love openeth his mouth with wisdom, and in his lips there is the law of kindness;[15] so he whose heart is full of prejudice, anger, suspicion, or any unkind temper, will surely open his mouth in a manner corresponding with the disposition of his mind. And hence will arise, if not lying and slandering (which yet will hardly be avoided), bitter words, talebearing, backbiting, and evil-speaking of every kind.

14. From evil words, from talebearing, backbiting, and evil-speaking, how many evil works will naturally flow! Anger, jealousy, envy, wrong tempers of every kind, do not vent themselves merely in words, but push men continually to all kind of ungodly and unrighteous actions. A plentiful harvest of all the works of darkness may be expected to spring from this source; whereby in the end thousands of souls—and not a few of those who once walked in the light of God's countenance—may be turned from the way of peace, and finally drowned in everlasting perdition.

15. Well might our blessed Lord say, 'Woe unto the world because of offences.' Yet 'it must needs be that offences will come.'[16] Yea, abundance of them will of necessity arise when a

[12] John 15:12.
[13] Cf. John 13:35.
[14] Matt. 12:34.
[15] See Prov. 31:26.
[16] Cf. Matt. 18:7.

breach of this sort is made, in any religious community; while they
that leave it endeavour to justify themselves by censuring those
they separate from; and these, on the other hand, retort[17] the
charge, and strive to lay the blame on them. But how mightily
5 does all this altercation grieve the Holy Spirit of God! How does it
hinder his mild and gentle operation in the souls both of one and
the other! Heresies and schisms (in the scriptural sense of those
words) will sooner or later be the consequence; parties will be
formed on one and the other side, whereby the love of many will
10 wax cold.[18] The hunger and thirst after righteousness,[19] after
either the favour or the full image of God, together with the
longing desires, wherewith so many were filled, of promoting the
work of God in the souls of their brethren, will grow languid, and
as offences increase will gradually die away. And as 'the fruit of
15 the Spirit'[20] withers away, 'the works of the flesh'[21] will again
prevail—to the utter destruction, first of the power, and then of
the very form of religion. These consequences are not imaginary,
are not built on mere conjectures, but on plain matter of fact. This
has been the case again and again within these last thirty or forty
20 years; these have been the fruits which we have seen over and over
to be consequent on such separation.

    16. And what a grievous stumbling-block must these things be
to those who are without! To those who are strangers to religion!
Who have neither the form nor the power of godliness![22] How will
25 they triumph over these once eminent Christians! How boldly
ask, 'What are they better than us?' How will they harden their
hearts more and more against the truth, and bless themselves in
their wickedness! From which possibly the example of the
Christians might have reclaimed them, had they continued
30 unblameable in their behaviour. Such is the complicated mischief
which persons separating from a Christian church or society do,
not only to themselves, but to that whole society, and to the world
in general.

    17. But perhaps such persons will say: 'We did not do this
35 willingly; we were constrained to separate from that society,
because we could not continue therein with a clear conscience;
we could not continue without sin. I was not allowed to continue

---

[17] See No. 42, 'Satan's Devices', §5 proem and n.
[18] See Matt. 24:12.
[19] Matt. 5:6.
[20] Gal. 5:22; Eph. 5:9.
[21] Gal. 5:19.
[22] See 2 Tim. 3:5.

therein without breaking a commandment of God.' If this was the
case you could not be blamed for separating from that society.
Suppose, for instance, you were a member of the Church of
Rome, and you could not remain therein without committing
idolatry, without worshipping of idols, whether images or saints 5
and angels; then it would be your bounden duty to leave that
community, totally to separate from it. Suppose you could not
remain in the Church of England without doing something which
the Word of God forbids, or omitting something which the Word
of God positively commands; if this were the case (but blessed be 10
God it is not) you ought to separate from the Church of England.
I will make the case my own. I am now, and have been from my
youth, a member and a minister of the Church of England. And I
have no desire nor design to separate from it till my soul separates
from my body. Yet if I was not permitted to remain therein 15
without omitting what God requires me to do, it would then
become meet, and right, and my bounden duty[23] to separate from
it without delay. To be more particular. I know God has
committed to me a dispensation of the gospel.[24] Yea, and my own
salvation depends upon preaching it: 'Woe is me, if I preach not 20
the gospel.'[25] If then I could not remain in the Church without
omitting this, without desisting from preaching the gospel, I
should be under a necessity of separating from it, or losing my
own soul. In like manner, if I could not continue united to any
smaller society, church, or body of Christians, without 25
committing sin, without lying and hypocrisy, without preaching to
others doctrines which I did not myself believe, I should be under
an absolute necessity of separating from that society. And in all
these cases the sin of separation, with all the evils consequent
upon it, would not lie upon me, but upon those who constrained 30
me to make that separation by requiring of me such terms of
communion as I could not in conscience comply with. But setting
aside this case, suppose the church or society to which I am now
united does not require me to do anything which the Scripture
forbids, or to omit anything which the Scripture enjoins, it is then 35
my indispensable duty to continue therein. And if I separate from
it without any such necessity I am justly chargeable (whether I
foresaw them or no) with all the evils consequent upon that
separation.

[23] An echo of the prayer before the Sanctus, BCP, Communion.
[24] See 1 Cor. 9:17.   [25] 1 Cor. 9:16.

18. I have spoke the more explicitly upon this head, because it is so little understood; because so many of those who profess much religion, nay, and really enjoy a measure of it, have not the least conception of this matter, neither imagine such a separation to be
5 any sin at all. They leave a Christian society with as much unconcern as they go out of one room into another. They give occasion to all this complicated mischief, and wipe their mouth, and say they have done no evil![26] Whereas they are justly chargeable before God and man both with an action that is evil in itself, and
10 with all the evil consequences which may be expected to follow, to themselves, to their brethren, and to the world.

19. I entreat you, therefore, my brethren—all that fear God and have a desire to please him, all that wish to have a conscience void of offence toward God and toward man[27]—think not so
15 slightly of this matter, but consider it calmly. Do not rashly tear asunder the sacred ties which unite you to any Christian society. This indeed is not of so much consequence to *you* who are only a *nominal* Christian. For you are not now vitally united to any of the members of Christ. Though you are called a Christian you are not
20 really a member of any Christian church. But if you are a living member, if you live the life that is hid with Christ in God,[28] then take care how you rend the body of Christ by separating from your brethren. It is a thing evil in itself. It is a sore evil in its consequences. O have pity upon yourself! Have pity on your
25 brethren! Have pity even upon the world of the ungodly![29] Do not lay more stumbling-blocks in the way of these for whom Christ died.

20. But if you are afraid, and that not without reason, of 'schism', improperly so called; how much more afraid will you be,
30 if your conscience is tender, of schism in the proper scriptural sense! O beware, I will not say of *forming,* but of *countenancing* or *abetting* any *parties* in a Christian society! Never encourage, much less cause either by word or action, any *division* therein. In the nature of things 'there must be heresies (divisions) among you;'[30]
35 but keep thyself pure. Leave off contention before it be meddled

---

[26] See Prov. 30:20.
[27] See Acts 24:16.
[28] See Col. 3:3.
[29] 2 Pet. 2:5.
[30] 1 Cor. 11:19.

with: shun the very beginning of strife.[31] Meddle not with them
that are given to dispute, with them that love contention. I never
knew that remark to fail, 'He that loves dispute does not love
God.'[32] Follow peace with all men,[33] without which you cannot
effectually follow holiness. Not only 'seek peace', but 'ensue it';[34]   5
if it seem to flee from you, pursue it nevertheless. 'Be not
overcome of evil, but overcome evil with good.'[35]

21. Happy is he that attains the character of a peacemaker in
the church of God. Why should not *you* labour after this? Be not
content not to stir up strife, but do all that in you lies to prevent or   10
quench the very first spark of it. Indeed it is far easier to prevent
the flame from breaking out than to quench it afterwards.
However, be not afraid to attempt even this: the God of peace is
on your side. He will give you acceptable words, and will send
them to the heart of the hearers. *Noli dissidere: noli discedere*, [36] says   15
a pious man: *Fac quod in te est; et Deus aderit bonae tuae
voluntati*[37]—'Do not distrust him that has all power, that has the
hearts of all men in his hand. Do what in thee lies, and God will be
present, and bring thy good desires to good effect.' Never be
weary of well-doing: in due time thou shalt reap if thou faint not.[38]   20

Newcastle-under-Lyme
March 30, 1786[39]

---

[31] See Prov. 17:14.

[32] π; source unidentified.

[33] Heb. 12:14.

[34] 1 Pet. 3:11.

[35] Rom. 12:21.

[36] Kempis, *Imitation*, III.xxxvii. The whole sentence may be translated: 'Wait on the
Lord, conduct thyself manfully and be of good courage: do not despond, do not fall away,
but constantly offer up both body and soul to God's glory.' In Wesley's translation of
Kempis (1735), this quotation appears in III.xxxv. See also the last paragraph of Wesley's
letter to 'Various Clergymen', Apr. 19, 1764.

[37] *Ibid.*, I.vii, where Kempis reads '. . . *bone voluntati tue*' ('Do what lieth in thy power
and God will assist thy good will'). Cf. also No. 85, 'On Working Out Our Own Salvation',
I.1-4, III.6-7.

[38] See Gal. 6:9.

[39] Place and date as in *AM*.

ON PERFECTION

AN INTRODUCTORY COMMENT

The single most consistent theme in Wesley's thought over the entire span of his ministry was 'holy living' and its cognate goal: perfection. His Plain Account of Christian Perfection *specifies 1725 as the beginning point of his formal interest in the doctrine of the experienced reality of perfection. In 1733 he had put the idea into a university sermon for Oxford (see No. 17, 'The Circumcision of the Heart'). In 1741 he had published his sermon on* Christian Perfection *(see No. 40), and yet another summary in the Preface to* Hymns and Sacred Poems, *1740. Later he would say of this preface: '(1) . . . this is the strongest account we ever gave of Christian perfection; indeed too strong in more than one particular . . . (2) . . . there is nothing which we have since advanced upon the subject, either in verse or prose, which is not either directly or indirectly contained in this preface. So that whether our present doctrine [i.e., 1766] be right or wrong, it is, however, the same which we had taught from the beginning.'[1]*

Meanwhile, he had been preaching the doctrine in season and out: eighteen times from Matt. 5:48 between 1740 and 1785, and fifty times from Heb. 6:1 between 1739 and 1785. There are important developments in nuance and emphasis (especially on the question of 'instantaneous sanctification' and 'entire sanctification'; cf. his letters to his brother, February 12, 1767, and to Lloyd's Evening Post, *March 5, 1767), but the main outlines of the doctrine remain constant. In 1766 (and then in five subsequent editions) he had published a full-length treatise,* A Plain Account of Christian Perfection . . . *in which he collected extracts from almost all he had ever written or said on the subject, and wove them into a sort of cumulative exposition, stressing the continuity and cruciality of the doctrine.*

What had grown clearer over the years, despite the endless confusions generated by this protracted discussion, was the doctrine's proper focus. Gradually it had dawned on Wesley that the whole question boiled

---

[1] *Plain Account*, §13; see also the Preface to *Hymns and Sacred Poems*, 1740, Vol. 12 of this edn.

*down to two issues: (1) the definition of 'perfection' in terms of a
Christian's* love of God and neighbour—*no less but also no more;
and (2) the definition of sin as deliberate. Thus, toward the end of the
climactic year of 1784, he decided to write out yet one more summary of
the idea as simply as possible and also as irenically. It was no laboured
effort; he seems to have written out the final draft of the whole sermon in
one afternoon, in Tunbridge Wells, in a brief interlude between other
activities on December 6.[2] One may guess that he was only setting down
on paper the gist of what he had already said so often for so long.*

This manuscript was published in the Arminian Magazine *the
following March and April (1785, VIII.125-35, 179-86), without a
title but numbered as 'Sermon XXVI'. It was then reprinted in* SOSO,
*VI.211-37, with its title. It seems not to have had other editions in
Wesley's lifetime. Was there some logical subtlety in its placement here
between 'On Schism' and 'Spiritual Worship'?*

On Perfection

Hebrews 6:1

Let us go on to perfection.

The whole sentence runs thus: 'Therefore leaving the
principles of the doctrine of Christ, let us go on unto perfection;   5
not laying again the foundation of repentance from dead works,
and of faith toward God'; which he had just before termed, 'the
first principles of the oracles of God',[1] and 'meat fit for babes',[2]
for such as have just tasted that the Lord is gracious.[3]

That the doing of this is a point of the utmost importance the   10
Apostle intimates in the next words: 'This will we do, if God
permit. For it is impossible for those who were once enlightened,
and have tasted of the good word of God, and the powers of the
world to come, and have fallen away, to renew them again unto

---

[2] Cf. JWJ and diary entries for that day.

---

[1] Heb. 5:12; cf. No. 5, 'Justification by Faith', §2 and n.
[2] Heb. 5:13-14.   [3] See 1 Pet. 2:3.

repentance.'⁴ As if he had said, 'If we do not "go on to perfection",⁵ we are in the utmost danger of "falling away". And if we do fall away,⁶ it is "impossible" (that is, exceeding hard) "to renew them again unto repentance".'

5   In order to make this very important Scripture as easy to be understood as possible I shall endeavour,

First, to show what perfection is;

Secondly, to answer some objections to it; and,

Thirdly, to expostulate a little with the opposers of it.

10   First, I will endeavour to show what perfection is.

[I.]1. And first, I do not conceive the perfection here spoken of to be the perfection of angels. As those glorious beings never 'left their first estate',⁷ never declined from their original perfection, all their native faculties are unimpaired, their understanding in
15   particular is still a lamp of light, their apprehension of all things clear and distinct, and their judgment always true. Hence, though their knowledge is limited (for they are creatures), though they are ignorant of innumerable things, yet they are not liable to mistake: their knowledge is perfect in its kind.⁸ And as their
20   affections are all constantly guided by their unerring understanding, so all their actions are suitable thereto; so they do every moment not their own will but the good and acceptable will of God.⁹ Therefore it is not possible for man, whose understanding is darkened, to whom mistake is as natural as ignorance, who
25   cannot think at all but by the mediation of organs which are weakened and depraved, like the other parts of his corruptible body; it is not possible, I say, for men always to think right, to apprehend things distinctly, and to judge truly of them. In consequence hereof his affections, depending on his under-
30   standing, are variously disordered. And his words and actions are influenced more or less by the disorder both of his understanding and affections. It follows that no man while in the body can possibly attain to *angelic perfection*.¹⁰

2. Neither can any man while he is in a corruptible body attain

---

⁴ Cf. Heb. 6:3-6.

⁵ Cf. No. 1, *Salvation by Faith*, II.4 and n.

⁶ *SOSO*, VI.214 reads: '. . . if we do *not* fall away . . .', but *AM* text reads: ' . . . if we *do* fall away . . .' (so does Jackson—and the clear sense of the context).

⁷ Cf. Jude 6.

⁸ Cf. Nos. 71, 'Of Good Angels', I.2-3; and 141, 'The Image of God', I.1-2.

⁹ See Rom. 12:2.   ¹⁰ Cf. No. 45, 'The New Birth', I.4 and n.

to Adamic perfection.[11] Adam before his fall was undoubtedly as pure, as free from sin, as even the holy angels. In like manner his understanding was as clear as theirs, and his affections as regular. In virtue of this, as he always judged right, so he was able always to speak and act right. But since man rebelled against God, the case 5 is widely different with him. He is no longer able to avoid falling into innumerable mistakes; consequently he cannot always avoid wrong affections; neither can he always think, speak, and act right. Therefore man, in his present state, can no more attain Adamic than angelic perfection. 10

3. The highest perfection which man can attain while the soul dwells in the body does not exclude ignorance and error, and a thousand other infirmities.[12] Now from wrong judgments wrong words and actions will often necessarily flow. And in some cases wrong affections also may spring from the same source. I may 15 judge wrong of *you:* I may think more or less highly of you than I ought to think. And this mistake in my judgment may not only occasion something wrong in my behaviour, but it may have a still deeper effect—it may occasion something wrong in my affection. From a wrong apprehension I may love and esteem you either 20 more or less than I ought. Nor can I be freed from a liableness[13] to such a mistake while I remain in a corruptible body. A thousand infirmities in consequence of this will attend my spirit till it returns to God who gave it.[14] And in numberless instances it comes short of doing the will of God as Adam did in paradise. 25 Hence the best of men may say from the heart,

> Every moment, Lord, I need
> The merit of thy death,[15]

for innumerable violations of the Adamic as well as the angelic law. It is well therefore for us that we are not now under these, but 30

---

[11] Cf. No. 5, 'Justification by Faith', I.4 and n.

[12] See Nos. 40, *Christian Perfection*, I.1-9; 41, *Wandering Thoughts*, I.2; 13, *On Sin in Believers* (intro., *et passim*); 8, 'The First-fruits of the Spirit' (intro.); and 9, 'The Spirit of Bondage and of Adoption', I.2. Note at the end of the paragraph, Wesley relates these to our continual liability 'to transgress' 'the Adamic law'. This, then, is his concession to the *simul justus et peccator*.

[13] A normal eighteenth-century usage; cf. OED, 'liability'.

[14] See Eccles. 12:7.

[15] Charles Wesley, 'And a Man shall be as an Hiding-place . . . Isaiah xxxii.2', *Hymns and Sacred Poems* (1742), p. 146 (*Poet. Wks.*, II.207); cf. No. 14, *The Repentance of Believers*, II.4 and n.

under the law of love. 'Love is now the fulfilling of the law',[16] which is given to fallen man. This is now, with respect to us, the perfect law. But even against this, through the present weakness of our understanding, we are continually liable to transgress.

5   Therefore every man living needs the blood of atonement, or he could not stand before God.

4. What is then the perfection of which man is capable while he dwells in a corruptible body? It is the complying with that kind command, 'My son, give me thy heart.'[17] It is the 'loving the Lord

10 his God with all his heart, and with all his soul, and with all his mind'.[18] This is the sum of Christian perfection: it is all comprised in that one word, love.[19] The first branch of it is the love of God: and as he that loves God loves his brother also,[20] it is inseparably connected with the second, 'Thou shalt love thy neighbour as

15 thyself'.[21] Thou shalt love every man as thy own soul, as Christ loved us. 'On these two commandments hang all the law and the prophets:'[22] these contain the whole of Christian perfection.

5. Another view of this is given us in those words of the great Apostle, 'Let this mind be in you, which was also in Christ

20 Jesus.'[23] For although this immediately and directly refers to the humility of our Lord, yet it may be taken in a far more extensive sense, so as to include the whole disposition of his mind, all his affections, all his tempers, both toward God and man. Now it is certain that as there was no evil affection in him, so no good

25 affection or temper was wanting. So that 'whatsoever things are holy, whatsoever things are lovely',[24] are all included in 'the mind that was in Christ Jesus'.

---

[16] Cf. Rom. 13:10.

[17] Cf. Prov. 23:26.

[18] Cf. Matt. 22:37, etc.

[19] A consistent restatement of frequent summaries of perfection (or holiness, or sanctification, or indeed true religion), beginning with No. 17, 'The Circumcision of the Heart', I.2 (cf.n.), and going across his entire career. As samplings from more than half a hundred such summations, cf. his letters to Bishop Gibson, June 11, 1747; to Thomas Olivers, Mar. 24, 1757; to Elizabeth Hardy, Apr. 5, 1758; to John Newton, May 14, 1765; and to Mrs. Woodhouse, Nov. 18, 1770. Or, see his 'Brief Thoughts on Christian Perfection', dated Jan. 27, 1767 (originally a letter to his brother Charles, printed in *AM*, 1783, VI.156-67). Or yet, again, cf. Nos. 43, *The Scripture Way of Salvation*, I.9; 83, 'On Patience', §14; and 114, *On the Death of John Fletcher*, I.14. Also his summaries in the succeeding edns. of *A Plain Account of Christian Perfection*.

[20] See 1 John 4:21.

[21] Lev. 19:18; Matt. 19:19, etc.

[22] Matt. 22:40.

[23] Phil. 2:5.   [24] Cf. Phil. 4:8.

6. St. Paul, when writing to the Galatians, places perfection in yet another view. It is the one undivided 'fruit of the Spirit', which he describes thus: 'The fruit of the Spirit is love, joy, peace; long-suffering, gentleness, goodness; fidelity (so the word should be translated here), 'meekness, temperance.'[25] What a glorious constellation of graces is here! Now suppose all these to be knit together in one, to be united together in the soul of a believer—this is Christian perfection.

7. Again. He writes to the Christians at Ephesus of 'putting on the new man, which is created after God in righteousness and true holiness'.[26] And to the Colossians of 'the new man, renewed after the image of him that created him';[27] plainly referring to the words in Genesis: 'So God created man in his own image.'[a] Now the moral image of God consists (as the Apostle observes) 'in righteousness and true holiness'. By sin this is totally destroyed. And we never can recover it till we are 'created anew in Christ Jesus'.[28] And this is perfection.

8. St. Peter expresses it in a still different manner, though to the same effect: 'As he that hath called you is holy, so be ye holy in all manner of conversation.'[b] According to this Apostle, then, perfection is another name for universal holiness—inward and outward righteousness—holiness of life arising from holiness of heart.[29]

9. If any expressions can be stronger than these they are those of St. Paul to the Thessalonians: 'The God of peace himself sanctify you wholly; and may the whole of you, the spirit, the soul, and the body' (this is the literal translation) 'be preserved blameless unto the coming of our Lord Jesus Christ.'[c]

10. We cannot show this sanctification in a more excellent way than by complying with that exhortation of the Apostle, 'I beseech

[a] Gen. 1:27.
[b] 1 Pet. 1:15.
[c] 1 Thess. 5:23.

[25] Gal. 5:22-23 (*Notes*). Cf. below, III.3; and No. 10, 'The Witness of the Spirit, I', II.12 and n.
[26] Cf. Eph. 4:24 (*Notes*).
[27] Col. 3:10.   [28] Cf. Eph. 2:10.
[29] Cf. *Notes* on 1 Thess. 4:3: 'Sanctification—entire holiness of heart and life'. See also, 'Thoughts Upon Methodism', §8, in *AM* (1787), X.155-56: 'The essence of [Methodism] is holiness of heart and life.' In his letter to Henry Venn, June 22, 1763, Wesley wrote, 'What I want is holiness of heart and life.'

you, brethren, by the mercies of God, that ye present your bodies' (yourselves, your souls and bodies)—a part put for the whole, by a common figure of speech—'a living sacrifice unto God;'[30] to whom ye were consecrated many years ago in baptism. When 5 what was then devoted is actually presented to God, then is the man of God perfect.

11. To the same effect St. Peter says, 'Ye are a holy priesthood, to offer up spiritual sacrifices, acceptable to God through Jesus Christ.'[d] But what sacrifices shall we offer now, seeing the Jewish 10 dispensation is at an end? If you have truly presented yourselves to God, you offer up to him continually all your thoughts, and words, and actions, through the Son of his love, as a sacrifice of praise and thanksgiving.

12. Thus you experience that he whose name is called Jesus 15 does not bear that name in vain; that he does in fact 'save his people from their sins',[31] the root as well as the branches. And this 'salvation from sin', from all sin, is another description of perfection, though indeed it expresses only the least, the lowest branch of it, only the negative part of the great salvation.

20   II. I proposed, in the second place, to answer some objections to this scriptural account of perfection.

1. One common objection to it is that there is no promise of it in the Word of God. If this were so we must give it up: we should have no foundation to build upon. For the promises of God are 25 the only sure foundation of our hope. But surely there is a very clear and full promise that we shall all love the Lord our God with all our hearts. So we read, 'Then will I circumcise thy heart, and the heart of thy seed, to love the Lord thy God with all thy heart and with all thy soul.'[e] Equally express is the word of our Lord, 30 which is no less a promise, though in the form of a command:[32] 'Thou shalt love the Lord thy God with all thy heart, and with all thy soul, and with all thy mind.'[f] No words can be more strong than these, no promise can be more express. In like manner,

---

[d] 1 Pet. 2:5.   [e] Deut. 30:6.   [f] Matt. 22:37.

---

[30] Cf. Rom. 12:1, and also its paraphrase in 'The Invocation', BCP, Communion.
[31] Matt. 1:21.
[32] For this crucial rule for biblical interpretation (*viz.*, that commands are covered promises), see below, II.11; and No. 25, 'Sermon on the Mount, V', II.2 and n. on Thomas Drayton.

'Thou shalt love thy neighbour as thyself'[33] is as express a promise
as a command.

2. And indeed that general and unlimited promise which runs
through the whole gospel dispensation, 'I will put my laws in their
minds, and write them in their hearts,'[34] turns all the commands 5
into promises; and consequently that, among the rest, 'Let this
mind be in you which was also in Christ Jesus.' The command
here is equivalent to a promise, and gives us full reason to expect
that he will work in us what he requires of us.

3. With regard to the fruit of the Spirit, the Apostle, 10
in affirming, 'The fruit of the Spirit is love, joy, peace;
long-suffering, gentleness, goodness, fidelity, meekness, temperance,' does in effect affirm that the Holy Spirit actually works
love and these other tempers in those that are led by him. So that
here also we have firm ground to tread upon, this Scripture 15
likewise being equivalent to a promise, and assuring us that all
these shall be wrought in us, provided we are led by the Spirit.

4. And when the Apostle says to the Ephesians: 'Ye have been
taught, as the truth is in Jesus, to be renewed in the spirit of your
mind, and to put on the new man, which is created after God' 20
(that is, after the image of God) 'in righteousness and true
holiness;'[g] he leaves us no room to doubt but God will thus
'renew' us 'in the spirit of our mind', and 'create us anew' in the
'image of God, wherein we were at first created'.[35] Otherwise it
could not be said that this is 'the truth as it is in Jesus'. 25

5. The command of God given by St. Peter, 'Be ye holy, as he
that hath called you is holy in all manner of conversation,' implies
a promise that we shall be thus holy if we are not wanting to
ourselves. Nothing can be wanting on God's part. As he has
called us to holiness he is undoubtedly willing, as well as able, to 30
work this holiness in us. For he cannot mock his helpless
creatures, calling us to receive what he never intends to give. That
he does call us thereto is undeniable; therefore he will give it, if
we are not disobedient to the heavenly calling.[36]

6. The prayer of St. Paul for the Thessalonians, that God 35
would 'sanctify them throughout', and 'that the whole of them,
the spirit, the soul, and the body might be preserved blameless',

[g] Eph. 4:21, [23-24].

---

[33] Matt. 19:19, etc.   [34] Cf. Heb. 10:16.
[35] Cf. Col. 3:10.   [36] See Acts 26:19.

will undoubtedly be heard in behalf of all the children of God, as
well as of those at Thessalonica. Hereby therefore all Christians
are encouraged to expect the same blessing from 'the God of
peace'; namely, that they also shall be 'sanctified throughout, in
5 spirit, soul, and body'; and that 'the whole of them shall be
preserved blameless unto the coming of our Lord Jesus Christ'.

   7. But the great question is whether there is any promise in
Scripture that we shall be 'saved from sin'. Undoubtedly there is.
Such is that promise, 'He shall redeem Israel from all his sins;'[37]
10 exactly answerable to those words of the angel, 'He shall save his
people from their sins.'[38] And surely 'he is able to save unto the
uttermost them that come unto God through him.'[39] Such is that
glorious promise given through the prophet Ezekiel in the
thirty-sixth chapter: 'Then will I sprinkle clean water upon you,
15 and ye shall be clean; from all your filthiness and from all your
idols will I cleanse you. A new heart also will I give you, and a new
spirit will I put within you; and I will take away the stony heart out
of your flesh, and I will give you a heart of flesh. And I will put my
Spirit within you, and cause you to walk in my statutes, and ye
20 shall keep my judgments, and do them.'[h] Such (to mention no
more) is that pronounced by Zechariah: 'The oath which he
sware to our father Abraham, that he would grant unto us, being
delivered out of the hand of our enemies' (and such doubtless are
all our sins) 'to serve him without fear, in holiness and
25 righteousness before him all the days of our life.'[i] The last part of
this promise is peculiarly worthy of our observation. Lest any
should say, 'True, we shall be saved from our sins when we die,'
that clause is remarkably added, as if on purpose to obviate this
pretence, 'all the days of our life'. With what modesty then can
30 anyone affirm that none shall enjoy this liberty *till* death?[40]

---

[h] [Ezek. 36:] Ver. 25-27.   [i] Luke 1:73-75.

---

[37] Ps. 130:8.   [38] Matt. 1:21.   [39] Cf. Heb. 7:25.
[40] There has been a general assumption in Latin Christianity that perfection is to be
sought and expected only in heaven, *in statu gloriae*. Cf. e.g., Thomas, *Summa Theologiae*,
I-II, Q.67 ('Of the Duration of Virtues after this Life'), Art. 3-6 (6, espec.); or *The
Westminster Confession* (1647), IX.iv, v (*non nisi in statu gloriae*). Wesley's contrary view had
been drawn largely from patristic Greek sources but had also been anticipated, in part, by
the Quakers (cf. the *Theses Theologicae* of 1675 [drafted by Robert Barclay], Propositions
Seventh, Eighth, and Ninth) and by such men as Thomas Drayton, *The Proviso or
Condition of the Promises* (1657), and Robert Gell, *An Essay Toward the Amendment of the
Last English Translation of the Bible* (1659): Appendix, No. 20, 'Some Saints not without
Sin for a Season', pp. 785 ff.

8. 'But', say some, 'this cannot be the meaning of the words; for the thing is impossible.' It is impossible to men; but the things impossible with men are possible with God.[41] 'Nay, but this is impossible in its own nature; for it implies a contradiction, that a man should be saved from all sin while he is in a sinful body.'

There is a great deal of force in this objection. And perhaps we allow most of what you contend for. We have already allowed that while we are in the body we cannot be wholly free from mistake. Notwithstanding all our care we shall still be liable to judge wrong in many instances. And a mistake in judgment will very frequently occasion a mistake in practice. Nay, a wrong judgment may occasion something in the temper or passions which is not strictly right. It may occasion needless fear, or illgrounded hope; unreasonable love, or unreasonable aversion. But all this is no way inconsistent with the perfection above described.

9. You say, 'Yes, it is inconsistent with the last article:[42] it cannot consist with salvation from sin.' I answer, It will perfectly well consist with salvation from sin, according to that definition of sin (which I apprehend to be the scriptural definition of it): 'a voluntary transgression of a known law'. 'Nay, but all transgressions of the law of God, whether voluntary or involuntary, are sin.[43] For St. John says, "All sin is a transgression of the law." '[44] True, but he does not say, 'All transgression of the law is sin.' This I deny: let him prove it that can.[45]

To say the truth, this a mere strife of words. You say none is saved from sin in *your* sense of the word; but I do not admit of that sense, because the word is never so taken in Scripture. And you cannot deny the possibility of being saved from sin in *my* sense of the word. And this is the sense wherein the word 'sin' is over and over taken in Scripture.

'But surely we cannot be saved from sin while we dwell in a *sinful body*.' A 'sinful body'? I pray, observe how deeply

---

[41] See Matt. 19:26, etc.

[42] I.e., with I.12, above.

[43] Cf. No. 13, *On Sin in Believers*, intro., III.1-9, and n.

[44] Cf. 1 John 3:4.

[45] That this distinction between sin as *voluntary* transgression and sin as pervasive is the crux of a tangled problem may be seen in C.F. Allison, *The Rise of Moralism* (1966). After a broad synopsis of seventeenth-century Anglican theology, he identifies this view of *deliberate* sin as a 'grotesque distinction which inevitably puts premiums on ignorance and suppression', and denounces Jeremy Taylor and other partisans of holy living for 'the development of their destructive doctrine' (p. xi).

ambiguous, how equivocal, this expression is! But there is no authority for it in Scripture: the word 'sinful body' is never found there. And as it is totally unscriptural, so it is palpably absurd. For no *body*, or matter of any kind, can be *sinful:* spirits alone are
5 capable of sin. Pray in what part of the body should sin lodge? It cannot lodge in the skin, nor in the muscles, or nerves, or veins, or arteries; it cannot be in the bones any more than in the hair or nails. Only the soul can be the seat of sin.[46]

10. 'But does not St. Paul himself say, "They that are in the
10 flesh cannot please God"?'[47] I am afraid the sound of these words has deceived many unwary souls, who have been told those words, 'they that are in the flesh', mean the same as they that are in the body. No, nothing less. 'The flesh' in this text no more means the body than it does the soul. Abel, Enoch, Abraham—
15 yea, all that cloud of witnesses[48] recited by St. Paul in the eleventh of the Hebrews—did actually please God while they were in the body, as he himself testifies. The expression, therefore, here means neither more nor less than they that are unbelievers, they that are in their natural state, they that are without God in the
20 world.[49]

11. But let us attend to the reason of the thing. Why cannot the Almighty sanctify the soul while it is in the body? Cannot he sanctify *you* while you are in this house, as well as in the open air? Can the walls of brick or stone hinder him? No more can these
25 walls of flesh and blood hinder him a moment from sanctifying you throughout. He can just as easily save you from all sin in the body as out of the body.

'But has he promised thus to save us from sin while we are in the body?' Undoubtedly he has; for a promise is implied in every
30 commandment of God;[50] consequently in that, 'Thou shalt love the Lord thy God with all thy heart, and with all thy soul, and with all thy mind.' For this and every other commandment is given, not to the dead, but to the living. It is expressed in the words above recited, that we should walk 'in holiness before him all the days of
35 our life'.[51]

[46] See No. 8, 'The First-fruits of the Spirit', II.6 and n. ('spirits alone are capable of sin . . .'). But cf. also No. 83, 'On Patience', §2, where Wesley is advocating a very different view.

[47] Rom. 8:8.   [48] Heb. 12:1.   [49] Eph. 2:12.

[50] See above, II.1, 2; also No. 25, 'Sermon on the Mount, V', II.2 and n.

[51] Luke 1:75.

I have dwelt the longer on this because it is the grand argument of those that oppose salvation from sin; and also because it has not been so frequently and so fully answered; whereas the arguments taken from Scripture have been answered a hundred times over.

12. But a still more plausible objection remains, taken from experience; which is, that there are no living witnesses of this salvation from sin. In answer to this I allow,

(1), that there are not many; even in this sense there are 'not many fathers'.[52] Such is our hardness of heart! Such our slowness to believe what both the prophets and apostles have spoke,[53] that there are few, exceeding few, true witnesses of the great salvation.

I allow, (2), that there are false witnesses, who either deceive their own souls, and speak of the things they know not, or 'speak lies in hypocrisy'.[54] And I have frequently wondered that we have not more of both sorts. It is nothing strange that men of warm imaginations should deceive themselves in this matter. Many do the same with regard to justification: they imagine they are justified, and are not. But though many imagine it falsely, yet there are some that are truly justified. And thus, though many imagine they are sanctified and are not, yet there are some that are really sanctified.

I allow, (3), that some who once enjoyed full salvation have now totally lost it. They once walked in glorious liberty, giving God their whole heart, 'rejoicing evermore, praying without ceasing, and in everything giving thanks'.[55] But it is past. They now are shorn of their strength, and become like other men.[56] Perhaps they do not give up their confidence; they still have a sense of his pardoning love. But even this is frequently assaulted by doubts and fears, so that they hold it with a trembling hand.

13. 'Nay, this' (say some pious and sensible men) 'is the very thing which we contend for. We grant it may please God to make some of his children for a time unspeakably holy and happy. We will not deny that they may enjoy all the holiness and happiness which you speak of. But it is only *for a time:* God never designed that it should continue to their lives' end. Consequently sin is only suspended: it is not destroyed.'

[52] 1 Cor. 4:15.
[53] See Luke 24:25.
[54] 1 Tim. 4:2.
[55] Cf. 1 Thess. 5:16-18.
[56] See Judg. 16:17.

This you affirm. But it is a thing of so deep importance that it cannot be allowed without clear and cogent proof. And where is the proof? We know that in general 'the gifts and calling of God are without repentance.'[57] He does not repent of any gifts which
5 he hath bestowed upon the children of men. And how does the contrary appear with regard to this particular gift of God? Why should we imagine that he will make an exception with respect to the most precious of all his gifts on this side heaven? Is he not as able to give it us always as to give it once? As able to give it for fifty
10 years as for one day? And how can it be proved that he is not willing to continue this his loving-kindness? How is this supposition, that he is not willing, consistent with the positive assertion of the Apostle? Who after exhorting the Christians at Thessalonica, and in them all Christians in all ages, 'to rejoice
15 evermore, pray without ceasing, and in everything give thanks', immediately adds (as if on purpose to answer those who denied, not the *power*, but the *will* of God to work this in them): 'For this is *the will* of God concerning you in Christ Jesus.'[58] Nay, and it is remarkable that after he had delivered that glorious promise
20 (such it properly is) in the twenty-third verse, 'The very God of peace shall sanctify you wholly: and the whole of you' (so it is in the original), 'the spirit, the soul, and the body shall be preserved blameless unto the coming of the Lord Jesus Christ'; he adds again, 'Faithful is he that hath called you, who also will do it.'[59] He
25 *will* not only sanctify you wholly, but will preserve you in that state until he comes to receive you unto himself.

14. Agreeable to this is the plain matter of fact. Several persons have enjoyed this blessing without any interruption for many years. Several enjoy it at this day. And not a few have enjoyed it
30 unto their death, as they have declared with their latest breath; calmly witnessing that God had saved them from all sin till their spirit returned to God.

15. As to the whole head of objections taken from experience I desire it may be observed farther: either the persons objected to
35 have attained Christian perfection, or they have not. If they have not, whatever objections are brought against them strike wide of the mark. For they are not the persons we are talking of: therefore whatever they are or do is beside the question. But if they have attained it, if they answer the description given under the nine

---

[57] Rom. 11:29.   [58] Cf. 1 Thess. 5:18.   [59] Cf. 1 Thess. 5:23-24.

preceding articles, no reasonable objection can lie against them. They are superior to all censure. And 'every tongue that riseth up against' them 'will they utterly condemn.'[60]

16. 'But I never saw one' (continues the objector) 'that answered my idea of perfection.' It may be so. And it is probable (as I observed elsewhere) you never will. For your idea includes abundantly too much—even freedom from those infirmities which are not separable from a spirit that is connected with flesh and blood. But if you keep to the account that is given above, and allow for the weakness of human understanding, you may see at this day undeniable instances of genuine, scriptural perfection.

III.1. It only remains, in the third place, to expostulate a little with the opposers of this perfection.

Now permit me to ask, Why are you so angry with those who profess to have attained this? And so mad (I cannot give it any softer title) against Christian perfection? Against the most glorious gift which God ever gave to the children of men upon earth? View it in every one of the preceding points of light, and see what it contains that is either odious or terrible; that is calculated to excite either hatred or fear in any reasonable creature.

What rational objection can you have to the loving the Lord your God with all your heart? Why should you have any aversion to it?[61] Why should you be afraid of it? Would it do you any hurt? Would it lessen your happiness either in this world or the world to come? And why should you be unwilling that others should give him their whole heart? Or that they should love their neighbours as themselves? Yea, 'as Christ hath loved us'?[62] Is this detestable? Is it the proper object of hatred? Or is it the most amiable thing under the sun? Is it proper to move terror? Is it not rather desirable in the highest degree?

2. Why are you so averse to having in you the whole 'mind which was in Christ Jesus'? All the affections, all the tempers and dispositions which were in him while he dwelt among men? Why should you be afraid of this? Would it be any worse for you were God to work in you this very hour all the mind that was in him? If not, why should you hinder others from seeking this blessing? Or be displeased at those who think they have attained it? Is anything

---

[60] Cf. Isa. 54:17.
[61] This sentence was deleted (inadvertently?) from *SOSO*, VI.232.
[62] Eph. 5:2.

more lovely? Anything more to be desired by every child of man?

3. Why are you averse to having the whole 'fruit of the spirit—love, joy, peace; long-suffering, meekness, gentleness; fidelity, goodness, temperance'? Why should you be afraid of
5 having all these planted in your inmost soul? As 'against these there is no law',[63] so there cannot be any reasonable objection. Surely nothing is more desirable than that all these tempers should take deep root in your heart; nay, in the hearts of all that name the name of Christ; yea, of all the inhabitants of the earth.
10 4. What reason have you to be afraid of, or to entertain any aversion to the being 'renewed in the whole image of him that created you'?[64] Is not this more desirable than anything under heaven? Is it not consummately amiable? What can you wish for in comparison of this, either for your own soul or for those for whom
15 you entertain the strongest and tenderest affection? And when you enjoy this, what remains but to be 'changed from glory to glory, by the spirit of the Lord'?[65]

5. Why should you be averse to universal holiness—the same thing under another name? Why should you entertain any
20 prejudice against this, or look upon it with apprehension?— whether you understand by that term the being inwardly conformed to the whole image and will of God, or an outward behaviour in every point suitable to that conformity. Can you conceive anything more amiable than this? Anything more
25 desirable? Set prejudice aside, and surely you will desire to see it diffused over all the earth.

6. Is perfection (to vary the expression) the being 'sanctified throughout in spirit, soul, and body'?[66] What lover of God and man can be averse to this, or entertain frightful apprehension of
30 it? Is it not in your best moments your desire to be all of a piece? All consistent with yourself? 'All faith, all meekness, and all love'?[67] And suppose you were once possessed of this glorious liberty, would not you wish to continue therein? To be preserved 'blameless unto the coming of our Lord Jesus Christ'?[68]

[63] Cf. Gal. 5:23.
[64] Cf. Col. 3:10.
[65] 2 Cor. 3:18.
[66] Cf. 1 Thess. 5:23.
[67] Cf. Charles Wesley, *Short Hymns on . . . the Holy Scriptures* (Bristol, 1762), II.49: 'All praise, all meekness, and all love.' Cf. also JWJ, June 9, 1777, where Wesley quotes the line correctly.
[68] 1 Thess. 5:23.

7. For what cause should you that are children of God be averse to or afraid of presenting yourselves, your souls and bodies, as a living sacrifice, holy, acceptable to God?[69] To God your Creator, your Redeemer, your Sanctifier? Can anything be more desirable than this entire self-dedication to him? And is it not your wish that all mankind should unite in this 'reasonable service'? Surely no one can be averse to this without being an enemy to all mankind.

8. And why should you be afraid of or averse to what is naturally implied in this? Namely, the offering up all our thoughts, and words, and actions, as a spiritual sacrifice to God, acceptable to him through the blood and intercession of his well-beloved Son. Surely you cannot deny that this is good and profitable to men, as well as pleasing to God. Should you not then devoutly pray that both you and all mankind may thus worship him in spirit and in truth?[70]

9. Suffer me to ask one question more. Why should any man of reason and religion be either afraid of, or averse to, salvation from all sin? Is not sin the greatest evil on this side hell? And if so, does it not naturally follow that an entire deliverance from it is one of the greatest blessings on this side heaven? How earnestly then should it be prayed for by all the children of God! By sin I mean 'a voluntary transgression of a known law'.[71] Are you averse to being delivered from this? Are you afraid of such a deliverance? Do you then love sin, that you are so unwilling to part with it? Surely no. You do not love either the devil or his works. You rather wish to be totally delivered from them, to have sin rooted out both of your life and your heart.

10. I have frequently observed, and not without surprise, that the opposers of perfection are more vehement against it when it is placed in this view than in any other whatsoever. They will allow all you say of the love of God and man, of the mind which was in Christ, of the fruit of the spirit, of the image of God, of universal holiness, of entire self-dedication, of sanctification in spirit, soul, and body; yea, and of the offering up all our thoughts, words, and actions, as a sacrifice to God. All this they will allow, so we will allow sin, a little sin, to remain in us till death.[72]

[69] See Rom. 12:1.
[70] John 4:24.   [71] As in II.9 above.
[72] An echo of Wesley's unresolved perplexities in his quandary over the 'remains of sin' and 'sinless perfection'.

11. Pray compare this with that remarkable passage in John Bunyan's *Holy War*. 'When Immanuel', says he, 'had driven Diabolus and all his forces out of the city of Mansoul, Diabolus preferred a petition to Immanuel, that he might have only a small
5 part of the city. When this was rejected, he begged to have only a little room within the walls. But Immanuel answered, "He should have no place at all, no, not to rest the sole of his foot."'[73]

Had not the good old man forgot himself? Did not the force of truth so prevail over him here as utterly to overturn his own
10 system? To assert perfection in the clearest manner? For if this is not salvation from sin I cannot tell what is.

12. 'No', says a great man, 'this is the error of errors: I hate it from my heart. I pursue it through all the world with fire and sword.'[74] Nay, why so vehement? Do you seriously think there is
15 no error under heaven equal to this? Here is something which I cannot understand. Why are those that oppose salvation from sin, few excepted, so eager? I had almost said furious? Are you fighting *pro aris et focis?*[75]—for God and your country! For all you have in the world? For all that is near and dear unto you? For your
20 liberty? Your life? In God's name, why are you so fond of sin? What good has it ever done you? What good is it ever likely to do you, either in this world or in the world to come? And why are you so violent against those that hope for deliverance from it! Have patience with us if we are in an error; yea, suffer us to enjoy our

---

[73] A quotation from memory of an incident in *The Holy War Made by Shaddai Upon Diabolus* (1682). Wesley had abridged it for the *Christian Lib.* (1753), XXXII.3-137. Mr. Loth-to-Stoop, on behalf of Diabolus and fearing victory by Immanuel (Shaddai's great captain) over Mansoul, makes a series of requests for Diabolus to retain a diminished relationship to Mansoul. The answers are emphatically negative: 'No: for if Mansoul come to be mine I shall not admit of, nor consent, that there should be the least scrap, shred, or dust of Diabolus left behind . . .'; cf. *Christian Lib.* XXXII.45-48. Wesley's irony here turns on the fact that Bunyan in *Grace Abounding* had denounced Richard Baxter and all others who allowed for any possibility of 'perfection in love' in this life.

[74] Count von Zinzendorf, in JWJ, Sept. 3, 1741: '*Nullam inhaerentem perfectionem in hac vita agnosco. Est hic error errorum. Eum per totum orbem igne et gladio persequor*' ('I acknowledge no inherent perfection whatsoever in this life. It is the error of errors; it should be harried over the whole globe with fire and sword.')

[75] A sarcastic use of a patriotic slogan (originally part of the oath administered to Roman soldiers), 'for our altars and our hearths'; cf. Cicero, *De Natura Deorum (On the Nature of the Gods)*, III.xl.(94), and Sallust, *The War with Catiline*, lix.5. Thomas Godwyn, in his *Romane Antiquities Expounded in English* (1648), after explaining the lexical background, had concluded: 'Whence arises that adage, *Pro aris et focis centare*, sounding as much as to fight for the defence of religion and one's estate, or (as our English proverb is) for God and our country' (I.i.20:24). Wesley had used this proverb without sarcasm in describing the motives of American revolutionaries in his letter to the Earl of Dartmouth, June 14, 1775.

error. If we should not attain it, the very expectation of this deliverance gives us present comfort. Yea, and ministers strength to resist those enemies which we expect to conquer. If you could persuade us to despair of that victory we should give over the contest. Now 'we are saved by hope:'[76] from this very hope a 5 degree of salvation springs. Be not angry at those who are

Felices errore suo[77]—

happy in their mistake. Else, be their opinion right or wrong, your temper is undeniably sinful. Bear then with *us*, as we do with *you;* and see whether the Lord will not deliver us;[78] whether he is not 10 able, yea, and willing 'to save them to the uttermost that come unto God through him'.[79]

Tunbridge Wells,
Dec. 6, 1784[80]

---

[76] Rom. 8:24.
[77] Lucan, *Civil War*, i.459.
[78] Cf. Wesley's Preface (1746), §9.
[79] Heb. 7:25.
[80] Place and date as in *AM*.

SPIRITUAL WORSHIP
SPIRITUAL IDOLATRY

AN INTRODUCTORY COMMENT

This is another pair of sermons that belong together. They were written in the same fortnight and on the same text, 1 John 5:20-21; they were then quickly published in sequence in the Arminian Magazine *as 'Sermons II and III'. Their shared theme is the very fundament of all Wesley's theology: the valid worship of the one true God incarnate in the Son, and the folly of 'spiritual idolatry', which is to say, any other focus of human devotion than God in Christ. Together, they add up to a single essay in a Christocentric doctrine of spirituality. What is not so clear, however, is their placement (along with their sequel 'On Dissipation') in* SOSO, VI, *very far past the point where they could have served a schematic purpose as an essay in fundamental theology.*

'Spiritual Worship', without that title, is dated in London on December 22, 1780. This, of course, would have been in the still tense aftermath of the tragic Gordon Riots of the previous June.[1] Wesley had been absent from London at the time of the riots, but his sympathies with Gordon and the Protestant Association are hard to reconcile with his repeated disavowals of any intention to persecute Catholics, since there is no denying that the riots themselves were savagely anti-Catholic.[2] The sermon itself, however, is a sermonic essay in theology proper: the reality of God in trinitarian terms, 'the essence of true religion' understood as 'our happy knowledge of God', with knowledge being defined less as acquaintance than as communion. There is a special stress on divine prevenience and many an echo from his earlier Oxford sermon, 'The Circumcision of the Heart'.

'Spiritual Idolatry' was dated January 5, 1781, also in London, and is clearly a sequel to 'Spiritual Worship'. It was also as clearly written for the Arminian Magazine *as one of two parts of a basic theme. This*

---

[1] See John Paul De Castro, *The Gordon Riots* (Oxford Univ. Press, 1926); George Rudé, *Hanoverian London, 1714–1808*, pp. 178-79, 221-26; and Leslie Stephen's article on Lord George Gordon ['agitator'] in *DNB*.

[2] Cf. JWJ, entries for Nov. 5 through Dec. 29, 1780, espec. Dec. 16, and his letter of Mar. 23, 1780, to *Freeman's Journal*, reprinted in *AM*, IV.295-300.

impression is reinforced by the fact that there is only a single reference to 1 John 5:21 as a preaching text before 1780 (and only two to 1 John 5:20). It moves beyond conventional notions to the classical view of idolatry as the 'idolizing of any human creature', or anything like supreme devotion to any other good than God. Then it focuses on Wesley's favourite text about sin: the famous triplex concupiscentia *of 1 John 2:16, and the folly of life on any other terms than wholehearted piety to God. For other references to idolatry, cf. Nos. 44,* Original Sin, *II.7; 127, 'On the Wedding Garment', §12; and 128, 'The Deceitfulness of the Human Heart', I.4; see also Wesley's letter to Samuel, Jun., for a comment on an early sermon on the idolatry of the Samaritans (December 5, 1726); and* A Word to a Protestant *(Bibliog, No. 113; Vol. 14 of this edn.).*

The two sermons were published in succession, without titles, in the first volume of the Arminian Magazine *to introduce Wesley's original sermons, 1781: in March and April for 'Spiritual Worship' (IV. 129-36, 184-89), and May and June for 'Spiritual Idolatry' (IV. 242-50, 300-3). Titles were supplied for their republication in* SOSO, *VI—'Spiritual Worship', pp. 239-60, and 'Spiritual Idolatry', pp. 261-80. There is no record of any other editions of them during Wesley's lifetime.*

SERMON 77

Spiritual Worship

1 John 5:20

This is the true God, and eternal life.

1. In this epistle St. John speaks, not to any particular church, but to all the Christians of that age; although more especially to them among whom he then resided. And in them he speaks to the whole Christian church in all succeeding ages.

2. In this letter, or rather tract (for he was present with those to whom it was more immediately directed, probably being not able to preach to them any longer, because of his extreme old age) he does not treat directly of faith, which St. Paul had done; neither of inward and outward holiness, concerning which both St. Paul, St. James, and St. Peter had spoken; but of the foundation of all, the

happy and holy communion which the faithful have with God the Father, Son, and Holy Ghost.

3. In the preface he describes the authority by which he wrote and spoke, and expressly points out the design of his present writing.[a] To the preface exactly answers the conclusion of the Epistle, more largely explaining the same design, and recapitulating the marks of our communion with God, by 'we know', thrice repeated.[b]

4. The tract itself treats,

First, severally, of communion with the Father, chapter one, verses 5-10; of communion with the Son, chapters two and three; of communion with the Spirit, chapter four.

Secondly, conjointly, of the testimony of the Father, Son, and Holy Ghost, on which faith in Christ, the being born of God, love to God and his children, the keeping his commandments, and victory over the world, are founded, chapter five, verses 1-12.

5. The recapitulation begins, chapter five, verse 18: 'We know that he who is born of God', who sees and loves God, 'sinneth not,' so long as this loving faith abideth in him. 'We know that we are of God', children of God, by the witness and the fruit of the Spirit; 'and the whole world', all who have not the Spirit, 'lieth in the wicked one.' They are, and live, and dwell in him, as the children of God do in the Holy One. 'We know that the Son of God is come; and hath given us a' spiritual 'understanding, that we may know the true one', the faithful and true witness. 'And we are in the true one', as branches in the vine. 'This is the true God, and eternal life.'

In considering these important words we may inquire,

First, how is he the true God?

Secondly, how is he eternal life?

I shall then, in the third place, add a few inferences.

I. [1.] And first we may inquire, how is he the true God?[1] He is 'God over all, blessed for ever'.[2] 'He was with God', with God the Father, 'from the beginning', from eternity, 'and was God.'[3] 'He and the Father are one;'[4] and consequently he 'thought it not robbery to be equal with God'.[5] Accordingly the inspired writers

---

[a] [1 John] Chap. 1, ver. 1-4.   [b] Chap. 5, ver. 18-20.

---

[1] Cf. John Deschner, *Wesley's Christology*, ch. I.   [2] Cf. Rom. 9:5.
[3] Cf. John 1:1-2.   [4] Cf. John 10:30.   [5] Phil. 2:6.

give him all the titles of the most high God. They call him over
and over by the incommunicable name, Jehovah, never given to
any creature. They ascribe to him all the attributes and all the
works of God. So that we need not scruple to pronounce him God
of God, Light of Light, very God of very God:[6] in glory equal with 5
the Father, in majesty coeternal.[7]

2. He is 'the true God', the only Cause, the sole Creator of all
things. 'By him', saith the Apostle Paul, 'were created all things
that are in heaven, and that are on earth'—yea, earth and heaven
themselves; but the inhabitants are named, because more noble 10
than the house—'visible and invisible'. The several species of
which are subjoined: 'Whether they be thrones, or dominions, or
principalities, or powers.'[8] So St. John, 'All things were made by
him, and without him was not anything made that was made.'[9]
And accordingly St. Paul applies to him those strong words of the 15
Psalmist, 'Thou, Lord, in the beginning hast laid the foundation
of the earth, and the heavens are the work of thy hands.'[10]

3. And as 'the true God' he is also the *Supporter* of all the things
that he hath made. He 'beareth', upholdeth, sustaineth, 'all'
created 'things by the word of his power',[11] by the same powerful 20
word which brought them out of nothing. As this was absolutely
necessary for the beginning of their existence, it is equally so for
the continuance of it: were his almighty influence withdrawn they
could not subsist a moment longer. Hold up a stone in the air; the
moment you withdraw your hand it naturally falls to the ground. 25
In like manner, were he to withdraw his hand for a moment the
creation would fall into nothing.

4. As 'the true God' he is likewise the *Preserver* of all things. He
not only keeps them in being, but preserves them in that degree of
well-being which is suitable to their several natures. He preserves 30
them in their several relations, connections, and dependences, so
as to compose one system of beings, to form one entire universe,
according to the counsel of his will. How strongly and beautifully

---

[6] From 'the Creed Commonly Called Nicene', BCP, Communion.

[7] A paraphrase from the *Quicunque Vult* ('commonly called the Creed of St.
Athanasius'), BCP (for Morning Prayer on thirteen special holy days). Orig.: 'But the
Godhead of the Father, of the Son, and of the Holy Ghost, is all one: the glory equal, the
majesty coeternal.'

[8] Col. 1:16.

[9] John 1:3.

[10] Ps. 102:25 (BCP).

[11] Cf. Heb. 1:3.

is this expressed! Τὰ πάντα ἐν αὐτῷ, συνέστηκεν[12]—'By him all things consist;' or, more literally, 'By and in him are all things compacted into one system.' He is not only the support but also the cement of the whole universe.[13]

5. I would particularly remark (what perhaps has not been sufficiently observed) that he is the true '*Author* of all' the *motion* that is in the universe. To spirits, indeed, he has given a small degree of self-moving power, but not to matter. All matter, of whatever kind it be, is absolutely and totally inert.[14] It does not, cannot in any case move itself; and whenever any part of it seems to move it is in reality moved by something else. See that log which, vulgarly speaking, *moves* on the sea! It is in reality *moved* by the water. The water is moved by the wind, that is, a current of air. And the air itself owes all its motion to the ethereal fire,[15] a particle of which is attached to every particle of it. Deprive it of that fire and it moves no longer: it is fixed; it is as inert as sand. Remove fluidity (owing to the ethereal fire intermixed with it) from water, and it has no more motion than the log. Impact fire into iron by hammering it when red hot, and it has no more motion than fixed air, or frozen water. But when it is unfixed, when it is in its most active state, what gives motion to fire? The very heathen will tell you. It is,

Magnam mens agitans molem, et vasto se corpore miscens.[16]

6. To pursue this a little farther: we say the moon moves round

---

[12] Col. 1:17. Wesley's translation of συνέστηκεν (from συνιστάνειν) is not 'more literal'; actually it is a paraphrase.
[13] Cf. Charles Wesley, 'Hymns on the Four Gospels', No. 1949, ver. 5, ll. 7-8:

> Cemented by thy blood alone,
> And one with unity divine.

(*Poet. Wks.*, XI.461.) Cf. also Johnson's definition (*Dictionary*, 1755) of 'cement' as 'the bond of union', and his quotation from Robert South: 'Look over the whole creation and you shall see that the cement that holds together all the parts of this great and glorious fabrick is gratitude.'
[14] A view consistently repeated; cf. No. 15, *The Great Assize*, III.3 and n.
[15] Another favourite notion, as also in the same sermon passage and n.
[16] Cf. Virgil, *Aeneid*, vi.726-27:

> *totamque infusa per artus*
> *Mens agitat molem et magno se corpore miscet.*

> The all-informing soul
> That fills, pervades, and actuates the whole.

See No. 74, 'Of the Church', §13 and n.

the earth, the earth and the other planets move round the sun, the sun moves round its own axis. But these are only vulgar expressions. For if we speak the truth of [them], neither the sun, moon, nor stars *move*. None of these move themselves. They are all *moved* every moment by the almighty hand that made them. 5

'Yes', says Sir Isaac, 'the sun, moon, and all the heavenly bodies do move, do gravitate toward each other.'[17] Gravitate! What is that? 'Why, they all *attract* each other, in proportion to the quantity of matter they contain.' 'Nonsense all over', says Mr. Hutchinson,[18] 'Jargon! self-contradiction! Can anything *act,* 10 *where it is not?* No, they are continually *impelled* toward each other.' Impelled, by what? 'By the subtle matter, the ether, or electric fire.' But remember! Be it ever so subtle, it is matter still. Consequently it is as inert in itself as either sand or marble. It cannot therefore move itself; but probably it is the first material 15 mover, the main spring whereby the Creator and Preserver of all things is pleased to move the universe.

7. 'The true God' is also the *Redeemer* of all the children of men. It pleased the Father to 'lay upon him the iniquities of us all',[19] that by the one oblation of himself once offered, when he 20 tasted death for every man, he might make a full and sufficient sacrifice, oblation, and satisfaction for the sins of the whole world.[20]

8. Again: the true God is the *Governor* of all things; 'his kingdom ruleth over all.'[21] 'The government' rests 'upon his 25 shoulder',[22] throughout all ages. He is the Lord and Disposer of the whole creation, and every part of it. And in how astonishing a manner does he govern the world! How far are his ways above human thought! How little do we know of his methods of government! Only this we know, *Ita praesides singulis sicut* 30

---

[17] Sir Isaac Newton; cf. *Opticks* (1721), p. 351, and elsewhere as one of Newton's prime hypotheses. Cf. No. 55, *On the Trinity*, §10 and n.

[18] John Hutchinson; see No. 57, 'On the Fall of Man', II.6 and n. Wesley has his own theological reasons for stressing the conflict between the views of the several natural philosophers. This quoted expostulation from Hutchinson is not exact; it does, however, reflect Hutchinson's indignant rejection of Newton's theory of gravitation; cf. *A Treatise of Power*, in *Works* (3rd edn., 1748–49), V.142, 145-46, 206-7; see also *Moses' Principia* (1724), Pt. I. On the other hand Wesley suggests in his *Address to the Clergy*, II.2(5), that all well-furnished ministers would have mastered Newton's *Principia Mathematica* (1687), and it was prescribed reading at Kingswood School, so listed in the Library Catalogue of 1789.

[19] Cf. Isa. 53:6.

[20] A paraphrase from the 'Prayer of Consecration', BCP, Communion.

[21] Ps. 103:19.   [22] Cf. Isa. 9:6.

universis, et universis sicut singulis![23]—thou presidest over each creature as if it were the universe, and over the universe as over each individual creature. Dwell a little upon this sentiment. What a glorious mystery does it contain! It is paraphrased in the words recited above.[24]

> Father, how wide thy glories shine!
> Lord of the universe—and mine:
> Thy goodness watches o'er the whole,
> As all the world were but one soul:
> Yet keeps my ev'ry sacred hair,
> As I remained thy single care![25]

9. And yet there is a difference, as was said before, in his providential government over the children of men. A pious writer[26] observes, there is a threefold circle of divine providence. The *outermost circle* includes all the sons of men—heathens, Mahometans, Jews, and Christians. He causeth his sun to rise upon all. He giveth them rain and fruitful seasons. He pours ten thousand benefits upon them, and fills their hearts with food and gladness. With an *interior circle* he encompasses the whole visible Christian church, all that name the name of Christ.[27] He has an additional regard to these, and a nearer attention to their welfare. But the *innermost circle* of his providence encloses only the invisible church of Christ—all real Christians, wherever dispersed in all corners of the earth; all that worship God (whatever denomination they are of) in spirit and in truth.[28] He keeps these as the apple of an eye: he hides them under the shadow of his wings.[29] And it is to these in particular that our Lord says, 'Even the hairs of your head are all numbered.'[30]

10. Lastly, being the true God he is the *End* of all things, according to that solemn declaration of the Apostle: 'Of him, and through him, and to him, are all things'c—*of him* as the Creator;

c Rom. 11:36.

[23] Cf. Augustine, *Confessions*, III.xi.19; see No. 37, 'The Nature of Enthusiasm', §28 and n.
[24] This sentence is added to the text in *SOSO* (1788).
[25] Charles Wesley, *Scripture Hymns*, II.158; see No. 54, 'On Eternity', §20 and n.
[26] Thomas Crane, *Isagoge ad Dei Providentiam, Or a Prospect of Divine Providence* (1672); see No. 67, 'On Divine Providence', §16 and n.
[27] See 2 Tim. 2:19. [28] See John 4:23.
[29] Ps. 17:8. [30] Luke 12:7.

through him as the Sustainer and Preserver; and *to him* as the ultimate End of all.

II. In all these senses Jesus Christ is 'the true God'. But how is he *'eternal life'?*

1. The thing directly intended in this expression is not that he *will be* eternal life—although this is a great and important truth, and never to be forgotten. 'He is the author of eternal salvation to all them that obey him.'[31] He is the purchaser of that 'crown of life' which will be given to all that are 'faithful unto death'.[32] And he will be the soul of all their joys to all the saints in glory.

> The flame of angelical love
> Is kindled at Jesus's face;
> And all the enjoyment above
> Consists in the rapturous gaze![33]

2. The thing directly intended is not that he is the resurrection; although this also is true, according to his own declaration, 'I am the resurrection and the life:'[34] agreeable to which are St. Paul's words, 'As in Adam all died, even so in Christ shall all be made alive.'[35] So that we may well say, 'Blessed be the God and Father of our Lord Jesus Christ, who hath begotten us again unto a lively hope by the resurrection of Christ from the dead, to an inheritance incorruptible and undefiled, and that fadeth not away.'[36]

3. But waiving what he *will be* hereafter, we are here called to consider what he *is now*. He is now the life of everything that lives in any kind or degree. He is the source of the lowest species of life, that of *vegetables;* as being the source of all the motion on which vegetation depends. He is the fountain of the life of *animals*, the power by which the heart beats, and the circulating juices flow. He is the fountain of all the life which man possesses in common with other animals. And if we distinguish the *rational* from the animal life, he is the source of this also.[37]

4. But how infinitely short does all this fall of the life which is here directly intended! And of which the Apostle speaks so explicitly in the preceding verses: 'This is the testimony, that God

---

[31] Cf. Heb. 5:9.   [32] Rev. 2:10.

[33] Charles Wesley, Hymn VIII, st. 5, last quatrain, in *Funeral Hymns* (1746), p. 12 (*Poet. Wks.*, VI.199), reading 'their enjoyment'.

[34] John 11:25.   [35] Cf. 1 Cor. 15:22.   [36] 1 Pet. 1:3-4.

[37] A more conventional (i.e., Aristotelian) schema here than that in the *Survey*.

hath given us eternal life; and this life is in his Son. He that hath
the Son *hath* life' (the eternal life here spoken of), 'and he that
hath not the Son of God, hath not this life.'ᵈ As if he had said,
'This is' the sum of 'the testimony which God hath' testified 'of
his Son, that God *hath* given us', not only a title to but the real
beginning of 'eternal life. And this life is' purchased by, and
treasured up 'in his Son', who has all the springs and the fullness
of it in himself, to communicate to his body, the church.

5. This eternal life then commences when it pleases the Father
to reveal his Son in our hearts; when we first know Christ, being
enabled to 'call him Lord by the Holy Ghost';³⁸ when we can
testify, our conscience bearing us witness in the Holy Ghost, 'the
life which I now live, I live by faith in the Son of God, who loved
me, and gave himself for me.'³⁹ And then it is that happiness
begins—happiness real, solid, substantial. Then it is that heaven
is opened in the soul, that the proper, heavenly state commences,
while the love of God, as loving us, is shed abroad in the heart,⁴⁰
instantly producing love to all mankind: general, pure benevolence, together with its genuine fruits, lowliness, meekness,
patience, contentedness in every state; an entire, clear, full
acquiescence in the whole will of God, enabling us to 'rejoice
evermore, and in everything to give thanks'.⁴¹

6. As our knowledge and our love of him increase by the same
degrees, and in the same proportion, the kingdom of an inward
heaven must necessarily increase also; while we 'grow up in all
things into him who is our head'.⁴² And when we are ἐν αὐτῷ
πεπληρωμένοι,⁴³ 'complete in him', as our translators render
it—but more properly when we are 'filled with him'; when 'Christ
in us, the hope of glory',⁴⁴ is our God and our all; when he has
taken the full possession of our heart; when he reigns therein,
without a rival, the Lord of every motion there;⁴⁵ when we dwell in

ᵈ [1 John 5:] Ver. 11, 12.

³⁸ Cf. 1 Cor. 12:3.   ³⁹ Cf. Gal. 2:20.   ⁴⁰ See Rom. 5:5.   ⁴¹ 1 Thess. 5:16, 18.
⁴² Eph. 4:15.   ⁴³ Col. 2:10.   ⁴⁴ Cf. Col. 1:27.
⁴⁵ See John Wesley, 'Divine Love. From the German' [of Gerhard Tersteegen], *Hymns and Sacred Poems* (1739), p. 79 (*Poet. Wks.*, I.72):

Is there a thing beneath the sun
That strives with thee my heart to share?
Ah, tear it thence, and reign alone,
The Lord of every motion there.

Christ, and Christ in us, we are one with Christ, and Christ with us; then we are completely happy; then we live all 'the life that is hid with Christ in God'.[46] Then, and not till then, we properly experience what that word meaneth, 'God is love; and whosoever dwelleth in love, dwelleth in God, and God in him.'[47]   5

III. I have now only to add a few inferences from the preceding observations.

1. And we may learn from hence, first, that as there is but one God in heaven above and in the earth beneath, so there is only one happiness for created spirits, either in heaven or earth. This 10 one God made our heart for himself; and it cannot rest till it resteth in him.[48] It is true that while we are in the vigour of youth and health; while our blood dances in our veins; while the world smiles upon us and we have all the conveniences, yea, and superfluities of life—we frequently have pleasing dreams and 15 enjoy a kind of happiness. But it cannot continue; it flies away like a shadow:[49] and even while it lasts it is not solid or substantial; it does not satisfy the soul. We still pant after something else, something which we have not. Give a man everything that this world can give, still, as Horace observed near two thousand years 20 ago,

Curtae nescio quid semper abest rei.[50]

Still

Amidst our plenty something still
To me, to thee, to him is wanting![51]   25

That *something* is neither more nor less than the knowledge and

In *A Plain Account of Christian Perfection* (1766), §7, Wesley reports that he wrote this quatrain in Savannah. Actually, as first published in *A Collection of Psalms and Hymns* (1738), p. 52, the couplet ran:

Ah, tear it thence, that thou alone
May'st reign unrivall'd monarch there.

(See also *Collection*, 1780, No. 335—7:493 of this edn.)

[46] Cf. Col. 3:3.   [47] Cf. 1 John 4:16.
[48] Yet another repetition of Augustine, *Confessions*, I.i; see No. 3, *'Awake, Thou That Sleepest'*, II.5 and n.
[49] See Job 14:2.
[50] Horace, *Odes*, III.xxiv.64: '. . . something is always lacking to make one's fortune incomplete.'
[51] Matthew Prior, 'The Ladle', ll. 162, 164; see No. 28, 'Sermon on the Mount, VIII', §20 and n.

love of God—without which no spirit[52] can be happy either in heaven or earth.

2. Permit me to cite my own experience in confirmation of this. I distinctly remember that even in my childhood, even when I was
5   at school, I have often said: 'They say the life of a schoolboy is the happiest in the world, but I am sure I am not happy. For I always want something which I have not; therefore I am not content, and so cannot be happy.' When I had lived a few years longer, being in the vigour of youth, a stranger to pain and sickness, and
10   particularly to lowness of spirits (which I do not remember to have felt one quarter of an hour since I was born),[53] having plenty of all things, in the midst of sensible and amiable friends who loved me, and I loved them; and being in the way of life which of all others suited my inclinations; still I was not happy! I wondered why I was
15   not, and could not imagine what the reason was. The reason certainly was: I did not know God, the source of present as well as eternal happiness. What is a clear proof that I was not then happy is that, upon the coolest reflection, I knew not one week which I would have thought it worthwhile to have lived over again; taking
20   it with every inward and outward sensation, without any variation at all.

3. But a pious man affirms, 'When I was young I was happy, though I was utterly without God in the world.'[54] I do not believe you; though I doubt not but you believe yourself. But you are
25   deceived, as I have been over and over. Such is the condition of human life!

> Flowerets and myrtles fragrant seem to rise;
> All is at distance fair; but near at hand,
> The gay deceit mocks the desiring eyes
30   > With thorns, and desert heath, and barren sand.[55]

Look forward on any distant prospect: how beautiful does it appear! Come up to it; and the beauty vanishes away, and it is rough and disagreeable. Just so is life! But when the scene is past it resumes its former appearance; and we seriously believe that we

---

[52] The *AM* text here reads 'creature'.

[53] A blurred memory; cf. his letter to his brother Charles, June 27, 1766, about his fear of 'falling into nothing'. Perhaps he was still focusing on his 'happy' youth and childhood.

[54] π; —but cf. Eph. 2:12.

[55] Cf. Samuel Wesley, Jun., 'The Battle of the Sexes', in *Poems on Several Occasions* (1736), p. 22; see also, John Wesley, *Moral and Sacred Poems*, III.20.

were then very happy, though in reality we were far otherwise. For as none is now, so none ever was happy without the loving knowledge of the true God.

4. We may learn hence, secondly, that this happy knowledge of the true God is only another name for *religion;* I mean *Christian* 5 *religion*, which indeed is the only one that deserves the name. Religion, as to the nature or essence of it, does not lie in this or that set of notions, vulgarly called 'faith'; nor in a round of duties, however carefully 'reformed' from error and superstition. It does not consist in any number of outward actions. No; it properly and 10 directly consists in the knowledge and love of God, as manifested in the Son of his love, through the eternal Spirit. And this naturally leads to every heavenly temper, and to every good word and work.[56]

5. We learn hence, thirdly, that none but a Christian is happy; 15 none but a real, inward Christian. A glutton, a drunkard, a gamester may be 'merry'; but he cannot be happy. The beau, the belle, may eat and drink, and rise up to play;[57] but still they feel they are not happy. Men or women may adorn their own dear persons with all the colours of the rainbow. They may dance and 20 sing, and hurry to and fro, and flutter hither and thither. They may roll up and down in their splendid carriages and talk insipidly to each other. They may hasten from one diversion to another; but happiness is not there. They are still 'walking in a vain shadow, and disquieting themselves in vain'.[58] One of their own 25 poets has truly pronounced concerning the whole life of these sons of pleasure:

> 'Tis a dull farce, and empty show:
> Powder, and pocketglass, and beau.[59]

I cannot but observe of that fine writer that he came near the 30 mark, and yet fell short of it. In his *Solomon* (one of the noblest poems in the English tongue) he clearly shows where happiness *is*

---

[56] 2 Thess. 2:17; cf. No. 24, 'Sermon on the Mount, IV', III.1 and n.
[57] See Exod. 32:6.   [58] Cf. Ps. 39:7 (BCP).
[59] Matthew Prior, 'An English Padlock', ll. 60-61. Prior was one of Wesley's favourites; see his 'Thoughts on the Character and Writings of Mr. Prior', in *AM*, V.600-3, 660-65 (Nov., Dec. 1782), where he ranks him above Pope and singles out *Solomon* for especial praise, as he does in this sermon. Both John and Charles had memorized the entire poem, and Charles required his children to commit it to memory; cf. his letter to his daughter, Sally, Oct. 1, 1778, in *The Journal of the Rev. Charles Wesley, M.A.*, ed. by Thomas Jackson (London, 1849), II.278, 280.

not; that it is not to be found in natural knowledge, in power, or in the pleasures of sense or imagination. But he does not show where it is to be found. He could not, for he did not know it himself. Yet he came near it when he said,

5   Restore, great Father, thy instructed son;
       And in my act may thy great will be done![60]

6. We learn hence, fourthly, that every Christian is happy, and that he who is not happy is not a Christian. If (as was observed above) religion is happiness, everyone that has it must be happy.
10 This appears from the very nature of the thing; for if religion and happiness are in fact the same, it is impossible that any man can possess the former without possessing the latter also. He cannot have religion without having happiness, seeing they are utterly inseparable.
15 And it is equally certain, on the other hand, that he who is not happy is not a Christian; seeing if he was a real Christian he could not but be happy. But I allow an exception here in favour of those who are under violent temptation; yea, and of those who are under deep nervous disorders, which are indeed a species of
20 insanity. The clouds and darkness which then overwhelm the soul suspend its happiness; especially if Satan is permitted to second those disorders by pouring in his fiery darts.[61] But excepting these cases the observation will hold, and it should be well attended to: whoever is not happy, yea, happy in God, is not a
25 Christian.

7. Are not *you* a living proof of this? Do not you still wander to and fro, seeking rest, but finding none?[62] Pursuing happiness, but never overtaking it? And who can blame you for pursuing it? It is the very end of your being. The great Creator made nothing to be
30 miserable, but every creature to be happy in its kind.[63] And upon a general review of the works of his hands he pronounced them all 'very good'; which they would not have been had not every intelligent creature—yea, everyone capable of pleasure and pain—been happy in answering the end of its creation. If *you* are
35 now unhappy, it is because you are in an unnatural state: and shall

[60] Prior, *Solomon*, iii.889-90 (the poem's closing lines). See also, Wesley, *A Collection of Moral and Sacred Poems* (1744), I.192.
[61] See Eph. 6:16.
[62] See Luke 11:24.
[63] Gen. 1:31.

you not sigh for deliverance from it? 'The whole creation', being now 'subject to vanity', 'groaneth and travaileth in pain together.'[64] I blame you only, or pity you, rather, for taking a wrong way to a right end: for seeking happiness where it never was and never can be found. You seek happiness in your fellow-creatures instead of your Creator. But these can no more make you happy than they can make you immortal. If you have ears to hear, every creature cries aloud, 'Happiness is not in *me*.'[65] All these are, in truth, 'broken cisterns, that can hold no water'.[66] O turn unto your rest! Turn to him in whom are hid all the treasures of happiness! Turn unto him 'who giveth liberally unto all men',[67] and he will give you 'to drink of the water of life freely'.[68]

8. You cannot find your long sought happiness in all the *pleasures of the world*. Are they not 'deceitful upon the weights'? Are they not 'lighter than vanity itself'?[69] How long will ye 'feed upon that which is not bread',[70] which may *amuse*, but cannot satisfy? You cannot find it in the *religion of the world*, either in opinions or a mere round of outward duties. Vain labour! Is not 'God a spirit'? And therefore to be 'worshipped in spirit and in truth'?[71] In this alone can you find the happiness you seek—in the union of your spirit with the Father of spirits; in the knowledge and love of him who is the fountain of happiness, sufficient for all the souls he has made.

9. But where is he to be found? Shall we 'go up into heaven' or 'down into hell' to seek him? Shall we 'take the wings of the morning' and search for him 'in the uttermost parts of the sea'?[72] Nay,

Quod petis, hic est![73]

What a strange word to fall from the pen of a heathen—'What you seek is here!' He is 'about your bed'! He is 'about your path'.[74] He

---

[64] Cf. Rom. 8:20, 22.
[65] Cf. Augustine, *Confessions*, XI. iv; and see No. 125, 'On a Single Eye', II.4. In the *Survey*, V.233, there is a comment on Job 28:14: 'The depth saith, it [i.e., wisdom] is not in *me*, and the sea saith, it is not in *me*.'
[66] Jer. 2:13.
[67] Cf. Jas. 1:5.
[68] Cf. Rev. 21:6; 22:17.
[69] Ps. 62:9 (BCP).
[70] Cf. Isa. 55:2.
[71] Cf. John 4:23-24.
[72] Cf. Ps. 139:8-9.
[73] Horace, *Epistles*, I.xi.29.
[74] Cf. Ps. 139:2 (BCP).

'besets you behind and before'. He 'lays his hand upon you'.[75] Lo! God is here! Not afar off![76] Now, believe and feel him near! May he now reveal himself in your heart! Know him! Love him! And you are happy.

5   10. Are you already happy in him? Then see that you 'hold fast'[77] 'whereunto you have attained'![78] 'Watch and pray,'[79] that you may never be 'moved from your steadfastness'.[80] 'Look unto yourselves, that ye lose not what you have gained, but that ye receive a full reward.'[81] In so doing, expect a continual growth in
10 grace, in the loving knowledge of our Lord Jesus Christ.[82] Expect that the power of the Highest shall suddenly overshadow you,[83] that all sin may be destroyed, and nothing may remain in your heart but holiness unto the Lord.[84] And this moment, and every moment, 'present yourselves a living sacrifice, holy, acceptable to
15 God,'[85] and 'glorify him with your body, and with your spirit, which are God's.'[86]

London,
Dec. 22, 1780[87]

---

[75] Cf. Ps. 139:5 (AV).
[76] See Jer. 23:23.
[77] 1 Thess. 5:21.
[78] Cf. 1 Tim. 4:6.
[79] Matt. 26:41.
[80] Cf. 2 Pet. 3:17.
[81] Cf. 2 John 8.
[82] See 2 Pet. 3:18.
[83] See Luke 1:35.
[84] Exod. 28:36, etc.
[85] Cf. Rom. 12:1.
[86] Cf. 1 Cor. 6:20.
[87] Place and date as in *AM*.

Spiritual Idolatry

1 John 5:21

Little children, keep yourselves from idols.

1. There are two words that occur several times in this epistle, παιδία[1] and τεκνία,[2] both of which our translators render by the same expression, 'little children'. But their meaning is very different. The former is very properly rendered 'little children'; for it means 'babes in Christ'—those that have lately tasted of his love and are as yet weak and unestablished therein. The latter might with more propriety be rendered 'beloved children'; as it does not denote any more than the affection of the speaker to those whom he had begotten in the Lord.[3]

2. An ancient historian relates that when the Apostle was so enfeebled by age as not to be able to preach he was frequently brought into the congregation in his chair, and just uttered, 'Beloved children, love one another.'[4] He could not have given a more important advice. And equally important is this which lies before us—equally necessary for every part of the Church of Christ: 'Beloved children, keep yourselves from idols.'

3. Indeed there is a close connection between them: one cannot subsist without the other. As there is no firm foundation for the love of our brethren except the love of God, so there is no possibility of loving God except we 'keep ourselves from idols'.

But what are the *idols* of which the Apostle speaks? This is the first thing to be considered. We may then, in the second place, inquire how shall we keep ourselves from them.

I.1. We are first to consider, What are the idols of which the Apostle speaks? I do not conceive him to mean, at least not

---

[1] 1 John 2:13, 18. [2] 1 John 3:10; 5:2.
[3] But consult the lexicons (cf., e.g., Arndt and Gingrich, *Greek-English Lexicon*, and Liddell and Scott, *Greek-English Lexicon*); Wesley's translation is barely possible, but certainly not obvious.
[4] Cf. Jerome, *Commentary on Galatians* (6:10), in Migne, *PL*, XXVI.462.

principally, the idols that were worshipped by the heathens. They
to whom he was writing, whether they had been Jews or heathens,
were not in much danger from these. There is no probability that
the Jews now converted had ever been guilty of worshipping
5   them. As deeply given to this gross idolatry as the Israelites had
been for many ages, they were hardly ever entangled therein after
their return from the Babylonish Captivity. From that period the
whole body of Jews had shown a constant, deep abhorrence of it.
And the heathens, after they had once turned to the living God,
10   had their former idols in the utmost detestation. They abhorred
to touch the unclean thing; yea, they chose to lay down their lives
rather than return to the worship of those gods whom they now
knew to be devils.

     2. Neither can we reasonably suppose that he speaks of those
15   idols that are now worshipped in the Church of Rome; whether
angels, or the souls of departed saints, or images of gold, silver,
wood, or stone. None of these idols were known in the Christian
Church till some centuries after the time of the apostles. Once,
indeed, St. John himself 'fell down to worship before the face of
20   an angel'[5] that spake unto him, probably mistaking him, from his
glorious appearance, for the great angel of the covenant.[6] But the
strong reproof of the angel, which immediately followed, secured
the Christians from imitating that bad example. 'See thou do it
not:' as glorious as I may appear, I am not thy Master. 'I am thy
25   fellow servant, and of thy brethren the prophets: worship God.'[a]

     3. Setting then pagan and Romish idols aside, what are those of
which we are here warned by the Apostle? The preceding words
show us the meaning of these. 'This is the true God'—the end of
all the souls he has made, the centre of all created spirits—'and
30   eternal life,'[7] the only foundation of present as well as eternal
happiness. To him therefore alone our heart is due. And he
cannot, he will not quit his claim, or consent to its being given to
any other. He is continually saying to every child of man, 'My son,
give me thy heart!'[8] And to give our heart to any other is plain
35   idolatry. Accordingly, whatever takes our heart from him, or

[a] Rev. 22:9.

---

[5] Cf. Rev. 22:8.
[6] I.e., St. Michael.
[7] 1 John 5:20.
[8] Prov. 23:26.

shares it with him, is an idol; or, in other words, whatever we seek happiness in, independent of God.

4. Take an instance that occurs almost every day: a person who has been long involved in the world, surrounded and fatigued with abundance of business, having at length acquired an easy 5 fortune, disengages himself from all business and retires into the country—to be happy. Happy in what? Why, in taking his ease. For he intends now,

> *Somno et inertibus horis*
> *Ducere sollicitae jucunda oblivia vitae.*[9]   10

> To sleep, and pass away,
> In gentle inactivity the day!

Happy in eating and drinking whatever his heart desires: perhaps more elegant fare than that of the old Roman who feasted his imagination[10] before the treat was served up, who before he left 15 the town consoled himself with the thought of 'fat bacon and cabbage too'!

> *Uncta satis pingui ponentur oluscula lardo!*[11]

Happy—in altering, enlarging, rebuilding, or at least decorating, the old mansion-house he has purchased; and likewise in 20 improving everything about it, the stables, outhouses, grounds. But meantime where does God come in? Nowhere at all. He did not think about him. He no more thought of the King of heaven than of the King of France. God is not in his plan. The knowledge and love of God are entirely out of the question. Therefore this 25 whole scheme of happiness in retirement is idolatry from beginning to end.

5. If we descend to particulars, the first species of this idolatry is what St. John terms 'the desire of the flesh'.[12] We are apt to take this in too narrow a meaning, as if it related to one of the senses 30

---

[9] Horace, *Satires*, II.vi.61-62: 'now with sleep and idle hours, to quaff sweet forgetfulness of life's cares'. Cf. also *An Earnest Appeal*, §41 (11:60 in this edn.), and *An Estimate of the Manners of the Present Times*, §1 (*Bibliog*, No. 426, Vol. 15 of this edn.).

[10] Cf. below, I.7, 8, 12; also No. 44, 'Original Sin', II.10 and n.

[11] Horace, *Satires*, II.vi.63-64: '*O quando faba, Pythagorae, cognata simulque uncta satis pingui ponentur oluscula lardo!*' 'O when shall beans, brethren of Pythagoras, be served me and, with them, greens [cabbage?] well larded with fat bacon!' Cf. Wesley's translation in JWJ, Nov. 5, 1766.

[12] The *triplex concupiscentia* again; see No. 7, 'The Way to the Kingdom', II.2 and n.

only. Not so: this expression equally refers to all the outward
senses. It means the seeking happiness in the gratification of any
or all of the external senses; although more particularly of the
three lower senses, tasting, smelling, and feeling. It means the
5 seeking happiness herein, if not in a gross, indelicate manner, by
open intemperance, by gluttony, or drunkenness, or shameless
debauchery; yet in a regular kind of epicurism,[13] in a genteel
sensuality, in such an elegant course of self-indulgence as does
not disorder either the head or the stomach, as does not at all
10 impair our health or blemish our reputation.

6. But we must not imagine this species of idolatry is confined
to the rich and great. In this also 'the toe of the peasant' (as our
poet speaks) 'treads upon the heel of the courtier.'[14] Thousands in
low as well as in high life sacrifice to this idol; seeking their
15 happiness (though in a more humble manner) in gratifying their
outward senses. It is true, their meat, their drink, and the objects
that gratify their other senses, are of a coarser kind. But still they
make up all the happiness they either have or seek, and usurp the
hearts which are due to God.

20 7. The second species of idolatry mentioned by the Apostle is
'the desire of the eye';[15] that is, the seeking happiness in gratifying
the imagination[16] (chiefly by means of the eyes)—that internal
sense which is as natural to men as either sight or hearing. This is
gratified by such objects as are either grand, or beautiful, or
25 uncommon. But as to grand objects, it seems they do not please
any longer than they are new.[17] Were we to survey the pyramids of
Egypt[18] daily for a year, what pleasure would they then give? Nay,
what pleasure does a far grander object than these,

The ocean rolling on the shelly shore,[19]

---

[13] For Epicurus as a sort of eponym, cf. No. 9, 'The Spirit of Bondage and of Adoption',
I.2 and n.

[14] Cf. Shakespeare, *Hamlet*, V.i.153: 'The age is grown so picked that the toe of the
peasant comes so near the heel of the courtier, he galls his kibe.' For other variations on
this quotation, see Wesley's letter to the Editor of *Lloyd's Evening Post*, Dec. 9, 1772, and
also his *Thoughts on the Present Scarcity of Provisions*, I.6 (*Bibliog*, No. 344, Vol. 15 of this
edn.).

[15] 1 John 2:16; see I.5, above.

[16] Cf. above, I.4 and n.

[17] For a continuing discussion of novelty, cf. the following paragraphs as well as No. 25,
'Sermon on the Mount, V', §1 and n.

[18] Cf. No. 54, 'On Eternity', §8 and n.

[19] Cf. Prior, *Solomon*, iii.160, 'The ocean rolling, and the shelly shore'; see also Wesley,
A Collection of Moral and Sacred Poems (1744), I.169.

give to one who has been long accustomed to it? Yea, what pleasure do we generally receive from the grandest object in the universe,

> Yon ample, azure sky,
> Terribly large, and wonderfully bright,   5
> With stars unnumbered, and unmeasured light?[20]

8. Beautiful objects are the next general source of the pleasures of the imagination—the works of nature in particular. So persons in all ages have been delighted

> With sylvan scenes, and hill and dale,   10
> And liquid lapse of murmuring streams.[21]

Others are pleased with adding art to nature, as in gardens with their various ornaments; others with mere works of art, as buildings and representations of nature, whether in statues or paintings. Many likewise find pleasure in beautiful *apparel* or 15 *furniture* of various kinds. But novelty must be added to beauty, as well as grandeur, or it soon palls upon the sense.

9. Are we to refer to the head of beauty the pleasure which many take in a *favourite animal*—suppose a sparrow, a parrot, a cat, a lap-dog? Sometimes it may be owing to this. At other times 20 none but the person pleased can find any beauty at all in the favourite. Nay, perchance it is in the eye of all other persons superlatively ugly. In this case the pleasure seems to arise from mere whim or caprice—that is, madness.

10. Must we not refer to the head of novelty, chiefly, the 25 pleasure found in most *diversions* and *amusements;* which, were we to repeat them daily but a few months would be utterly flat and insipid? To the same head we may refer the pleasure that is taken in *collecting curiosities;*[22] whether they are natural or artificial,

---

[20] Cf. Prior, *Solomon*, i.638-40, beginning 'This fair half-round, this ample azure sky'. See also Wesley, *A Collection of Moral and Sacred Poems* (1744), I.115; and No. 103, 'What is Man? Ps. 8:3-4', §2.

[21] Cf. Milton, *Paradise Lost*, iv.140 ('a sylvan scene'), and viii.262-63:

> Hill, dale, and shady woods, and sunny plains,
> And liquid lapse of murmuring streams. . . .

See No. 56, 'God's Approbation of His Works', I.4 and n.

[22] An echo from a recent *Journal* entry (for Dec. 22, 1780): 'At the desire of some of my friends, I accompanied them to the British Museum. What an immense field is here for curiosity to range! One large room is filled from top to bottom with things brought from

whether old or new. This sweetens the labour of the virtuoso, and makes all his labour light.

11. But it is not chiefly to novelty that we are to impute the pleasure we receive from *music.* Certainly this has an intrinsic beauty, as well as frequently an intrinsic grandeur. This is a beauty and grandeur of a peculiar kind, not easy to be expressed; nearly related to the sublime and the beautiful in *poetry*, which give an exquisite pleasure.[23] And yet it may be allowed that novelty heightens the pleasure which arises from any of these sources.

12. From the study of *languages*, from *criticism*, and from *history*, we receive a pleasure of a mixed nature. In all these there is always something new; frequently something beautiful or sublime. And history not only gratifies the imagination[24] in all these respects, but likewise pleases us by touching our passions, our love, desire, joy, pity. The last of these gives us a strong pleasure, though strangely mixed with a kind of pain. So that one need not wonder at the exclamation of a fine poet,

> What is all mirth but turbulence unholy,
> When to the charms compared of heavenly melancholy?[25]

13. The love of novelty is immeasurably gratified by *experimental philosophy;* and, indeed, by every branch of *natural philosophy*, which opens an immense field for still new discoveries. But is there not likewise a pleasure therein, as well as in *mathematical* and *metaphysical* studies, which does not result from the imagination, but from the exercise of the understanding? Unless we will say that the newness of the discoveries which we make by mathematical or metaphysical researches is one reason

Otaheite [Tahiti]; two or three more with things dug out of the ruins of Herculaneum [first excavated in 1738]. Seven huge apartments are filled with curious books, five with manuscripts, two with fossils of all sorts, and the rest with various animals. But what account will a man give to the Judge of the quick and dead for a life spent in collecting all these?'

[23] An echo from Edmund Burke's famous *Philosophical Inquiry into the Origins of Our Ideas of the Sublime and the Beautiful* (1756), which Wesley had read.

[24] Cf. above, I.4 and n.

[25] Cf. James Beattie, 'The Minstrel', I.1v.8-9:

> Ah! what is mirth but turbulence unholy
> When with the charm compared of heavenly melancholy?

In JWJ, Dec. 16, 1775, Wesley adjudges Beattie (1735–1803) as 'certainly one of the best poets of the age. He wants only the ease and simplicity of Mr. Pope. I know one, and only one, that has it.' This one, presumably, would have been his brother Charles. Beattie's 'Retirement' and 'Hermit' appeared in *AM*, Dec. 1778 and Oct. 1786.

at least, if not the chief, of the pleasure we receive therefrom. 14. I dwell the longer on these things because so very few see them in the true point of view. The generality of men, and more particularly men of sense and learning, are so far from suspecting that there is, or can be, the least harm in them, that they seriously 5 believe it is matter of great praise to 'give ourselves wholly to them'.[26] Who of them, for instance, would not admire and commend the indefatigable industry of that great philosopher[27] who says: 'I have been now eight and thirty years at my parish of Upminster. And I have made it clear that there are no less than 10 three and fifty species of butterflies therein. But if God should spare my life a few years longer, I do not doubt but I should demonstrate there are five and fifty!' I allow that most of these studies have their use, and that it is possible to *use* without *abusing*[28] them. But if we seek our happiness in any of these 15 things, then it commences an *idol*. And the enjoyment of it, however it may be admired and applauded by the world, is condemned of God as neither better nor worse than damnable *idolatry*.

15. The third kind of 'love of the world' the Apostle speaks of 20 under that uncommon expression, ἡ ἀλαζονεία τοῦ βίου.[29] This is rendered by our translators, 'the pride of life'. It is usually supposed to mean the pomp and splendour of those that are in high life. But has it not a more extensive sense? Does it not rather mean the seeking happiness in the praise of men, which above all 25 things engenders pride? When this is pursued in a more pompous way, by kings or illustrious men, we call it thirst for glory; when it is sought in a lower way, by ordinary men, it is styled, taking care of our reputation. In plain terms, it is seeking the honour that cometh of men instead of that which 'cometh of God only'.[30] 30

---

[26] 1 Tim. 4:15.

[27] William Derham (1657–1735), rector of Upminster in Essex (1689–1735), Fellow of the Royal Society, Canon of Windsor (1716–35). His *Physico-Theology* (1713) and *Astro-Theology* (1715) greatly influenced William Paley, and Wesley claimed to have included the substance of Derham's work in his own *Survey*; cf. his letter to Miss M. Lewen in *AM* (1780), pp. 602-4. Wesley's quotation from Derham may have come to him from oral tradition since it does not appear in Derham's published writings, or in Leslie Stephen's life of Derham in the *DNB*, or in Eleazar Albin's *Natural History of English Insects* (1724), to which Derham contributed notes. Incidentally, *The Victoria History of the Counties of England: Essex* (1903-56), I.136-43, lists fifty-four species of butterflies as having been identified in Essex, at the turn of the twentieth century.

[28] Cf. No. 20, *The Lord Our Righteousness*, II.20 and n.

[29] 1 John 2:16; see I.5, above.   [30] John 5:44.

16. But what creates a difficulty here is this: we are required, not only to 'give no offence to anyone',[31] and to 'provide things honest in the sight of all men',[32] but to 'please all men for their good to edification'.[33] But how difficult is it to do this with a single eye to God! We ought to do all that in us lies to prevent 'the good that is in us from being evil spoken of'.[34] Yea, we ought to value a clear reputation, if it be given us, only less than a good conscience. But yet, if we seek our happiness therein, we are liable to perish in our idolatry.

17. To which of the preceding heads is 'the love of money'[35] to be referred? Perhaps sometimes to one and sometimes to another, as it is a means of procuring gratifications either for 'the desire of the flesh', for 'the desire of the eyes', or for 'the pride of life'. In any of these cases money is only pursued in order to a farther end. But it is sometimes pursued for its own sake, without any farther view. One who is properly a miser loves and seeks money for its own sake. He looks no farther, but places his happiness in the acquiring or the possessing of it. And this is a species of idolatry distant[36] from all the preceding and, indeed, the lowest, basest idolatry of which the human soul is capable. To seek happiness either in gratifying this or any other of the desires above mentioned is effectually to renounce the true God, and to set up an idol in his place. In a word, so many objects as there are in the world wherein men seek happiness instead of seeking it in God, so many *idols* they set up in their hearts; so many species of *idolatry* they practise.

18. I would take notice of only one more, which, though it in some measure falls in with several of the preceding, yet in many respects is distinct from them all, I mean the idolizing any human creature. Undoubtedly it is the will of God that we should all love one another. It is his will that we should love our relations and our Christian brethren with a peculiar love; and those in particular whom he has made particularly profitable to our souls. These we are commanded to 'love fervently'—yet still 'with a pure heart'.[37]

---

[31] Cf. 2 Cor. 6:3.
[32] Rom. 12:17.
[33] Cf. Rom. 15:2.
[34] Cf. Rom. 14:16.
[35] 1 Tim. 6:10.
[36] The texts in *AM* and in *SOSO*, VI, read 'distant', and no alteration is made in the printed errata or Wesley's own copy of the former. Jackson (1825) altered it to read 'distinct', however, and this *may* have come from Wesley's revised copy of *SOSO*, VI, now missing. The original text does read 'distinct' in the opening sentence of I.18.
[37] Cf. 1 Pet. 1:22.

But is not this 'impossible with man'?[38] To retain the strength and tenderness of affection, and yet without any stain to the soul, with unspotted purity? I do not mean only unspotted by lust. I know this is possible. I know a person may have an unutterable affection for another without any desire of this kind. But is it without idolatry? Is it not loving the creature more than the Creator?[39] Is it not putting a man or woman in the place of God? Giving them your heart? Let this be carefully considered, even by those whom God has joined together[40]—by husbands and wives, parents and children. It cannot be denied that these ought to love one another tenderly: they are commanded so to do. But they are neither commanded nor permitted to love one another idolatrously! Yet how common is this! How frequently is a husband, a wife, a child, put in the place of God! How many that are accounted good Christians fix their affections on each other so as to leave no place for God! They seek their happiness in the creature, not in the Creator. One may truly say to the other,

> I view thee, lord and end of my desires.[41]

That is: 'I desire nothing more but thee! Thou art the thing that I long for! All my desire is unto thee, and unto the remembrance of thy name.' Now if this is not flat idolatry I cannot tell what is!

II. Having largely considered what those *idols* are of which the Apostle speaks, I will come now to inquire (which may be done more briefly) how we may 'keep ourselves from them'.

1. In order to this I would advise you, first, be deeply convinced that none of them bring happiness; that no thing, no person under the sun—no, nor the amassment of all together—can give any solid, satisfactory happiness to any child of man. The world itself, the giddy, thoughtless world, acknowledge this unawares, while they allow, nay, vehemently maintain, 'No man upon earth is contented.' The very same observation was made near two thousand years ago.

---

[38] Cf. Matt. 19:26.

[39] See Rom. 1:25.

[40] Matt. 19:6.

[41] Cf. Prior, 'Henry and Emma', 710. Wesley had published this poem in the Sept. issue of *AM* (1779), II.481-96. Some of his readers complained that it 'was not strictly religious'. Wesley's extended response to such a criticism is an interesting reflection of his own theology of culture (see 'To the Reader', *AM*, 1780, III.iv-v).

Nemo quam sibi sortem
Seu ratio dederit, seu fors, objecerit, illa
Contentus vivat:[42]

Let fortune, or let choice the station give
5   To man, yet none on earth contented live.

And if no man upon earth is contented, it is certain no man is
happy. For whatever station we are in, discontent is incompatible
with happiness.

2. Indeed not only the giddy but the thinking part of the world
10 allow that no man is contented, the melancholy proofs of which
we see on every side, in high and low, rich and poor. And
generally, the more understanding they have, the more
discontented they are. For,

They know with more distinction to complain,
15   And have superior sense in feeling pain.[43]

It is true, everyone has (to use the cant term of the day—and an
excellent one it is) his 'hobby-horse'![44] Something that pleases the
great boy for a few hours or days, and wherein he *hopes* to be
happy! But though

20   Hope blooms eternal in the human breast;
        Man never *is*, but always *to be* blest.[45]

Still he is walking in a vain shadow which will soon vanish
away![46] So that universal experience, both our own and that of all
our friends and acquaintance, clearly proves that as God made
25 our hearts for himself, so they cannot rest till they rest in him;[47]

---

[42] Horace, *Satires*, I.i.1-3. Is the translation here Wesley's own? It is neither Pope's nor
Dryden's. Loeb translates: 'No man living is content with the lot which either his choice
has given him or chance has thrown in his way.'

[43] Matthew Prior, *Solomon*, iii.345-46, beginning 'To know'; cf. Wesley, *A Collection of
Moral and Sacred Poems* (1744), I.174. See also, Sermon 125, 'On a Single Eye', II.5,
where Wesley again quotes these lines as well as the two preceding.

[44] I.e., a child's plaything; cf. Horace, *Satires*, II. iii. 247-49, and Erasmus, *In Praise of
Folly* ('Epistle to More'), p. xviii. But Wesley also uses the term to mean 'a chamber horse'
for exercise: 'If you have no other [horse] you should daily ride a wooden horse, which is
only a double plank nine or ten feet long, properly placed upon two tressels. This has
removed many distempers and saved abundance of lives' (cf. letters to Mrs. Christian, July
17, 1785; Samuel Bradburn, Mar. 13, 1788; and Sarah Wesley, Aug. 18, 1790).

[45] Cf. Pope, *Essay on Man*, i.95-96. Cf. also Wesley, *A Collection of Moral and Sacred
Poems* (1744), I.305, with the footnote added: 'Yes, blessed is the man whose iniquity is
forgiven, and his sin covered' (cf. Ps. 32:1).

[46] See Ps. 39:7.

[47] See Augustine, *Confessions*, I.i; cf. also No. 3, '*Awake, Thou That Sleepest*', II.5 and n.

that till we *acquaint* ourselves with him we cannot be at peace. As 'a scorner' of the wisdom of God 'seeketh wisdom and findeth it not,'[48] so a scorner of happiness in God seeketh happiness but findeth none.

3. When you are thoroughly convinced of this I advise you, secondly, stand and consider what you are about. Will you be a fool and a madman all your days? Is it not high time to come to your senses? At length awake out of sleep, and shake yourself from the dust! Break loose from this miserable idolatry, and 'choose the better part.'[49] Steadily resolve to seek happiness where it may be found—where it cannot be sought in vain. Resolve to seek it in the true God, the fountain of all blessedness! And cut off all delay. Straightway put in execution what you have resolved! Seeing 'all things are ready,'[50] 'acquaint thyself now with him, and be at peace.'[51]

4. But do not either resolve or attempt to execute your resolution trusting in your own strength. If you do you will be utterly foiled. You are not able to contend with the evil world, much less with your own evil heart, and least of all with the powers of darkness. Cry therefore to the Strong for strength.[52] Under a deep sense of your own weakness and helplessness, 'trust thou in the Lord Jehovah, in whom is everlasting strength.'[53] I advise you to cry to him for repentance in particular, not only for a full consciousness of your own impotence, but for a piercing sense of the exceeding guilt, baseness, and madness of the idolatry that has long swallowed you up. Cry for a thorough knowledge of yourself, of all your sinfulness and guiltiness. Pray that you may be fully discovered to yourself, that you may know yourself as also you are known.[54] When once you are possessed of this genuine conviction, all your idols will lose their charms. And you will wonder how you could so long lean upon those broken reeds which had so often sunk under you.

5. What should you ask for next?

> Jesus, now I have lost my all,
> Let me upon thy bosom fall![55]

---

[48] Prov. 14:6.   [49] Cf. Luke 10:42.   [50] Matt. 22:4.
[51] Cf. Job 22:21.   [52] See No. 48, 'Self-denial', III.4 and n.   [53] Cf. Isa. 26:4.
[54] See 1 Cor. 13:12. For Wesley's notion of repentance as self-knowledge, cf. No. 7, 'The Way to the Kingdom', II.1 and n.
[55] Cf. John and Charles Wesley, 'Come, Lord Jesus!', st. 9, ll. 3-4, in *Hymns and Sacred Poems* (1742), p. 205 (*Poet. Wks.*, II.259). See also, *A Collection of Hymns* (1780), No. 157 (7:277 of this edn.).

Now let me see thee in thy vesture dipped in blood!

> Now stand in all thy wounds confest,
> And wrap me in thy crimson vest![56]

Hast thou not said, 'If thou canst believe',[57] 'thou shalt see the
5 glory of God'?[58] 'Lord, I *would* believe! Help thou mine
unbelief !'[59] And help me *now!* Help me now to enter into the rest
that remaineth for the people of God![60] For those who give thee
their heart, their whole heart! Who receive thee as their God and
their all! O thou that art fairer than the children of men, full of
10 grace are thy lips![61] Speak, that I may see thee! And as the
shadows flee before the sun, so let all my idols vanish at thy
presence!

6. From the moment that you begin to experience this, fight the
good fight of faith;[62] take the kingdom of heaven by violence![63]
15 Take it as it were by storm. Deny yourself every pleasure that you
are not divinely conscious brings you nearer to God. Take up
your cross daily.[64] Regard no pain if it lies in your way to him. If
you are called thereto, scruple not to pluck out the right eye and to
cast it from you.[65] Nothing is impossible to him that believeth:[66]
20 you can do all things through Christ that strengtheneth you.[67] Do
valiantly, and stand fast in the liberty wherewith Christ hath made
you free.[68] Yea, go on in his name and in the power of his might,[69]
till you 'know all that love of God that passeth knowledge'.[70] And
then you have only to wait till he shall call you into his everlasting
25 kingdom.

London, Jan. 5, 1781[71]

[56] Cf. Charles Wesley, Hymn 161, in *Hymns for a Family* (1767), p. 171 (*Poet. Wks.*,
VII.194). Wesley has conflated lines from two verses:

> Come then, and to my soul reveal
> The heights and depths of grace,
> Those wounds which all my sorrows heal,
> That dear disfigured face.

> Before my eyes of faith confessed
> Stand forth a slaughter'd Lamb,
> And wrap me in thy crimson vest,
> And tell me all thy name.

[57] Mark 9:23.   [58] Cf. John 11:40.   [59] Cf. Mark 9:24.
[60] See Heb. 4:9.   [61] See Ps. 45:2 (BCP).   [62] 1 Tim. 6:12.
[63] See Matt. 11:12.   [64] See Luke 9:23.   [65] See Matt. 5:29.
[66] See Mark 9:23.   [67] See Phil. 4:13.   [68] See Gal. 5:1.
[69] Eph. 6:10.   [70] Eph. 3:19.   [71] The date and place are added only in *AM*.

ON DISSIPATION

AN INTRODUCTORY COMMENT

This sermon is yet another variation on the same theme as its two predecessors: that life centred in God is valid and secure, whereas life that is uncentred from God generates 'every possible evil temper, evil word, or evil action'. The interesting thing here about Wesley's sensitivity to current rhetorical fashion is his deliberate borrowing of what he knows to be 'a cant word of the day' and turning its newly acquired pejorative connotation into a theological definition, 'the uncentring of the soul from God'.

He was well aware that the word 'dissipation' had not appeared in any of the English translations of ἀπερισπάστως (itself a singular usage in 1 Cor. 7:35), so that it takes some straining to get from its common interpretation, 'distraction', with its traditionally neutral connotation of 'scattered attention' or 'overburden' (impedimenta in the Vulgate), to his desired meaning for it of self-centredness and, therefore, self-indulgence. Such a shift, however, had already begun to happen in then current English usage (see below, §1 and n.), and it is typical that Wesley pitches on that for his own homiletical purposes. Indeed, his first recorded use of 1 Cor. 7:35 for oral preaching does not come until 1751 (once); then he uses it twice in 1760 and six times in 1783. There is a clear connection here with his discovery of a recent SPCK pamphlet (1772) by Sir James Stonhouse, M.D., physician and rector of Little and Great Cheverell near Devizes, in which the doctor denounced 'drunkenness, swearing, etc.' under the pejorative label of 'dissipation'.[1] This prompted Wesley to write a tract of his own for the Arminian Magazine, *entitled 'Thoughts Upon Dissipation', dated at* Hilton Park, *'March 26, 1783', and published two years later.[2]*

He also wrote out this sermon on 1 Cor. 7:35 as a sort of expansion of that tract. But he then published the sermon before the tract, in the Arminian Magazine *(Vol. VII), with its biblical text but no title, in the instalments for January and February 1784, pp. 7-13, 66-70,*

[1] JWJ, Mar. 24-26, 1783.
[2] AM, Dec. 1785, VIII.643-46.

numbered as 'Sermon XIX'. Later, he would place it in a different sequence in SOSO, *VI. 281-97, where it appeared, now with a title, as a sequel to 'Spiritual Worship' and 'Spiritual Idolatry'. Although it was not reprinted elsewhere in Wesley's lifetime, the topic reappears again and again in his last years, as in his 1788 definition of 'dissipation' as 'the art of forgetting God . . . ; a total studied inattention to the whole invisible and eternal world'.*[3]

On Dissipation

1 Corinthians 7:35

This I speak . . . that ye may attend upon the Lord without distraction.

5   1. Almost in every part of our nation, more especially in the large and populous towns, we hear a general complaint among sensible persons of the still increasing 'dissipation'. It is observed to diffuse itself more and more in the court, the city, and the country. From the continual mention which is made of this, and 10 the continual declamations against it, one would naturally imagine that a word so commonly used was perfectly understood. Yet it may be doubted whether it be or no. Nay, we may very safely affirm that few of those who frequently use the term understand what it means. One reason of this is that although the thing has 15 been long among us, especially since the time of King Charles II (one of the most dissipated mortals that ever breathed)[1] yet the word is not of long standing.[2] It was hardly heard of fifty years ago;

---

[3] Nos. 119, 'Walking by Sight and Walking by Faith', §§20-21; and 128, 'The Deceitfulness of the Human Heart', I.3.

---

[1] See No. 68, 'The Wisdom of God's Counsels', §12 and n.
[2] See *OED* on this point; its earliest instance is 1545. Johnson in his *Dictionary* had defined the term in its two current meanings: 'dispersion' and 'scattered attention'. The first instance given in the *OED* for 'waste of moral and physical powers by undue or vicious indulgence, etc.' is from William Cowper's *The Task*, II.770, in 1784. But James Beattie had used it thus in *The Minstrel*, II.27, in 1744 ('In the giddy storm of dissipation toss'd'), and Anthony Godeau had used it as early as 1703 in Wesley's exact sense ('the soul of man . . . as being removed from its proper centre, from the knowledge of Almighty God')

and not much before the present reign. So lately has it been imported: and yet it is so in everyone's mouth that it is already worn threadbare, being one of the cant words of the day.

2. Another reason why it is so little understood may be that among the numberless writers that swarm about us there is not 5 one (at least whom I have seen) that has published so much as a sixpenny pamphlet concerning it. We have indeed one short essay upon the subject; but exceeding few have seen it, as it stands in the midst of a volume of essays, the author of which is little known in the world.[3] And even this is so far from going to the bottom of 10 the subject that it only slightly glances over it; and does not so much as give us one definition of dissipation (which I looked narrowly for) from the beginning to the end.

3. We are accustomed to speak of dissipation as having respect chiefly, if not wholly, to the outward behaviour—to the manner of 15 life. But it is within before it appears without: it is in the heart before it is seen in the outward conversation. There must be a dissipated spirit before there is a dissipated manner of life. But what is dissipation of spirit? This is the first and the grand inquiry.

4. God created all things for himself; more especially all 20 intelligent spirits. (And indeed it seems that intelligence, in some kind or degree, is inseparable from spiritual beings, that intelligence is as essential to spirits as extension is to matter.)[4] He made those more directly for himself, to know, love, and enjoy him. As the sun is the centre of the solar system, so (as far as we 25 may compare material things with spiritual) we need not scruple to affirm that God is the centre of spirits. And as long as they are united to him, created spirits are at rest: they are at rest so long, and no longer, as they 'attend upon the Lord without distraction'.

---

in his *Pastoral Instructions and Meditations*, p. 1. Wesley's more immediate source, however, was Sir James Stonhouse, 'Admonitions against Swearing, Sabbath-breaking, and Drunkenness', an eleven-page pamphlet, published in 1772 as a tract for *The Society for Promoting Christian Knowledge* (popular enough to run through fifteen edns. by 1800).

[3] This author, quite probably, was Dr. Stonhouse, despite the fact that he was 'known [well enough] in the world' to rate an entry in the *DNB*. But it could have been Hannah More, whom Wesley would have reckoned as 'little known in the world' of *his* readers. She and Dr. Stonhouse were friends; and the first of her *Essays on Various Subjects, principally designed for Young Ladies* (1777) is entitled 'On Dissipation' (cf. her *Works*, 1847, II.552-54). Wesley wrote his own 'Thoughts Upon Dissipation' and published the tract in *AM* (1785), VIII.643. For some of Wesley's other comments on 'dissipation', see Nos. 81, 'In What Sense we are to Leave the World', §16; 108, 'On Riches', II.1; 119, 'Walking by Sight and Walking by Faith', §20; and 128, 'The Deceitfulness of the Human Heart', I.3.

[4] An echo of Descartes's distinction between matter as *res extensa* and spirit as *res cogitans*.

5. This expression of the Apostle (not to encumber ourselves at present with the particular occasion of his speaking) is exceeding peculiar: πρὸς τὸ εὐπρόσεδρον τῷ κυρίῳ.[5] The word which we render 'attend upon' literally means sitting in a good posture for hearing. And therein St. Paul undoubtedly alluded to Mary sitting at the Master's feet, Luke 10:39. Meantime Martha was 'cumbered' with much serving, was *distracted, dissipated—περιε-σπᾶτο*.[6] It is the very expression from whence St. Paul takes the word which we render 'without distraction'.[7]

6. And even as much serving dissipated the thoughts of Martha, and distracted her from attending to her Lord's words, so a thousand things which daily occur are apt to dissipate our thoughts, and distract us from attending to his voice who is continually speaking to our hearts—I mean, to all that listen to his voice. We are encompassed on all sides with persons and things that tend to draw us from our centre.[8] Indeed every creature, if we are not continually on our guard, will draw us from our Creator. The whole visible world, all we see, hear, or touch, all the objects either of our senses or understanding, have a tendency to dissipate our thoughts from the invisible world, and to distract our minds from attending to him who is both the author and end of our being.

7. This is the more easily done because we are all by nature 'atheists in the world';[9] and that in so high a degree that it requires no less than an almighty power to counteract that tendency to dissipation which is in every human spirit, and restore the capacity of attending to God, and fixing itself on him. For this cannot be done till we are new creatures, till we are created anew

---

[5] 1 Cor. 7:35. Modern critical texts read εὐπάρεδρον ('attentive') in place of εὐπρόσεδρον ('constant'), as in the *TR* that served Wesley as his text.

[6] Luke 10:40.

[7] ἀπερισπάστως, 1 Cor. 7:35.

[8] This image of the soul centred in God is basic in Wesley's thought; cf. Nos. 84, *The Important Question*, III.7 ('we are unhinged from our proper centre'); and 108, 'On Riches', II.1 (uncentring from God'). It had been a favourite of his mother (see Moore, *Wesley*, I.328) and derives from the mystical tradition of Christian Platonism; cf. John Norris, *A Collection of Miscellanies* (1692), pp. 239, 323, 327 (where Plotinus is cited as describing the union of the soul with God as a 'joining of centre to centre').

[9] Eph. 2:12, an overly literal translation of ἄθεοι ('godless'), an epithet used by Christians referring to the pagans, as here, or in *Logia Jesu*, 1:5, and in *Martyrdom of Polycarp*, 9:2ᵇ; alternatively by pagans with reference to the Christians, as in *ibid.*, 9:2ᵃ, and in Justin Martyr, *The First Apology*, chs. 6, 13, etc.; see also No. 44, *Original Sin*, II.3 and n.

in Christ Jesus,[10] till the same power which made the world 'make us a clean heart', and 'renew a right spirit within us'.[11]

8. But who is he that is thus renewed? He that believeth in the name of the Son of God. He alone that believeth on the Lord Jesus Christ is thus 'born of God'.[12] It is by this faith alone that he is 'created anew in' or *through* 'Christ Jesus', that he is restored to the image of God wherein he was created, and again centred in God, or, as the Apostle expresses it, 'joined to the Lord' in 'one spirit'.[13] Yet even then the believer may find in himself the remains of that 'carnal mind',[14] that natural tendency to rest in created good, to acquiesce in visible things, which, without continual care, will press down his soul, and draw him from his Creator. Herein the world—the men that know not God—will never fail to join; at some times with design, and at other times perhaps without design: for their very spirit is infectious, and insensibly changes ours into its own likeness. And we may be well assured, the prince of this world, the devil, will assist them with all his might. He will labour with all his strength, and, what is far more dangerous, with all his subtlety, if by any means he may draw us away from our 'simplicity towards Christ';[15] from our simple adherence to him, from our union with him, through whom we are also united in one spirit to the Father.

9. But nothing is more certain than this, that though he may tempt the strongest believer to give up his 'simplicity toward Christ', and scatter his thoughts and desires among worldly objects; yet he cannot force even the weakest, for the grace of God is still sufficient for him. The same grace which at first united him to God is able to continue that happy union, in spite of all the rage, and all the strength, and all the subtlety of the enemy. God has never left himself without witness that he has power to deliver them that trust in him, as out of every temptation that can assault them, so out of this in particular. He has still a little flock who do in fact 'attend upon him without distraction'; who, cleaving to him with full purpose, are not dissipated from him; no, not for a moment, but 'rejoice evermore, pray without ceasing, and in everything give thanks'.[16]

---

[10] See Eph. 2:10.
[12] 1 John 3:9, etc.
[14] Rom. 8:7.
[15] Cf. 2 Cor. 11:3.
[16] 1 Thess. 5:16-18.

[11] Cf. Ps. 51:10 (BCP).
[13] 1 Cor. 6:17.

10. But so far as anyone yields to this temptation, so far he is 'dissipated'. The original word properly signifies to 'disperse' or 'scatter'. So the sun dissipates, that is, scatters, the clouds; the wind dissipates or scatters the dust. And by an easy metaphor our thoughts are said to be dissipated when they are irregularly scattered up and down. In like manner our desires are dissipated when they are unhinged from God, their proper centre, and scattered to and fro among the poor, perishing, unsatisfying things of the world. And indeed it may be said of every man that is a stranger to the grace of God, that all his passions are dissipated.

Scattered o'er all the earth abroad,
Immeasurably far from God.[17]

11. 'Distraction', in St. Paul's sense, is nearly allied to, or rather the same with, dissipation; consequently, to attend upon the Lord 'without distraction' is the same as to attend upon the Lord 'without dissipation'. But whenever the mind is unhinged from God it is so far dissipated or distracted. Dissipation then, in general, may be defined, the uncentring the soul from God. And whatever uncentres the mind from God does properly dissipate us.

12. Hence we may easily learn what is the proper, direct meaning of that common expression, a 'dissipated man'. He is a man that is separated from God, that is disunited from his centre, whether this be occasioned by hurry of business, by seeking honour or preferment, or by fondness for diversions, for silly pleasures, so called, or for any trifle under the sun. The vulgar, it is true, commonly confine this character to those who are violently attached to women, gaming, drinking; to dancing, balls, races, or the poor, childish diversion of 'running foxes and hares out of breath'.[18] But it equally belongs to the serious fool who forgets God by a close attention to any worldly employment, suppose it were of the most elegant or the most important kind. A man may be as much dissipated from God by the study of the mathematics or astronomy as by fondness for cards or hounds. Whoever is habitually inattentive to the presence and will of his Creator, he is a 'dissipated' man.

---

[17] John and Charles Wesley, 'Psalm 139:23', *Hymns and Sacred Poems* (1739), p. 98 (*Poet. Wks.*, I.88).

[18] William Law, *A Practical Treatise Upon Christian Perfection* (1726), *Works*, III.38; cf. No. 89, 'The More Excellent Way', V.4 and n.

13. Hence we may likewise learn that a 'dissipated life' is not barely that of a powdered beau, of a petit-maître, a gamester, a woman-hunter, a playhouse-hunter, a fox-hunter, or a shatter-brain[19] of any kind; but the life of an honourable statesman, a gentleman, or a merchant, that is 'without God in the world'.[20] Agreeably to this a 'dissipated age' (such as is the present, perhaps beyond all that ever were—at least that are recorded in history) is an age wherein God is generally forgotten. And a 'dissipated nation' (such as England is at present in a superlative degree) is a nation a vast majority of which have not 'God in all their thoughts'.[21]

14. A plain consequence of these observations is (what some may esteem a paradox) that 'dissipation', in the full, general meaning of the word, is the very same thing with *ungodliness*. The name is new, but the thing is undoubtedly almost as old as the creation. And this is at present the peculiar glory of England, wherein it is not equalled by any nation under heaven. We therefore speak an unquestionable truth when we say, there is not on the face of the earth another *nation* (at least that we ever heard of) so perfectly *dissipated* and *ungodly;* not only so totally without God in the world, but so openly setting him at defiance. There never was an *age* that we read of in history, since Julius Caesar, since Noah, since Adam, wherein dissipation or ungodliness did so generally prevail, both among high and low, rich and poor.

15. But still, blessed be God!

> All are not lost! There be who faith prefer
> And piety to God![22]

There are some, I trust more than 'seven thousand', yea, or ten times that number, in England, 'who have not' yet 'bowed' either 'their knee'[23] or their heart to the god of this world; who, cleaving close to the God of heaven, are not borne away by the flood, by the general, the almost universal torrent of dissipation or ungodliness. They are not of the mind of gentle Crispus,

[19] Cf. *OED*, where this instance is cited: 'a giddy, thoughtless person'. 'Scatter-brain', with the same meaning, is first cited as of 1790.

[20] Eph. 2:12.

[21] Cf. Ps. 10:4 (BCP).

[22] Cf. Milton, *Paradise Lost*, vi.143-44; see also No. 52, *The Reformation of Manners*, II.1 and n.

[23] Rom. 11:4.

Qui nunquam direxit brachia contra torrentem[24]—

'who never attempted to swim against the stream'. They dare
swim against the stream. Each of them can truly say,

> . . . *non me, qui cetera, vincit*
> 5   *Impetus, et rapido contrarius evehor orbi.*[25]

If they cannot turn the tide back, they can at least bear an open
testimony against it. They are therefore free from the blood of
their ungodly countrymen: it must be upon their own head.

16. But by what means may we avoid the being carried away by
10 the overflowing stream of dissipation? It is not difficult for those
who believe the Scripture to give an answer to this question. Now
I really believe the Bible to be the Word of God; and on that
supposition I answer: the radical cure of all dissipation is the 'faith
that worketh by love'.[26] If therefore you would be free from this
15 evil disease, first 'continue steadfast in the faith;'[27] in that faith
which brings 'the spirit of adoption, crying in your heart, Abba,
Father;'[28] whereby you are enabled to testify, 'The life which I
now live, I live by faith in the Son of God, who loved me, and gave
himself for me.'[29] By this faith you 'see him that is invisible',[30] and
20 'set the Lord always before you'.[31] Next, 'building yourselves up
in your most holy faith, keep yourselves in the love of God,
waiting for the mercy of our Lord Jesus Christ, unto everlasting
life.'[32] And as long as you walk by this rule, you will be superior to
all dissipation.

25   17. How exactly does this agree (though there is a difference in
the expression) with that observation of pious Kempis:
'Simplicity and purity are the two wings which lift the soul up to
heaven. Simplicity is in the intention, purity in the affection'![33]

---

[24] Cf. Juvenal, *Satires*, iv.89-90: 'So Crispus never struck out those arms of his against
the torrent' (Loeb).

[25] Cf. Ovid, *Metamorphoses*, ii.72-73: 'nor does this swift motion which overcomes all
else overcome me; but I drive [forward] clear contrary to the swift circuit of the universe'
(Loeb).

[26] Gal. 5:6; cf. No. 2, *The Almost Christian*, II.6 and n.

[27] Cf. Acts 2:42.   [28] Cf. Rom. 8:15.

[29] Cf. Gal. 2:20.   [30] Cf. Heb. 11:27.

[31] Cf. Ps. 16:8 (AV).

[32] Cf. Jude 20-21.

[33] Kempis, *Imitation*, II.iv.1-3. Cf. No. 125, 'On a Single Eye', §1, where Wesley
repeats this quotation. For other references to Kempis, cf. No. 55, *On the Trinity*, §1 and n.
For 'simplicity' cf. No. 12, 'The Witness of Our Own Spirit', §11 and n.

For what is this but (in the Apostle's language) simple 'faith working by love'? By that simplicity you always see God, and by purity you love him! What is it but having (as one of the ancients speaks) 'the loving eye of the soul fixed upon God'?[34] And as long as your soul is in this posture, dissipation can have no place. 5

18. It is with great judgment, therefore, that great and good Bishop Taylor, in his *Rules of Holy Living and Dying* (of whom Bishop Warburton, a person not very prone to commend, used to say, 'I have no conception of a greater genius on earth than Dr. Jeremy Taylor'[35]), premises to all his other rules those concerning 10 purity of intention.[36] And has he not the authority of our Lord himself so to do?—who lays it down as an universal maxim, 'If thine eye be single, thy whole body shall be full of light.'[37] Singly aim at God. In every step thou takest, eye him alone. Pursue one thing: happiness in knowing, in loving, in serving God. Then shall 15 thy soul be full of light; full of the light of the glory of God, of his glorious love shining upon thee from 'the face of Jesus Christ'.[38]

19. Can anything be a greater help to universal holiness than the continually seeing the light of his glory? It is no wonder, then, that so many wise and good men have recommended, to all who 20 desire to be truly religious, the exercise of the presence of God. But in doing this some of those holy men seem to have fallen into one mistake (particularly an excellent writer of our own country, in his letters concerning *The Spirit of Prayer*).[39] They put men wholly unawakened, unconvinced of sin, upon this exercise at 25 their very entrance into religion; whereas this certainly should not be first, but rather one of the last things. They should begin with repentance, the knowledge of themselves,[40] of their sinfulness, guilt, and helplessness. They should be instructed next to seek peace with God, through our Lord Jesus Christ.[41] Then let them 30

[34] Cf. No. 81, §17, for 'the eyes of the soul'. The 'ancient' has not been identified.
[35] In William Warburton's letter to Bishop Richard Hurd in *Directions for the Study of Theology* (1750), in *Works* (1811), IX-X.368, he speaks of 'the very masterly manner of Bishop Taylor's'. For other references by Wesley to Warburton cf. No. 100, 'On Pleasing All Men', I.2 and n.
[36] Cf. Jeremy Taylor, *The Rule and Exercises of Holy Living* (1650), and *The Rule and Exercises of Holy Dying* (1651), *Works* (1844), I.399-604. Actually, Taylor lists 'Purity of Intention' as 'the *second* general instrument in holy living'; cf. *Holy Living*, I.ii.
[37] Matt. 6:22.   [38] 2 Cor. 4:6.
[39] William Law, *The Spirit of Prayer* (1749, 1750), *Works*, VII. 3-143. In a comment on this, Wesley deplores Law's 'method of converting deists by giving up the very essence of Christianity' (see JWJ, July 27, 1749).
[40] Cf. No. 7, 'The Way to the Kingdom', II.1 and n.   [41] Rom. 5:11.

be taught to retain what they have received, to 'walk in the light of his countenance';[42] yea, to 'walk in the light, as he is in the light', without any darkness at all, till 'the blood of Jesus Christ cleanseth' them 'from all sin'.[43]

5   20. It was from a full conviction of the absolute necessity there is of a Christian's setting the Lord always before him that a set of young gentlemen in Oxford,[44] who many years ago used to spend most of their evenings together in order to assist each other in working out their salvation, placed that question first in their
10 scheme of daily self-examination: 'Have I been *simple* and *recollected* in all I said or did? Have I been *simple?* That is, setting the Lord always before me, and doing everything with a single view of pleasing him? *Recollected*; that is, quickly gathering in my scattered thoughts, recovering my simplicity, if I had been in any
15 wise drawn from it by men or devils or my own evil heart.'[45] By this means they were preserved from dissipation, and were enabled each of them to say: 'By the grace of God "this one thing I do"[46] (at least, it is my constant aim): I see God; I love God; I serve God; I glorify him with my body and with my spirit.'

20   21. The same thing seems to be intended by two uncommon words which are frequently found in the writings of those pious men who are usually styled mystics. I mean 'introversion' and 'extroversion'.[47] 'Examine yourselves,' says St. Paul to the Corinthians, and in them to the Christians of all ages; 'Know ye
25 not that Christ is in you, except ye be reprobates?'[48]—that is, unbelievers, unable to bear the touchstone of God's word. Now the attending to the voice of Christ within you is what they term 'introversion'. The turning the eye of the mind from him to outward things they call 'extroversion'.[49] By this your thoughts

---

[42] Cf. Ps. 89:15.

[43] 1 John 1:7.

[44] Cf. No. 53, *On the Death of George Whitefield*, III.2 and n.

[45] Cf. 'A Scheme of Self-examination used by the first Methodists in Oxford', *AM*, IV.319 (June 1781). (See Vol. 9 of this edn.)

[46] Phil. 3:13.

[47] Cf. Johann Arndt, *True Christianity* (1712, 1714), III.i.2 (abridged in the *Christian Lib.*, I.155-290, II.5-206). *OED* cites Thomas Gataker, *A Discours Apologetical . . .* (1654), 68, Robert Barclay, *Apology* (1678), XI, §16, and this sermon of Wesley's as using 'introversion' to connote radical subjectivity. See also Thomas Blount, *Glossographia; Or, a Dictionary Interpreting All Such Hard Words, Whether Hebrew, Greek, Latin . . . As Are Now Used in Our Refined English Tongue* (1656), for 'extroversion' in the sense of 'mystical divinity, . . . a scattering of one's thoughts upon exterior objects'.

[48] 2 Cor. 13:5.   [49] Cf. Arndt, *op. cit.*

wander from God, and you are properly dissipated; whereas by introversion you may be always sensible of his loving presence. You continually hearken to whatever it pleases your Lord to say to your heart. And if you continually listen to his inward voice you will be kept from all dissipation. 5

22. We may, lastly, learn hence, what judgment to form of what is frequently urged in favour of the English nation, and of the present age; namely, that in other respects England stands on a level with other nations, and the present age stands upon a level with any of the preceding. Only it is allowed we are more 10 'dissipated' than our neighbours, and this age is more dissipated than the preceding ages. Nay, if this is allowed, all is allowed. It is allowed that this nation is worse than any of the neighbouring nations; and that this age is worse, essentially worse, than any of the preceding ages. For as dissipation or ungodliness is the parent 15 of all sin, of all unrighteousness; of unmercifulness, injustice, fraud, perfidy; of every possible evil temper, evil word, or evil action; so it in effect comprises them all. Whatsoever things are impure, whatsoever things are of evil report, whatsoever things are unholy; if there be any vice, all these are included in 20 ungodliness, usually termed dissipation.[50] Let not therefore any lover of virtue and truth say one word in favour of this monster; let no lover of mankind once open his mouth to extenuate the guilt of it. Abhor it, as you would abhor the devil, whose offspring and likeness it is. Abhor it, as you would abhor the extinction of all 25 virtue, and the universal prevalence of an earthly, sensual, devilish spirit;[51] and flee from it as you would flee (if you saw it open before you) the 'lake of fire burning with brimstone'.[52]

[50] A parody on Phil. 4:8.
[51] Jas. 3:15.
[52] Rev. 19:20.

ON FRIENDSHIP WITH THE WORLD

AN INTRODUCTORY COMMENT

This is another sermon written on the run, finished in Wakefield on the morning of May 1, 1786, just before Wesley's departing by chaise for Leeds at 11 a.m. (see JWJ and diary for April 30–May 4). Its central thesis is that all friendship with 'the world' is enmity against God. This, of course, required a special definition of ὁ κόσμος, not as the whole created order (as in Rom. 1:20; 1 Cor. 5:10; Eph. 1:4, etc.) but rather as the Christian's environing society: all human beings who are 'out of God' and who are, as a consequence, willing subjects of *'the Evil One'.*

What is so odd about this thesis is Wesley's stress on the novelty of his definition and on the paucity of literature on the subject, since he had grown up in the contemptus mundi *tradition and had been strongly reinforced in this by the mystics—pre-eminently, Thomas à Kempis and William Law. A probable clue to such a puzzle is Wesley's belated 'discovery' that 'the world', in this new sense, is less the theatre of 'worldly pleasures' than it is the aggregate of quite ordinary people (most of them professing Christians in his culture) who are, nevertheless, 'enemies of God'. This had somehow refocused the problem of Christian living: how can a Christian live and work in such a society? This sermon is an answer to that question. That it was for him a relatively new variation on the conventional theme of 'disdaining the world' is suggested by the fact that he himself had preached from Jas. 4:4 just once before, in London on December 11, 1784.*

He then published his new sermon in a single instalment in the Arminian Magazine *(August 1786, IX.404-17), the only instance of a whole sermon of Wesley's in a single issue. Without a title, it was numbered 'Sermon XXXIII'. The title was added when it was reprinted in* SOSO, *VI.299-322. It was not republished thereafter in Wesley's lifetime; nor did he return again to Jas. 4:4 for a preaching text as far as we know. The sermon must, however, have reminded the Methodists of the ominous temptations posed for them by their enhanced respectability in this same world and by their increasing affluence—an obvious by-product of their accommodations to such a world. In this sense, it is a reassertion of Wesley's lifelong emphasis upon an asceticism within the daily round (cf. No. 81, 'In What Sense we are to Leave the World', especially §23).*

On Friendship with the World

James 4:4

Ye adulterers and adulteresses, know ye not that the friendship of this world is enmity with God? Whosoever therefore desireth to be a friend of the world is an enemy of God.

1. There is a passage in St. Paul's Epistle to the Romans which has been often supposed to be of the same import with this: 'Be not conformed to this world.'[a] But it has little or no relation to it; it speaks of quite another thing. Indeed the supposed resemblance arises merely from the use of the word 'world' in both places. This naturally leads us to think that St. Paul means by 'conformity to the world' the same which St. James means by 'friendship with the world'; whereas they are entirely different things, as the words are quite different in the original (for St. Paul's word is $\alpha i\omega\nu$, St. James's is $\kappa\acute{o}\sigma\mu os$[1]). However the words of St. Paul contain an important direction to the children of God. As if he had said, Be not conformed to either the wisdom, or the spirit, or the fashions 'of the age'—of either the unconverted Jews or the heathens among whom ye live. You are called to show, by the whole tenor of your life and conversation, that you are 'renewed in the spirit of your mind',[2] 'after the image of him that created you',[3] and that

[a] [Rom.] Chap. 12, ver. 2.

---

[1] $\acute{o}$ $\kappa\acute{o}\sigma\mu os$ is defined below, §§5-7, as 'the enemies of God', the domain of 'the wicked one'; cf. Wesley's *Notes, loc. cit.* But see also Herman Sasse's article on $\kappa\acute{o}\sigma\mu os$ in Gerhard Kittel, ed., *Theological Dictionary of the New Testament* (Grand Rapids, Michigan, Wm. B. Eerdmans Publishing Company, 1965), III.868, where only one out of the four basic senses of $\kappa\acute{o}\sigma\mu os$ in the New Testament can be understood in the satanocratic sense adopted here.

[2] Eph. 4:23.   [3] Cf. Col. 3:10.

your rule is, not the example or will of man, but 'the good, and acceptable, and perfect will of God'.[4]

2. But it is not strange that St. James's caution against 'friendship with the world' should be so little understood, even
5   among Christians. For I have not been able to learn that any author, ancient or modern, has wrote upon the subject;[5] no, not (so far as I have observed) for sixteen or seventeen hundred years. Even that excellent writer Mr. Law, who has treated so well many other subjects, has not in all his practical treatises wrote one
10 chapter upon it.[6] No, nor said one word, that I remember, or given one caution against it. I never heard one sermon preached upon it either before the university or elsewhere. I never was in any company where the conversation turned explicitly upon it, even for one hour.

15 3. Yet are there very few subjects of so deep importance; few that so nearly concern the very essence of religion, the life of God in the soul, the continuance and increase, or the decay, yea, extinction of it. From the want of instruction in this respect the most melancholy consequences have followed. These indeed
20 have not affected those who were still dead in trespasses and sins;[7] but they have fallen heavy upon many of those who were truly alive to God. They have affected many of those called Methodists in particular, perhaps more than any other people. For want of understanding this advice of the Apostle (I hope, rather than from
25 any contempt of it) many among them are sick, spiritually sick, and many sleep who were once thoroughly awakened. And it is well if they awake any more till their souls are required of them. It has appeared difficult to me to account for what I have frequently observed: many who were once greatly alive to God, whose
30 conversation was in heaven,[8] who had their affections on things

---

[4] Cf. Rom. 12:2.

[5] And yet Henry's note on this text had already spelled out Wesley's main line here, and Wesley had once known Henry's *Exposition* very well. See also Poole's comment in *Annotations, loc. cit.*: 'world' means 'inordinate affection to . . . the things, or the men of the world'.

[6] Another curious comment, since *contemptus mundi* is one of William Law's most pervasive themes; cf. *A Serious Call to a Devout and Holy Life* (*Works*, IV.11-12) and *Christian Perfection* (*Works*, III.36-48, 68, 72, 74-75). Cf. also Jeremy Taylor, *Holy Living, Works*, I.408-9; Robert Gell, *Remaines: Or Several Select Scriptures of the New Testament* (1676), p. 16; and John Cardinal Bona, *Precepts and Practical Rules for a Truly Christian Life* (1678), xiv. 41. As for never having heard the topic in Oxford, Wesley can only mean that *contemptus mundi* was not treated in the satanocratic sense he had come to adopt.

[7] See Eph. 2:1.   [8] See Phil. 3:20.

above, not on things of the earth;[9] though they walked in all the ordinances of God,[10] though they still abounded in good works,[11] and abstained from all known sin, yea, and from the appearance of evil; yet they gradually and insensibly decayed (like Jonah's gourd when the worm ate the root of it),[12] insomuch that they are 5 less alive to God now than they were ten, twenty, or thirty years ago. But it is easily accounted for if we observe that as they increased in goods they increased in 'friendship with the world'; which indeed must always be the case unless the mighty power of God interpose.[13] But in the same proportion as they increased in 10 this, the life of God in their soul decreased.

4. Is it strange that it should decrease, if those words are really found in the oracles of God?[14]—'Ye adulterers and adulteresses, know ye not that the friendship of the world is enmity with God?' What is the meaning of these words? Let us seriously consider. 15 And may God open the eyes of our understanding, that in spite of all the mist wherewith the wisdom of the world would cover us we may discern what is the good and acceptable will of God.[15]

5. Let us first consider what it is which the Apostle here means by 'the world'. He does not here refer to this outward frame of 20 things, termed in Scripture, 'heaven and earth', but to the inhabitants of the earth, the children of men—or at least the greater part of them. But what part? This is fully determined both by our Lord himself and by his beloved disciple. First, by our Lord himself. His words are: 'If the world hateth you, ye know 25 that it hated me before it hated you. If ye were of the world, the world would love its own; but because ye are not of the world, but I have chosen you out of the world, therefore the world hateth you. If they have persecuted me, they will also persecute you. And all these things will they do unto you because they know not him 30 that sent me.'[b] You see here 'the world' is placed on one side, and 'those who are not of the world' on the other. They whom God has 'chosen out of the world', namely by 'sanctification of the Spirit and belief of the truth',[16] are set in direct opposition to those

[b] John 15:18-21.

---

[9] See Col. 3:2.   [10] See Luke 1:6.

[11] See 2 Cor. 9:8.   [12] Jonah 4:7.

[13] For earlier denunciations of surplus accumulation, see No. 50, 'The Use of Money', intro.

[14] See No. 5, 'Justification by Faith', §2 and n.

[15] See Rom. 12:2.   [16] 2 Thess. 2:13.

whom he hath not so chosen. Yet again, those who know not him that sent me, saith our Lord, who know not God, they are 'the world'.

6. Equally express are the words of the beloved disciple. 'Marvel not, my brethren, if the world hate you; we know that we have passed from death unto life, because we love the brethren.'[c] As if he had said, You must not expect any should love you but those that have 'passed from death unto life'. It follows, those that are not passed from death unto life, that are not alive to God, are 'the world'. The same we may learn from those words in the fifth chapter, verse 19: 'We know that we are of God, and the whole world lieth in the wicked one.' Here 'the world' plainly means those that are not of God, and who consequently 'lie in the wicked one'.

7. Those on the contrary 'are of God' who love God, or at least 'fear him, and keep his commandments'.[17] This is the lowest character of those that 'are of God', who are not properly sons, but servants;[18] who 'depart from evil',[19] and study to do good, and walk in all his ordinances,[20] because they have the fear of God in their heart, and a sincere desire to please him. Fix in your heart this plain meaning of the term 'the world'—those who do not thus fear God. Let no man deceive you with vain words: it means neither more nor less than this.

8. But, understanding the term in this sense, what kind of friendship may we have with 'the world'? We may, we ought to love them as ourselves (for they also are included in the word 'neighbour'); to bear them real goodwill; to desire their happiness as sincerely as we desire the happiness of our own souls; yea, we are in a sense to honour them (seeing we are directed by the Apostle to 'honour all men')[21] as the creatures of God; nay, as immortal spirits who are capable of knowing, of loving, and of enjoying him to all eternity. We are to honour them as redeemed by his blood who 'tasted death for every man'.[22] We are to bear them tender compassion when we see them forsaking their own

---

[c] 1 John 3:13[-14].

---

[17] Deut. 13:4.

[18] A basic distinction, especially in the later Wesley; cf. Nos. 106, 'On Faith, Heb. 11:6', I.2; and 117, 'On the Discoveries of Faith', §§14-15.

[19] Job 28:28.

[20] A summary of the *General Rules*; see No. 24, 'Sermon on the Mount, IV', IV.1 and n.

[21] 1 Pet. 2:17.   [22] Cf. Heb. 2:9.

mercies, wandering from the path of life, and hastening to
everlasting destruction. We are never willingly to grieve their
spirits or give them any pain; but on the contrary to give them all
the pleasure we innocently can; seeing we are to 'please all men
for their good'.[23] We are never to aggravate their faults, but 5
willingly to allow all the good that is in them.

9. We may, and ought, to speak to them on all occasions in the
most kind and obliging manner we can. We ought to speak no evil
of them when they are absent, unless it be absolutely necessary,
unless it be the only means we know of preventing their doing 10
hurt; otherwise we are to speak of them with all the respect we
can, without transgressing the bounds of truth. We are to behave
to them when present with all courtesy, showing them all the
regard we can, without countenancing them in sin. We ought to
do them all the good that is in our power, all they are willing to 15
receive from us; following herein the example of the universal
Friend, our Father which is in heaven, who, till they will
condescend to receive greater blessings, gives them such as they
are willing to accept, 'causing his sun to rise on the evil and the
good, and sending his rain on the just and on the unjust'.[24] 20

10. But what kind of friendship is it which we may not have with
the world? May we not converse with ungodly men at all? Ought
we wholly to avoid their company? By no means: the contrary of
this has been allowed already. If we were not to converse with
them at all, 'we must needs go out of the world.'[25] Then we could 25
not show them those offices of kindness which have been already
mentioned. We may doubtless converse with them, first, on
business, in the various purposes of this life, according to that
station therein, wherein the providence of God has placed us;
secondly, when courtesy requires it—only we must take great 30
care not to carry it too far; thirdly, when we have a reasonable
hope of doing them good. But here too we have an especial need
of caution, and of much prayer; otherwise we may easily burn
ourselves in striving to pluck other brands out of the burning.[26]

11. We may easily hurt our own souls by sliding into a close 35
attachment to any of them that know not God. This is the
'friendship' which is 'enmity with God': we cannot be too jealous
over ourselves, lest we fall into this deadly snare; lest we contract,

[23] Cf. 1 Cor. 10:33.   [24] Cf. Matt. 5:45.   [25] Cf. 1 Cor. 5:10.
[26] See Amos 4:11; Zech. 3:2; cf. No. 4, *Scriptural Christianity*, II.2 and n.

or ever we are aware, a love of *complacence* or *delight* in them. Then
only do we tread upon sure ground when we can say with the
Psalmist, 'All my delight is in the saints that are upon earth, and in
such as excel in virtue.'[27] We should have no *needless conversation*
5 with them. It is our duty and our wisdom to be no oftener and no
longer with them than is strictly necessary. And during the whole
time we have need to remember and follow the example of him
that said, 'I kept my mouth as it were with a bridle while the
ungodly was in my sight.'[28] We should enter into no sort of
10 connection with them farther than is absolutely necessary. When
Jehoshaphat forgot this, and formed a connection with Ahab,
what was the consequence? He first lost his substance: 'the ships'
they sent out 'were broken at Ezion-geber.'[29] And when he was
not content with this warning, as well as that of the prophet
15 Micaiah, but would go up with him to Ramoth-Gilead, he was on
the point of losing his life.[30]

12. Above all we should tremble at the very thought of entering
into a marriage covenant, the closest of all others, with any person
who does not love, or at least, fear God. This is the most horrid
20 folly, the most deplorable madness, that a child of God can
possibly plunge into, as it implies every sort of connection with the
ungodly which a Christian is bound in conscience to avoid. No
wonder then it is so flatly forbidden of God; that the prohibition is
so absolute and peremptory: 'Be not unequally yoked with an
25 unbeliever.'[31] Nothing can be more express. Especially if we
understand by the word 'unbeliever' one that is so far from being
a believer in the gospel sense—from being able to say, 'The life
which I now live, I live by faith in the Son of God, who loved me
and gave himself for me'[32]—that he has not even the faith of a
30 servant: he does not 'fear God and work righteousness'.[33]

13. But for what reasons is the friendship of the world so
absolutely prohibited? Why are we so strictly required to abstain
from it? For two general reasons: first, because it is a sin in itself;
secondly, because it is attended with most dreadful conse-
35 quences.

[27] Cf. Ps. 16:3 (BCP).
[28] Cf. Ps. 39:2 (BCP).
[29] 1 Kgs. 22:48.
[30] See 1 Kgs. 22:1-36.
[31] Cf. 2 Cor. 6:14.
[32] Cf. Gal. 2:20.   [33] Cf. Acts 10:35.

First, it is a sin in itself; and indeed a sin of no common dye. According to the oracles of God,[34] 'friendship with the world' is no less than spiritual adultery. All who are guilty of it are addressed by the Holy Ghost in those terms, 'ye adulterers and adulteresses'. It is plainly [the] violating of our marriage contract 5 with God, by loving the creature more than the Creator[35]—in flat contradiction to that kind command, 'My son, give me thine heart.'[36]

14. It is a sin of the most heinous nature, as not only implying ignorance of God, and forgetfulness of him, or inattention to him, 10 but positive 'enmity against God'. It is openly, palpably such. 'Know ye not,' says the Apostle, can ye possibly be ignorant of this so plain, so undeniable a truth, 'that the friendship of the world is enmity against God?' Nay, and how terrible is the inference which he draws from hence! 'Therefore whosoever will be a friend of 15 the world' (the words properly rendered are, 'Whosoever desireth to be a friend of the world', of the men who know not God), whether he attain it or no, is *ipso facto* 'constituted an enemy of God'. This very desire, whether successful or not, gives him a right to that appellation. 20

15. And as it is a sin, a very heinous sin in itself, so it is attended with the most dreadful consequences. It frequently entangles men again in the commission of those sins from which they 'were clean escaped'.[37] It generally makes them 'partakers of other men's sins',[38] even those which they do not commit themselves. It 25 gradually abates their abhorrence and dread of sin in general, and thereby prepares them for falling an easy prey to any strong temptation. It lays them open to all those sins of omission whereof their worldly acquaintance are guilty. It insensibly lessens their exactness in private prayer, in family duty, in fasting, in attending 30 public service, and partaking of the Lord's Supper. The indifference of those that are near them with respect to all these will gradually influence them; even if they say not one word (which is hardly to be supposed) to recommend their own practice, yet their example speaks, and is many times of more 35 force than any other language. By this example they are unavoidably betrayed, and almost continually, into unprofitable,

---

[34] Cf. No. 5, 'Justification by Faith', §2 and n.
[35] Rom. 1:25.
[36] Prov. 23:26.
[37] 2 Pet. 2:18.   [38] 1 Tim. 5:22.

yea, and uncharitable conversation, till they no longer 'set a watch before their mouth, and keep the door of their lips',[39] till they can join in backbiting, talebearing, and evil-speaking without any check of conscience, having so frequently grieved the Holy Spirit
5 of God that he no longer reproves them for it; insomuch that their discourse is not now, as formerly, 'seasoned with salt',[40] and 'meet to minister grace to the hearers'.[41]

16. But these are not all the deadly consequences that result from familiar intercourse with unholy men. It not only hinders
10 them from ordering their conversation aright, but directly tends to corrupt the heart. It tends to create or increase in us all that pride and self-sufficiency, all that fretfulness and resentment,[42] yea, every irregular passion and wrong disposition which are indulged by their companions. It gently leads them into habitual
15 self-indulgence, and unwillingness to deny themselves; into unreadiness to bear or take up any cross; into a softness and delicacy; into evil shame, and the fear of man that brings numberless snares. It draws them back into the love of the world, into foolish and hurtful desires,[43] into the desire of the flesh, the
20 desire of the eyes, and the pride of life,[44] till they are swallowed up in them. So that in the end the last state of these men is far worse than the first.[45]

17. If the children of God will connect themselves with the men of the world, though the latter should not endeavour to make
25 them like themselves (which is a supposition by no means to be made)—yea, though they should neither design nor desire it—yet they will actually do it, whether they design it and whether they endeavour it, or no. I know not how to account for it, but it is a real fact that their very spirit is infectious. While you are near them
30 you are apt to catch their spirit, whether they will or no. Many physicians have observed that not only the plague, and putrid or malignant fevers, but almost every disease men are liable to are more or less infectious.[46] And undoubtedly so are all spiritual

---

[39] Cf. Ps. 141:3.   [40] Col. 4:6.   [41] Cf. Eph. 4:29.

[42] Orig., 'fretfulness to resent', altered in Wesley's annotated copy of *AM*.

[43] 1 Tim. 6:9.

[44] 1 John 2:16; cf. No. 7, 'The Way to the Kingdom', II.2 and n.

[45] See Matt. 12:45.

[46] Cf. Chambers's *Cyclopaedia*, on 'Plague', where Sydenham, Lister, and Mr. Boyle are cited; also entries on 'fevers', 'infection', 'contagion'. See also Wesley's note on avoiding an 'infectious fever' in *Primitive Physick*, which seems first to have been included in the edn. of 1755, No. 303, and changed numbers frequently during following edns.

diseases—only with great variety. The infection is not so swiftly communicated by some as it is by others. In either case the person already diseased does not desire or design to infect another. The man who has the plague does not desire or intend to communicate his distemper to you. But you are not therefore 5 safe; so keep at a distance, or you will surely be infected. Does not experience show that the case is the same with the diseases of the mind? Suppose the proud, the vain, the passionate, the wanton, do not desire or design to infect *you* with their own distempers; yet it is best to keep at a distance from them: you are not safe if you 10 come too near them. You will perceive (it is well if it be not too late) that their very breath is infectious. It has been lately discovered that there is an atmosphere surrounding every human body, which naturally affects everyone that comes within the limits of it.[47] Is there not something analogous to this with regard 15 to a human spirit?[48] If you continue long within their atmosphere (so to speak) you can hardly escape the being infected. The contagion spreads from soul to soul,[49] as well as from body to body, even though the persons diseased do not intend or desire it. But can this reasonably be supposed? Is it not a notorious truth 20 that men of the world (exceeding few excepted) eagerly desire to make their companions like themselves? Yea, and use every means, with their utmost skill and industry, to accomplish their desire. Therefore fly for your life! Do not play with the fire, but escape before the flames kindle upon you. 25

18. But how many are the pleas for 'friendship with the world'! And how strong are the temptations to it! Such of these as are the most dangerous, and at the same time most common, we will consider.

To begin with one that is the most dangerous of all others, and 30 at the same time by no means uncommon. 'I grant', says one, 'the person I am about to marry is not a religious person. She does not make any pretensions to it. She has little thought about it. But she is a beautiful creature. She is extremely agreeable, and I think will make me a lovely companion.' 35

---

[47] Cf. Robert Boyle (1627–91), *A Continuation of New Experiments . . . Whereto is Annext a Short Discourse of the Atmospheres of Consistent Bodies* (1669), and *Essays of the Strange Subtilty . . . of Effluviums . . .* (1673). See also Chambers's *Cyclopaedia*, on 'Effluvium'. In a letter to Jonathan Swift, Alexander Pope confesses that he is 'so atmospherical a creature'; see Swift's *Works* (1761), VIII.85.

[48] Cf. No. 69, 'The Imperfection of Human Knowledge', I.13 and n.

[49] Cf. No. 81, 'In What Sense we are to Leave the World', §§13, 14.

This is a snare indeed! Perhaps one of the greatest that human nature is liable to. This is such a temptation as no power of man is able to overcome. Nothing less than the mighty power of God can make a way for you to escape from it. And this can work a
5   complete deliverance: his grace is sufficient for you.[50] But not unless you are a worker together with him;[51] not unless you deny yourself and take up your cross.[52] And what you do, you must do at once! Nothing can be done by degrees. Whatever you do in this important case must be done at one stroke. If it be done at all, you
10   must at once cut off the right hand and cast it from you![53] Here is no time for conferring with flesh and blood![54] At once, conquer or perish![55]

19. Let us turn the tables. Suppose a woman that loves God is addressed by an agreeable man, genteel, lively, entertaining,
15   suitable to her in all other respects, though not religious. What should she do in such a case? What she *should* do, if she believes the Bible, is sufficiently clear. But what *can* she do? Is not this

A test for human frailty too severe?[56]

Who is able to stand in such a trial? Who can resist such a
20   temptation? None but one that holds fast the shield of faith,[57] and earnestly cries to the Strong for strength.[58] None but one that gives herself to watching and prayer, and continues therein with all perseverance. If she does this she will be a happy witness in the midst of an unbelieving world that as 'all things are possible with
25   God,'[59] so 'all things are possible to' her 'that believeth'.[60]

20. But either a man or woman may ask: 'What if the person who seeks my acquaintance be a person of a strong natural understanding, cultivated by various learning? May not I gain much useful knowledge by a familiar intercourse with him? May I
30   not learn many things from him, and much improve my own

---

[50] See 2 Cor. 12:9.   [51] See 2 Cor. 6:1.   [52] See Matt. 16:24.
[53] See Matt. 5:30.   [54] See Gal. 1:16.
[55] Cf. Plutarch, *Moralia*, III, 'Sayings of the Spartan Women', 241-F, 16, 17: '[Come back from battle] with your shield or upon it.'
[56] Samuel Wesley, Jun., 'The Battle of the Sexes', in *Poems* (1736), p. 40, 'The test for human frailty too severe'. See Wesley, *A Collection of Moral and Sacred Poems* (1744), III.33; also his letter to Mrs. Cousins, Nov. 1, 1778.
[57] Eph. 6:16.
[58] See Job 9:19; cf. also No. 48, 'Self-denial', III.4 and n.
[59] Cf. Matt. 19:26.
[60] Mark 9:23.

understanding?' Undoubtedly you may improve your own understanding, and you may gain much knowledge. But still, if he has not at least the fear of God, your loss will be far greater than your gain. For you can hardly avoid decreasing in holiness as much as you increase in knowledge. And if you lose one degree of 5 inward or outward holiness, all the knowledge you gain will be no equivalent.

21. 'But his fine and strong understanding, improved by education, is not his chief recommendation. He has more valuable qualifications than these: he is remarkably good 10 humoured; he is of a compassionate, humane spirit, and has much generosity in his temper.' On these very accounts, if he does not fear God, he is infinitely more dangerous. If you converse intimately with a person of this character you will surely drink into his spirit. It is hardly possible for you to avoid stopping 15 just where he stops. I have found nothing so difficult in all my life as to converse with men of this kind ('good sort of men',[61] as they are commonly called) without being hurt by them. O beware of them! Converse with them just as much as business requires, and no more! Otherwise (though you do not feel any present harm, 20 yet) by slow and imperceptible degrees they will attach you again to earthly things, and damp the life of God in your soul.

22. It may be the persons who are desirous of your acquaintance, though they are not experienced in religion, yet understand it well, so that you frequently reap advantage from 25 their conversation. If this be really the case (as I have known a few instances of the kind) it seems you may converse with them; only very sparingly and very cautiously. Otherwise you will lose more of your spiritual life than all the knowledge you gain is worth.

23. 'But the persons in question are useful to me in carrying on 30 my temporal business. Nay, on many occasions they are necessary to me, so that I could not well carry it on without them.' Instances of this kind frequently occur. And this is doubtless a sufficient

---

[61] A phrase to denote nominal Christians and especially the affluent ones; cf. Wesley's letter to Bishop William Warburton, Nov. 1762: 'By this [phrase], "good sort of men", I mean persons who have a liking to but no sense of religion, no real fear or love of God, no truly Christian tempers . . .;' they are, says Wesley, 'the bane of all religion'. See also Nos. 81, 'In What Sense we are to Leave the World', §13 (where Wesley equates the term with 'worthy'); 83, 'On Patience', §2; 108, 'On Riches', II.4; 125; 'On a Single Eye', II.2; 131, 'The Danger of Increasing Riches', I.6; 147, 'Wiser than the Children of Light', I, II; and 150, 'Hypocrisy in Oxford', I.9. The phrase also occurs in the sense in which Wesley uses it in Richard Graves, *Spiritual Quixote* (1772), II.21, 26, 30, 89.

reason for having some intercourse, perhaps frequently, with men that do not fear God. But even this is by no means a reason for your contracting an intimate acquaintance with them. And you here need to take the utmost care 'lest even by that converse
5 with them which is necessary, while your fortune in the world increases, the grace of God should decrease in your soul.'[62]

24. There may be one more plausible reason given for some intimacy with an unholy man. You may say: 'I have been helpful to him. I have assisted him when he was in trouble. And he
10 remembers it with gratitude. He esteems and loves *me*, though he does not love God. Ought I not then to love *him?* Ought I not to return love for love? Do not even heathens and publicans so?'[63] I answer, you should certainly return love for love; but it does not follow that you should have any intimacy with him. That would be
15 at the peril of your soul. Let your love give itself vent in constant and fervent prayer; wrestle with God for him. But let not your love for him carry you so far as to weaken, if not destroy, your own soul.

25. 'But must I not be intimate with my relations? And that
20 whether they fear God or not? Has not his providence recommended these to me?' Undoubtedly it has: but there are relations nearer or more distant. The nearest relations are husbands and wives. As these have taken each other for better for worse,[64] they must make the best of each other; seeing as God has
25 joined them together, none can put them asunder[65]—unless in case of adultery, or when the life of one or the other is in imminent danger. Parents are almost as nearly connected with their children. You cannot part with them while they are young; it being your duty to 'train them up' with all care 'in the way wherein
30 they should go'.[66] How frequently you should converse with them when they are grown up is to be determined by Christian prudence. This also will determine how long it is expedient for children, if it be at their own choice, to remain with their parents.

---

[62] Wesley may be paraphrasing himself; cf. §§3 (end), 10,20 (end).

[63] See Matt. 5:46.

[64] An echo of the troth in 'The Solemnization of Matrimony' in the BCP: '. . . for better for worse, for richer for poorer, in sickness and in health'.

[65] See Matt. 19:6; Mark 10:9; also repeated by the priest in 'The Solemnization of Matrimony', *ibid*. But note Wesley's added ground for divorce here; there is no precedent for it in Anglican canon law or Caroline divinity (cf. More and Cross, *Anglicanism*, pp. 661-66).

[66] Cf. Prov. 22:6.

In general, if they do not fear God, you should leave them as soon as is convenient. But wherever you are, take care (if it be in your power) that they do not want the necessaries or conveniences of life. As for all other relations, even brothers or sisters, if they are of the world you are under no obligation to be intimate with them: you may be civil and friendly at a distance.

26. But allowing that 'the friendship of the world is enmity against God', and consequently that it is the most excellent way, indeed the only way to heaven, to avoid all intimacy with worldly men; yet who has resolution to walk therein? Who even of those that love or fear God? For these only are concerned in the present question. A few I have known who even in this respect were lights in a benighted land; who did not and would not either contract or continue any acquaintance with persons of the most refined and improved understanding, and the most engaging tempers, merely because they were of the world, because they were not alive to God. Yea, though they were capable of improving them in knowledge, or of assisting them in business. Nay, though they admired and esteemed them for that very religion which they did not themselves experience: a case one would hardly think possible, but of which there are many instances at this day. Familiar intercourse even with these they steadily and resolutely refrain from, for conscience' sake.

27. Go thou and do likewise,[67] whosoever thou art that art a child of God by faith.[68] Whatever it cost, flee spiritual adultery. Have no friendship with the world. However tempted thereto by profit or pleasure, contract no intimacy with worldly-minded men. And if thou hast contracted any such already, break it off without delay. Yea, if thy ungodly friend be dear to thee as a right eye or useful as a right hand, yet confer not with flesh and blood,[69] but pluck out the right eye, cut off the right hand, and cast them from thee![70] It is not an indifferent thing. Thy life is at stake—eternal life, or eternal death. And is it not better to go into life having one eye or one hand than having both to be cast into hell-fire?[71] When thou knewest no better, the times of ignorance God winked at.[72] But now thine eyes are opened, now the light is

[67] See Luke 10:37.
[68] Gal. 3:26.
[69] See Gal. 1:16.
[70] See Matt. 5:29.
[71] See Matt. 18:8-9.
[72] See Acts 17:30.

come; walk in the light.[73] Touch not pitch lest thou be defiled.[74] At all events 'keep thyself pure'![75]

28. But whatever others do, whether they will hear or whether they will forbear,[76] hear this, all ye that are called Methodists.
5 However importuned or tempted thereto, have no friendship with the world. Look round and see the melancholy effects it has produced among your brethren! How many of the mighty are fallen![77] How many have fallen by this very thing! They would take no warning: they *would* converse, and that intimately, with
10 earthly-minded men, till 'they measured back their steps to earth again'![78] O 'come out from among them', from all unholy men, however harmless they may appear, 'and be ye separate'![79]—at least so far as to have no intimacy with them. As 'your fellowship is with the Father, and with his Son Jesus Christ',[80] so let it be with
15 those, and those only, who at least seek the Lord Jesus Christ in sincerity. So 'shall ye be', in a peculiar sense, 'my sons and my daughters, saith the Lord Almighty'.[81]

Wakefield, May 1, 1786[82]

---

[73] 1 John 1:7.

[74] See Ecclus. 13:1.

[75] 1 Tim. 5:22.

[76] Ezek. 2:5, 7; 3:11.

[77] See 2 Sam. 1:19, 25, 27.

[78] Cf. Thomas Parnell, 'The Hermit', l.227: 'And measured back his steps to earth again.' Cf. Wesley, *A Collection of Moral and Sacred Poems* (1744), I.275. See also Nos. 71, 'Of Good Angels', I.7; 81, 'In What Sense we are to Leave the World', §11; and 88, 'On Dress', §25; also Wesley's letters to Lady Rawdon, Mar. 18, 1760; and the Earl of Dartmouth, July 26, 1764.

[79] 2 Cor. 6:17.

[80] Cf. 1 John 1:3.

[81] Cf. 2 Cor. 6:18.

[82] Place and date as in *AM*.

IN WHAT SENSE WE ARE TO LEAVE
THE WORLD

AN INTRODUCTORY COMMENT

This is the first sermon in the seventh volume of SOSO *(1788) and is a logical sequel to the last one in* SOSO, *VI. It argues the same practical conclusion—i.e., Christian discipline 'requires us to keep at a distance, as far as is practicable, from all ungodly men' (§4), and it is in this sense that we are 'to leave the world'. It was, however, written almost two years earlier and in a very different setting (July 17, 1784). Wesley had already recorded his optimistic reflections on his eighty-first birthday, in the midst of an arduous itinerary through the West Country, Wales, Ireland, Scotland, and now the north of England: 'Today I entered on my eighty-second year, and found myself just as strong to labour and as fit for any exercise of body or mind as I was forty years ago.' (JWJ, June 28, 1784). The* Journal *entry for July 15 is terse: 'I retired to Otley and rested two days.' The diary for the 17th records that he spent that morning writing a sermon; that it was this one is confirmed by its postscript in the* Arminian Magazine *(VII.632): 'Otley, July 17, 1784'.*

What is not mentioned, either here or elsewhere in the Journal *or diary, was a momentous crisis looming over the Methodist movement as a whole. By this time, Wesley had decided to provide his movement with a new structure in the form of a Deed of Declaration, to be proposed to the Conference in Leeds, July 27-August 3. One would never know from Wesley how deeply this move toward autonomy for the Conference had stirred the emotions of many, or how decisively it had marked the point of no return in the evolution of Methodism toward eventual separation from the Church of England.[1]*

In such a crisis it would have been important for Wesley to reject the conventional Nonconformist interpretations of 2 Cor. 6:17-18—which

---

[1] See Curnock's understated note, VII.5-6, where he comments that 'the manner in which the Deed was devised and executed, and the names selected for the constitution of the first Legal Conference, gave offence to some;' see also Baker, *John Wesley and the Church of England*, chs. 13–15.

had served so long as their scriptural warrant for separation from the Established Church. Wesley had never intended any such separation, and steadfastly denied that separation was inevitable or even 'expedient'. Thus, he could lay an even heartier stress on his very different interpretation of the same Scripture as the basis for that asceticism-in-the-world to which he would return in 'On Friendship with the World'. His ideal was a revival that helped renew the church without leaving it, and a Christian discipline that would 'leave the world' without fleeing from it.

This Otley sermon was published in the Arminian Magazine, *without title, in the November and December issues of 1784 (VII.569-77, 626-32), and numbered as 'Sermon XXIV'. Then in 1788 he could invert the chronological order and use this sermon with a somewhat cumbersome title added to it for the opening message in the third volume of his 'original sermons'. It was not reprinted in Wesley's lifetime, but it serves both as a variation of a constant theme and as something of a mirroring of Wesley's basic character: a man who had himself 'left the world' long since, and who never ceased to call on others to follow in his train.*

In What Sense we are to Leave the World

2 Corinthians 6:17-18

Come out from among them, and be ye separate, saith the Lord, and touch not the unclean thing; and I will receive you;

And I will be to you a Father, and ye shall be my sons and daughters, saith the Lord Almighty.

1. How exceeding few in the religious world have duly considered these solemn words! We have read them over and
10 over, but never laid them to heart, or observed that they contain as plain and express a command as any in the whole Bible. And it is to be feared, there are still fewer that understand the genuine meaning of this direction. Numberless persons in England have interpreted it as a command to come out of the Established
15 Church. And in the same sense it has been understood by

thousands in the neighbouring kingdoms.[1] Abundance of sermons have been preached and of books wrote upon this supposition. And indeed many pious men have grounded their separation from the Church chiefly on this text. 'God himself,' say they, 'commands us, "Come out from among them, and be ye 5 separate." And it is only upon this condition that he "will receive" us, and we "shall be the sons and daughters of the Lord Almighty".'

2. But this interpretation is totally foreign to the design of the Apostle, who is not here speaking of this or that church, but on 10 quite another subject. Neither did the Apostle himself or any of his brethren draw any such inference from the words. Had they done so it would have been a flat contradiction both to the example and precept of their Master. For although the Jewish church was then full as 'unclean', as unholy both inwardly and 15 outwardly, as any Christian church now upon earth, yet our Lord constantly attended the service of it. And he directed his followers in this, as in every other respect, to 'tread in his steps'.[2] This is clearly implied in that remarkable passage: 'The scribes and Pharisees sit in Moses' seat; all therefore whatsoever they bid you 20 observe, that observe and do; but do not ye after their works; for they say and do not.'[a] Even though they themselves 'say and do not', though their lives contradict their doctrines, though they were ungodly men, yet our Lord here not only permits but requires his disciples to hear them. For he requires them to 25 'observe and do what they say'; but this could not be if they did not hear them. Accordingly the apostles, as long as they were at Jerusalem, constantly attended the public service. Therefore it is certain these words have no reference to a separation from the Established Church. 30

3. Neither have they any reference to the direction given by the Apostle in his first Epistle to the Corinthians. The whole passage

---

[a] Matt. 23:2-3.

---

[1] In England this included both the Independents and the Nonconformists; cf. H.W. Clark, *History of English Nonconformity* (2 vols.; 1911-13), II.244-86. They regarded conformity to the Church of England as sinful and appealed to the arguments of Milton's *Consideration Touching the Likeliest Means to Remove Hirelings Out of the Church* (1659). In Scotland disestablishment sentiments were strong; in Ireland it was the Roman Catholics who were the disestablishmentarians. And, at the time of this writing, Wesley had just come from preaching visits to all of these 'neighbouring kingdoms'.

[2] Cf. 1 Pet. 2:21.

runs thus: 'I wrote unto you in an epistle, not to company with fornicators. Yet not altogether with the fornicators of this world, or with the covetous, or extortioners, or with idolaters; for then must ye needs go out of the world. But now I have written unto
5   you, not to [keep]³ company, if *any man that is called a brother* be a fornicator, or covetous, or an idolater, or a railer, or a drunkard, or an extortioner; with such an one, no not to eat.'ᵇ This wholly relates to them that are members of the same Christian community. The Apostle tells them expressly, he does not give
10   this direction not to company with such and such persons, with regard to the heathens or to men in general; and adds this plain reason: 'For then must ye needs go out of the world'—you could transact no business in it. 'But if any man that is called a brother', that is connected with you in the same religious society, 'be a
15   fornicator, or covetous, or an idolater, or a railer, or a drunkard, or an extortioner; with such an one, no not to eat.' How important a caution is this! But how little is it observed even by those that are in other respects conscientious Christians! Indeed some parts of it are not easy to be observed, for a plain reason—they are not
20   easy to be understood. I mean, it is not easy to be understood to whom the characters belong. It is very difficult, for instance, to know, unless in some glaring cases, to whom the character of an 'extortioner' or of a 'covetous' man belongs. We can hardly know one or the other without seeming (at least) to be 'busybodies in
25   other men's matters'.⁴ And yet the prohibition is as strong concerning converse with these as with fornicators or adulterers. We can only act in the simplicity of our hearts, without setting up for infallible judges (still willing to be better informed), according to the best light we have.
30   4. But although this direction relates only to our Christian brethren (such at least by outward profession), that in the text is of a far wider extent: it unquestionably relates to all mankind. It clearly requires us to keep at a distance, as far as is practicable, from all ungodly men. Indeed it seems the word which we render

---

ᵇ 1 Cor. 5:9-11. [In the *Notes* Wesley had translated this: 'I wrote to you an epistle not to converse with lewd persons; . . . not to converse with such an one, no, not to eat with him.']

---

³ Wesley here is quoting the AV of 1 Cor. 5:11, which reads 'not to *keep* company', etc. His omission, however, is in line with the translations of Tyndale, Cranmer, and the Geneva Bible, and good English—cf. the next sentence but one.
⁴ Cf. 1 Pet. 4:15.

'unclean thing', τοῦ ἀκαθάρτου, might rather be rendered 'unclean person', probably alluding to the ceremonial law which forbade *touching* one that was legally unclean.[5] But even here, were we to understand the expression literally, were we to take the words in the strictest sense, the same absurdity would follow: we must needs, as the Apostle speaks, 'go out of the world'. We should not be able to abide in those callings which the providence of God has assigned us. Were we not to converse at all with men of those characters it would be impossible to transact our temporal business. So that every conscientious Christian would have nothing to do but to flee into the desert. It would not suffice to turn recluses, to shut ourselves up in monasteries or nunneries; for even then we must have some intercourse with ungodly men in order to procure the necessaries of life.

5. The words therefore must necessarily be understood with considerable restriction. They do not prohibit our conversing with any man, good or bad, in the way of worldly business. A thousand occasions will occur whereon we must converse with them, in order to transact those affairs which cannot be done without them. And some of these may require us to have frequent intercourse with drunkards or fornicators; yea, sometimes it may be requisite for us to spend a considerable time in their company; otherwise we should not be able to fulfil the duties of our several callings. Such conversation therefore with men, holy or unholy, is no way contrary to the Apostle's advice.

6. What is it then which the Apostle forbids? First, the conversing with ungodly men when there is no necessity, no providential call, no business, that requires it; secondly, the conversing with them more frequently than business necessarily requires; thirdly, the spending more time in their company than is necessary to finish our business; above all, fourthly, the choosing ungodly persons, however ingenious or agreeable, to be our ordinary companions, or to be our familiar friends. If any instance of this kind will admit of less excuse than others it is that which the Apostle expressly forbids elsewhere, the being 'unequally yoked with an unbeliever'[6] in marriage—with any person that has not the love of God in their heart, or at least the fear of God before their eyes.[7] I do not know anything that can justify this;

[5] See Lev. 5:2-3, etc.
[7] Rom. 3:18.

[6] Cf. 2 Cor. 6:14.

neither the sense, wit, or beauty of the person; nor temporal advantage; nor fear of want; no, nor even the command of a parent. For if any parent command what is contrary to the Word of God, the child ought to obey God rather than man.[8]

5   7. The ground of this prohibition is laid down at large in the preceding verses: 'What fellowship hath righteousness with unrighteousness? What communion hath light with darkness? And what concord hath Christ with Belial? Or what part hath he that believeth with an unbeliever?' (Taking that word in the

10 extensive sense for him that hath neither the love nor the fear of God.) 'Ye are the temple of the living God: as God hath said, I will dwell in them and walk in them; and I will be their God, and they shall be my people.' It follows, 'Wherefore come out from among them'—the unrighteous, the children of darkness, the sons of

15 Belial, the unbelievers—'and be ye separate, and touch not the unclean thing (or person), and I will receive you.'[9]

     8. Here is the sum of this prohibition—to have any more intercourse with unholy men than is absolutely necessary. There can be no profitable 'fellowship' between the righteous and the

20 unrighteous; as there can be no 'communion' between light and darkness (whether you understand this of natural or of spiritual darkness). As Christ can have no 'concord' with Belial, so a believer in him can have no concord with an unbeliever. It is absurd to imagine that any true union or concord should be

25 between two persons while one of them remains in darkness and the other walks in the light. They are subjects not only of two separate, but of two opposite kingdoms. They act upon quite different principles: they aim at quite different ends. It will necessarily follow that frequently, if not always, they will walk in

30 different paths. How can they walk together till they are agreed?[10] Until they both serve either Christ or Belial?

     9. And what are the consequences of our not obeying this direction? Of our not coming out from among unholy men? Of not being separate from them, but contracting or continuing a

35 familiar intercourse with them? It is probable it will not immediately have any apparent visible ill consequences. It is hardly to be expected that it will immediately lead us into any outward sin. Perhaps it may not presently occasion our neglect of

---

[8] Acts 5:29; cf. No. 96, 'On Obedience to Parents', §§5-6.
[9] 2 Cor. 6:14-17.   [10] See Amos 3:3.

any outward duty. It will first sap the foundations of our religion; it will by little and little damp our zeal for God; it will gently cool that fervency of spirit which attended our first love. If they do not openly oppose anything we say or do, yet their very spirit will by insensible degrees affect our spirit, and transfuse into it the same lukewarmness and indifference toward God and the things of God. It will weaken all the springs of our soul, destroy the vigour of our spirit, and cause us more and more to slacken our pace in running the race that is set before us.[11]

10. By the same degrees all needless intercourse with unholy men will weaken our divine evidence and conviction of things unseen;[12] it will dim the eyes of the soul, whereby we see him that is invisible, and weaken our confidence in him. It will gradually abate our 'taste of the powers of the world to come',[13] and deaden that hope which before made us 'sit in heavenly places with Christ Jesus'.[14] It will imperceptibly cool that flame of love which before enabled us to say: 'Whom have I in heaven but thee? And there is none upon earth that I desire beside thee!'[15] Thus it strikes at the root of all vital religion, of our fellowship with the Father and with the Son.

11. By the same degrees, and in the same secret and unobserved manner, it will prepare us to 'measure back our steps to earth again'.[16] It will lead us softly to relapse into the love of the world from which we were clean escaped; to fall gently into 'the desire of the flesh', the seeking happiness in the pleasures of sense; 'the desire of the eye', the seeking happiness in the pleasure of imagination;[17] 'and the pride of life',[18] the seeking it in pomp, in riches, or in the praise of man. And all this may be done, by the assistance of the spirit who 'beguiled Eve through his subtlety',[19] before we are sensible of his attack, or are conscious of any loss.

12. And it is not only the love of the world in all its branches which necessarily steals upon us while we converse with men of a worldly spirit farther than duty requires, but every other evil

---

[11] See Heb. 12:1.   [12] See Heb. 11:1.

[13] Cf. Heb. 6:5.   [14] Cf. Eph. 2:6.

[15] Ps. 73:25 (AV).

[16] Thomas Parnell, 'The Hermit', l. 227; cf. No. 80, 'On Friendship with the World', §28 and n.

[17] Cf. No. 44, *Original Sin*, II.10 and n.

[18] 1 John 2:16; cf. No. 7, 'The Way to the Kingdom', II.2 and n.

[19] 2 Cor. 11:3.

passion and temper of which the human soul is capable: in particular pride, vanity, censoriousness, evil surmising, proneness to revenge; while on the other hand levity, gaiety, and dissipation, steal upon us and increase continually. We know how
5   all these abound in the men that know not God. And it cannot be but they will insinuate themselves into all who frequently and freely converse with them: they insinuate most deeply into those who are not apprehensive of any danger; and most of all if they have any particular affection, if they have more love than duty
10 requires, for those who do not love God, with whom they familiarly converse.

13. Hitherto I have supposed that the persons with whom you converse are such as we use to call 'good sort of people'; such as are styled in the cant term of the day men of 'worthy'
15 characters—one of the silliest insignificant[20] words that ever came into fashion. I have supposed them to be free from cursing, swearing, profaneness; from sabbath-breaking and drunkenness; from lewdness either in word or action; from dishonesty, lying, and slandering—in a word, to be entirely clear from open vice of
20 every kind. Otherwise whoever has even the fear of God must in any wise keep at a distance from them. But I am afraid I have made a supposition which hardly can be admitted. I am afraid some of the persons with whom you converse more than business necessarily requires do not deserve even the character of 'good
25 sort of men'; are not 'worthy' of anything but shame and contempt. Do not some of them live in open sin? In cursing and swearing, drunkenness, or uncleanness? You cannot long be ignorant of this; for they take little pains to hide it. Now is it not certain, all vice is of an infectious nature?[21] For who can touch
30 pitch and not be defiled?[22] From these therefore you ought undoubtedly to flee, as from the face of a serpent.[23] Otherwise how soon may 'evil communications corrupt good manners'![24]

14. I have supposed likewise that those unholy persons with whom you frequently converse have no desire to communicate
35 their own spirit to *you*, or to induce *you* to follow their example.

---

[20] I.e., 'meaningless', as in Samuel Johnson's first definition. In *SOSO* (1788), the text reads, 'one of the most silly, insignificant words, . . . ' as in Johnson's second sense of 'unimportant'; cf. No. 80, 'On Friendship with the World', §21 and n.
[21] Cf. No. 80, 'On Friendship with the World', §17.
[22] See Ecclus. 13:1.
[23] See Rev. 12:14.   [24] 1 Cor. 15:33.

But this also is a supposition which can hardly be admitted. In many cases their interest may be advanced by your being a partaker of their sins. But supposing interest to be out of the question, does not every man naturally desire and more or less endeavour to bring over his acquaintance to his own opinion or party? So that as all good men desire and endeavour to make others good like themselves, in like manner all bad men desire and endeavour to make their companions as bad as themselves.

15. But if they do not, if we allow this almost impossible supposition, that they do not desire or use any endeavours to bring you over to their own temper and practice, still it is dangerous to converse with them. I speak not only of openly vicious men, but of all that do not love God, or at least fear him, and sincerely seek the kingdom of God and his righteousness.[25] Admit such companions do not endeavour to make you like themselves, does this prove you are in no danger from them? See that poor wretch that is ill of the plague! He does not desire, he does not use the least endeavour to communicate his distemper to you. Yet have a care! Touch him not! Nay, go not near him, or you know not how soon you may be in just the same condition. To draw the parallel: though we should suppose the man of the world does not desire, design, or endeavour to communicate his distemper to you, yet touch him not! Come not too near him. For it is not only his reasonings or persuasions that may infect your soul, but his very breath is infectious—particularly to those who are apprehensive of no danger.

16. If conversing freely with worldly-minded men has no other ill effect upon you, it will surely, by imperceptible degrees, make you less heavenly-minded. It will give a bias to your mind which will continually draw your soul to earth. It will incline you, without your being conscious of it, instead of being wholly transformed in the renewing of your mind,[26] to be again conformed to this world, in its spirit, in its maxims, and in its vain conversation. You will fall again into that levity and dissipation of spirit[27] from which you had before clean escaped, into that superfluity of apparel, and into that foolish, frothy, unprofitable conversation, which was an abomination to you when your soul was alive to God. And you will daily decline from that simplicity both of speech and behaviour

---

[25] Matt. 6:33.   [26] See Rom. 12:2.
[27] Cf. No. 79, 'On Dissipation', §1 and n.

whereby you once adorned the doctrine of God our Saviour.

17. And if you go thus far in conformity to the world, it is hardly to be expected you will stop here. You will go farther in a short time; having once lost your footing, and begun to slide down, it is
5 a thousand to one you will not stop till you come to the bottom of the hill; till you fall yourself into some of those outward sins which your companions commit before your eyes or in your hearing. Hereby the dread and horror which struck you at first will gradually abate, till at length you are prevailed upon to follow
10 their example.[28] But suppose they do not lead you into outward sin, if they infect your spirit with pride, anger, or love of the world, it is enough: it is sufficient, without deep repentance, to drown your soul in everlasting perdition; seeing (abstracted from all outward sin) 'to be carnally minded is death'.[29]

15 18. But as dangerous as it is to converse familiarly with men that know not God, it is more dangerous still for men to converse with women of that character; as they are generally more insinuating than men, and have far greater power of persuasion; particularly if they are agreeable in their persons, or pleasing in
20 their conversation. You must be more than man if you can converse with such and not suffer any loss. If you do not feel any foolish or unholy desire—and who can promise that you shall not?—yet it is scarce possible that you should not feel more or less of an improper softness, which will make you less willing and less
25 able to persist in that habit of denying yourself, and taking up your cross daily,[30] which constitute the character of a good soldier of Jesus Christ.[31] And we know that not only fornicators and adulterers, but even 'the soft and effeminate',[32] the delicate followers of a self-denying Master, 'shall have no part in the
30 kingdom of Christ and of God'.[33]

19. Such are the consequences which must surely, though perhaps slowly, follow the mixing of the children of God with the

---

[28] Cf. Addison's essay on the effects of custom, in *The Spectator*, No. 447, Aug. 2, 1712: '[We must] take particular care how we too frequently indulge ourselves in the most innocent diversions and entertainments, since the mind may insensibly fall off from the relish of virtuous actions and, by degrees, exchange that pleasure which takes in the performance of its duty for delights of a much more inferior and unprofitable nature.'
[29] Rom. 8:6.　　　　　　　　　　　　　　　　　　　　　　　[30] Luke 9:23.
[31] 2 Tim. 2:3.
[32] Cf. 1 Cor. 6:9—μαλακοί (i.e., 'soft') as in Matt. 11:8 and Luke 7:25. In the *General Rules*, §4, Wesley inveighs against 'softness and needless self-indulgence'.
[33] Cf. Eph. 5:5.

men of the world. And by this means more than by any other, yea, than by all others put together, are the people called Methodists[34] likely to lose their strength and become like other men.[35] It is indeed with a good design, and from a real desire of promoting the glory of God, that many of them admit of familiar 5 conversation with men that know not God. You have a hope of awakening them out of sleep, and persuading them to seek the things that make for their peace. But if after a competent time of trial you can make no impression upon them, it will be your wisdom to give them up to God. Otherwise you are more likely to 10 receive hurt from them than to do them any good. For if you do not raise their hearts up to heaven, they will draw yours down to earth. Therefore retreat in time, and 'come out from among them, and be ye separate.'

20. But how may this be done? What is the most easy and 15 effectual method of separating ourselves from unholy men? Perhaps a few advices will make this plain to those that desire to know and do the will of God.

First, invite no unholy person to your house unless on some very particular occasion. You may say, 'But civility requires this; 20 and sure, religion is no enemy to civility. Nay, the Apostle himself directs us to "be courteous", as well as to "be pitiful".'[36] I answer, You may be civil, sufficiently civil, and yet keep them at a proper distance. You may be courteous in a thousand instances; and yet stand aloof from them. And it was never the design of the Apostle 25 to recommend any such courtesy as must necessarily prove a snare to the soul.

21. Secondly, on no account accept any invitation from an unholy person. Never be prevailed upon to pay a visit unless you wish it to be repaid. It may be a person desirous of your 30 acquaintance will repeat the visit twice or thrice. But if you steadily refrain from returning it the visitant will soon be tired. It is not improbable he will be disobliged; and perhaps he will show marks of resentment. Lay your account with this,[37] that when anything of the kind occurs you may neither be surprised nor 35

---

[34] For other comments on Methodist 'triumphalism', cf. No. 102, 'Of Former Times', §22 and n.

[35] A remembrance of Samson as in Judg. 16:7-17.

[36] 1 Pet. 3:8.

[37] Cf. Joseph Wright, *The English Dialect Dictionary* (1896–1905), *loc.cit.* This is a Scottish phrase meaning, 'to expect and be prepared for', as in Wesley's letter to his preachers, Aug. 4, 1769, §3, where he gives a similar forewarning.

discouraged. It is better to please God and displease man than to please man and displease God.

22. Thirdly, it is probable you were acquainted with men of the world before you yourself knew God. What is best to be done with
5 regard to these? How may you most easily drop their acquaintance? First, allow a sufficient time to try whether you cannot by argument and persuasion, applied at the soft times of address, induce them to choose the better part.[38] Spare no pains. Exert all your faith and love, and wrestle with God in their behalf.
10 If after all you cannot perceive that any impression is made upon them, it is your duty gently to withdraw from them, that you be not entangled with them. This may be done in a short time, easily and quietly, by not returning their visits. But you must expect they will upbraid you with haughtiness and unkindness, if not to your face,
15 yet behind your back. And this you can suffer for a good conscience. It is properly the reproach of Christ.[39]

23. When it pleased God to give *me* a settled resolution to be not a *nominal* but a *real* Christian (being then about two and twenty years of age)[40] my acquaintance were as ignorant of God as
20 myself. But there was this difference: I knew my own ignorance; they did not know theirs. I faintly endeavoured to help them; but in vain. Meantime I found by sad experience that even their *harmless*[41] conversation (so called) damped all my good resolutions. But how to get rid of them was the question, which I
25 resolved in my mind again and again. I saw no possible way, unless it should please God to remove me to another college. He did so, in a manner utterly contrary to all human probability. I was elected fellow of a college[42] where I knew not one person. I

---

[38] See Luke 10:42.   [39] Heb. 11:26.

[40] I.e., in 1725, which would coincide with Wesley's account in JWJ, May 24, 1738, §4 ('When I was about twenty-two . . . I began to see that true religion was seated in the heart.'), and also with his report in *A Plain Account of Christian Perfection*, §2 ('In the year 1725 . . . I met with Bishop Taylor's "Rule and Exercises of Holy Living and Dying" . . . and I instantly resolved to dedicate *all* my life to God.'). Then follows (in both accounts) the successive 'moments' of Wesley's conversion from a 'nominal' to a 'real' Christian. But both these accounts and Wesley's remembrance here are in conflict with the public 'confession' in No. 2, *The Almost Christian*, I.13, 'that all this time [he was in Oxford] I was but almost a Christian', and also with the familiar stereotype in Wesleyan biography that he was no better than a nominal Christian until Aldersgate. It is interesting how Wesley's memories (and perspective) had changed over the years.

[41] Cf. No. 32, 'Sermon on the Mount, XII', II.2 and n.

[42] Lincoln, where he had been elected in 1726 as one of the College's twelve Fellows; cf. V. H. H. Green, *The Young Mr. Wesley*, pp. 100-23. Here, Wesley's recollections agree with his earlier *Journal* memoir (May 24, 1738, §5).

foresaw abundance of people would come to see me, either out of
friendship, civility, or curiosity; and that I should have offers of
acquaintance, new and old: but I had now fixed my plan. Entering
now, as it were, into a new world, I resolved to have no
acquaintance by chance, but by choice; and to choose such only as   5
I had reason to believe would help me on in my way to heaven. In
consequence of this I narrowly observed the temper and
behaviour of all that visited me. I saw no reason to think that the
greater part of these truly loved or feared God. Such
acquaintance therefore I did not choose: I could not expect they   10
would do me any good. Therefore when any of these came to see
me, I behaved as courteously as I could. But to the question,
'When will you come to see me?' I returned no answer. When they
had come a few times, and found I still declined returning the
visit, I saw them no more. And I bless God this has been my   15
invariable rule for about threescore years. I knew many
reflections would follow; but that did not move me, as I knew full
well it was my calling to go 'through evil report and good report'.[43]

24. I earnestly advise all of you who resolve to be not 'almost,
but altogether Christians',[44] to adopt the same plan, however   20
contrary it may be to flesh and blood. Narrowly observe which of
those that fall in your way are like minded with yourself. Who
among them have you reason to believe fears God and works
righteousness?[45] Set them down as worthy of your acquaintance;
gladly and freely converse with them at all opportunities. As to all   25
who do not answer that character, gently and quietly let them
drop. However good-natured and sensible they may be, they will
do you no real service. Nay, if they did not lead you into outward
sin, yet they would be a continual clog to your soul,[46] and would
hinder your running with vigour and cheerfulness the race that is   30
set before you.[47] And if any of your friends that did once run well
'turn back from the holy commandment once delivered to
them',[48] first use every method that prudence can suggest to bring
them again into the good way. But if you cannot prevail, let them

---

[43] 2 Cor. 6:8 (*Notes*).

[44] The 'almost Christian' here is presumed to be a worldling. In No. 2, *The Almost
Christian*, he had been portrayed as very 'religious' without, however, being a real *Christian*
(see espec. I.1-12).

[45] Acts 10:35.

[46] Cf. No. 24, 'Sermon on the Mount, IV', III.5 and n.

[47] See Heb. 12:1.

[48] Cf. 2 Pet. 2:21.

go; only still commending them unto God in prayer. Drop all familiar intercourse with them, and save your own soul.[49]

25. I advise you, fourthly, walk circumspectly with regard to your relations. With your parents, whether religious or not, you must certainly converse if they desire it; and with your brothers and sisters—more especially if they want your service. I do not know that you are under any such obligation with respect to your more distant relations. Courtesy, indeed, and natural affection, may require that you should visit them sometimes. But if they neither know nor seek God, it should certainly be as seldom as possible. And when you are with them you should not stay a day longer than decency requires. Again, whichsoever of them you are with at any time, remember that solemn caution of the Apostle: 'Let no corrupt communication (conversation) come out of your mouth; but that which is good, to the use of edifying, that it may minister grace to the hearers.'[50] You have no authority to vary from this rule; otherwise you 'grieve the Holy Spirit of God'.[51] And if you keep closely to it, those who have no religion will soon dispense with your company.

26. Thus it is that those who fear or love God should 'come out from among' all that do not fear him. Thus in a plain scriptural sense you should 'be separate' from them, from all unnecessary intercourse with them. Yea, 'Touch not', saith the Lord, 'the unclean thing' or person, any farther than necessity requires; 'and I will receive you' into the family and household of God. 'And I will be unto you a Father', will embrace you with paternal affection, 'and ye shall be unto me sons and daughters, saith the Lord Almighty.' The promise is express to all that renounce the company of ungodly men, provided their spirit and conversation are in other respects also suitable to their duty. God does here absolutely engage to give them all the blessings he has prepared for his beloved children, both in time and eternity. Let all those therefore who have any regard for the favour and the blessing of God, first, beware how they contract any acquaintance or form any connection with ungodly men, any farther than necessary business or some other providential call requires; and secondly, with all possible speed, all that the nature of the thing will admit, break off all such acquaintance already contracted, and all such

[49] See Ezek. 33:9.
[50] Cf. Eph. 4:29.
[51] Eph. 4:30.

connections already formed. Let no pleasure resulting from such acquaintance, no gain found or expected from such connections, be of any consideration when laid in the balance against a clear, positive command of God. In such a case, 'pluck out the right eye,' tear away the most pleasing acquaintance, 'and cast it from thee:' give up all thought, all design of seeking it again. 'Cut off the right hand,' absolutely renounce the most profitable connection, 'and cast it from thee.'[52] 'It is better for thee to enter into life with one eye', or one hand, 'than having two, to be cast into hell-fire.'[53]

Otley, July 17, 1784[54]

---

[52] Cf. Matt. 5:29-30.
[53] Matt. 18:9.
[54] Place and date as in *AM*.

ON TEMPTATION

AN INTRODUCTORY COMMENT

There would seem to have been no special occasion for this sermon except for the regular demands that the Arminian Magazine *had come to place on Wesley for an 'original sermon' in each two successive instalments. It was written by an eighty-three-year-old man in the midst of a busy autumnal itinerary in 1786 and finished during a stopover in London on October 7; cf. his* Journal *entry for the preceding June 28, the conclusion of the last* Journal *extract published in Wesley's lifetime, and a birthday comment on his vigour: 'I am a wonder to myself. It is now twelve years since I have felt any such sensation as weariness,' etc.*

His theme here may have been suggested by the continuing clash between Wesleyan and Calvinist notions as to the proper terms of Christian confidence—a further complication of the older debates about assurance. The fifth of the 'Five Points' of Calvinism was the affirmation of the perseverance of the saints, based on the trustworthiness of God's indefectible grace. Wesley had always come at this problem of assurance from its other end: viz., the power of the Spirit's prevenient and *accompanying grace to deliver the faithful soul not from but in temptation, and to 'make a way of escape' for anyone whose faith and trust are unfaltering. That this particular nuance on a lifelong view had evolved more or less recently is suggested by the fact that of the nine times Wesley records using 1 Cor. 10:13 as a sermon text, the first is in 1763, and the second in 1771; but there are three instances for 1784, one more in 1785, and three again in 1786.*

The written sermon was published in the first two issues of the Arminian Magazine *for 1787 (January and February), X.8-13, 61-67, without title and numbered as 'Sermon XXXVII'. In the following year it was included in* SOSO, *VII.27-45. It was not thereafter reprinted in Wesley's lifetime.*

On Temptation

1 Corinthians 10:13

There hath no temptation taken you but such as is common to man. And God is faithful, who will not suffer you to be tempted above that ye are able; but will with the temptation also make a way to escape, that ye may be able to bear it.

1. In the foregoing part of the chapter the Apostle has been reciting, on the one hand, the unparalleled mercies of God to the Israelites; and, on the other, the unparalleled ingratitude of that disobedient and gainsaying people.[1] And all these things, as the Apostle observes, 'wcre written for our ensample';[2] that we might take warning from them, so as to avoid their grievous sins, and escape their terrible punishment. He then adds that solemn and important caution, 'Let him that thinketh he standeth, take heed lest he fall.'[3]

2. But if we observe these words attentively, will there not appear a considerable difficulty in them? 'Let him that thinketh he standeth take heed lest he fall.' If a man only *thinks he stands* he is in no danger of falling. It is not possible that anyone should fall if he only *thinks he stands*. The same difficulty occurs, according to our translation, in those well-known words of our Lord (the importance of which we may easily learn from their being repeated in the Gospel no less than eight times), 'To him that hath shall be given; but from him that hath not shall be taken away even *what he seemeth to have.*'[4] That which he *seemeth to have!*' Nay, if he only 'seems to have it', it is impossible it should be taken away. None can take away from another what he only 'seems to have'. What a man only 'seems to have' he cannot possibly lose. This difficulty may at first appear impossible to be surmounted. It is really so; it cannot be surmounted if the common translation be

[1] Rom. 10:21.
[2] Cf. 1 Cor. 10:11 (AV marginal n.: 'Or, type').
[3] 1 Cor. 10:12.
[4] Cf. Luke 8:18; 'eight times' here refers to cognates of the verb δοκεῖν; cf. Alfred Schmoller, ed., *Handkonkordanz zum griechischen Neuen Testament* (Stuttgart, 9th edn., 1951).

allowed. But if we observe the proper meaning of the original word the difficulty vanishes away. It may be allowed that the word δοκεῖ does (sometimes, at least in some authors) mean no more than to *seem*. But I much doubt whether it ever bears that meaning
5 in any part of the inspired writings. By a careful consideration of every text in the New Testament wherein this word occurs I am fully convinced that it nowhere lessens but everywhere strengthens the sense of the word to which it is annexed.[5] Accordingly ὁ δοκεῖ ἔχειν does not mean 'what he seems to
10 have', but on the contrary, 'what he assuredly hath'. And so ὁ δοκῶν ἑστάναι, not 'he that seemeth to stand', or he that 'thinketh he standeth', but 'he that assuredly standeth'; he who standeth so fast that he does not appear to be in any danger of falling; he that saith, like David, 'I shall never be moved; thou,
15 Lord, hast made my hill so strong.'[6] Yet at that very time, thus saith the Lord, 'Be not high-minded, but fear; else shalt thou be cut off,'[7] else shalt thou also be moved from thy steadfastness. The strength which thou assuredly hast shall be taken away. As firmly as thou didst really stand thou wilt fall into sin, if not into
20 hell.

3. But lest any should be discouraged by the consideration of those who once ran well and were afterwards overcome by temptation; lest the fearful of heart should be utterly cast down, supposing it impossible for them to stand, the Apostle subjoins to
25 that serious exhortation these comfortable words: 'There hath no temptation taken you but such as is common to man. But God is faithful, who will not suffer you to be tempted above that ye are able; but will with the temptation also make a way to escape, that ye may be able to bear it.'

30 I. 1. Let us begin with the observation which ushers in this comfortable promise, 'There hath no temptation taken you but such as is common to man.' Our translators seem to have been sensible that this expression, 'common to man', does by no means reach the force of the original word. Hence they substitute

---

[5] A repetition of a lexical opinion already expressed in Wesley's *Notes* on Luke 8:18 and 1 Cor. 10:12; cf. No. 43, *The Scripture Way of Salvation*, §1 and n. The point, however, had already been interpreted differently by Poole in his *Annotations* on Matt. 13:12; Luke 8:18; Jas. 1:26. It is equally doubtful in such cases as 1 Cor. 3:18; Phil. 3:4; and Heb. 12:11. Cf. Arndt and Gingrich, *Greek-English Lexicon*, on δοκέω, and Alfred Plummer, *The Gospel According to St. Luke* in *The International Critical Commentary*, on 8:18.
[6] Ps. 30:6 (BCP).   [7] Rom. 11:20, 22.

another in the margin, 'moderate'.[8] But this seems to be less significant than the other, and farther from the meaning of it. Indeed it is not easy to find any single word in the English tongue which answers the word ἀνθρώπινος. I believe the sense of it can only be expressed by some such circumlocution as this: 'Such as 5 is suited to the nature and circumstances of man; such as every man may reasonably expect if he considers the nature of his body and his soul, and his situation in the present world.' If we duly consider these we shall not be surprised at any temptation that hath befallen us; seeing it is no other than such a creature, in such 10 a situation, has all reason to expect.

2. Consider, first, the nature of that body with which your soul is connected.[9] How many are the evils which it is every day, every hour liable to! Weakness, sickness, and disorders of a thousand kinds, are its natural attendants. Consider the inconceivably 15 minute fibres, threads abundantly finer than hair (called from thence capillary vessels) whereof every part of it is composed; consider the innumerable multitude of equally fine pipes and strainers, all filled with circulating juice! And will not the breach of a few of these fibres, or the obstruction of a few of these tubes, 20 particularly in the brain, or heart, or lungs, destroy our ease, health, strength, if not life itself?[10] Now if we observe that all pain implies temptation, how numberless must the temptations be which will beset every man, more or less, sooner or late, while he dwells in this corruptible body! 25

3. Consider, secondly, the present state of the soul as long as it inhabits the house of clay.[11] I do not mean in its unregenerate state, while it lies in darkness and the shadow of death; under the

[8] This appears as a marginal note in the folio edition of the AV in 1611 and again thereafter in all its annotated editions throughout the seventeenth and eighteenth centuries. Wesley, of course, used smaller, unannotated Bibles in his travels and for his preaching. One of his prized possessions at his death was a small Bible printed by John Field (1653; 24mo.); it is still in use and is passed on in annual succession from President to President of the British Methodist Conference.

[9] For more on Wesley's body-soul dualism, see No. 41, *Wandering Thoughts*, III.5 and n.; but see also, No. 141, 'The Image of God', II.1.

[10] Cf. Addison, *The Spectator*, No. 115, July 12, 1711: 'I consider the body as a system of tubes and glands, or to use a more rustick phrase, a bundle of pipes and strainers, fitted to one another after so wonderful a manner as to make a proper engine for the soul to work with. This description does not only comprehend the bowels, bones, tendons, veins, nerves, arteries, but every muscle, and every ligature, which is a composition of fibres that are so many imperceptible tubes or pipes interwoven on all sides with invisible glands or strainers.'

[11] Job 4:19; cf. also No. 28, 'Sermon on the Mount, VIII', §21 and n.

dominion of the prince of darkness, without hope, and without God in the world.[12] No: look upon men who are raised above that deplorable state. See those who have tasted that the Lord is gracious.[13] Yet still how weak is their understanding! How limited 5 its extent! How confused, how inaccurate our apprehensions of even the things that are round about us! How liable are the wisest of men to mistake! To form false judgments! To take falsehood for truth, and truth for falsehood! Evil for good, and good for evil! What starts, what wanderings of imagination are we continually 10 subject to! In how many instances does the corruptible body press down the soul![14] And how many are the temptations which we have to expect, even from these innocent infirmities![15]

4. Consider, thirdly, what is the present situation of even those that fear God. They dwell in the ruins of a disordered world, 15 among men that know not God, that care not for him, and whose heart is fully set in them to do evil. How many are forced to cry out, 'Woe is me that I am constrained to dwell with Mesech; to have my habitation among the tents of Kedar,'[16] among the enemies of God and man! How immensely outnumbered are 20 those that would do well by them that neither fear God nor regard man.[17] And how striking is Cowley's observation: If a man that was armed cap-à-pie was closed in by a thousand naked Indians, their number would give them such advantage over him that it would be scarce possible for him to escape. What hope then 25 would there be for a naked, unarmed man to escape, who was surrounded by a thousand armed men! Now this is the case of every good man. He is not armed either with force or fraud, and is turned out naked as he is among thousands that are armed with the whole armour of Satan, and provided with all the weapons 30 which the prince of this world can supply out of the armoury of hell.[18] If then he is not destroyed, yet how must a good man be tempted in the midst of this evil world!

[12] Eph. 2:12.
[13] 1 Pet. 2:3.
[14] Cf. Wisd. 9:15; and see No. 41, *Wandering Thoughts*, II.3 and n.
[15] *SOSO*, VII.33-34, omits 'instances does . . . how many', obviously a compositorial error. In his own copy of these *Sermons* Wesley deleted 'In', thus making sense but also changing the original sense by at least a little.
[16] Ps. 120:4 (BCP, but note Wesley's preference for the AV spelling of 'Mesech').
[17] See Luke 18:4.
[18] A misreading of Abraham Cowley's *Several Discourses by Way of Essays*, VIII, 'The Dangers of an Honest Man in Much Company': 'If twenty thousand naked Americans were not able to resist the assaults of but twenty well armed Spaniards, I see but little

5. But is it only from wicked men that temptations arise to them that fear God? It is very natural to imagine this; and almost everyone thinks so. Hence how many of us have said in our hearts: 'Oh! if my lot were but cast among good men, among those that loved or even feared God, I should be free from all these temptations.' Perhaps you would; probably you would not find the same sort of temptations which you have now to encounter. But you would surely meet with temptations of some other kind, which you would find equally hard to bear. For even good men in general, though sin has not dominion over them, yet are not freed from the remains of it.[19] They have still the remains of an evil heart, ever prone to 'depart from the living God'.[20] They have the seeds of pride, of anger, of foolish desire; indeed of every unholy temper. And any of these, if they do not continually watch and pray, may, and naturally will spring up and trouble not themselves only, but all that are round about them. We must not therefore depend upon finding no temptation from those that fear, yea, in a measure, love God. Much less must we be surprised if some of those who once loved God in sincerity should lay greater temptations in our way than many of those that never knew him.

6. 'But can we expect to find any temptation from those that are "perfected in love"?'[21] This is an important question, and deserves a particular consideration. I answer, first, You may find every kind of temptation from those who *suppose* they are perfected when indeed they are not; and so you may, secondly, from those who once really were so, but are now moved from their steadfastness. And if you are not aware of this, if you think they are still what they were once, the temptation will be harder to bear. Nay, thirdly, even those who 'stand fast in the liberty wherewith Christ has made them free',[22] who are now really perfect in love, may still be an occasion of temptation to *you*. For they are still encompassed with infirmities. They may be dull of

---

possibility for one honest man to defend himself against twenty thousand knaves, who are all furnished cap-à-pie, with the defensive arms of worldly prudence, and the offensive too of craft and malice. He will find no less odds than this against him if he have much to do in human affairs' (*Works*, 7th edn., 1681, p. 132). An extract of this appears in the *Christian Lib.*, XXXIII.286-91; see also Wesley's *Doctrine of Original Sin*, Pt. I, II.9.

[19] For Wesley's wrestlings with the problem of 'the remains of sin', cf. No. 13, *On Sin in Believers*, intro., III.1-9, and n.

[20] Cf. Heb. 3:12.

[21] Cf. 1 John 2:5; 4:12, 18.

[22] Cf. Gal. 5:1.

apprehension; they may have a natural heedlessness, or a treacherous memory; they may have too lively an imagination: and any of these may cause little improprieties, either in speech or behaviour, which though not sinful in themselves may try all the grace you have. Especially if you impute to perverseness of will (as it is very natural to do) what is really owing to defect of memory or weakness of understanding; if these appear to you to be voluntary mistakes which are really involuntary. So proper was the answer which a saint of God (now in Abraham's bosom) gave me some years ago when I said: 'Jenny, surely now your mistress and you can neither of you be a trial to the other, as God has saved you both from sin.' 'O sir,' said she, 'if we are saved from sin, we still have infirmities enough to try all the grace that God has given us.'[23]

7. But besides evil men, do not evil spirits also continually surround us on every side? Do not Satan and his angels continually go about seeking whom they may devour?[24] Who is out of the reach of their malice and subtlety? Not the wisest or the best of the children of men. 'The servant is not above his Master.'[25] If then they tempted him, will they not tempt us also? Yea, it may be, should God see good to permit, more or less to the end of our lives. 'No temptation' therefore 'hath taken us' which we had not reason to expect, either from our body or soul, either from evil spirits or evil men, yea, or even from good men, till our spirits return to God that gave them.[26]

II. 1. Meantime what a comfort it is to know, with the utmost certainty, that 'God is faithful, who will not suffer us to be tempted above that we are able.' He knoweth what our ability is, and cannot be mistaken. 'He knoweth' precisely 'whereof we are made; he remembereth that we are but dust.'[27] And he will suffer no temptation to befall us but such as is proportioned to our strength. Not only his justice requires this, which could not punish us for not resisting any temptation if it was so disproportioned to our strength that it was impossible for us to

[23] Probably Jane Cooper (1738–62); cf. Wesley's references to her in JWJ, including her funeral, Nov. 25, 1762. In 1764 he published a small volume of *Letters Wrote by Jane Cooper* (*Bibliog*, No. 260).
[24] See 1 Pet. 5:8.
[25] Cf. Matt. 10:24.
[26] See Eccles. 12:7.
[27] Ps. 103:14 (BCP).

resist it; not only his mercy, that tender mercy which is over us, as well as over all his works;[28] but above all his faithfulness, seeing all his words are faithful and true, and the whole tenor of his promises altogether agrees with that declaration, 'As thy day, so thy strength shall be.'[29]

2. In that execrable slaughter-house, the Romish Inquisition[30] (most unfortunately called 'the house of mercy'!), it is the custom of those holy butchers, while they are tearing a man's sinews upon the rack, to have the physician of the house standing by. His business is from time to time to observe the eyes, the pulse, and other circumstances of the sufferer, and to give notice when the torture has continued so long as it can without putting an end to his life; that it may be preserved long enough for him to undergo the residue of their tortures. But notwithstanding all the physician's care, he is sometimes mistaken, and death puts a period to the patient's sufferings before his tormentors are aware. We may observe something like this in our own case. In whatever sufferings or temptations we are, our great Physician never departs from us. He is about our bed and about our path.[31] He observes every symptom of our distress, that it may not rise above our strength. And he cannot be mistaken concerning us. He knows the souls and bodies which he has given us. He sees exactly how much we can endure with our present degree of strength. And if this is not sufficient he can increase it to whatever degree it pleases him. Nothing therefore is more certain than that in consequence of his wisdom, as well as his justice, mercy, and faithfulness, he never will, he never can suffer us to be tempted above that we are able—above the strength which he either hath given already, or will give as soon as we need it.

III. 1. 'He will with the temptation also' (this is the third point we are to consider) 'make a way to escape, that we may be able to bear it.'

The word ἔκβασιν, which we render 'a way to escape', is extremely significant. The meaning of it is nearly expressed by the English word 'outlet'; but more exact by the old word 'outgate', still frequently used by the Scottish writers. It literally means 'a way out'.[32] And this God will either find or make: which he that hath all wisdom, as well as all power in heaven and earth, can never be at a loss how to do.

2. Either he 'makes a way to escape' out of the temptation, by 5 removing the occasion of it, or *in the temptation;* that is, the occasion remaining as it was, it is a temptation no longer. First, he makes a way to escape out of the temptation, by removing the occasion of it. The histories of mankind, of the church in particular, afford us numberless instances of this. And many have 10 occurred in our own memory, and within the little circle of our acquaintance. One of many I think it worth while to relate, as a memorable instance of the faithfulness of God in making a way to escape out of temptation: Elizabeth Chadsey, then living in London (whose daughter is living at this day, and is no dishonour 15 to her parent), was advised to administer [33] to her husband, who was supposed to leave much substance behind him. But when a full inquiry into his circumstances was made, it appeared that this supposition was utterly destitute of foundation, and that he not only left nothing at all behind him, but also was very considerably 20 in debt. It was not long after his burial that a person came to her house and said, 'Mrs. Chadsey, you are much indebted to your landlord, and he has sent me to demand the rent that is due to him.' She answered, 'Sir, I have not so much money in the world; indeed I have none at all!' 'But', said he, 'have you nothing that 25 will fetch money?' She replied: 'Sir, you see all that I have. I have nothing in the house but these six little children.' 'Then', said he, 'I must execute my writ and carry you to Newgate. But it is a hard case. I will leave you here till tomorrow, and will go and try if I cannot persuade your landlord to give you time.' He returned the 30 next morning and said: 'I have done all I can. I have used all the arguments I could think of, but your landlord is not to be moved. He vows, if I do not carry you to prison without delay I shall go thither myself.' She answered, 'You have done *your* part. The will of the Lord be done!' He said, 'I will venture to make one trial 35 more, and will come again in the morning.' He came in the morning, and said: 'Mrs. Chadsey, God has undertaken your

---

[32] Cf. Liddell and Scott, *Greek-English Lexicon*, for ἔκβασις (i.e., 'exit', etc.); for 'outgate', cf. *OED* ('a way of escape or deliverance'). See also Thomas Boston, *Human Nature in Its Fourfold State* (1720: Edinburgh, 1812), State IV, Head VI, p. 442: 'It is an entry without an out-gate.'

[33] I.e., had undertaken to serve as executor of his estate; cf. *OED* for this usage of 'administer'.

cause. None can give you any trouble now; for your landlord died last night. But he has left no will, and no one knows who is heir to the estate.'[34]

3. Thus God is able to deliver out of temptations, by removing the occasion of them. But are there not temptations, the occasions of which cannot be taken away? Is it not a striking instance of this kind which we have in a late publication? 'I was walking' (says the writer of the letter) 'over Dover cliffs, in a calm, pleasant evening, with a person whom I tenderly loved, and to whom I was to be married in a few days. While we were engaged in earnest conversation her foot slipped, she fell down, and I saw her dashed in pieces on the beach. I lifted up my hands, and cried out: "This evil admits of no remedy. I must now go mourning all my days! My wound is incurable. It is impossible I should ever find such another woman! One so every way fitted for me." I added in an agony, "This is such an affliction as even God himself cannot redress!" And just as I uttered the words I awoke; for it was a dream!'[35] Just so can God remove any possible temptation! Making it like a dream when one waketh!

4. Thus is God able to deliver out of temptation by taking away the very ground of it. And he is equally able to deliver in the temptation, which perhaps is the greatest deliverance of all. I mean, suffering the occasion to remain as it was, he will take away the bitterness of it; so that it shall not be a temptation at all, but

---

[34] This Mrs. Chadsey does not appear elsewhere in Wesley's *Works*, nor in *Gent's Mag.* (1731–86), nor in the indices of *AM* and Charles Wesley's *Letters*.

[35] This story is adapted from *The Tatler*, No. 117, Jan. 7, 1710, by Addison: 'When I was a youth in a part of the army which was then quartered at Dover, I fell in love with an agreeable young woman, of a good family in those parts, and had the satisfaction of seeing my addresses kindly received, which occasioned the perplexity I am going to relate. We were in a calm evening diverting ourselves upon the top of the cliff with the prospect of the sea, and trifling away the time in such little fondnesses as are most ridiculous to people in business, and most agreeable to those in love. In the midst of these our innocent endearments, she snatched a paper of verses out of my hand, and ran away with them. I was following her, when on a sudden the ground, though at a considerable distance from the verge of the precipice, sunk under her, and threw her down from so prodigious an height upon such a range of rocks, as would have dashed her into ten thousand pieces, had her body been made of adamant. It is much easier for my reader to imagine my state of mind upon such an occasion, than for me to express it. I said to myself, it is not in the power of heaven to relieve me! when I awaked, equally transported and astonished, to see myself drawn out of an affliction which, the very moment before, appeared to me altogether inextricable.'

Dr. James Beattie in his *Dissertations, Moral and Critical* (1783) speaks of this as 'one of the finest moral tales I ever read, which though it has every appearance of a real dream, comprehends a moral so sublime and so interesting that I question whether any man who attends to it, can ever forget it.'

only an occasion of thanksgiving. How many proofs of this have
the children of God, even in their daily experience! How
frequently are they encompassed with trouble! Or visited with
pain or sickness! And when they cry unto the Lord, at some times
5 he takes away the cup from them;[36] he removes the trouble, or
sickness, or pain, and it is as though it never had been. At other
times he does not make any outward change—outward trouble,
or pain, or sickness continue—but the consolations of the Holy
One so increase as to overbalance them all. And they can boldly
10 declare,

> Labour is rest, and pain is sweet,
> When thou, my God, art here.[37]

5. An eminent instance of this kind of deliverance is that which
occurs in the life of that excellent man, the Marquis de Renty.
15 When he was in a violent fit of the rheumatism, a friend asked
him, 'Sir, are you in much pain?' He answered: 'My pains are
extreme; but through the mercy of God I give myself up, not to
them, but to him.'[38] It was in the same spirit that my own father
answered, though exhausted with a severe illness (an ulcer in the
20 bowels, which had given him little rest day or night for upwards of
seven months). When I asked, 'Sir, are you in pain now?' he
answered with a strong and loud voice: 'God does indeed chasten
me with pain; yea, all my bones with strong pain. But I thank him
for all; I bless him for all; I love him for all.'[39]
25 6. We may observe one more instance of a somewhat similar
kind in the life of the Marquis de Renty. When his wife, whom he
very tenderly loved, was exceeding ill, and supposed to be near
death, a friend took the liberty to inquire how he felt himself on

[36] Cf. Matt. 26:39 and parallels.
[37] John and Charles Wesley, 'On a Journey'; cf. No. 52, *The Reformation of Manners*, III.7 and n.
[38] Cf. Saint-Jure, *The Holy Life of Monsr. De Renty, A Late Nobleman of France and Sometimes Councellor to King Lewis the 13th*, p. 96: 'My pains are great, even to crying out, and swouning [sic]; but although I feel them in the greatest extremity; yet through God's grace, I yield not up myself to them, but to him.' Cf. also Wesley's *Extract of the Life of Monsieur De Renty*, London, Strahan, 1741, iv. 3-4 (p. 21). The quotation is repeated in his letter to Ann Bolton, Jan. 14, 1780; cf. also No. 14, *The Repentance of Believers*, I.15 and n.
[39] John and Charles heard that their father was ill and on Sunday, Mar. 30, 1735, they started walking from Oxford to Epworth, where they arrived on Apr. 4 (Good Friday). The old man died on Apr. 25, with John and Charles present at his deathbed. Cf. John's Savannah sermon, 'On Love', III.7 (No. 149), and also his letter to 'John Smith', Mar. 22, 1748, §6.

the occasion. He replied: 'I cannot but say that this trial affects me in the most tender part. I am exquisitely sensible of my loss. I feel more than it is possible to express. And yet I am so satisfied that the will of God is done, and not the will of a vile sinner, that were it not for fear of giving offence to others I could dance and sing!'[40] Thus the merciful, the just, the faithful God, will in one way or other, in every 'temptation make a way to escape, that we may be able to bear it'.

7. This whole passage is fruitful of instruction. Some of the lessons which we may learn from it are:

First, 'Let him that most assuredly standeth, take heed lest he fall'[41] into *murmuring;* lest he say in his heart, 'Surely no one's case is like mine: no one was ever tried like *me.*' Yea, ten thousand. 'There has no temptation taken you but such as is common to man;' such as you might reasonably expect if you considered *what you are*—a sinner born to die, a sinful inhabitant of a mortal body, liable to numberless inward and outward sufferings—and *where you are*, in a shattered, disordered world, surrounded by evil men and evil spirits. Consider this, and you will not repine at the common lot, the general condition of humanity.

8. Secondly, let him that standeth 'take heed lest he fall', lest he 'tempt God',[42] by thinking or saying: 'This is insupportable; this is too hard; I can never get through it; my burden is heavier than I can bear.' Not so; unless something is too hard for God. He will not suffer you to be 'tempted above that ye are able'. He proportions the burden to your strength. If you want more strength, ask and it shall be given you.[43]

9. Thirdly, 'Let him that standeth take heed lest he fall,' lest he 'tempt God' *by unbelief,* by distrusting his faithfulness. Hath he said, in every temptation he will make a way to escape? And shall he not do it? Yea, verily:

> Far, far above thy thought
> His counsel shall appear,
> When fully he the work hath wrought,
> That caused thy needless fear.[44]

[40] Again, cf. Saint-Jure, *De Renty*, p. 270; the reference to dancing and singing is an addition of Wesley's.

[41] Cf. 1 Cor. 10:12 (*Notes*).   [42] Mal. 3:15.   [43] Matt. 7:7; Luke 11:9.

[44] John Wesley, A hymn from the German, 'Trust in Providence', st. 14, *Hymns and Sacred Poems* (1739), p. 143 (*Poet. Wks.*, I.127). *SOSO* (1788) alters to 'And far above thy thought'. See also Wesley's letter to the Revd. Mr. Heath, May 18, 1787.

10. Let us then receive every trial with calm resignation,[45] and with humble confidence that he who hath all power, all wisdom, all mercy, and all faithfulness, will first support us in every temptation, and then deliver us out of all; so that in the end all
5 things shall work together for good,[46] and we shall happily experience that all these things were for our profit, 'that we might be partakers of his holiness'.[47]

London, October 7, 1786[48]

---

[45] See No. 69, 'The Imperfection of Human Knowledge', IV.[3] and n.
[46] See Rom. 8:28.
[47] Heb. 12:10.
[48] Place and date as in *AM*.

ON PATIENCE

AN INTRODUCTORY COMMENT

This sermon first appeared in the Arminian Magazine *for 1784 (March and April, VII.121-27, 178-82), without a title, numbered 'Sermon XX'. There is a single diary reference to an oral sermon on Jas. 1:4, 5, on December 16, 1740, in Bristol. Wesley's* Journal *states: 'In the afternoon I preached on, "Let patience have her perfect work."')—proof enough that this text was not one of his favourites. The sermon has no internal clues as to its date or provenance other than the retrospective datings in §12, which suggest that it was not written before 1783.*

The sermon's present title was added when it was included in SOSO, *VII.47-63, and is not altogether apt. Clearly, the sermon's main theme is not 'patience' (ὑπομονή) but rather 'perfection' as a requisite virtue in one's further progress on the way to Christian maturity. In this sense, what we have here is yet another sermon in the line of his two previous ones: Nos. 40,* Christian Perfection, *and 76, 'On Perfection'. In §10, echoes from the continuing Calvinist debates may be heard; 'final perseverance' is rejected yet again. But the sermon's argument and rhetoric come to a climax in §14, where we have the strongest emphasis to be found anywhere in the corpus on what later evolved into the Methodist doctrines of 'entire sanctification as a second and separate work of grace'. (Cf. John L. Peters,* Christian Perfection and American Methodism.)

The sermon was not reprinted in Wesley's lifetime, and one wonders how widely and carefully it might have been read. Even so, it helps define the line of development that follows from the doctrinal premises of those earlier interrogations of Methodist preachers: 'Are you going on to perfection?' and 'Do you expect to be made perfect in love in this life?'

On Patience

James 1:4

Let patience have its perfect work, that ye may be perfect and entire, wanting nothing.

5   1. 'My brethren,' says the Apostle in the preceding verse, 'count it all joy when ye fall into divers temptations.'[1] At first view this may appear a strange direction; seeing most temptations are, 'for the present, not joyous, but grievous'.[2] Nevertheless ye know by your own experience that 'the trying of your faith worketh 10 patience:' and if 'patience have its perfect work, ye shall be perfect and entire, wanting nothing'.

    2. It is not to any particular person or church that the Apostle gives this instruction; but to all who are partakers of like precious faith,[3] and are seeking after that common salvation.[4] For as long as 15 any of us are upon earth we are in the region of temptation. He who came into the world to save his people from their sins did not come to save them from temptation. He himself 'knew no sin';[5] yet while he was in this vale of tears 'he suffered, being tempted;'[6] and herein also 'left us an example, that we should tread in his 20 steps'.[7] We are liable to a thousand temptations from the corruptible body variously affecting the soul.[8] The soul itself, encompassed as it is with infirmities, exposes us to ten thousand more. And how many are the temptations which we meet with even from the good men[9] (such at least they are in part, in their 25 general character) with whom we are called to converse from day to day! Yet what are these to the temptations we may expect to meet with from an evil world! Seeing we all, in effect, 'dwell with

---

[1] Jas. 1:2.
[2] Cf. Heb. 12:11.
[3] See 2 Pet. 1:1.
[4] Jude 3.
[5] 2 Cor. 5:21.
[6] Heb. 2:18.   [7] Cf. 1 Pet. 2:21.
[8] See Wisd. 9:15; cf. No. 41, *Wandering Thoughts*, II.3 and n. Cf. also No. 76, 'On Perfection', II.9, where Wesley makes the point that *no* body or matter of any kind can be sinful, that only spirits are capable of sin—a very different statement.
[9] Cf. No. 80, 'On Friendship with the World', §21 and n.

Mesech, and have our habitation in the tents of Kedar'![10] Add to this that the most dangerous of our enemies are not those that assault us openly. No:

> Angels our march oppose,
> Who still in strength excel,
> Our secret, sworn, eternal foes,
> Countless, invisible![11]

For is not our 'adversary the devil, as a roaring lion', with all his infernal legions, 'still going about seeking whom he may devour'?[12] This is the case with all the children of men. Yea, and with all the children of God, as long as they sojourn in this strange land. Therefore if we do not wilfully and carelessly rush into them, yet we shall surely 'fall into divers temptations'—temptations innumerable as the stars of heaven, and those varied and complicated a thousand ways. But instead of counting this a loss, as unbelievers would do, 'count it all joy; knowing that the trial of your faith', even when it is 'tried as by fire',[13] 'worketh patience'. But 'let patience have its perfect work, and ye shall be perfect and entire, wanting nothing.'

3. But what is 'patience'?[14] We do not now speak of a heathen virtue; neither of a natural indolence; but of a gracious temper wrought in the heart of a believer by the power of the Holy Ghost. It is a disposition to suffer whatever pleases God, in the manner and for the time that pleases him.[15] We thereby hold the middle way,[16] neither ὀλιγωροῦντες,[17] 'despising' our sufferings, 'making little' of them, passing over them lightly, as if they were owing to chance, or second causes; nor, on the other hand,

---

[10] Cf. Ps. 120:4 (BCP).

[11] Charles Wesley, 'Hymns for the Watch-night', No. 8, st. 7, ll. 1-4, in *Hymns and Sacred Poems* (1749), II.130 (*Poet. Wks.*, V.272). The pronouns have been altered from 'your' to 'our'. See also No. 72, 'Of Evil Angels', II.3, where the last four lines of this stanza appear.

[12] Cf. 1 Pet. 5:8. [13] Cf. 1 Pet. 1:7.

[14] ὑπομονή: 'endurance' or 'perseverance' rather than passive resignation; cf. Aristotle's *Nicomachean Ethics*, III.6-7; and R. C. Trench, *Synonyms of the New Testament* (1880), *loc. cit.*

[15] Johnson, *Dictionary*, had defined patience as 'the power of suffering', and quotes Bishop Sprat to this effect. Wesley, in a letter to Hannah Ball, Feb. 27, 1774, offers a further distinction: 'There are two general ways wherein it pleases God to lead his children to perfection—doing and suffering.' But in another letter to John Valton, Jan. 18, 1782, Wesley comments that for all his holiness the Apostle John 'seems to have suffered very little'.

[16] Cf. No. 27, 'Sermon on the Mount, VII', §4 and n. [17] Heb. 12:5.

ἐκλυόμενοι,[18] affected too much, unnerved, dissolved, sinking under them. We may observe, the proper object of patience is suffering, either in body or mind. Patience does not imply the not *feeling* this; it is not apathy or insensibility. It is at the utmost 5 distance from stoical stupidity! yea, and at an equal distance from fretfulness and dejection. The patient believer is preserved from falling into either of these extremes by considering who is the Author of all his suffering, even God his Father. What is the *motive* of his *giving us* to suffer? Not so properly his justice as his 10 love. And what is the *end* of it? 'Our profit, that we may be partakers of his holiness.'[19]

4. Very nearly related to patience is *meekness;*[20] if it be not rather a species of it. For may it not be defined, patience of injuries, particularly affronts, reproach, or unjust censure? This teaches 15 not to return evil for evil, or railing for railing; but contrariwise, blessing. Our blessed Lord himself seems to place a peculiar value upon this temper. This he peculiarly calls us to 'learn of him', if we would 'find rest for our souls'.[21]

5. But what may we understand by the 'work of patience'[22]—'let 20 patience have its perfect work'? It seems to mean, let it have its full fruit or effect. And what is the fruit which the Spirit of God is accustomed to produce hereby in the heart of a believer? One immediate fruit of patience is peace—a sweet tranquillity of mind, a serenity of spirit, which can never be found unless where 25 patience reigns. And this peace often rises into joy. Even in the midst of various temptations those that are enabled 'in patience to possess their souls'[23] can witness not only quietness of spirit, but triumph and exultation. This both

30
Lays the rough paths of peevish nature even,
And opens in each breast a little heaven.[24]

6. How lively is the account which the Apostle Peter gives, not only of the peace and joy, but of the hope and love which God

[18] Heb. 12:3.
[19] Heb. 12:10 (*Notes*).
[20] Cf. No. 22, 'Sermon on the Mount, II', I.4 and n.
[21] Cf. Matt. 11:29.
[22] Cf. Jas. 1:3. For other references to 'patience' cf. Nos. 22, 'Sermon on the Mount, II', I.12; 92, 'On Zeal', II.3; 108, 'On Riches', I.6-7; and 114, *On the Death of John Fletcher*, III.12 (where Wesley is quoting Mrs. Fletcher's account of her husband).
[23] Cf. Luke 21:19.
[24] Prior, 'Charity', ll. 7-8. See also, *An Earnest Appeal*, §8 (11:47 in this edn.).

works in those patient sufferers 'who are kept by the power of God through faith unto salvation'![25] Indeed he appears herein to have an eye to this very passage of St. James: 'Though ye are grieved for a season with manifold temptations' (the very word ποικίλοις πειρασμοῖς[26]); 'that the trial of your faith' (the same expression which was used by St. James)[27] 'may be found to praise, and honour, and glory, at the revelation of Jesus Christ; whom having not seen ye love; in whom, though ye see him not, yet believing, ye rejoice with joy unspeakable, and full of glory.'[28] See here the peace, the joy, and the love, which, through the mighty power of God, are the fruit or 'work of patience'!

7. And as peace, hope, joy, and love, are the fruits of patience, both springing from and confirmed thereby, so is also rational, genuine courage, which indeed cannot subsist without patience. The brutal courage, or rather fierceness, of a lion, may probably spring from impatience. But true fortitude, the courage of a man, springs from just the contrary temper. Christian *zeal* is likewise confirmed and increased by patience. And so is *activity* in every good work, the same spirit inciting us to be

Patient in bearing ill, and doing well,[29]

making us equally willing to do and suffer the whole will of God.

8. But what is the 'perfect work' of patience? Is it anything less than the 'perfect love of God',[30] constraining us to love every soul of man, 'even as Christ loved us'?[31] Is it not the whole of religion, the whole 'mind which was also in Christ Jesus'?[32] Is it not the 'renewal of our soul in the image of God, after the image of him that created us'?[33] And is not the fruit of this the constant resignation of ourselves, body, and spirit, to God—entirely giving up all we are, all we have, and all we love, as a holy sacrifice, acceptable unto God through the Son of his love? It seems this is the 'perfect work of patience', consequent upon the trial of our faith.

[25] 1 Pet. 1:5.
[26] 1 Pet. 1:6; Jas. 1:2.
[27] Cf. another parallel: 1 Pet. 1:7; Jas. 1:3.
[28] 1 Pet. 1:7-8.
[29] Samuel Wesley, Jun., 'The Battle of the Sexes', st. xxxv, *Poems* (1736), p. 38; cf. No. 53, *On the Death of George Whitefield*, II.7 and n.
[30] Cf. 1 John 2:5.   [31] Cf. Eph. 5:2.
[32] Cf. Phil. 2:5.
[33] Cf. Col. 3:10.

9. But how does this work differ from that gracious work which is wrought in every believer when he first finds redemption in the blood of Jesus, even the remission of his sins? Many persons that are not only upright of heart, but that fear, nay, and love God,
5 have not spoken warily upon this head, not according to the oracles of God. They have spoken of the work of sanctification, taking the word in its full sense, as if it were quite of another kind, as if it differed entirely from that which is wrought in justification.[34] But this is a great and dangerous mistake, and has a
10 natural tendency to make us undervalue that glorious work of God which was wrought in us when we were justified; whereas in that moment when we are justified freely by his grace, when we are accepted through the Beloved,[35] we are born again, born from above, born of the Spirit.[36] And there is as great a change wrought
15 in our souls when we are born of the Spirit as was wrought in our bodies when we were born of a woman.[37] There is in that hour a general change from inward sinfulness to inward holiness. The love of the creature is changed into the love of the Creator, the love of the world into the love of God. Earthly desires, the desire
20 of the flesh, the desire of the eyes, and the pride of life,[38] are in that instant changed by the mighty power of God into heavenly desires. The whirlwind of our will is stopped in its mid-career, and sinks down into the will of God. Pride and haughtiness subside into lowliness of heart; as does anger, with all turbulent
25 and unruly passions, into calmness, meekness, and gentleness. In a word, the earthly, sensual, devilish[39] mind gives place to 'the mind that was in Christ Jesus'.[40]

10. 'Well, but what more than this can be implied in entire sanctification?' It does not imply any new *kind* of holiness: let no
30 man imagine this. From the moment we are justified till we give up our spirits to God, love is the fulfilling of the law[41]—of the

---

[34] Cf. Wesley's other references to the antinomians such as William Cudworth, James Relly, *et al.*; cf. *A Short History of Methodism* (1765), §§12ff., and *A Blow at the Root* (1762). This, of course, represented a persisting tendency running back into the seventeenth century (e.g., Tobias Crisp, John Saltmarsh, John Eaton, *et al.*).

[35] See Eph. 1:6.

[36] John 3:6-8; cf. No. 14, *The Repentance of Believers*, III.2 and n.

[37] For the changes wrought by the new birth, cf. No. 19, 'The Great Privilege of those that are Born of God', I.1 and n.

[38] 1 John 2:16 (*Notes*); cf. No. 7, 'The Way to the Kingdom', II.2 and n.

[39] Jas. 3:15.   [40] Cf. Phil. 2:5.

[41] Rom. 13:10; see the trilogy on 'the Law' (Nos. 34, 35, 36, 'The Original, Nature, Properties, and Use of the Law', and 'The Law Established through Faith', Discourses I and II, and nn.).

whole evangelical law, which took [the] place of the Adamic law when the first promise of 'the seed of the woman'[42] was made. Love is the sum of Christian sanctification:[43] it is the one *kind* of holiness which is found, only in various *degrees*, in the believers who are distinguished by St. John into 'little children, young men, and fathers'.[44] The difference between one and the other properly lies in the degree of love. And herein there is as great a difference in the spiritual as in the natural sense between fathers, young men, and babes. Everyone that is born of God, though he be as yet only 'a babe in Christ',[45] has the love of God in his heart, the love of his neighbour, together with lowliness, meekness, and resignation. But all of these are then in a low degree, in proportion to the degree of his faith. The faith of a babe in Christ is weak, generally mingled with doubts or fears; with doubts whether he has not deceived himself; or fear that he shall not endure to the end. And if in order to prevent those perplexing doubts, or to remove those tormenting fears, he catches hold of the opinion that a true believer cannot 'make shipwreck of the faith',[46] experience will sooner or later show that it is only the staff of a broken reed,[47] which will be so far from sustaining him that it will only enter into his hand and pierce it. But to return. In the same proportion as he grows in faith, he grows in holiness: he increases in love, lowliness, meekness, in every part of the image of God; till it pleases God, after he is thoroughly convinced of inbred sin, of the total corruption of his nature, to take it all away, to purify his heart and cleanse him from all unrighteousness;[48] to fulfil that promise which he made first to his ancient people, and in them to the Israel of God in all ages, 'I will circumcise thy heart and the heart of thy seed, to love the Lord thy God, with all thy heart and with all thy soul.'[49] It is not easy to conceive what a

[42] A complex metaphor of covenant theology involving the first 'promise' to Eve in Gen. 3:16-19, to the 'first' and 'second Adam' theme of Gal. 3-4, and to the eschatological vision of 1 Cor. 15:21-28.

[43] Cf. No. 17, 'The Circumcision of the Heart', I.2 and n.

[44] Cf. 1 John 2:12-14; and No. 13, *On Sin in Believers*, III.2 and n. For the *kinds* of holiness, see No. 85, 'On Working Out Our Own Salvation', I.2, 3; for *degrees* of holiness, see No. 40, *Christian Perfection*, I.9 and n. For references to inward holiness (the love of God) and outward holiness (love of neighbour), cf. No. 7, 'The Way to the Kingdom', I.10 and n.

[45] Cf. 1 Cor. 3:1.   [46] 1 Tim. 1:19.

[47] See Isa. 36:6.

[48] See 1 John 1:9.

[49] Cf. Deut. 30:6.

difference there is between that which he experiences now, and that which he experienced before. Till this universal change was wrought in his soul, all his holiness was *mixed*. He was humble, but not entirely; his humility was mixed with pride. He was meek;
5 but his meekness was frequently interrupted by anger, or some uneasy and turbulent passion. His love of God was frequently damped by the love of some creature; the love of his neighbour by evil surmising, or some thought, if not temper, contrary to love. His will was not wholly melted down into the will of God; but
10 although in general he could say, 'I come "not to do my own will but the will of him that sent me",'[50] yet now and then nature rebelled, and he could not clearly say, 'Lord, not as I will, but as thou wilt.'[51] His whole soul is now consistent with itself: there is no jarring string. All his passions flow in a continued stream, with
15 an even tenor to God. To him that is entered into this rest[52] you may truly say,

> Calm thou ever art within,
> All unruffled, all serene![53]

There is no mixture of any contrary affections—all is peace and
20 harmony. After being filled with love, there is no more interruption of it than of the beating of his heart.[54] And continual love bringing continual joy in the Lord, he rejoices evermore. He converses continually with the God whom he loves, unto whom in everything he gives thanks. And as he now loves God with all his
25 heart, and with all his soul, and with all his mind, and with all his strength,[55] so Jesus now reigns alone in his heart, the Lord of every motion there.[56]

11. But it may be inquired, In what manner does God work this entire, this universal change in the soul of the believer? This
30 strange work, which so many will not believe, though we declare it unto them? Does he work it gradually, by slow degrees? Or

---

[50] John 6:38.   [51] Cf. Matt. 26:39.
[52] See Ps. 95:11.
[53] Charles Wesley, Hymn VIII, 'The Beatitudes', st. 8, ll. 9,10, in *Hymns and Sacred Poems* (1749), I.37. See also Wesley's letter of Feb. 21, 1759, to an unidentified woman.
[54] Orig., '. . . harmony after. Being filled. . . .', altered in Wesley's MS errata in his copy of *SOSO*. These MS errata also revert to the text of *AM* at the end of this sentence, which *SOSO* had altered to read, '. . . his heart and continual love . . .'.
[55] See Mark 12:30.
[56] For this phrase, an allusion to one of his hymns, see No. 77, 'Spiritual Worship', II.6 and n.

instantaneously, in a moment? How many are the disputes upon this head, even among the children of God! And so there will be, after all that ever was or ever can be said upon it. For many will still say, with the famous Jew, *Non persuadebis, etiamsi persuaseris:* that is, 'Thou shalt not persuade me, though thou dost persuade 5 me.'[57] And they will be the more resolute herein because the Scriptures are silent upon the subject; because the point is not determined—at least, not in express terms—in any part of the oracles of God. Every man therefore may abound in his own sense, provided he will allow the same liberty to his neighbour; 10 provided he will not be angry at those who differ from his opinion, nor entertain hard thoughts concerning them. Permit me likewise to add one thing more. Be the change instantaneous or gradual, see that you never rest till it is wrought in your own soul, if you desire to dwell with God in glory. 15

12. This premised, in order to throw what light I can upon this interesting question I will simply relate what I have seen myself in the course of many years. Four or five and forty years ago (when I had no distinct views of what the Apostle meant by exhorting us to 'leave the principles of the doctrine of Christ,' and 'go on to 20 perfection'),[58] two or three persons in London whom I knew to be truly sincere desired to give me an account of their experience. It appeared exceeding strange, being different from any that I had heard before; but exactly similar to the preceding account of entire sanctification. The next year two or three more persons at 25 Bristol, and two or three in Kingswood, coming to me severally, gave me exactly the same account of their experience. A few years after I desired all those in London who made the same profession to come to me all together at the Foundery, that I might be thoroughly satisfied. I desired that man of God, Thomas Walsh,[59] 30 to give us the meeting there. When we met, first one of us and then the other asked them the most searching questions we could devise. They answered every one without hesitation, and with the utmost simplicity, so that we were fully persuaded they did not

---

[57] The 'famous Jew' here was probably Agrippa (as in Acts 26:28: ἐν ὀλίγῳ με πείθεις χριστιανὸν ποιῆσαι). Cf. Aristophanes, *Plutus*, 600: οὐ γὰρ πείσις, οὔ᾽δὴν πείσῃς. As for the Latin version, see No. 4, *Scriptural Christianity*, IV.2 and n.

[58] Cf. Heb. 6:1.

[59] Thomas Walsh (1730–59) was Irish, a convert from Roman Catholicism, who became one of Wesley's most trusted assistants. Though he served chiefly in Ireland, he made three visits to London, the last (referred to here) from Sept. 1756 to early 1757. Cf. James Morgan, *The Life and Death of Mr. Thomas Walsh* (1762).

deceive themselves. In the years 1759, 1760, 1761, and 1762, their numbers multiplied exceedingly, not only in London and Bristol, but in various parts of Ireland as well as England. Not trusting to the testimony of others, I carefully examined most of
5 these myself; and in London alone I found six hundred and fifty-two members of our society who were exceeding clear in their experience, and of whose testimony I could see no reason to doubt. I believe no year has passed since that time wherein God has not wrought the same work in many others; but sometimes in
10 one part of England or Ireland, sometimes in another, as 'the wind bloweth where it listeth'.[60] And every one of these (after the most careful inquiry I have not found one exception either in Great Britain or Ireland) has declared that his deliverance from sin was *instantaneous*, that the change was wrought in a moment.
15 Had half of these, or one-third, or one in twenty, declared it was *gradually* wrought in *them*, I should have believed this with regard to *them*, and thought that *some* were gradually sanctified and some instantaneously. But as I have not found in so long a space of time a single person speaking thus—as all who believe they are
20 sanctified declare with one voice that the change was wrought in a moment—I cannot but believe that sanctification is commonly, if not always, an *instantaneous* work.

13. But however that question be decided—whether sanctification, in the full sense of the word, be wrought instantaneously
25 or gradually—how may *we* attain to it? 'What shall we do', said the Jews to our Lord, 'that we may work the works of God?'[61] His answer will suit those that ask, 'What shall we do that this work of God may be wrought in us?'—'This is the work of God, that ye believe on him whom he hath sent.'[62] On this one work all the
30 others depend. Believe on the Lord Jesus Christ, and all his wisdom, and power, and faithfulness, and mercy are engaged on thy side. In this, as in all other instances, 'by grace we are saved through faith.'[63] Sanctification, too, is 'not of works, lest any man should boast'.[64] 'It is the gift of God,'[65] and is to be received by
35 plain, simple faith. Suppose you are now labouring to 'abstain from all appearance of evil',[66] 'zealous of good works',[67] and walking diligently and carefully in all the ordinances of God;

[60] John 3:8; Wesley's point here is that the work of sanctification was uniquely the office of the Holy Spirit.
[61] John 6:28 (*Notes*).   [62] John 6:29.   [63] Cf. Eph. 2:8.
[64] Eph. 2:9.   [65] Eph. 2:8.   [66] 1 Thess. 5:22.
[67] Titus 2:14.

there is then only one point remaining—the voice of God to your soul is, 'Believe and be saved.'ᵃ First, believe that God has promised to save you from all sin, and to fill you with all holiness. Secondly, believe that he is 'able' thus 'to save to the uttermost all those that come unto God through him'.[68] Thirdly, believe that he is *willing*, as well as able, to save *you* to the uttermost; to purify you from all sin, and fill up all your heart with love. Believe, fourthly, that he is not only able, but willing to do it *now!* Not when you come to die; not at any distant time; not tomorrow, but *today*. He will then enable you to believe, *it is done*, according to his word. And then 'patience shall have its perfect work, that ye may be perfect and entire, wanting[69] nothing.'

14. Ye shall then be *perfect*. The Apostle seems to mean by this expression, τέλειοι,[70] ye shall be wholly delivered from every evil work, from every evil word, from every sinful thought; yea, from every evil desire, passion, temper, from all inbred corruption, from all remains of the carnal mind, from the whole body of sin: and ye shall be renewed in the spirit of your mind,[71] in every right temper, after the image of him that created you,[72] in righteousness and true holiness.[73] Ye shall be entire, ὁλόκληροι—the same word which the Apostle uses to the Christians in Thessalonica.[74] This seems to refer not so much to the kind as to the degree of holiness. As if he had said, 'Ye shall enjoy as high a degree of holiness as is consistent with your present state of pilgrimage.' And ye shall 'want nothing'; the Lord being your Shepherd, your Father, your Redeemer, your Sanctifier, your God, and your all, will feed you with the bread of heaven, and give you meat enough. He will lead you forth beside the waters of comfort,[75] and 'keep you every moment';[76] so that loving him with all your heart (which is the sum of all perfection) you will 'rejoice evermore, pray without ceasing', and 'in everything give thanks',[77] 'till an abundant entrance is ministered unto you, into his everlasting kingdom'![78]

ᵃ See the Sermon on *The [Scripture] Way of Salvation* [cf. No. 43, but note the different reading of Eph. 2:8].

---

[68] Cf. Heb. 7:25.   [69] Orig. (*AM*), 'lacking'.   [70] Jas. 1:4.
[71] Eph. 4:23.   [72] See Col. 3:10.   [73] See Eph. 4:24.
[74] Jas. 1:4 and 1 Thess. 5:23; thus Wesley takes τέλειος and ὁλόκληρος as synonyms, both meaning 'whole' or 'complete'.
[75] Ps. 23:2 (BCP).   [76] Cf. Isa. 27:3.
[77] 1 Thess. 5:16-18.   [78] Cf. 2 Pet. 1:11.

The Important Queſtion:

A

SERMON,

PREACHED

In TAUNTON, *Somerſetſhire,*

On Monday, Sept. 12, 1775.

By *JOHN WESLEY*, M. A.

Publiſhed at the Requeſt of many of the Hearers, for the Benefit of a public Charity.

LONDON:

Printed by I. MOORE and Co. in Queen-Street, near Upper-Moorfields.

[*Price* SIX-PENCE.]

THE IMPORTANT QUESTION

AN INTRODUCTORY COMMENT

In August and September 1775 Wesley was itinerating through Wales, Cornwall, and Somerset. On Wednesday, August 30, he 'preached in the great Presbyterian meeting-house at Taunton', and in the same place on Monday, September 11, when he 'pressed that important question, "What is a man profited if he should gain the whole world and lose his own soul?"' (See the Journal *for those dates and note the discrepancy between the date given in the* Journal *for the oral sermon and the date on the title-page for the published sermon.)*

The occasion for the Taunton sermon was 'for the benefit of a public charity' (i.e., ad aulam*); this may account for the noticeable increase in rhetorical ornamentation and length over what we have seen in most of his sermons* ad populum. *It was written out in Bristol, September 30, 1775, and then printed in London as a separate pamphlet before the end of the year. It proceeded to go through six further separate editions in Wesley's lifetime in addition to being included in* SOSO, *VII.67-91. For further details as to its publishing history and a list of variant readings in its successive editions, see Appendix, Vol. 4, and* Bibliog, *No. 355.*

This sermon is unusual in yet another interesting way that helps illuminate the relationship between Wesley's oral preaching and his published sermons. Of all the texts for his published sermons, Matt. 16:26 is the one he had used most often in his oral preaching and by a fairly wide margin (one hundred seventeen times between 1747 and 1790). This in itself would seem to be a sufficient comment on the familiar but misleading generalization that Wesley was less interested in eschatology than in soteriology. There is a sense in which this is true; but the much more crucial fact is that, for Wesley, soteriology and eschatology were actually two sides of the same mystery of God's proffered grace to man.

The Important Question

Matthew 16:26

What is a man profited if he shall gain the whole world, and lose his own soul?

5   1. There is a celebrated remark to this effect (I think in the works of Mr. Pascal), that if a man of low estate would speak of high things, as of what relates to kings or kingdoms, it is not easy for him to find suitable expressions, as he is so little acquainted with things of this nature. But if one of royal parentage speaks of
10 royal things, of what concerns his own or his father's kingdom, his language will be free and easy, as these things are familiar to his thoughts.[1] In like manner, if a mere inhabitant of this lower world speaks concerning the great things of the kingdom of God, hardly is he able to find expressions suitable to the greatness of the
15 subject. But when the Son of God speaks of the highest things, which concern his heavenly kingdom, all his language is easy and unlaboured, his words natural and unaffected: inasmuch as known unto him are all these things from all eternity.

  2. How strongly is this remark exemplified in the passage now
20 before us! The Son of God, the great King of heaven and earth, here uses the plainest and easiest words; but how high and deep are the things which he expresses therein! None of the children of men can fully conceive them till, emerging out of the darkness of the present world, he commences an inhabitant of eternity.

25   3. But we may conceive a little of these deep things if we consider, first, what is implied in that expression, a man's 'gaining the whole world'; secondly, what is implied in 'losing his own soul'; we shall then, thirdly, see in the strongest light 'what he is profited who gains the whole world, and loses his own soul'.

---

[1] This would seem to be a recollection from a Pascalian fragment preserved in Basil Kennett's Preface to his translation of *Thoughts on Religion* (1727), p. xxiv: 'A mechanic speaking of riches [speaks incompetently]; a solicitor speaking of war or of a regal state [does likewise]. But the rich discourse well of riches; a king speaks coldly of a vast present which he is about to make; and God discourseth well of God.' The same idea recurs in the first of 'Three Discourses by Pascal on the Station of Noblemen', in *Great Shorter Works of Pascal*, translated by Emile Cailliet and John C. Blankennagel (Philadelphia, The Westminster Press, 1948), pp. 211-13. Cf. Robert South, *Sermons on Several Occasions*

I. 1. We are, first, to consider what is implied in a man's 'gaining the whole world'. Perhaps at the first hearing this may seem to some equivalent with conquering the whole world. But it has no relation thereto at all; and indeed that expression involves a plain absurdity;[2] for it is impossible, any that is born of a woman should ever conquer the whole world, were it only because the short life of man could not suffice for so wild an undertaking. Accordingly no man ever did conquer the half, no, nor the tenth part of the world. But whatever others might do, there was no danger that any of our Lord's hearers should have any thought of this. Among all the sins of the Jewish nation the desire of universal empire was not found. Even in their most flourishing times they never sought to extend their conquests beyond the river Euphrates. And in our Lord's time all their ambition was at an end—'the sceptre was departed from Judah'[3]—and Judea was governed by a Roman procurator, as a branch of the Roman empire.

2. Leaving this, we may find a far more easy and natural sense of the expression. To gain the whole world may properly enough imply, to gain all the pleasures which the world can give.[4] The man we speak of may therefore be supposed to have gained all that will gratify his senses. In particular, all that can increase his pleasure of tasting,[5] all the elegancies of meat and drink. Likewise, whatever can gratify his smell, or touch—all that he can enjoy in common with his fellow-brutes. He may have all the plenty and all the variety of these objects which the world can afford.

3. We may farther suppose him to have gained all that gratifies 'the desire of the eyes';[6] whatever (by means of the eye chiefly) conveys any pleasure to the imagination.[7] The pleasures of imagination arise from three sources: grandeur, beauty, and novelty. Accordingly we find by experience our own imagination

(Oxford, 1823), I.38: 'It is difficult for a peasant . . . to fancy in his mind the unseen splendours of a court.' See also Seneca, *Epistles*, xciv.14.

[2] For Wesley's rule that the literal sense of Scripture is to be preferred unless it 'involves a plain absurdity', see No. 21, 'Sermon on the Mount, I', §6 and n.

[3] Cf. Gen. 49:10.

[4] A somewhat different nuance for the term 'world' than above in Nos. 80, 'On Friendship with the World'; and 81, 'In What Sense we are to Leave the World'.

[5] Cf. William Law, as in No. 50, 'The Use of Money', II.2 and n.

[6] 1 John 2:16 (*Notes*). The *concupiscientia triplex* again; see No. 7, 'The Way to the Kingdom', II.2 and n. See also, below, III.10.

[7] Cf. No. 44, *Original Sin*, II.10 and n.

is gratified by surveying either grand, or beautiful, or uncommon objects. Let him be encompassed then with the most grand, the most beautiful, and the newest things that can anywhere be found. For all this is manifestly implied in a man's gaining the
5 whole world.

4. But there is also another thing implied herein, which men of the most elevated spirits have preferred before all the pleasures of sense and of imagination put together; that is, honour, glory, renown:

10   *Virum volitare per ora.*[8]

It seems that hardly any principle in the human mind is of greater force than this. It triumphs over the strongest propensities of nature, over all our appetites and affections. If Brutus sheds the blood of his own children;[9] if we see another Brutus, in spite of
15 every possible obligation, in defiance of all justice and gratitude,

Cringing while he stabs his friend;[10]

if a far greater man than either of these, Paschal Paoli,[11] gave up ease, pleasure, everything, for a life of constant toil, pain, and alarms; what principle could support them? They might talk of
20 *amor patriae*, the love of their country; but this would never have carried them through had there not been also the

Laudum immensa cupido[12]—

[8] Virgil, *Georgics*, iii.9: '[To have one's fame] flying about on the lips of men'.

[9] Lucus Junius Brutus, nephew of Tarquinius Superbus (last of the Roman kings) and one of the first two consuls of the new Republic. He sentenced his own two sons to death for treason; cf. Livy, *Annals*, I.59, II.3; see also Voltaire, *Le Brutus* (1731).

[10] Samuel Wesley, Jun., 'On Mr. Hobbes', ver. 1, ll. 5-6, in *Poems* (1736), p. 102:

'Twill task a Cowley's genius to commend
False Brutus cringing while he stabs his friend.

Cf. also John Wesley, *A Collection of Moral and Sacred Poems* (1744), III.66. The reference here is to 'another Brutus', Marcus Junius, one of the assassins of Julius Caesar. Note the casual playing off here of two like and unlike classical references.

[11] Pasquale Paoli (1725–1807), a Corsican liberator who after his defeat by the French (1769) fled to England and was still living there as a popular hero at the time of this sermon. Wesley records two visits with him during 1784 (JWJ, Feb. 19 and Nov. 6): '. . . the modern Hannibal, . . . probably the most accomplished general that is now in the world . . .'. A fulsome plaque in his honour in Westminster Abbey stands directly opposite the more modest memorial there to the brothers Wesley. There are numerous admiring references to Paoli in Boswell's *Life of Johnson*.

[12] Virgil, *Aeneid*, vi.823: *laudumque immensa cupido*, a familiar theme in Latin literature. Cf. *ibid.*, v. 138; *Georgics*, iii.112; Tacitus, *Histories*, IV.vi., etc. Cf. also Nos. 62, 'The End of Christ's Coming', §2; and 14, *The Repentance of Believers*, I.7 and n.

the immense thirst of *praise*. Now the man we speak of has gained abundance of this; he is praised, if not admired, by all that are round about him. Nay, his name is gone forth into distant lands, as it were to the ends of the earth.[13]

5. Add to this that he has gained abundance of wealth; that there is no end of his treasures; that he has laid up silver as the dust, and gold as the sand of the sea.[14] Now when a man has obtained all these pleasures, all that will gratify either the senses or the imagination; when he has gained an honourable name, and also laid up much treasure for many years; then he may be said, in an easy, natural sense of the word, to have 'gained the whole world'.

II. 1. The next point we have to consider is what is implied in a man's 'losing his own soul'. And here we draw a deeper scene, and have need of a more steady attention. For it is easy to sum up all that is implied in a man's 'gaining the whole world'. But it is not so easy to understand all that is implied in his 'losing his own soul'. Indeed none can fully conceive this until he has passed through time into eternity.

2. The first thing which it undeniably implies is the losing all the present pleasures of religion; all those which it affords to truly religious men, even in the present life. 'If there be any consolation in Christ; if any comfort of love',[15] in the love of God, and of all mankind; if any 'joy in the Holy Ghost';[16] if there be a peace of God, a peace that passeth all understanding;[17] if there be any rejoicing in the testimony of a good conscience toward God;[18] it is manifest, all this is totally lost by the man that loses his own soul.

3. But the present life will soon be at an end: we know it passes away like a shadow.[19] The hour is at hand when the spirit will be summoned to return to God that gave it.[20] In that awful moment,

> Leaving the old, both worlds at once they view,
> Who stand upon the threshold of the new.[21]

[13] See Ps. 48:10 (AV).
[14] See Job 27:16; Zech. 9:3.
[15] Phil. 2:1.
[16] Rom. 14:17.
[17] Phil. 4:7.   [18] See Acts 23:1.
[19] See Ps. 144:4 (BCP). Cf. also Wisd. 5:9-13, and Wesley's Preface (1746), §5.
[20] See Eccles. 12:7.
[21] Cf. the last two lines of Edmund Waller's 'On the Foregoing Divine Poems', *Works* (1729), p. 317.

And whether he looks backward or forward, how pleasing is the
prospect to him that saves his soul! If he looks back, he has 'the
calm remembrance of the life well spent'. [22] If he looks forward,
there is an inheritance incorruptible, undefiled, and that fadeth
5   not away,[23] and he sees the convoy of angels ready to carry him
into Abraham's bosom.[24] But how is it in that solemn hour with
the man that *loses* his soul? Does he look back? What comfort is
there in this? He sees nothing but scenes of horror, matter of
shame, remorse, and self-condemnation, a foretaste of 'the worm
10 that never dieth'.[25] If he looks forward, what does he see? No joy,
no peace! No gleam of hope from any point of heaven! Some
years since, one who turned back as a dog to his vomit[26] was struck
down in his mid-career of sin. A friend visiting him prayed,
'Lord, have mercy upon those who are just stepping out of the
15 body, and know not which shall meet them at their entrance into
the other world, an angel or a fiend.' The sick man shrieked out
with a piercing cry, 'A fiend! a fiend!' and died. Just such an end,
unless he die like an ox, may any man expect who loses his own
soul.
20   4. But in what situation is the spirit of a good man at his
entrance into eternity? See,

> The convoy attends,
> The minist'ring host of invisible friends.[27]

They receive the new-born spirit, and conduct him safe into
25 Abraham's bosom, into the delights of paradise, the garden of
God,[28] where the light of his countenance perpetually shines. It is
but one of a thousand commendations of this antechamber of
heaven[29] that 'there the wicked cease from troubling, there the
weary are at rest.'[30] For there they have numberless sources of

---

[22] Cf. Samuel Wesley, Jun., 'To the Memory of the Right Reverend Francis Gastrell', l.
106, in *Poems* (1736), p. 130; see also John Wesley, *A Collection of Moral and Sacred Poems*
(1744), III.81. Cf. 'Dr. Arbuthnot's Character Versified', in *AM* (1783), VI.448, for a
similar line. As a motto for his *Guardian*, No. 18 (June 13, 1713), Richard Steele quotes
Cicero for this basic human aspiration: *'Quiete et pure atque eleganter actae aetatis placida ac
lenis recordatio'* ('Placid and soothing is the remembrance of a life passed in quiet,
innocence and elegance'). Cf. *De Senectute*, v.13; see also iii.9.
[23] 1 Pet. 1:4.   [24] See Luke 16:22.
[25] Cf. Mark 9:44, 46, 48.   [26] See Prov. 26:11; 2 Pet. 2:22.
[27] Cf. Charles Wesley, *Funeral Hymns* (1746), No. 15 (*Poet. Wks.*, VI.211); cf. also No.
71, 'Of Good Angels', II.7 and n.
[28] Ezek. 28:13; 31:8, 9.   [29] Cf. No. 115, 'Dives and Lazarus', I.3 and n.
[30] Cf. Job 3:17.

happiness which they could not have upon earth. There they meet with 'the glorious dead of ancient days'. [31] They converse with Adam, first of men; with Noah, first of the new world; with Abraham, 'the friend of God';[32] with Moses and the prophets; with the apostles of the Lamb; with the saints of all ages; and above all, they 'are with Christ'.

5. How different, alas! is the case with him who loses his own soul! The moment he steps into eternity he meets with the devil and his angels. Sad convoy into the world of spirits! Sad earnest of what is to come! And either he is bound with chains of darkness, and reserved unto the judgment of the great day;[33] or at best he wanders up and down, seeking rest, but finding none.[34] Perhaps he may seek it (like the 'unclean spirit cast out of the man') in dry, dreary, desolate places;[35] perhaps

> Where nature all in ruins lies,
> And owns her sovereign, death![36]

And little comfort can he find here, seeing everything contributes to increase, not remove, the fearful expectation of fiery indignation which will devour the ungodly![37]

6. For even this is to him but the beginning of sorrows.[38] Yet a little while, and he will see 'the great white throne coming down from heaven, and him that sitteth thereon, from whose face the heavens and the earth flee away, and there is found no place for them'. And 'the dead, small and great, stand before God, and are judged, everyone according to his works.'[39] 'Then shall the King say to them on his right hand' (God grant he may say so to you!): 'Come, ye blessed of my Father, inherit the kingdom prepared for you from the foundation of the world.'[40] And the angels shall tune their harps and sing, 'Lift up your heads, O ye gates, and be ye lift up, ye everlasting doors, that the heirs of glory may come in.'[41] And then shall they 'shine as the brightness of the firmament, and as the stars for ever and ever.'[42]

---

[31] Is this a misremembrance of Isaac Watts's line, 'Thy glorious deeds of ancient date' (*Works*, IV.137)? See also No. 117, 'On the Discoveries of Faith' §8; and cf. Wesley's variant in No. 132, 'On Faith, Heb. 11:1', §11: 'the *illustrious* dead of ancient *days*'.

[32] Jas. 2:23.   [33] Jude 6.   [34] See Luke 11:24.   [35] *Ibid.*

[36] Cf. Watts, 'Death and Eternity', st. 1, ll. 3-4, *Horae Lyricae*, Bk. I (*Works*, IV.343). Cf. also John Wesley, *A Collection of Moral and Sacred Poems* (1744), I.194. See also No. 82, 'On Temptation', I.4.

[37] See Heb. 10:27.   [38] Matt. 24:8.   [39] Cf. Rev. 20:11-12.

[40] Matt. 25:34.   [41] Cf. Ps. 24:7.   [42] Dan. 12:3.

7. How different will be the lot of him that loses his own soul! No joyful sentence will be pronounced on him, but one that will pierce him through with unutterable horror (God forbid that ever it should be pronounced on any of you that are here before God!): 'Depart ye cursed, into everlasting fire, prepared for the devil and his angels!'[43] And who can doubt but those infernal spirits will immediately execute the sentence, will instantly drag those forsaken of God into their own place of torment![44] Into those

> Regions of sorrow, doleful shades; where joy,
> Where peace can never come! Hope never comes,
> That comes to all![45]—

all the children of men who are on this side eternity. But not to them: the gulf is now fixed, over which they cannot pass.[46] From the moment wherein they are once plunged into the lake of fire, burning with brimstone,[47] their torments are not only without intermission, but likewise without end. For 'they have no rest, day or night, but the smoke of their torment ascendeth up for ever and ever.'[48]

III. Upon ever so cursory a view of these things would not anyone be astonished that a man, that a creature endued with reason, should voluntarily choose (I say *choose;* for God forces no man into inevitable damnation: he never yet

> Consigned one unborn soul to hell,
> Or damned him from his mother's womb)[49]—

should choose thus to lose his own soul, though it were to gain the whole world! For what shall a man be profited thereby upon the whole of the account?

But a little to abate our astonishment at this, let us observe the suppositions which a man generally makes before he can reconcile himself to this fatal choice.

---

[43] Matt. 25:41.   [44] Luke 16:28.

[45] Cf. Milton, *Paradise Lost*, i.65-69; see also Nos. 73, 'Of Hell', III.3; and 124, 'Human Life a Dream', §12.

[46] See Luke 16:26; cf. above, I.4 and n.

[47] See Rev. 19:20.

[48] Cf. Rev. 14:11.

[49] Cf. John and Charles Wesley, 'Universal Redemption', *Hymns and Sacred Poems* (1740), p. 133 (*Poet. Wks.*, III.33). See No. 54, 'On Eternity', §14, where Wesley quotes the entire stanza; and cf. his letter to James Hervey, Oct. 15, 1756.

1. He supposes, first, that a life of religion is a life of misery. That religion is misery! How is it possible that anyone should entertain so strange a thought! Do any of *you* imagine this? If you do, the reason is plain; you know not what religion is. 'No! But I do, as well as you.' What is it then? 'Why, the doing no harm.' Not 5 so; many birds and beasts do no harm, yet they are not capable of religion. 'Then it is going to church and sacrament.' Indeed it is not. This may be an excellent help to religion; and everyone who desires to save his soul should attend them at all opportunities; yet it is possible you may attend them all your days, and still have no 10 religion at all. Religion is an higher and deeper thing than any outward ordinance whatever.

2. 'What is religion, then?' It is easy to answer if we consult the oracles of God. According to these it lies in one single point: it is neither more nor less than love—it is love which 'is the fulfilling 15 of the law',[50] 'the end of the commandment'.[51] Religion is the love of God and our neighbour—that is, every man under heaven.[52] This love, ruling the whole life, animating all our tempers and passions, directing all our thoughts, words, and actions, is 'pure religion and undefiled'.[53] 20

3. Now will anyone be so hardy as to say that love is misery? Is it misery to love God? To give him my heart who alone is worthy of it? Nay, it is the truest happiness, indeed the only true happiness which is to be found under the sun. So does all experience prove the justness of that reflection which was made long ago: 'Thou 25 hast made us for thyself; and our heart cannot rest until it resteth in thee.'[54] Or does anyone imagine the love of our neighbour is misery, even the loving every man as our own soul? So far from it that next to the love of God this affords the greatest happiness of which we are capable. Therefore, 30

> Let not the stoic boast his mind unmoved,
> The brute-philosopher, who ne'er has proved
> The joy of loving, or of being loved.[55]

---

[50] Rom. 13:10. [51] 1 Tim. 1:5.

[52] An oft-repeated definition; cf. No. 7, 'The Way to the Kingdom', I.8 and n.; for 'inward holiness' (love of God) and 'outward holiness' (love of neighbour), cf. *ibid.*, I.10 and n.

[53] Jas. 1:27.

[54] Augustine, *Confessions*, I.i; see No. 3, *'Awake, Thou That Sleepest'*, II.5 and n.

[55] *OED* ('brute'), on Johnson's authority, cites this as from Alexander Pope. Actually, it is a nearly exact quotation from Nicholas Rowe's first play, *The Ambitious Step-Mother* (1701), Prologue, ll. 6-8. Cf. Wesley's earlier reference to 'brute philosophers', in No. 22, 'Sermon on the Mount, II', I.2.

4. So much every reasonable man must allow. But he may object: 'There is more than this implied in religion. It implies not only the love of God and man (against which I have no objection) but also a great deal of doing and suffering. And how can this be
5 consistent with happiness?'

There is certainly some truth in this objection. Religion does imply both doing and suffering. Let us then calmly consider whether this impairs or heightens our happiness.

Religion implies, first, the doing many things. For the love of
10 God will naturally lead us at all opportunities to converse with him we love; to speak to him in (public or private) prayer, and to hear the words of his mouth, which 'are dearer to us than thousands of gold and silver'.[56] It will incline us to lose no opportunity of receiving

15   The dear memorials of his dying love;[57]

to continue instant in thanksgiving; at morning, evening, and noonday to praise him. But suppose we do all this, will it lessen our happiness? Just the reverse. It is plain, all these fruits of love are means of increasing the love from which they spring; and of
20 consequence they increase our happiness in the same proportion. Who then would not join in that wish:

> Rising to sing my Saviour's praise,
>   Thee may I publish all day long,
>   And let thy precious word of grace
25   Flow from my heart, and fill my tongue;
>   Fill all my life with purest love,
>   And join me to thy church above![58]

[56] Ps. 119:72 (BCP).

[57] Cf. John and Charles Wesley, Hymn 54, *Hymns on the Lord's Supper* (1745, *Poet. Wks.*, III.253), beginning:

> Why did my dying Lord ordain
> This dear memorial of his love?

In *SOSO* (1788), VII.79, the quotation is altered to 'The dear memorials of our dying Lord.' The Wesleys may be indebted to Isaac Watts in this instance. Cf. his 'Our Lord Jesus at His Own Table', st. 1, l. 1, in Bk. III, Hymn XV (*Works*, IV.263): 'The mem'ry of our dying Lord'. See also Watts, 'To the Memory of T. Gunston, Esq.', l. 88 (*ibid.*, p. 440), 'That dear memorial of the best-loved name!' See also, Edmund Spenser, *Faerie Queene*, I.i-ii:

> But on his breast a bloody cross he bore,
> The dear remembrance of his dying Lord.

[58] Charles Wesley, 'Hymn on Deut. 6:7', in *Short Hymns on Select Passages of the Holy Scriptures* (1762), I.93 (*Poet. Wks.*, IX.95).

5. It must also be allowed that as the love of God naturally leads to works of piety, so the love of our neighbour naturally leads all that feel it to works of mercy. It inclines us to feed the hungry, to clothe the naked, to visit them that are sick or in prison;[59] to be as eyes to the blind and feet to the lame;[60] an husband to the widow, a father to the fatherless.[61] But can you suppose that the doing this will prevent or lessen your happiness? Yea, though you did so much as to be like a guardian angel to all that are round about you? On the contrary, it is an infallible truth that

> All worldly joys are less
> Than that one joy of doing kindnesses.[62]

A man of pleasure was asked some years ago, 'Captain, what was the greatest pleasure you ever had?' After a little pause he replied: 'When we were upon our march in Ireland, in a very hot day, I called at a cabin on the road, and desired a little water. The woman brought me a cup of milk. I gave her a piece of silver; and the joy that poor creature expressed gave me the greatest pleasure I ever had in my life.'[63] Now if the doing good gave so much pleasure to one who acted merely from natural generosity, how much more must it give to one who does it on a nobler principle, the joint love of God and his neighbour? It remains, that the doing all which religion requires will not lessen, but immensely increase our happiness.

6. 'Perhaps this also may be allowed. But religion implies, according to the Christian account, not only doing but *suffering*. And how can suffering be consistent with happiness?' Perfectly well. Many centuries ago it was remarked by St. Chrysostom: 'The Christian has his sorrows as well as his joys; but his sorrow is sweeter than joy.'[64] He may accidentally suffer loss, poverty, pain; but in all these things he is more than conqueror:[65] he can testify,

> Labour is rest, and pain is sweet,
> While thou, my God, art here.[66]

---

[59] See Matt. 25:35-36, 38.   [60] Job 29:15.   [61] See Ps. 68:5.

[62] Cf. George Herbert, *The Temple*, 'The Church Porch', st. 55, ll. 5-6; see No. 59, 'God's Love to Fallen Man', I.9 and n.

[63] Would this have belonged to an oral tradition? No literary source has yet been located.

[64] Cf. Chrysostom, Homily XVIII, §8(*NPNF*, *II*, IX.461). See also, Kempis, *Imitation*, III.xxx.

[65] See Rom. 8:37.

[66] Cf. John and Charles Wesley, *Hymns and Sacred Poems* (1740), p. 127 (*Poet. Wks.*, I.304). See No. 52, *The Reformation of Manners*, III.7 and n.

He can say: 'The Lord gave; the Lord taketh away: blessed be the name of the Lord!'[67] He *must* suffer more or less reproach; for 'the servant is not above his master;'[68] but so much the more does the Spirit of glory and of Christ rest upon him.[69] Yea, love itself
5 will on several occasions be the source of suffering: the love of God will frequently produce

> . . . the pleasing smart,
> The meltings of a broken heart.[70]

And the love of our neighbour will give rise to sympathizing
10 sorrow: it will lead us to visit the fatherless and widow in their affliction,[71] to be tenderly concerned for the distressed, and 'to mix our pitying tear with those that weep'.[72] But may we not well say, these are 'tears that delight, and sighs that waft to heaven'?[73] So far then are all these sufferings from either preventing or
15 lessening our happiness, that they greatly contribute thereto, and indeed constitute no inconsiderable part of it. So that upon the whole there cannot be a more false supposition than that a life of religion is a life of misery; seeing true religion, whether considered in its nature or its fruits, is true and solid happiness.
20   7. The man who chooses to gain the world by the loss of his soul supposes, secondly, that a life of wickedness is a life of happiness! That wickedness is happiness! Even an old heathen poet could have taught him better. Even Juvenal discovered,

Nemo malus felix[74]—

25 no wicked man is happy! And how expressly does God himself declare, 'There is no peace to the wicked'[75]—no peace of mind; and without this there can be no happiness.
    But not to avail ourselves of authority, let us weigh the thing in

---

[67] Cf. Job 1:21.
[68] Cf. Matt. 10:24.
[69] See 1 Pet. 4:14.
[70] Charles Wesley, 'The Invitation', in *Hymns on the Great Festivals* (1746), p. 46 *(Poet. Wks.*, V.64). For other lines from this hymn, cf. Nos. 63, 'The General Spread of the Gospel', §12; and 123, 'On Knowing Christ after the Flesh', §12.
[71] Jas. 1:27.
[72] π; but cf. Pope, 'Eloise to Abelard', l. 22 ('And pitying saints, whose statues learn to weep') and a line from 'The Rape of the Lock', Canto V.1 ('. . . the pitying audience melt in tears').
[73] Pope, 'Eloise to Abelard', l. 214.
[74] Juvenal, *Satires*, iv.8; see No. 45, 'The New Birth', III.3 and n.
[75] Isa. 57:21.

the balance of reason.[76] I ask, 'What can make a wicked man happy?' You answer, 'He has "gained the whole world".' We allow it; and what does this imply? He has gained all that gratifies the senses: in particular, all that can please the taste, all the delicacies of meat and drink. True; but can eating and drinking make a man happy? They never did yet; and certain it is they never will. This is too coarse food for an immortal spirit. But suppose it did give him a poor kind of happiness during those moments wherein he was swallowing, what will he do with the residue of his time?[77] Will it not hang heavy upon his hands? Will he not groan under many a tedious hour, and think swift-winged time flies too slow? If he is not fully employed, will he not frequently complain of lowness of spirits?—an unmeaning expression, which the miserable physician usually no more understands than his miserable patient. We know there are such things as nervous disorders. But we know likewise that what is commonly called 'nervous lowness' is a secret reproof from God, a kind of consciousness that we are not in our place; that we are not as God would have us to be; we are unhinged from our proper centre.[78]

8. To remove, or at least soothe, this strange uneasiness, let him add the pleasures of imagination.[79] Let him bedaub himself with silver and gold, and adorn himself with all the colours of the rainbow. Let him build splendid palaces, and furnish them in the most elegant as well as costly manner. Let him lay out walks and gardens, beautified with all that nature and art can afford. And how long will these give him pleasure? Only as long as they are new. As soon as ever the novelty is gone, the pleasure is gone also. After he has surveyed them a few months, or years, they give him no more satisfaction. The man who is saving his soul has the advantage of him in this very respect. For he can say:

> In the pleasures the rich man's possessions display,
>   Unenvied I challenge my part;
> While every fair object my eye can survey,
>   Contributes to gladden my heart.[80]

---

[76] The obverse of 'the balance of the sanctuary'; cf. No. 10, 'The Witness of the Spirit, I', II.8 and n. See also No. 147, 'Wiser than the Children of Light', III.2.

[77] Cf. No. 50, 'The Use of Money', I.7 and n.

[78] Cf. No. 79, 'On Dissipation', §6 and n.

[79] Cf. No. 44, *Original Sin*, II.10 and n.

[80] Cf. Thomas Fitzgerald, 'An Ode', st. 4, *Poems* (1733), pp. 12-13; see also John Wesley, *A Collection of Moral and Sacred Poems* (1744), II.142.

9. 'However, he has yet another resource: applause, glory. And will not this make him happy?' It will not; for he cannot be applauded by all men; no man ever was. Some will praise; perhaps many, but not all. It is certain some will blame; and he that is fond
5 of applause will feel more pain from the censure of one than pleasure from the praise of many. So that whoever seeks happiness in applause will infallibly be disappointed, and will find, upon the whole of the account, abundantly more pain than pleasure.

10. But to bring the matter to a short issue. Let us take an
10 instance of one who had gained more of this world than probably any man alive, unless he be a sovereign prince. But did all he had gained make him happy? Answer for thyself. Then said Haman, 'Yet all this profiteth me nothing, while I see Mordecai sitting in the gate.'[81] Poor Haman! One unholy temper, whether pride,
15 envy, jealousy, or revenge, gave him more pain, more vexation of spirit, than all the world could give pleasure. And so it must be in the nature of things; for all unholy tempers are unhappy tempers. Ambition, covetousness, vanity, inordinate affection, malice, revengefulness, carry their own punishment with them, and
20 avenge themselves on the soul wherein they dwell. Indeed what are these, more especially when they are combined with an awakened conscience, but the dogs of hell[82] already gnawing the soul, forbidding happiness to approach! Did not even the heathens see this? What else means their fable of Tityus, chained
25 to a rock with a vulture continually tearing up his breast and feeding upon his liver?[83] *Quid rides?* Why do you smile? Says the poet:

> *Mutato nomine, de te*
> *Fabula narratur.*[84]

30 It is another name: but thou art the man! Lust, foolish desire, envy, malice, or anger, is now tearing thy breast: love of money, or of praise, hatred, or revenge, is now feeding on thy poor spirit. Such happiness is in vice! So vain is the supposition that a life of wickedness is a life of happiness![85]

[81] Cf. Esther 5:13.   [82] Cf. No. 15, *The Great Assize*, III.1 and n.
[83] Homer, *Odyssey*, xi.576-81; cf. No. 73, 'Of Hell', II.2 and n.
[84] Cf. Horace, *Satires*, I.i.68-70: 'Tantalus, racked by thirst, reaches for the streams flowing by his lips. But why do you laugh at this? *Change but the name and this tale can be told of you.*' Cf. No. 87, 'The Danger of Riches', I.6.
[85] A negative of Wesley's correlation of holiness and happiness; cf. I.3 above, and No. 7, 'The Way to the Kingdom', II.2 and n.

11. But he makes a third supposition, that he shall certainly live forty or fifty or threescore years. Do *you* depend upon this? On living threescore years? Who told you that you should? It is no other than the enemy of God and man: it is the murderer of souls. Believe him not: he was a liar from the beginning;[86] from the beginning of his rebellion against God. He is eminently a liar in this; for he would not give you life if he could. Would God permit, he would make sure work, and just now hurry you to his own place. And he cannot give you life if he would: the breath of man is not in his hands. He is not the disposer of life and death—that power belongs to the Most High. It is possible, indeed, God may, on some occasions, permit him to inflict death. I do not know but it was an evil angel who smote an hundred fourscore and five thousand Assyrians in one night;[87] and the fine lines of our poet are as applicable to an evil as to a good spirit:

> So when an angel, by divine command,
> Hurls death and terror o'er a guilty land—
> He, pleased th' Almighty's order to perform,
> Rides in the whirlwind, and directs the storm.[88]

But though Satan may sometimes inflict death, I know not that he could ever give life. It was one of his most faithful servants that shrieked out some years ago: 'A week's life! A week's life! Thirty thousand pounds for a week's life!'[89] But he could not purchase a day's life. That night God required his soul of him! And how soon may he require it of *you*? Are you sure of living threescore years?

---

[86] See John 8:44.
[87] See 2 Kgs. 19:35; Isa. 37:36.
[88] Cf. Addison, 'The Campaign', 286-91:

> So when an angel, by divine command
> With rising tempests shakes the guilty land,
> Such as of late o'er pale Britannia passed,
> Calm and serene he drives the furious blasts;
> And, pleased th' Almighty's order to perform,
> Rides in the whirlwind, and directs the storm.

This was written as part of the celebration of the Duke of Marlborough's triumphal return to London (Dec. 21, 1704) after his victory at Blenheim (Aug. 13, 1704).

[89] Was this an oral tradition about someone such as Lord Chesterfield (d. 1773)? Later, Wesley tells a similar story about Voltaire's death (cf. JWJ, Sept. 13, 1778); see also his letter of Jan. 4, 1779, to an unidentified man. In *AM* (1783), VI.645, Wesley printed the account of Voltaire's death which he had recently read in the *Gent's Mag.* (Nov. 1782), LII.529.

Are you sure of living one year? One month? One week? One day? O make haste to live! Surely the man that may die tonight, should live today.

12. So absurd are all the suppositions made by him who gains
5 the world and loses his soul! But let us for a moment imagine that religion is misery, that wickedness is happiness, and that he shall certainly live threescore years; and still I would ask, '*What is he profited* if he gain the whole world for threescore years, and then lose his soul eternally?'

10   Can such a choice be made by any that considers what eternity is? Philip Melanchthon, the most learned of all the German reformers, gives the following relation. (I pass no judgment upon it, but set it down nearly in his own words.) 'When I was at Würtemberg, as I was walking out one summer evening with
15 several of my fellow-students, we heard an uncommon singing, and following the sound saw a bird of an uncommon figure. One stepping up asked, "In the name of the Father, Son, and Holy Ghost, what art thou?" It answered, "I am a damned spirit;" and in vanishing away pronounced these words: "O eternity, eternity!
20 Who can tell the length of eternity!" '⁹⁰ And how soon will this be the language of him who sold his soul for threescore years' pleasure!⁹¹ How soon will he cry out, 'O eternity, eternity! Who can tell the length of eternity!'

13. In how striking a manner is this illustrated by one of the
25 ancient fathers! 'Supposing there were a ball of sand as big as the whole earth. Suppose a grain of this to be annihilated in a thousand years. Which would be more eligible, to be happy while

⁹⁰ Wesley's misattribution of this story to Melanchthon himself is interesting. Actually, it was one of Melanchthon's published anecdotes about a reported incident from the Council of Basel (not Würtemberg) concerning a group of learned members strolling together one evening and being astonished by the sound of a speaking bird. One of the bolder men (*animosior*) accosted the bird with the demand: 'I adjure you, by the Son of God . . . , tell me who you are?' Whereupon the bird responded *in Latin:* 'I am a damned spirit, and I have been stationed here as my destiny until the last days.' Then he flew away, calling out, *in German,* 'Eternity, eternity, eternity! How long is eternity.' The original appears in Melanchthon's *Historiae Quaedam Recitatae Inter Publicas Lectiones*, CXLIII, in *Opera* (Brunsvigae, 1854), *Corpus Reformatorum*, 20:554-55: '*In concilio Basiliensi quidam docti viri (cum nunc ibi essent) deambulationis gratia exiverunt in proximum nemus; audiunt ibi suavissime canentem aviculam et inusitatos sonos edentem; mirantur, quid sit. Ibi unus inter illos animosior, qui suspicatus est non esse veram avem, accessit et alloquitur: Adiuro te, inquit, per filium Dei, Dominum nostrum Iesum Christum, ut dicas mihi, qui sis. Respondit: Ego sum damnatus spiritus, et est mihi hos domicilium destinatum usque ad novissimum diem. Postea avolavit et clamavit:* EWIG EWIG EWIG WIE LANG IST DAS! *Isti perterrefacti domini iverunt et coeperunt aegrotare ex consternatione, et aliqui etiam mortui sunt.*'
⁹¹ Cf. No. 142, 'The Wisdom of Winning Souls', II.

this ball was wasting away at the rate of one grain in a thousand years, and miserable ever after? Or to be miserable while it was wasting away at that proportion, and happy ever after?'[92] A wise man, it is certain, could not pause one moment upon the choice; seeing all the time wherein this ball would be wasting away bears infinitely less proportion to eternity than a drop of water to the whole ocean, or a grain of sand to the whole mass. Allowing then that a life of religion were a life of misery, that a life of wickedness were a life of happiness, and that a man were assured of enjoying that happiness for the term of threescore years; yet what would he be profited if he were then to be miserable to all eternity?

14. But it has been proved that the case is quite otherwise, that religion is happiness, that wickedness is misery, and that no man is assured of living threescore days: and if so, is there any fool, any madman[93] under heaven, who can be compared to him that casts away his own soul, though it were to gain the whole world? For what is the real state of the case? What is the choice which God proposes to his creatures? It is not: 'Will you be happy threescore years, and then miserable for ever; or, will you be miserable threescore years, and then happy for ever?' It is not: 'Will you have first a temporary heaven, and then hell eternal; or, will you have first a temporary hell, and then heaven eternal?' But it is simply this: Will you be miserable threescore years, and miserable ever after; or, will you be happy threescore years, and happy ever after? Will you have a foretaste of heaven now, and then heaven for ever; or will you have a foretaste of hell now and then hell for ever? Will you have two hells, or two heavens?

15. One would think there needed no great sagacity to answer this question. And this is the very question which I now propose to *you* in the name of God. Will you be happy here and hereafter—in the world that now is, and in that which is to come? Or will you be miserable here and hereafter, in time and in eternity? What is your choice? Let there be no delay: now take one or the other. I take heaven and earth to record this day that I set before you life and death, blessing and cursing. O choose life![94] The life of peace and love now; the life of glory for ever. By the grace of God now choose that better part, which shall never be taken from you.[95] And having once fixed your choice, never draw

---

[92] Cyprian: see No. 54, 'On Eternity', §10 and n.
[93] No. 4, *Scriptural Christianity*, IV.2 and n.
[94] See Deut. 30:19.
[95] See Luke 10:42.

back; adhere to it at all events. Go on in the name of the Lord whom ye have chosen, and in the power of his might![96] In spite of all opposition, from nature, from the world, from all the powers of darkness, still fight the good fight of faith, and lay hold on eternal
5   life![97] And then there is laid up for you a crown, which the Lord, the righteous Judge, will give you at that day![98]

Bristol, Sept. 30, 1775

[96] Eph. 6:10.
[97] 1 Tim. 6:12.
[98] See 2 Tim. 4:8.

ON WORKING OUT OUR OWN SALVATION

AN INTRODUCTORY COMMENT

This must be considered as a landmark sermon, for it stands as the late Wesley's most complete and careful exposition of the mystery of divine-human interaction, his subtlest probing of the paradox of prevenient grace and human agency. If there were ever a question as to Wesley's alleged Pelagianism, this sermon alone should suffice to dispose of it decisively.

There is no indication of its date or provenance; but Wesley's recorded use of Phil. 2:12-13 as a preaching text shows an interesting configuration. He used it four times at Oxford (twice in 1732 and twice in 1734) and only once thereafter, at Norwich (February 13, 1781). The written version appeared in the Arminian Magazine *(September and October 1785), VIII. 450-54, 506-11, with no title but numbered as 'Sermon XXIX'. It later appeared in* SOSO, *VII.93-109, between* The Important Question *and* A Call to Backsliders; *the question as to the progression here must be left open. Nor was it reprinted in Wesley's lifetime. And yet, in any dozen of his sermons most crucial for an accurate assay of Wesley's theology, this one would certainly deserve inclusion.*

On Working Out Our Own Salvation

Philippians 2:12-13

Work out your own salvation with fear and trembling; for it is God that worketh in you, both to will and to do of his good pleasure.

1. Some great truths, as the being and attributes of God, and 5
the difference between moral good and evil, were known in some
measure to the heathen world; the traces of them are to be found
in all nations; so that in some sense it may be said to every child of
man: 'He hath showed thee, O man, what is good; even to do

justly, to love mercy, and to walk humbly with thy God.'[1] With this truth he has in some measure 'enlightened everyone that cometh into the world'.[2] And hereby they that 'have not the law', that have no written law, 'are a law unto themselves'.[3] They show 'the work of the law', the substance of it, though not the letter, 'written in their hearts', by the same hand which wrote the commandments on the tables of stone; 'their conscience also bearing them witness',[4] whether they act suitably thereto or not.

2. But there are two grand heads of doctrine, which contain many truths of the most important nature, of which the most enlightened heathens in the ancient world were totally ignorant; as are also the most intelligent heathens that are now on the face of the earth: I mean those which relate to the eternal Son of God, and the Spirit of God—to the Son, giving himself to be 'a propitiation for the sins of the world',[5] and to the Spirit of God, renewing men in that image of God wherein they were created.[6] For after all the pains which ingenious and learned men have taken (that great man the Chevalier Ramsay[7] in particular), to find some resemblance of these truths in the immense rubbish of heathen authors, the resemblance is so exceeding faint as not to be discerned but by a very lively imagination. Beside that even this resemblance, faint as it was, is only to be found in the discourses of a very few, and those were the most improved and deeply thinking men in their several generations; while the innumerable multitudes that surrounded them were little better for the knowledge of the philosophers, but remained as totally ignorant, even of these capital truths, as were the beasts that perish.

3. Certain it is that these truths were never known to the vulgar,

---

[1] Note the correlation here between Mic. 6:8 and a definition of 'natural religion'.

[2] Cf. John 1:9.

[3] Rom. 2:14.

[4] Cf. Rom. 2:15.

[5] Cf. 1 John 2:2.

[6] See Col. 3:10; cf. No. 44, *Original Sin*, III.5 and n.

[7] Andrew Michael Ramsay (1686–1743), a Scottish philosopher who, under the influence of Poiret and Fénelon, converted to Roman Catholicism and was made a Knight of the Order of St. Lazarus (thus 'Le Chevalier'). Wesley's annotated copy of Ramsay's *Philosophical Principles of Natural and Revealed Religion* (1749) is preserved in the John Rylands Library; see also his comments on it in JWJ, Sept. 14, 1753, and in his letter to Dr. John Robertson, Sept. 24, 1753 (see 26:515-24 in this edn.). Wesley also admired Ramsay's *The Travels of Cyrus* (1727); it was prescribed reading (in French?) for the scholars at Kingswood School; see also his reference in a letter to Mary Bishop, Aug. 18, 1784. Ramsay was more widely read and admired in France and Scotland than he ever was in England.

the bulk of mankind, to the generality of men in any nation, till they were brought to light by the gospel.[8] Notwithstanding a spark of knowledge glimmering here and there, the whole earth was covered with darkness till the Sun of Righteousness arose[9] and scattered the shades of night. Since this Day-spring from on high has appeared, a great light hath shined unto those who till then sat in darkness and in the shadow of death.[10] And thousands of them in every age have known, 'that God so loved the world' as to 'give his only Son, to the end that whosoever believeth on him should not perish, but have everlasting life.'[11] And being entrusted with the oracles of God,[12] they have known that 'God hath also given us his Holy Spirit,'[13] who 'worketh in us both to will and to do of his good pleasure'.[14]

4. How remarkable are those words of the Apostle which precede these! 'Let this mind be in you, which was also in Christ Jesus: who, being in the form of God', the incommunicable nature of God from eternity, 'counted it no act of robbery' (that is the precise meaning of the word), no invasion of any other's prerogative, but his own unquestionable right, 'to be equal with God.'[15] The word implies both the *fullness* and the supreme *height* of the Godhead. To which are opposed the two words, he 'emptied', and he 'humbled himself'. He 'emptied himself' of that divine fullness, veiled his fullness from the eyes of men and angels, 'taking'—and by that very act emptying himself—'the form of a servant, being made in the likeness of man', a real man like other men.[16] 'And being found in fashion as a man', a common man, without any peculiar beauty or excellency, 'he humbled himself' to a still greater degree, 'becoming obedient' to God, though equal with him, 'even unto death, yea the death of

---

[8] See 2 Tim. 1:10.

[9] See Mal. 4:2.

[10] See Luke 1:78-79.

[11] Cf. John 3:16.

[12] See Rom. 3:2.

[13] 1 Thess. 4:8.

[14] Cf. Phil. 2:13.

[15] Cf. Phil. 2:5-6 (*Notes*).

[16] Note the stress here (rare in Wesley) on the full humanity of Jesus Christ. Cf. William Tilly's sermon on John 3:19, in *Sermons on Several Occasions* (1712), pp. 139-40: '. . . . To suppose our Saviour a mere man like ourselves would be very much to weaken the awe and authority of his laws . . . .' See also John Deschner, *Wesley's Christology*, pp. 24 ff., 40-41, 132-33, 146, 159-60, 165, 191. Wesley's problem with the full and real humanity of Jesus Christ had a long history; see his letter to his mother, Feb. 28, 1732: 'We cannot allow Christ's human nature to be present [in the Eucharist] without allowing either con- or trans-substantiation.' See also Nos. 20, *The Lord Our Righteousness*, I.1-2; and 139, 'On the Sabbath', II.2.

the cross'[17]—the greatest instance both of humiliation and obedience.

Having proposed the example of Christ, the Apostle exhorts them to secure the salvation which Christ hath purchased for
5 them: 'Wherefore work out your own salvation with fear and trembling; for it is God that worketh in you both to will and to do of his good pleasure.'

In these comprehensive words we may observe,

First, that grand truth, which ought never to be out of our
10 remembrance, 'It is God that worketh in us, both to will and to do of his own good pleasure;'

Secondly, the improvement we ought to make of it: 'Work out your own salvation with fear and trembling;'

Thirdly, the connection between them: 'It is God that worketh
15 in you;' therefore 'work out your own salvation.'

I.1. First, we are to observe that great and important truth which ought never to be out of our remembrance, 'It is God that worketh in us both to will and to do of his good pleasure.'[18] The meaning of these words may be made more plain by a small
20 transposition of them: 'It is God that of his good pleasure worketh in you both to will and to do.' This position of the words, connecting the phrase of 'his good pleasure' with the word 'worketh', removes all imagination of merit from man, and gives God the whole glory of his own work. Otherwise we might have
25 had some room for boasting, as if it were our own desert, some goodness in us, or some good thing done by us, which first moved God to work. But this expression cuts off all such vain conceits, and clearly shows his motive to work lay wholly in himself—in his own mere grace, in his unmerited mercy.

30 2. It is by this alone he is impelled to work in man both to will and to do. The expression is capable of two interpretations, both of which are unquestionably true. First, 'to will' may include the whole of inward, 'to do' the whole of outward religion. And if it be thus understood, it implies that it is God that worketh both
35 inward and outward holiness.[19] Secondly, 'to will' may imply every good desire, 'to do' whatever results therefrom. And then the

---

[17] Phil. 2:7-8 (*Notes*).
[18] Cf. below, III.6-7.
[19] For the love of God as the substance of inward holiness and the love of neighbour as the substance of outward holiness, cf. No. 7, 'The Way to the Kingdom', I.10 and n.

sentence means, God breathes into us every good desire, and brings every good desire to good effect.

3. The original words τὸ θέλειν and τὸ ἐνεργεῖν,[20] seem to favour the latter construction; τὸ θέλειν, which we render 'to will', plainly including every good desire, whether relating to our tempers, words, or actions, to inward or outward holiness. And τὸ ἐνεργεῖν, which we render 'to do', manifestly implies all that power from on high; all that energy which works in us every right disposition, and then furnishes us for every good word and work.[21]

4. Nothing can so directly tend to hide pride from man as a deep, lasting conviction of this. For if we are thoroughly sensible that we have nothing which we have not received, how can we glory as if we had not received it?[22] If we know and feel that the very first motion of good is from above, as well as the power which conducts it to the end—if it is God that not only infuses every good desire, but that accompanies and follows it, else it vanishes away—then it evidently follows that 'he who glorieth must glory in the Lord.'[23]

II.1. Proceed we now to the second point: if God 'worketh in you', then 'work out your own salvation.' The original word rendered, 'work out', implies the doing a thing thoroughly. 'Your own'—for you yourselves must do this, or it will be left undone for ever. 'Your *own salvation*'—salvation begins with what is usually termed (and very properly) 'preventing grace';[24] including the first wish to please God, the first dawn of light concerning his will, and the first slight, transient conviction of having sinned against him. All these imply some tendency toward

---

[20] Phil. 2:13.

[21] 2 Thess. 2:17.

[22] See 1 Cor. 4:7.

[23] Cf. 1 Cor. 1:31.

[24] 'Preventing' and 'prevenient' had long since become synonyms denoting the Holy Spirit's activity in moving or drawing the will in advance of any conscious resolve. In III.4, below, Wesley relates it to natural conscience even while denying that anything natural is good in and of itself alone. Cf. Thomas Manton, *Works* (1681), I.181: 'There is *gratia praeveniens, operans,* and *co-operans;* there is preventing grace, working grace and co-working grace. Preventing grace that is when God converts us, when the Lord turns us to himself and doth plant grace in the soul at first. Working grace that is when God strengthens the habit. Co-working grace when God stirs up the act and helps us in the exercise of the grace we have.' Cf. William Tilly's first sermon on Phil. 2:12, 13 (Sermon VIII, in *Sermons,* pp. 245 ff.), where he uses the same term; and see No. 43, *The Scripture Way of Salvation,* I.2 and n.

life, some degree of salvation, the beginning of a deliverance from a blind, unfeeling heart, quite insensible of God and the things of God. Salvation is carried on by 'convincing grace',[25] usually in Scripture termed 'repentance', which brings a larger measure of
5   self-knowledge, and a farther deliverance from the heart of stone.[26] Afterwards we experience the proper Christian salvation, whereby 'through grace' we 'are saved by faith',[27] consisting of those two grand branches, justification and sanctification. By justification we are saved from the guilt of sin, and restored to the
10 favour of God: by sanctification we are saved from the power and root of sin, and restored to the image of God.[28] All experience, as well as Scripture, shows this salvation to be both instantaneous and gradual. It begins the moment we are justified, in the holy, humble, gentle, patient love of God and man. It gradually
15 increases from that moment, as a 'grain of mustard seed, which at first is the least of all seeds, but' gradually 'puts forth large branches',[29] and becomes a great tree; till in another instant the heart is cleansed from all sin, and filled with pure love to God and man. But even that love increases more and more, till we 'grow up
20 in all things into him that is our head',[30] 'till we attain the measure of the stature of the fullness of Christ'.[31]

     2. But how are we to 'work out' this salvation? The Apostle answers, 'With fear and trembling'. There is another passage of St. Paul wherein the same expression occurs, which may give
25 light to this: 'Servants, obey your masters according to the flesh,' according to the present state of things, although sensible that in a little time the servant will be free from his master, 'with fear and trembling'. This is a proverbial expression, which cannot be understood literally. For what master could bear, much less
30 require, his servant to stand trembling and quaking before him?

---

[25] Cf. Tilly's alternate phrase (*ibid.*), 'assisting grace'. For Wesley this is equivalent to 'the grace of repentance'; cf. No. 14, *The Repentance of Believers*, II.6, and Wesley's *Notes* on Luke 23:40.

[26] See Ezek. 11:19.

[27] Eph. 2:8.

[28] Cf. Bishop Francis Gastrell (whose death Samuel Wesley, Jun. commemorated in his *Poems* [1736], p. 130; see No. 84, *The Important Question*, II.3 and n.), *The Certainty and Necessity of Religion in General* (1697), pp. 315, 317, 336. See also No. 6, 'The Righteousness of Faith', II.9: 'The best end of any fallen creature is the recovery of the favour [justification] and image [sanctification] of God;' cf. No. 1, *Salvation by Faith*, §1 and n.

[29] Cf. Matt. 13:31-32.   [30] Cf. Eph. 4:15.

[31] Cf. Eph. 4:13.

And the following words utterly exclude this meaning: 'in singleness of heart', with a single eye to the will and providence of God, 'not with eye-service, as men-pleasers, but as servants of Christ, doing the will of God from the heart'; doing whatever they do as the will of God, and therefore with their might.[a] It is easy to see that these strong expressions of the Apostle clearly imply two things: first, that everything be done with the utmost earnestness of spirit, and with all care and caution—perhaps more directly referring to the former word, μετὰ φόβου, 'with fear'; secondly, that it be done with the utmost diligence, speed, punctuality, and exactness—not improbably referring to the latter word, μετὰ τρόμου, 'with trembling'.[32]

3. How easily may we transfer this to the business of life, the working out our own salvation! With the same temper and in the same manner that Christian servants serve their masters that are upon earth, let other Christians labour to serve their Master that is in heaven: that is, first, with the utmost earnestness of spirit, with all possible care and caution; and, secondly, with the utmost diligence, speed, punctuality, and exactness.

4. But what are the steps which the Scripture directs us to take, in the working out of our own salvation? The prophet Isaiah gives us a general answer touching the first steps which we are to take: 'Cease to do evil; learn to do well.'[33] If ever you desire that God should work in you that faith whereof cometh both present and eternal salvation, by the grace already given, fly from all sin as from the face of a serpent; carefully avoid every evil word and work; yea, abstain from all appearance of evil. And 'learn to do well'; be zealous of good works,[34] of works of piety, as well as works of mercy. Use family prayer, and cry to God in secret. Fast in secret, and 'your Father which seeth in secret, he will reward you openly.'[35] 'Search the Scriptures;'[36] hear them in public, read them in private, and meditate therein. At every opportunity be a partaker of the Lord's Supper. 'Do this in remembrance of him,'[37]

[a] Eph. 6:5-6.

---

[32] The Greek text reads μετὰ φόβου καὶ τρόμου.

[33] Isa. 1:16-17; cf. this and the first and second of the *General Rules,* and note that Wesley can speak both positively and negatively of these rules, depending always upon the context. For other positive instances, cf. No. 24, 'Sermon on the Mount, IV', IV.1 and n.; and for negative instances, cf. No. 22, 'Sermon on the Mount, II', II.4 and n.

[34] Titus 2:14.   [35] Cf. Matt. 6:4, 6, 18.

[36] John 5:39.   [37] Cf. Luke 22:19; 1 Cor. 11:24.

and he will meet you at his own table. Let your conversation be with the children of God, and see that it 'be in grace, seasoned with salt'.[38] As ye have time, do good unto all men,[39] to their souls and to their bodies. And herein 'be ye steadfast, unmovable, always abounding in the work of the Lord.'[40] It then only remains that ye deny yourselves and take up your cross daily.[41] Deny yourselves every pleasure which does not prepare you for taking pleasure in God, and willingly embrace every means of drawing near to God, though it be a cross, though it be grievous to flesh and blood. Thus when you have redemption in the blood of Christ, you will 'go on to perfection';[42] till, 'walking in the light, as he is in the light',[43] you are enabled to testify that 'he is faithful and just', not only 'to forgive your sins', but 'to cleanse you from all unrighteousness.'[44]

III. 1. 'But', say some, 'what connection is there between the former and the latter clause of this sentence? Is there not rather a flat opposition between the one and the other? If it is God that worketh in us both to will and to do, what need is there of our working? Does not his working thus supersede the necessity of our working at all? Nay, does it not render our working impracticable, as well as unnecessary? For if we allow that God does all, what is there left for us to do?'

2. Such is the reasoning of flesh and blood. And at first hearing it is exceeding plausible. But it is not solid, as will evidently appear if we consider the matter more deeply. We shall then see there is no opposition between these—'God works; therefore do ye work'—but on the contrary the closest connection, and that in two respects. For, first, God works; therefore you *can* work. Secondly, God works; therefore you *must* work.

3. First, God worketh in you; therefore you can work—otherwise it would be impossible. If he did not work it would be impossible for you to work out your own salvation. 'With man this is impossible—', saith our Lord, 'for a rich man to enter into the kingdom of heaven.'[45] Yea, it is impossible for any man; for any that is born of a woman, unless God work in him. Seeing all men

---

[38] Cf. Col. 4:6.
[39] See Gal. 6:10, with 'time' once more in place of the AV's 'opportunity'.
[40] 1 Cor. 15:58.   [41] See Luke 9:23, etc.
[42] Heb. 6:1.   [43] Cf. 1 John 1:7.
[44] Cf. 1 John 1:9.
[45] Cf. Matt. 19:23, 26.

are by nature not only sick, but 'dead in trespasses, and sins',[46] it is not possible for them to do anything well till God raises them from the dead. It was impossible for Lazarus to 'come forth'[47] till the Lord had given him life. And it is equally impossible for us to 'come' out of our sins, yea, or to make the least motion toward it, till he who hath all power in heaven and earth calls our dead souls into life.

4. Yet this is no excuse for those who continue in sin, and lay the blame upon their Maker by saying: 'It is God only that must quicken us; for we cannot quicken our own souls.' For allowing that all the souls of men are dead in sin by *nature*, this excuses none, seeing there is no man that is in a state of mere nature; there is no man, unless he has quenched the Spirit, that is wholly void of the grace of God.[48] No man living is entirely destitute of what is vulgarly called 'natural conscience'.[49] But this is not natural; it is more properly termed 'preventing grace'. Every man has a greater or less measure of this, which waiteth not for the call of man. Everyone has sooner or later good desires, although the generality of men stifle them before they can strike deep root or produce any considerable fruit. Everyone has some measure of that light, some faint glimmering ray, which sooner or later, more or less, enlightens every man that cometh into the world.[50] And everyone, unless he be one of the small number whose conscience is seared as with a hot iron,[51] feels more or less uneasy when he acts contrary to the light of his own conscience. So that no man sins because he has not grace, but because he does not use the grace which he hath.[52]

5. Therefore inasmuch as God works in you, you are now able to work out your own salvation. Since he worketh in you of his own good pleasure, without any merit of yours, both to will and to do, it is possible for you to fulfil all righteousness.[53] It is possible for you to 'love God, because he hath first loved us',[54] and to 'walk

---

[46] Eph. 2:1.
[47] John 11:43.
[48] For a summary of the Reformed doctrines of the state of fallen human nature, cf. Heppe, *Reformed Dogmatics*, XV.13-39; cf. also No. 14, *The Repentance of Believers*, I.17 and n.
[49] Cf. II.1, above; also No. 129, 'Heavenly Treasure in Earthen Vessels', I.1.
[50] John 1:9.
[51] 1 Tim. 4:2; cf. No. 12, 'The Witness of Our Own Spirit', §19 and n.
[52] Cf. No. 98, 'On Visiting the Sick', §1, and Wesley's counsel to Miss March, Oct. 13, 1765: 'To use the grace we have, and now to expect all we want, is the grand secret.'
[53] See Matt. 3:15.
[54] Cf. 1 John 4:19.

in love',[55] after the pattern of our great Master. We know indeed
that word of his to be absolutely true, 'Without me ye can do
nothing.'[56] But on the other hand we know, every believer can say,
'I can do all things through Christ that strengtheneth me.'[57]

5   6. Meantime let us remember that God has joined these
together in the experience of every believer. And therefore we
must take care not to imagine they are ever to be put asunder.[58]
We must beware of that mock humility which teacheth us to say,
in excuse for our wilful disobedience, 'Oh, I can do nothing,' and
10 stops there, without once naming the grace of God. Pray think
twice. Consider what you say. I hope you wrong yourself. For if it
be really true that you can do nothing, then you have no faith. And
if you have not faith you are in a wretched condition. Surely it is
not so. You can do something, through Christ strengthening
15 you.[59] Stir up the spark of grace which is now in you, and he will
give you more grace.[60]

     7. Secondly, God worketh in you; therefore you *must* work: you
must be 'workers together with him'[61] (they are the very words of
the Apostle); otherwise he will cease working. The general rule
20 on which his gracious dispensations invariably proceed is this:
'Unto him that hath shall be given; but from him that hath not',
that does not improve the grace already given, 'shall be taken away
what he assuredly hath'[62] (so the words ought to be rendered).[63]
Even St. Augustine, who is generally supposed to favour the
25 contrary doctrine, makes that just remark, *Qui fecit nos sine nobis,
non salvabit nos sine nobis:*[64] 'he that made us without ourselves, will
not save us without ourselves.' He will not save us unless we 'save

[55] Eph. 5:2.
[56] John 15:5.
[57] Cf. Phil. 4:13.
[58] See Matt. 19:6.
[59] See Phil. 4:13.
[60] The essence of Wesley's synergism; every human action is a reaction to prevenient grace. Cf. I.1, above; and No. 90, 'An Israelite Indeed', I.5; also Thomas Crane, *Isagoge ad Dei Providentiam*, p. 275: 'Men come not into the inmost circle of divine providence because they cannot but because they will not.' See also Samuel Annesley's sermon 'On Conscience', in *The Morning-Exercise at Cripplegate* (1661), p. 13: 'Do what you know, and God will teach you what to do. Do what you know to be your present duty and God will acquaint you with your future duty as it comes to be present.'
[61] 2 Cor. 6:1.
[62] Luke 8:18 (*Notes*). Cf. Nos. 43, *The Scripture Way of Salvation*, §1 and n.; and 82, 'On Temptation', §2 and n.
[63] Another instance of Wesley's insistence that ὁ δοκεῖ does *not* mean 'appearance' (as it does in most lexicons).
[64] Augustine, Sermon 169, xi (13); cf. No. 63, 'The General Spread of the Gospel', §12 and n.

ourselves from this untoward generation';[65] unless we ourselves 'fight the good fight of faith, and lay hold on eternal life';[66] unless we 'agonize to enter in at the strait gate,'[67] 'deny ourselves, and take up our cross daily',[68] and labour, by every possible means, to 'make our own calling and election sure'.[69]

8. 'Labour' then, brethren, 'not for the meat that perisheth, but for that which endureth to everlasting life.'[70] Say with our blessed Lord, though in a somewhat different sense, 'My Father worketh hitherto, and I work.'[71] In consideration that he still worketh in you, be never 'weary of well-doing'.[72] Go on, in virtue of the grace of God preventing, accompanying, and following you, in 'the work of faith, in the patience of hope, and in the labour of love'.[73] 'Be ye steadfast and immovable; always abounding in the work of the Lord.'[74] And 'the God of peace, who brought again from the dead the great Shepherd of the sheep',—Jesus—'make you perfect in every good work to do his will, working in you what is well-pleasing in his sight, through Jesus Christ, to whom be glory for ever and ever!'[75]

[65] Cf. Acts. 2:40.
[66] 1 Tim. 6:12.
[67] Cf. Luke 13:24.
[68] Cf. Luke 9:23.
[69] Cf. 2 Pet. 1:10.
[70] John 6:27 (*Notes*).
[71] John 5:17.
[72] Cf. Gal. 6:9; 2 Thess. 3:13.
[73] Cf. 1 Thess. 1:3.
[74] Cf. 1 Cor. 15:58.
[75] See Heb. 13:20-21 (*Notes*). Note that the benediction in Hebrews serves here as an ascription. For Wesley's rare usage of ascriptions, cf. No. 1, *Salvation by Faith*, III.9 and n.

A CALL TO BACKSLIDERS

AN INTRODUCTORY COMMENT

With this sermon we move seven years back in time, over to Ireland and to a quite different issue: the problems of religious despair and the valid grounds of Christian assurance and reassurance. We know its place and date only from its separate editions: 'Sligo, May 20, 1778'. A decade later it was included in SOSO, *VII.111-37; it also appeared in three other editions in Wesley's lifetime. For further details of its publishing history and a list of variant readings, see Vol. 4, Appendix A, and* Bibliog, *No. 388. For an account of Wesley's trip to Sligo, see* Journal *for March 17-21, 1778.*

It was Wesley's way to emphasize the continuities in his thought even as he was quietly nuancing his earlier statements of complex questions. We have seen how, in the earliest stages of the Revival, he insisted on clear-cut experiences of conscious assurance, and was not particularly sensitive to the tendency of such an insistence toward religious despair in some cases (see No. 3, 'Awake, Thou That Sleepest', *III.6 and n.). We have also noticed his quiet de-emphasis upon such a stark disjunction. Here, we have a careful analysis of religious despair and a comforting statement of a doctrine of degrees of assurance on the one hand and an encouraging 'call to backsliders' on the other. It is interesting to note that the only other record of Wesley's use of Ps. 77:7-8 is from the* Journal, *August 23, 1768 (at Cullompton): 'In the evening I preached to the poor backsliders at Cullompton on "Will the Lord be no more entreated?"' Thus we can see a maturer Wesley amending his earlier views even as he disavows any rejection of his positive intentions in them: viz., of emphasizing in full seriousness his doctrine of conscious Christian experiences of pardon and assurance.*

A Call to Backsliders

Psalm 77:7-8

Will the Lord absent himself for ever? And will he be no more entreated? Is his mercy clean gone for ever? And is his promise come utterly to an end for evermore?[1]

1. Presumption is one grand snare of the devil, in which many of the children of men are taken. They so presume upon the mercy of God as utterly to forget his justice. Although he has expressly declared, 'Without holiness no man shall see the Lord,'[2] yet they flatter themselves that in the end God will be better than his word. They imagine they may live and die in their sins, and nevertheless 'escape the damnation of hell'.[3]

2. But although there are many that are destroyed by *presumption*, there are still more that perish by *despair*. I mean by want of hope; by thinking it impossible that they should escape destruction. Having many times fought against their spiritual enemies, and always been overcome, they lay down their arms; they no more contend, as they have no hope of victory. Knowing by melancholy experience that they have no power of themselves to help themselves, and having no expectation that God will help them, they lie down under their burden. They no longer strive; for they suppose it is impossible they should attain.

3. In this case, as in a thousand others, 'the heart knoweth its own bitterness, but a stranger intermeddleth not with its grief.'[4] It is not easy for those to know it who never felt it. For 'who knoweth the things of a man, but the spirit of a man that is in him?'[5] Who knoweth, unless by his own experience, what this sort of 'wounded spirit'[6] means! Of consequence there are few that know how to sympathize with them that are under this sore temptation. There are few that have duly considered the case, few that are not

---

[1] Usually, Wesley quotes his sermon texts from the AV; here he has reverted to his lifelong preference for the BCP Psalter.
[2] Cf. Heb. 12:14.
[3] Matt. 23:33.
[4] Cf. Prov. 14:10.
[5] Cf. 1 Cor. 2:11.
[6] Prov. 18:14.

deceived by appearances. They see men go on in a course of sin, and take it for granted, it is out of mere presumption; whereas in reality it is from the quite contrary principle—it is out of mere despair. Either they have no hope at all, and while that is the case
5 they do not strive at all; or they have some intervals of hope, and while that lasts, 'strive for the mastery'.[7] But that hope soon fails. They then cease to strive, and are 'taken captive' of Satan 'at his will'.[8]

4. This is frequently the case with those that began to run well,
10 but soon tired in the heavenly road; with those in particular who once saw 'the glory of God in the face of Jesus Christ',[9] but afterwards grieved his Holy Spirit, and made shipwreck of the faith.[10] Indeed many of these rush into sin as an horse into battle.[11] They sin with so high an hand as utterly to quench the Holy Spirit
15 of God; so that he gives them up to their own heart's lusts, and lets them follow their own imaginations.[12] And those who are thus given up may be quite stupid, without either fear, or sorrow, or care; utterly easy and unconcerned about God, or heaven, or hell—to which the god of this world contributes not a little by
20 blinding and hardening their hearts.[13] But still even these would not be so careless were it not for despair. The great reason why they have no sorrow or care is because they have no hope. They verily believe they have so provoked God that 'he will be no more entreated'.

25 5. And yet we need not utterly give up even these. We have known some, even of the careless ones, whom God has visited again, and restored to their first love. But we may have much more hope for those backsliders who are not careless, who are still uneasy; those who fain would escape out of the snare of the
30 devil,[14] but think it is impossible. They are fully convinced they cannot save themselves, and believe God *will* not save them. They believe he has irrevocably 'shut up his loving-kindness in displeasure'.[15] They fortify themselves in believing this by abundance of reasons. And unless those reasons are clearly
35 removed they cannot hope for any deliverance.

---

[7] Cf. 1 Cor. 9:25.
[8] 2 Tim. 2:26.
[9] 2 Cor. 4:6.
[10] 1 Tim. 1:19.   [11] See Jer. 8:6.
[12] Ps. 81:13, as in the BCP Psalter. Cf. Rom. 1:21, 26, 28; and also 1 John 2:16, and No. 7, 'The Way to the Kingdom', II.2 and n.
[13] See John 12:40.   [14] 2 Tim. 2:26.   [15] Ps. 77:9 (BCP).

It is in order to relieve these hopeless, helpless souls that I propose, with God's assistance:

First, to inquire what the chief of those reasons are, some or other of which induce so many backsliders to cast away hope, to suppose that God hath 'forgotten to be gracious';[16] and, secondly, to give a clear and full answer to each of those reasons.

I. I am, first, to inquire what the chief of those reasons are which induce so many backsliders to think that God 'hath forgotten to be gracious'. I do not say *all* the reasons—for innumerable are those which either their own evil hearts or that old serpent will suggest—but the chief of them; those that are most plausible, and therefore most common.

1.[17]The first argument which induces many backsliders to believe that 'the Lord will be no more entreated' is drawn from the very reason of the thing. 'If ', say they, 'a man rebel against an earthly prince, many times he dies for the first offence, he pays his life for the first transgression. Yet possibly if the crime be extenuated by some favourable circumstance, or if strong intercession be made for him, his life may be given him. But if after a full and free pardon he were guilty of rebelling a second time, who would dare to intercede for him? He must expect no farther mercy. Now if one rebelling against an earthly king, after he has been freely pardoned once, cannot with any colour of reason hope to be forgiven a second time,[18] what must be the case of him that after having been freely pardoned for rebelling against the great King of heaven and earth, rebels against him again?

---

[16] *Ibid.*

[17] There is a difficult problem here with respect to this sermon's proper divisions. The heads are clear enough: I, a list of reasons why backsliders lose hope; II, answers to these reasons. But the order of the subdivisions was not clear and was still further obscured in the second edition of *SOSO*. Different schemes of enumeration were adopted in the 2nd and 3rd edns. of Wesley's *Works* by Joseph Benson (1809–13) and Thomas Jackson (1829–31). The format adopted here represents a return to the order of the first edition with revisions designed to clarify the complex relationship of the divisions, subdivisions, and sub-subdivisions under each of the two main heads, thus: I.1; 2(1)-(6); 3. II.1; 2(1) i-v; 2(2); 2(3) i-iii; 2(4); 2(5) i-ii; 2(6); 3(1)-(8).

[18] A problem that had troubled the second- and third-century theologians and ethicists; cf. Reinhold Seeberg, *History of Doctrines*, I.61, 175, 196. See espec. *The Shepherd of Hermas*, 'Mandates', 4:3:1; 4:1:8; and Tertullian, *On a Second Repentance*. In its first form the question of a 'second repentance and forgiveness' had been correlated with baptism; in radical Protestantism and the Evangelical Revival, it was correlated with conversion.

What can be expected but that "vengeance will come upon him to the uttermost"?"[19]

2. (1). This argument drawn from reason they enforce by several passages of Scripture. One of the strongest of these is that which occurs in the First Epistle of St. John: 'If any man see his brother sin a sin which is not unto death, he shall ask, and God shall give him life for them that sin not unto death. There is a sin unto death. I do not say that he shall pray for it.'[a]

Hence they argue: 'Certainly "I do not say that he shall pray for it" is equivalent with "I say he shall not pray for it." So the Apostle supposes him that has committed this sin to be in a desperate state indeed! So desperate that we may not even pray for his forgiveness; we may not ask life for him! And what may we more reasonably suppose to be a sin unto death than wilful rebellion after a full and free pardon?'

(2). 'Consider, secondly', say they, 'those terrible passages in the Epistle to the Hebrews, one of which occurs in the sixth chapter, the other in the tenth. To begin with the latter: "If we sin wilfully after we have received the knowledge of the truth, there remaineth no other sacrifice for sin, but a certain looking for of judgment and fiery indignation, which shall devour the adversaries. He that despised Moses' law died without mercy: of how much sorer punishment, suppose ye, shall he be thought worthy who hath trodden under foot the Son of God, [and] counted the blood of the covenant, wherewith he was sanctified, an unholy thing, and done despite to the Spirit of grace? For we know him that hath said, Vengeance is mine; I will recompense, saith the Lord. It is a fearful thing to fall into the hands of the living God!"[b] Now is it not here expressly declared by the Holy Ghost that our case is desperate? Is it not declared that "if after we have received the knowledge of the truth", after we have experimentally known it, "we sin wilfully", which we have undoubtedly done, and that over and over, "there remaineth no other sacrifice for sin, but a certain looking for of judgment and fiery indignation, which shall devour the adversaries"?'

(3). 'And is not that passage in the sixth chapter exactly parallel with this? "It is impossible for those that were once enlightened,

[a] [1 John] 5:16 [cf. *Notes*, 5:16-18, and also for Matt. 12:31].
[b] [Heb. 10:] Ver. 26-31.

[19] Cf. 1 Thess. 2:16.

and have tasted of the heavenly gift, and were made partakers of the Holy Ghost, . . . if they fall away (literally—and have fallen away),[20] to renew them again unto repentance; seeing they crucify to themselves the Son of God afresh, and put him to an open shame." [c]

5

(4). 'It is true, some are of opinion that those words, "it is impossible", are not to be taken literally as denoting an absolute impossibility, but only a very great difficulty. But it does not appear that we have any sufficient reason to depart from the literal meaning, as it neither implies any absurdity, nor contradicts any 10 other Scriptures.[21] Does not this then', they say, 'cut off all hope, seeing we have undoubtedly "tasted of the heavenly gift, and been made partakers of the Holy Ghost"? How is it possible to "renew us again to repentance", to an entire change both of heart and life? Seeing we "have crucified" to ourselves "the Son of God 15 afresh, and put him to an open shame"?'

(5). 'A yet more dreadful passage, if possible, than this, is that in the twelfth chapter of St. Matthew: "All manner of sin and blasphemy shall be forgiven unto men: but the blasphemy against the Holy Ghost shall not be forgiven unto men. And whosoever 20 speaketh a word against the Son of man, it shall be forgiven him. But whosoever speaketh against the Holy Ghost, it shall not be forgiven him, neither in this world, nor in the world to come." [d] Exactly parallel to these are those words of our Lord which are recited by St. Mark: "Verily I say unto you, all sins shall be 25 forgiven unto the sons of men, and blasphemies wherewith soever they blaspheme. But he that shall blaspheme against the Holy Ghost shall never be forgiven, but is in danger of eternal damnation." [e]

(6). It has been the judgment of some that all these passages 30 point at one and the same sin; that not only the words of our Lord, but those of St. John, concerning the 'sin unto death', and those of St. Paul concerning 'crucifying to themselves the Son of God afresh', 'treading underfoot the Son of God, and doing despite to

[c] Ver. 4, 6.
[d] Ver. 31-32.   [e] Chap. 3, ver. 28-29.

---

[20] For this peculiar translation of παραπεσόντας, see No. 1, *Salvation by Faith*, II.4 and n.; Wesley is at least consistent in his minority opinion on this point.
[21] Another version of the hermeneutic rule that literal interpretations are to be preferred; cf. No. 21, 'Sermon on the Mount, I', §6 and n.

the Spirit of grace', all refer to the blasphemy against the Holy Ghost—the only sin that shall never be forgiven. Whether they do or no, it must be allowed that this blasphemy is absolutely unpardonable; and that consequently, for those who have been
5 guilty of this, God 'will be no more entreated'.

3. To confirm those arguments drawn from reason and Scripture they appeal to matter of fact. They ask, 'Is it not a fact that those who fall away from justifying grace, "who make shipwreck of the faith",[22] that faith whereof cometh present
10 salvation, perish without mercy? How much less can any of those escape who fall away from sanctifying grace? Who make shipwreck of that faith whereby they were cleansed from all pollution of flesh and spirit? Has there ever been an instance of one or the other of these being "renewed again to repentance"?[23]
15 If there be any instances of that, one would be inclined to believe that thought of our poet not to be extravagant:

> E'en Judas struggles his despair to quell,
> Hope almost blossoms in the shades of hell.'[24]

II. These are the principal arguments, drawn from reason,
20 from Scripture, and from fact, whereby backsliders are wont to justify themselves in casting away hope; in supposing that God hath utterly 'shut up his loving-kindness in displeasure'. I have proposed them in their full strength, that we may form the better judgment concerning them, and try whether each of them may
25 not receive a clear, full, satisfactory answer.

1. I begin with that argument which is taken from the nature of the thing. 'If a man rebel against an earthly prince, he may possibly be forgiven the first time. But if after a full and free pardon he should rebel again, there is no hope of obtaining a
30 second pardon: he must expect to die without mercy. Now if he that rebels again against an earthly king can look for no second pardon, how can he look for mercy who rebels a second time against the great King of heaven and earth?'[25]

---

[22] Cf. 1 Tim. 1:19.   [23] Cf. Heb. 6:6.

[24] Young, *The Last Day* (1713), II.38; however, these lines and the preceding eight were dropped from later editions of Young's *Works*. Wesley had published an extract in *A Collection of Moral and Sacred Poems*, II.71-99, and later in No. 115, 'Dives and Lazarus', I.7, will borrow a phrase from this same couplet and use it without quotation marks.

[25] An echo of the ancient rigorism summarized by Tertullian in *De Pudicitia* (*Of Purity*)—the distinction between *peccata remissibilia* and *irremissibilia*—and illustrated by Constantine's decision to postpone his own baptism lest he should lapse before death into

I answer: this argument, drawn from the analogy between earthly and heavenly things, is plausible, but it is not solid; and that for this plain reason: analogy has no place here. There can be no analogy or proportion between the mercy of any of the children of men and that of the most high God. 'Unto whom will ye liken me, saith the Lord?'[26] Unto whom either in heaven or earth? Who, 'what is he among the gods, that shall be compared unto the Lord?'[27] 'I have said, Ye are gods,'[28] saith the Psalmist, speaking to supreme magistrates. Such is your dignity and power, compared to that of common men. But what are they to the God of heaven? As a bubble upon the wave.[29] What is their power in comparison of his power? What is their mercy compared to his mercy? Hence that comfortable word: 'I am God, and not man;[30] therefore the house of Israel is not consumed.'[31] Because he is God and not man, 'therefore his compassions fail not'.[32] None then can infer that because an earthly king will not pardon one that rebels against him a second time, therefore the King of heaven will not. Yea, he will: not until seven times only, or seventy times seven.[33] Nay, were your rebellions multiplied as the stars of heaven, were they more in number than the hairs of your head; yet 'return unto the Lord, and he will have mercy upon you, and to our God, and he will abundantly pardon.'[34]

2. (1). i. 'But does not St. John cut us off from this hope by what he says of the "sin unto death"?'[35] Is not, "I do not say that he shall pray for it" equivalent with "I say he shall not pray for it"? And does not this imply that God has determined not to hear that prayer? That he will not give life to such a sinner, no, not through the prayer of a righteous man?'

ii. I answer: 'I do not say that he shall pray for it' certainly means 'He shall not pray for it.' And it doubtless implies that God will not give life unto them that have sinned this sin; that their sentence is passed, and God has determined it shall not be

---

an unpardonable sin. The teaching of other fathers was generally more lenient, as in Anthony's letter to the archimandrite Theodore (*c.* A.D. 340), and in Origen (*In Lev. hom.* 2, 4; *De orat.* 28; and *Contra Celsum* 3, 50). See also Chrysostom (Hom. in *Hebr.* 9 and *De sacerdotio* 3, 6) and Cyprian (*Ep. to Antonianus*, No. 55).

[26] Cf. Isa. 40:18, 25.
[27] Cf. Ps. 86:8.
[28] Ps. 82:6.
[29] Cf. No. 36, 'The Law Established through Faith, II', III.5 and n.
[30] Hos. 11:9.
[31] Lam. 3:22.
[32] Cf. *ibid.*
[33] See Matt. 18:22.
[34] Cf. Isa. 55:7.
[35] 1 John 5:16; cf. I.2 (1), above.

revoked. It cannot be altered even by that 'effectual fervent prayer' which in other cases 'availeth much'.[36]

iii. But I ask, first, what is 'the sin unto death'? And secondly, what is the 'death' which is annexed to it?

5 And first, what is the 'sin unto death'? It is now many years since, being among a people the most experienced in the things of God of any I had ever seen, I asked some of them 'What do you understand by the "sin unto death" mentioned in the First Epistle of St. John?'[37] They answered, '"If anyone is sick among" us, he "sends for the elders of the church"; and they pray over
10 him, and the "prayer of faith saves the sick, and the Lord raises him up. And if he hath committed sins", which God was punishing by that sickness, "they are forgiven him."[38] But sometimes none of us can pray that God would "raise him up".
15 And we are constrained to tell him, "We are afraid that you have sinned 'a sin unto death', a sin that God has determined to punish with death—we cannot pray for your recovery." And we have never yet known an instance of such a person recovering.'[39]

iv. I see no absurdity at all in this interpretation of the word. It
20 seems to be one meaning (at least) of the expression, 'a sin unto death'—a sin which God has determined to punish by the death of the sinner. If therefore you have sinned a sin of this kind, and your sin has overtaken you; if God is chastising you by some severe disease, it will not avail to pray for your life; you are
25 irrevocably sentenced to die. But observe! This has no reference to eternal death. It does by no means imply that you are condemned to die the second death.[40] No; it rather implies the contrary—the body is destroyed that the soul may escape destruction. I have myself, during the course of many years, seen
30 numerous instances of this. I have known many sinners (chiefly notorious backsliders from high degrees of holiness, and such as had given great occasion to the enemies of religion to blaspheme) whom God has cut short in the midst of their journey, yea, before

[36] Jas. 5:16.
[37] Is this a memory of his experiences at Herrnhut and Marienborn in July and Aug. 1738? No explicit reference to it appears in Wesley's account of his conversations with Michael Linner, Christian David, *et al.*, in JWJ, but it does echo a familiar Moravian perspective.
[38] Cf. Jas. 5:14-15.
[39] Cf. JWJ, June 25, 1776: 'I visited a poor backslider. . . . I fear he has sinned a sin unto death; a sin which God has determined to punish by death.'
[40] Cf. Rev. 20:6.

they had lived out half their days. These, I apprehend, had sinned 'a sin unto death'; in consequence of which they were cut off, sometimes more swiftly, sometimes more slowly, by an unexpected stroke. But in most of these cases it has been observed that 'mercy rejoiced over judgment'.[41] And the persons themselves were fully convinced of the goodness as well as justice of God. They acknowledged that he destroyed the body in order to save the soul. Before they went hence he healed their backsliding. So they died that they might live for ever.

v. A very remarkable instance of this occurred many years ago. A young collier in Kingswood, near Bristol, was an eminent sinner, and afterwards an eminent saint. But by little and little he renewed his acquaintance with his old companions, who by degrees wrought upon him till he dropped all his religion, and was twofold more a child of hell than before. One day he was working in the pit with a serious young man, who suddenly stopped and cried out: 'O Tommy, what a man was you once! How did your words and example provoke many to love and to good works! And what are you now? What would become of you if you were to die as you are?' 'Nay, God forbid,' said Thomas, 'for then I should fall into hell headlong! O let us cry to God!' They did so for a considerable time, first the one, and then the other. They called upon God with strong cries and tears, wrestling with him in mighty prayer. After some time Thomas broke out: 'Now I know God hath healed my backsliding.[42] I know again that my Redeemer liveth,[43] and that he hath washed me from my sins in his own blood.[44] I am willing to go to him.' Instantly part of the pit calved[45] in, and crushed him to death in a moment. Whosoever thou art that hast sinned 'a sin unto death', lay this to heart! It may be, God will require thy soul of thee in an hour when thou lookest not for it! But if he doth, there is mercy in the midst of judgment; thou shalt not die eternally.

(2). 'But what say you to that other Scripture, namely, the tenth of the Hebrews? Does that leave any hope to notorious backsliders that they shall not die eternally? That they can ever

---

[41] Cf. Jas. 2:13. For other references to Wesley's body-soul dualism, cf. No. 41, *Wandering Thoughts*, III.5 and n.

[42] See Hos. 14:4.

[43] Cf. Job 19:25.

[44] See Rev. 1:5.

[45] I.e., 'caved in'; cf. *OED* for eighteenth-century usages of 'calved' for 'caved'.

recover the favour of God, or escape the damnation of hell? "If we
sin wilfully, after we have received the knowledge of the truth,
there remaineth no other sacrifice for sins, but a certain fearful
looking for of judgment and fiery indignation, which shall devour
5 the adversaries. He that despised Moses' law died without mercy:
of how much sorer punishment, suppose ye, shall he be thought
worthy, who hath trodden under foot the Son of God, and
counted the blood of the covenant, wherewith he was sanctified,
an unholy thing, and done despite unto the Spirit of grace?"'
10   (3). i. 'And is not the same thing, namely, the desperate,
irrecoverable state of wilful backsliders, fully confirmed by that
parallel passage in the sixth chapter? "It is impossible for those
who were once enlightened, and have tasted of the heavenly gift,
and were made partakers of the Holy Ghost, . . . and have fallen
15 away (so it is in the original), to renew them again unto
repentance; seeing they crucify to themselves the Son of God
afresh, and put him to an open shame."'
   ii. These passages do seem to me parallel to each other, and
deserve our deepest consideration. And in order to understand
20 them it will be necessary to know, (i), who are the persons here
spoken of; and (ii), what is the sin they had committed which
made their case nearly, if not quite desperate.
   As to the first, it will be clear to all who impartially consider and
compare both these passages that the persons spoken of herein
25 are those and those only that have been justified. It was when they
were justified that the eyes of their understanding were opened
and 'enlightened', to see the light of the glory of God in the face of
Jesus Christ. These only 'have tasted of the heavenly gift',
remission of sins, eminently so called. These 'were made
30 partakers of the Holy Ghost', both of the witness and the fruit of
the Spirit. This character cannot with any propriety be applied to
any but those that have been justified.
   And they had been sanctified, too; at least in the first degree, as
far as all are who receive remission of sins.[46] So the second
35 passage expressly: 'Who hath counted the blood of the covenant,
wherewith he was *sanctified*, an unholy thing.'
   iii. Hence it follows that this Scripture concerns those alone
who have been *justified*, and, at least in part, *sanctified*. Therefore

---

[46] Note a new twist here, with 'remission of sins' considered as a *degree* in the process of
sanctification. Since 1738, certainly, Wesley had not linked justification and pardon so
directly to sanctification as he does here.

all of you, who never were thus 'enlightened' with the light of the
glory of God; all who never did 'taste of the heavenly gift', who
never received remission of sins; all who never 'were made
partakers of the Holy Ghost', of the witness and fruit of the
Spirit—in a word, all you who never were *sanctified* by the blood of 5
the everlasting covenant[47]—you are not concerned here.
Whatever other passages of Scripture may condemn you, it is
certain you are not condemned either by the sixth or the tenth of
the Hebrews. For both those passages speak wholly and solely of
apostates from the faith which you never had. Therefore it was 10
not possible that you should lose it, for you could not lose what
you had not. Therefore whatever judgments are denounced in
these Scriptures, they are not denounced against *you*. You are not
the persons here described, against whom only they are
denounced.   15

(4). Inquire we next, What was the sin which the persons here
described were guilty of? In order to understand this, we should
remember that whenever the Jews prevailed on a Christian to
apostatize, they required him to declare in express terms, and that
in the public assembly, that Jesus of Nazareth was an impostor; 20
that he was a deceiver of the people; and that he had suffered no
more punishment than his crimes justly deserved. This is the sin
which St. Paul in the first passage terms emphatically 'falling
away; crucifying the Son of God afresh, and putting him to an
open shame'. This is that which he terms in the second, 'counting 25
the blood of the covenant an unholy thing, treading under foot the
Son of God, and doing despite to the Spirit of grace'. Now which
of you has thus 'fallen away'? Which of you has thus 'crucified the
Son of God afresh'? Not one; nor has one of you thus 'put him to
an open shame'. If you had thus formally renounced that only 30
'sacrifice for sin', there had 'no other sacrifice remained'; so that
you must have perished without mercy. But this is not your case.
Not one of you has thus renounced that sacrifice by which the
Son of God made a full and perfect satisfaction for the sins of the
whole world.[48] Bad as you are, you shudder at the thought; 35
therefore that *sacrifice* still remains for you. Come then, cast away
your needless fears! 'Come boldly to the throne of grace.'[49] The

[47] Heb. 13:20.
[48] BCP, Communion, 'The Prayer of Consecration'.
[49] Heb. 4:16.

way is still open. You shall again 'find mercy and grace to help in time of need'.[50]

(5). i. 'But do not the well-known words of our Lord himself cut us off from all hope of mercy? Does he not say: "All manner of
5 sin and blasphemy shall be forgiven unto men: but the blasphemy against the Holy Ghost shall not be forgiven unto men. And whosoever speaketh a word against the Son of Man, it shall be forgiven him. But whosoever speaketh a word against the Holy Ghost, it shall never be forgiven him, neither in this world, nor in
10 the world to come." Therefore it is plain, if we have been guilty of this sin, there is no room for mercy. And is not the same thing repeated by St. Mark, almost in the same words? "Verily I say unto you" (a solemn preface, always denoting the great importance of that which follows), "all sins shall be forgiven unto
15 the sons of men, and blasphemies wherewith soever they shall blaspheme: but he that shall blaspheme against the Holy Ghost hath never forgiveness, but is under the sentence of eternal damnation."'

ii. How immense is the number in every nation throughout the
20 Christian world of those who have been more or less distressed on account of this Scripture! What multitudes in this kingdom have been perplexed above measure upon this very account! Nay, there are few that are truly convinced of sin, and seriously endeavour to save their souls, who have not felt some uneasiness,
25 for fear they had committed or should commit this unpardonable sin. What has frequently increased their uneasiness was that they could hardly find any to comfort them. For their acquaintances, even the most religious of them, understood no more of the matter than themselves. And they could not find any writer who
30 had published anything satisfactory upon the subject. Indeed in the *Seven Sermons* of Mr. Russell,[51] which are common among us, there is one expressly written upon it. But it will give little

---

[50] *Ibid.*

[51] This was Robert Russell, a seventeenth-century Baptist preacher at Wadhurst in Sussex. His sermon, *Of the Unpardonable Sin Against the Holy Ghost, or the Sin Unto Death* (on 1 John 5:16), had first been published, separately, in 1692. It had then been included as 'Sermon I' in *Seven Sermons* (the earliest edition which I have seen is the thirteenth, dated 1705); Wesley records having read it on Sept. 18, 1725. That these *Seven Sermons* were indeed still 'common among us' (in 1778) is suggested by the fact that their fiftieth edition is dated 1774. Wesley's disparaging remarks about such a familiar and popular sermon are puzzling; as a matter of fact, Russell's arguments and conclusions are reasonably close to Wesley's own, and there must have been some of Wesley's readers who would have known this.

satisfaction to a troubled spirit. He talks 'about it and about it',[52] but makes nothing out. He takes much pains, but misses the mark at last.

(6). But was there ever in the world a more deplorable proof of the littleness of human understanding, even in those that have 5 honest hearts, and are desirous of knowing the truth? How is it possible that anyone who reads his Bible can one hour remain in doubt concerning it, when our Lord himself, in the very passage cited above, has so clearly told us what that blasphemy is? 'He that blasphemeth against the Holy Ghost, hath never forgiveness; 10 because they said, He hath an unclean spirit.'[f] This then, and this alone (if we allow our Lord to understand his own meaning), is the blasphemy against the Holy Ghost: 'the saying he had an unclean spirit'; the affirming that Christ wrought his miracles by the power of an evil spirit; or, more particularly, that 'he cast out 15 devils by Beelzebub, the prince of the devils.'[53] Now have *you* been guilty of this? Have *you* affirmed that he cast out devils by the prince of devils? No more than you have cut your neighbour's throat, and set his house on fire. How marvellously then have you been afraid, where no fear is? Dismiss that vain terror; let your 20 fear be more rational for the time to come. Be afraid of giving way to pride, be afraid of yielding to anger, be afraid of loving the world or the things of the world, be afraid of foolish and hurtful desires. But never more be afraid of committing the blasphemy against the Holy Ghost! You are in no more danger of doing this 25 than of pulling the sun out of the firmament.

3. (1). Ye have then no reason from Scripture for imagining that 'the Lord hath forgotten to be gracious.'[54] The arguments drawn from thence, you see, are of no weight, are utterly inconclusive. Is there any more weight in that which has been 30 drawn from experience or matter of fact?[55]

[f] [Mark 3:] ver. 29-30.

---

[52] Cf. Pope, *Dunciad*, IV.251-52:

> For thee explain a thing till all men doubt it,
> And write about it, goddess, and about it.

See also John Byrom, 'Verses Contributed to the *Chester Courant*', No. XII, in *The Poems of John Byrom* (1894), I.310: 'He writes about it, and about it writes.' Cf. also JWJ, Mar. 13, 1747.

[53] Cf. Luke 11:15.   [54] Cf. Ps. 77:9.

[55] See I.3, above.

(2). This is a point which may exactly be determined; and that with the utmost certainty. If it be asked, 'Do any real apostates find mercy from God? Do any that "have made shipwreck of faith and a good conscience",[56] recover what they have lost? Do you
5 know, have you seen any instance, of persons who found redemption in the blood of Jesus, and afterwards fell away, and yet were restored? "Renewed again to repentance"?' Yea, verily. And not one, or an hundred only; but, I am persuaded, several thousands. In every place where the arm of the Lord has been
10 revealed,[57] and many sinners converted to God, there are several found who 'turn back from the holy commandment delivered to them'. For a great part of these 'it had been better never to have known the way of righteousness.'[58] It only increases their damnation, seeing they die in their sins. But others there are who
15 'look unto him whom they have pierced, and mourn',[59] refusing to be comforted. And sooner or later he surely lifts up the light of his countenance upon them.[60] He strengthens the hands that hung down, and confirms the feeble knees.[61] He teaches them again to say, 'My soul doth magnify the Lord, and my spirit rejoiceth in
20 God my Saviour.'[62] Innumerable are the instances of this kind, of those who had fallen but now stand upright. Indeed it is so far from being an uncommon thing for a believer to fall and be restored, that it is rather uncommon to find any believers who are not conscious of having been backsliders from God, in an higher
25 or lower degree, and perhaps more than once, before they were established in faith.

(3). 'But have any that had fallen from sanctifying grace[63] been restored to the blessing they had lost?' This also is a point of experience; and we have had the opportunity of repeating our
30 observations during a considerable course of years, and from the one end of the kingdom to the other.

(4). And, first, we have known a large number of persons, of every age and sex, from early childhood to extreme old age, who have given all the proofs which the nature of the thing admits that
35 they were 'sanctified throughout',[64] 'cleansed from all pollution

---

[56] Cf. 1 Tim. 1:19.
[58] Cf. 2 Pet. 2:21.
[60] See Ps. 4:6 (AV).
[61] See Isa. 35:3.
[62] Luke 1:46-47.
[63] See Gal. 5:4.
[64] Cf. 1 Thess. 5:23 (*Notes*).

[57] Isa. 53:1; John 12:38.
[59] Cf. Zech. 12:10.

both of flesh and spirit';[65] that they 'loved the Lord their God with all their heart, and mind, and soul, and strength';[66] that they continually presented their souls and bodies 'a living sacrifice, holy, acceptable to God':[67] in consequence of which they 'rejoiced evermore, prayed without ceasing, and in everything gave 5 thanks'.[68] And this, and no other, is what we believe to be true, scriptural sanctification.

(5). Secondly, it is a common thing for those who are thus sanctified to believe they cannot fall; to suppose *themselves* 'pillars in the temple of God, that shall go out no more'.[69] Nevertheless 10 we have seen some of the strongest of them after a time moved from their steadfastness. Sometimes suddenly, but oftener by slow degrees, they have yielded to temptation; and pride, or anger, or foolish desires have again sprung up in their hearts. Nay, sometimes they have utterly lost the life of God, and sin hath 15 regained dominion over them.

(6). Yet, thirdly, several of these, after being thoroughly sensible of their fall, and deeply ashamed before God, have been again filled with his love, and not only 'perfected' therein, but 'stablished, strengthened, and settled'.[70] They have received the 20 blessing they had before, with abundant increase. Nay, it is remarkable that many who had fallen either from justifying or from sanctifying grace, and so deeply fallen that they could hardly be ranked among the servants of God, have been restored (but seldom till they had been shaken, as it were, over the mouth of 25 hell), and that very frequently in an instant, to all that they had lost. They have at once recovered both a consciousness of his favour and the experience of the pure love of God. In one moment they received anew both remission of sins and a lot among them that were sanctified. 30

(7). But let not any man infer from this long-suffering of God that he hath given anyone a licence to sin. Neither let any dare to continue in sin because of these extraordinary instances of divine mercy. This is the most desperate, the most irrational presumption, and leads to utter, irrecoverable destruction. In all 35 my experience I have not known one who fortified himself in sin by a presumption that God would save him at the last, that was not

[65] 2 Cor. 7:1 (*Notes*).   [66] Cf. Mark 12:30.
[67] Rom. 12:1.   [68] Cf. 1 Thess. 5:16-18.
[69] Cf. Rev. 3:12.
[70] Cf. 1 Pet. 5:10.

miserably disappointed, and suffered to die in his sins.[71] To turn the grace of God into an encouragement to sin is the sure way to the nethermost hell.

(8). It is not for these desperate children of perdition that the preceding considerations are designed, but for those who feel 'the remembrance of our sins is grievous unto us, the burden of them is intolerable.'[72] We set before these an open door of hope: let them go in, and give thanks unto the Lord.[73] Let them know that 'the Lord is gracious and merciful, long-suffering and of great goodness.'[74] 'Look how high the heavens are from the earth! So far will he set their sins from them.'[75] 'He will not always be chiding; neither keepeth he his anger for ever.'[76] Only settle it in your heart, 'I will give all for all,' and the offering shall be accepted. Give him all your heart! Let all that is within you continually cry out, 'Thou art my God, and I will thank thee: thou art my God, and I will praise thee.'[77] 'This God is my God for ever and ever. He shall be my guide even unto death.'[78]

Sligo, May 20, 1778[79]

---

[71] Another echo of Benjamin Calamy's warning (itself an Anglican commonplace) against deathbed repentance; cf. No. 29, 'Sermon on the Mount, IX', §25 and n.
[72] Cf. BCP, Communion, Confession.
[73] See Ps. 118:19.
[74] Ps. 145:8 (BCP).
[75] Cf. Ps. 103:11 (BCP).
[76] Ps. 103:9 (BCP).
[77] Ps. 118:28 (BCP).
[78] Cf. Ps. 48:14 (AV).
[79] Place and date as in *AM*.

THE DANGER OF RICHES

AN INTRODUCTORY COMMENT

Wesley's followers were intensely loyal and, by and large, obedient. They revered him as founder, patriarch, even as cult-hero. They had responded to his gospel of salvation by faith; they had accepted most of his demands for disciplined Christian living (good works as the fruit and proof of faith). Moreover, given his stress on a self-denying moral rigorism, together with the general economic expansion in the Hanoverian era, it was natural enough that more than a few Methodists moved upward on the economic scale from erstwhile poverty toward modest affluence. In such a setting Wesley's first two rules about 'The Use of Money' ('gaining' and 'saving') made eminently good sense.

It was the third rule against surplus accumulation ('giving') that made for trouble. Many, if not most, of the newly rich Methodists were stubbornly, though quietly, unconvinced that their affluence, in and of itself, was a fatal inlet to sin. Thus it was that they simply ignored Wesley's insistence that they part with all but their 'necessaries and conveniences'. Moreover, their views had lately been fortified by the immense influence of Adam Smith's Wealth of Nations *(1776). This turn of events was, for Wesley, both perplexing and frustrating.*

Something of this mood is suggested by the fact that the very first 'original sermon' published in the Arminian Magazine *is this one ('Sermon I'). It had been written in the late autumn of 1780 and appeared in the January and February instalments of Vol. IV (1781), pp. 15-23, 73-81, without a title. That was subsequently added when he included it in* SOSO, VII. 139-66. *On April 16, 1783, in Dublin, he preached from the same text. In 1788, he wrote and published yet another sermon, 'On Riches' (see No. 108). Then, in the very last year of his life, he wrote out yet another anguished warning on, 'The Danger of Increasing Riches' (see No. 131). If this trio of 'late sermons' is added to Nos. 28, 'Sermon on the Mount, VIII'; 50, 'The Use of Money'; and 51,* The Good Steward; *and if these are then placed alongside the other frequent blasts against riches in other sermons and other writings, an interesting generalization suggests itself: surplus accumulation leads Wesley's inventory of sins in praxis. It was, in his eyes, an offence before*

God and man, an urgent and dire peril to any Christian's profession and hope of salvation. This is in clear contrast to the notion, proffered by the Puritans, but approved by others, that honestly earned wealth is a sign and measure of divine favour. What is interesting is that Wesley's economic radicalism on this point has been ignored, not only by most Methodists, but by the economic historians as well.

The Danger of Riches

1 Timothy 6:9

They that will be rich fall into temptation and a snare, and into many foolish and hurtful desires, which drown men in destruction and perdition.

1. How innumerable are the ill consequences which have followed from men's not knowing or not considering this great truth! And how few are there even in the Christian world that either know or duly consider it! Yea, how small is the number of
10 those, even among real Christians, who understand and lay it to heart! Most of these too pass it very lightly over, scarce remembering there is such a text in the Bible. And many put such a construction upon it as makes it of no manner of effect. '"They that will be rich"', say they, 'that is, will be rich at all events, who
15 will be rich right or wrong, that are resolved to carry their point, to compass this end, whatever means they use to attain it—"they fall into temptation," and into all the evils enumerated by the Apostle.' But truly if this were all the meaning of the text it might as well have been out of the Bible.
20   2. This is so far from being the whole meaning of the text that it is no part of its meaning. The Apostle does not here speak of gaining riches unjustly, but of quite another thing: his words are to be taken in their plain, obvious sense, without any restriction or qualification whatsoever.[1] St. Paul does not say, 'They that will be
25 rich *by evil means*', by theft, robbery, oppression, or extortion; they

---

[1] Another affirmation of the principle of literal interpretation; cf. No. 21, 'Sermon on the Mount, I', §6 and n.

that will be rich by fraud, or dishonest art; but simply, 'they that will be rich'; these, allowing, supposing the means they use to be ever so innocent, 'fall into temptation, and a snare, and into many foolish and hurtful desires, which drown men in destruction and perdition.'   5

3. But who believes that? Who receives it as the truth of God? Who is deeply convinced of it? Who preaches this? Great is the company of preachers at this day, regular and irregular. But who of them all openly and explicitly preaches this strange doctrine? It is the keen observation of a great man, 'The pulpit is a fearful   10 preacher's stronghold.'[2] But who, even in his stronghold, has the courage to declare so unfashionable a truth? I do not remember that in threescore years I have heard one sermon preached upon this subject. And what author within the same term has declared it from the press? At least in the English tongue? I do not know   15 one. I have neither seen nor heard of any such author.[3] I have seen two or three who just touch upon it, but none that treats of it professedly. I have myself frequently touched upon it in preaching, and twice in what I have published to the world: once in explaining our Lord's Sermon on the Mount, and once in the   20 discourse on the 'mammon of unrighteousness'.[4] But I have never yet either published or preached any sermon expressly upon the subject. It is high time I should, that I should at length speak as strongly and explicitly as I can, in order to leave a full and clear testimony behind me whenever it pleases God to call me hence.   25

---

[2] Cf. A. H. Francke, *Nicodemus: Or, A Treatise Against the Fear of Man* (1706). No. 19 among Francke's list of seventy-four 'signs and effects' of 'the fear of man' reads: 'The pulpit is a fearful preacher's stronghold and castle; but when he has to speak face to face and bear witness to the truth, then he is very supple and complaisant.' Cf. No. 14, *The Repentance of Believers*, I.7 and n.

[3] It is not easy to understand here why Wesley ignores a series of condemnations of riches in the literature that he almost certainly had seen. For example, there were Bishop Joseph Hall's complaints in his *Meditations and Vows*, XIV ('Century II'), in his *Select Works* (London, 1811), III.28. Or what of the even more vivid denunciations in Simon Patrick, *Fifteen Sermons Upon Contentment and Resignation to the Will of God* (1729)? In his Preface to *SOSO*, V (1788), Wesley praises 'Dr. [William] Bates'; but what of Bates's series of sermons, all on Prov. 1:32, under the general title, 'The Dangers of Prosperity', in *Whole Works* (1st edn., 1700; (1815), Vol. II? He knew and might have cited John Tillotson's four sermons on 'Covetousness' (Sermons XXXVI-XXXIX), in *Works* (1722), I.253-74, where Tillotson defines and denounces riches in similar terms to those of Hall, Bates, South—and Wesley. One might guess that what Wesley has in mind here was the huge popularity of Adam Smith's case for economic self-interest and the lack of an adequate current critique from clergy and other opinion-makers.

[4] I.e., Nos. 28, 'Sermon on the Mount, VIII', §§9-28 (and n.); and 50, 'The Use of Money', II.2-8, III.3-7; see also No. 122, 'Causes of the Inefficacy of Christianity', §8.

4. O that God would give me to speak *right* and *forcible* words! And you to receive them in honest and humble hearts! Let it not be said: 'They sit before thee as my people, and they hear thy words; but they will not do them. Thou art unto them as one that
5 hath a pleasant voice, and can play well on an instrument; for they hear thy words, but they do them not!'[5] O that ye may 'not be forgetful hearers, but doers of the word, that ye may be blessed in your deed'![6] In this hope I shall endeavour:

First, to explain the Apostle's words. And,
10 Secondly, to apply them.

But Oh! 'Who is sufficient for these things?'[7] Who is able to stem the general torrent? To combat all the prejudices, not only of the vulgar, but of the learned and the religious world? Yet nothing is too hard for God! Still his grace is sufficient for us.[8] In his
15 name, then, and by his strength I will endeavour,

I. To explain the words of the Apostle.

1. And, first, let us consider what it is to 'be rich'. What does the Apostle mean by this expression?

The preceding verse fixes the meaning of this: 'Having food
20 and raiment' (literally 'coverings', for the word includes *lodging* as well as *clothes*) 'let us be therewith content.[9] But they that will be rich . . . '—that is, who will have more than these, more than 'food and coverings'. It plainly follows, whatever is more than these is, in the sense of the Apostle, *riches*—whatever is above the
25 plain necessaries or (at most) conveniences of life. Whoever has sufficient food to eat and raiment to put on, with a place where to lay his head, and something over, is *rich*.[10]

2. Let us consider, secondly, what is implied in that expression, 'they that will be rich'. And does not this imply, first, 'they that
30 desire to be rich', to have more than 'food and coverings'; they that seriously and deliberately desire more than food to eat and

---

[5] Ezek. 33:31-32.
[6] Cf. Jas. 1:25.
[7] 2 Cor. 2:16.
[8] See 2 Cor. 12:9.
[9] See 1 Tim. 6:8 (*Notes;* 'coverings, that is, raiment and a house to cover us'); but cf. Arndt and Gingrich, *Greek-English Lexicon* (σκεπάσματα): 'chiefly clothing but also house (as in Aristotle, *Metaphysics*, 7, etc.)'.
[10] A leaner definition of riches than Tillotson's or Hall's but one which Wesley uses consistently, early and late; cf. below, II.3; also Nos. 50, 'The Use of Money', intro.; 28, 'Sermon on the Mount, VIII', §§11-12; 108, 'On Riches', §4; 115, 'Dives and Lazarus', II.1; and 131, 'The Danger of Increasing Riches', I.1.

raiment to put on, and a place where to lay their head; more than the plain necessaries and conveniences of life? All, at least, who allow themselves in this desire, who see no harm in it, 'desire to be rich'.

3. And so do, secondly, all those that calmly, deliberately, and 5 of set purpose *endeavour* after more than 'food and coverings'; that aim at and endeavour after, not only so much worldly substance as will procure them the necessaries and conveniences of life,[11] but more than this, whether to lay it up, or lay it out in superfluities. All these undeniably prove their 'desire to be rich' 10 by their endeavours after it.

4. Must we not, thirdly, rank among those 'that desire to be rich' all that in fact 'lay up treasures on earth'[12]—a thing as expressly and clearly forbidden by our Lord as either adultery or murder. It is allowed, (1), that we are to provide necessaries and 15 conveniences for those of our own household; (2), that men in business are to lay up as much as is necessary for the carrying on of that business; (3), that we are to leave our children what will supply them with necessaries and conveniences after we have left the world; and (4), that we are to provide things honest in the sight 20 of all men, so as to 'owe no man anything'.[13] But to lay up any more, when this is done, is what our Lord has flatly forbidden. When it is calmly and deliberately done, it is a clear proof of our desiring to be rich. And thus to lay up money is no more consistent with good conscience than to throw it into the sea.[14] 25

5. We must rank among them, fourthly, all who *possess* more of this world's goods than they use according to the will of the Donor—I should rather say of the Proprietor, for he only *lends* them to us; or, to speak more strictly, *entrusts* them to us as stewards, reserving the property of them to himself. And indeed 30 he cannot possibly do otherwise, seeing they are the work of his hands; he is and must be the Possessor of heaven and earth.[15] This is his inalienable right, a right he cannot divest himself of. And together with that portion of his goods which he hath lodged in our hands he has delivered to us a writing, specifying the 35 purposes for which he has entrusted us with them. If therefore we

---

[11] Cf. No. 30, 'Sermon on the Mount, X', §26 and n.
[12] Cf. Matt. 6:19.   [13] Rom. 13:8.
[14] An echo of Horace, *Odes*, III.xxiv.47: '*In mare proximum . . .*'; cf. No. 50, 'The Use of Money', §2 and n.
[15] Gen. 14:19, 22.

keep more of them in our hands than is necessary for the preceding purposes, we certainly fall under the charge of 'desiring to be rich'. Over and above that we are guilty of burying our Lord's talent in the earth, and on that account are liable to be
5 pronounced 'wicked', because 'unprofitable servants'.[16]

6. Under this imputation of 'desiring to be rich' fall, fifthly, all 'lovers of money'.[17] The word properly means those that *delight in money*, those that take pleasure in it, those that seek their happiness therein, that brood over their gold and silver, bills or
10 bonds. Such was the man described by the fine Roman painter, who broke out into that natural soliloquy,

> . . . *Populus me sibilat, at mihi plaudo*
> *Ipse domi quoties nummos contemplor in arca.*[18]

15   If there are any vices which are not natural to man, I should imagine this is one; as money of itself does not seem to gratify any natural desire or appetite of the human mind; and as, during an observation of sixty years, I do not remember one instance of a man given up to the love of money till he had neglected to employ
20 this precious talent according to the will of his master. After this, sin was punished by sin, and this evil spirit was permitted to enter into him.

7. But beside this gross sort of covetousness, 'the love of money',[19] there is a more refined species of covetousness, termed
25 by the great Apostle, πλεονεξία,[20] which literally means 'a desire of having more'—more than we have already. And those also

---

[16] Matt. 25:26, 30.   [17] 2 Tim. 3:2 (*Notes*).
[18] Cf. Horace, *Satires*, I.i.66-67:

> . . . *populus me sibilat, at mihi plaudo*
> *ipse domi, simul ac nummos contemplor in arca.*

The people hiss, but at home I congratulate myself even as I gaze on the moneys in my treasure chest.

In No. 84, *The Important Question*, III.10, Wesley had cited this same passage and more. This favourable reference to Horace as 'the fine Roman painter' connotes the vividness of his *language;* it is unusual for Wesley and reflects his strong feelings here. But he had many precedents for such an estimate, as in Abraham Cowley, 'Ode Upon Occasion of a Copy of Verses of My Lord Broghill's', *Works* (11th edn., 1710), II.547; Philip Dormer Stanhope, Earl of Chesterfield, Letter XLIV (written between Aug. 14–Oct. 20, 1740), *Letters . . . to His Son* (London, 1774), I.112; William Warburton, *Works*, VIII.299, 301; and William Law, *An Humble, Earnest, and Affectionate Address to the Clergy* (1761), in *Works*, IX.53.
[19] 1 Tim. 6:10.
[20] Rom. 1:29; but see also 2 Cor. 9:5; Eph. 4:19; 5:3; Col. 3:5 (*Notes*).

come under the denomination of 'they that will be rich'. It is true that this desire, under proper restrictions, is innocent; nay, commendable. But when it exceeds the bounds (and how difficult is it not to exceed them!) then it comes under the present censure.

8. But who is able to receive these hard sayings? Who can 5 believe that they are the great truths of God? Not many wise, not many noble,[21] not many famed for learning; none indeed who are not taught of God. And who are they whom God teaches? Let our Lord answer: 'If any man be willing to do his will, he shall know of the doctrine whether it be of God.'[22] Those who are otherwise 10 minded will be so far from receiving it that they will not be able to understand it. Two as sensible men as most in England sat down together, some time since, to read over and consider that plain discourse on, 'Lay not up for yourselves treasures upon earth.'[23] After much deep consideration one of them broke out: 15 'Positively, I cannot understand it. Pray, do *you* understand it, Mr. L.?' Mr. L. honestly replied: 'Indeed, not I. I cannot conceive what Mr. W[esley] means. I can make nothing at all of it.' So utterly blind is our natural understanding touching the truth of God!

9. Having explained the former part of the text, 'they that will 20 be rich', and pointed out in the clearest manner I could the persons spoken of, I will now endeavour, God being my helper, to explain what is spoken of them: 'They fall into temptation, and a snare, and into many foolish and hurtful desires, which drown men in destruction and perdition.' 25

'They fall into temptation.' This seems to mean much more than simply, 'they are tempted.' They 'enter into the temptation':[24] they fall plump down[25] into it. The waves of it compass them about, and cover them all over. Of those who thus enter into temptation very few escape out of it. And the few that do are 30 sorely scorched by it, though not utterly consumed. If they escape at all it is with the skin of their teeth,[26] and with deep wounds that are not easily healed.

10. They fall, secondly, 'into a snare', the snare of the devil,[27]

---

[21] 1 Cor. 1:26.
[22] John 7:17 (*Notes*).
[23] I.e., No. 28, 'Sermon on the Mount, VIII', on Matt. 6:19-23.
[24] Cf. Mark 14:38, etc.
[25] Cf. Johnson, *Dictionary:* 'to fall like a stone into the water'.
[26] Job 19:20.
[27] 1 Tim 3:7; 2 Tim. 2:26.

which he hath purposely set in their way. I believe the Greek word[28] properly means a gin, a steel trap,[29] which shows no appearance of danger. But as soon as any creature touches the spring it suddenly closes, and either crushes its bones in pieces or 5 consigns it to inevitable ruin.

11. They fall, thirdly, 'into many foolish and hurtful desires': ἀνοήτους, silly, senseless, fantastic; as contrary to reason, to sound understanding, as they are to religion; 'hurtful', both to body and soul, tending to weaken, yea, destroy every gracious and 10 heavenly temper; destructive of that faith which is of the operation of God; of that hope which is full of immortality;[30] of love to God and to our neighbour, and of every good word and work.[31]

12. But what desires are these? This is a most important 15 question, and deserves the deepest consideration.

In general they may all be summed up in one—the desiring happiness out of God.[32] This includes, directly or remotely, every foolish and hurtful desire. St. Paul expresses it by 'loving the creature more than the Creator';[33] and by being 'lovers of 20 pleasure more than lovers of God'.[34] In particular they are (to use the exact and beautiful enumeration of St. John) 'the desire of the flesh, the desire of the eyes, and the pride of life':[35] all of which 'the desire of riches' naturally tends both to beget and to increase.

13. 'The desire of the flesh' is generally understood in far too 25 narrow a meaning. It does not, as is commonly supposed, refer to one of the senses only, but takes in all the pleasures of sense, the gratification of any of the outward senses. It has reference to the *taste* in particular. How many thousands do we find at this day in whom the ruling principle is the desire to enlarge the pleasure of 30 *tasting*?[36] Perhaps they do not gratify this desire in a gross manner, so as to incur the imputation of intemperance; much less so as to

---

[28] παγίς: 'trap, snare', as in Rom. 11:9; 1 Tim. 3:7; 6:9; 2 Tim. 2:26. The Vulgate reads *laqueus*, which also means 'fetters' or 'chains'. Cf. *Notes;* also Nos. 131, 'The Danger of Increasing Riches', II.16; and 24, 'Sermon on the Mount, IV', §4, proem.

[29] An example not noted in *OED;* Wesley hyphenated the word.

[30] See Wisd. 3:4. Cf. below, II.12; also No. 72, 'Of Evil Angels', II.4 and n.

[31] 2 Thess. 2:17.

[32] The shadow side of Wesley's eudaemonism; cf. No. 6, 'The Righteousness of Faith', II.9 and n.

[33] Rom. 1:25.

[34] 2 Tim. 3:4.

[35] 1 John 2:16; cf. No. 7, 'The Way to the Kingdom', II.2 and n.

[36] Here following William Law again; cf. No. 50, 'The Use of Money', II.2 and n.

violate health or impair their understanding by gluttony or drunkenness. But they live in a genteel, regular sensuality; in an elegant epicurism,[37] which does not hurt the body, but only destroys the soul, keeping it at a distance from all true religion.

14. Experience shows that the imagination is gratified chiefly by means of the eye. Therefore 'the desire of the eyes', in its natural sense, is the desiring and seeking happiness in gratifying the imagination. Now the imagination is gratified either by grandeur, by beauty, or by novelty—chiefly by the last, for neither grand nor beautiful objects please any longer than they are new.

15. Seeking happiness in *learning*, of whatever kind, falls under 'the desire of the eyes'; whether it be in history, languages, poetry, or any branch of natural or experimental philosophy; yea, we must include the several kinds of learning, such as geometry, algebra, and metaphysics. For if our supreme delight be in any of these, we are herein gratifying 'the desire of the eyes'.

16. 'The pride of life' (whatever else that very uncommon expression ἡ ἀλαζονεία τοῦ βίου may mean)[38] seems to imply chiefly the *desire of honour*, of the esteem, admiration, and applause of men; as nothing more directly tends both to beget and cherish pride than the honour that cometh of men. And as *riches* attract much admiration, and occasion much applause, they proportionably minister food for pride, and so may also be referred to this head.

17. *Desire of ease* is another of these foolish and hurtful desires; desire of avoiding every cross, every degree of trouble, danger, difficulty; a desire of slumbering out of life, and going to heaven (as the vulgar say) upon a feather-bed.[39] Everyone may observe how riches first beget and then confirm and increase this desire, making men more and more soft and delicate, more unwilling, and indeed more unable, to 'take up' their 'cross daily',[40] to 'endure hardship as good soldiers of Jesus Christ',[41] 'and to take the kingdom of heaven by violence'.[42]

---

[37] Cf. No. 9, 'The Spirit of Bondage and of Adoption', I.2 and n.

[38] It must have sounded 'uncommon' indeed in Wesley's ears because ἀλαζονεία in classical Greek commonly means 'false pretension', 'imposture', etc. (cf. Liddell and Scott, *Greek-English Lexicon*); cf. also No. 14, *The Repentance of Believers*, I.7 and n.

[39] See Sir Thomas More (quoted as from Nicholas Harpsfield's *Life* . . . , p. 75, in *The Oxford Dictionary of English Proverbs*): 'We may not look . . . to go to heaven in feather-beds.' Cf. Isaac Watts, 'Must I be carried to the skies on flowery beds of ease . . .', in 'A Hymn for Sermon XXXI', in *Works*, I.341.

[40] Cf. Luke 9:23.   [41] Cf. 2 Tim. 2:3.   [42] Cf. Matt. 11:12.

18. Riches, either desired or possessed, naturally lead to some or other of these foolish and hurtful desires; and by affording the means of gratifying them all, naturally tend to increase them. And there is a near connection between unholy desires and every other unholy passion and temper. We easily pass from these to pride, anger, bitterness, envy, malice, revengefulness; to an headstrong, unadvisable, unreprovable spirit—indeed to every temper that is earthly, sensual, or devilish.[43] All these the desire or possession of riches naturally tends to create, strengthen, and increase.

19. And by so doing, in the same proportion as they prevail, they 'pierce men through with many sorrows';[44] sorrows from remorse, from a guilty conscience; sorrows flowing from all the evil tempers which they inspire or increase; sorrows inseparable from those desires themselves, as every unholy desire is an uneasy desire; and sorrows from the contrariety of those desires to each other, whence it is impossible to gratify them all. And in the end 'they drown' the body in pain, disease, 'destruction', and the soul in everlasting 'perdition'.

II. 1. I am, in the second place, to apply what has been said. And this is the principal point. For what avails the clearest knowledge, even of the most excellent things, even of the things of God, if it go no farther than speculation, if it be not reduced to practice? He that hath ears to hear, let him hear![45] And what he hears, let him instantly put in practice. O that God would give me the thing which I long for—that before I go hence and am no more seen,[46] I may see a people wholly devoted to God, crucified to the world, and the world crucified to them![47] A people truly given up to God, in body, soul, and substance! How cheerfully should I then say, 'Now lettest thou thy servant depart in peace!'[48]

2. I ask, then, in the name of God, who of *you* 'desire to be rich'? Which of *you* (ask your own hearts in the sight of God) seriously and deliberately desire (and perhaps applaud yourselves for so doing, as no small instance of your *prudence*) to have more than food to eat, and raiment to put on, and a house to cover you? Who of you desires to have more than the plain necessaries and conveniences of life? Stop! Consider! What are you doing? Evil is

---

[43] See Jas. 3:15.   [44] Cf. 1 Tim. 6:10.
[45] Matt. 11:15, etc.   [46] Ps. 39:15 (BCP).
[47] See Gal. 6:14.
[48] Luke 2:29.

before you! Will you rush upon the point of a sword? By the grace of God, turn and live!

3. By the same authority I ask, who of you are *endeavouring* to be rich? To procure for yourselves more than the plain necessaries and conveniences of life?[49] Lay, each of you, your hand to your 5 heart, and seriously inquire, Am I of that number? Am I labouring, not only for what I want, but for more than I want? May the Spirit of God say to everyone whom it concerns, 'Thou art the man!'[50]

4. I ask, thirdly, who of you are in fact 'laying up for yourselves 10 treasures upon earth'?[51] Increasing in goods? Adding, as fast as you can, house to house, and field to field?[52] 'As long as thou' thus 'dost well unto thyself, men will speak good of thee.'[53] They will call thee a 'wise', a 'prudent' man! A man that 'minds the main chance'.[54] Such is, and always has been, the wisdom of the world. 15 'But God saith unto' thee, 'Thou fool!'[55] Art thou not 'treasuring up to thyself wrath against the day of wrath', and 'revelation of the righteous judgment of God'?[56]

5. Perhaps you will ask, 'But do not you yourself advise, To gain all we can, and to save all we can?[57] And is it possible to do 20 this without both "desiring" and "endeavouring to be rich"? Nay, suppose our endeavours are successful, without actually "laying up treasures upon earth"?'

I answer, it is possible. You may gain all you can without hurting either your soul or body; you may save all you can, by 25 carefully avoiding every needless expense, and yet never 'lay up treasures on earth', nor either desire or endeavour so to do.

6. Permit me to speak as freely of myself as I would of another man. I 'gain all I can' (namely, by writing) without hurting either

---

[49] Cf. above, I.3; see also, No. 30, 'Sermon on the Mount, X', §26 and n.
[50] 2 Sam. 12:7.
[51] Cf. Matt. 6:19.
[52] Cf. Isa. 5:8.
[53] Ps. 49:18 (BCP).
[54] A proverbial motto for self-serving, running back at least to Persius, *Satires*, vi.158 (in Dryden's translation, 'Be careful still of the main chance, my son'). But see also John Lyly, *Euphues* (1579; Arbor's Reprint, p. 104): 'Lette mee stande to thee maine chaunce'; Samuel Butler, *Hudibras*, Pt. II, Canto II, ll. 501-2 ('have a care of the main chance'); and John Tillotson, *Works*, I.293 ('secure the main chance'). Wesley uses the phrase in Nos. 90, 'An Israelite Indeed', I.1; and 95, 'On the Education of Children', §19.
[55] Luke 12:20.
[56] Cf. Rom. 2:5.
[57] See No. 50, 'The Use of Money', I.1 and n.; also II.1.

my soul or body. I 'save all I can', not willingly wasting anything, not a sheet of paper, not a cup of water. I do not lay out anything, not a shilling, unless as a sacrifice to God. Yet by 'giving all I can'[58] I am effectually secured from 'laying up treasures upon earth'.
5 Yea, and I am secured from either desiring or endeavouring it as long as I 'give all I can'. And that I do this I call all that know me, both friends and foes, to testify.

7. But some may say, 'Whether you endeavour it or no, you are undeniably *rich*. You have more than the necessaries of life.' I
10 have. But the Apostle does not fix the charge barely on *possessing* any quantity of goods, but on possessing more than we employ according to the will of the Donor.

Two and forty years ago, having a desire to furnish poor people with cheaper, shorter, and plainer books than any I had seen, I
15 wrote many small tracts, generally a penny apiece; and afterwards several larger. Some of these had such a sale as I never thought of; and by this means I unawares became rich.[59] But I never desired or endeavoured after it. And now that it is come upon me

[58] This, of course, is the third division of Wesley's sermon on 'The Use of Money', noted above.

[59] Tyerman (*JW*), III. 615-16, observes that Wesley was the 'proprietor of a large publishing and book concern from which he derived considerable profits . . . , but of these he literally spent none upon himself except for an occasional suit of clothes.' John Hampson, *Memoirs of the Late Rev. John Wesley* (1791), III.185-86, says that Wesley was 'Perhaps the most charitable man in England. His liberality to the poor knew no bounds. He gave away, not merely a certain part of his income, but all he had. We are persuaded, upon a moderate calculation, he gave away in about fifty years, twenty or thirty thousand pounds' (cf. also John Whitehead, *Life of John Wesley*, II. 481-82). Moore, *Wesley*, II. 433-34, raises that figure: '[Mr. Wesley's] accounts lie before me . . . and I am persuaded that Mr. Hampson might have increased the supposed sum to several thousands more.' Naturally enough, an income of this magnitude gave rise to numerous accusations of hypocrisy and worse. For example, in a letter of Sept. 3, 1756, to an unidentified man, Wesley refutes such a charge: '[You say that] I who have written so much against the hoarding up money have put out £700 to interest.' I never put sixpence out to interest since I was born; nor had I ever an hundred pounds together my own since I came into the world.' In June 1760, he rejects the assertion of one John Baily that he 'was as fond of riches as the most worldly clergyman.'

Actually, because of his indifference, the fiscal affairs of the movement and his publishing interests were chaotic; cf. JWJ, Sept. 8-9, 1756; Nov. 6, 1752; Aug. 21, 1773; Feb. 21, 1783; Jan. 1789; see also the letter to Robert Lindsay, Oct. 7, 1781. On July 16, 1790, he broke off his lifelong habit of keeping a monthly financial 'Account' with a characteristic comment: 'For upwards of eighty-six years I have kept my accounts exactly. I will not attempt it any longer, being satisfied with the continual conviction that I save all I can, and give all I can, that is, all I have.' Eighty-six years is either an exaggeration or else an inversion of 'sixty-eight', which would take us back to four years before his earliest recorded 'account', dated Sept. 1726. For more on Wesley's money matters, see Tyerman (*JW*), III.614-17.

unawares I lay up no treasures upon earth: I lay up nothing at all. My desire and endeavour in this respect is to 'wind my bottom round the year'.[60] I cannot help leaving my books behind me whenever God calls me hence. But in every other respect my own hands will be my executors.   5

8. Herein, my brethren, let you that are rich be even as I am. Do you that possess more than food and raiment ask: 'What shall we do? Shall we throw into the sea what God hath given us?'[61] God forbid that you should! It is an excellent talent: it may be employed much to the glory of God. Your way lies plain before 10 your face; if you have courage, walk in it. Having 'gained' (in a right sense) 'all you can', and 'saved all you can'; in spite of nature, and custom, and worldly prudence, 'give all you can'. I do not say, 'Be a good Jew,' giving a tenth of all you possess. I do not say, 'Be a good Pharisee,' giving a fifth of all your substance.[62] I 15 dare not advise you to give half of what you have; no, nor three-quarters—but all! Lift up your hearts and you will see clearly in what sense this is to be done.

If you desire to be a 'faithful and a wise steward',[63] out of that portion of your Lord's goods which he has for the present lodged in your hands, but with the 20 right of resumption whenever it pleaseth him, (1), provide things needful for yourself—food to eat, raiment to put on, whatever nature moderately requires for preserving you both in health and strength; (2), provide these for your wife, your children, your servants, or any others who pertain to your household. If when this is done there is an overplus left, then do good to 'them that are of the 25 household of faith'.[64] If there be an overplus still, 'as you have opportunity, do good unto all men'.[65] In so doing, you *give all you can;* nay, in a sound sense, all you have. For all that is laid out in this manner is really given to God. You render unto God the things that are God's,[66] not only by what you give to the poor, but

---

[60] Cf. Prior, 'An Epitaph', l. 48; see also No. 89, 'The More Excellent Way', VI.4, and Wesley's circular letter of June 20, 1766. *OED* defines the phrase as 'bringing an affair to a final settlement'. Wesley might have borrowed the expression from a sermon of his grandfather Annesley (and therefore before Prior); cf. his extract of 'On the Sovereignty of God', in the *Christian Lib.*, XLIV.303.

[61] Cf. No. 50, 'The Use of Money', §2.

[62] A reference to the rabbinical tradition of the '*two* tithes' which, between them, added up to 'a fifth'; cf. *Encyclopaedia Judaica, loc. cit.* (see also the tractates in the Mishnah: *Terumoth, Ma'aseroth,* and *Ma'aser Sheni*).

[63] Luke 12:42. For other comments on stewardship, see Nos. 88, 'On Dress', §17; 89, 'The More Excellent Way', VI (proem); and 131, 'The Danger of Increasing Riches', I.7.

[64] Gal. 6:10.

[65] *Ibid.*

[66] Matt. 22:21.

also by that which you expend in providing things needful for yourself and your household.[a]

9. O ye Methodists,[67] hear the word of the Lord! I have a message from God to all men; but to *you* above all. For above forty years I have been a servant to you and to your fathers. And I have not been as a reed shaken with the wind:[68] I have not varied in my testimony. I have testified to you the very same thing from the first day even until now. But 'who hath believed our report?'[69] I fear, not many rich. I fear there is need to apply to some of *you* those terrible words of the Apostle: 'Go to, now, ye rich men! Weep and howl for the miseries which shall come upon you. Your gold and silver is cankered, and the rust of them shall witness against you, and shall eat your flesh, as it were fire.'[70] Certainly it will, unless ye both save all you can and give all you can. But who of you hath considered this since you first heard the will of the Lord concerning it? Who is now determined to consider and practise it? By the grace of God begin today!

10. O ye 'lovers of money', hear the word of the Lord! Suppose ye that money, though multiplied as the sand of the sea, can give happiness? Then you are 'given up to a strong delusion, to believe a lie';[71] a palpable lie, confuted daily by a thousand experiments. Open your eyes! Look all around you! Are the richest men the happiest? Have those the largest share of content who have the largest possessions? Is not the very reverse true? Is it not a common observation that the richest of men are in general the most discontented, the most miserable? Had not the far greater part of them more content when they had less money? Look into your breasts. If you are increased in goods, are you proportionably increased in happiness? You have more substance; but have you more content? You know the contrary. You know that in seeking

---

[a] Works [1771], Vol. 4, p. 56 [i.e., No. 50 'The Use of Money', III.3, with minor rephrasings].

---

[67] Another use of the term 'Methodists' without some qualifier; this suggests extra emphasis, for §§9-16 constitute Wesley's most explicit and direct condemnation of Methodists for their involvement in the accumulation of capital. There is nothing to match this sort of thing in any other English preacher in the century. See also No. 50, 'The Use of Money', intro.

[68] Matt. 11:7.

[69] Isa. 53:1; John 12:38.

[70] Cf. Jas. 5:1, 3.

[71] Cf. 2 Thess. 2:11.

happiness from riches you are only striving to drink out of empty cups. And let them be painted and gilded ever so finely, they are empty still.

11. O ye that 'desire' or endeavour 'to be rich',[72] hear ye the word of the Lord! Why should ye be stricken any more? Will not even experience teach you wisdom? Will ye leap into a pit with your eyes open? Why should you any more 'fall into temptation'? It cannot be but temptation will beset you as long as you are in the body. But though it should beset you on every side, why will you *enter into* it? There is no necessity for this; it is your own voluntary act and deed. Why should you any more plunge yourselves 'into a snare', into the trap Satan has laid for you, that is ready to break your bones in pieces, to crush your soul to death? After fair warning, why should you sink any more into 'foolish and hurtful desires'? Desires as foolish, as inconsistent with reason as they are with religion itself! Desires that have done you more hurt already than all the treasures upon earth can countervail.

12. Have they not hurt you already, have they not wounded you in the tenderest part, by slackening, if not utterly destroying your 'hunger and thirst after righteousness'?[73] Have you now the same longing that you had once for the whole image of God? Have you the same vehement desire as you formerly had of 'going on unto perfection'?[74] Have they not hurt you by weakening your *faith*? Have you now faith's 'abiding impression, realizing things to come'?[75] Do you endure in all temptations from pleasure or pain, 'seeing him that is invisible'?[76] Have you every day, and every hour, an uninterrupted sense of his presence? Have they not hurt you with regard to your *hope*? Have you now a hope full of immortality?[77] Are you still big with earnest expectation of all the great and precious promises?[78] Do you now 'taste the powers of the world to come'?[79] Do you 'sit in heavenly places with Christ Jesus'?[80]

[72] 1 Tim. 6:9 (*Notes*).
[73] Matt. 5:6.
[74] Cf. Heb. 6:1.
[75] Cf. Heb. 11:1, and Charles Wesley's 'Faith lends its realizing light' (1780 *Collection*, Hymn 92:21; see 7:195 in this edn.)—though these do not constitute a clear source for the quotation.
[76] Heb. 11:27 (*Notes*).
[77] Wisd. 3:4. Cf. above, I.11; also No. 72, 'Of Evil Angels', II.4 and n.
[78] 2 Pet. 1:4.
[79] Heb. 6:5.
[80] Cf. Eph. 2:6.

13. Have they not so hurt you as to stab your religion to the heart? Have they not cooled (if not quenched) your *love of God?* This is easily determined. Have you the same delight in God which you once had? Can you now say,

5

> I nothing want beneath, above:
> Happy, happy in thy love![81]

I fear not. And if your love of God is in any wise decayed, so is also your love of your neighbour. You are then hurt in the very life and spirit of your religion! If you lose love, you lose all.

10   14. Are not you hurt with regard to your *humility?* If you are increased in goods, it cannot well be otherwise. Many will think you a better, because you are a richer man; and how can you help thinking so yourself? Especially considering the commendations which some will give you in simplicity, and many with a design to
15 serve themselves of you.

If you are hurt in your humility it will appear by this token: you are not so teachable as you were, not so advisable; you are not so easy to be convinced, not so easy to be persuaded. You have a much better opinion of your own judgment, and are more
20 attached to your own will. Formerly one might guide you with a thread; now one cannot turn you with a cart-rope.[82] You were glad to be admonished or reproved; but that time is past. And you now account a man your enemy because he tells you the truth. O let each of you calmly consider this, and see if it be not your own
25 picture!

15. Are you not equally hurt with regard to your *meekness?* You had once learned an excellent lesson of him that was meek as well as lowly in heart.[83] When you were reviled, you reviled not again.[84] You did not return railing for railing, but contrariwise, blessing.[85]
30 Your love was 'not provoked',[86] but enabled you on all occasions to overcome evil with good.[87] Is this your case now? I am afraid not. I fear you cannot 'bear all things'.[88] Alas, it may rather be said

---

[81] Cf. John and Charles Wesley, *A Collection of Psalms and Hymns*, 2nd edn. (1743), p. 95 (*Poet. Wks.*, VIII.247), on Ps. 131. See also Wesley's letters to Sarah Pywell, Apr. 23, 1771, and to Miss Cummins, June 8, 1773.

[82] See Isa. 5:18; 'cart-ropes' as in the harness of strong 'cart-horses'; cf. instances in *OED.*

[83] See Matt. 11:29.   [84] See 1 Pet. 2:23.

[85] 1 Pet. 3:9.   [86] 1 Cor. 13:5.

[87] Rom. 12:21.

[88] Cf. 1 Cor. 13:7.

you can bear nothing—no injury, nor even affront! How quickly are you ruffled! How readily does that occur: 'What! to use *me* so! What insolence is this! How did he dare to do it! I am not now what I was once. Let him know I am now able to defend myself.' You mean, to revenge yourself. And it is much if you are not 5 willing as well as able; if you do not take your fellow servant by the throat.

16. And are you not hurt in your *patience* too? Does your love now 'endure all things'?[89] Do you still 'in patience possess your soul',[90] as when you first believed? O what a change is here! You 10 have again learnt to be frequently out of humour. You are often fretful; you feel, nay, and give way to peevishness. You find abundance of things go so cross that you cannot tell how to bear them!

Many years ago I was sitting with a gentleman in London who 15 feared God greatly, and generally gave away, year by year, nine-tenths of his yearly income. A servant came in and threw some coals on the fire. A puff of smoke came out. The baronet threw himself back in his chair and cried out, 'Oh! Mr. Wesley, these are the crosses I meet with daily!' Would he not have been 20 less impatient if he had had fifty, instead of five thousand pounds a year?[91]

17. But to return. Are not you who have been successful in your endeavours to increase in substance, insensibly sunk into softness of mind, if not of body too? You no longer rejoice to 'endure 25 hardship, as good soldiers of Jesus Christ'.[92] You no longer 'rush into the kingdom of heaven, and take it as by storm'.[93] You do not

---

[89] *Ibid.*   [90] Cf. Luke 21:19.

[91] Sir John Phillips (*c.* 1701-64) of Picton Castle, County Pembroke (Wales). Wesley repeats this recollection from the days of the Holy Club in No. 108, 'On Riches', II.8, and mentions it in a letter to Joseph Benson, Nov. 5, 1769 ('You put me in mind of Sir John Phillips's exclamation when a puff of smoke came out of the chimney . . .'). Cf. John Clayton's letter to Wesley at Epworth, Sept. 4, 1732, and Sir John Thorold's letter to Wesley, May 24, 1736, for examples of Sir John Phillips's benefactions to the Holy Club (Curnock, VIII.278-80, 301).

[92] Cf. 2 Tim. 2:3.

[93] Cf. Charles Wesley, *Short Hymns on Select Passages of the Holy Scriptures* (1762), II.160, on Matt. 11:12(*Poet. Wks.*, X.249):

> O might thy powerful word
> Inspire a feeble worm
> To rush into thy kingdom, Lord,
> And take it as by storm.

(Cf. *A Collection of Hymns* (1780), No. 257, Vol. 7 of this edn.)

cheerfully and gladly 'deny yourselves', and 'take up your cross daily'.[94] You cannot deny yourself the poor pleasure of a little sleep, or of a soft bed, in order to hear the word that is able to save your souls! Indeed, you 'cannot go out so early in the morning;

5   besides it is dark; nay, cold; perhaps rainy too. Cold, darkness, rain—all these together. I can never think of it.' You did not say so when you were a poor man. You then regarded none of these things. It is the change of circumstances which has occasioned this melancholy change in your body and mind; you are but the

10 shadow of what you were. What have riches done for you?

'But it cannot be expected I should do as I have done; for I am now grown old.' Am not I grown old as well as you? Am not I in my seventy-eighth year? Yet by the grace of God I do not slack my pace yet. Neither would *you*, if you were a poor man still.

15   18. You are so deeply hurt that you have wellnigh lost your zeal for works of mercy, as well as of piety.[95] You once pushed on, through cold or rain, or whatever cross lay in your way, to see the poor, the sick, the distressed. You went about doing good, and found out those who were not able to find you. You cheerfully

20 crept down into their cellars, and climbed up into their garrets, to

> Supply all their wants,
> And spend and be spent in assisting his saints.[96]

You found out every scene of human misery, and assisted according to your power:

25   Each form of woe your generous pity moved;
            Your Saviour's face you saw, and seeing, loved.[97]

Do you now tread in the same steps? What hinders? Do you fear spoiling your silken coat? Or is there another lion in the way?[98] Are you afraid of catching vermin? And are you not afraid lest the

30 roaring lion should catch *you*?[99] Are you not afraid of him that hath said, 'Inasmuch as ye have not done it unto the least of these, ye have not done it unto me'?[100] What will follow? 'Depart,

---

[94] Cf. Luke 9:23.
[95] For more on this distinction, see No. 14, *The Repentance of Believers*, I.13 and n.
[96] Charles Wesley, *Hymns and Sacred Poems* (1749), II.281 (*Poet. Wks.*, V.424; see also No. 482 in *A Collection of Hymns* (1780), Vol. 7 of this edn.).
[97] π; author not identified so far.
[98] See Prov. 26:13.
[99] See 1 Pet. 5:8.   [100] Cf. Matt. 25:45.

ye cursed, into everlasting fire prepared for the devil and his angels.'[101]

19. In time past how mindful were you of that word: 'Thou shalt not hate thy brother in thy heart. Thou shalt in any wise reprove thy brother, and not suffer sin upon him.'[102] You *did* reprove, directly or indirectly, all those that sinned in your sight. And happy consequences quickly followed. How good was a word spoken in season![103] It was often as an arrow from the hand of a giant.[104] Many a heart was pierced. Many of the stout-hearted, who scorned to hear a sermon,

> Fell down before his cross subdued,
> And felt his arrows dipped in blood.[105]

But which of you now has that compassion for the ignorant, and for them that are out of the way? They may wander on for *you*, and plunge into the lake of fire without let or hindrance. Gold hath steeled your hearts. You have something else to do.

> Unhelped, unpitied let the wretches fall.[106]

20. Thus have I given you, O ye gainers, lovers, possessors of riches, one more (it may be the last) warning.[107] O that it may not be in vain! May God write it upon all your hearts! Though 'it is easier for a camel to go through the eye of a needle, than for a rich man to enter into the kingdom of heaven,'[108] yet the things

---

[101] Matt. 25:41. [102] Cf. Lev. 19:17.
[103] See Prov. 15:23. [104] See Ps. 127:5 (BCP).
[105] Cf. John and Charles Wesley, Ps. 45, in *A Collection of Psalms and Hymns* (1743), p. 74 (*Poet. Wks.*, VIII.103):

> Fall down before thy cross subdued,
> And feel thine arrows dipped in blood.

[106] Cf. Samuel Wesley, Jun., 'The Battle of the Sexes', xxvii. 8, 'Unaided, friendless, let the wretches fall' (*Poems*, 1736, p. 34; cf. John Wesley, *A Collection of Moral and Sacred Poems* (1744), III.29).

[107] There is a hint of self-pity and frustration in this valedictory word. Actually, Wesley would live another decade and would fill it with further denunciations of riches; cf. Nos. 61, 'The Mystery of Iniquity', §12 (1783); 94, 'On Family Religion', III.16, 17 (1783); 63, 'The General Spread of the Gospel', §20 (1783); 68, 'The Wisdom of God's Counsels', §§8, 16 (1784); 90, 'An Israelite Indeed', I.1 (1785); 80, 'On Friendship with the World', §3 (1786); 89, 'The More Excellent Way', VI.4 (1787); 108, 'On Riches', §4 (1788); 115, 'Dives and Lazarus', II.1 (1788); 122, 'Causes of the Inefficacy of Christianity', §12 (1789); 126, 'On Worldly Folly', I.4, II.8 (1790); and 131, 'The Danger of Increasing Riches', I, II.16 (1790).

[108] Cf. Matt. 19:24.

impossible with men are possible with God.[109] Lord, speak! And even the rich men that hear these words shall enter thy kingdom! Shall 'take the kingdom of heaven by violence';[110] shall 'sell all for the pearl of great price':[111] Shall be 'crucified to the world',[112] 'and
5 count all things dung, that they may win Christ'![113]

[109] Luke 18:27 (*Notes*).
[110] Cf. Matt. 11:12.
[111] Cf. Matt. 13:46.
[112] Cf. Gal. 6:14.
[113] Cf. Phil. 3:8.

ON DRESS

AN INTRODUCTORY COMMENT

This sermon is a sequel to 'The Danger of Riches' in the sense that it focuses on a particular extravagance which at least some affluent Methodists had fallen into: wearing 'gay and costly apparel', and even defending such a practice as licit for Christians. Twenty-six years before (1760), he had added an Advice to the People called Methodists with regard to Dress *to the sermons in* SOSO, IV.151-68 *(see* Bibliog, No. 131.iii). *None of the numerous editions of this little essay lists an author, but it reads very much like Wesley, and Thomas Jackson included it as Wesley's in his edition of the* Works *(1830), XI.466-77. The idea of frugality and plainness in dress was both a Quaker and Puritan commonplace; Wesley had taken up Robert Barclay and Richard Baxter and made their ideas on dress his own.*

Now, in 1786, he returns to the same topic with very few alterations in substance and style. 'On Dress' was published in the March and April *instalments of the* Arminian Magazine *(1787), X.117-22, 172-80, without a title but numbered 'Sermon XXXVIII'. There is a postscript: 'North-Green, Dec. 30, 1786'. Wesley's diary indicates that he visited North Green occasionally between 1786 and 1790. Thomas Rankin, who had retired in 1783, lived there, and Wesley moved his printing operation from the Foundery to North Green around 1788.*

A title was added in the year following when the sermon was published in SOSO, VII.167-89. *A further qualifying comment on this topic was published in 1788, entitled 'Thoughts upon Dress'; this was a postscript to an extract from* The Refined Courtier *which Wesley had published in the* Arminian Magazine *(1788), XI.196-97.*

On Dress

1 Peter 3:3-4

Whose adorning, let it not be that outward adorning of . . . wearing of gold, or of putting on of apparel. But let it be the hidden man of the heart, in that which is not corruptible, even the ornament of a meek and quiet spirit, which is in the sight of God of great price.

1. St. Paul exhorts all those who desire to 'be transformed by the renewal of their minds', and to 'prove what is that good, and acceptable, and perfect will of God', not to be 'conformed to this world'.[1] Indeed this exhortation relates more directly to the *wisdom* of the world, which in all its branches is 'foolishness with God',[2] and to the spirit of the world, which is totally opposite to his 'good, and acceptable, and perfect will'. But it likewise has a reference even to the *manners* and *customs* of the world, which naturally flow from its wisdom and spirit, and are exactly suitable thereto. And it was not beneath the wisdom of God to give us punctual[3] directions in this respect also.

2. Some of these, particularly that in the text, descend even to the apparel of Christians. And both this text and the parallel one of St. Paul are as express as possible. St. Paul's words are: 'I will that women adorn themselves in modest apparel; not . . . with gold, or pearls, or costly array; but (which becometh women professing godliness) with good works.'[a]

3. But is it not strange, say some, that the all-wise Spirit of God should condescend to take notice of such trifles as these? To take notice of such insignificant trifles? Things of so little moment? Or rather of none at all? For what does it signify, provided we take care of the soul, what the body is covered with? Whether in silk or sackcloth? What harm can there be in the wearing of gold, or silver, or precious stones? Or any other of those beautiful things with which God has so amply provided us? May we not apply to

---

[a] [Cf.] 1 Tim. 2:8-10[ver. 9-10].

[1] Cf. Rom. 12:2.
[2] 1 Cor. 3:19.
[3] I.e., 'exact' as in Johnson, *Dictionary, loc. cit.*

this what St. Paul has observed on another occasion, that 'every creature of God is good, and nothing to be rejected'?[4]

4. It is certain that many who sincerely fear God have cordially embraced this opinion. And their practice is suitable thereto: they make no scruple of conformity to the world by putting on, as often as occasion offers, either gold, or pearls, or costly apparel. And indeed they are not well-pleased with those that think it their duty to reject them; the using of which they apprehend to be one branch of Christian liberty. Yea, some have gone considerably farther; even so far as to make it a point to bring those who had refrained from them for some time to make use of them again, assuring them that it was mere superstition to think there was any harm in them. Nay, farther still, a very respectable person has said in express terms, 'I do not desire that any who "dress plain" should be in our society.'[5] It is therefore certainly worth our while to consider this matter thoroughly; seriously to inquire whether there is any harm in the putting on of gold, or jewels, or costly apparel.

5. But before we enter on the subject, let it be observed that slovenliness is no part of religion; that neither this nor any text of Scripture condemns neatness of apparel; certainly this is a duty, not a sin. 'Cleanliness is indeed next to godliness.'[6] Agreeably to this, good Mr. Herbert advises everyone that fears God:

> Let thy mind's sweetness have its operation
> Upon thy person, clothes, and habitation.[7]

---

[4] 1 Tim. 4:4 (*Notes*); cf. 'Thoughts Upon Dress' for a reply to complaints about a rule he had quoted approvingly in *AM* (1788), XI.196-97: 'Let everyone, when he appears in public, be decently clothed according to his age and the custom of the place where he lives.'

[5] Apparently this is not a quotation from a printed source, but a comment from some unknown Methodist.

[6] Cf. 'The Song of Songs' in the *Midrash Rabbah*, I.1:9, where Rabbi Phinehas ben-Yair affirms a long sorites that begins with zeal ('zeal leads to cleanliness') and continues on to 'purity' or 'godliness'. In Bartlett, *Familiar Quotations*, the adage is credited to Wesley, as derived from 'the Hebrew fathers'. But Bartlett quotes Rabbi A. S. Bettelheim as citing Phinehas ben-Yair as having summarized 'the doctrines of religion as carefulness, . . . abstemiousness next to cleanliness, cleanliness next to godliness'. See also No. 98, 'On Visiting the Sick', II.6, where the saying is quoted as from 'a pious man'. Thus, it had passed into its proverbial form before Wesley. See his advice to his assistants in *Minutes*, June 25, 1744, etc., *Q.* 41(6), and his *Advice to the People called Methodists with Regard to Dress*, II.2 (*Bibliog*, No. 131.iii), where he says, 'Cleanliness is one great branch of frugality.'

[7] Cf. George Herbert, *The Temple*, 'The Church Porch', ll. 371-72:

> Let thy mind's sweetness have his operation
> Upon thy body, clothes, and habitation.

And surely everyone should attend to this if he would not have the good that is in him evil spoken of.[8]

6. Another mistake with regard to apparel has been common in the religious world. It has been supposed by some that there ought to be no difference at all in the apparel of Christians. But neither these texts nor any other in the Book of God teach any such thing, or direct that the dress of the master or mistress should be nothing different from that of their servants. There may undoubtedly be a moderate difference of apparel between persons of different stations. And where the eye is single this will easily be adjusted by the rules of Christian prudence.

7. Yea, it may be doubted whether any part of Scripture forbids (at least I know not any) those in any nation that are invested with supreme authority to be arrayed in gold and costly apparel; or to adorn their immediate attendants, or magistrates, or officers with the same. It is not improbable that our blessed Lord intended to give countenance to this custom when he said, without the least mark of censure or disapprobation, 'Behold, those that wear gorgeous (splendid) apparel are in kings' courts.'[b]

8. What is then the meaning of these Scriptures? What is it which they forbid? They manifestly forbid ordinary Christians, those in the lower or middle ranks of life, to be adorned with gold, or pearls, or costly apparel. But why? What harm is there therein? This deserves our serious consideration. But it is highly expedient, or rather absolutely necessary for all who would consider it to any purpose, as far as is possible to divest themselves of all prejudice, and to stand open to conviction. Is it not necessary likewise in the highest degree that they should earnestly beseech the Father of lights that 'by his holy inspiration they may think the things that are right, and by his merciful guidance perform the same'?[9] Then they will not say, no, not in their hearts (as I fear too many have done), what the famous Jew

---

[b] Luke 7:25.

Cf. John Wesley, *A Collection of Moral and Sacred Poems* (1744), I.30. See also, Wesley's letter to Richard Steel, Apr. 24, 1769.

[8] See Rom. 14:16.

[9] Cf. BCP, Collect for Rogation Sunday (Fifth Sunday after Easter): 'O Lord, from whom all good things do come; Grant to us thy humble servants, that by thy holy inspiration we may think those things that be good, and by thy merciful guiding may perform the same, through our Lord Jesus Christ. Amen.'

said to the Christian, *Non persuadebis, etiamsi persuaseris*—'Thou shalt not persuade me, though thou hast persuaded me.'[10]

9. The question is, What harm does it do to adorn ourselves with gold, or pearls, or costly array? Suppose you can *afford* it? That is, suppose it does not hurt or impoverish your family? The first harm it does is, it engenders *pride*,[11] and where it is already, increases it. Whoever narrowly observes what passes in his own heart will easily discern this. Nothing is more natural than to think ourselves better because we are dressed in better clothes. And it is scarce possible for a man to wear costly apparel without in some measure valuing himself upon it. One of the old heathens was so well apprised of this that when he had a spite to a poor man, and had a mind to turn his head, he made him a present of a suit of fine clothes:

> *Eutrapelus, cuicunque nocere volebat,*
> *Vestimenta dabat pretiosa.*[12]

He could not then but imagine himself to be as much better as he was finer than his neighbour. And how many thousands, not only lords and gentlemen in England, but honest tradesmen, argue the same way—inferring the superior value of their persons from the value of their clothes!

10. 'But may not one man be as proud, though clad in sackcloth, as another is, though clad in cloth of gold?' As this argument meets us at every turn, and is supposed to be unanswerable, it will be worth while to answer it once for all, and to show the utter emptiness of it. 'May not then one clad in sackcloth', you ask, 'be as proud as he that is clad in cloth of gold?' I answer, Certainly he may: I suppose no one doubts of it. And what inference can you draw from this? Take a parallel case. One man that drinks a cup of wholesome wine[13] may be as sick as another that drinks poison. But does this prove that the poison has no more tendency to hurt a man than the wine? Or does it excuse any man for taking what has a natural tendency to make

---

[10] Cf. Acts. 26:28; and see No. 4, *Scriptural Christianity*, IV.2 and n.

[11] Cf. No. 14, *The Repentance of Believers*, I.3 and n.

[12] Horace, *Epistles*, I.xviii.31-32: 'Eutrapelus, if he wished to injure someone, would present him with fancy and expensive clothes.'

[13] Cf. Wesley's Preface to his *Extract From Dr. Cadogan's Dissertation on Gout* (1774), and his comment in JWJ, Sept. 9, 1771—both disavowing Dr. Cadogan's condemnation of the use of wine, *'toto genere'*. See also his inquiry to his wife, Apr. 24, 1757: '. . . Sister Hacket was to have a cag [small keg] of the elder wine. Has she had it?'

him sick? Now to apply—experience shows that fine clothes have
a natural tendency to make a man sick of pride. Plain clothes have
not. Although it is true you may be sick of pride in these also, yet
they have no natural tendency either to cause or increase this
5 sickness. Therefore let all that desire to be clothed with humility[14]
abstain from that poison.

11. Secondly, the wearing gay or costly apparel naturally tends
to breed and to increase *vanity*. By vanity I here mean the love and
desire of being admired and praised. Every one of you that is fond
10 of dress has a witness of this in your own bosom. Whether you will
confess it before man or no, you are convinced of this before God.
You know in your hearts, it is with a view to be admired that you
thus adorn yourselves, and that you would not be at the pains were
none to see you but God and his holy angels. Now the more you
15 indulge this foolish desire, the more it grows upon you. You have
vanity enough by nature, but by thus indulging it you increase it a
hundredfold. O stop! Aim at pleasing God alone, and all these
ornaments will drop off.

12. Thirdly, the wearing of gay and costly apparel naturally
20 tends to beget *anger*, and every turbulent and uneasy passion. And
it is on this very account that the Apostle places this 'outward
adorning' in direct opposition to 'the ornament of a meek and
quiet spirit'. How remarkably does he add, 'which is in the sight of
God of great price':

25   Than gold and pearls more precious far,
                And brighter than the morning star.[15]

None can easily conceive, unless himself were to make the sad
experiment, the contrariety there is between that 'outward
adorning' and this 'inward quietness of spirit'. You never can
30 thoroughly enjoy this while you are fond of the other. It is only
while you sit loose[16] to that 'outward adorning' that you can 'in
patience possess your soul'. Then only, when you have cast off
your fondness for dress, will the peace of God reign in your
hearts.

35   13. Fourthly, gay and costly apparel directly tends to create and

---

[14] 1 Pet. 5:5.
[15] John Wesley, 'A Morning Dedication of Ourselves to Christ', st. 6, last two lines,
translated from Joachim Lange, in John and Charles Wesley, *Hymns and Sacred Poems*
(1739), p. 180 *(Poet. Wks.,* I.160).
[16] For this vernacular phrase, see No. 44, *Original Sin,* II.9 and n.

inflame lust. I was in doubt whether to name this brutal appetite. Or, in order to spare delicate ears, to express it by some gentle circumlocution. (Like the Dean who some years ago told his audience at Whitehall, 'If you do not repent, you will go to a place which I have too much manners to name before this good 5 company.')[17] But I think it best to speak out; since the more the word shocks your ears, the more it may arm your heart. The fact is plain and undeniable: it has this effect both on the wearer and the beholder. To the former our elegant poet, Cowley, addresses those fine lines: 10

> Th' adorning thee with so much art
> Is but a barb'rous skill;
> 'Tis like the pois'ning of a dart,
> Too apt before to kill.[18]

That is (to express the matter in plain terms, without any 15 colouring), 'You poison the beholder with far more of this base appetite than otherwise he would feel.' Did you not *know* this would be the natural consequence of your elegant adorning? To push the question home, did you not *desire*, did you not *design* it should? And yet all the time, how did you 20

> set to public view
> A specious face of innocence and virtue.[19]

Meanwhile you do not yourself escape the snare which you spread for others. The dart recoils, and you are infected with the

[17] This story was a well-known eighteenth-century anecdote. Cf. Richard Steele, *The Guardian*, No. 17 (Mar. 31, 1713), who remembers having heard it 'about thirty years ago'; Pope, *Moral Essays* (1731), IV.49-50 and n.('. . . soft Dean . . . who never mentions Hell to ears polite'); and Richard Graves, *Spiritual Quixote*, I.102. John Butt, in his 1963 edn. of Pope (p. 593), identifies 'the soft dean' as Knightly Chetwood but this seems conjectural. Basil Williams, *The Whig Supremacy*, p. 92, tells the story as of White Kennett (afterwards Bishop of Peterborough), but Kennett's dates do not jibe with Steele's. There is a variation of this anecdote in Wesley's letter to 'John Smith' (July 10, 1747): '. . . an eminent man, who preaching at St. James's said, "If you do not repent, you will go to a place which I shall not name before this audience" '; cf. also CWJ, Sept. 24, 1738. See also *AM*, II.46, where another version is printed (in an unidentified poem which quotes Pope's lines).
[18] Abraham Cowley, 'The Waiting-Maid', ver. 4, in *The Mistress*.
[19] Cf. Nicholas Rowe, *The Fair Penitent* (1703), Act II, sc. 1:

> . . . and set to public view
> A specious face of innocence and beauty.

Cf. Rowe's *Works* (1766), I.232.

same poison with which you infected them. You kindle a flame which at the same time consumes both yourself and your admirers. And it is well if it does not plunge both you and them into the flames of hell.

5   14. Fifthly, the wearing costly array is directly opposite to the being 'adorned with good works'. Nothing can be more evident than this; for the more you lay out on your own apparel, the less you have left to clothe the naked, to feed the hungry, to lodge the strangers, to relieve those that are sick and in prison, and to lessen 10 the numberless afflictions to which we are exposed in this vale of tears. And here is no room for the evasion used before, 'I may be as *humble* in cloth of gold as in sackcloth.' If you could be as *humble* when you choose costly as when you choose plain apparel (which I flatly deny), yet you could not be as *beneficent*, as 15 plenteous in good works. Every shilling which you save from your own apparel you may expend in clothing the naked, and relieving the various necessities of the poor, whom ye 'have always with you'.[20] Therefore every shilling which you needlessly spend on your apparel is in effect stolen from God and the poor.[21] And how 20 many precious opportunities of doing good have you defrauded yourself of? How often have you disabled yourself from doing good by purchasing what you did not want? For what end did you buy these ornaments? To please God? No; but to please your own fancy; or to gain the admiration and applause of those that were 25 no wiser than yourself. How much good might you have done with that money! And what an irreparable loss have you sustained by not doing it, if it be true that the day is at hand when 'every man shall receive his own reward according to his own labour'![22]

    15. I pray consider this well. Perhaps you have not seen it in this 30 light before. When you are laying out that money in costly apparel which you could have otherwise spared for the poor, you thereby deprive them of what God, the Proprietor of all, had lodged in your hands for their use. If so, what you put upon yourself you are, in effect, tearing from the back of the naked; as the costly and 35 delicate food which you eat you are snatching from the mouth of the hungry. For mercy, for pity, for Christ's sake, for the honour of his gospel, stay your hand. Do not throw this money away. Do not lay out on nothing, yea, worse than nothing, what may clothe your poor, naked, shivering fellow-creature!

---

[20] Cf. Mark 14:7.   [21] Cf. No. 50, 'The Use of Money', II.3.   [22] 1 Cor. 3:8.

16. Many years ago, when I was at Oxford, in a cold winter's day, a young maid (one of those we kept at school) called upon me. I said: 'You seem half starved. Have you nothing to cover you but that thin linen gown?' She said, 'Sir, this is all I have!' I put my hand in my pocket; but found I had scarce any money left, having 5 just paid away what I had. It immediately struck me, will not thy Master say, ' "Well done, good and faithful steward!" '[23] Thou hast adorned thy walls with the money which might have screened this poor creature from the cold!' O justice! O mercy! Are not these pictures the blood of this poor maid![24] See thy expensive 10 apparel in the same light—thy gown, hat, head-dress! Everything about thee which cost more than Christian duty required thee to lay out is the blood of the poor! O be wise for the time to come! Be more merciful! More faithful to God and man! More abundantly 'adorned (like men and women professing godliness) with good 15 works'.

17. It is true, great allowance is to be made for those who have never been warned of these things, and perhaps do not know that there is a word in the Bible which forbids costly apparel. But what is *that* to *you?* You have been warned over and over;[25] yea, in the 20 plainest manner possible. And what have you profited thereby? Do not you still dress just like other people of the same fortune? Is not your dress as gay, as expensive as theirs, who never had any such warning? As expensive as it would have been if you had never heard a word said about it? O how will you answer this when you 25 and I stand together at the judgment seat of Christ?[26] Nay, have

[23] Matt. 25:23.
[24] The Oxford diaries suggest a possible identification here with Katherine Jervas's daughter, Sarah; cf. Feb. 1, 1734. Earlier entries in Oct. and Dec. 1731, specify Wesley's interest in the Jervas family and a gift of eight shillings 'for Sarah [J.'s] gown and petticoat'. As for 'adorning his walls', there are five different entries for pictures and framing, amounting to £1.10s. between Apr. 1732 and July 1733.
Wesley recalls: 'I used to be fond of pictures containing Scripture pieces. At that time, I was one day walking the streets of London, when I met an old servant. I was distressed to see her in such poor attire. Knowing I had put half a guinea in my pocket, I put my hand in, intending to give it to her, that she might buy a new gown, but it was gone. Then I recollected that I had called at the stationers and laid it out in pictures. How much more good should I have done if I had given it to that needy woman;' cf. John B. Dyson, *The History of Wesleyan Methodism in the Congleton Circuit* (London, Leeds, 1856), p. 105; also Benjamin Smith, *Methodism in Macclesfield* (London, 1875), p. 205. Thus, we have two stories quite similar, of Wesley's recollections of his own dilemmas in Christian stewardship. See also No. 122, 'Causes of the Inefficacy of Christianity', §9, where he climaxes his appeal to Christian generosity with, 'See that poor member of Christ's [Body] pinched with hunger, shivering with cold, half-naked!'
[25] Cf. No. 87, 'The Danger of Riches', II.20.   [26] Rom. 14:10.

not many of you grown finer as fast as you have grown richer? As you increased in substance have you not increased in dress? Witness the profusion of ribbands, gauze, or linen about your heads! What have you profited then by bearing the reproach of
5   Christ?[27] By being called Methodists? Are you not as fashionably dressed as others of your rank that are no Methodists? Do you ask, 'But may we not as well buy fashionable things as unfashionable?' I answer, Not if they give you a bold, immodest look (as those huge hats, bonnets, head-dresses do). And not if
10 they cost more. 'But I can *afford* it.' O lay aside for ever that idle, nonsensical word! No Christian can *afford* to waste any part of the substance which God has entrusted him with.[28] How long are you to stay here? May not you tomorrow, perhaps tonight, be summoned to arise and go hence, in order to give an account of
15 this and all your talents to the Judge of quick and dead?[29]

     18. How then can it be that after so many warnings you persist in the same folly? Is it not hence? There are still among you some that neither profit themselves by all they hear, nor are willing that others should; and these, if any of you are almost persuaded to
20 dress as Christians, reason, and rally, and laugh you out of it. O ye pretty triflers, I entreat you not to do the devil's work any longer! Whatever ye do yourselves, do not harden the hearts of others. And you that are of a better mind, avoid these tempters with all possible care. And if you come where any of them are, either beg
25 them to be silent on the head, or quit the room.

     19. Sixthly, the putting on of costly apparel is directly opposite to what the Apostle terms 'the hidden man of the heart'; that is, to the whole 'image of God'[30] wherein we were created, and which is stamped anew upon the heart of every Christian believer; it is
30 opposite to 'the mind which was in Christ Jesus',[31] and the whole nature of inward holiness. All the time you are studying this 'outward adorning', the whole inward work of the Spirit stands still; or rather goes back, though by very gentle and almost imperceptible degrees. Instead of growing more heavenly-minded, you
35 are more and more earthly-minded. If you once had fellowship

[27] Heb. 11:26.
[28] Cf. No. 87, 'The Danger of Riches', II.8 and n.
[29] Acts 10:42; many of Wesley's readers would have associated this phrase with their recital of it in The Apostles' Creed.
[30] Gen. 1:27; 9:6; 2 Cor. 4:4.
[31] Cf. Phil. 2:5.

with the Father and the Son,³² it now gradually declines; and you insensibly sink deeper and deeper into the spirit of the world, into foolish and hurtful desires,³³ and grovelling appetites. All these evils, and a thousand more, spring from that one root—indulging yourself in costly apparel.

20. Why then does not everyone that either loves or fears God flee from it as from the face of a serpent?³⁴ Why are *you* still so conformable to the irrational, sinful customs of a frantic world? Why do you still despise the express commandment of God, uttered in the plainest terms? You see the light: why do not you follow the light of your own mind? Your conscience tells you the truth: why do you not obey the dictates of your own conscience?

21. You answer, 'Why, universal custom³⁵ is against me; and I know not how to stem the mighty torrent!' Not only the profane, but the religious world, run violently the other way. Look into, I do not say, the theatres, but the churches, nay, and the meetings of every denomination (except a few old-fashioned Quakers, or the people called Moravians); look into the congregations in London or elsewhere of those that are styled 'gospel ministers';³⁶ look into Northampton Chapel, yea, into the Tabernacle, or the chapel in Tottenham Court Road; nay, look into the chapel in West Street or that in the City Road;³⁷ look at the very people that

³² See 1 John 1:3. ³³ 1 Tim. 6:9 (*Notes*).
³⁴ See Rev. 12:14.
³⁵ Cf. No. 25, 'Sermon on the Mount, V', IV.3 and n.
³⁶ Cf. No. 35, 'The Law Established through Faith, I', I.12 and n.
³⁷ Wesley is here identifying the principal preaching places of London Methodists (those in connexion with the Countess of Huntingdon and his own). Northampton Chapel had once been a place of entertainment called The Pantheon in Spa Fields, Clerkenwell. It had been renovated by the Revd. John Ryland of Northampton and dedicated as a chapel in 1777. In 1779 it came under the control of Lady Huntingdon and was renamed 'Spa Fields Chapel' (and was the place of the first public ordinations in her 'Connexion' in 1783). Wesley remembers it here under its older name.

The Tabernacle, first built in 1741, was Whitefield's stronghold in Moorfields within sight (and sound) of Wesley's Foundery. In 1753 it was rebuilt as a brick chapel and continued in use into the twentieth century.

The Chapel on Tottenham Court Road (opened in 1756) was Whitefield's other London centre built by Lady Huntingdon and her friends; in its time it was one of the largest auditoriums of its kind in Britain. A rebuilt church and an active congregation are still there.

The Chapel in West Street (one of the streets opening into Seven Dials) had been the church for the London Huguenots whose lease Wesley acquired in 1743. Thereafter it served Wesley as a consecrated church in west-central London where he and Charles could serve Holy Communion as well as preach.

'The New Chapel' on City Road was Wesley's replacement for the Foundery; it was built in 1778. See No. 112, *On Laying the Foundation of the New Chapel*.

congregation full as plain dressed as a Quaker congregation.[48] Only be more consistent with yourselves. Let your dress be *cheap* as well as plain. Otherwise you do but trifle with God and me, and your own souls. I pray, let there be no costly silks among you, how
5 grave soever they may be. Let there be no *Quaker-linen*,[49] proverbially so called for their exquisite fineness; no Brussels lace, no elephantine hats or bonnets, those scandals of female modesty. Be all of a piece, dressed from head to foot as persons 'professing godliness';[50] professing to do everything small and
10 great with the single view of pleasing God.

27. Let not any of you who are rich in this world endeavour to excuse yourselves from this by talking nonsense. It is stark, staring nonsense to say, 'Oh, I can *afford* this or that.' If you have regard to common sense, let that silly word never come out of
15 your mouth. No man living can 'afford' to waste any part of what God has committed to his trust. None can 'afford' to throw any part of that food and raiment into the sea which was lodged with him on purpose to feed the hungry and clothe the naked. And it is far worse than simple waste to spend any part of it in gay or costly
20 apparel. For this is no less than to turn wholesome food into deadly poison. It is giving so much money to poison both yourself and others, as far as your example spreads, with pride, vanity, anger, lust, love of the world, and a thousand 'foolish and hurtful desires', which tend to 'pierce' them 'through with many
25 sorrows'.[51] And is there no harm in all this? O God, arise, and maintain thy own cause![52] Let not men or devils any longer put out our eyes, and lead us blindfold into the pit of destruction.[53]

28. I beseech you, every man that is here present before God, every woman, young or old, married or single, yea, every child
30 that knows good from evil, take this to yourself. Each of you, for

---

[48] For other admiring references to Quaker modesty, cf. Nos. 97, 'On Obedience to Pastors', III.10; and 122, 'Causes of the Inefficacy of Christianity', §12. See also Wesley's *Advice to the People called Methodists with Regard to Dress*, I.3-II.4; and his letters to Miss March, Sept. 15, 1770, and to Kitty Warren, Aug. 26, 1779.

[49] Cf. *OED*, where this is the sole instance cited for this phrase.

[50] Cf. Wesley's letter to Richard Steel, Apr. 24, 1769: 'Whatever clothes you wear, let them be whole. . . . Let none ever see a ragged Methodist.'

[51] Cf. 1 Tim. 6:9-10 (*Notes*).

[52] See Ps. 74:23 (BCP). Is there an echo here of the historic denunciation of Martin Luther in Pope Leo X's *Exsurge Domine* (1520), the first papal encyclical against the great reformer?

[53] See Ps. 55:23 (AV).

one, take the Apostle's advice: at least, hinder not others from taking it. I beseech you, O ye parents, do not hinder your children from following their own convictions, even though you might think they would 'look prettier' if they were adorned with such gewgaws as other children wear. I beseech you, O ye husbands, 5 do not hinder your wives: you, O ye wives, do not hinder your husbands, either by word or deed, from acting just as they are persuaded in their own minds. Above all, I conjure you, ye half Methodists, you that trim between us and the world, you that frequently, perhaps constantly, hear our preaching, but are in no 10 farther connexion with us; yea, and all you that were once in full connexion with us but are not so now: whatever ye do yourselves, do not say one word to hinder others from recovering and practising the advice which has been now given! Yet a little while, and we shall not need these poor coverings; for this corruptible 15 body shall put on incorruption. Yet a few days hence, and this mortal body shall put on immortality.[54] In the meantime, let this be our only care, to 'put off the old man', our old nature, 'which is corrupt', which is altogether evil; and to 'put on the new man, which after God is created in righteousness and true holiness'.[55] 20 In particular, 'put on, as the elect of God, bowels of mercies, kindness, gentleness, long-suffering.'[56] Yea, to sum up all in one word, 'put on Christ,'[57] 'that when he shall appear, ye may appear with him in glory.'[58]

North-Green, Dec. 30, 1786 25

---

[54] Cf. 1 Cor. 15:54.
[55] Eph. 4:22, 24.
[56] Cf. Col. 3:12.
[57] Gal. 3:27; cf. Rom. 13:14.
[58] Cf. Col. 3:4.

THE MORE EXCELLENT WAY

AN INTRODUCTORY COMMENT

This is a practical essay in Christian ethics that also illustrates how far the later Wesley had moved away from his earlier exclusivist standards of true faith and salvation. It should be read alongside The Almost Christian; *the startling contrast between the two reflects a half-century's experience as leader of a revival movement and also a significant change in his mind and heart. Here, more explicitly than anywhere else in his writings, we see Wesley's acceptance of an older notion of 'two orders of Christians', each with its legitimate hope of salvation.*

His particular concern in this essay is to encourage 'the lower order of Christians' (i.e., 'the generality of Christians') to a more earnest striving for the shared goal of both 'orders': 'the more excellent way', a pure love of God and an humble 'love of all men for God's sake'. This is the presupposition of his pastoral counsel on such mundane problems as the Christian's regulation of sleep, his daily round of prayer, his diligence in 'business', grace before and cheerfulness at meals, allowable 'diversions' and, as always, the proper 'use of money'. None of Wesley's lifelong aspirations to holiness is compromised here, nor is there any betrayal of his soteriological premise of justification by 'faith alone'. But there is a different spirit; there is an implied admission that he has changed his mind on this and other important points in his understanding of the Christian ordo salutis.

The sermon itself provides no definite clues as to date and provenance. It first appeared in the Arminian Magazine *(July and August 1787, X.341-46, 398-406), without a title (numbered 'Sermon XL'), and then reappeared the year following in* SOSO, *VII.191-214, with its present title. It was not reprinted in Wesley's lifetime.*

The More Excellent Way

1 Corinthians 12:31

Covet earnestly the best gifts; and yet I show unto you a more excellent way.

1. In the preceding verses St. Paul has been speaking of the extraordinary gifts of the Holy Ghost,[1] such as healing the sick, prophesying (in the proper sense of the word; that is, foretelling things to come), speaking with strange tongues, such as the speaker had never learned, and the miraculous interpretation of tongues. And these gifts the Apostle allows to be desirable; yea, he exhorts the Corinthians, at least the teachers among them (to whom chiefly, if not solely, they were wont to be given in the first ages of the church) to 'covet' them 'earnestly', that thereby they might be qualified to be more useful either to Christians or heathens. 'And yet', says he, 'I show unto you a more excellent way'—far more desirable than all these put together, inasmuch as it will infallibly lead you to happiness both in this world and in the world to come; whereas you might have all those gifts, yea, in the highest degree, and yet be miserable both in time and eternity.

2. It does not appear that these extraordinary gifts of the Holy Ghost were common in the church for more than two or three centuries. We seldom hear of them after that fatal period when the Emperor Constantine[2] called himself a Christian, and from a vain imagination of promoting the Christian cause thereby heaped riches, and power, and honour, upon the Christians in general; but in particular upon the Christian clergy. From this time they almost totally ceased; very few instances of the kind were found. The cause of this was not (as has been vulgarly supposed) 'because there was no more occasion for them'[3] because all the world was become Christian. This is a miserable

---

[1] Cf. No. 4, *Scriptural Christianity*, §4 and n.
[2] Cf. No. 61, 'The Mystery of Iniquity', §§27-28 and n.
[3] An echo from Richard Graves, *The Spiritual Quixote?* Cf. I.55: 'They [our modern itinerant reformers] are planting the gospel in a Christian country; they are combating the shadow of popery where the protestant religion is established; and declaiming against good works in an age which they usually represent as abounding in every evil work.'

mistake: not a twentieth part of it was then nominally Christian.[4] The real cause was: 'the love of many'—almost of all Christians, so called—was 'waxed cold.'[5] The Christians had no more of the Spirit of Christ than the other heathens. The Son of man, when
5 he came to examine his church, could hardly 'find faith upon earth'.[6] This was the real cause why the extraordinary gifts of the Holy Ghost were no longer to be found in the Christian church—because the Christians were turned heathens again, and had only a dead form left.[7]

10 3. However, I would not at present speak of these, of the extraordinary gifts of the Holy Ghost, but of the ordinary; and these likewise we may 'covet earnestly', in order to be more useful in our generation. With this view we may covet 'the gift of *convincing* speech', in order to 'sound the unbelieving heart';[8] and
15 the gift of *persuasion* to move the affections, as well as enlighten the understanding. We may covet *knowledge*, both of the word and of the works of God, whether of providence or grace. We may desire a measure of that faith which on particular occasions, wherein the glory of God or the happiness of men is nearly
20 concerned, goes far beyond the power of natural causes. We may desire an easy elocution, a pleasing address,[9] with resignation to the will of our Lord; yea, whatever would enable us, as we have opportunity, to be useful wherever we are. These gifts we may innocently desire: but there is a more excellent way.

25 4. The way of love, of loving all men for God's sake, of humble, gentle, patient love, is that which the Apostle so admirably describes in the ensuing chapter. And without this, he assures us, all eloquence, all knowledge, all faith, all works, and all

[4] Cf. No. 15, *The Great Assize*, II.4 and n.
[5] Cf. Matt. 24:12.
[6] Luke 18:8 (*Notes*).
[7] An interesting note here that the possibility of 'the extraordinary gifts of the Holy Ghost' stands open, in principle, in any age of the church.
[8] Cf. John Wesley, 'On the Descent of the Holy Ghost at Pentecost', *Hymns and Sacred Poems* (1739), p. 186 (*Poet. Wks.*, I.166). This was altered from Henry More's poem in *Divine Dialogues* (1668) which Wesley had read in 1733. Later, Wesley prepared two hymns from this poem for his *Collection* of 1780 (Nos. 444-45; see 7:623-25 in this edn.). The quotation is from st. 8:

> The spirit of convincing speech,
> Of pow'r demonstrative impart,
> Such as may ev'ry conscience reach
> And sound the unbelieving heart.

[9] Cf. *Directions for Pronunciation and Gesture* (*Bibliog*, No. 161, Vol. 15 of this edn.).

sufferings, are of no more value in the sight of God than sounding brass or a rumbling cymbal;[10] and are not of the least avail toward our eternal salvation. Without this all we know, all we believe, all we do, all we suffer, will profit us nothing in the great day of accounts.

5. But at present I would take a different view of the text, and point out a more excellent way in another sense. It is the observation of an ancient writer that there have been from the beginning two orders of Christians.[11] The one lived an innocent life, conforming in all things not sinful to the customs and fashions of the world, doing many good works, abstaining from gross evils, and attending the ordinances of God. They endeavoured in general to have a conscience void of offence[12] in their outward behaviour, but did not aim at any particular strictness, being in most things like their neighbours.[13] The other sort of Christians not only abstained from all appearance of evil, were zealous of good works[14] in every kind, and attended all the ordinances of God; but likewise used all diligence to attain the whole mind that was in Christ,[15] and laboured to walk in every point as their beloved Master. In order to this they walked in a constant course of universal self-denial, trampling on every pleasure which they were not divinely conscious prepared them for taking pleasure in God. They took up their cross daily.[16] They strove, they agonized without intermission, to enter in at the strait gate.[17] This one thing they did;[18] they spared no pains to arrive at the summit of Christian holiness: 'leaving the first principles of the doctrine of Christ, to go on to perfection';[19] 'to know all that

[10] See 1 Cor. 13:1; but see *Notes, loc. cit.*, where Wesley had followed the consensus of Wycliffe, Tyndale, Cranmer, Geneva, Rheims, and the AV in translating ἀλαλάζον as 'tinkling'. In No. 36, 'The Law Established through Faith, II', III.1, we find 'tinkling', but in No. 91, 'On Charity', III.1, Wesley uses 'rumbling' again. Wesley had no precedent for this in Poole's *Annotations*, or Henry's *Exposition*—and has had no imitators in later translations. See also Arndt and Gingrich, and Liddell and Scott, *Greek-English Lexicons*.

[11] This distinction is at least as old as *The Shepherd of Hermas*, but was developed more explicitly by Clement of Alexandria; cf. *The Instructor*, I.i-vii, and *Stromateis*, II.xix-xx, IV.xxi-xxii, V.i-iv. It was then summed up by Eusebius in his *Demonstratio Evangelica*, I.viii.

[12] Acts 24:16.

[13] Still another deprecating reference to the *General Rules*. Cf. No. 22, 'Sermon on the Mount, II', II.4 and n.

[14] Titus 2:14.

[15] See 1 Cor. 2:16, and Phil. 2:5.

[16] See Luke 9:23.

[17] Luke 13:24; cf. No. 17, 'The Circumcision of the Heart', II.7 and n.

[18] See Phil. 3:13.   [19] Cf. Heb. 6:1.

love of God which passeth knowledge, and to be filled with all the fullness of God'.[20]

6. From long experience and observation I am inclined to think that whoever finds redemption in the blood of Jesus, whoever is justified, has then the choice of walking in the higher or the lower path. I believe the Holy Spirit at that time sets before him the more excellent way, and incites him to walk therein, to choose the narrowest path in the narrow way, to aspire after the heights and depths of holiness, after the entire image of God. But if he does not accept this offer, he insensibly declines into the lower order of Christians. He still goes on in what may be called a good way, serving God in his degree, and finds mercy in the close of life, through the blood of the covenant.[21]

7. I would be far from quenching the smoking flax,[22] from discouraging those that serve God in a low degree. But I would not wish them to stop here: I would encourage them to come up higher,[23] without thundering hell and damnation in their ears, without condemning the way wherein they were, telling them it is the way that leads to destruction.[24] I will endeavour to point out to them what is in every respect a more excellent way.

8. Let it be well remembered, I do not affirm that all who do not walk in this way are in the high road to hell. But thus much I must affirm: they will not have so high a place in heaven as they would have had if they had chosen the better part.[25] And will this be a small loss? The having so many fewer stars in your crown of glory?[26] Will it be a little thing to have a lower place than you might have had in the kingdom of your Father? Certainly there will be no sorrow in heaven: there all tears will be wiped from our eyes.[27] But if it were possible grief could enter there, we should grieve at that irreparable loss! Irreparable then, but not now! Now, by the grace of God, we may choose the 'more excellent way'. Let us now compare this in a few particulars with the way wherein most Christians walk.

[20] Cf. Eph. 3:19.
[21] See Heb. 13:20.
[22] See Isa. 42:3.
[23] See Luke 14:10.
[24] For another example of this striking change in the doctrine of assurance, cf. No. 106, 'On Faith, Heb. 11:6', I.11.
[25] See Luke 10:42.
[26] Cf. No. 57, 'On the Fall of Man', II.8 and n.
[27] See Rev. 7:17; 21:4.

I. To begin at the beginning of the day. It is the manner of the generality of Christians, if they are not obliged to work for their living, *to rise*, particularly in winter, at eight or nine in the morning, after having lain in bed eight or nine, if not more hours. I do not say now (as I should have been very apt to do fifty years 5 ago) that all who indulge themselves in this manner are in the way to hell. But neither can I say they are in the way to heaven, denying themselves, and taking up their cross daily.[28] Sure I am, there is a more excellent way to promote health both of body and mind. From an observation of more than sixty years I have learnt 10 that men in health require, at an average, from six to seven hours' sleep, and healthy women a little more, from seven to eight, in four and twenty hours. I know this quantity of sleep to be most advantageous to the body as well as the soul. It is preferable to any medicine which I have known, both for preventing and removing 15 nervous disorders.[29] It is therefore undoubtedly the most excellent way, in defiance of fashion and custom, to take just so much sleep as experience proves our nature to require; seeing this is indisputably most conducive both to bodily and spiritual health. And why should not you walk in this way? Because it is 20 difficult? Nay, with men it is impossible. But all things are possible with God;[30] and by his grace all things will be possible to *you*. Only continue instant in prayer, and you will find this not only possible, but easy; yea, and it will be far easier to rise early constantly than to do it sometimes. But then you must begin at the 25 right end: if you rise early, you must sleep early. Impose it upon yourself, unless when something extraordinary occurs, to go to bed at a fixed hour. Then the difficulty of it will soon be over; but the advantage of it will remain for ever.

II. The generality of Christians, as soon as they rise, are 30 accustomed to use some kind of *prayer;* and probably to use the same form still which they learned when they were eight or ten years old. Now I do not condemn those who proceed thus (though many do) as mocking God, though they have used the same form, without any variation, for twenty or thirty years together. But 35

---

[28] See Luke 9:23.
[29] Cf. 'Thoughts on Nervous Disorders', §7, *AM* (1786), IX.94-95, where Wesley discusses intemperance in sleep being one cause of 'lowness of spirits'; see also No. 93, 'On Redeeming the Time', *passim*.
[30] See Matt. 19:26.

surely there is a more excellent way of ordering our private devotions. What if you were to follow the advice given by that great and good man, Mr. Law,[31] on this subject? Consider both your outward and inward state, and vary your prayers accordingly.

5   For instance: suppose your outward state is prosperous; suppose you are in a state of health, ease, and plenty, having your lot cast among kind relations, good neighbours, and agreeable friends, that love you and you them; then your outward state manifestly calls for praise and thanksgiving to God. On the other hand, if you

10 are in a state of adversity; if God has laid trouble upon your loins;[32] if you are in poverty, in want, in outward distress; if you are in any imminent danger; if you are in pain and sickness: then you are clearly called to pour out your soul before God in such prayer as is suited to your circumstances. In like manner you may suit

15 your devotions to your inward state, the present state of your mind. Is your soul in heaviness either from a sense of sin or through manifold temptations?[33] Then let your prayer consist of such confessions, petitions, and supplications, as are agreeable to your distressed situation of mind. On the contrary, is your soul in

20 peace? Are you rejoicing in God? Are his consolations not small with you?[34] Then say with the Psalmist: 'Thou art my God, and I will thank thee; thou art my God, and I will praise thee.'[35] You may likewise, when you have time, add to your other devotions a little reading and meditation, and perhaps a psalm of praise, the

25 natural effusion of a thankful heart. You must certainly see that this is a more excellent way than the poor dry form which you used before.

III. 1. The generality of Christians, after using some prayer, usually apply themselves to the *business* of their calling. Every man

30 that has any pretence to be a Christian will not fail to do this;

---

[31] The reference here is to *A Serious Call*, ch. xiv, and Wesley's own published *Extract* of it (see *Bibliog*, No. 86). But Law had also published *The Spirit of Prayer*, and for Wesley's comment on it see JWJ, July 20, 1749. Wesley's estimates of Law varied according to circumstances and contexts; e.g., his attitude here represents a mellowing of the late Wesley. For his earlier criticisms of Law, cf. Wesley's letter to him, May 14, 1738, as well as a later one, Jan. 6, 1756; and see the letter to Dorothy Furly, May 18, 1757: 'Mr. Law . . . betrays deep ignorance both of Scripture and the inward work of God. You are more liable to receive hurt from his late writings than from any other which I know.' Cf. also No. 20, *The Lord Our Righteousness*, II.16.

[32] See Ps. 66:10 (BCP).

[33] 1 Pet. 1:6.

[34] See Job 15:11.   [35] Ps. 118:28 (BCP).

seeing it is impossible that an idle man can be a good man, sloth being inconsistent with religion.[36] But with what view? For what end do you undertake and follow your worldly business? 'To provide things necessary for myself and my family.' It is a good answer as far as it goes; but it does not go far enough. For a Turk 5 or a heathen goes so far, does his work for the very same ends. But a Christian may go abundantly farther: his end in all his labour is to please God; to do, not his own will, but the will of him that sent him into the world—[37] for this very purpose, to do the will of God on earth as angels do in heaven.[38] He works for eternity. He 10 'labours not for the meat that perisheth'—this is the smallest part of his motive—'but for that which endureth to everlasting life'.[39] And is not this 'a more excellent way'?

2. Again: in what *manner* do you transact your worldly business? I trust, with *diligence*, whatever your hand findeth to do, doing it 15 with your might;[40] in justice, rendering to all their due,[41] in every circumstance of life; yea, and in mercy, doing unto every man what you would he should do unto you.[42] This is well; but a Christian is called to go still farther—to add piety to justice; to intermix prayer, especially the prayer of the heart, with all the 20 labour of his hands. Without this all his diligence and justice only show him to be an honest heathen—and many there are who profess the Christian religion that go no farther than honest heathenism.

3. Yet again: in what *spirit* do you go through your business? In 25 the spirit of the world, or the Spirit of Christ? I am afraid thousands of those who are called good Christians do not understand the question. If you act in the Spirit of Christ you carry the end you at first proposed through all your work from first to last. You do everything in the spirit of sacrifice, giving up 30 your will to the will of God, and continually aiming, not at ease, pleasure, or riches; not at anything this short enduring world can give; but merely at the glory of God. Now can anyone deny that this is the most excellent way of pursuing worldly business?

IV. 1. But these tenements of clay[43] which we bear about us 35 require constant reparation, or they will sink into the earth from

---

[36] Cf. No. 111, *National Sins and Miseries*, II.6 and n.
[37] See John 6:38.   [38] See Matt. 6:10.   [39] Cf. John 6:27.
[40] See Eccles. 9:10.   [41] See Rom. 13:7.   [42] See Matt. 7:12.
[43] Cf. No. 28, 'Sermon on the Mount, VIII', §21 and n.

which they were taken, even sooner than nature requires. Daily food is necessary to prevent this, to repair the constant decays of nature. It was common in the heathen world when they were about to use this, to take meat or even drink, *libare pateram Jovi*,[44]
5 to pour out a little to the honour of their god—although the gods of the heathens were but devils, as the Apostle justly observes.[45] 'It seems', says a late writer, 'there was once some such custom as this in our own country. For we still frequently see a gentleman before he sits down to dinner in his own house, holding his hat
10 before his face, and perhaps seeming to say something; though he generally does it in such a manner that no one can tell what he says.'[46] Now what if instead of this, every head of a family, before he sat down to eat and drink, either morning, noon, or night (for the reason of the thing is the same at every hour of the day), was
15 seriously to ask a blessing from God on what he was about to take; yea, and afterward seriously to return thanks to the Giver of all his blessings. Would not this be a more excellent way than to use that dull farce which is worse than nothing, being in reality no other than mockery both of God and man?
20   2. As to the *quantity* of their food, good sort of men do not usually eat to excess. At least not so far as to make themselves sick with meat, or to intoxicate themselves with drink. And as to the manner of taking it, it is usually innocent, mixed with a little mirth, which is said to help digestion. So far, so good. And
25 provided they take only that measure of plain, cheap, wholesome food, which most promotes health both of body and mind, there will be no cause of blame. Neither can I require you to take that advice of Mr. Herbert, though he was a good man:

30   Take thy meat; think it dust; then eat a bit,
        And say with all, 'Earth to earth I commit.'[47]

This is too melancholy: it does not suit with that cheerfulness[48] which is highly proper at a Christian meal. Permit me to illustrate

---

[44] 'To pour out a libation bowl to Jove'; cf. Virgil, *Aeneid*, vii.133: '. . . *nunc pateras libate Jovi*'.
[45] See 1 Cor. 10:20.
[46] A vague recollection of an anecdote from Law, *Serious Call* (*Works*, IV.41); cf. another anecdote in this same vein in *The Spectator*, No. 380, May 16, 1712.
[47] Cf. George Herbert, *The Temple*, 'The Church Porch', ll. 131-32.
[48] In Wesley's 'holiness-happiness' equation cheerfulness is emphatically included; cf. the younger Wesley's letter to Mrs. Chapman, Mar. 29, 1737 ('. . . holiness cannot be without cheerfulness . . .'), and the older Wesley's letter to his niece, Sarah, Aug. 18, 1790

this subject with a little story. The King of France one day, pursuing the chase, outrode all his company, who after seeking him some time found him sitting in a cottage eating bread and cheese. Seeing them, he cried out: 'Where have I lived all my time? I never before tasted so good food in my life!' 'Sire', said 5 one of them, 'you never had so *good sauce* before; for you were never hungry.'[49] Now it is true, hunger is a good sauce:[50] but there is one that is better still; that is, thankfulness. Sure that is the most agreeable food which is seasoned with this. And why should not yours at every meal? You need not then fix your eye on death, but 10 receive every morsel as a pledge of life eternal. The Author of your being gives you in this food, not only a reprieve from death, but an earnest that in a little time 'death shall be swallowed up in victory.'[51]

3. The time of taking our food is usually a time of *conversation* 15 also, as it is natural to refresh our minds while we refresh our bodies. Let us consider a little in what manner the generality of Christians usually converse together. What are the ordinary subjects of their conversation? If it is harmless (as one would hope it is), if there be nothing in it profane, nothing immodest, nothing 20 untrue, or unkind; if there be no talebearing, backbiting, or evil-speaking, they have reason to praise God for his restraining grace. But there is more than this implied in 'ordering our conversation aright'.[52] In order to this it is needful, first, that 'your communication', that is, discourse or conversation, 'be good',[53] 25 that it be materially good, on good subjects; not fluttering about anything that occurs. For what have you to do with courts and kings? It is not your business to

Fight o'er the wars, reform the state,[54]

unless when some remarkable event calls for the acknowledge- 30 ment of the justice or mercy of God. We *must* indeed sometimes talk of worldly things; otherwise we may as well go out of the

('Perpetual cheerfulness is the temper of a Christian, . . . which is in one sense to rejoice evermore').
[49] π; source unidentified.
[50] Quoted by Cervantes in *Don Quixote*, II.5; and earlier in Cicero, *De Finibus [bonorum et malorum] (On the Purpose of Good and Evil)*, II.xxviii.90, where it is credited to Socrates.
[51] Cf. 1 Cor. 15:54.
[52] Cf. Ps. 50:23.
[53] Cf. Matt. 5:37; Eph. 4:29.
[54] Prior, 'The Ladle', l. 96.

world.[55] But it should only be so far as is needful; then we should return to a better subject. Secondly, let your conversation be 'to the use of edifying';[56] calculated to edify either the speaker or the hearers or both; to build them up, as each has particular need,
5 either in faith, or love, or holiness. Thirdly, see that it not only gives entertainment, but, in one kind or other, 'ministers grace to the hearers'.[57] Now is not this a more excellent way of *conversing* than the harmless way above mentioned?

V. 1. We have seen what is the more excellent way of ordering
10 our conversation, as well as our business. But we cannot be always intent upon business; both our bodies and minds require some relaxation. We need intervals of diversion from business. It will be necessary to be very explicit upon this head, as it is a point which has been much misunderstood.
15   2. Diversions are of various kinds. Some are almost peculiar to men, as the sports of the field—hunting, shooting, fishing—wherein not many women (I should say, ladies) are concerned. Others are indifferently used by persons of both sexes; some of which are of a more public nature, as races, masquerades, plays,
20 assemblies, balls. Others are chiefly used in private houses, as cards, dancing, and music; to which we may add the reading of plays, novels, romances, newspapers, and fashionable poetry.
  3. Some diversions indeed which were formerly in great request are now fallen into disrepute. The nobility and gentry (in
25 England at least) seem totally to disregard the once fashionable diversion of *hawking*; and the vulgar themselves are no longer diverted by men hacking and hewing each other in pieces at *broadsword*. The noble game of *quarterstaff* likewise is now exercised by very few. Yea, *cudgelling* has lost its honour, even in
30 Wales itself. *Bear-baiting* also is now very seldom seen, and *bull-baiting* not very often. And it seems *cock-fighting* would totally cease in England, were it not for two or three right honourable patrons.
  4. It is not needful to say anything more of these foul 'remains
35 of Gothic barbarity'[58] than that they are a reproach, not only to all

[55] See 1 Cor. 5:10.
[56] Eph. 4:29.   [57] *Ibid.*
[58] Pope, in *The Guardian*, No. 61 (May 21, 1713), had used this phrase as from the Abbé Claude Fleury's *Les Moeurs des Israélites* in the context of Fleury's comparison of the ancient Israelites with those of *'les Francs'*. The pejorative use of the adjective 'Gothic' had, however, already become a commonplace (cf. *OED*).

religion, but even to human nature. One would not pass so severe a censure on the sports of the field. Let those who have nothing better to do, still run foxes and hares out of breath.[59] Neither need much be said about horse-races,[60] till some man of sense will undertake to defend them. It seems a great deal more may be said in defence of seeing a serious *tragedy*. I could not do it with a clear conscience; at least not in an English theatre, the sink of all profaneness and debauchery;[61] but possibly others can. I cannot say quite so much for *balls* or *assemblies*, which are more reputable than *masquerades*, but must be allowed by all impartial persons to have exactly the same tendency. So undoubtedly have all public dancings. And the same tendency they must have, unless the same caution obtained among modern Christians which was observed among the ancient heathens. With them men and women never danced together, but always in separate rooms. This was always observed in ancient Greece, and for several ages at Rome,[62] where a woman dancing in company with men would have at once been set down for a prostitute. Of playing at *cards* I say the same as of seeing plays.[63] I could not do it with a clear conscience. But I am not obliged to pass sentences on those that are otherwise minded.[64] I leave them to their own Master: to him let them stand or fall.

5. But supposing these, as well as the reading of plays, novels, newspapers, and the like, to be quite 'innocent diversions', yet are there not 'more excellent ways' of diverting themselves for those that love or fear God? Would men of fortune divert themselves in the open air? They may do it by cultivating and improving their

[59] This had appeared in quotation marks in No. 79, 'On Dissipation', §12; cf. n. there.
[60] Cf. No. 143, 'Public Diversions Denounced', III.2.
[61] In his Oxford days Wesley 'had a passionate interest in plays and in the theatre. . . . There was a histrionic streak in his character' (Green, *Wesley*, pp. 72, 114). And his delight in plays continued even after he had come round to the views of Jeremy Collier *(A Defence of the Short View of the Profaneness and Immorality of the English Stage* [1699]) and William Law *(The Absolute Unlawfulness of the Stage-Entertainment Fully Demonstrated* [1726]); cf., e.g., his comment on John Home's recent tragedy, *Douglas* (JWJ, June 9, 1757). Notice the extraordinary range of his quotations from various dramas; his reading in them was extensive (clearly, he distinguished 'seeing' plays in a theatre from *reading* them). Cf. George Farquhar's description of a typical 'first night' in his *The Inconstant: Or, the Way to Win Him* (1702), Act IV, sc. 3; see also No. 94, 'On Family Religion', III.14.
[62] A doubtful inference from Lucian, 'The Dance'; Athenaeus, *Deipnosophistae*, I.14-22; and Plato, *The Laws*, VII.814E-816D; cf. Chambers's *Cyclopaedia, loc. cit.*
[63] The young Wesley had also played cards; cf. diary, Dec. 30, 1736 ('played at ombre'); Jan. 7, 1727 ('played loo'); Jan. 10, 1727 ('played cards and lost'); on June 20, 1729, he played cards and lost twelve shillings.
[64] More evidence of the mellowing late Wesley; cf. No. 39, 'Catholic Spirit'.

lands, by planting their grounds, by laying out, carrying on, and perfecting their gardens and orchards. At other times they may visit and converse with the most serious and sensible of their neighbours; or they may visit the sick, the poor, the widows, and
5   fatherless in their affliction.[65] Do they desire to divert themselves in the house? They may read useful history, pious and elegant poetry, or several branches of natural philosophy. If you have time, you may divert yourself by music, and perhaps by philosophical experiments.[66] But above all, when you have once
10 learned the use of prayer, you will find that as

> that which yields or fills
> All space, the ambient air, wide interfused
> Embraces round this florid earth;[67]

so will this, till through every space of life it be interfused with all
15 your employments, and wherever you are, whatever you do, embrace you on every side. Then you will be able to say boldly:

> With me no melancholy void,
> No moment lingers unemployed,
> Or unimproved below;
20   My weariness of life is gone,
> Who live to serve my God alone,
> And only Jesus know.[68]

VI. One point only remains to be considered; that is, the use of money.[69] What is the way wherein the generality of Christians
25 employ this? And is there not a more excellent way?

[65] See Jas. 1:27.
[66] Cf. Chambers's *Cyclopaedia*, 'Experimental': 'Experiments are of the last [i.e., highest] importance in philosophy. . . . In effect, experiments within these past fifty or sixty years, are come into such vogue that nothing will pass in philosophy [i.e., natural science] but what is founded on experiment or confirmed by experiment. . . . The new philosophy is almost altogether experimental.' The chief sponsor of this new philosophy was The Royal Society of London for Improving Natural Knowledge, which was founded in 1660; cf. Thomas Sprat, *History of the Royal Society* (1667).
[67] Cf. Milton, *Paradise Lost*, vii.88-90; No. 55, *On the Trinity*, §9 and n.
[68] Cf. Charles Wesley, *Hymns and Sacred Poems* (1749), II.136 (*Poet. Wks.*, V.279), which was reprinted separately in *Hymns for the Watch-night:*

> With us no melancholy void,
> No moment lingers unemployed,
> Or unimproved below;
> Our weariness of life is gone,
> Who live to serve our God alone,
> And only thee to know.

[69] See No. 87, 'The Danger of Riches', II.8 and n.

1. The generality of Christians usually set apart something yearly, perhaps a tenth or even one-eighth part of their income, whether it arise from yearly revenue, or from trade, for charitable uses. A few I have known who said like Zaccheus, 'Lord, the half of my goods I give to the poor.'[70] O that it would please God to 5 multiply these friends of mankind, these general benefactors! But,

2. Besides those who have a stated rule, there are thousands who give large sums to the poor; especially when any striking instance of distress is represented to them in lively colours.   10

3. I praise God for all of you who act in this manner. May you never be weary of well-doing! May God restore what you give sevenfold into your own bosom! But yet I show unto you a more excellent way.

4. You may consider yourself as one in whose hands the 15 Proprietor of heaven and earth and all things therein has lodged a part of his goods, to be disposed of according to his direction. And his direction is, that you should look upon yourself as one of a certain number of indigent persons who are to be provided for out of that portion of his goods wherewith you are entrusted. You 20 have two advantages over the rest: the one, that 'it is more blessed to give than to receive;'[71] the other, that you are to serve yourself first, and others afterwards. This is the light wherein you are to see yourself and them. But to be more particular: first, if you have no family, after you have provided for yourself, give away all that 25 remains; so that

> Each Christmas you accounts may clear,
> And wind your bottom round the year.[72]

This was the practice of all the young men at Oxford who were called 'Methodists'.[73] For example: one of them had thirty pounds 30 a year. He lived on twenty-eight and gave away forty shillings. The next year receiving sixty pounds, he still lived on

---

[70] Luke 19:8.
[71] Acts 20:35.
[72] Cf. Prior, 'An Epitaph', ll. 47-48:

> Each Christmas they accounts did clear,
> And wound their bottom round the year.

Orig., 'your accounts', altered by Wesley's errata; see also No. 87, 'The Danger of Riches', II.7 and n.
[73] Cf. No. 53, *On the Death of George Whitefield*, III.2 and n.

twenty-eight, and gave away two and thirty. The third year he received ninety pounds, and gave away sixty-two. The fourth year he received a hundred and twenty pounds. Still he lived as before on twenty-eight, and gave to the poor ninety-two.[74] Was not this a
5 more excellent way? Secondly, if you have a family, seriously consider before God how much each member of it wants in order to have what is needful for life and godliness. And in general do not allow them less, nor much more, than you allow yourself. Thirdly, this being done, fix your purpose to 'gain no more'. I
10 charge you in the name of God, do not increase your substance![75] As it comes daily or yearly, so let it go; otherwise you 'lay up treasures upon earth'.[76] And this our Lord as flatly forbids as murder and adultery. By doing it, therefore, you would 'treasure up to yourselves wrath against the day of wrath and revelation of
15 the righteous judgment of God'.[77]

5. But suppose it were not forbidden, how can you on principles of reason spend your money in a way which God may *possibly forgive*, instead of spending it in a manner which he will *certainly reward*? You will have no reward in heaven for what you
20 *lay up;* you will for what you *lay out.* Every pound you put into the earthly bank is sunk: it brings no interest above.[78] But every pound you give to the poor is put into the bank of heaven. And it will bring glorious interest; yea, and such as will be accumulating to all eternity.

25 6. Who then is a wise man, and endued with knowledge among you?[79] Let him resolve this day, this hour, this moment, the Lord

---

[74] Tyerman regarded this as Wesley's reference to himself; cf. *JW*, I.71-72. But see Green's comments on Wesley's income at Oxford in *Wesley*, pp. 100-1, 320-21. Thus, this is either a romanticized memory of those early days or, just possibly, a reference to some other member of the Holy Club (John Clayton?).

[75] Another flat prohibition of surplus accumulation; see No. 50, 'The Use of Money', intro., I.1, and n.

[76] Matt. 6:19.

[77] Cf. Rom. 2:5.

[78] A notable contradiction of the famous 'Weber-Tawney' thesis that it was the Protestant work ethic that served as the prime sponsor of capitalism and its presuppositions as to the legitimacy of capital accumulation by means of interest. By contrast, Wesley here reaffirms his agreement with the classical and medieval condemnation of 'interest'; cf. the summation of that tradition in Thomas, *Summa Theologica*, II-II, Q. 78, Arts. 1-4. Clearly, there is a need for a more careful and complete study of Wesley's economic notions and for a more careful critique of the 'Weber-Tawney' thesis itself; cf. Max Weber, *The Protestant Ethic and the Spirit of Capitalism* (London, G. Allen and Unwin, 1930), and R. H. Tawney, *Religion and the Rise of Capitalism* (London, J. Murray, 1926).

[79] Jas. 3:13.

assisting him, to choose in all the preceding particulars the 'more excellent way'; and let him steadily keep it, both with regard to sleep, prayer, work, food, conversation, and diversions; and particularly with regard to the employment of that important 'talent', *money*. Let *your* heart answer to the call of God: 'From   5 this moment, God being my helper, I will lay up no more treasure upon earth; this one thing I will do, I will lay up treasure in heaven;[80] I will render unto God the things that are God's;[81] I will give him all my goods and all my heart.'

---

[80] See Matt. 6:19-20.
[81] Matt. 22:21.

AN ISRAELITE INDEED

AN INTRODUCTORY COMMENT

This is another sermon prepared expressly for the Arminian Magazine. *We have no other data about its context except the interesting fact that Wesley seems to have used John 1:47 as a preaching text but twice—once in 1728 (see No. 138A, 'On Dissimulation') and again in 1755. In a way more probing than 'The More Excellent Way', this sermon is a discussion of a Christian's inner motivations and aims, and his outward expressions of Christian benevolence; the illuminating metaphor for all this is Nathanael's* guilelessness. *The sermon also serves as Wesley's belated refutation of the naturalist ethics of Francis Hutcheson and Hutcheson's claim (along with the deists generally) that the virtues of human benevolence are innate and universal in human nature itself. (See No. 12, 'The Witness of Our Own Spirit', §5 and n.) One may suppose that Hutcheson's influence had continued to grow, and Wesley had concluded that a formal rejection was needed, since on Hutcheson's ground one could dispense with the supernatural aspects of biblical revelation. The sermon first appeared in the* Arminian Magazine *(July and August 1785), VIII.349-54, 393-98, with no title but numbered as 'Sermon XXVIII'. It was then included in* SOSO, *VII.215-31, with its present title apparently lifted from the text. It was not reprinted in Wesley's lifetime.*

An Israelite Indeed

John 1:47

Behold an Israelite indeed, in whom is no guile.

1. Some years ago a very ingenious man, Professor Hutcheson of Glasgow,[1] published two treatises, on *The Original of our Ideas of* 5 *Beauty and Virtue*. In the latter of these he maintains that the very essence of virtue is the love of our fellow-creatures. He endeavours to prove that virtue and benevolence are one and the same thing; that every temper is only so far virtuous as it partakes of the nature of benevolence; and that all our words and actions 10 are then only virtuous when they spring from the same principle. 'But does he not suppose gratitude or the love of God to be the foundation of this benevolence?' By no means: such a supposition as this never entered into his mind. Nay, he supposes just the contrary; he does not make the least scruple to aver that if any 15 temper or action be produced by any regard to God, or any view to a reward from him, it is not virtuous at all; and that if an action spring partly from benevolence and partly from a view to God, the more there is in it of a view to God, the less there is of virtue.[2]

2. I cannot see this beautiful essay of Mr. Hutcheson's in any 20 other light than as a decent, and therefore more dangerous, attack upon the whole of the Christian revelation;[3] seeing this asserts the

[1] Texts in both the *AM* and *SOSO* read 'Hutchinson', but this is obviously a printer's error. The reference is to Francis Hutcheson (1694–1746); see above No. 12, 'The Witness of Our Own Spirit', §5 and n. Wesley secured a copy of *An Inquiry into the Original of Our Ideas of Beauty and Virtue* in the year of its publication (1725); a copy of the third edn. (1729) initialled 'J. W. 1772. Kingswood' is still in the library of the Kingswood School where, along with Hutcheson's *Essay on the Nature and Conduct of the Passions and Affections with Illustrations Upon the Moral Sense* (1726), it had been used as a text.

[2] This is a caricature of Hutcheson's argument (Pt. II, Concerning Moral Good and Evil); Hutcheson had repeatedly asserted that both virtue and the love of God are fixed in us by our divine Creator; cf. No. 12, 'The Witness of Our Own Spirit', §5 and n.

[3] The quarrel between Wesley and Hutcheson turns upon the issue of the prime motivation for human benevolence (i.e., what *is* 'the first and great commandment'?); and Hutcheson does deny that our primary ethical concern is to seek or earn God's approval of our moral actions. Yet he insists (against Shaftesbury, Mandeville, Hobbes, and the deists) that even on naturalistic grounds, 'Christianity . . . gives us the truest idea of virtue and recommends the love of God and of mankind as the sum of true religion' (*Inquiry*, xix-xx); cf. No. 105, 'On Conscience', I.8-10.

279

love of God to be the true foundation both of the love of our
neighbour and all other virtues; and accordingly places this as 'the
first and great commandment',[4] on which all the rest depend—
'Thou shalt love the Lord thy God will all thy heart, and with all
5   thy mind, and with all thy soul, and with all thy strength.'[5] So that
according to the Bible, benevolence, or the love of our neighbour,
is only the second commandment. And suppose the Scripture be
of God, it is so far from being true that benevolence alone is both
the foundation and the essence of all virtue, that benevolence
10 itself is no virtue at all, unless it spring from the love of God.
    3. Yet it cannot be denied that this writer himself has a
marginal note in favour of Christianity. 'Who would not wish',
says he, 'that the Christian revelation could be proved to be of
God? Seeing it is unquestionably the most benevolent institution
15 that ever appeared in the world.'[6] But is not this, if it be
considered thoroughly, another blow at the very root of that
revelation? Is it more or less than to say: 'I wish it could; but in
truth it cannot be proved.'
    4. Another ingenious writer advances an hypothesis totally
20 different from this. Mr. Wollaston, in the book which he entitles
The Religion of Nature Delineated, endeavours to prove that 'truth is
the essence of virtue', or conformableness to truth.[7] But it seems

---

[4] Matt. 22:38.

[5] Cf. Mark 12:30.

[6] No such sentence appears in Hutcheson's published writings; it is, apparently, a
tenuous paraphrase by Wesley from Hutcheson's rare allusions to Christianity as such. Cf.
Inquiry, p. 151: 'Whoever would appeal to the general strain of Christian exhortations will
find *disinterested love* [i.e., benevolence] more inculcated and *motives of gratitude* more
frequently suggested than any others.' See also pp. 275-76 (1st edn.) and sect. 3, xv. Cf.
Nos. 128, 'The Deceitfulness of the Human Heart', II.8; and 12, 'The Witness of Our
Own Spirit', §5 and n.

[7] William Wollaston (1660–1724), a moral philosopher whose fame rests on one book
(privately printed in 1722 and first published in 1724). It was yet another variation on the
rationalistic ethics of Samuel Clarke, but with a distinctive emphasis on 'the truth' as the
prime norm for all judgments 'of moral good and evil' (sect. I, Theses IV-X). Wollaston's
home was in Charterhouse Square, and Wesley 'remembers to have seen [him] when I was
at school, attending the public service at the Charterhouse chapel' (No. 106, 'On Faith,
Heb. 11:6', II.2). His alleged quotation does not appear in Wollaston's text but is a
reasonably accurate over-simplification of the basic argument. For example, Wollaston's
second 'Thesis' (p. 8) asserts that 'those [moral propositions] are true which express things
as they are. . . . Truth is the conformity of those words or signs by which things are
exprest, to the things themselves.' If one treats a post as if it were a man, or vice versa, this
is more than a mistake; it is morally wrong (p. 15). But this presupposes that rational
creatures are competent judges of 'truth', without any necessary aid of God's self-revealed
will or 'law'—and this is what Wesley objects to. Even so, he kept copies of *The Religion of
Nature Delineated* (which he had read first in 1733) in the preaching-house libraries in

Mr. Wollaston goes farther from the Bible than Mr. Hutcheson himself. For Mr. Hutcheson's scheme sets aside only one of the two great commandments, namely, 'Thou shalt love the Lord thy God;'[8] whereas Mr. Wollaston sets aside both—for his hypothesis does not place the essence of virtue in either the love 5 of God or of our neighbour.

5. However, both of these authors agree, though in different ways, to put asunder what God has joined. But St. Paul unites them together in teaching us to 'speak the truth in love'.[9] And undoubtedly both truth and love were united in him to whom he 10 who knows the hearts of all men gives this amiable character, 'Behold an Israelite indeed, in whom is no guile.'

6. But who is it concerning whom our blessed Lord gives this glorious testimony? Who is this Nathanael, of whom so remarkable an account is given in the latter part of the chapter 15 before us? Is it not strange that he is not mentioned again in any part of the New Testament? He is not mentioned again under this name; but probably he had another, whereby he was more commonly called. It was generally believed by the ancients that he is the same person who is elsewhere termed Bartholomew, one of 20 our Lord's apostles, and one that in the enumeration of them, both by St. Matthew and St. Mark, is placed immediately after St. Philip, who first brought him to his Master. It is very probable that his proper name was Nathanael—a name common among the Jews—and that his other name, Bartholomew, meaning only the 25 son of Ptolemy, was derived from his father, a custom which was then exceeding common among the Jews, as well as the heathens.[10]

7. By what little is said of him in the context he appears to have been a man of an excellent spirit; not hasty of belief, and yet open 30 to conviction, and willing to receive the truth from whencesoever

London, Bristol, and Newcastle (cf. *Minutes*, Aug. 3, 1745), and he includes it in a list of recommended readings in his edition of John Norris, *Reflections Upon the Conduct of Human Life* (1741; *Bibliog*, No. 3). For other references to Wollaston, cf. No. 120, 'The Unity of the Divine Being', §18; and JWJ, July 9, 1737. For 'natural religion', see No. 1, *Salvation by Faith*, I.2 and n.

[8] Deut. 6:5; Matt. 22:37.   [9] Cf. Eph. 4:15.

[10] Cf. Wesley's *Notes* for John 1:45: '. . . Nathanael was probably the same with Bartholomew;' he is here following Bengel's *Gnomon, loc. cit.*, and an ancient tradition that thus reconciles John 1:45; John 21:2; Matt. 10:3; and Acts 1:13. But see R. B. Y. Scott, 'Who Was Nathanael?' In *Expository Times*, XXXVIII, No. 2 (Nov. 1926), pp. 93-94, and U. Holzmeister, '*Nathanael, fuitne idem ac S. Bartholomaeus apostolus?*' in *Biblica*, XXI (1940). 28-39.

to be rendered 'what he assuredly hath'.[24] And it may be observed that the word δοκέω, in various places of the New Testament, does not lessen but strengthens the sense of the word joined with it. Accordingly, whoever improves the grace he has already
5 received, whoever increases in the love of God, will surely retain it. God will continue, yea, will give it more abundantly; whereas whoever does not improve this talent cannot possibly retain it.[25] Notwithstanding all he can do, it will infallibly be taken away from him.

10 II.1. Meantime, as the heart of him that is 'an Israelite indeed' is true to God, so his words are suitable thereto. And as there is no guile lodged in his heart, so there is none 'found in his lips'.[26] The first thing implied herein is *veracity*, the speaking the truth from his heart; the putting away all wilful lying, in every kind and
15 degree. A lie, according to a well-known definition of it, is, *falsum testimonium cum intentione fallendi*[27]—a falsehood, known to be such by the speaker, and uttered with an intention to deceive. But even the speaking a falsehood is not a lie, if it be not spoken with an intent to deceive.
20 2. Most casuists, particularly those of the Church of Rome, distinguish lies into three sorts: the first sort is malicious lies; the second, harmless lies; the third, officious lies[28]—concerning which they pass a very different judgment. I know not any that are so hardy as even to excuse, much less defend, *malicious* lies; that
25 is, such as are told with a design to hurt anyone. These are condemned by all parties. Men are more divided in their

---

[24] Luke 8:18 (*Notes*). Cf. Nos. 43, *The Scripture Way of Salvation*, §1 and n.; and 82, 'On Temptation', §2 and n. See also Wesley's *Notes* for 1 Cor. 10:12.
[25] Cf. No. 85, 'On Working Out Our Own Salvation', III.6 and n.
[26] Mal. 2:6; cf. 1 Pet. 3:10.
[27] Cf. Augustine, *De Mendacio*, iv.5 (Migne, *PL*, XL.491), or 'On Lying', §5, in *NPNF*, I, III.460.
[28] Cf. Thomas, *Summa Theologica*, II-II, Q.110, Art. 2: 'Whether lies are rightly divided into *Officious*, *Jocose*, and *Mischievous* lies?' His answer is affirmative, and in Art. 3 he proceeds to the conclusion that 'every lie is a sin, as also Augustine declares (*Contra Mendac.* xiv)'. Cf. Bishop Ezekiel Hopkins, *Exposition on the Ten Commandments*, which Wesley extracted and printed in 1759 (*Bibliog*, No. 234): 'Now lies are usually distinguished into three kinds: the jocular, officious, and pernicious . . .' . See also Thomas Manton, *One Hundred and Ninety Sermons on the 119th Psalm* (1681), p. 187: 'There are three sorts of lies: *mendacium jocosum, officiosum, et perniciosum*. There's the sporting lie, tending to our recreation and delight; there's the officious lie, tending to our own and others' profit; and there's the pernicious and hurtful lie, tending to our neighbour's prejudice.' Cf. Steele, *The Spectator*, No. 234, Nov. 28, 1711; and John Tillotson, *Works*, I.562.

judgment with regard to *harmless* lies, such as are supposed to do neither good nor harm. The generality of men, even in the Christian world, utter them without any scruple, and openly maintain that if they do no harm to anyone else, they do none to the speaker. Whether they do or no, they have certainly no place 5 in the mouth of him that is 'an Israelite indeed'. He cannot tell lies in jest, any more than in earnest; nothing but truth is heard from his mouth. He remembers the express command of God to the Ephesian Christians: 'Putting away' all '*lying*, speak every man truth to his neighbour.'[b]   10

3. Concerning *officious* lies, those that are spoken with a design to do good, there have been numerous controversies in the Christian church. Abundance of writers, and those men of renown for piety as well as learning, have published whole volumes upon the subject, and in despite of all opposers, not only 15 maintained them to be innocent, but commended them as meritorious.[29] But what saith the Scripture? One passage is so express that there does not need any other. It occurs in the third chapter of the Epistle to the Romans, where the very words of the Apostle are: 'If the truth of God hath more abounded through my 20 lie unto his glory, why am I yet judged as a sinner?' (Will not that lie be excused from blame, for the good effect of it?) 'And not rather (as we are slanderously reported, and as some affirm that we say), Let us do evil, that good may come? Whose damnation is just.'[c] Here the Apostle plainly declares: (1), that the good effect 25 of a lie is no excuse for it; (2), that it is a mere slander upon Christians to say, 'They teach men to do evil that good may come;' (3), that if any in fact do this, either teach men to do evil that good may come, or do so themselves, their damnation is just. This is peculiarly applicable to those who tell lies in order to do 30 good thereby. It follows that officious lies, as well as all others, are

[b] Eph. 4:25.
[c] Ver. 7-8.

---

[29] Cf. Jeremy Taylor, *Ductor Dubitantium; Or, the Rule of Conscience* (1660) Bk. III, ch. ii, 'Of Laws Penal and Tributary', Rule V, §§7-11. In §10, Taylor tells of a young Christian in Jerusalem who (by confessing to a deed of which he was not guilty) saved the larger community from execution 'by an officious and charitable lie. . . . Himself indeed was put to death . . . but he saved the lives of all the rest; who, I doubt not, believed that young man to have in heaven a great reward for his piety, and no reproof for his innocent and pious lie;' cf. Taylor, *Works*, III.429. The burden of Taylor's general argument, however, lies heavily against any self-serving form of lying.

exclude the using any *compliments?* A vile word, the very sound of which I abhor; quite agreeing with our poet,

> It never was a good day
> Since lowly fawning was called compliment.[38]

5 I advise men of sincerity and simplicity never to take that silly word in their mouth; but labour to keep at the utmost distance both from the name and the thing.

9. Not long before that remarkable time,

> When statesmen sent a prelate cross the seas,
> 10   By long famed Act of Pains and Penalties,[39]

several bishops attacked Bishop Atterbury at once, then Bishop of Rochester, and asked: 'My lord, why will you not suffer your servants to deny you, when you do not care to see company? It is not a lie for them to say your lordship is not at home; for it 15 deceives no one. Everyone knows it means only, your lordship is busy.' He replied, 'My lords, if it is (which I doubt) consistent

---

[38] Cf. Shakespeare, *Twelfth Night*, III.i.109-10:

> 'Twas never a merry world
> Since lowly *feigning* was call'd compliment.

Wesley repeats his emendation of Shakespeare in No. 111, *National Sins and Miseries*, II.3.

[39] Another conflation, this one from a poem by his brother, Samuel Wesley, Jun., preserved in Adam Clarke, *Memoirs of the Wesley Family* (1823), p. 382, and somehow omitted from *Poems* (1736). Samuel, Jun. was a protégé of Bishop Francis Atterbury and a critic of Sir Robert Walpole; the reference is to Atterbury's banishment because of his opposition (1715–23) to the new Whig government; cf. Williams, *The Whig Supremacy, 1714–1760*, pp. 144-45, 174-76. Here is Samuel's poem with John's epigrams picked out:

> When patriots sent a Bishop 'cross the seas,
> They met to fix the pains and penalties;
> While true-blue blood-hounds on his death were bent,
> Thy mercy, Walpole, voted banishment!
> Or, forc'd thy sov'reign's orders to perform,
> Or, proud to govern, as to raise the storm.
> Thy goodness shewn in such a dangerous day,
> He only who receiv'd it can repay:
> Thou never justly recompens'd can be,
> Till banish'd Francis do the same for thee.

> * * *

> Tho' some would give Sir Bob no quarter,
> But long to hang him in his garter;
> Yet sure he will deserve to have
> Such mercy as in power he gave:
> Send him abroad to take his ease,
> By Act of pains and penalties:
> But if he e'er comes here again,
> Law, take thy course, and hang him then.

with sincerity, yet I am sure it is not consistent with that simplicity which becomes a Christian bishop.'[40]

10. But to return. The sincerity and simplicity of him in whom is no guile have likewise an influence on his whole behaviour; they give a colour to his whole outward conversation; which though it 5 be far remote from everything of clownishness, and ill breeding, of roughness and surliness, yet is plain and artless, and free from all disguise, being the very picture of his heart. The truth and love which continually reign there produce an open front, and a serene countenance. Such as leave no pretence for anyone to say, with 10 that arrogant King of Castile, 'When God made man, he left one capital defect: he ought to have set a window in his breast;'[41] for he opens a window in his own breast by the whole tenor of his words and actions.

11. This then is real, genuine, solid virtue. Not truth alone, nor 15 conformity to truth. This is a property of real virtue, not the essence of it. Not love alone, though this comes nearer the mark; for 'love' in one sense 'is the fulfilling of the law'.[42] No: truth and love united together are the essence of virtue or holiness.[43] God indispensably requires 'truth in the inward parts',[44] influencing all our words and 20 actions. Yet truth itself, separate from love, is nothing in his sight. But let the humble, gentle, patient love of all mankind be fixed on its right foundation, namely, the love of God, springing from faith, from a full conviction that God hath given his only Son to die for *my* sins; and then the whole will resolve into that grand conclusion, 25 'worthy of all men to be received':[45] 'Neither circumcision availeth anything, nor uncircumcision, but faith that worketh by love.'[46]

---

[40] All the Wesleys were partisans of Bishop Francis Atterbury (1662–1732) and of his Tory churchmanship and politics; they were saddened and outraged by Walpole's ruthless treatment of him. This anecdote does not appear in Atterbury's writings or in J. H. Overton's biography in *DNB*. One supposes that it was heard and preserved in the family's painful memories of the tragedy of 1723.

[41] The 'arrogant King of Castile' was probably Alphonso X (*El Sabio*); see No. 56, 'God's Approbation of His Works', II.1 and n. The allusion here to a window in the human breast is an echo of the story of Momus, the Greek god of wit, who was supposed to have said of the human creature fashioned by Prometheus that 'this new being should have had a window in his breast so that his thoughts might be seen.' Cf. No. 4, *Scriptural Christianity*, III.5 and n.

[42] Rom. 13:10.

[43] Wesley's definition of 'the essence of virtue', *contra* Hutcheson (see above, §2 proem). Note especially this correlation of 'truth and love united' with 'virtue or holiness', as if taken together they were working synonyms.

[44] Ps. 51:6.   [45] 1 Tim. 1:15 (BCP, Communion, Comfortable Words).

[46] Cf. Gal. 5:6. Cf. above II.4; and No. 2, *The Almost Christian*, II.6 and n.

ON CHARITY

AN INTRODUCTORY COMMENT

More often than not, Wesley's published sermons were from texts infrequently used in his oral preaching. This sermon, however, is an interesting exception: it was written in London, October 15, 1784 (a year in which he used it a dozen times for oral sermons). It then appeared in the first two instalments of 'Original Sermons by the Rev. John Wesley, M.A.' in the Arminian Magazine *of 1785, VIII.8-16, 70-76, without a title but numbered as 'Sermon XXV'. Three years later (1788), it reappeared in* SOSO, *VII.233-56.*

In the interval he continued to use 1 Cor. 13:1-3 (eight times in 1785; three times in 1787). And, by a happy accident, we can compare his written sermon with an oral sermon on the same text which is remarkably close to the written text. There is in the Drew University Library a unique manuscript précis of a 'Charity Sermon' by 'John Westley', preached in the church of St. John's Clerkenwell (near The Charterhouse and not far from Wesley's New Chapel on City Road; in 1787 it was a prominent parish church, but in 1962 was restored to its original status as the local priory church of the Knights Templar). This memoir deserves publication here as the only instance on record where we have a full report of an oral sermon and its written counterpart. Moreover, it is a careful report by an obviously well-educated and attentive hearer (maybe the rector?) who is evidently one of 'Mr. Westley's' admirers but not, as it would appear, a Methodist himself:

> *Minutes of a Sermon preach'd at St. John's Clerkenwell by Mr. John Westley, Dec. 16, 1787. Mr. Westley was then 85 years of age.*

The text was 1 Cor. 13, v. 3 [quoted from the AV].

Mr. Westley began his discourse by defining the true religion which, he said, did not consist in opinion but in a proper temper and disposition of mind towards God and man. He then adverted to the word 'charity' in the text. In all the old translations of the Bible, he said, the word ἀγάπη was translated 'love': in the Bishops' Bible published in the time of Henry the Eighth, in all the editions printed in the reigns of Queen Elizabeth, King Edward the Sixth, and James the First. The first edition where the word 'charity' occurs, he said, was that printed by Roger Daniel in 1647; later editions have adopted the same word, which is neither English nor good Latin. By 'love' he understood love towards our neighbour: a spirit of universal goodwill and benevolence. He then proceeded to show more particularly the nature and excellence of this 'love', and its superiority over the other virtues and qualities mentioned in the text and the preceding verses.

In mentioning the properties of love when he came to the passage, 'is not easily provoked', he observed that in all the translations of the Bible which he had seen in foreign languages, in the Dutch, German, French, and Italian, the word 'easily' was entirely left out. The English was the only translation which had that expression which was by no means justified by the original οὐ παροξύνεται. Why then, says he, did the translators of the Bible introduce this word? From very good motives, I doubt not; recollecting St. Paul's conduct as recorded in the Acts of the Apostles, they were unwilling that that conduct should seem contrary to his own rules. But, says he (quoting the passage, Acts 15, v. 36-39), it appears from hence that the anger was on the side of Barnabas and not of Paul. Away, then, with the word 'easily', and rest on the original meaning without any modification.

Speaking of the superiority of charity or love over prophecy, he told the following story: 'During the last continental war, it was rumoured here in England that a soldier in Flanders had prophesied some strange things which fell out just as he had foretold. I suspended my belief till ---- returned (mentioning some person on whose veracity he could depend [i.e., John Haime]). He confirmed these reports and said that the officers had sent for the man, who persisted before them in the truth of his prophecies, which were relative to the events of the war, and said that he would give them three signs of his veracity. The first was that on the morrow morning there would be a very terrible storm of thunder and lightning. The second was that they should have a general engagement with the French within three days (an event very little expected) and [the third was] that if he was a false prophet he should be killed; if not, he should only receive a musket ball in the calf of his leg. All this happened as foretold. The next morning there was such a storm of thunder and lightning as had not been known in the memory of man. Within three days, the obstinate Duke of Cumberland, without sense or reason, brought his troops to an engagement and the Battle of Fontenoy ensued. And this soldier advancing in the front line received a musket ball in the calf of his leg. Now this man, says Mr. W., when he came to England, was sent for by the Countess of Stair and many of the nobility, to whom he related the story, till at last he absolutely became mad with pride and was obliged to be confined till within these two years when, having a small glimmering of reason, he praised God and died. What was this man the better for his prophecy? It elated his heart and he narrowly escaped dying in his sins.'

To illustrate the passage in the text, 'Tho' I give my body to be burned', he said that if the poor sufferers burnt at an auto-da-fé *by command of the Inquisition, instead of praying for their persecutors and following the example of Christ, are full of malice and revenge against them, tho' they die in the flames, I will not say that they will go to God.*

Having summed up all by saying that whatever we do, whatever we hope, whatever we believe, yet if love be wanting, we shall not be meet partakers of the Kingdom of Heaven, he adverted to the subject of the day (it was a 'Charity Sermon'). When he was a boy, he said, there were only two hospitals in London: St. Thomas's and St. Bartholomew's. A child, going along Deans's Yard [Westminster], picked up a French book giving an account of the great hospital at Paris [L'Hôtel de Dieu]. He carried it to his father who showed it to Mr. Wesley's father (or uncle) who was then head usher at Westminster School [i.e., his brother, Samuel Wesley, Jun.]. 'Come', says Mr. W., 'let us *found an hospital.' The other gentleman said, 'You are jocular.' Mr. W. assured him he was serious, and the very next day they went about soliciting contributions, in which they succeeded so well that the Hyde Park Hospital [i.e., St. George's] was soon after built. Mr. Wesley then briefly mentioned the number of charitable institutions which are now established, and concluded with a fine exhortation to induce his audience to contribute upon the present occasion [to the Finsbury Dispensary; cf. JWJ, Dec. 16, 1787].*

Soon after Mr. Westley had begun his discourse, he made a pause and said: 'This I learned of a good man, Mr. Romaine, to pause every now and then, especially in the wintertime, that those who happen to be troubled with coughs may have an opportunity of easing themselves without interrupting the congregation.'

N.B. Mr. Westley's sermon was 45 minutes in delivery. He preached without notes and had a small Bible in his hand.

Wesley's printed text can be read through, at a homiletical pace, in thirty-five minutes; but note that it omits the story about Samuel Wesley, Jun.'s role in helping to found St. George's and also John's 'fine exhortation to induce the audience to contribute upon the present occasion', as well as the pauses allowed for coughing.

On Charity

1 Corinthians 13:1-3

Though I speak with the tongues of men and of angels, and have not charity, I am become as sounding brass, or a tinkling cymbal.

And though I have the gift of prophecy, and understand all mysteries, and all knowledge; and though I have all faith, so as to remove mountains, and have not charity, I am nothing.

And though I bestow all my goods to feed the poor, and give my body to be burned, and have not charity, it profiteth me nothing.

10 We know, 'All Scripture is given by inspiration of God,'[1] and is therefore true and right concerning all things. But we know, likewise, that there are some Scriptures which more immediately commend themselves to every man's conscience. In this rank we may place the passage before us; there are scarce any that object 15 to it. On the contrary, the generality of men very readily appeal to

[1] 2 Tim. 3:16.

it. Nothing is more common than to find even those who deny the authority of the Holy Scriptures yet affirming, 'This is my religion—that which is described in the thirteenth chapter of the Corinthians.' Nay, even a Jew, Dr. Nunes,[2] a Spanish physician, then settled at Savannah, in Georgia, used to say with great 5 earnestness: 'That Paul of Tarsus was one of the finest writers I have ever read. I wish the thirteenth chapter of his first letter to the Corinthians were wrote in letters of gold. And I wish every Jew were to carry it with him wherever he went.' He judged (and herein he certainly judged right) that this single chapter 10 contained the whole of true religion. It contains 'whatsoever things are just, whatsoever things are pure, whatsoever things are lovely; if there be any virtue, if there be any praise',[3] it is all contained in this.

In order to see this in the clearest light, we may consider, 15
First, what the charity here spoken of is;
Secondly, what those things are which are usually put in the place of it. We may then,
Thirdly, observe that neither any of them, nor all of them put together, can supply the want of it.   20

I.1. We are first to consider what this charity is. What is the nature, and what are the properties of it?

St. Paul's word is ἀγάπη, exactly answering to the plain English word 'love'.[4] And accordingly it is so rendered in all the old translations of the Bible. So it stood in William Tyndale's 25 Bible, which I suppose was the first English translation of the whole Bible. So it was also in the Bible published in London by the authority of King Henry VIII.[5] So it was likewise in all the

---

[2] Samuel Nuñez arrived in Savannah, July 10, 1733, and in the following December was awarded lot 43 in the new town; cf. E. Merton Coulter and Albert B. Sayre, eds., *A List of the Early Settlers of Georgia* (Athens, Univ. of Georgia Press, 1949), p. 91. He left Aug. 30, 1740. There are several references to Dr. Nuñez in Wesley's diary; JWJ, Apr. 4, 1737, has this entry: 'I began learning Spanish in order to converse with my Jewish parishioners [some eight in all]; some of whom seem nearer the mind that was in Christ than many of those who call him Lord.' William Stephens (in 1737) also speaks of 'Henriquez Nuñis, a Jew inhabitant', as being 'one of the greatest substance in Savannah'; cf. *A Journal of the Proceedings in Georgia* (1742), I.21.

[3] Phil. 4:8.

[4] For Wesley's preference for 'love' as the translation of ἀγάπη, see No. 17, 'The Circumcision of the Heart', I.2 and n.

[5] The first English translation (Wycliffe, 1380) had 'charity'; successive translations (Tyndale, 1534; Coverdale, 1535; Cranmer, 1539; and the Geneva Bible, 1557) have 'love', as does the first edition of the Bishops' Bible (1568). But, curiously enough, the

editions of the Bible that were successively published in England
during the reign of King Edward VI, Queen Elizabeth, and King
James I. Nay, so it is found in the Bibles of King Charles I's
reign—I believe, to the period of it. The first Bibles I have seen
5 wherein the word was changed were those printed by Roger
Daniel and John Field, printers to the Parliament, in the year
1649. Hence it appears, that the alteration was made during the
reign of the Long Parliament; then it was that the Latin word
'charity' was put in the place of the plain English word 'love'.[6] It
10 was in an unhappy hour this alteration was made; the ill effects of
it remain to this day; and these may be observed not only among
the poor and illiterate; not only thousands of common men and
women no more understand the word charity than they do the
original Greek, but the same miserable mistake has diffused itself
15 among men of education and learning. Thousands of these also
are misled thereby, and imagine that the charity treated of in this
chapter refers chiefly, if not wholly, to outward actions, and to
mean little more than almsgiving. I have heard many sermons
preached upon this chapter, particularly before the University of
20 Oxford. And I never heard more than one wherein the meaning of
it was not totally misrepresented. But had the old and proper
word 'love' been retained, there would have been no room for
misrepresentation.

    2. But what kind of love is that whereof the Apostle is speaking
25 throughout the chapter? Many persons of eminent learning and

---

second (and subsequent) edition of the Bishops' Bible (1572) reads 'charity', the first
known instance of this usage since Wycliffe. The moving spirit behind this revision was
Giles Lawrence, friend of John Jewel and professor of Greek at Oxford; cf. T. H. Darlow
and H. F. Moule, *Historical Catalogue of Printed Editions of the English Bible* (1903), revised
by A. S. Herbert (1968), Nos. 125 and 132. All the Douai-Rheims editions (1st, 1582)
read 'charity', but note that they had been anticipated by Lawrence. In the 1599 edition of
the Geneva Bible the text reads 'love', but there is an extended marginal annotation that
amounts to a short homily 'On *Charity*'. Thus, the translators of the AV (1611) had a
precedent for their preference for 'charity' over 'love' in this chapter.

   [6] Wesley is more cautious in his text of 1788: 'Hence it seems probable that the
alteration was made during the sitting of the Long Parliament [1640–48]; probably it was
then that the Latin word "charity" was put in the place of the English word "love".' But
the facts are otherwise. None of a dozen representative editions of the AV (between 1611
and 1658) has 'love'; it was not the Presbyterians who were responsible for the alteration;
the first solo printing of the Bible by Roger Daniel is dated 1645 (and reads 'charity') and
John Field's first Bible is dated 1648; neither printed a Bible in 1649, nor did they ever
collaborate on a joint edition. Wesley's heavy stress on 'love' as *the* proper translation of
ἀγάπη (cf. his translation of 1 Cor. 13 in *Notes* [1755]) was, therefore, more innovative
than he seems to have realized, despite the older traditions to which he appeals. Even so,
he had the backing of both Poole and Henry in this preference for 'love' over 'charity'.

piety apprehend that it is the love of God. But from reading the whole chapter numberless times, and considering it in every light, I am thoroughly persuaded that what St. Paul is here directly speaking of is the love of our neighbour. I believe whoever carefully weighs the whole tenor of his discourse will be fully 5 convinced of this. But it must be allowed to be such a love of our neighbour as can only spring from the love of God. And whence does this love of God flow? Only from that faith which is of the operation of God;[7] which whoever has, has a direct evidence that 'God was in Christ, reconciling the world unto himself.'[8] When 10 this is particularly applied to his heart, so that he can say with humble boldness, 'The life which I now live, I live by the faith of the Son of God, who loved me and gave himself for me;'[9] then, and not till then, 'the love of God is shed abroad in his heart.'[10] And this love sweetly constrains him to love every child of man 15 with the love which is here spoken of; not with a love of esteem or of complacence—for this can have no place with regard to those who are (if not his personal enemies, yet) enemies to God and their own souls—but with a love of benevolence, of tender goodwill to all the souls that God has made.[11] 20

3. But it may be asked: 'If there be no true love of our neighbour but that which springs from the love of God; and if the love of God flows from no other fountain than faith in the Son of God; does it not follow that the whole heathen world is excluded from all possibility of salvation? Seeing they are cut off from faith; 25 for faith cometh by hearing.[12] And how shall they hear without a preacher?'[13] I answer, St. Paul's words, spoken on another occasion, are applicable to this: 'What the law speaketh, it speaketh to them that are under the law.'[14] Accordingly that sentence, 'He that believeth not shall be damned,'[15] is spoken of 30 them to whom the gospel is preached. Others it does not concern;

---

[7] See Col. 2:12.
[8] 2 Cor. 5:19.
[9] Gal. 2:20.
[10] Cf. Rom. 5:5.
[11] A general eighteenth-century theme, as in Joseph Butler's *Fifteen Sermons Preached at the Rolls Chapel* (1726), Law's *Serious Call* (*Works*, xx.220): 'Benevolence to all our fellow creatures as creatures of God and for his sake. . . . This love that loves all things in God as his creatures', and in Johnson, *Dictionary* ('charity'). See No. 94, 'On Family Religion', I.3.
[12] Rom. 10:17.
[13] Rom. 10:14.
[14] Cf. Rom. 3:19.
[15] Mark 16:16.

and we are not required to determine anything touching their final state.[16] How it will please God, the Judge of all, to deal with *them*, we may leave to God himself. But this we know, that he is not the God of the Christians only, but the God of the heathens 5 also; that he is 'rich in mercy to all that call upon him',[17] 'according to the light they have';[18] and that 'in every nation he that feareth God and worketh righteousness is accepted of him.'[19]

4. But to return. This is the *nature* of that love whereof the 10 Apostle is here speaking. But what are the properties of it, the fruits which are inseparable from it? The Apostle reckons up many of them; but the principal of them are these:

First, 'Love is not puffed up.'[20] As is the measure of love, so is the measure of humility. Nothing humbles the soul so deeply as 15 love: it casts out all 'high conceits, engendering pride',[21] all arrogance and overweaning, makes us little, and poor, and base, and vile in our own eyes. It abases us both before God and man; makes us willing to be the least of all, and the servants of all, and teaches us to say, 'A mote in the sunbeam is little, but I am 20 infinitely less in the presence of God.'[22]

5. Secondly, 'Love is not provoked.'[23] Our present English translation renders it, 'is not easily provoked'.[24] But how did the word 'easily' come in? There is not a tittle of it in the text: the words of the Apostle are simply these, οὐ παροξύνεται.[25] Is it not

---

[16] For other references to the salvability of the heathen (as yet another implication of Wesley's 'catholic spirit'), cf. Nos. 106, 'On Faith, Heb. 11:16', I.4; 127, 'On the Wedding Garment', §17; 130, 'On Living without God', §14; cf. also No. 44, *Original Sin*, I.5 and n. See Michael Hurley, S.J., 'Salvation Today and Wesley Today', in Kenneth E. Rowe, ed., *The Place of Wesley in the Christian Tradition*, pp. 101-12.

[17] Cf. Rom. 10:12.

[18] Cf. Rom. 12:6. Note Wesley's casual reiteration here of the medieval theme of divine-human synergism (*in se est*).

[19] Cf. Acts 10:35.

[20] 1 Cor. 13:4 (*Notes*).

[21] Milton, *Paradise Lost*, iv.809.

[22] A recollection from de Renty; cf. Edward Sheldon's translation of Saint-Jure, *The Holy Life of Monsr. de Renty*, p. 59: 'He said, "A mote in the sun is very little, but yet I am far less in the presence of God, for I am not any thing." '

[23] 1 Cor. 13:5 (*Notes*); cf. No. 22, 'Sermon on the Mount, II', III.10 and n.

[24] Here, Wesley has all the precedents with him, including Douai-Rheims. 'Easily' first appears in 1611.

[25] παροξίζω is the root verb from which 'paroxysm' is derived and more often connotes exasperation, 'acute provocation', than mere 'provocation'; cf. Liddell and Scott, *Greek-English Lexicon*, and NEB, 'not quick to take offence'. *The Twentieth Century New Testament* agrees with Wesley and his predecessors: 'Love is never provoked.'

probable it was inserted by the translators with a design to excuse St. Paul, for fear his practice should appear to contradict his doctrine? For we read:

And some days after, Paul said unto Barnabas, Let us go again and visit our brethren in every city where we have preached the word of the Lord, and see 5
how they do. And Barnabas determined to take with them John, whose surname was Mark. But Paul thought not good to take him with them who departed from the work. And the contention was so sharp between them that they departed asunder one from the other; and so Barnabas took Mark, and sailed unto Cyprus; and Paul chose Silas, and departed, being recommended by the 10
brethren unto the grace of God. And he went through Syria and Cilicia, confirming the churches.[a]

6. Would not anyone think on reading these words that they were both equally sharp? That Paul was just as hot as Barnabas, and as much wanting in love as he? But the text says no such thing, as will 15 be plain if we consider first the occasion. When St. Paul proposed that they should 'again visit the brethren in every city where they had preached the word', so far they were agreed. 'And Barnabas determined to take with him John,' because he was his sister's son, without receiving or asking St. Paul's advice. 'But Paul 20 thought [it] not good to take him with them who had departed from them from Pamphylia' (whether through sloth or cowardice) 'and went not with them to the work.' And undoubtedly he thought right: he had reason on his side. The following words are, καὶ ἐγένετο παροξυσμός;[26] literally, 'and there was a fit of 25 anger.' It does not say in St. Paul; probably it was in Barnabas alone, who thus supplied the want of reason with passion, so 'that they departed asunder'. 'And Barnabas', resolved to have his own way, did as his nephew had done before, 'departed from the work, took Mark with him, and sailed to Cyprus'. But Paul went on in 30 his work, 'being recommended by the brethren to the grace of God' (which Barnabas seems not to have stayed for). 'And he went through Syria and Cilicia, confirming the churches.' From the whole account, it does not appear that St. Paul was in any fault; that he either felt any temper, or spoke any word contrary to 35

---

[a] Acts 15, ver. 36 and seq.

[26] Acts 15:39. Wesley is here quoting from memory; the text actually reads ἐγένετο δὲ παροξυσμός. This incident interested Wesley very much; cf. No. 22, 'Sermon on the Mount, II', III.10 and n.

the law of love. Therefore not being in any fault, he does not need any excuse.

7. Certainly he who is full of love is 'gentle towards all men'.[27] He 'in meekness instructs those that oppose themselves',[28] that oppose what he loves the most, even the truth of God, or that holiness without which no man shall see the Lord;[29] not knowing but 'God peradventure may bring them to the knowledge of the truth.'[30] However provoked, he does 'not return evil for evil, or railing for railing'.[31] Yea, he 'blesses those that curse him, and does good to them that despitefully use him and persecute him'.[32] He 'is not overcome of evil, but' always 'overcomes evil with good'.[33]

8. Thirdly, 'love is long-suffering.'[34] It 'endures' not a few affronts, reproaches, injuries, but 'all things'[35] which God is pleased to permit either men or devils to inflict. It arms the soul with inviolable patience; not harsh, stoical patience, but yielding as the air, which, making no resistance to the stroke, receives no harm thereby. The lover of mankind remembers him who suffered for us, 'leaving us an example, that we might tread in his steps'.[36] Accordingly, 'if his enemy hunger, he feeds him;' if he thirst, he 'gives him drink'; and by so doing he heaps coals of fire, of melting love, upon his head.[37] And 'many waters cannot quench' this 'love;' 'neither can' even 'the floods' of ingratitude 'drown it.'[38]

II.1. We are, secondly, to inquire what those things are which it is commonly supposed will supply the place of love. And the first of these is eloquence—a faculty of talking well, particularly on religious subjects. Men are generally inclined to think well of one that talks well. If he speaks properly and fluently of God and the things of God, who can doubt of his being in God's favour? And it is very natural for him to think well of himself, to have as favourable an opinion of himself as others have.

---

[27] 2 Tim. 2:24 (*Notes*).   [28] Cf. 2 Tim. 2:25.
[29] Heb. 12:14.   [30] Cf. 2 Tim. 2:25.
[31] Cf. 1 Pet. 3:9.   [32] Matt. 5:44 (*Notes*).
[33] Cf. Rom. 12:21.   [34] Cf. 1 Cor. 13:4.
[35] 1 Cor. 13:7.
[36] Cf. 1 Pet. 2:21.
[37] Cf. Rom. 12:20. Poole's *Annotations* on this text cite his parallel comment on Prov. 25:22: 'Thou shalt melt him into repentance, inflame him with love and kindness to thee for so unexpected and undeserved a favour.'
[38] Cf. S. of S. 8:7.

2. But men of reflection are not satisfied with this: they are not content with a flood of words; they prefer thinking before talking, and judge, one that knows much is far preferable to one that talks much. And it is certain, knowledge is an excellent gift of God; particularly knowledge of the Holy Scriptures, in which are 5 contained all the depths of divine knowledge and wisdom. Hence it is generally thought that a man of much knowledge, knowledge of Scripture in particular, must not only be in the favour of God, but likewise enjoy a high degree of it.

3. But men of deeper reflection are apt to say: 'I lay no stress 10 upon any other knowledge but the knowledge of God by faith. Faith is the only knowledge which in the sight of God is of great price.[39] "We are saved by faith;"[40] by faith alone: this is the one thing needful. He that believeth, and he alone, shall be saved everlastingly.' There is much truth in this: it is unquestionably 15 true that 'we are saved by faith;' consequently, that 'he that believeth shall be saved; and he that believeth not shall be damned.'[41]

4. But some men will say, with the Apostle James, 'Show me thy faith without thy works' (if thou canst; but indeed it is impossible), 20 'and I will show thee my faith by my works.'[42] And many are hereby induced to think that good works, works of piety and mercy,[43] are of far more consequence than faith itself, and will supply the want of every other qualification for heaven. Indeed, this seems to be the general sentiment, not only of the members of 25 the Church of Rome, but of Protestants also; not of the giddy and thoughtless, but the serious members of our own Church.

5. And this cannot be denied, our Lord himself hath said, 'Ye shall know them by their fruits:'[44] by their works ye know them that believe, and them that believe not. But yet it may be doubted 30 whether there is not a surer proof of the sincerity of our faith than even our works; that is, our willingly suffering for righteousness' sake;[45] especially if after suffering reproach, and pain, and loss of friends and substance, a man gives up life itself, yea, by a shameful and painful death, by giving his body to be burned,[46] 35

---

[39] See 1 Pet. 3:4; and cf. No. 88, 'On Dress', §12, which quotes the same passage from its text, 1 Pet. 3:3-4.
[40] Cf. Eph. 2:8.   [41] Cf. Mark 16:16.   [42] Jas. 2:18.
[43] Cf. No. 14, *The Repentance of Believers*, I.13 and n.
[44] Matt. 7:16.
[45] Cf. Matt. 5:10; 1 Pet. 3:14.
[46] Cf. 1 Cor. 13:3.

rather than he would give up faith and a good conscience by neglecting his known duty.

6. It is proper to observe here, first, what a beautful gradation there is, each step rising above the other in the enumeration of those several things which some or other of those that are called Christians, and are usually accounted so, really believe will supply the absence of love. St. Paul begins at the lowest point, 'talking well', and advances step by step, every one rising higher than the preceding, till he comes to the highest of all. A step above eloquence is knowledge; faith is a step above this. Good works are a step above that faith. And even above this, is suffering for righteousness' sake. Nothing is higher than this but Christian love[47]—the love of our neighbour flowing from the love of God.

7. It may be proper to observe, secondly, that whatever passes for religion in any part of the Christian world (whether it be a part of religion, or no part at all, but either folly, superstition, or wickedness) may with very little difficulty be reduced to one or other of these heads. Everything which is supposed to be religion, either by Protestants or Romanists, and is not, is contained under one or another of these five particulars. Make trial, as often as you please, with anything that is called religion, but improperly so called, and you will find the rule to hold without any exception.

III.1. I am now, in the third place, to demonstrate to all who have ears to hear, who do not harden themselves against conviction, that neither any one of these five qualifications, nor all of them together, will avail anything before God without the love above described.

In order to do this in the clearest manner we may consider them one by one. And first, 'though I speak with the tongues of men and of angels'[48]—with an eloquence such as never was found in men, concerning the nature, attributes, and works of God, whether of creation or providence; though I were not herein a whit behind the chief of the apostles, preaching like St. Peter and

---

[47] Cf. Richard Lucas, *Enquiry After Happiness* (1717), III.410: 'Love is the last round in the scale of perfection,' and Robert Barclay's comment on Rom. 8:30, in his *Apology* (1736 edn.), Prop. VII, 'Of Justification', pp. 220, 224: 'This [gradation] is commonly called *The Golden Chain*, as being acknowledged to comprehend the method and order of salvation.' For other comments of Wesley on the instrumentality of faith to love, see No. 36, 'The Law Established through Faith, II', II.1-2.

[48] 1 Cor. 13:1.

praying like St. John; yet unless humble, gentle, patient love be the ruling temper of my soul, I am no better in the judgment of God 'than sounding brass, or a rumbling cymbal'.[49] The highest eloquence, therefore, either in private conversation or in public ministrations; the brightest talent, either for preaching or prayer, if it was not joined with humble, meek, and patient resignation, might sink me the deeper into hell, but will not bring me one step nearer heaven.

2. A plain instance may illustrate this. I knew a young man, between fifty and sixty years ago, who during the course of several years never endeavoured to convince anyone of a religious truth but he *was* convinced; and he never endeavoured to persuade anyone to engage in a religious practice but he was persuaded.[50] What then? All that power of convincing speech, all that force of persuasion, if it was not joined with meekness and lowliness, with resignation and patient love, would no more qualify him for the fruition of God than a clear voice, or a fine complexion. Nay, it would rather procure him a hotter place in the everlasting burnings.[51]

3. Secondly, 'though I have the gift of prophecy',[52] of foretelling those future events which no creature can foresee; and 'though I understand all' the 'mysteries' of nature, of providence, and of the Word of God; and 'all knowledge' of things divine or human that any mortal ever attained to; though I could explain the most mysterious passages of Daniel, of Ezekiel, and the Revelation; yet if I have not humility, gentleness, and resignation, I 'am nothing'[53] in the sight of God.

[49] *Ibid.* For Wesley's preference for 'rumbling' over the consensus translation, 'tinkling', cf. No. 89, 'The More Excellent Way', §4, proem, and n.
[50] But cf. the young Wesley's letter to his mother, Jan. 25, 1727, reporting his successful effort to persuade Robin Griffiths to a more decisive Christian commitment. 'He [i.e., Griffiths] turned exceedingly serious and kept something of that disposition ever since. Yesterday was a fortnight he died of a consumption. I saw him three days before he died, and on the Sunday following . . . preach[ed] his funeral sermon;' cf. No. 136, 'On Mourning for the Dead', which Wesley preached Jan. 11, 1727.
[51] Isa. 33:14.
[52] Especially among the Puritans, the 'gift of prophecy' had come to mean the gifts of preaching. Cf. William Perkins, *The Art of Prophesying* (1613); also Henry Smith, *Sermons* (1657), p. 137: 'prophesying doth signify preaching.' See also, Wesley's *Notes* on 1 Thess. 5:20: 'For the Apostle here is not speaking of extraordinary gifts. Prophesying or preaching it seems is one means of grace and is put in this place for all the means of grace' (cf. No. 121, 'Prophets and Priests', §6). Here, however, Wesley is following the older usage of *foretelling* and gnostic wisdom.
[53] 1 Cor. 13:2.

A little before the conclusion of the late war in Flanders,[54] one who came from thence gave us a very strange relation. I knew not what judgment to form of this; but waited till John Haime[55] should come over, of whose veracity I could no more doubt than of his understanding. The account he gave was this: 'Jonathan Pyrah was a member of our Society in Flanders. I knew him some years, and knew him to be a man of unblameable character. One day he was summoned to appear before the Board of General Officers. One of them said: "What is this which we hear of you? We hear you are turned prophet, and that you foretell the downfall of the bloody House of Bourbon, and the haughty House of Austria. We should be glad if you were a real prophet, and if your prophecies came true. But what sign do you give to convince us that you are so, and that your predictions will come to pass?" He readily answered: "Gentlemen, I give you a sign. Tomorrow at twelve o'clock you shall have such a storm of thunder and lightning as you never had before since you came into Flanders. I give you a second sign: as little as any of you expect any such thing, as little appearance of it as there is now, you shall have a general engagement with the French within three days. I give you a third sign: I shall be ordered to advance in the first line. If I am a false prophet, I shall be shot dead at the very first discharge. But if I am a true prophet I shall only receive a musket ball in the calf of my left leg." At twelve the next day there was such thunder and lightning as they never had before in Flanders. On the third day, contrary to all expectations, was the general battle of Fontenoy.[56] He was ordered to advance in the first line. And at the very first discharge, he did receive a musket ball in the calf of his left leg.'

4. And yet all this profited him nothing, either for temporal or eternal happiness. When the war was over he returned to England; but the story was got before him: in consequence of

[54] The so-called 'War of the Austrian Succession', 1740–48; the campaigns in Flanders ran from 1742 to 1745. Cf. Charles Grant Robertson, *England Under the Hanoverians*, pp. 91-94.

[55] See his autobiography in *AM* (1780), III.207-17, 255-73, 307-13, for an account of the religious society Haime had organized among the soldiers; it mentions the Battle of Fontenoy (§39) but not Jonathan Pyrah. After his military discharge, Haime became one of Wesley's trusted veterans.

[56] May 11, 1745, one of the most famous battles of the eighteenth century in terms of the classical patterns of military strategy and tactics—and a defeat for the Anglo-Allied armies; cf. Williams, *The Whig Supremacy, 1714–1760*, pp. 237-39; and Charles Grant Robertson, *op. cit.*, 97-98.

which he was sent for by the Countess of St[air]s,[57] and several other persons of quality, who were desirous to receive so surprising an account from his own mouth. He could not bear so much honour. It quite turned his brain. In a little time he ran stark mad. And so he continues to this day, living still, as I apprehend, on Wibsey Moorside,[58] within a few miles of Leeds.[b]

5. And what would it profit a man to 'have all knowledge', even that which is infinitely preferable to all other, the knowledge of the Holy Scripture? I knew a young man about twenty years ago who was so thoroughly acquainted with the Bible that if he was questioned concerning any Hebrew word in the Old or any Greek word in the New Testament, he would tell, after a little pause, not only how often the one or the other occurred in the Bible, but also what it meant in every place. His name was Thomas Walsh.[c] Such a master of biblic knowledge I never saw before, and never expect to see again. Yet if with all his knowledge he had been void of love, if he had been proud, passionate, or impatient, he and all his knowledge would have perished together, as sure as ever he was born.

6. 'And though I have all faith, so that I could remove mountains.'[59] The faith which is able to do this cannot be the fruit of vain imagination, a mere madman's dream, a system of opinions; but must be a real work of God. Otherwise it could not have such an effect. Yet if this faith does not work by love, if it does not produce universal holiness, if it does not bring forth lowliness, meekness, and resignation, it will profit me nothing. This is as certain a truth as any that is delivered in the whole

[b] At the time of writing this sermon [i.e., 1784]. He is since dead [this footnote added in *Sermons* (1788), VII.250].

[c] His Journal, written by himself, is extant [It was used by James Morgan for his *Life and Death of Mr. Thomas Walsh* (London, 1762). Wesley published extracts from this in *Works* (1772), Vol. XI; cf. *Bibliog*, No. 252].

[57] The Countess of Stair was Eleanor, daughter of the second Earl of Loudoun and widow of Viscount James Primrose. She is the heroine in Sir Walter Scott's novel, 'My Aunt Margaret's Mirror', in *Chronicles of the Canongate* (1827). Lord Stair (John Dalrymple, second Earl of Stair [1673–1747]) distinguished himself in the battles of Dettingen and Fontenoy; 'his countess survived him by twelve years and remained till her death the most striking figure in Edinburgh society' (*DNB, loc. cit.*). John Hampson, *Memoirs of the Late Rev. John Wesley*, II.142, refers to her and also spells the name Stair*s* as Wesley has done.

[58] The text in both *AM* and *SOSO* here reads 'Websey'; Wibsey is two miles south of Bradford and Wibsey Moorside about a mile farther south.

[59] 1 Cor. 13:2.

One of the persons who was then brought out for execution, having been confined in the dungeons of the Inquisition, had not seen the sun for many years. It proved a bright, sunshiny day. Looking up, he cried out in surprise, 'O how can anyone who sees
5   that glorious luminary worship any but the God that made it!'[69] A friar standing by ordered them to run an iron gag through his lips, that he might speak no more. Now what did that poor man feel within when this order was executed? If he said in his heart, though he could not utter it with his lips, 'Father, forgive them;
10 for they know not what they do;'[70] undoubtedly the angels of God were ready to carry his soul into Abraham's bosom.[71] But if instead of this he cherished the resentment in his heart which he could not express with his tongue, although his body was consumed by the flames, I will not say his soul went into paradise.
15   11. The sum of all that has been observed is this: whatever I speak, whatever I know, whatever I believe, whatever I do, whatever I suffer; if I have not the faith that worketh by love,[72] that produces love to God and all mankind, I am not in the narrow way which leadeth to life, but in the broad road that leadeth to
20 destruction.[73] In other words: whatever eloquence I have, whether natural or supernatural knowledge; whatever faith I have received from God; whatever works I do, whether of piety or mercy; whatever sufferings I undergo for conscience' sake, even though I resist unto blood—all these things put together, however
25 applauded of men, will avail nothing before God unless I am meek and lowly in heart,[74] and can say in all things, 'Not as I will, but as thou wilt.'[75]
        12. We conclude from the whole (and it can never be too much inculcated, because all the world votes on the other side), that
30 true religion, in the very essence of it, is nothing short of *holy tempers*. Consequently all other religion, whatever name it bears, whether pagan, Mahometan, Jewish, or Christian; and whether popish or Protestant, Lutheran or Reformed, without these is lighter than vanity[76] itself.

[69] Cf. No. 28, 'Sermon on the Mount, VIII', §5.
[70] Luke 23:34.
[71] See Luke 16:22.
[72] See Gal. 5:6; cf. above, No. 2, *The Almost Christian*, II.6 and n.
[73] See Matt. 7:13-14.
[74] Matt. 11:29.
[75] Matt. 26:39.
[76] Ps. 62:9.

13. Let every man therefore that has a soul to be saved see that he secure this one point. With all his eloquence, his knowledge, his faith, works, and sufferings, let him hold fast this 'one thing needful'.[77] He that through the power of faith endureth to the end in[78] humble, gentle, patient love; he, and he alone, shall, through 5 the merits of Christ, 'inherit the kingdom prepared from the foundation of the world'.[79]

London, October 15, 1784[80]

---

[77] Luke 10:42.
[78] See Matt. 10:22.
[79] Matt. 25:34.
[80] Place and date as in *AM*.

ON ZEAL

AN INTRODUCTORY COMMENT

This sermon, written three years earlier than No. 91, 'On Charity', is thematically subsequent to it, so its place here is fitting. It is further comment on love *in a single, crucial aspect. Thus, Wesley focuses on the much misunderstood impulse labelled 'religious zeal', and then proceeds to show that* true *'zeal' is actually an expression of love or else it is both false and destructive ('Christian zeal is all love,' etc.; I.2). This allows him then to distinguish between the zeal which fuels the fires of controversy and persecution and that special quality of holy love which is, as he says, 'the queen of all graces' (III.12). That this idea was a favourite in his mid-career is suggested by the fact that Gal. 4:18 is mentioned eighteen times as a preaching text between 1758 and 1779.*

The written sermon first appeared in the September and October issues of the Arminian Magazine *for 1781 (IV.463-69, 520-25), numbered 'Sermon V', without a title but with a postscript: 'Haverford West, May 6, 1781'. This fits with his account in the* Journal *(April 29–May 7) of his visit for that year to Wales, where Haverford West is located as 'seventeen measured miles from St. David's': 'In the evening [of April 29th] I preached at Haverford West to the liveliest congregation I have seen in Wales.'*

The sermon was then placed directly after 'On Charity' in SOSO, *VII.257-76. It was not thereafter reprinted in Wesley's lifetime.*

On Zeal

Galatians 4:18

It is good to be always zealously affected in a good thing.

1. There are few subjects in the whole compass of religion that
5 are of greater importance than this. For without zeal it is impossible either to make any considerable progress in religion

ourselves, or to do any considerable service to our neighbour, whether in temporal or spiritual things. And yet nothing has done more disservice to religion, or more mischief to mankind, than a sort of zeal which has for several ages prevailed, both in pagan, Mahometan, and Christian nations. Insomuch that it may truly be 5 said: pride, covetousness, ambition, revenge, have in all parts of the world slain their thousands, but zeal its ten thousands.[1] Terrible instances of this have occurred in ancient times, in the most civilized heathen nations. To this chiefly were owing the inhuman persecutions of the primitive Christians; and in later 10 ages the no less inhuman persecutions of the Protestants by the Church of Rome. It was zeal that kindled fires in our nation during the reign of bloody Queen Mary.[2] It was zeal that soon after made so many provinces of France a field of blood. It was zeal that murdered so many thousand unresisting Protestants in 15 the never to be forgotten massacre of Paris.[3] It was zeal that occasioned the still more horrid massacre in Ireland;[4] the like whereof, both with regard to the number of the murdered, and the shocking circumstances wherewith many of those murders

---

[1] See 1 Sam. 18:7.

[2] Cf. No. 23, 'Sermon on the Mount, III', III.5 and n.

[3] The bloodiest single episode of its kind in French history. The 'Massacre' had begun on St. Bartholomew's Eve, Aug. 22, 1572, and had raged in and around Paris for a full week by order, or at least by the connivance, of the queen mother (Catherine de Medici) and King Charles IX. Estimates of the total number of its victims (in the sources readily available to Wesley) varied from the 100,000 of Beaumont de Péréfixe (Archbishop of Paris, 1662–71) to J. L. von Mosheim's and Samuel Pufendorf's 30,000. Cf. Mosheim, *Institutiones historiae ecclesiastiae* (1726; Eng. trans. by J. Murdock, 1841), p. 667: 'The bloody scene began at midnight at the signal of the tolling of the great bell of the palace. . . . Six thousand Protestants were butchered in Paris alone. . . . More than thirty thousand—some say seventy thousand—perished by the hands of the royal assassins, and the pope ordered a jubilee throughout Christendom.' See also Pufendorf, *Introduction to the History of the Principal Kingdoms and States of Europe* (rev. edn. 1764), I.260-61: 'The example set at Paris being followed in many other cities, above 30,000 Protestants were massacred. . . . This horrid business, which is commonly called *the Wedding at Paris*, has been scandalously represented by Gabriel Maude as a masterpiece of policy.'

[4] 'The Rising of 1641', the beginning of the first large scale rebellion of the Irish against English rule, leading to the Ulster 'plantation' of Scottish colonists in Northern Ireland. This tragic struggle dragged on until Cromwell's decisive reconquest in 1649-50. The sober truth about this horror was soon lost in partisan legends with estimates of the victims of 'the great Popish Massacre' ranging from Milton's 'hundreds of thousands' to Cromwell's Commission's Report (2,109 murders in ten years of war). Ferdinand Warner, *History of the Irish Rebellion* (1767; 2nd edn., 1770), calculated that 4,028 Protestants were killed within the first two years of the rebellion and 8,000 died of 'ill-usage'. For all his love of the Irish, Wesley had no sympathy for their nationalism and had come to accept the Miltonian exaggeration. For example, in JWJ, Aug. 14, 1747, he records having read Sir John Temple's *The Irish Rebellion; or an history of the beginning and*

were perpetrated, I verily believe never occurred before, since the world began. As to the other parts of Europe, an eminent German writer has taken immense pains to search both the records in various places, and the most authentic histories, in order to gain
5 some competent knowledge of the blood which has been shed since the Reformation; and computes that, partly by private persecution, partly by religious wars in the course of forty years, reckoning from the year 1520, above forty millions of persons have been destroyed.[5]
10 2. But is it not possible to distinguish right zeal from wrong? Undoubtedly it is possible. But it is difficult—such is the deceitfulness of the human heart! So skilfully do the passions justify themselves.[6] And there are exceeding few treatises on the subject; at least in the English language. To this day I have seen or
15 heard of only one sermon; and that was wrote above a hundred years ago by Dr. Sprat, then Bishop of Rochester, so that it is now exceeding scarce.[7]

3. I would gladly cast in my mite, by God's assistance, toward the clearing up this important question, in order to enable
20 well-meaning men who are desirous of pleasing God to

first progresse of the general rebellion raised within the Kingdom of Ireland upon the . . . 23 October, 1641 (1646), with the following comment: 'I procured a genuine account of the great Irish massacre in 1641. Surely never was there such a transaction before, from the beginning of the world! More than two hundred thousand men, women, and children butchered within a few months, in cool blood, and with such circumstances of cruelty as make one's blood run cold! It is well if God has not a controversy with the nation, on this very account, to this day.'

For a careful and comparatively objective account of this rebellion, see Edmund Borlase, *The History of the Execrable Irish Rebellion . . . to the Grand Eruption* (London, 1680), pp. 109-25. This 'appendix' is an inventory, county by county, of English and Scots slain in the Insurrection of 1641–42; the total adds up to 9,350.

[5] Wesley's apparent source here is Bengel, *Gnomon*, Apocalypse 18:24. Bengel cites Matthias Hoë von Hoenegg, *Commentariorum in beati Apostoli et evangelistae Joannis Apocalypsin* (2 pt.; Lipsiae, 1610-11), Apoc. XVII, Q. 234; and also G. D. Seyler, whose estimate is put at 900,000. Bengel's own judgment is that 'neither of these calculations is probable. . . . The true number, whatever it is, is stupendous;' cf. Fausset's edn. of the *Gnomon* (1877), 4:360. Cf. also Nos. 102, 'Of Former Times', §14; and 22, 'Sermon on the Mount, II', III.18 and n.

[6] Cf. Nos. 49, 'The Cure of Evil-speaking', §4 and n.; and 12, 'The Witness of Our Own Spirit', §5 and n.

[7] Thomas Sprat (1635–1713), Bishop of Rochester, 1684–1713. The sermon, on Gal. 4:18, was preached 'before the King at Whitehall', Dec. 22, 1678, when Sprat was not 'then Bishop of Rochester' but still Chaplain to the King; cf. *Sermons Preached on Several Occasions* (London, 1722), pp. 143-90. In Sept. 1733 Wesley read William Reeves's *Fourteen Sermons Preached on Several Occasions* (1729); No. 4 in that volume is entitled 'On Zeal for the Faith Requisite for a Christian.'

distinguish true Christian zeal from its various counterfeits. And this is more necessary at this time than it has been for many years. Sixty years ago there seemed to be scarce any such thing as religious zeal left in the nation. People in general were wonderfully cool and undisturbed about 'that trifle, religion'.[8] But since then, it is easy to observe, there has been a very considerable alteration. Many thousands almost in every part of the nation have felt a real desire to save their souls. And I am persuaded there is at this day more religious zeal in England than there has been for a century past.

4. But has this zeal been of the right or the wrong kind? Probably both the one and the other. Let us see if we cannot separate these, that we may avoid the latter and cleave to the former. In order to this, I would first inquire what is the nature of true Christian zeal; secondly, what are the properties of it; and thirdly, draw some practical inferences.

I. And first, what is the nature of zeal in general, and of true Christian zeal in particular?

1. The original word, in its primary signification, means *heat*, such as the heat of boiling water. When it is figuratively applied to the mind it means any warm emotion or affection. Sometimes it is taken for *envy*. So we render it, Acts 5:17, where we read, 'The high priest and all that were with him were filled with envy'—ἐπλήσθησαν ζήλου (although it might as well be rendered were filled with *zeal*.)[9] Sometimes it is taken for anger and indignation; sometimes for vehement desire. And when any of our passions are strongly moved on a religious account, whether for anything good, or against anything which we conceive to be evil, this we term, 'religious zeal'.

2. But it is not all that is called religious zeal which is worthy of that name. It is not properly religious or Christian zeal if it be not joined with charity. A fine writer (Bishop Sprat) carries the matter farther still. 'It has been affirmed', says that great man, 'no zeal is right which is not charitable. But this is not saying enough. I affirm that true zeal is not only charitable, but is mostly so. Charity or love is not only one ingredient, but the chief

<hr />

[8] π; source unidentified.
[9] Wesley's translation (*Notes*), following Poole's *Annotations, loc. cit.* The AV reads 'indignation', which is more literal; the NEB reads 'jealousy'.

ingredient, in its composition.'[10] May we not go farther still? May we not say that true zeal is not mostly charitable, but wholly so? That is, if we take charity in St. Paul's sense, for love—the love of God and our neighbour. For it is a certain truth (although little 5 understood in the world) that Christian zeal is all love. It is nothing else. The love of God and man fills up its whole nature.

3. Yet it is not every degree of that love to which this appellation is given. There may be some love, a small degree of it, where there is no zeal. But it is properly love in a higher degree. It is 10 'fervent love'.[11] True Christian zeal is no other than *the flame of love*. This is the nature, the inmost essence of it.

II.1. From hence it follows that the properties of love are the properties of zeal also. Now one of the chief properties of love is *humility*—'love is not puffed up.'[12] Accordingly this is a property 15 of true zeal: humility is inseparable from it. As is the degree of zeal, such is the degree of humility: they must rise and fall together. The same love which fills a man with zeal for God makes him little, and poor, and vile in his own eyes.

2. Another of the properties of love is *meekness:*[13] consequently 20 it is one of the properties of zeal. It teaches us to be meek as well as lowly; to be equally superior to anger and pride. Like as the wax melteth at the fire,[14] so before this sacred flame all turbulent passions melt away, and leave the soul unruffled and serene.

3. Yet another property of love, and consequently of zeal, is 25 unwearied *patience;* for 'love endureth all things'.[15] It arms the soul with entire resignation to all the disposals of divine providence, and teaches us to say in every occurrence, 'It is the Lord; let him do what seemeth him good.'[16] It enables us, in whatever state we are, therewith to be content;[17] to repine at nothing; to murmur at 30 nothing; but 'in everything to give thanks'.[18]

4. There is a fourth property of Christian zeal, which deserves

---

[10] A misquotation from Sprat, whose text here (p. 166) reads: 'Whereas no religion is true that is not peaceable, . . . no zeal is spiritual that is not also charitable, nay, chiefly so.'
[11] 1 Pet. 4:8 (*Notes*).
[12] 1 Cor. 13:4 (*Notes*); see also No. 21, 'Sermon on the Mount, I', I.7 and n.
[13] Cf. No. 22, 'Sermon on the Mount, II', I.4 and n.
[14] See Ps. 68:2 (BCP).
[15] 1 Cor. 13:7 (*Notes*). For other comments on patience, cf. No. 83, 'On Patience', §5 and n.
[16] 1 Sam. 3:18.
[17] Phil. 4:11.
[18] Cf. 1 Thess. 5:18.

to be more particularly considered. This we learn from the very words of the Apostle: 'It is good to be zealously affected' (not to have transient touches of zeal, but a steady, rooted disposition) 'in a good thing'—in that which is good; for the proper object of zeal is good in general, that is, everything that is good, really such, in 5 the sight of God.

5. But what is good in the sight of God? What is that religion wherewith God is always well pleased? How do the parts of this rise one above another? And what is the comparative value of them? 10

This is a point exceeding little considered, and therefore little understood. Positive divinity many have some knowledge of. But few know anything of comparative divinity. I never saw but one tract wrote upon this head; a sketch of which it may be of use to subjoin.[19] 15

In a Christian believer *love* sits upon the throne, which is erected in the inmost soul; namely, love of God and man, which fills the whole heart, and reigns without a rival. In a circle near the throne are all *holy tempers:* long-suffering, gentleness, meekness, goodness, fidelity, temperance[20]—and if any other is comprised in 20 'the mind which was in Christ Jesus'.[21] In an exterior circle are all the *works of mercy,*[22] whether to the souls or bodies of men. By these we exercise all holy tempers; by these we continually improve them, so that all these are real *means of grace,* although this is not commonly adverted to. Next to these are those that are 25 usually termed *works of piety:*[23] reading and hearing the Word, public, family, private prayer, receiving the Lord's Supper, fasting or abstinence. Lastly, that his followers may the more effectually provoke one another to love, holy tempers, and good works,[24] our blessed Lord has united them together in one—*the* 30 *church,* dispersed all over the earth; a little emblem of which, of

---

[19] James Garden (1647–1726), Scottish disciple of Antoinette Bourignon, brother to a more famous divine, George Garden (1649–1733), had written a tract entitled *Comparative Theology, or the True and Solid Grounds of a Pure and Peaceable Theology* (1700), which Wesley regarded highly enough to extract and include in the *Christian Lib.,* XXII.243-87. But if this is Wesley's source here, he is taking large liberties with Garden's text, for the metaphor of 'love seated on the throne' is not in Garden. However, the essential idea here of concentric circles of the Christian virtues and tempers, with love as their centre and peak, is reminiscent of both the Gardens and Bourignon—and William Law as well.

[20] See Gal. 5:22-23.   [21] Cf. Phil. 2:5.
[22] Cf. below, III.7, 12; also No. 14, *The Repentance of Believers,* I.13 and n.
[23] *Ibid.*   [24] See Heb. 10:24.

the church universal, we have in every particular Christian congregation.

6. This is that religion which our Lord has established upon earth, ever since the descent of the Holy Ghost on the day of
5 Pentecost. This is the entire, connected system of Christianity: and thus the several parts of it rise one above another, from that lowest point, 'the assembling ourselves together',²⁵ to the highest, love enthroned in the heart. And hence it is easy to learn the comparative value of every branch of religion. Hence also we
10 learn a fifth property of true zeal—that as it is always exercised ἐν καλῷ,²⁶ 'in that which is good', so it is always *proportioned* to that good, to the degree of goodness that is in its object.

7. For example: every Christian ought undoubtedly to be zealous for *the church*, bearing a strong affection to it, and
15 earnestly desiring its prosperity and increase. He ought to be thus zealous, as for the church universal, praying for it continually, so especially for that particular church or Christian society whereof he himself is a member. For this he ought to wrestle with God in prayer; meantime using every means in his power to enlarge its
20 borders, and to strengthen his brethren, that they may adorn the doctrine of God our Saviour.²⁷

8. But he should be more zealous for the *ordinances of Christ* than for the church itself: for prayer in public and private, for the Lord's Supper, for reading, hearing, and meditating on his Word;
25 and for the much neglected duty of fasting. These he should earnestly recommend, first, by his example, and then by advice, by argument, persuasion, and exhortation, as often as occasion offers.

9. Thus should he show his zeal for works of piety; but much
30 more for *works of mercy;* seeing 'God will have mercy and not sacrifice'²⁸—that is, rather than sacrifice. Whenever, therefore, one interferes with the other, works of mercy are to be preferred. Even reading, hearing, prayer, are to be omitted, or to be postponed, 'at charity's almighty call'²⁹—when we are called to
35 relieve the distress of our neighbour, whether in body or soul.

10. But as zealous as we are for all good works, we should be

²⁵ Heb. 10:25.   ²⁶ Gal. 4:18.
²⁷ Titus 2:10.
²⁸ Cf. Hos. 6:6; Matt. 9:13; 12:7.
²⁹ Samuel Wesley, Jun., 'Upon These Two Verses of Mr. Oldham', in *Poems* (1736), p. 121.

still more zealous for *holy tempers;*[30] for planting and promoting both in our souls, and in all we have any intercourse with, lowliness of mind, meekness, gentleness, long-suffering, contentedness, resignation unto the will of God, deadness to the world and the things of the world, as the only means of being truly 5 alive to God. For these proofs and fruits of living faith we cannot be too zealous. We should 'talk of them as we sit in our house, and when we walk by the way, and when we lie down, and when we rise up'.[31] We should make them continual matter of prayer, as being far more excellent than any outward works whatever; seeing 10 those will fail when the body drops off, but these will accompany us into eternity.

11. But our choicest zeal should be reserved for *love* itself, the end of the commandment,[32] the fulfilling of the law.[33] The church, the ordinances, outward works of every kind, yea, all other holy 15 tempers, are inferior to this, and rise in value only as they approach nearer and nearer to it. Here then is the great object of Christian zeal. Let every true believer in Christ apply with all fervency of spirit to the God and Father of our Lord Jesus Christ, that his heart may be more and more enlarged in love to God and 20 to all mankind. This one thing let him do: let him 'press on to this prize of our high calling of God in Christ Jesus'.[34]

III. It remains only to draw some practical inferences from the preceding observations.

1. And, first, if zeal, true Christian zeal, be nothing but the 25 flame of love, then *hatred*, in every kind and degree, then every sort of *bitterness* toward them that oppose us, is so far from deserving the name of zeal that it is directly opposite to it. If zeal be only fervent love, then it stands at the utmost distance from *prejudice*, jealousy, evil surmising; seeing 'love thinketh no evil'.[35] 30 Then *bigotry* of every sort, and above all the spirit of *persecution*, are totally inconsistent with it.[36] Let not, therefore, any of these unholy tempers screen themselves under that sacred name. As all these are the works of the devil,[37] let them appear in their own

---

[30] Cf. No. 91, 'On Charity', III.8 and n.
[31] Cf. Deut. 6:7.
[32] 1 Tim. 1:5.
[33] Rom. 13:10.
[34] Cf. Phil. 3:14.   [35] Cf. 1 Cor. 13:5 (*Notes*).
[36] Cf. Nos. 38, 'A Caution against Bigotry'; and 39, 'Catholic Spirit'.
[37] 1 John 3:8.

shape, and no longer under that specious disguise deceive the unwary children of God.

2. Secondly; if lowliness be a property of zeal, then pride is inconsistent with it. It is true some degree of pride may remain 5 after the love of God is shed abroad in the heart;[38] as this is one of the last evils that is rooted out when God creates all things new. But it cannot reign, nor retain any considerable power, where fervent love is found. Yea, were we to give way to it but a little, it would damp that holy fervour; and if we did not immediately fly 10 back to Christ, would utterly quench the Spirit.[39]

3. Thirdly; if meekness be an inseparable property of zeal, what shall we say of those who call their anger by that name? Why, that they mistake the truth totally; that they in the fullest sense put darkness for light, and light for darkness.[40] We cannot be too 15 watchful against this delusion, because it spreads over the whole Christian world. Almost in all places zeal and anger pass for equivalent terms; and exceeding few persons are convinced that there is any difference between them. How commonly do we hear it said, 'See how zealous the man is!' Nay, he cannot be zealous: 20 that is impossible; for he is in a passion. And passion is as inconsistent with zeal as light with darkness, or heaven with hell.

It were well that this point were thoroughly understood. Let us consider it a little farther. We frequently observe one that bears the character of a religious man vehemently angry at his 25 neighbour. Perhaps he calls his brother 'Raca', or 'Thou fool':[41] he brings a railing accusation against him.[42] You mildly admonish him of his warmth. He answers, 'It is my zeal!' No, it is your sin; and unless you repent of it, will sink you lower than the grave. There is much such zeal as this in the bottomless pit. Thence all 30 zeal of this kind comes. And thither it will go, and you with it, unless you are saved from it before you go hence.

4. Fourthly; if patience, contentedness, and resignation, are the properties of zeal, then murmuring, fretfulness, discontent, impatience, are wholly inconsistent with it. And yet how ignorant 35 are mankind of this! How often do we see men fretting at the ungodly, or telling you they are 'out of patience' with such or such

[38] See Rom. 5:5. For other references to pride, cf. No. 14, *The Repentance of Believers*, I.3 and n.
[39] See 1 Thess. 5:19.   [40] Isa. 5:20.
[41] Matt. 5:22; cf. No. 7, 'The Way to the Kingdom', II.4 and n.
[42] See Jude 9.

things, and terming all this their zeal! O spare no pains to
undeceive them! If it be possible, show them what zeal is; and
convince them that all murmuring, or fretting at sin, is a species of
sin, and has no resemblance of, or connection with, the true zeal
of the gospel.

5. Fifthly; if the object of zeal be 'that which is good',[43] then
fervour for any *evil thing* is not Christian zeal. I instance in
idolatry—worshipping of angels, saints, images, the cross.
Although therefore a man were so earnestly attached to any kind
of idolatrous worship that he would even 'give his body to be
burned'[44] rather than refrain from it, call this bigotry or
superstition if you please, but call it not zeal. That is quite another
thing.

From the same premises it follows that fervour for *indifferent
things* is not Christian zeal. But how exceedingly common is this
mistake too! Indeed one would think that men of understanding
could not be capable of such weakness. But alas! the history of all
ages proves the contrary. Who were men of stronger understandings than Bishop Ridley and Bishop Hooper?[45] And how
warmly did these and other great men of that age dispute about
the *sacerdotal vestments?* How eager was the contention for almost
a hundred years for and against wearing a *surplice!* O shame to
man! I would as soon have disputed about a straw or a
barley-corn! And this, indeed, shall be called zeal! And why was it
not rather called wisdom or holiness?

6. It follows also from the same premises that fervour for
opinions is not Christian zeal. But how few are sensible of this!

---

[43] See II.7, above.

[44] Cf. 1 Cor. 13:3.

[45] Nicholas Ridley (*c.* 1500–55) and John Hooper (d. 1555). Ridley, Bishop of London,
was a moderate reformer whereas Hooper, Bishop of Gloucester-Worcester, was an
aggressive 'puritan' who regarded vestments as vestiges of popery and, therefore,
'impious' and 'idolatrous'. Archbishop Cranmer refused to consecrate him as bishop
without the traditional vestments and appointed Bishop Ridley to debate the issue with
Hooper (cf. *DNB*). John Strype reports that the debate was bitter and angry; cf. *Historical
Memorials, Chiefly Ecclesiastical as such as Concern Religion and the Reformation of It and the
Progress Made Therein, Under the Reign and Influence of King Edward VI* (London, 1721),
II.224-27. Hooper later agreed to a vested consecration but carried his zeal over into his
episcopal ministry. He was martyred in Gloucester in 1555 during the same period that
saw Ridley, Hugh Latimer, and Archbishop Cranmer burned in Oxford. Thomas Fuller,
Church History of Britain (1656), XVI.21, says that 'of all the Marian martyrs . . . Bishop
Ridley was the profoundest scholar, ... Archbishop Cranmer of the mildest, meekest
temper, Bishop Hooper of the sternest and austerest nature, . . . and Mr. Latimer had the
plainest, simplest heart. . . .'

And how innumerable are the mischiefs which even this species of false zeal has occasioned in the Christian world! How many thousand lives have been cast away by those who were zealous for the Romish opinions! How many of the excellent ones of the earth 5 have been cut off by zealots for the senseless opinion of transubstantiation! But does not every unprejudiced person see that this zeal is 'earthly, sensual, devilish'?[46] And that it stands at the utmost contrariety to the zeal which is here recommended by the Apostle?

10   What an excess of charity is it then which our great poet expresses in his poem on the last day! Where he talks of meeting in heaven,

> Those who by mutual wounds expired,
> By *zeal* for their distinct persuasions fired?[47]

15 Zeal indeed! What manner of zeal was this which led them to cut one another's throats? Those who were *fired* with this spirit, and died therein, will undoubtedly have their portion, not in heaven—only love is there—but in 'the fire that never shall be quenched'.[48]

20   7. Lastly, if true zeal be always proportioned to the degree of goodness which is in its object, then should it rise higher and higher according to the scale mentioned above; according to the comparative value of the several parts of religion. For instance, all that truly fear God should be zealous for the *church:* both for the 25 catholic or universal church, and for that part of it whereof they are members. This is not the appointment of men, but of God. He saw 'it was not good for men to be alone',[49] even in this sense, but that the whole body of his children should be 'knit together, and strengthened, by that which every joint supplieth'.[50] At the same 30 time they should be more zealous for the *ordinances* of God: for public and private prayer, for hearing and reading the Word of

---

[46] Jas. 3:15.
[47] Cf. Young, *The Last Day*, ll. 113-16:

> Some who, perhaps, by mutual wounds expired,
> With zeal for their distinct persuasions fired,
> In mutual friendship their long slumber break,
> And hand in hand their Saviour's love partake.

See also John Wesley, *A Collection of Moral and Sacred Poems* (1744), II.78.
[48] Mark 9:43, 45.
[49] Cf. Gen. 2:18.   [50] Cf. Eph. 4:16.

God, and for fasting, and the Lord's Supper. But they should be more zealous for 'works of mercy' than even for works of piety. Yet ought they to be more zealous still for *holy tempers*—lowliness, meekness, resignation; but most zealous of all for that which is the sum and the perfection of religion—the *love* of God and man. 5

8. It remains only to make a close and honest application of these things to our own souls. We all know the general truth that 'it is good to be always zealously affected in a good thing.' Let us now, every one of us, apply it to his own soul in particular.

9. Those indeed who are still dead in trespasses and sins[51] have 10 neither part nor lot in this matter;[52] nor those that live in any open sin, such as drunkenness, sabbath-breaking, or profane swearing. These have nothing to do with zeal; they have no business at all even to take the word in their mouth. It is utter folly and impertinence for any to talk of zeal for God while he is doing the 15 works of the devil. But if you have renounced the devil and all his works, and have settled it in your heart, I will 'worship the Lord my God, and him only will I serve',[53] then beware of being neither cold nor hot;[54] then be zealous for God! You may begin at the lowest step. Be zealous for *the church;* more especially for that 20 particular branch thereof wherein your lot is cast. Study the welfare of this, and carefully observe all the rules of it, for conscience' sake. But in the meantime take heed that you do not neglect any of the *ordinances* of God; for the sake of which, in a great measure, the church itself was constituted; so that it would 25 be highly absurd to talk of zeal for the church if you were not more zealous for them. But are you more zealous for 'works of mercy' than even for works of piety? Do *you* follow the example of your Lord, and prefer mercy even before sacrifice? Do you use all diligence in feeding the hungry, clothing the naked, visiting them 30 that are sick and in prison?[55] And above all, do you use every means in your power to save souls from death? If, as you have time, 'you do good unto all men', though 'especially to them that are of the household of faith',[56] your zeal for the church is pleasing to God; but if not, if you are not 'careful to maintain good 35 works',[57] what have you to do with the church? If you have not

---

[51] Eph. 2:1. [52] See Acts 8:21.
[53] Cf. Matt. 4:10. [54] See Rev. 3:15-16.
[55] See Matt. 25:35-36. [56] Cf. Gal. 6:10.
[57] Titus 3:8. Note Wesley's reversal here of the third General Rule (using the means of grace) and the second ('do all the good you can').

'compassion on your fellow-servants',[58] neither will your Lord have pity on *you*. 'Bring no more vain oblations.'[59] All your service is 'an abomination to the Lord'.[60]

10. Are you better instructed than to put asunder what God has
5   joined?[61] Than to separate works of piety from works of mercy? Are you uniformly zealous of both? So far you walk acceptably to God: that is, if you continually bear in mind that God 'searcheth the heart and reins';[62] that 'He is a Spirit, and they that worship him, must worship him in spirit and in truth;'[63] that consequently
10   no outward works are acceptable to him unless they spring from *holy tempers*, without which no man can have a place in the kingdom of Christ and of God.

11. But of all holy tempers, and above all others, see that you be most zealous for *love!* Count all things loss in comparison of this,
15   the love of God and all mankind. It is most sure that if you give all your goods to feed the poor, yea, and your body to be burned, and have not humble, gentle, patient love, it profiteth you nothing.[64] O let this be deep engraven upon your heart: all is nothing without love.

20   12. Take then the whole of religion together, just as God has revealed it in his Word, and be uniformly zealous for every part of it, according to its degree of excellence, grounding all your zeal on the one foundation, 'Jesus Christ and him crucified';[65] holding fast this one principle, 'The life I now live, I live by faith in the Son
25   of God who loved *me*, and gave himself for *me;*'[66] proportion your zeal to the value of its object. Be calmly zealous therefore, first, for the *church*—'the whole state of Christ's church militant here on earth',[67] and in particular for that branch thereof with which you are more immediately connected. Be more zealous for all
30   those *ordinances* which our blessed Lord hath appointed to continue therein to the end of the world. Be more zealous for those *works of mercy*, those 'sacrifices wherewith God is well pleased',[68] those marks whereby the Shepherd of Israel will know

---

[58] Cf. Matt. 18:33.
[59] Isa. 1:13.
[60] Deut. 7:25, etc.
[61] See Matt. 19:6.
[62] Cf. Rev. 2:23.
[63] Cf. John 4:24.   [64] See 1 Cor. 13:3.
[65] 1 Cor. 2:2.   [66] Cf. Gal. 2:20.
[67] Cf. BCP, Communion, Prayer for the Church Militant.
[68] Cf. Heb. 13:16.

his sheep at the last day. Be more zealous still for *holy tempers*, for 'long-suffering, gentleness, goodness, meekness, lowliness, and resignation';[69] but be most zealous of all for *love*, the queen of all graces,[70] the highest perfection in earth or heaven, the very image of the invisible God, as in men below, so in angels above. For 'God is love; and he that dwelleth in love, dwelleth in God and God in him.'[71]

Haverford West, May 6, 1781[72]

---

[69] Cf. Gal. 5:22-23.
[70] Cf. 'Charity the queen of virtues' (βασιλὶς τῶν ἀρετῶν), cited in Francis Atterbury, *Fourteen Sermons Preached on Several Occasions* (1708), p. 58, as from Chrysostom, 'Tom. VI.193'. But see Lampe, *Patristic Greek Lexicon*, βασιλίς, No. 5.
[71] 1 John 4:16.
[72] Place and date as in *AM*, IV.525.

ON REDEEMING THE TIME

AN INTRODUCTORY COMMENT

Here Wesley turns abruptly from his praise of love to a moralistic admonition against 'sleeping overmuch'. The unobvious notion of grounding such a counsel on Eph. 5:16 may have come to Wesley from Richard Baxter who, in his Christian Directory *(1673), Pt. I, ch. 5, 'Directions for Redeeming or Well Improving Time', had taken Eph. 5:15, 16 for his text; but Baxter's comments range over all the different ways in which time may be 'redeemed' or wasted. In Title 4 ('The Thieves or Time-wasters to be watchfully avoided'), the second 'thief' or 'time-waster' is 'excess of sleep'. Here Baxter makes Wesley's point one hundred years before him, although without the same specific references to a proper daily ration of sleep.*

There is no hint of the idea in the extensive comments of Matthew Poole's Annotations *on this verse or Matthew Henry's* Exposition *of it. The discussion, or course, is part of Wesley's insistence upon the Christian stewardship of* time *as an aspect of the Christian ethic which aims at 'universal self-denial . . . in a full pursuit of . . . inward and outward holiness' (III.7).*

Wesley had already spoken to this same point in his earlier sermon, No. 89, 'The More Excellent Way', I.1 (see n.). We know of eleven usages of Eph. 5:16 as a sermon text between 1750 and 1788. In 1782 (January 20) in London, he undertook to summarize the idea in writing. The result appeared shortly thereafter in the Arminian Magazine, *March and April 1782 (V.117-22, 173-79), numbered as 'Sermon VIII'. The following year it was reprinted in Cambridge by an anonymous editor who had been 'much struck with the force and propriety of its reasoning'. This unknown admirer abridged the original (the great abridger abridged!), supplied it 'with small additions from* Law's Serious Call *and two or three notes', and entitled his pamphlet* The Duty and Advantage of Early Rising. *In apparent approval, Wesley reissued this edited pamphlet under its title in four separate editions in his lifetime (and there were many subsequent editions thereafter). When, however, he decided to include the sermon in* SOSO

(VII.277-94), he reverted to the original text and gave it the ambiguous title it has carried ever since. (Actually the half-title [p.(277)], is 'On Redeeming Time', while the opening page (p. 279) is headed by the title 'Ephesians V.16', below which is the scriptural text, 'Redeeming the Time'.)

For a stemma illustrating its publishing history and all substantive variant readings, see Appendix, Vol. 4; see also Bibliog, *No. 375.i.*

On Redeeming the Time

Ephesians 5:16

Redeeming the time.

1. 'See that ye walk circumspectly', says the Apostle in the preceding verse, 'not as fools, but as wise men: redeeming the time;'[1] saving all the time you can for the best purposes; buying up every fleeting moment out of the hands of sin and Satan, out of the hands of sloth, ease, pleasure, worldly business; the more diligently because the present 'are evil days', days of the grossest ignorance, immorality, and profaneness.

2. This seems to be the general meaning of the words. But I purpose at present to consider only one particular way of 'redeeming the time', namely, from sleep.

3. This appears to have been exceeding little considered, even by pious men. Many that have been eminently conscientious in other respects have not been so in this. They seemed to think it an indifferent thing whether they slept more or less, and never saw it in the true point of view, as an important branch of Christian temperance.

That we may have a more just conception hereof, I will endeavour to show,

    I.   What it is to 'redeem the time' from sleep;

    II.   The evil of not redeeming it; and

    III. The most effectual manner of doing it.

---

[1] Cf. Henry's comment here: ' "Redeeming the time", literally "buying the opportunity". It is a metaphor taken from merchants and traders who diligently observe and improve the seasons for merchandise and trade, etc.'; see also Poole, *Annotations, loc. cit.*

I.1. And, first, what is it to 'redeem the time' from sleep? It is, in general, to take that measure of sleep every night which nature requires, and no more; that measure which is the most conducive to the health and vigour both of the body and mind.

5   2. But it is objected, 'One measure will not suit all men: some require considerably more than others. Neither will the same measure suffice even the same persons at one time as at another. When a person is sick, or if not actually so, yet weakened by preceding sickness, he certainly wants more of this natural 10 restorative than he did when in perfect health. And so he will when his strength and spirits are exhausted by hard or long-continued labour.'

   3. All this is unquestionably true, and confirmed by a thousand experiments. Whoever therefore they are that have attempted to 15 fix one measure of sleep for all persons did not understand the nature of the human body, so widely different in different persons; as neither did they who imagined that the same measure would suit even the same person at all times. One would wonder therefore that so great a man as Bishop Taylor should have 20 formed this strange imagination; much more that the measure which he has assigned for the general standard should be only three hours in four and twenty.[2] That good and sensible man, Mr. Baxter, was not much nearer the truth; who supposes four hours in four and twenty will suffice for any man.[3] I knew an extremely 25 sensible man who was absolutely persuaded that no one living needed to sleep above five hours in twenty-four. But when he made the experiment himself, he quickly relinquished the opinion. And I am fully convinced, by an observation continued for more than fifty years, that whatever may be done by 30 extraordinary persons, or in some extraordinary cases (wherein persons have subsisted with very little sleep for some weeks or

---

[2] In his *Holy Living*, which greatly influenced Wesley's devotional discipline, including the maintaining of a diary and early rising, Taylor urged: 'Let your sleep be necessary and healthful, not idle and expensive of time, beyond the needs and convenience of nature . . .', which Wesley summarized for himself as, 'sleep not immoderately', but the restriction to three hours only is not found in this context (Jeremy Taylor, *Works*, Heber, ed. (1844), III.10; cf. Heitzenrater, p. 60).

[3] In *Christian Directory*, Pt. I, ch. viii (*Works*, I.228-41), Richard Baxter has a set of 'Directions Against Sinful Excess of Sleep': 'To some five hours is enough; to the ordinary sort of beautiful persons six hours is enough; to many weak, valetudinary persons seven hours is needful; to sick persons I am not to give directions.'

even months) a human body can scarce continue in health and vigour without at least six hours' sleep in four and twenty. Sure I am, I never met with such an instance: I never found either man or woman that retained vigorous health for one year with a less quantity of sleep than this.[4]

4. And I have long observed that women in general want a little more sleep than men; perhaps because they are in common of a weaker as well as a moister habit of body.[5] If therefore one might venture to name one standard (though liable to many exceptions and occasional alterations) I am inclined to think this would come near the mark: healthy men, in general, need a little above six hours' sleep, healthy women, a little above seven, in four and twenty. I myself want six hours and a half, and I cannot well subsist with less.

5. If anyone desires to know exactly what quantity of sleep his own constitution requires, he may very easily make the experiment which I made about sixty years ago.[6] I then waked every night about twelve or one, and lay awake for some time. I readily concluded that this arose from my lying longer in bed than nature required. To be satisfied I procured an alarum, which waked me the next morning at seven (near an hour earlier than I rose the day before), yet I lay awake again at night. The second morning I rose at six; but notwithstanding this I lay awake the second night. The third morning I rose at five; but nevertheless I lay awake the third night. The fourth morning I rose at four (as, by the grace of God, I have done ever since); and I lay awake no more.[7] And I do not now lie awake (taking the year round) a quarter of an hour together in a month. By the same experiment,

---

[4] Cf. No. 89, 'The More Excellent Way', I.1.

[5] An echo of the distinctions in medieval physiology between the 'temperaments' or 'humours' of the body; cf. Chambers's *Cyclopaedia*, 'Temperament' and 'Humours' for comments that seemed commonplace in Wesley's time.

[6] I.e., about 1722, in his undergraduate days in Christ Church.

[7] A conveniently oversimplified recollection. The early diaries, however, show that Wesley was still experimenting with various diurnal patterns as late as 1729; it was in Aug. 1730 that he seems to have settled on a regular awakening hour between 4:00 and 5:00 a.m. What is not mentioned here is the fact that Wesley often took daytime cat naps whenever it was convenient; cf. A. H. S. Pask, in WHS, XXIX.95-96 (1953). In John Foster's *Life and Correspondence* (posthumously in Bohn's Library, 1846, I.301) there is a report from Samuel Bradburn, (but possibly Joseph Bradford is intended, who was one of Wesley's frequent travelling companions), that in addition to his six hours of regular sleep, 'Wesley slept several hours in the course of the day' (i.e., after he switched from riding horseback to carriage); see also J. C. Adlard, 'Notes', in WHS, XI.96 (1917).

rising earlier and earlier every morning, may anyone find how much sleep he really wants.

II.1. 'But why should anyone be at so much pains? What need is there of being so scrupulous? Why should we make ourselves so
5 particular? What harm is there in doing as our neighbours do?—suppose in lying from ten till six or seven in summer, and till eight or nine in winter?'

2. If you would consider this question fairly you will need a good deal of candour and impartiality, as what I am about to say
10 will probably be quite new; different from anything you ever heard in your life; different from the judgment, at least from the example, of your parents and your nearest relations; nay, and perhaps of the most religious persons you ever were acquainted with. Lift up therefore your heart to the Spirit of truth,[8] and beg of
15 him to shine upon it, that without respecting any man's person you may see and follow the truth as it in Jesus.[9]

3. Do you really desire to know what harm there is in not redeeming all the time you can from sleep? Suppose in spending therein an hour a day more than nature requires? Why, first, it
20 *hurts your substance*. It is throwing away six hours a week which might turn to some temporal account. If you can do any work, you might earn something in that time, were it ever so small. And you have no need to throw even this away. If you do not want it yourself, give it to them that do: you know some of them that are
25 not far off. If you are of no trade, still you may so employ the time that it will bring money, or money's worth, to yourself or others.

4. The not redeeming all the time you can from sleep, the spending more time therein than your constitution necessarily requires, in the second place, *hurts your health*. Nothing can be
30 more certain than this, though it is not commonly observed. It is not commonly observed because the evil steals on you by slow and insensible degrees. In this gradual and almost imperceptible manner it lays the foundation of many diseases. It is the chief, real (though unsuspected) cause of all nervous diseases in particular.
35 Many inquiries have been made why nervous disorders are so much more common among us than among our ancestors. Other causes may frequently concur; but the chief is, we lie longer in

[8] John 14:17.
[9] See Eph. 4:21.

bed. Instead of rising at four, most of us who are not obliged to work for our bread lie till seven, eight, or nine. We need inquire no farther. This sufficiently accounts for the large increase of these painful disorders.[10]

5. It may be observed that most of these arise, not barely from sleeping too long, but even from what we imagine to be quite harmless—the lying too long in bed. By *soaking* (as it is emphatically called) so long between warm sheets the flesh is, as it were, parboiled, and becomes soft and flabby.[11] The nerves in the meantime are quite unstrung, and all the train of melancholy symptoms—faintness, tremors, lowness of spirits (so called)—come on, till life itself is a burden.

6. One common effect of either sleeping too long, or lying in bed, is weakness of sight, particularly that weakness which is of the nervous kind. When I was young my sight was remarkably weak. Why is it stronger now than it was forty years ago?[12] I impute this principally to the blessing of God, who fits us for whatever he calls us to. But undoubtedly the outward means which he has been pleased to bless was the rising early in the morning.

7. A still greater objection to the not rising early, the not redeeming all the time we can from sleep, is, it *hurts the soul* as well as the body; it is a sin against God. And this indeed it must necessarily be, on both the preceding accounts. For we cannot waste or (which comes to the same thing) not improve any part of our worldly substance, neither can we impair our own health, without sinning against him.

8. But this fashionable intemperance does also hurt the soul in a more direct manner. It sows the seeds of foolish and hurtful desires:[13] it dangerously inflames our natural appetites, which a person stretching and yawning in bed is just prepared to gratify. It breeds and continually increases sloth, so often objected to [in] the English nation. It opens the way and prepares the soul for every other kind of intemperance. It breeds an universal softness and faintness of spirit, making us afraid of every little

---

[10] Cf. 'Thoughts on Nervous Disorders', *AM* (1786), IX.52-54, 94-97. For other references to intemperance in sleep, cf. *Notes* on Luke 21:38, and Wesley's letter to his niece, Sarah Wesley, July 17, 1781. See also No. 89, 'The More Excellent Way', I.1.

[11] Cf. Steele, *The Spectator*, No. 65 (May 15, 1771): 'Because it is vulgar to lie and soak together, we have each of us separate settle-beds.'

[12] Cf. the memoir of Sophie de la Roche, *Sophie in London, 1786*, Eng. trans. by Clare Williams (1933), p. 78. See above, Vol. 1 (this edn.), pp. 71-72.

[13] 1 Tim. 6:9 (*Notes*).

inconvenience, unwilling to deny ourselves any pleasure, or to take up or bear any cross. And how then shall we be able (without which we must drop into hell) to 'take the kingdom of heaven by violence'?[14] It totally unfits us for 'enduring hardship as good
5   soldiers of Jesus Christ';[15] and consequently for 'fighting the good fight of faith, and laying hold on eternal life'.[16]

9. In how beautiful a manner does that great man, Mr. Law, treat this important subject! Part of his words I cannot but here subjoin for the use of every sensible reader:

10   I take it for granted that every Christian who is in health is up early in the morning; for it is much more reasonable to suppose a person is up early because he is a Christian, than because he is a labourer or a tradesman or a servant.
We conceive an abhorrence of a man that is in bed when he should be at his labour. We cannot think good of him who is such a slave to drowsiness as to
15   neglect his business for it.
Let this therefore teach us to conceive how odious we must appear to God if we are in bed, shut up in sleep, when we should be praising God; and are such slaves to drowsiness as to neglect our devotions for it.
Sleep is such a dull, stupid state of existence that even among mere animals
20   we despise them most which are most drowsy. He therefore that chooses to enlarge the slothful indolence of sleep rather than be early at his devotions, chooses the dullest refreshment of the body before the noblest employment[17] of the soul. He chooses that state which is a reproach to mere animals before that exercise which is the glory of angels.
25   10. Besides, he that cannot deny himself this drowsy indulgence is no more prepared for prayer when he is up than he is prepared for fasting or any other act of self-denial. He may indeed more easily read over a form of prayer than he can perform these duties; but he is no more disposed for the spirit of prayer than he is disposed for fasting. For sleep, thus indulged, gives a softness to all our
30   tempers, and makes us unable to relish anything but what suits an idle state of mind, as sleep does. So that a person who is a slave to this idleness is in the same temper when he is up. Everything that is idle or sensual pleases him. And everything that requires trouble or self-denial is hateful to him, for the same reason that he hates to rise.
35   11. It is not possible for an epicure to be truly devout. He must renounce his sensuality before he can relish the happiness of devotion. Now he that turns sleep into an idle indulgence does as much to corrupt his soul, to make it a slave to bodily appetites, as an epicure does. It does not disorder his life,[18] as notorious acts of intemperance do; but like any more moderate course of indulgence it

---

[14] Cf. Matt. 11:12 (*Notes*).
[15] Cf. 2 Tim. 2:3.
[16] Cf. 1 Tim. 6:12.
[17] Law's term; Wesley or his printer had misread this as 'enjoyments'.
[18] Again, Law's term; Wesley's text in *AM* reads 'life'; *SOSO* (1788), VII.288, has it 'health'.

silently and by smaller degrees wears away the spirit of religion, and sinks the soul into dullness and sensuality.

Self-denial of all kinds is the very life and soul of piety; but he that has not so much of it as to be able to be early at his prayers cannot think that he has taken up his cross, and is following Christ.   5

What conquest has he got over himself? What right hand has he cut off? What trials is he prepared for? What sacrifice is he ready to offer to God, who cannot be so cruel to himself as to rise to prayer at such a time as the drudging part of the world are content to rise to their labour?

12. Some people will not scruple to tell you that they indulge themselves in   10 sleep because they have nothing to do; and that if they had any business to rise to they would not lose so much of their time in sleep. But they must be told that they mistake the matter; that they have a great deal of business to do; they have a hardened heart to change; they have the whole spirit of religion to get. For surely he that thinks he has nothing to do because nothing but his prayers want him,   15 may justly be said to have the whole spirit of religion to seek.

You must not therefore consider how small a fault it is to rise late, but how great a misery it is to want the spirit of religion; and to live in such softness and idleness as makes you incapable of the fundamental duties of Christianity.

If I was to desire you not to study the gratification of your palate I would not   20 insist upon the sin of wasting your money, though it is a great one, but I would desire you to renounce such a way of life because it supports you in such a state of sensuality as renders you incapable of relishing the most essential doctrines of religion.

For the same reason I do not insist much upon the sin of wasting your time in   25 sleep, though it be a great one; but I desire you to renounce this indulgence because it gives a softness and idleness to your soul, and is so contrary to that lively, zealous, watchful, self-denying spirit, which was not only the spirit of Christ and his apostles, and the spirit of all the saints and martyrs that have ever been among men, but must be the spirit of all those who would not sink in the   30 common corruption of the world.

13. Here therefore we must fix our charge against this practice. We must blame it, not as having this or that particular evil, but as a general habit that extends itself through our whole spirit, and supports a state of mind that is wholly wrong.   35

It is contrary to piety; not as accidental slips or mistakes in life are contrary to it, but in such a manner as an ill state of body is contrary to health.

On the other hand, if you was to rise early every morning as an instance of self-denial, as a method of renouncing indulgence, as a means of redeeming your time and fitting your spirit for prayer, you would soon find the advantage.   40 This method, though it seems but a small circumstance, might be a means of great piety. It would constantly keep it in your mind that softness and idleness are the bane of religion. It would teach you to exercise power over yourself, and to renounce other pleasures and tempers that war against the soul. And what is so planted and watered, will certainly have an increase from God.[19]   45

---

[19] An untypically long quotation; it is from Law's *Serious Call* (*Works*, IV.128-34), which Wesley had extracted and published in 1744 (*Bibliog*, No. 86), pp. 118-22, and is here still further revised. One remembers that in the early days of the Revival Wesley had turned

III.1. It now only remains to inquire, in the third place, how we may redeem the time, how we may proceed in this important affair. In what manner shall we most effectually practise this important branch of temperance?

5   I advise all of you who are thoroughly convinced of the unspeakable importance of it, suffer not that conviction to die away, but instantly begin to act suitably to it. Only do not depend on your own strength. If you do, you will be utterly baffled. Be deeply sensible that as you are not able to do anything good of 10 yourselves, so here in particular all your strength, all your resolution, will avail nothing. Whoever trusts in himself will be confounded. I never found an exception. I never knew one who trusted in his own strength that could keep this resolution for a twelvemonth.

15   2. I advise you, secondly, cry to the Strong for strength.[20] Call upon him that hath all power in heaven and earth; and believe that he will answer the prayer that goeth not out of feigned lips.[21] As you cannot have too little confidence in yourself, so you cannot have too much in him. Then set out in faith; and surely his 20 strength shall be made perfect in your weakness.[22]

3. I advise you, thirdly, add to your faith, prudence: use the most rational means to attain your purpose. Particularly begin at the right end, otherwise you will lose your labour.[23] If you desire to rise early, sleep early[24]—secure this point at all events. In spite of 25 the most dear and agreeable companions, in spite of their most earnest solicitations, in spite of entreaties, railleries, or reproaches, rigorously keep your hour. Rise up precisely at your time; and retire without ceremony. Keep your hour, notwithstanding the most pressing business: lay all things by till the

against Law with severe reproaches which Law, in turn, had shrugged off; cf. Wesley's letter to Law, May 14, 1738, and Law's reply in the same month and year (see 25:540-46 in this edn.). In later years Wesley's references to Law are mixed. For example, cf. his letter to Law, Jan. 6, 1756. But in 1770 and the years following, there are several letters in which he speaks of Law approvingly; cf. the letters to Mrs. Marston, Aug. 26, 1770; to Richard Locke, Sept. 14, 1770; to Philothea Briggs, May 2, 1771; to Elizabeth Ritchie, Nov. 29, 1774; and to Ann Taylor, Mar. 8, 1787. See also the letter to Ann Bolton, Jan. 9, 1789. In No. 79, 'On Dissipation', §19, Wesley speaks of Law as 'an excellent writer'; and in No. 125, 'On a Single Eye', §1, as 'the strong and elegant writer, Mr. Law'.

[20] See Job 9:19; see also No. 48, 'Self-denial', III.4 and n.
[21] Ps. 17:1.
[22] See 2 Cor. 12:9.
[23] Cf. No. 65, 'The Duty of Reproving our Neighbour', I.3 and n.
[24] Cf. No. 89, 'The More Excellent Way', I.1.

morning. Be it ever so great a cross, ever so great self-denial, keep your hour, or all is over.

4. I advise you, fourthly, be steady. Keep your hour of rising, without intermission. Do not rise two mornings, and lie in bed the third; but what you do once, do always. 'But my head aches.' Do not regard that. It will soon be over. 'But I am uncommonly drowsy; my eyes are quite heavy.' Then you must not parley—otherwise it is a lost case—but start up at once.[25] And if your drowsiness does not go off, lie down for awhile an hour or two after. But let nothing make a breach upon this rule: rise and dress yourself at your hour.

5. Perhaps you will say: 'The advice is good; but it comes too late: I have made a breach already. I did rise constantly, and for a season nothing hindered me. But I gave way by little and little, and I have now left it off for a considerable time!' Then in the name of God begin again! Begin tomorrow; or rather tonight, by going to bed early, in spite of either company or business. Begin with more self-diffidence than before, but with more confidence in God. Only follow these few rules, and—my soul for yours—God will give you the victory. In a little time the difficulty will be over; but the benefit will last for ever.

6. If you say: 'But I cannot do now as I did then; for I am not what I was. I have many disorders, my spirits are low, my hands shake: I am all relaxed.'[26] I answer, all these are nervous symptoms; and they all partly arise from your taking too much sleep; nor is it probable they will ever be removed unless you remove the cause. Therefore on this very account (not only to punish yourself for your folly and unfaithfulness, but) in order to recover your health and strength, resume your early rising. You have no other way: you have nothing else to do. You have no other possible means of recovering, in any tolerable degree, your health both of body and mind. Do not murder yourself outright. Do not run on in the path that leads to the gates of death! As I said before, so I say again: in the name of God, this very day, set out anew. True, it will be more difficult than it was at the beginning. But

---

[25] Is there a possible echo here of a once familiar satire of the difficulties of early rising in Edward Ward, *The Wooden World Dissected* . . . (1707)? In 'character No. 14' (a sailor) much is made of this, and on p. 76 there is a reference to the effect of the boatswain's 'whistling . . ., and you have a hundred or more *Cartesian Puppets* pop up upon deck . . .'.

[26] I.e., 'enfeebled'; cf. *OED* for instances.

bear the difficulty which you have brought upon yourself, and it will not last long. The Sun of righteousness will soon arise again, and will heal both your soul and your body.[27]

7. But do not imagine that this single point, rising early, will 5 suffice to make you a Christian. No: although that single point, the not rising, may keep you a heathen, void of the whole Christian spirit; although this alone (especially if you had once conquered it) will keep you cold, formal, heartless, dead, and make it impossible for you to get one step forward in vital 10 holiness: yet this alone will go but a little way to make you a real Christian. It is but one step out of many; but it is one. And having taken this, go forward. Go on to universal self-denial, to temperance in all things,[28] to a firm resolution of taking up daily every cross[29] whereto you are called. Go on, in a full pursuit of all 15 the mind that was in Christ,[30] of inward, and then outward holiness; so shall you be not almost, but altogether, a Christian;[31] so shall you finish your course with joy:[32] you shall awake up after his likeness, and be satisfied.[33]

London, Jan. 20, 1782[34]

---

[27] See Mal. 4:2.
[28] See 1 Cor. 9:25.
[29] See Luke 9:23.
[30] See Phil. 2:5.
[31] See No. 2, *The Almost Christian*, on Acts 26:28.
[32] See Acts 20:24.
[33] See Ps. 17:16 (BCP); cf. also No. 3, *'Awake, Thou That Sleepest'*.
[34] Place and date as in *AM*.

ON FAMILY RELIGION

AN INTRODUCTORY COMMENT

On May 25, 1783, Wesley was in Nottingham where, as he reports in the Journal, 'I had an easy day's work, as Mr. Bayley assisted me by reading prayers and delivering the wine at the Lord's Table.' He remained there over the following Monday and wrote out this sermon on Josh. 24:15, a text used sparingly heretofore in his oral preaching (three times up to mid-1783). The theme of 'family religion', however, was an old favourite with the Puritans; Wesley had already collected many extracts on the subject; see Christian Library 2nd edn. (1819-27); e.g., VIII.72-85, Isaac Ambrose on 'Family Duties', 'Duties of Parents', 'Duties of Children' (Prima, Media, & Ultima [1674], Treatise II, ch. 10, sects. 1, 2, 4, 7, pp. 228-29, 231-33, 236-37); XXVIII.292-306, 'Life of Philip Henry'; XXIX.399-400, 'Bishop Hopkins' Exposition of the Ten Commandments'; XXX.193 ff.; Jonathan Edwards, 'Faithful Narrative . . .'; see also John Shower (a schoolmate of Samuel Wesley, Sen.), Family Religion . . . (1694). Indeed, four of the seven essays added to the sermons in SOSO, IV (1760)— viz., 'The Duties of Husbands and Wives', 'Directions to Children', 'Directions to Servants', and 'Christian Instructions'—had been focused on 'family religion'. Now in 1783, however, Wesley was aware that the Methodist Revival had already outlasted the normal life span of such movements, and that its future depended quite crucially on 'family religion', 'the education of children', 'obedience to parents', 'obedience to pastors', etc. Hence the sequence of Nos. 94-97.

This particular sermon first appeared in the Arminian Magazine (September and October 1783), VI.452-58, 508-14, without a title but numbered as 'Sermon XVII'. It was then included as the last sermon in SOSO, VII.295-315, and not printed elsewhere in Wesley's lifetime.

On Family Religion

Joshua 24:15

As for me and my house, we will serve the Lord.

1. In the foregoing verses we read that Joshua, now grown old,
5 'gathered the tribes of Israel to Shechem, and called for the elders
of Israel, for their heads, for their judges, and officers, and they
presented themselves before the Lord.'[a] And Joshua rehearsed to
them the great things which God had done for their fathers,[b]
concluding with the strong exhortation: 'Now therefore fear the
10 Lord, and serve him in sincerity and truth; and put away the gods
which your fathers served on the other side the flood (Jordan),
and in Egypt.'[c] Can anything be more astonishing than this! That
even in Egypt, yea, and in the wilderness, where they were daily
fed, and both day and night guided by miracle, the Israelites in
15 general should worship idols, in flat defiance of the Lord their
God! He proceeds: 'If it seemeth evil to you to serve the Lord,
choose ye this day whom ye will serve: whether the gods your
fathers served on the other side of the flood, or the gods of the
Amorites in whose land ye dwell. But as for me and my house, we
20 will serve the Lord.'
2. A resolution this worthy of a hoary-headed saint, who had
had large experience from his youth up of the goodness of the
Master to whom he had devoted himself, and the advantages of
his service. How much is it to be wished that all who have tasted
25 that the Lord is gracious,[1] all whom he has brought out of the land
of Egypt, out of the bondage of sin; those especially who are
united together in Christian fellowship, would adopt this wise
resolution! Then would the work of the Lord prosper in our land;
then would his word run and be glorified. Then would multitudes
30 of sinners in every place stretch out their hands unto God, until
'the glory of the Lord covered the land, as the waters cover the
sea.'[2]

---

[a] Ver. 1. [b] Ver. 2-13.
[c] Ver. 14 [AV reads, 'on the other side of the flood, and in Egypt'; Wesley inserts
'Jordan' without the parentheses supplied].

---

[1] 1 Pet. 2:3. [2] Cf. Hab. 2:14.

3. On the contrary, what will the consequence be if they do not adopt this resolution? If family religion be neglected? If care be not taken of the rising generation? Will not the present revival of religion in a short time die away? Will it not be, as the historian speaks of the Roman state in its infancy, *res unius aetatis*, an event 5 that has its beginning and end within the space of one generation?[3] Will it not be a confirmation of that melancholy remark of Luther's that 'a revival of religion never lasts longer than one generation'?[4] By a generation (as he explains himself) he means thirty years. But, blessed be God, this remark does not 10 hold with regard to the present instance; seeing this revival, from its rise in the year 1729, has already lasted above fifty years.[5]

4. Have we not already seen some of the unhappy consequences of good men's not adopting this resolution? Is there not a generation arisen, even within this period, yea, and 15 from pious parents, that know not the Lord? That have neither his love in their hearts, nor his fear before their eyes?[6] How many of them already 'despise their fathers, and mock at the counsel of their mothers'?[7] How many are utter strangers to real religion—to the life and power of it? And not a few have shaken off all religion, 20 and abandoned themselves to all manner of wickedness! Now although this may sometimes be the case, even of children educated in a pious manner, yet this case is very rare. I have met with some, but not many instances of it: the wickedness of the children is generally owing to the fault or neglect of their parents. 25 For it is a general, though not universal rule, though it admits of some exceptions, 'Train up a child in the way he should go, and when he is old he will not depart from it.'[8]

---

[3] Cf. *Minutes*, Aug. 16, 1768, *Q.* 23, *A.* 10: 'Unless we take care . . . , the present revival will be *res unius aetatis* ['a matter of a single generation']; it will last only the age of a man.' Cf. Cicero, *De Re Publica* (*The Republic*), I.viii, *unius aetatis* ('a single short period . . .').

[4] Cf. No. 63, 'The General Spread of the Gospel', §16 and n. For other references to Luther, cf. No. 14, *The Repentance of Believers*, I.9 and n.

[5] This dating reflects several conflations of Wesley's memories. 'Above fifty years' before 1783 would mean 'before 1733'; the year 1729 was the origin of the Holy Club, and Wesley has other places where he dates the Revival from 1729 (cf. No. 107, 'On God's Vineyard', proem, I.1; and his letter to William Black, Nov. 26, 1786). This conflicts with the *Journal* evidence, the preface to the *General Rules*, etc., that the Revival, as a popular movement, was not really active before 1739. Cf. Wesley's *Plain Account of the People called Methodists* (written in 1748; published in 1749) and his *Short History of Methodism* (1765).

[6] See Rom. 3:18.

[7] Cf. Prov. 30:17.

[8] Prov. 22:6.

5. But what is the purport of this resolution, 'I and my house will serve the Lord'? In order to understand and practise this, let us first inquire what it is to 'serve the Lord'; secondly, who are included in that expression, 'my house'; and thirdly, what can we do, that 'we and our house' may 'serve the Lord'.

I.1. We may inquire, first, what it is to 'serve the Lord', not as a Jew, but as a Christian. Not only with an outward service (though some of the Jews undoubtedly went farther than this) but with inward; with the service of the heart, 'worshipping him in spirit and in truth'.[9] The first thing implied in this service is faith—believing in the name of the Son of God.[10] We cannot perform an acceptable service to God till we believe on Jesus Christ whom he hath sent.[11] Here the spiritual worship of God begins. As soon as anyone has the witness in himself, as soon as he can say, 'The life that I now live, I live by faith in the Son of God, who loved me and gave himself for me,'[12] he is able truly to 'serve the Lord'.

2. As soon as he believes, he loves God, which is another thing implied in 'serving the Lord'. 'We love him, because he first loved us'[13]—of which faith is the evidence. The love of a pardoning God 'is shed abroad in our hearts by the Holy Ghost which is given unto us'.[14] Indeed this love may admit of a thousand degrees; but still everyone, as long as he believes, may truly declare before God, 'Lord, thou knowest that I love thee.'[15] Thou knowest that 'my desire is unto thee, and unto the remembrance of thy name'.[16]

3. And if any man truly love God he cannot but love his brother also. Gratitude to our Creator will surely produce benevolence to our fellow-creatures.[17] If we love him, we cannot but love one another, as Christ loved us. We feel our souls enlarged in love toward every child of man. And toward all the children of God we put on 'bowels of kindness, gentleness, long-suffering, forgiving

---

[9] Cf. John 4:24.
[10] See 1 John 5:13.
[11] See John 17:3.
[12] Cf. Gal. 2:20.
[13] 1 John 4:19.   [14] Rom. 5:5.
[15] John 21:15, 16, 17.   [16] Cf. Isa. 26:8.
[17] Note that Wesley has a place for benevolence in Christian ethics as a consequence of Christian gratitude to God (cf. No. 91, 'On Charity', I.2 and n.). His quarrel with Hutcheson and others was their thesis that benevolence was a primal human disposition independent of divine endowment and grace; see No. 12, 'The Witness of Our Own Spirit', §5 and n.

one another',[18] if we have a complaint against any, 'even as God for Christ's sake hath forgiven us'.[19]

4. One thing more is implied in 'serving the Lord', namely, the obeying him; the steadily walking in all his ways, the doing his will from the heart. Like those 'his servants' above 'who do his 5 pleasure', who 'keep his commandments, and hearken unto the voice of his words',[20] these his servants below hearken unto his voice, diligently keep his commandments, carefully avoid whatever he has forbidden, and zealously do whatever he has enjoined; studying always to have a conscience void of offence 10 toward God and toward man.[21]

II. 'I and my house will serve the Lord,' will every real Christian say. But who are included in that expression, 'my house'? This is the next point to be considered.

1. The person in your house that claims your first and nearest 15 attention is undoubtedly your wife; seeing you are to love her even as Christ loved the Church,[22] when he laid down his life for it, that he might 'purify it unto himself',[23] 'not having spot or wrinkle or any such thing'.[24] The same end is every husband to pursue in all his intercourse with his wife, to use every possible means that she 20 may be freed from every spot, and may walk unblameable in love.

2. Next to your wife are your children: immortal spirits whom God hath for a time entrusted to your care, that you may train them up in all holiness, and fit them for the enjoyment of God in eternity. This is a glorious and important trust; seeing one soul is 25 of more value than all the world beside.[25] Every child therefore you are to watch over with the utmost care, that when you are called to give an account of each to the Father of Spirits, you may give your accounts with joy and not with grief.

[18] Cf. Col. 3:12, 13.
[19] Cf. Eph. 4:32.
[20] Cf. Ps. 103:21, 20 (BCP).
[21] See Acts 24:16.   [22] See Eph. 5:25.
[23] Cf. Titus 2:14.   [24] Eph. 5:27.
[25] See Young, *Night Thoughts*, vii. 994-97:

> Behold this midnight glory: worlds on worlds!
> Amazing pomp! Redouble this amaze!
> Ten thousand add, add twice ten thousand more;
> Then weigh the whole: one soul outweighs them all.

See also Charles Wesley, 'As all the world were but one soul', several times quoted by Wesley, as in No. 54, 'On Eternity', §20.

3. Your servants of whatever kind you are to look upon as a kind of *secondary children*;[26] these likewise God has committed to your charge, as one that must give account; for everyone under your roof that has a soul to be saved is under your care; not only
5 indented[27] servants, who are legally engaged to remain with you for a term of years; not only hired servants, whether they voluntarily contract for a longer or shorter time; but also those who serve you by the week or day; for these too are in a measure delivered into your hands. And it is not the will of *your* Master
10 who is in heaven that any of these should go out of your hands before they have received from you something more valuable than gold or silver. Yea, and you are in a degree accountable even for 'the stranger that is within your gates'.[28] As you are particularly required to see that he does 'no manner of work'[29] on the Lord's
15 day, while he is within your gates; so, by parity of reason, you are required to do all that is in your power to prevent his sinning against God in any other instance.

III. Let us inquire, in the third place, what can we do that all these may 'serve the Lord'?
20   1. May we not endeavour, first, to *restrain* them from all outward sin? From profane swearing; from taking the name of God in vain; from doing any needless work, or taking any pastime on the Lord's day? This labour of love you owe even to your visitants; much more to your wife, children, and servants. The
25 former, over whom you have the least influence, you may restrain by argument or mild persuasion. If you find that after repeated trials they will not yield, either to one or the other, it is your bounden duty to set ceremony aside, and to dismiss them from your house. Servants also, whether by the day or for a longer
30 space, if you cannot reclaim either by reasoning added to your example, or by gentle or severe reproofs, though frequently repeated, you must in any wise dismiss from your family, though it should be ever so inconvenient.

---

[26] Cf. *OED* (usage 'c'), citing John Brown, Minister of the Gospel at Haddington, *Compendious View of Natural and Revealed Religion* (1782), I.i.24: 'Servants in families ought to be considered as secondary children and have due instruction . . . .' See also Law, *Christian Perfection* (*Works*, III.223). The same point is made by J. H. Plumb in *The First Four Georges*, p. 31; see No. 50, 'The Use of Money', III.3 and n.
[27] An archaic form of 'indentured'.
[28] Cf. Exod. 20:10; Deut. 5:14; 31:12.
[29] Exod. 12:16; Lev. 23:31.

2. But you cannot dismiss your wife unless for the cause of fornication,[30] that is, adultery. What then can be done if she is habituated to any other open sin? I cannot find in the Bible that a husband has authority to strike his wife on any account—even suppose she struck him first—unless his life were in imminent 5 danger. I never have known one instance yet of a wife that was mended thereby. I have heard indeed of some such instances; but as I did not see them, I do not believe them.[31] It seems to me, all that can be done in this case is to be done partly by example, partly by argument or persuasion, each applied in such a manner as is 10 dictated by Christian prudence. If evil can ever be overcome, it must be 'overcome by good'.[32] It cannot be overcome by evil: we cannot beat the devil with his own weapons. Therefore if this evil cannot be overcome by good, we are called to suffer it. We are then called to say: 'This is the cross which God hath chosen for 15 me. He surely permits it for wise ends: "Let him do what seemeth him good."[33] Whenever he sees it to be best, he will remove this cup from me.'[34] Meantime continue in earnest prayer, knowing that with God no word is impossible; and that he will either in due time take the temptation away or make it a blessing to your soul. 20

3. Your children, while they are young, you may restrain from evil not only by advice, persuasion, and reproof, but also by correction; only remembering that this means is to be used last—not till all other have been tried, and found to be ineffectual. And even then you should take the utmost care to avoid the very 25 appearance of passion. Whatever is done should be done with mildness; nay, indeed, with kindness too. Otherwise your own spirit will suffer loss, and the child will reap little advantage.

4. But some will tell you: 'All this is lost labour; a child need not be corrected at all. Instruction, persuasion, and advice will be 30 sufficient for any child, without correction; especially if gentle reproof be added, as occasion may require.' I answer, there may be particular instances wherein this method may be successful. But you must not in any wise lay this down as an universal rule; unless you suppose yourself wiser than Solomon, or, to speak 35

---

[30] See Matt. 19:9.

[31] Note that, for Wesley, the logic of empirical evidence cuts both ways; cf. JWJ, May 25, 1768, where the question is whether Wesley had ever seen an apparition himself. 'No', says he, 'nor did I ever see a murder; yet I believe there is such a thing. . . . The testimony of unexceptional witnesses fully convinces me both of the one and the other.'

[32] Cf. Rom. 12:21.

[33] 1 Sam. 3:18.   [34] Luke 22:42.

more properly, wiser than God. For it is God himself, who best knoweth his own creatures, that has told us expressly, 'He that spareth the rod hateth the child; but he that loveth him chasteneth him betimes.'[d] And upon this is grounded that plain command-
5 ment, directed to all that fear God, 'Chasten thy son while there is hope; and let not thy soul spare for his crying.'[e]

5. May we not endeavour, secondly, to *instruct* them? To take care that every person who is under our roof have all such knowledge as is necessary to salvation? To see that our wife,
10 servants, and children be taught all those things which belong to their eternal peace? In order to this, you should provide that not only your wife, but your servants also may enjoy all the public means of instruction. On the Lord's day, in particular, you should so forecast what is necessary to be done at home that they may
15 have an opportunity of attending all the ordinances of God. Yea, and you should take care that they have some time every day for reading, meditation, and prayer. And you should inquire whether they do actually employ that time in the exercises for which it is allowed. Neither should any day pass without family prayer,
20 seriously and solemnly performed.

6. You should particularly endeavour to instruct your children, early, plainly, frequently, and patiently. Instruct them *early*, from the first hour that you perceive reason begins to dawn. Truth may then begin to shine upon the mind, far earlier than we are apt to
25 suppose. And whoever watches the first openings of the understanding may by little and little supply fit matter for it to work upon, and may turn the eye of the soul toward good things, as well as toward bad or trifling ones. Whenever a child begins to speak, you may be assured reason begins to work. I know no cause
30 why a parent should not just then begin to speak of the best things, the things of God. And from that time no opportunity should be lost of instilling all such truths as they are capable of receiving.

7. But the speaking to them early will not avail, unless you
35 likewise speak to them *plainly*. Use such words as little children may understand, just such as they use themselves. Carefully observe the few ideas which they have already, and endeavour to graft what you say upon them. To take a little example: bid the

[d] Prov. 13:24.
[e] Chap. 19:18.

child look up, and ask, 'What do you see there?' 'The sun.' 'See, how bright it is! Feel how warm it shines upon your hand! Look, how it makes the grass and the flowers grow, and the trees and everything look green! But God (though you cannot see him) is above the sky, and is a deal brighter than the sun! It is he, it is 5 God, that made the sun, and you and me, and everything. It is he that makes the grass and the flowers grow; that makes the trees green, and the fruit to come upon them! Think what he can do! He can do whatever he pleases. He can strike me or you dead in a moment. But he loves you; he loves to do you good. He loves to 10 make you happy. Should not you then love *him!* You love *me*, because I love you and do you good. But it is God that makes me love you. Therefore you should love him. And he will teach you how to love him.'[35]

8. While you are speaking in this, or some such manner, you 15 should be continually lifting up your heart to God, beseeching him to open the eyes of their understanding, and to pour his light upon them. He and he alone can make them to differ herein from the beasts that perish. He alone can apply your words to their hearts; without which all your labour will be in vain. But whenever 20 the Holy Ghost teaches, there is no delay in learning.[36]

9. But if you would see the fruit of your labour, you must teach them not only early and plainly, but *frequently* too. It would be of little or no service to do it only once or twice a week. How often do you feed their bodies? Not less than three times a day. And is the 25 soul of less value than the body? Will you not then feed this as often? If you find this a tiresome task, there is certainly something wrong in your own mind. You do not love them enough; or you do not love him who is your Father and their Father. Humble yourself before him! Beg that he would give you more love; and 30 love will make the labour light.

---

[35] Cf. No. 95, 'On the Education of Children', §14. See also Samuel Lee, 'What Means May be Used Towards the Conversion of Our Carnal Relations', Sermon 8 in *The Morning-Exercise at Cripplegate* (1661), pp. 193 ff.

[36] Cf. the Elizabethan 'Homily for Whitsunday', Pt. I, p. 412: 'So true is the saying of Bede: "Where the Holy Ghost doth instruct and teach, there is no delay at all in learning." ' The marginal note here reads 'Hom. 9 sup. Lucam.', but the quotation itself has not been located in any of the homilies of Bede numbered nine in Migne, *PL*, XCIV, *Sectio Prima—Homiliae*. But cf. *Homilia II* ('*In Festo Visitationis Beatae Mariae*') [on Luke 1:44], Migne, *PL*, XCIV, col. 17: '*Et quam miranda, quam cita sancti Spiritus operatio! Nulla quippe in discendo mora est, ubi Spiritus sanctus doctor adest.*' See *A Farther Appeal*, Pt.I, V.25 (11:168 in this edn.).

10. But it will not avail to teach them both early, plainly, and frequently, unless you *persevere* therein. Never leave off, never intermit your labour of love, till you see the fruit of it. But in order to this you will find the absolute need of being endued with power

5   from on high; without which, I am persuaded, none ever had or will have patience sufficient for the work. Otherwise the inconceivable dullness of some children, and the giddiness or perverseness of others, would induce them to give up the irksome task, and let them follow their own imagination.

10   11. And suppose after you have done this—after you have taught your children from their early infancy, in the plainest manner you could, omitting no opportunity, and persevering therein—you did not presently see any fruit of your labour, you must not conclude that there will be none. Possibly the 'bread

15   which you have cast upon the waters' may be 'found after many days'.[37] The seed which has long remained in the ground may at length spring up into a plentiful harvest. Especially if you do not restrain prayer before God, if you continue instant herein with all supplication. Meantime, whatever the effect of this be upon

20   others, your reward is with the Most High.

12. Many parents, on the other hand, presently see the fruit of the seed they have sown, and have the comfort of observing that their children grow in grace in the same proportion as they grow in years. Yet they have not done all. They have still upon their

25   hands another task, sometimes of no small difficulty. Their children are now old enough to go to school. But to what school is it advisable to send them?

13. Let it be remembered that I do not speak to the wild, giddy, thoughtless world, but to those that fear God. I ask, then, 'For

30   what end do you send your children to school?' 'Why, that they may be fit to live in the world.' In which world do you mean? This or the next? Perhaps you thought of this world only; and had forgot that there is a world to come—yea, and one that will last for ever! Pray take this into your account, and send them to such

35   masters as will keep it always before their eyes. Otherwise to send them to school (permit me to speak plainly) is little better than sending them to the devil. At all events, then, send your boys, if you have any concern for their souls, not to any of the large public

---

[37] Cf. Eccles. 11:1.

schools (for they are nurseries of all manner of wickedness)[38] but a private school kept by some pious man who endeavours to instruct a small number of children in religion and learning together.

14. 'But what shall I do with my girls?' By no means send them to a large boarding-school. In these seminaries, too, the children teach one another pride, vanity, affectation, intrigue, artifice, and in short everything which a Christian woman ought not to learn. Suppose a girl were well inclined, yet what would she do in a crowd of children not one of whom has any thought of God, or the least concern for her soul? Is it likely, is it possible, she should retain any fear of God or any thought of saving her soul in such company? Especially as their whole conversation points another way, and turns upon things which one would wish she should never think of. I never yet knew a pious, sensible woman that had been bred at a large boarding-school who did not aver one might as well send a young maid to be bred in Drury Lane.[39]

15. 'But where then shall I send my girls?' If you cannot breed them up yourself (as my mother did, who bred up seven daughters to years of maturity), send them to some mistress that truly fears God, one whose life is a pattern to her scholars, and who has only so many that she can watch over each as one that must give account to God. Forty years ago I did not know such a mistress in England; but you may now find several.[40] You may find such a mistress and such a school at Highgate,[41] at Deptford,[42] near Bristol,[43] in Chester,[44] or near Leeds.[45]

[38] Steele in *The Guardian*, No. 94 (June 29, 1713), had spoken of the universities as 'public nurseries', and Bishop Edward Stillingfleet in *Sermons on Several Occasions* (1696), I.31, had characterized 'the houses of great men in too many places' as 'public schools of debauchery . . .'. Cf. also Charles Wesley's 'Commemorative Hymn' (*Poet. Wks.*, VIII.393): 'The public schools of sin'.

[39] The then centre of the London theatre district (with the Theatre Royal and Covent Garden). Wesley's low opinion of theatres and theatrical people was widely shared; see No. 89, 'The More Excellent Way', V.4 and n.

[40] On May 22, 1781, in a letter to Mary Bishop, he could think of only two.

[41] Linden House, Hornsey Lane; its headmistress was Mary Teulon, daughter of Melchior Teulon (1734–1806), a prominent Methodist class-leader for twenty-four years.

[42] No such reference to Deptford in JWJ, *Letters*, or in the autobiography of Sampson Staniforth, 'the father of Deptford Methodism', in *AM* (1783). There are, however, references to a boarding-school presided over by a Mrs. Edwards in Lambeth; cf. JWJ, Dec. 11, 1778; and Dec. 29, 1787.

[43] Mary Bishop's school near Keynsham.

[44] No other references to this in JWJ, *Letters*, or in F. F. Bretherton, *Early Methodism in and Around Chester* (Chester, Phillipson, and Golder, 1903), pp. 225-33.

[45] Cross Hall, where Mary Bosanquet, who later married John Fletcher, had been headmistress; cf. No. 114, *On the Death of John Fletcher*, III.11.

16. We may suppose your sons have now been long enough at school, and you are thinking of some business for them. Before you determine anything on this head, see that your eye be single.[46] Is it so? Is it your view to please God herein? It is well if you take
5 him into your account. But surely if you love or fear God yourself this will be your first consideration: in what business will your son be most likely to love and serve God? In what employment will he have the greatest advantage for laying up treasures in heaven?[47] I have been shocked above measure in observing how little this is
10 attended to, even by pious parents! Even these consider only how he may get most money; not how he may get most holiness! Even these, upon this glorious motive, send him to a heathen master, and into a family where there is not the very form, much less the power of religion![48] Upon this motive they fix him in a business
15 which will necessarily expose him to such temptations as will leave him not a probability, if a possibility, of serving God. O savage parents! Unnatural, diabolical cruelty!—if you believe there is another world.

'But what shall I do?' Set God before your eyes, and do all
20 things with a view to please him. Then you will find a master, of whatever profession, that loves, or at least fears God; and you will find a family wherein is the form of religion, if not the power also.[49] Your son may nevertheless serve the devil if he will; but it is probable he will not. And do not regard if he gets less money, and
25 provided he gets more holiness. It is enough, though he have less of earthly goods, if he secure the possession of heaven.

17. There is one circumstance more wherein you will have great need of the wisdom from above. Your son or your daughter is now of age to marry, and desires your advice relative to it. Now
30 you know what the world calls a 'good match'[50]—one whereby

---

[46] See Matt. 6:22; Luke 11:34.   [47] Cf. No. 50, 'The Use of Money', intro.
[48] See 2 Tim. 3:15.   [49] *Ibid.*
[50] Cf. Johnson, *The Rambler*, No. 182, p. 4:'a wealthy match'. See also the Epilogue to James Thomson's *Edward and Eleanora* ('written by a friend'), ll. 9-14:

> Look round this town—the question is not whether
> Spouse dies for spouse: but who will live together?
> Of old, they say, a husband was a lover,
> But, thank our stars! these foolish days are over:
> To such substantial prudence we are come,
> We wed not heart to heart—but plumb to plumb [i.e.,
>   fortune to fortune].

Cf. Nos. 125, 'On a Single Eye', III.4; and 131, 'The Danger of Increasing Riches', I.6 and n.

much money is gained. Undoubtedly it is so, if it be true that
money always brings happiness. But I doubt it is not true; money
seldom brings happiness, either in this world or the world to
come. Then let no man deceive you with vain words—riches and
happiness seldom dwell together.[51] Therefore if you are wise you
will not seek riches for your children by their marriage. See that
your eye be single in this also: aim simply at the glory of God, and
the real happiness of your children, both in time and eternity. It is
a melancholy thing to see how Christian parents rejoice in selling
their son or their daughter to a wealthy heathen! And do you
seriously call this *'a good match'!* Thou fool, by a parity of reason
thou mayst call hell a 'good lodging' and the devil a 'good master'.
O learn a better lesson from a better master. 'Seek ye first the
kingdom of God and his righteousness,' both for *thyself and thy
children*, 'and all other things shall be added unto you.'[52]

18. It is undoubtedly true that if you are steadily determined to
walk in this path; to endeavour by every possible means that you
and your house may thus serve the Lord; that every member of
your family may worship him, not only in form, but in spirit, and
in truth; you will have need to use all the grace, all the courage, all
the wisdom which God has given you. For you will find such
hindrances in the way as only the mighty power of God can enable
you to break through. You will have all the 'saints of the world'[53] to
grapple with, who will think you carry things too far. You will have
all the powers of darkness against you, employing both force and
fraud; and above all the deceitfulness of your own heart, which if
you will hearken to it will supply you with many reasons why you
should be a *little more* conformable to the world. But as you have
begun, go on in the name of the Lord, and in the power of his
might![54] Set the smiling and the frowning world, with the prince
thereof, at defiance. Follow reason and the oracles of God;[55] not
the fashions and customs[56] of men. 'Keep thyself pure.'[57]
Whatever others do, let you and your house 'adorn the doctrine of

---

[51] Repeated in No. 95, 'On the Education of Children', §21 ('riches cannot give
happiness').
[52] Cf. Matt. 6:33.
[53] Juán de Valdés; see No. 4, *Scriptural Christianity*, II.5 and n.
[54] Eph. 6:10.
[55] Cf. No. 5, 'Justification by Faith', §2 and n.
[56] Cf. No. 25, 'Sermon on the Mount, V', IV.3 and n.
[57] 1 Tim. 5:22.

God our Saviour'.[58] Let you, your yokefellow, your children, and your servants be all on the Lord's side; sweetly drawing together in one yoke, walking in all his commandments and ordinances,[59] till every one of you 'shall receive his own reward, according to his
5 own labour'.[60]

Nottingham, May 26, 1783[61]

---

[58] Titus 2:10.
[59] See Luke 1:6.
[60] 1 Cor. 3:8.
[61] Place and date as in *AM*.

ON THE EDUCATION OF CHILDREN

AN INTRODUCTORY COMMENT

This sermon is a sequel, both in logic and in time, to 'On Family Religion'. It was written shortly after Wesley's return from a refreshing 'little excursion' to Holland (cf. JWJ, June 11–July 12, 1783) and was published in the Arminian Magazine *in the November and December instalments (VI.566-74, 628-35). Some of its problems had already been anticipated in the July issue of the* Magazine *in a personally initialled 'Thought on the Manner of Educating Children', pp. 380-83; indeed, this sermon can be read as a further reflection upon that 'Thought'. It is also interesting as a retrospective on his own experiences of Christian nurture in the Epworth parsonage and his early encounters with William Law.*

The Magazine *text had no title but was numbered 'Sermon XVIII'. When Wesley included it as the first item in* SOSO, *VIII.3-27(1788), he had supplied the title as above. From 1748 to 1783 there are only seven notices of his use of Prov. 22:6 in his oral preaching; it may be significant that he reverted to it eleven times in the five years between 1785 and 1789.*

On the Education of Children

Proverbs 22:6

Train up a child in the way wherein he should go; and when he is old he will not depart from it.

1. We must not imagine that these words are to be understood 5
in an absolute sense, as if no child that had been trained up in the
way wherein he should go had ever departed from it. Matter of
fact will by no means agree with this. So far from it that it has been
a common observation, 'some of the best parents have had the

worst children.' It is true this might sometimes be the case because good men have not always a good understanding. And without this it is hardly to be expected that they will know how to train up their children. Besides, those who are in other respects
5 good men have often too much easiness of temper; so that they go no farther in restraining their children from evil than old Eli did, when he said gently, 'Nay, my sons, the report I hear of you is not good.'[1] This then is no contradiction to the assertion; for their children are not 'trained up in the way wherein they should go'.
10 But it must be acknowledged, some have been trained up therein with all possible care and diligence; and yet before they were old, yea, in the strength of their years, they did utterly depart from it.

2. The words, therefore, must be understood with some limitation, and then they contain an unquestionable truth. It is a
15 general though not an universal promise, and many have found the happy accomplishment of it. As this is the most probable method for making their children pious which any parents can take, so it generally, although not always, meets with the desired success. The God of their fathers is with their children; he
20 blesses their endeavours; and they have the satisfaction of leaving their religion, as well as their worldly substance, to those that descend from them.

3. But what is 'the way wherein a child should go'? And how shall we 'train him up' therein? The ground of this is admirably
25 laid down by Mr. Law in his *Serious Call to a Devout Life*. Part of his words are:

Had we continued perfect, as God created the first man, perhaps the perfection of our nature had been a sufficient self-instructor for everyone. But as sickness and diseases have created the necessity of medicines and physicians,
30 so the disorders of our rational nature have introduced the necessity of education and tutors.

And as the only end of a physician is to restore nature to its own state, so the only end of education is to restore our rational nature to its proper state. Education therefore is to be considered as reason borrowed at second hand, which is, as far as it can, to supply the loss of original perfection. And as physic
35 may justly be called the art of restoring health, so education should be considered in no other light than as the art of recovering to man his rational perfection.

This was the end pursued by the youths that attended upon Pythagoras,
40 Socrates, and Plato. Their everyday lessons and instructions were so many lectures upon the nature of man, his true end, and the right use of his faculties;

---

[1] Cf. 1 Sam. 2:24; cf. also No. 96, 'On Obedience to Parents', II.5.

upon the immortality of the soul, its relation to God; the agreeableness of virtue to the divine nature; upon the necessity of temperance, justice, mercy, and truth; and the folly of indulging our passions.

Now as Christianity has, as it were, new created the moral and religious world, and set everything that is reasonable, wise, holy, and desirable in its true 5 point of light; so one would expect the education of children should be as much mended by Christianity as the doctrines of religion are.

As it has introduced a new state of things, and so fully informed us of the nature of man and the end of his creation; as it has fixed all our goods and evils, taught us the means of purifying our souls, of pleasing God, and being happy 10 eternally; one might naturally suppose that every Christian country abounded with schools, not only for teaching a few questions and answers of a catechism, but for the forming, training, and practising children in such a course of life as the sublimest doctrines of Christianity require.

An education under Pythagoras or Socrates had no other end but to teach 15 children to think, judge, and act as Pythagoras and Socrates used.

And is it not reasonable to suppose that a Christian education should have no other end but to teach them how to think, and judge, and act according to the strictest rules of Christianity?

At least one would suppose that in all Christian schools the teaching them to 20 begin their lives in the spirit of Christianity, in such abstinence, humility, sobriety, and devotion as Christianity requires, should not only be more, but a hundred times more regarded than any or all things else.

For those that educate us should imitate our guardian angels, suggest nothing to our minds but what is wise and holy; help us to discover every false judgment 25 of our minds, and to subdue every wrong passion of our hearts.

And it is as reasonable to expect and require all this benefit from a Christian education as to require that physic should strengthen all that is right in our nature and remove all our diseases.[2]

4. Let it be carefully remembered all this time that God, not 30 man, is the Physician of souls; that it is he, and none else, who 'giveth medicine to heal' our natural 'sickness';[3] that all 'the help which is done upon earth, he doth it himself;'[4] that none of all the children of men is able to 'bring a clean thing out of an unclean';[5] and in a word that 'it is God who worketh in us, both to will and to 35 do of his good pleasure.'[6] But it is generally his pleasure to work by his creatures: to help man by man. He honours men to be, in this sense, 'workers together with him'.[7] By this means the reward is ours, while the glory redounds to him.

[2] Abridged and revised from Law, *Serious Call* (*Works*, IV.180-82); cf. Wesley's published abridgement of 1744, ch. 14, pp. 154-56.
[3] Ps. 147:3 (BCP).
[4] Cf. Ps. 74:13 (BCP).
[5] Job 14:4.
[6] Cf. Phil. 2:13.
[7] 2 Cor. 6:1.

5. This being premised, in order to see distinctly what is the way wherein we should train up a child, let us consider, What are the diseases of his nature? What are those spiritual diseases which everyone that is born of a woman brings with him into the world?[8]

5   Is not the first of these *atheism?* After all that has been so plausibly written concerning 'the innate idea of God';[9] after all that has been said of its being common to all men in all ages and nations; it does not appear that man has naturally any more idea of God than any of the beasts of the field: he has no knowledge of
10 God at all, no fear of God at all, neither is God in all his thoughts.[10] Whatever change may afterwards be wrought (whether by the grace of God, or by his own reflection, or by education) he is by nature a mere atheist.[11]

6. Indeed, it may be said that every man is by nature, as it were,
15 his own god. He worships himself. He is, in his own conception, absolute Lord of himself. Dryden's hero speaks only according to nature when he says, 'Myself am king of *me.*'[12] He seeks himself in all things. He pleases himself. And why not? Who is Lord over him? *His own will* is his only law; he does this or that because it is
20 his good pleasure. In the same spirit as the son of the morning said of old time, 'I *will* sit upon the sides of the north,'[13] he says, 'I *will* do thus or thus.' And do we not find sensible men on every side who are of the selfsame spirit? Who, if asked, 'Why did you do this?' will readily answer, 'Because I had a mind to it.'

25   7. Another evil disease which every human soul brings into the world with him is *pride*—a continual proneness to think of himself more highly than he ought to think.[14] Every man can discern more or less of this disease in everyone—but himself. And indeed, if he could discern it in himself it would subsist no longer; for he would
30 then in consequence think of himself just as he ought to think.

8. The next disease natural to every human soul, born with every man, is *love of the world.* Every man is by nature a lover of the

---

[8] Cf. No. 45, 'The New Birth', I.4 and n.

[9] A commonplace thesis of Christian Platonism; cf. No. 69, 'The Imperfection of Human Knowledge', I.4 and n.

[10] See Ps. 10:4.

[11] See Eph. 2:3 (*Notes*).

[12] Almanzor in John Dryden, *The Conquest of Granada* (1672), Pt. I, I.i.28:'. . . But know that I alone am king of me.' In No. 128, 'The Deceitfulness of the Human Heart', II.8, Wesley quotes a similar line from John Davies: 'I know I'm one of nature's little kings.'

[13] Cf. Isa. 14:13.

[14] Rom. 12:3.

creature instead of the Creator;[15] 'a lover of pleasure' in every kind 'more than a lover of God'.[16] He is a slave to foolish and hurtful desires in one kind or another; either to the 'desire of the flesh, the desire of the eyes', or 'the pride of life'.[17] 'The desire of the flesh' is a propensity to seek happiness in what gratifies one or more of the outward senses. 'The desire of the eyes' is a propensity to seek happiness in what gratifies the internal sense, the imagination, either by things grand, or new, or beautiful. 'The pride of life' seems to mean a propensity to seek happiness in what gratifies the sense of honour. To this head is usually referred 'the love of money',[18] one of the basest passions that can have place in the human heart. But it may be doubted whether this be not an acquired rather than a natural distemper.

9. Whether this be a natural disease or not, it is certain *anger* is. The ancient philosopher defines it, 'a sense of injury received, with a desire of revenge'.[19] Now, was there ever anyone born of a woman who did not labour under this? Indeed, like other diseases of the mind, it is far more violent in some than in others. But it is *furor brevis*,[20] as the poet speaks; it is a real, though short, madness wherever it is.

10. A deviation from *truth* is equally natural to all the children of men. One said in his haste, 'All men are liars';[21] but we may say, upon cool reflection, All natural men will, upon a close temptation, vary from or disguise the truth. If they do not offend against *veracity*, if they do not say what is false, yet they frequently offend against *simplicity*.[22] They use art; they hang out false colours; they practise either simulation or dissimulation.[23] So that

---

[15] See Rom. 1:25. [16] Cf. 2 Tim. 3:4.

[17] Cf. 1 John 2:16 (*Notes*). See also §19, below; and No. 7, 'The Way to the Kingdom', II.2 and n.

[18] 1 Tim. 6:10.

[19] This root idea comes from Aristotle, *Rhetoric*, II.2, but it is repeated by Cicero in his *Tusculan Disputations*, IV.ix.(21): '*Ira sit libido poeniendi eius qui videatur laesisse injuria*' ('Anger is the desire to punish someone who is thought to have inflicted an undeserved injury'); cf. also Seneca, *De Ira* I.1-3. See also Steele, *The Guardian*, No. 129 (Aug. 8, 1713): 'The moralists have defined anger as "a desire of revenge for some injury offered." '

[20] Horace, *Epistles*, I.ii.62: '*Ira furor brevis est*' ('Anger is a momentary madness').

[21] Cf. Ps. 116:11 (AV).

[22] Cf. No. 12, 'The Witness of Our Own Spirit', §11 and n.

[23] One of Wesley's earliest themes, as in No. 138A, 'On Dissimulation', and the fragment on the same topic (No. 138B). Cf. also No. 24, 'Sermon on the Mount, IV', IV.3 and n.; and match these with Lemuel Gulliver's unflattering description of human nature in *Gulliver's Travels* (Heritage Press reprint of George Faulkner's 1st edn. of *The Works of J[onathan] S[wift]* (1735), III.265, 271).

you cannot say truly of any person living, till grace has altered nature, 'Behold an Israelite indeed, in whom is no guile!'[24]

11. Everyone is likewise prone by nature to speak or act contrary to *justice*. This is another of the diseases which we bring
5 with us into the world. All human creatures are naturally partial to themselves, and when opportunity offers have more regard to their own interest or pleasure than strict justice allows. Neither is any man by nature *merciful* as our heavenly Father is merciful;[25] but all more or less transgress that glorious rule of mercy as well
10 as justice, 'Whatsoever ye would that men should do unto you, the same do unto them.'[26]

12. Now if these are the general diseases of human nature, is it not the grand end of education to cure them? And is it not the part of all those to whom God has entrusted the education of children
15 to take all possible care, first, not to increase, not to feed any of these diseases (as the generality of parents constantly do), and next, to use every possible means of healing them?

13. To come to particulars. What can parents do, and mothers more especially, to whose care our children are necessarily
20 committed in their tender years, with regard to the *atheism* that is natural to all the children of men? How is this fed by the generality of parents, even those that love, or at least, fear God, while in spending hours, perhaps days, with their children, they hardly name the name of God? Meantime they talk of a thousand
25 other things in the world that is round about them. Will not then the things of the present world, which surround these children on every side, naturally take up their thoughts, and set God at a greater distance from them (if that be possible) than he was before? Do not parents feed the atheism of their children farther
30 by ascribing the works of creation to *nature*? Does not the common way of talking about nature leave God quite out of the question? Do they not feed this disease whenever they talk in the hearing of their children of anything *happening* so or so? Of things coming by *chance*? Of good or ill *fortune*? As also when they ascribe
35 this or that event to the wisdom or power of men; or indeed to any other second causes, as if these governed the world? Yea, do they not feed it unawares while they are talking of their own wisdom or goodness, or power to do this or that, without expressly

[24] John 1:47; cf. No. 90, 'An Israelite Indeed' (espec.II.7-8).
[25] See Luke 6:36.
[26] Cf. Matt. 7:12.

mentioning that all these are the gift of God? All this tends to confirm the atheism of their children, and to keep God out of their thoughts.

14. But we are by no means clear of their blood if we only go thus far, if we barely do not feed their disease. What can be done to cure it? From the first dawn of reason continually inculcate, God is in this and every place. God made you, and me, and the earth, and the sun, and the moon, and everything. And everything is his: heaven and earth and all that is therein.[27] God orders all things: he makes the sun shine, and the wind blow, and the trees bear fruit. Nothing comes by chance: that is a silly word: there is no such thing as chance.[28] As God made the world, so he governs the world, and everything that is in it. Not so much as a sparrow falls to the ground[29] without the will of God. And as he governs all things, so he governs all men, good and bad, little and great. He gives them all the power and wisdom they have. And he overrules all. He gives us all the goodness we have: every good thought, and word, and work are from him. Without him we can neither think anything right, or do anything right. Thus it is we are to inculcate upon them that God is all in all.[30]

15. Thus may we counteract, and, by the grace of God assisting us, gradually cure the natural atheism of our children. But what can we do to cure their *self-will*? It is equally rooted in their nature, and is indeed the original idolatry, which is not confined to one age or country, but is common to all the nations under heaven. And how few parents are to be found even among Christians, even among them that truly fear God, who are not guilty in this matter? Who do not continually feed and increase this grievous distemper in their children? To let them have their own will does this most effectually. To let them take their own way is the sure method of increasing their self-will sevenfold. But who has the resolution to do otherwise? One parent in a hundred? Who can be so singular, so cruel, as not more or less to *humour* her child? 'And why should you not? What harm can there be in this, which everybody does?' The harm is that it strengthens their

---

[27] Jer. 51:48.
[28] Wesley rarely forewent an opportunity to deny randomness; cf. No. 69, 'The Imperfection of Human Knowledge', II.1 and n.
[29] See Matt. 10:29.
[30] Cf. No. 94, 'On Family Religion', III.7.

will more and more, till it will neither bow to God nor man. To humour children is, as far as in us lies, to make their disease incurable. A wise parent, on the other hand, should begin to break their will the first moment it appears.[31] In the whole art of
5 Christian education there is nothing more important than this. The will of the parent is to a little child in the place of the will of God. Therefore studiously teach them to submit to this while they are children, that they may be ready to submit to his will when they are men. But in order to carry this point you will need
10 incredible firmness and resolution. For after you have once begun you must never more give way. You must hold on still in an even course: you must never intermit your attention for one hour; otherwise you lose your labour.[32]

16. If you are not willing to lose all the labour you have been at,
15 to break the will of your child, to bring his will into subjection to yours that it may be afterward subject to the will of God, there is one advice which, though little known, should be particularly attended to. It may seem a small circumstance; but it is of more consequence than one can easily imagine. It is this: never, on any
20 account, give a child anything that it cries for. For it is a true observation (and you may make the experiment as often as you please), if you give a child what he cries for you *pay him for crying;* and then he will certainly cry again. 'But if I do not give it to him when he cries, he will scream all day long.' If he does it is your
25 own fault; for it is in your power effectually to prevent it. For no mother need suffer a child to cry aloud after it is a year old. 'Why, it is impossible to hinder it.' So many suppose; but it is an entire mistake. I am a witness of the direct contrary; and so are many others. My own mother had ten children, each of whom had spirit
30 enough.[33] Yet not one of them was ever heard to cry aloud after it was a year old. A gentlewoman of Sheffield (several of whose children I suppose are alive still) assured me she had the same

---

[31] An oft-repeated thesis; cf. No. 96, 'On Obedience to Parents', I.9 ff., where its source (a letter from his mother) is quoted at length. For references to 'will' and 'liberty', cf. No. 60, 'The General Deliverance', I.4 and n.

[32] Cf. No. 65, 'The Duty of Reproving our Neighbour', I.3 and n.

[33] Susanna Wesley bore nineteen children but only ten survived their infancy—seven daughters (Emilia, Susanna, Mary, Mehetabel [Hetty], Anne, Martha, and Kezia [Kezzy]), and three sons (Samuel, Jun., John, and Charles); cf. Adam Clarke, *Memoirs of the Wesley Family,* pp. 362 ff. See also Robert Bolton, *On the Employment of Time* (1750), which Wesley had read. In Essay I, pp. 37-54, there is a discourse on the proper education of children by an idealized mother called Emilia; Bolton's views are strikingly similar to Susanna's—and John's.

success with regard to her eight children. When some were objecting to the possibility of this, Mr. Parson Greenwood[34] (well-known in the north of England) replied, 'This cannot be impossible: I have had the proof of it in my own family. Nay, of more than this. I had six children by my former wife. And she suffered none of them to cry aloud after they were ten months old. And yet none of their spirits were so broken as to unfit them for any of the offices of life.' This therefore may be done by any woman of sense, who may thereby save herself abundance of trouble, and prevent that disagreeable noise, the squalling of young children, from being heard under her roof. But I allow, none but a woman of sense will be able to effect this. Yea, and a woman of such patience and resolution as only the grace of God can give. However, this is doubtless the more excellent way;[35] and she that is able to receive it, let her receive it![36]

[17.] It is hard to say whether self-will or *pride* be the more fatal distemper. It was chiefly pride that threw down so many of the stars of heaven and turned angels into devils.[37] But what can parents do in order to check this until it can be radically cured?

First, beware of adding fuel to the flame, of feeding the disease which you should cure. Almost all parents are guilty of doing this by praising their children to their face. If you are sensible of the folly and cruelty of this, see that you sacredly abstain from it. And in spite of either fear or complaisance, go one step farther. Not only do not encourage, but do not suffer others to do what you dare not do yourself. How few parents are sufficiently aware of this! Or at least sufficiently resolute to practise it! To check everyone, at the first word, that would praise them before their face. Even those who would not on any account 'sit attentive to their own applause',[38] nevertheless do not scruple to sit attentive to the applause of their children. Yea, and that to their face! Oh! consider! Is not this the spreading a net for their feet?[39] Is it not a

---

[34] Parson Greenwood joined Wesley as an assistant in 1762, retired in 1793, and died in 1811; see his obituary in *MM* (Sept. 1811), XXXIV.354.

[35] 1 Cor. 12:31.

[36] See Matt. 19:12.

[37] See No. 72, 'Of Evil Angels', I.3.

[38] Cf. Pope, 'Epistle to Dr. Arbuthnot', ll. 209-10:

> Like Cato, give his little Senate laws,
> And sit attentive to his own applause.

[39] See Prov. 29:5; Lam. 1:13.

grievous incentive to pride, even if they are praised for what is truly praiseworthy? Is it not doubly hurtful if they are praised for things not truly praiseworthy? Things of an indifferent nature, as sense, good breeding, beauty, elegance of apparel! This is liable
5   not only to hurt their heart, but their understanding also. It has a manifest and direct tendency to infuse pride and folly together; to pervert both their taste and judgment, teaching them to value what is dung and dross in the sight of God.

     18. If, on the contrary, you desire without loss of time to strike
10   at the root of their pride, teach your children as soon as possibly you can that they are fallen spirits; that they are fallen short of that glorious image of God wherein they were at first created; that they are not now, as they were once, incorruptible pictures of the God of glory; bearing the express likeness of the wise, the good,
15   the holy Father of spirits; but more ignorant, more foolish, and more wicked, than they can possibly conceive. Show them that in pride, passion, and revenge, they are now like the devil. And that in foolish desires and grovelling appetites they are like the beasts of the field. Watch over them diligently in this respect, that
20   whenever occasion offers you may 'pride in its earliest motions find',[40] and check the very first appearance of it.

     If you ask, 'But how shall I encourage them when they do well, if I am never to commend them?' I answer, I did not affirm this. I did not say, 'You are *never* to commend them.' I know many
25   writers assert this, and writers of eminent piety. They say, to commend man is to rob God, and therefore condemn it altogether. But what say the Scriptures? I read there that our Lord himself frequently commended his own disciples; and the great Apostle scruples not to commend the Corinthians,
30   Philippians, and divers others to whom he writes. We may not therefore condemn this altogether. But I say, use it exceeding sparingly. And when you use it let it be with the utmost caution, directing them at the same moment to look upon all they have as the free gift of God, and with the deepest self-abasement to say,
35   'Not unto us! Not unto us! But unto thy name give the praise!'[41]

     19. Next to self-will and pride, the most fatal disease with which we are born is *love of the world.* But how studiously do the generality of parents cherish this in its several branches! They

---

[40] John and Charles Wesley, 'Watch in All Things', in *Hymns and Sacred Poems* (1742), p. 218 (*Poet. Wks.*, II.273); see also No. 12, 'The Witness of Our Own Spirit', §19 and n.
[41] Ps. 115:1 (BCP).

cherish 'the desire of the flesh',[42] that is, the tendency to seek happiness in pleasing the outward senses, by studying to 'enlarge the pleasure of tasting'[43] in their children to the uttermost; not only giving them before they are weaned other things beside milk, the natural food of children, but giving them both before and after 5 any sort of meat or drink that they will take. Yea, they entice them, long before nature requires it, to take wine or strong drink; and provide them with comfits,[44] gingerbread, raisins, and whatever fruit they have a mind to. They feed in them 'the desire of the eyes',[45] the propensity to seek happiness in pleasing the 10 imagination, by giving them pretty playthings, glittering toys, shining buckles or buttons, fine clothes, red shoes, laced hats, needless ornaments, as ribbons, necklaces, ruffles;[46] yea, and by proposing any of these as *rewards* for doing their duty, which is stamping a great value upon them. With equal care and attention 15 they cherish in them the third branch of the love of the world, 'the pride of life', the propensity to seek their happiness in 'the honour that cometh of men'.[47] Nor is the love of money forgotten; many an exhortation do they hear on 'securing the main chance';[48] many a lecture exactly agreeing with that of the old heathen, 20

Si possis, recte; si non, quocumque modo rem[49]—

get money honestly if you can; but if not, get money. And they are carefully taught to look on riches and honour as the reward of all their labours.

20. In direct opposition to all this, a wise and truly kind parent 25 will take the utmost care not to cherish in her children the desire of the flesh, their natural propensity to seek happiness in gratifying the outward senses. With this view she will suffer them

[42] 1 John 2:16.
[43] See William Law, as in No. 50, 'The Use of Money', II.2 and n. For this phrase and theme in this paragraph and those following, cf. Law's *Serious Call* (*Works*, IV.191 ff.).
[44] Johnson, *Dictionary*, defines this as 'a dry sweetmeat' and derives it from 'the Dutch', *konfit*; cf. *OED*.
[45] 1 John 2:16; see §8 above, and n.
[46] Repeated almost verbatim in §21, below.
[47] Cf. John 5:41.
[48] Cf. No. 87, 'The Danger of Riches', II.4 and n.
[49] Horace, *Epistles*, I.i.65-66. Cf. Nos. 111, *National Sins and Miseries*, II.2; and 87, 'The Danger of Riches', §1. See also Ben Jonson, *Every Man in His Humour*, II.iii.49-51:

> Get money, boy;
> No matter by what means; money will do
> More, boy, than my lord's letter. . . .

to taste no food but milk till they are weaned (which a thousand experiments show is most safely and easily done at the end of the seventh month). And then accustom them to the most simple food, chiefly of vegetables. She may inure them to taste only one
5 food, beside bread, at dinner, and constantly to breakfast and sup on milk, either cold or heated, but not boiled. She may use them to sit by her at meals and ask for nothing, but take what is given them. She need never, till they are at least nine or ten years old, let them know the taste of tea, or use any other drink at meals but
10 water or small beer. And they will never desire to taste either meat or drink between meals if not accustomed thereto. If fruit, comfits, or anything of the kind be given them, let them not touch it but at meals. And never propose any of these as a reward; but teach them to look higher than this.
15 But herein a difficulty will arise which it will need much resolution to conquer. Your servants, who will not understand your plan, will be continually giving little things to your children, and thereby undoing all your work. This you must prevent, if possible, by warning them when they first come into your house,
20 and repeating the warning from time to time. If they *will* do it notwithstanding, you must turn them away. Better lose a good servant than spoil a good child.

Possibly you may have another difficulty to encounter, and one of a still more trying nature. Your mother, or your husband's
25 mother, may live with you; and you will do well to show her all possible respect. But let her on no account have the least share in the management of your children. She would undo all that you had done; she would give them their own will in all things. She would humour them to the destruction of their souls, if not of
30 their bodies too. In fourscore years I have not met with one woman that knew how to manage grandchildren. My own mother, who governed her children so well, could never govern one grandchild. In every other point obey your mother. Give up your will to hers. But with regard to the management of your
35 children, steadily keep the reins in your own hands.

21. A wise and kind parent will be equally cautious of feeding 'the desire of the eyes' in her children. She will give them no pretty playthings, no glittering toys, shining buckles or buttons, fine or gay clothes; no needless ornaments of any kind; nothing
40 that can attract the eye. Nor will she suffer any other person to give them what she will not give them herself. Anything of the

kind that is offered may be either civilly refused, or received and laid by. If they are displeased at this, you cannot help it. Complaisance, yea, and temporal interest, must needs be set aside when the eternal interest of your children is at stake.

Your pains will be well requited if you can inspire them early 5 with a contempt of all finery; and, on the other hand, with a love and esteem for neat plainness of dress. Teach them to associate the ideas of plainness and modesty; and those of a fine and a loose woman. Likewise instil into them as early as possible a fear and contempt of pomp and grandeur, an abhorrence and dread of the 10 love of money, and a deep conviction that riches cannot give happiness.[50] Wean them therefore from all these false ends; habituate them to make God their end in all things, and inure them in all they do to aim at knowing, loving, and serving God.

22. Again, the generality of parents feed *anger* in their children; 15 yea, the worst part of it, that is, revenge. The silly mother says, 'What hurt my child? Give me a blow for it.' What horrid work is this! Will not the old murderer[51] teach them this lesson fast enough? Let the Christian parent spare no pains to teach them just the contrary. Remind them of the words of our blessed Lord: 20 'It was said of old, An eye for an eye, and a tooth for a tooth. But I say unto you, that ye resist not evil;'[52] not by returning evil for evil. Rather than this, 'if a man take away thy cloak, let him take thy coat also.'[53] Remind him of the words of the great Apostle: 'Dearly beloved, avenge not yourselves. For it is written, 25 Vengeance is mine; I will repay, saith the Lord.'[54]

23. The generality of parents feed and increase the natural *falsehood* of their children. How often may we hear that senseless word: 'No, it was not *you;* it was not my child that did it: say, it was the cat.' What amazing folly is this! Do you feel no remorse while 30 you are putting a lie in the mouth of your child, before it can speak plain? And do not you think it will make good proficiency when it comes to years of discretion? Others teach them both dissimulation and lying by their unreasonable severity; and yet others by admiring and applauding their ingenious lies and 35 cunning tricks. Let the wise parent, on the contrary, teach them to 'put away all lying',[55] and both in little things and great, in jest or

---

[50] Cf. No. 94, 'On Family Religion', III.17 and n.
[51] I.e., the devil; see John 8:44.
[52] Matt. 5:38-39.
[53] Cf. Matt. 5:40.
[54] Rom. 12:19.
[55] Cf. Eph. 4:25; cf. also No. 138A, 'On Dissimulation'.

earnest, speak the very truth from their heart. Teach them that
the author of all falsehood is the devil, who 'is a liar and the father
of it'.[56] Teach them to abhor and despise, not only all lying, but all
equivocating, all cunning and dissimulation. Use every means to
5 give them a love of truth: of veracity, sincerity, and simplicity, and
of openness both of spirit and behaviour.

24. Most parents increase the natural tendency to *injustice* in
their children by conniving at their wronging each other, if not
laughing at, or even applauding, their witty contrivances to cheat
10 one another. Beware of everything of this kind; and from their
very infancy sow the seeds of justice in their hearts, and train
them up in the exactest practice of it. If possible, teach them the
love of justice, and that in the least things as well as the greatest.
Impress upon their mind the old proverb, 'He that will steal a
15 penny will steal a pound.'[57] Habituate them to render unto all
their due, even to the uttermost farthing.[58]

25. Many parents connive likewise at the *ill nature* of their
children, and thereby strengthen it. But truly affectionate parents
will not indulge them in any kind or degree of *unmercifulness*.
20 They will not suffer them to vex their brothers or sisters either by
word or deed. They will not allow them to hurt or give pain to
anything that has life. They will not permit them to rob birds'
nests, much less to kill anything without necessity; not even
snakes, which are as innocent as worms, or toads, which,
25 notwithstanding their ugliness, and the ill name they lie under,
have been proved over and over to be as harmless as flies. Let
them extend in its measure the rule of doing as they would be
done by to every animal whatsoever. Ye that are truly kind
parents, in the morning, in the evening, and all the day beside,
30 press upon all your children to 'walk in love, as Christ also loved
us, and gave himself for us';[59] to mind that one point, 'God is love;
and he that dwelleth in love, dwelleth in God, and God in him.'[60]

London, July 12, 1783[61]

---

[56] John 8:44.

[57] Cf. G. L. Apperson, *English Proverbs and Proverbial Phrases; A Historical Dictionary*
(1929), p. 496: 'He that will steal a pin will steal a better thing.' He cites R. Whitford,
Werke for Householders (1537), 'The chylde that begineth to pike at a pynne or a poynte wyl
after pyke a penny or a pound.' There are numerous variations; cf., e.g., George Herbert,
Jacula Prudentium, No. 1090: 'He that will steal an egg will steal an ox.'

[58] See Matt. 5:26.   [59] Cf. Eph. 5:2.

[60] 1 John 4:16.   [61] Place and date as in *AM*.

ON OBEDIENCE TO PARENTS

AN INTRODUCTORY COMMENT

There is no record of Wesley's having preached from Col. 3:20 in public. But his series of sermonic essays on 'family religion' required something about 'obedience to parents', and Wesley provided it in this sermon in the September and October issues of the Arminian Magazine *(1784), VII.457-64, 514-18—a year's interval after No. 94. There was no title and no indication of its date or occasion of writing, but it was numbered 'Sermon XXIII'. Its present title was supplied when he included it, in sequence, in* SOSO, *VIII.29-48. It was not printed elsewhere in his lifetime.*

It is worth noting that besides his abundant offerings of practical wisdom he also finds an opportunity to discuss certain larger speculative issues (e.g., the presence or absence of innate moral ideas in children, and the relation between the personal will of a reigning king and the binding laws of his kingdom—'the will of the king is not *a law for the subject'). Thus, we have still another instance of Wesley's range of interests and his unfaltering impulse to combine current theoretical questions with perennial practical problems, even if in simplified forms that served his aims of effective communication.*

On Obedience to Parents

Colossians 3:20

Children, obey your parents in all things.

1. It has been a subject of controversy for many years, whether there are any innate principles in the mind of man.[1] But it is 5 allowed on all hands, if there be any practical principles naturally implanted in the soul, that 'we ought to honour our parents' will

---

[1] A long disputed question between the philosophical idealists (Malebranche, the Cambridge Platonists, John Norris, *et al.*) and the empiricists (pre-eminently John Locke). In his 'Remarks' on Locke's *Essay on Human Understanding* (in *AM*, Vols. V, VI, VII)

claim this character almost before any other.[2] It is enumerated among those universal principles by the most ancient authors, and is undoubtedly found even among savages in the most barbarous nations. We may trace it through all the extent of
5 Europe and Asia, through the wilds of Africa, and the forests of America. And it is not less, but more observable in the most civilized nations. So it was first in the eastern parts of the world, which were for so many ages the seat of empire, of learning and politeness, as well as of religion. So it was afterwards in all the
10 Grecian states, and throughout the whole Roman Empire. In this respect, it is plain, they that 'have not the' written 'law are a law *unto themselves';* showing 'the work (the substance) of the law' to be 'written in their hearts'.[3]

2. And wherever God has revealed his will to man this law has
15 been a part of that revelation. It has been herein opened afresh, considerably enlarged, and enforced in the strongest manner. In the Jewish revelation the notorious breakers thereof were punishable with death. And this was one of the laws which our blessed Lord did not come to destroy, but to fulfil.[4] Accordingly
20 he severely reproved the scribes and Pharisees for making it void through their traditions;[5] clearly showing that the obligation thereof extended to all ages. It is the substance of this which St. Paul delivers to the Ephesians: 'Children, obey your parents in the Lord;'[a] and again in those words to the Colossians, 'Children,
25 obey your parents in all things.'[6]

3. It is observable that the Apostle enforces this duty by a threefold encouragement. First, to the Ephesians he adds: 'For this is right'[7]—it is an instance of justice as well as mercy. It is no

---

[a] Chap. 6, ver. 1.

Wesley professes to have been convinced by Locke's arguments that there are no such innate principles. But it turns out that this applies to empirical objects and processes only, and not to our powers of transempirical intuition. Reverence for parents is, therefore, regarded here as such an intuition. See also No. 69, 'The Imperfection of Human Knowledge', I.4 and n.

[2] See also, below, I.4; and cf. Wesley's letter to Mary Smith, Nov. 20, 1789. Also Bishop Ezekiel Hopkins, *Exposition on the Ten Commandments,* which Wesley extracted and published in 1759 (see *Bibliog,* No. 234), and John Flavell, *Husbandry Spiritualized* (1669), which Wesley published in the *Christian Lib.,* XLIV.5-192.

[3] Cf. Rom. 2:14-15; see also No. 10, 'The Witness of the Spirit, I', I.12 and n.

[4] Matt. 5:17.

[5] See Matt. 15:3-6; Mark 7:9-13; it is the specific command, 'Honour thy father and mother,' that is in question.

[6] Col. 3:20.

[7] Eph. 6:1.

more than their due; it is what we owe to them for the very being which we have received from them. Secondly, 'This is acceptable to the Lord;'[8] it is peculiarly pleasing to the great Father of men and angels that we should pay honour and obedience to the fathers of our flesh.[9] Thirdly, it is 'the first commandment with promise;'[10] the first to the performance whereof a peculiar promise is annexed, 'that it may be well with thee',[11] and 'that thy days may be long in the land which the Lord thy God giveth thee'.[12] This promise has been generally understood to include health and temporal blessings, as well as long life. And we have seen innumerable proofs that it belongs to the Christian as well as the Jewish dispensation: many remarkable instances of its accomplishment occur even at this day.

But what is the meaning of these words, 'Children, obey your parents in all things'? I will endeavour by the assistance of God, first, to explain, and then to apply them.

I.1. First, I will endeavour to explain these words; and the rather because so few people seem to understand them. Look round into the world—not the heathen, but the Christian world; nay, the reformed part of it. Look among those that have the Scriptures in their own tongue: and who is there that appears even to have heard of this? Here and there a child obeys the parent out of fear, or perhaps out of natural affection. But how many children can you find that obey their fathers and mothers out of a sense of duty to God? And how many parents can you find that duly inculcate this duty upon their children? I doubt, a vast majority both of parents and children are totally ignorant of the whole affair. For the sake of these I will make it as plain as I can: but still I am thoroughly sensible, those that are not willing to be convinced will no more understand what I say than if I was talking Greek or Hebrew.

2. You will easily observe that by 'parents' the Apostle means both fathers and mothers, as he refers us to the fifth commandment, which names both the one and the other. And however human laws may vary herein, the law of God makes no difference; but lays us under the same obligation of obeying both the one and the other.

---

8 Cf. Eph. 5:10.   9 Heb. 12:9.
10 Eph. 6:2.   11 Eph. 6:3.
12 Exod. 20:12; cf. Eph. 6:3.

3. But before we consider how we are to obey our parents it may be inquired how long we are to obey them. Are children to obey only till they run alone? Till they go to school? Till they can read and write? Or till they are as tall as their parents? Or, attain to
5 years of discretion? Nay, if they obey only because they cannot help it, only because they fear to be beaten, or because otherwise they cannot procure food and raiment, what avails such obedience? Those only who obey their parents when they can live without them, and when they neither hope nor fear anything from
10 them, shall have praise from God.

4. 'But is a man that is at age, or a woman that is married, under any farther obligation to obey their parents?' With regard to marriage, although it is true that a man is to leave father and mother and cleave unto his wife;[13] and by parity of reason, she is to
15 leave father and mother and cleave unto her husband (in consequence of which there may be some particular cases wherein conjugal duty must take [the] place[14] of filial), yet I cannot learn either from Scripture or reason that marriage either cancels or lessens the general obligation of filial duty. Much less does it
20 appear that it is either cancelled or lessened by our having lived one and twenty years. I never understood it so in my own case. When I had lived upwards of thirty years I looked upon myself to stand just in the same relation to my father as I did when I was ten years old.[15] And when I was between forty and fifty I judged
25 myself full as much obliged to obey my mother in everything lawful as I did when I was in my hanging-sleeve coat.[16]

5. But what is implied in 'Children, obey your parents in all things'? Certainly the first point of obedience is to do nothing which your father or mother forbids, whether it be great or small.
30 Nothing is more plain than that the prohibition of a parent binds every conscientious child; that is, except the thing prohibited is clearly enjoined of God. Nor indeed is this all: the matter may be

---

[13] See Matt. 19:5.

[14] For the obsolete usage without the article see *OED*, 'place', 9, 13.b, and 27.c.

[15] And yet, in Dec. 1734, Wesley had firmly rejected his father's importunate request that he apply for the Epworth living so as to provide much needed support for his aged parents and sisters. How close to 'disobedience' had this been?

[16] In *SOSO* (1788), VIII.35, this reads 'leading-strings'. But see James Hervey, *Theron and Aspasio*, I.530: 'In this respect, Theron, men are but children of larger growth. We may leave the vest or hanging-sleeve coat but we shall still find the follies of the child.' *OED* definition (dated from 1659, 1683, and 1742): 'a loose open sleeve hanging from the arm', by which small children are held from falling.

carried a little farther still. A tender parent may totally disapprove what he does not care flatly to forbid. What is the duty of a child in this case? How far is that disapprobation to be regarded? Whether it be equivalent to a prohibition or not, a person who would have a conscience void of offence[17] should undoubtedly keep on the safe side,[18] and avoid what may perhaps be evil. It is surely the more excellent way[19] to do nothing which you know your parents disapprove. To act otherwise seems to imply a degree of disobedience which one of a tender conscience would wish to avoid.

6. The second thing implied in this direction is: do everything which your father or mother bids, be it great or small, provided it be not contrary to any command of God.[20] Herein God has given a power to parents which even sovereign princes have not. The King of England, for instance, is a sovereign prince; yet he has not power to bid me do the least thing unless the law of the land requires me so to do; for he has no power but to execute the law. The will of the king is no law to the subject.[21] But the will of the parent is a law to the child, who is bound in conscience to submit thereto unless it be contrary to the law of God.

7. It is with admirable wisdom that the Father of spirits has

---

[17] Acts 24:16.

[18] A much earlier instance of this phrase than the citation in the *Oxford Dictionary of English Proverbs*.

[19] 1 Cor. 12:31.

[20] See Acts 5:29; cf. No. 81, 'In What Sense we are to Leave the World', §6.

[21] A basic constitutional thesis; cf. JWJ, June 1, 1777, 'The will of the king does not bind any English subject, unless it is seconded by an express law.' See also the letter to his brother Charles, June 8, 1780. This aphorism was a distillate of at least one great tradition of English law; it may be inferred from the Magna Charta, from Sir John Fortescue's proposed limitations on regal power after the death of Elizabeth I (1603), and from Sir Edward Coke's *Institutes*, III. It is an equally licit inference from Richard Hooker, *Laws of Ecclesiastical Polity*, I.i, VIII.ii; and from Offspring Blackall, *Works*, II.849. Back of all this would have been the pervasive influence of Juan de Marianna's famous *De rege et regis institutione* (Toledo, 1599); there are more than two hundred references to Marianna's thesis on the limitations of regal power in the English and Scottish debates of the seventeenth century on divine right and the right and wrongs of tyrannicide. On the other side, cf. Sir John Suckling, *The Sad One; A Tragedy* (1659), Act III, sc. 5; Jeremy Taylor, *Ductor Dubitantium*, III.iii (Rule II, §§2-18: *Princeps legibus solutus est*, 'the prince is not bound by the laws'), and William Saywell, *Evangelical and Catholick Unity . . .* (1682), p. 113.

Something very close to Wesley's exact words may be found in a tract of 1680 entitled, *English Liberties: Or, the Free-Born Subject's Inheritance*, attributed in some catalogues (e.g., McAlpin) to one 'Henry Care' but identified by Winthrop Hudson, as more probably from William Penn himself; cf. Hudson, 'William Penn's *English Liberties:* A Tract for Several Times', in *William & Mary Quarterly* (1969), XXVI.578-85.

given this direction, that as the strength of the parents supplies the want of strength, and the understanding of the parents the want of understanding, in their children, till they have strength and understanding of their own, so the will of the parents should
5 guide that of their children, till they have wisdom and experience to guide themselves. This therefore is the very first thing which children have to learn: that they are to obey their parents, to submit to their will in all things. And this they may be inured to [22] long before they understand the reason of it. And, indeed, long
10 before they are capable of understanding any of the principles of religion. Accordingly St. Paul directs all parents to bring up their children 'in the discipline and doctrine of the Lord'.[23] For their will may be broke by proper discipline, even in their early infancy; whereas it must be a considerable time after before they are
15 capable of instruction. This therefore is the first point of all: bow down their wills from the very first dawn of reason; and by habituating them to submit to your will, prepare them for submitting to the will of their Father which is in heaven.[24]

8. But how few children do we find, even of six or eight years
20 old, that understand anything of this? Indeed how should they understand it, seeing they have none to teach them? Are not their parents, father as well as mother, full as ignorant of the matter as themselves? Whom do you find, even among religious people, that have the least conception of it? Have not you seen the proof of
25 it with your own eyes! Have not you been present when a father or mother has said, 'My child, do so or so'? The child, without any ceremony, answered peremptorily, 'I won't.' And the parent quietly passes it by, without any further notice. And does he or she not see that by this cruel indulgence they are training up their
30 child, by flat rebellion against their parents, to rebellion against God? Consequently they are training him up for the everlasting fire prepared for the devil and his angels![25] Did they duly consider this they would neither eat, nor drink, nor sleep, till they had taught him a better lesson, and made him thoroughly afraid of
35 ever giving that diabolical answer again.

---

[22] Johnson, *Dictionary*, first usage: 'to habituate; to make ready and willing by practice and custom . . .'.
[23] Cf. Eph. 6:4; in his *Notes* Wesley adds, '. . . both in Christian knowledge and practice'.
[24] Matt. 7:21; 12:50; 18:14.
[25] Matt. 25:41.

9. Let me reason this case a little farther with you parents that fear God. If you *do* fear God, how dare you suffer a child above a year old to say, '*I will do* what you forbid;' or, '*I won't do* what you bid,' and to go unpunished? Why do not you stop him at once, that he may never dare to say so again? Have you no bowels, no compassion for your child? No regard for his salvation or destruction? Would you suffer him to curse or swear in your presence, and take no notice of it? Why, disobedience is as certain a way to damnation as cursing and swearing. Stop him, stop him at first, in the name of God. Do not 'spare the rod, and spoil the child'.[26] If you have not the heart of a tiger, do not give up your child to his own will, that is, to the devil. Though it be pain to yourself, yet pluck your offspring out of the lion's teeth.[27] Make them submit, that they may not perish. Break their will, that you may save their soul.[28]

10. I cannot tell how to enforce this point sufficiently. To fix it upon your minds more strongly, permit me to add part of a letter on the subject, printed some years ago:

In order to form the minds of children, the first thing to be done is to conquer their will. To inform their understanding is a work of time, and must proceed by slow degrees; but the subjecting the will is a thing which must be done at once—and the sooner the better. For by our neglecting timely correction they contract a stubbornness which is hardly ever to be conquered, and never without using that severity which would be as painful to us as to the children. Therefore I call those cruel parents who pass for kind and indulgent, who permit their children to contract habits which they know must be afterwards broken.

I insist upon conquering the wills of children betimes, because this is the only foundation for a religious education. When this is thoroughly done, then a child is capable of being governed by the reason of its parent, till its own understanding comes to maturity.

I cannot yet dismiss this subject. As self-will is the root of all sin and misery, so whatever cherishes this in children ensures their after-wretchedness and irreligion; and whatever checks and mortifies it promotes their future happiness and piety. This is still more evident if we consider that religion is nothing else but the doing the will of God, and not our own; and that self-will being the grand impediment to our temporal and eternal happiness, no indulgence of it can be

[26] A proverb derived from Prov. 13:24, phrased by Samuel Butler, *Hudibras*, II.i.843-44:

> Love is a boy, by poets styled,
> Then spare the rod and spoil the child.

[27] See Ps. 22:21.
[28] See No. 95, 'On the Education of Children', §15.

trivial; no denial of it unprofitable. Heaven or hell depends on this alone. So that the parent who studies to subdue it in his children works together with God in the saving of a soul. The parent who indulges it does the devil's work, makes religion impracticable, salvation unattainable, and does all that in him lies to
5 damn his child, soul and body, for ever!

This therefore I cannot but earnestly repeat, break their wills betimes. Begin this great work before they can run alone, before they can speak plain, or perhaps speak at all. Whatever pains it cost, conquer their stubbornness: break the will, if you would not damn the child. I conjure you not to neglect, not to
10 delay this! Therefore, (1), let a child from a year old be taught to fear the rod and to cry softly. In order to this, (2), let him have nothing he cries for, absolutely nothing, great or small; else you undo your own work. (3). At all events, from that age, make him do as he is bid, if you whip him ten times running to effect it: let none persuade you it is cruelty to do this; it is cruelty not to do it. Break his
15 will now, and his soul will live, and he will probably bless you to all eternity.[29]

11. On the contrary, how dreadful are the consequences of that accursed kindness which gives children their own wills, and does not bow down their necks from their infancy. It is chiefly owing to this that so many religious parents bring up children that have no
20 religion at all; children that when they are grown up have no regard for them; perhaps set them at naught, and are ready to pick out their eyes![30] Why is this, but because their wills were not broken at first, because they were not inured from their early infancy to obey their parents in all things, and to submit to their
25 wills as to the will of God? Because they were not taught from the very first dawn of reason that the will of their parents was to them the will of God; that to resist it was rebellion against God, and an inlet to all ungodliness.[31]

II.1. This may suffice for the explication of the text: I proceed
30 to the application of it. And permit me first to apply to you that are parents, and as such concerned to teach your children. Do you know these things yourselves? Are *you* thoroughly convinced of these important truths? Have you laid them to heart? And have you put them in practice with regard to your own children? Have
35 you inured them to discipline before they were capable of

---

[29] From a letter written by his mother already abridged and printed in JWJ, Aug. 1, 1742. However, the last paragraph of the present quotation is not included in the *Journal* extract, which suggests that Wesley had preserved the original text for some five decades.

[30] *Oxford Dictionary of English Proverbs:* 'He hath brought up a bird to pick [peck] out his own eyes.'

[31] See Richard Baxter, 'our senses are the inlets of sin', in *The Saints' Everlasting Rest*, Pt.I, ch.VII, sect. xvi. 8 (*Works*, III. 58). See also Francis Atterbury, *Sermons* (1708), p. 310: 'our senses are the greatest inlets of temptation.'

instruction? Have you broken their wills from their earliest infancy? And do you still continue so to do, in opposition both to nature and custom? Did you explain to them, as soon as their understanding began to open, the reasons of your proceeding thus? Did you point out to them the will of God as the sole law of every intelligent creature? And show them it is the will of God that they should obey you in all things? Do you inculcate this over and over again till they perfectly comprehend it? O never be weary of this labour of love; and your labour will not always be in vain.[32]

2. At least do not teach them to disobey by rewarding them for disobedience. Remember! This you do every time you give them anything because they cry for it. And herein they are apt scholars: if you reward them for crying they will certainly cry again. So that there is no end, unless you make it a sacred rule to give them nothing which they cry for. And the shortest way to do this is, never suffer them to cry aloud. Train them up to obedience in this one instance, and you will easily bring them to obey in others. Why should you not begin today? Surely you see what is the most excellent way; best for your child, and best for your own soul. Why then do you disobey? Because you are a coward; because you want resolution. And doubtless it requires no small resolution to begin and persist herein. It certainly requires no small patience, more than nature ever gave. But the grace of God is sufficient for you;[33] you can do all things through Christ that strengtheneth you.[34] This grace is sufficient to give you diligence, as well as resolution; otherwise laziness will be as great a hindrance as cowardice. For without much pains you cannot conquer: nothing can be done with a slack hand; labour on; never tire; lay line upon line,[35] till patience has its perfect work.[36]

3. But there is another hindrance that is full as hard to be conquered as either laziness or cowardice. It is called fondness, and is usually mistaken for love: but Oh, how widely different from it! It is real hate; and hate of the most mischievous kind, tending to destroy both body and soul in hell! O give not way to it any longer, no not for a moment. Fight against it with your might! For the love of God; for the love of your children; for the love of your own soul!

---

[32] See No. 65, 'The Duty of Reproving our Neighbour', I.3 and n.
[33] See 2 Cor. 12:9.
[34] See Phil. 4:13.
[35] See Isa. 28:10.   [36] See Jas. 1:4.

4. I have one word more to say to parents—to mothers in particular. If, in spite of all the Apostle can say, you encourage your children by your example to 'adorn' themselves 'with gold, or pearls, or costly apparel',[37] you and they must drop into the pit[38] together. But if they do it though you set them a better example, still it is yours as well as their fault. For if you did not put any ornament on your little child that you would not wear yourself (which would be utter distraction, and far more inexcusable than putting it on your own arms or head), yet you did not inure them to obey you from their infancy, and teach them the duty of it from at least two years old. Otherwise they would not have dared to do anything, great or small, contrary to your will. Whenever therefore I see the fine-dressed daughter of a plain-dressed mother, I see at once the mother is defective either in knowledge or religion. Either she is ignorant of her own or her child's duty; or she has not practised what she knows.

5. I cannot dismiss this subject yet.[39] I am pained continually at seeing religious parents suffer their children to run into the same folly of dress as if they had no religion at all. In God's name, why do you suffer them to vary a hair's breadth from *your* example? 'Why, they will do it'? They will! Whose fault is that? Why did not you break their will from their infancy? At least do it now; better late than never. It should have been done before they were two years old. It may be done at eight or ten, though with far more difficulty. However, do it now; and accept that difficulty as the just reward for your past neglect. Now at least carry your point, whatever it costs. Be not mealy-mouthed; say not, like foolish Eli, 'Nay, my children; it is no good report which I hear of you,'[40] instead of restraining them with a strong hand; but speak (though as calmly as possible, yet) firmly and peremptorily, 'I will have it so;' and do as you say. Instil diligently into them the love of plain dress, and hatred of finery. Show them the reason of your own plainness of dress, and show it is equally reasonable for them. Bid defiance to indolence, to cowardice, to foolish fondness, and at all events carry your point; if you love their souls, make and keep them just as plain as yourselves. And I charge you, grandmothers, before God, do not hinder your daughters herein. Do not dare to

[37] Cf. 1 Tim. 2:9.
[38] See Rev. 9:11; 20:1; cf. No. 32, 'Sermon on the Mount, XII', I.7 and n.
[39] Notice this repetition of his mother's rhetorical device (in I.10, above).
[40] Cf. 1 Sam. 2:24; and No. 95, 'On the Education of Children', §1.

give the child anything which the mother denies. Never take the part of the children against their parent; never blame her before them. If you do not strengthen her authority, as you ought to do, at least do not weaken it; but if you have either sense or piety left, help her on in the work of real kindness.   5

6. Permit me now to apply myself to you, children; particularly you that are the children of religious parents. Indeed if you have no fear of God before your eyes,[41] I have no concern with you at present; but if you have, if you really fear God, and have a desire to please him, you desire to understand all his commandments, 10 the fifth in particular. Did you ever understand it yet? Do you now understand what is your duty to your father and mother? Do you know, at least do you consider, that by the divine appointment *their* will is law to *you*? Have you ever considered the extent of that obedience to your parents which God requires? 'Children, obey 15 your parents *in all things*.' No exception, but of things unlawful. Have you practised your duty in this extent? Did you ever so much as intend it?

7. Deal faithfully with your own souls. Is your conscience now clear in this matter? Do you do nothing which you know to be 20 contrary to the will either of your father or mother? Do you never do anything (though ever so much inclined to it) which he or she forbids? Do you abstain from everything which they dislike, as far as you can in conscience? On the other hand, are you careful to do whatever a parent bids? Do you study and contrive how to please 25 them? To make their lives as easy and pleasant as you can? Whoever you are that add this to your general care to please God in all things, blessed art thou of the Lord! 'Thy days shall be long in the land which the Lord thy God giveth thee.'[42]

8. But as for you who are little concerned about this matter, 30 who do not make it a point of conscience to obey your parents in all things, but sometimes obey them, as it happens, and sometimes not; who frequently do what they forbid or disapprove, and neglect what they bid you do—suppose you awake out of sleep, that you begin to feel yourself a sinner, and begin to cry to 35 God for mercy, is it any wonder that you find no answer while you are under the guilt of unrepented sin? How can you expect mercy

---

[41] See Rom. 3:18.
[42] Cf. Exod. 20:12.

from God till you obey your parents? But suppose you have, by an uncommon miracle of mercy, tasted of the pardoning love of God, can it be expected, although you hunger and thirst after righteousness,[43] after the perfect love of God, that you should
5 ever attain it, ever be satisfied therewith, while you live in outward sin, in the wilful transgression of a known law of God, in disobedience to your parents? Is it not rather a wonder that he has not withdrawn his Holy Spirit from you? That he still continues to strive with you, though you continually grieve his Spirit? O grieve
10 him no more! By the grace of God obey them in all things from this moment! As soon as you come home, as soon as you set foot within the door, begin an entirely new course; look upon your father and mother with new eyes; see them as representing your Father which is in heaven. Endeavour, study, rejoice to please, to
15 help, to obey them in all things. Behave not barely as their child, but as their servant for Christ's sake. O how will you then love one another! In a manner unknown before. God will bless you to them and them to you: all around will feel that God is with you of a truth. Many shall see it and praise God; and the fruit of it will
20 remain when both you and they are lodged in Abraham's bosom.

---

[43] Matt. 5:6.

ON OBEDIENCE TO PASTORS

AN INTRODUCTORY COMMENT

The problem of the relationships between the Methodists and their Anglican pastors (and sometimes also with their own pastors) had long been linked in Wesley's mind with his paradoxical concern to hold his societies within the Church of England and yet also to maintain their qualified autonomy. He was equally concerned with his pastoral conviction that every Christian needs a spiritual director in the course of his spiritual growth and development. In 1784 he had altered the character of his 'annual conference' from a personal convocation with his preachers into a quasi-public, legal entity, maintaining, however, that this should not be construed as 'separation'. Also in 1784, he had turned to Heb. 13:17 as the text for a sermon in London. In March 1785, and almost certainly as a comment on the controversy stirred by the events of 1784, he wrote out this sermon as a sort of guideline by which Christians might rightly gauge their duties of 'obedience' to their 'pastors'. There is no record of this in the Journal *and only a casual reference in the diary for March 18; clearly, he was simply setting down his summary of an extended discussion.*

The sermon first appeared in the Arminian Magazine *for May and June 1785 (VIII.236-41, 291-97), without a title but numbered 'Sermon XXVII'. It was then included with its present title in* SOSO, *VIII.49-66. We have no record of its being printed elsewhere in Wesley's lifetime.*

On Obedience to Pastors

Hebrews 13:17

Obey them that have the rule over you, and submit yourselves; for they watch over your souls, as they that shall give account; that they may do this with joy, and not with grief; for that is unprofitable for you.

1. Exceeding few, not only among nominal Christians, but among truly religious men, have any clear conception of that important doctrine which is here delivered by the Apostle. Very many scarce think of it, and hardly know that there is any such direction in the Bible. And the greater part of those who know it is there, and imagine they follow it, do not understand it, but lean too much either to the right hand or to the left, to one extreme or the other. It is well known to what an extravagant height the Romanists in general carry this direction. Many of them believe an implicit faith is due to the doctrines delivered by those that rule over them, and that implicit obedience ought to be paid to whatever commands they give: and not much less has been insisted on by several eminent men of the Church of England.[1] Although it is true that the generality of Protestants are apt to run to the other extreme, allowing their pastors no authority at all, but making them both the creatures and the servants of their congregations.[2] And very many there are of our own Church who agree with them herein; supposing the pastors to be altogether dependent upon the people, who in their judgment have a right to direct as well as to choose their ministers.

2. But is it not possible to find a medium between these two extremes?[3] Is there any necessity for us to run either into one or

---

[1] Chief among these would have been William Laud (1573–1645), Archbishop of Canterbury (1633–45), whose doctrines of divine regal and ecclesiastical authority required both implicit obedience and explicit conformity. His canons of 1640 required a so-called 'etcetera oath', 'never to give their consent to alter the [episcopal] government of this church [of England] . . . , etc.' Thus he became a prime target for the Puritans and another of their victims after their execution of the first Earl of Strafford in 1641.

[2] I.e., the Baptists and Congregationalists. Note Wesley's own unavowed Anglican presuppositions here (as generally).

[3] See No. 27, 'Sermon on the Mount, VII', §4 and n. 9.

into the other? If we set human laws out of the question, and simply attend to the oracles of God, we may certainly discover a middle path in this important matter. In order thereto, let us carefully examine the words of the Apostle above recited. Let us consider,   5

First, who are the persons mentioned in the text, 'they that rule over us'?

Secondly, who are they whom the Apostle directs to 'obey and submit themselves' to them?

Thirdly, what is the meaning of this direction? In what sense 10 are they to 'obey and submit themselves'? I shall then endeavour to make a suitable application of the whole.

I.1. Consider we, first, who are the persons mentioned in the text, 'they that have the rule over you'? I do not conceive that the words of the Apostle are properly translated; because this 15 translation makes the sentence little better than tautology.[4] If they 'rule over you' you are certainly ruled by them; so that according to this translation you are only enjoined to do what you do already—to obey those whom you do obey. But there is another meaning of the Greek word which seems abundantly more 20 proper: it means to 'guide', as well as to rule. And thus, it seems, it should be taken here. The direction then, when applied to our spiritual guides, is plain and pertinent.

2. This interpretation seems to be confirmed by the seventh verse, which fixes the meaning of this. 'Remember them which 25 have the rule over you, who have spoken unto you the word of God.'[5] The Apostle here shows, by the latter clause of the sentence, whom he meant in the former. Those that 'were over them' were the same persons 'who spoke unto them the word of God'; that is, they were their pastors, those who guided and fed 30 this part of the flock of Christ.[6]

3. But by whom are these guides to be appointed? And what are they supposed to do in order to be entitled to the obedience which is here prescribed?

Volumes upon volumes have been wrote on that knotty 35 question, 'By whom are guides of souls to be appointed?' I do not

---

[4] Cf. Wesley's translation and *Notes* for Heb. 13:17.

[5] Heb. 13:7.

[6] An echo here of Poole, *Annotations (loc. cit.)* and the rule he propounds there for pastoral guidance in spiritual things.

intend here to enter at all into the dispute concerning church government; neither to debate whether it be advantageous or prejudicial to the interest of true religion that the church and the state should be blended together, as they have been ever since the
5   time of Constantine[7] in every part of the Roman Empire where Christianity has been received. Waiving all these points (which may find employment enough for men that abound in leisure), by them that guide you I mean them that do it, if not by your choice, at least by your consent; them that you willingly accept of to be
10   your guides in the way to heaven.

     4. But what are they supposed to do in order to entitle them to the obedience here prescribed?

     They are supposed to go before the flock (as is the manner of the eastern shepherds to this day) and to guide them in all the
15   ways of truth and holiness; they are to 'nourish them with the words of eternal life',[8] to feed them with 'the pure milk of the word';[9] applying it continually 'for doctrine',[10] teaching them all the essential doctrines contained therein; 'for reproof',[11] warning them if they turn aside from the way to the right hand or to the
20   left; 'for correction',[12] showing them how to amend what is amiss, and guiding them back into the way of peace; and 'for instruction in righteousness',[13] training them up in inward and outward holiness, 'until they come to a perfect man, to the measure of the stature of the fullness of Christ'.[14]
25   5. They are supposed to 'watch over your souls, as those that shall give account'. 'As those that shall give account'! How unspeakably solemn and awful are those words! May God write them upon the heart of every guide of souls!

     'They watch', waking while others sleep, over the flock of
30   Christ;[15] over the souls that he has bought with a price,[16] that he has purchased with his own blood.[17] They have them in their hearts both by day and by night; regarding neither sleep nor food in comparison of them. Even while they sleep their heart is waking, full of concern for their beloved children. 'They watch'
35   with deep earnestness, with uninterrupted seriousness, with unwearied care, patience, and diligence, as they that are about to

---

[7] Cf. No. 61, 'The Mystery of Iniquity', §27 and n.
[8] Cf. 1 Tim. 4:6; John 6:68.   [9] Cf. 1 Pet. 2:2.
[10] 2 Tim. 3:16.   [11] *Ibid.*   [12] *Ibid.*
[13] *Ibid.*   [14] Cf. Eph. 4:13.   [15] See Luke 2:8.
[16] 1 Cor. 6:20; 7:23.   [17] Acts 20:28.

give an account of every particular soul to him that standeth at the door,[18] to the Judge of quick and dead.[19]

II.1. We are, secondly, to consider who those are whom the Apostle directs to obey them that have the rule over them. And in order to determine this with certainty and clearness, we shall not appeal to human institutions, but simply (as in answering the preceding question) appeal to that decision of it which we find in the oracles of God. Indeed we have hardly occasion to go one step farther than the text itself. Only it may be proper, first, to remove out of the way some popular opinions which have been almost everywhere taken for granted, but can in no wise be proved.

2. It is usually supposed, first, that the Apostle is here directing *parishioners* to obey and submit themselves to the *minister* of their parish. But can anyone bring the least shadow of proof for this from the Holy Scripture? Where is it written that we are bound to obey any minister because we live in what is called his parish? 'Yes', you say, 'we are bound to "obey every ordinance of man for the Lord's sake".'[20] True, in all things indifferent; but this is not so; it is exceeding far from it. It is far from being a thing indifferent to *me* who is the guide of *my* soul. I dare not receive one as my guide to heaven that is himself in the high road to hell. I dare not take a wolf for my shepherd, that has not so much as sheep's clothing; that is a common swearer, an open drunkard, a notorious sabbath-breaker. And such (the more is the shame, and the more the pity!) are many parochial ministers at this day.

3. 'But are you not properly members of that congregation to which your parents belong?' I do not apprehend that I am; I know no Scripture that obliges me to this. I owe all deference to the commands of my parents, and willingly obey them in all things lawful.[21] But it is not lawful to 'call them Rabbi',[22] that is, to believe or obey them implicitly. Everyone must give an account of himself to God. Therefore every man must judge for himself; especially

---

[18] See Jas. 5:9.   [19] Acts 10:42; cf. The Apostles' Creed.

[20] Cf. 1 Pet. 2:13.

[21] Cf. No. 96, 'On Obedience to Parents', I.4.

[22] Cf. Matt. 23:8-10 and *Notes:* 'Our Lord, therefore, by forbidding us either to give or receive the title of Rabbi (Master or Father) forbids us either to receive any such reverence or to pay any such to any but God.' See also his criticism of the Moravians for their calling Zinzendorf 'Rabbi' (JWJ, Sept. 3, 1741). Cf. his letters to the Moravian Church, §9, June 24, 1744, §9; to Micaiah Towgood, Jan. 10, 1758; his first Preface to the *Christian Lib.*, I.v, §10; Nos. 123, 'On Knowing Christ after the Flesh', §8; and 150, 'Hypocrisy in Oxford', I.4.

in a point of so deep importance as this is, the choice of a guide for his soul.

4. But we may bring this matter to a short issue by recurring to the very words of the text. They that have voluntarily connected 5 themselves with such a pastor as answers the description given therein; such as do in fact watch over their souls, as they that shall give account; such as do nourish them up with the words of eternal life;²³ such as feed them as with the pure milk of the word,²⁴ and constantly apply it to them for doctrine, for reproof, 10 for correction, and for instruction in righteousness:²⁵ all who have found and chosen guides of this character, of this spirit and behaviour, are undoubtedly required by the Apostle to 'obey and submit themselves' to them.

III.1. But what is the meaning of this direction? This remains to 15 be considered. In what sense, and how far, does the Apostle direct them to 'obey and submit to their' spiritual guides?

If we attend to the proper sense of the two words here used by the Apostle, we may observe that the former of them (πείθεσθε, from πείθω, to persuade) refers to the understanding, the latter, 20 ὑπείκετε,²⁶ to the will, and outward behaviour. To begin with the former. What influence ought our spiritual guides to have over our understanding? We dare no more call our spiritual fathers Rabbi, than the 'fathers of our flesh'.²⁷ We dare no more yield implicit faith to the former than to the latter. In this sense 'one is 25 our Master' (or rather 'Teacher'), 'who is in heaven.'²⁸ But whatever submission, of even our understanding, is short of this, we may, nay, we ought to yield to them.

2. To explain this a little farther. St. James uses a word which is nearly allied to the former of these. 'The wisdom which is from 30 above is' εὐπειθής, 'easy to be convinced,' or 'to be persuaded'.²⁹ Now if we ought to have and to show this wisdom toward all men; we ought to have it in a more eminent degree, and to show it upon every occasion, toward those that 'watch over our souls'. With regard to these, above all other men, we should be 'easy to be

---

²³ See John 6:68; and n.8 above.   ²⁴ See 1 Pet. 2:2.
²⁵ 2 Tim. 3:16.
²⁶ Cf. the Greek orig. of Heb. 13:17: πείθεσθε τοῖς ἡγουμένοις ὑμῶν καὶ ὑπείκετε. . . .
²⁷ Heb. 12:9.
²⁸ Cf. Matt. 23:8-9 (*Notes*).
²⁹ Jas. 3:17; cf. No. 10, 'The Witness of the Spirit, I', II.6 and n.

entreated'; easily convinced of any truth, and easily persuaded to anything that is not sinful.

3. A word of nearly the same import with this is frequently used by St. Paul; namely, ἐπιεικής.[30] In our translation it is more than once rendered 'gentle'. But perhaps it might be more properly 5 rendered (if the word may be allowed) 'yielding'; ready to yield, to give up our own will, in everything that is not a point of duty. This amiable temper every real Christian enjoys, and shows in his intercourse with all men. But he shows it in a peculiar manner toward those that watch over his soul. He is not only willing to 10 receive any instruction from them, to be convinced of anything which he did not know before; lying open to their advice, and being glad to receive admonition, or reproof; but is ready to give up his own will, whenever he can do it with a clear conscience. Whatever they desire him to do, he does; if it be not forbidden in 15 the Word of God. Whatever they desire him to refrain from, he does so; if it be not enjoined in the Word of God. This is plainly implied in those words of the Apostle, 'Submit yourselves to them'—'yield to them'[31]—give up your own will. This is meet, and right, and your bounden duty,[32] if they do indeed watch over 20 your souls as they that shall give account. If you do thus 'obey and submit yourselves to them', they will give an account of you 'with joy; not with groaning', as they must otherwise do; for although they should be clear of your blood, yet 'that would be unprofitable to you'; yea, a prelude to eternal damnation. 25

4. How acceptable to God was an instance of obedience somewhat similar to this! You have a large and particular account of it in the thirty-fifth chapter of Jeremiah. 'The word of the Lord came to Jeremiah, saying, Go unto the house of the Rechabites, and give them wine to drink. Then I took the whole house of the 30 Rechabites' (all the heads of their families) 'and set before them pots full of wine, and said unto them, Drink ye wine. But they said, We will drink no wine: for Jonadab', a great man in the reign of Jehu, 'the son of Rechab', from whom we are named, being the father of our family, 'commanded us, Ye shall drink no wine, 35

---

[30] The text in James has ἐπιεικής and εὐπειθής. In the *Notes* Wesley translates ἐπιεικής 'gentle' and then explains it: 'soft, mild, yielding, not rigid'. His dubious point is that St. Paul also uses ἐπιεικής in the same sense as St. James (as in Phil. 4:5; 1 Tim. 3:3; Titus 3:2). The only other cognate usage is 2 Cor. 10:1, ἐπιείκεια; cf. No. 108, 'On Riches', I.8 and n.

[31] Cf. Rom. 6:13.

[32] An echo of the Preface to the Sanctus in BCP, Communion.

neither ye nor your sons for ever. And we have obeyed the voice of Jonadab our father, in all that he charged us.'[33] We do not know any particular reason why Jonadab gave this charge to his posterity. But as it was not sinful they gave this strong instance of gratitude to their great benefactor. And how pleasing this was to the Father of their spirits we learn from the words that follow. 'And Jeremiah said unto the Rechabites, Because ye have obeyed the voice of Jonadab your father, therefore thus saith the Lord of hosts, Jonadab shall not want a man to stand before my face for ever.'[34]

5. Now it is certain Christians owe full as much gratitude and obedience to those that watch over their souls as ever the house of the Rechabites owed to Jonadab the son of Rechab. And we cannot doubt but he is as well pleased with our obedience to these as ever he was with their obedience to Jonadab. If he was so well pleased with the gratitude and obedience of this people to their temporal benefactor, have we not all reason to believe he is full as well pleased with the gratitude and obedience of Christians to those who derive far greater blessings to them than ever Jonadab conveyed to his posterity?

6. It may be of use yet again to consider, In what instances is it the duty of Christians to obey and submit themselves to those that watch over their souls? Now the things which they enjoin must be either enjoined of God, or forbidden by him, or indifferent. In things forbidden of God we dare not obey them; for we are to obey God rather than man. In things enjoined of God we do not properly obey them, but our common Father. Therefore if we are to obey them at all it must be in things indifferent. The sum is: it is the duty of every private Christian to obey his spiritual pastor, by either doing or leaving undone anything of an indifferent nature—anything that is in no way determined in the Word of God.

7. But how little is this understood in the Protestant world! At least in England and Ireland! Who is there, even among those that are supposed to be good Christians, who dreams there is such a duty as this? And yet there is not a more express command either in the Old or New Testament. No words can be more clear and plain; no command more direct and positive. Therefore certainly

---

[33] Cf. Jer. 35:1-3, 5-6, 8.
[34] Cf. Jer. 35:18-19.

none who receive the Scripture as the Word of God can live in the habitual breach of this and plead innocence. Such an instance of wilful, or at least careless disobedience, must grieve the Holy Spirit of God. It cannot but hinder the grace of God from having its full effect upon the heart. It is not improbable that this very disobedience may be one cause of the deadness of many souls; one reason of their not receiving those blessings which they seek with some degree of sincerity.

8. It remains only to make a short application of what has now been delivered.

You that read this, do you apply it to yourself? Do you examine yourself thereby? Do not *you* stop your own growth in grace, if not by wilful disobedience to this command, yet by a careless inattention to it, by not considering it, as the importance of it deserves? If so, you defraud yourself of many blessings which you might enjoy. Or, are you of a better mind, of a more excellent spirit? Is it your fixed resolution and your constant endeavour 'to obey them that have the rule over you' in the Lord? To 'submit yourself' as cheerfully to your spiritual as to your natural parents? Do you ask, 'Wherein should I submit to them?' The answer has been given already: not in things enjoined of God; not in things forbidden by him; but in things indifferent—in all that are not determined one way or the other by the oracles of God. It is true this cannot be done in some instances without a considerable degree of self-denial, when they advise you to refrain from something that is agreeable to flesh and blood. And it cannot be obeyed in other instances without taking up your cross; without suffering some pain or inconvenience that is not agreeable to flesh and blood. For that solemn declaration of our Lord has place here, as well as on a thousand other occasions, 'Except a man deny himself, and take up his cross daily, he cannot be my disciple.'[35] But this will not affright you, if you resolve to be not only almost, but altogether, a Christian;[36] if you determine to fight the good fight of faith, and lay hold on eternal life.[37]

9. I would now apply myself in a more particular manner to *you* who desire *me* to watch over your souls. Do *you* make it a point of conscience to *obey* me, for my Master's sake? To 'submit

---

[35] Cf. Luke 9:23; 14:27.
[36] See No. 2, *The Almost Christian*, on Acts 26:28.
[37] 1 Tim. 6:12.

yourselves' to *me* in things indifferent, things not determined in the Word of God? In all things that are not enjoined, nor yet forbidden in Scripture? Are you 'easy to be entreated', as by men in general, so by me in particular? Easy to be convinced of any
5 truth, however contrary to your former prejudices? And easy to be persuaded to do or forbear any indifferent thing at *my* desire? You cannot but see that all this is clearly contained in the very words of the text. And you cannot but acknowledge that it is highly reasonable for you so to do, if I do employ all my time, all my
10 substance, all my strength both of body and soul, not in seeking my own hónour, or pleasure; but in promoting your present and eternal salvation; if I do indeed 'watch over your souls as one that must give account'.

10. Do you then take my advice (I ask in the presence of God
15 and all the world) with regard to *dress?* I published that advice above thirty years ago:[38] I have repeated it a thousand times since. I have advised you not to be conformable to the world herein; to lay aside all needless ornaments; to avoid all needless expense; to be patterns of plainness to all that are round about you. Have you
20 taken this advice? Have you all, men and women, young and old, rich and poor, laid aside all those needless ornaments which I particularly objected to? Are you all exemplarily plain in your apparel? As plain as Quakers (so called) or Moravians?[39] If not, if you are still dressed like the generality of people of your own rank
25 and fortune, you declare hereby to all the world that you will not obey them that are over you in the Lord. You declare, in open defiance of God and man, that you will not 'submit yourselves' to them. Many of you carry your sins on your forehead, openly and in the face of the sun. You harden your hearts against instruction
30 and against conviction; you harden one another; especially those of you that were once convinced, and have now stifled your convictions. You encourage one another to stop your ears against the truth, and shut your eyes against the light, lest haply you should see that you are fighting against God and against your own
35 souls. If I were now called to give an account of you, it would be 'with groans, and not with joy'.[40] And sure that would

---

[38] Cf. *Advice to the People called Methodists with regard to Dress.* See No. 88, intro. Briefer 'advices' on dress had appeared as early as 1744 in 'Directions given to the Band Societies' (Dec. 25), and also in *Advice to the People called Methodists* (1745).
[39] Cf. No. 88, 'On Dress', §26 and n.
[40] Cf. Heb. 13:17 (*Notes*).

be 'unprofitable for you':[41] the loss would fall upon your own head.

11. I speak all this on supposition (though that is a supposition not to be made) that the Bible was silent on this head; that the Scripture said nothing concerning *dress*, and left it to everyone's own discretion. But if all other texts were silent, this is enough, 'Submit yourselves to them that are over you in the Lord.' I bind this upon your consciences, in the sight of God. Were it only in obedience to this direction, you cannot be clear before God unless you throw aside all needless ornaments, in utter defiance of that tyrant of fools, fashion;[42] unless you seek only to be adorned with good works, as men and women professing godliness.[43]

12. Perhaps you will say, 'This is only a little thing: it is a mere trifle.' I answer, If it be, you are the more inexcusable before God and man. What! Will you disobey a plain commandment of God for 'a mere trifle'? God forbid! Is it a trifle to sin against God? To set his authority at nought? Is this a little thing? Nay, remember, there can be no little sin, till we can find a little god! Meantime be assured of one thing: the more conscientiously you obey your spiritual guides, the more powerfully will God apply the word which they speak in his name to your heart! The more plentifully will he water what is spoken with the dew of his blessing:[44] and the more proofs will you have, it is not only they that speak, but the Spirit of your Father who speaketh in them.[45]

Bristol, March 18, 1785[46]

---

[41] *Ibid.*
[42] Cf. No. 25, 'Sermon on the Mount, V', IV.3 and n.
[43] 1 Tim. 2:10.
[44] See Deut. 32:1-2.
[45] See Matt. 10:20.
[46] Place and date as in *AM*.

ON VISITING THE SICK

AN INTRODUCTORY COMMENT

Mid-May of 1786 found Wesley on his travels from north-west England (Westmorland, Cumberland) to Scotland. 'In my way . . . I looked over Lord Bacon's Ten Centuries of Experiments [Sylva Sylvarum: Or, a Natural History. In Ten Experiments *(an unfinished work intended as a section for the* Instauratio Magna*), published posthumously in 1627]. Many of them are extremely curious, and many may be highly useful. Afterwards I read Dr. [James] Anderson's* Account of the Hebrides [An Account of the Present State of the Hebrides and Western Coasts of Scotland . . . being the Substance of the West Coasts of Scotland, with hints for encouraging the Report to the Lords of the Treasury . . . together er with the evidence given before the Committee of Fisheries . . . , *Edinburgh, 1785]. How accurate and sensible a writer!' (JWJ, May 11). On his journey from Carlisle to Edinburgh to Dundee to Arbroath to Aberdeen, he seems to have been working, in snatches, on a written sermon, 'On Visiting the Sick', which he completed in Aberdeen on May 23. The diary suggests that he gave most of Tuesday, the 23rd, to this task; the* Journal *has no entry for that day.*

The sermon is a practical comment on one of those 'works of mercy' which are the natural fruit of active love: viz., 'visiting the sick'. He seems never to have used Matt. 25:26 as a sermon text except this once. In the sermon there are no unexpected turns in the argument or rhetoric and no speculative flights. Even so, it is an interesting mirror of the concerns of the ageing evangelist—a single Christian 'duty' expounded in the larger context of good works in the true spirit of love as an efficacious means of grace.

It was first published in the Arminian Magazine *in September and October, 1786 (IX.469-75, 525-31), without a title but numbered as 'Sermon XXXIV'. Two years later it was included in* SOSO, *VIII. 67-88, with its present title; it was not printed elsewhere in Wesley's lifetime.*

On Visiting the Sick

Matthew 25:36

I was sick, and ye visited me.

1. It is generally supposed that 'the means of grace' and 'the ordinances of God' are equivalent terms. We usually mean by that expression those that are usually termed 'works of piety',[1] namely, hearing and reading the Scripture, receiving the Lord's Supper, public and private prayer, and fasting. And it is certain these are the ordinary channels which convey the grace of God to the souls of men. But are they the only means of grace? Are there no other means than these whereby God is pleased, frequently, yea, ordinarily to convey his grace to them that either love or fear him? Surely there are works of mercy, as well as works of piety, which are real means of grace. They are more especially such to those that perform them with a single eye. And those that neglect them do not receive the grace which otherwise they might. Yea, and they lose, by a continued neglect, the grace which they had received.[2] Is it not hence that many who were once strong in faith are now weak and feeble-minded? And yet they are not sensible whence that weakness comes, as they neglect none of the ordinances of God.[3] But they might see whence it comes were they seriously to consider St. Paul's account of all true believers. 'We are his workmanship, created anew in Christ Jesus unto good works, which God hath before prepared, that we might walk therein.'[a]

2. The walking herein is essentially necessary, as to the continuance of that faith whereby we 'are' already 'saved by

[a] Eph. 2:10. [Another text that seems not to have been in Wesley's sermon repertory; there is a single reference (1748) to Eph. 2:11-13. On the other hand, Eph. 2:8 was a prime favourite (more than a hundred recorded usages).]

---

[1] Here, the 'works of piety' are nearly identical with 'the means of grace' as defined in the third General Rule. In No. 92, 'On Zeal', I.4, the two were more sharply distinguished; cf. also No. 14, *The Repentance of Believers*, I.13 and n.

[2] The obverse of an aphorism in No. 85, 'On Working Out Our Own Salvation', III.6: 'stir up the spark of grace which is now in you and God will give you more grace.'

[3] Cf. No. 22, 'Sermon on the Mount, II', II.4 and n.

grace',[4] so to the attainment of everlasting salvation. Of this we cannot doubt, if we seriously consider that these are the very words of the great Judge himself: 'Come, ye blessed children of my Father, inherit the kingdom prepared for you from the
5 foundation of the world. For I was hungry, and ye gave me meat, thirsty, and ye gave me drink. I was a stranger, and ye took me in; naked, and ye clothed me; I was sick, and ye visited me; I was in prison, and ye came unto me.'[b] 'Verily I say unto you, inasmuch as ye have done it unto one of the least of these my brethen, ye have
10 done it unto me.' If this does not convince you that the continuance in works of mercy is necessary to salvation, consider what the Judge of all says to those on the left hand: 'Depart, ye cursed, into everlasting fire, prepared for the devil and his angels. For I was hungry, and ye gave me no meat: thirsty, and ye gave me
15 no drink: I was a stranger, and ye took me not in: naked, and ye clothed me not: sick and in prison, and ye visited me not. Inasmuch as ye have not done it unto one of the least of these, neither have ye done it unto me.' You see, were it for this alone, they must 'depart' from God 'into everlasting punishment'.[5]
20   3. Is it not strange that this important truth should be so little understood, or at least should so little influence the practice even of them that fear God? Suppose this representation be true, suppose the Judge of all the earth speaks right, those and those only that feed the hungry, give drink to the thirsty, clothe the
25 naked, relieve the stranger, visit those that are sick and in prison, according to their power and opportunity, shall 'inherit the everlasting kingdom'. And those that do not shall 'depart into everlasting fire, prepared for the devil and his angels'.[6]
     4. I purpose at present to confine my discourse to one article of
30 these, 'visiting the sick'; a plain duty, which all that are in health may practise in a higher or lower degree; and which nevertheless is almost universally neglected, even by those that profess to love God. And touching this I would inquire, first, what is implied in visiting the sick? Secondly, how is it to be performed? And thirdly,
35 by whom?

---

[b] Matt. 25:34, etc.

---

[4] Cf. Eph. 2:5, 8.
[5] Cf. Matt. 25:40-46.
[6] Matt. 25:41.

I. First, I would inquire, What is the nature of this duty? What is implied in 'visiting the sick'?

1. By the sick I do not mean only those that keep their bed, or that are sick in the strictest sense. Rather I would include all such as are in a state of affliction, whether of mind or body; and that whether they are good or bad, whether they fear God or not. 5

[2.] 'But is there need of visiting them in person? May we not relieve them at a distance? Does it not answer the same purpose if we send them help as if we carry it ourselves?' Many are so circumstanced that they cannot attend the sick in person; and 10 where this is the real case it is undoubtedly sufficient for them to send help, being the only expedient they can use. But this is not properly 'visiting the sick'; it is another thing. The word which we render 'visit' in its literal acceptation means to 'look upon'.[7] And this, you well know, cannot be done unless you are present with 15 them. To send them assistance is therefore entirely a different thing from visiting them. The former then ought to be done, but the latter not left undone.[8]

'But I send a physician to those that are sick; and he can do them more good than I can.' He can in one respect: he can do 20 them more good with regard to their bodily health. But he cannot do them more good with regard to their souls, which are of infinitely greater importance. And if he could, this would not excuse *you:* his going would not fulfil *your* duty. Neither would it do the same good to *you,* unless you saw them with your own eyes. 25 If you do not, you lose a means of grace; you lose an excellent means of increasing your thankfulness to God, who saves you from this pain and sickness, and continues your health and strength; as well as of increasing your sympathy with the afflicted, your benevolence, and all social affections. 30

3. One great reason why the rich in general have so little sympathy for the poor is because they so seldom visit them. Hence it is that, according to the common observation, one part of the world does not know what the other suffers.[9] Many of them

---

[7] I.e., ἐπισκέπτεσθαι, as in Matt. 25:36, 43; Luke 1:68; 7:16; Acts 6:3; 7:23; 15:14, 36; Heb. 2:6; and Jas. 1:27. It is a familiar usage in classical Greek and occurs frequently in the Septuagint as a translation of פָּקַד (*paqad*) and its cognates; cf. Hatch and Redpath, *Concordance to the Septuagint,* I.527-28.

[8] An echo of BCP, General Confession.

[9] Rabelais has the proverb as 'one half of the world knoweth not how the other half liveth;' cf. *Works* (1532), II.xxxii. Bishop Joseph Hall, *Holy Observations* (1607), No. XVII,

do not know, because they do not care to know: they keep out of the way of knowing it—and then plead their voluntary ignorance as an excuse for their hardness of heart. 'Indeed, sir' (said a person of large substance), 'I am a very compassionate man. But 5 to tell you the truth, I do not know anybody in the world that is in want.' How did this come to pass? Why, he took good care to keep out of their way. And if he fell upon any of them unawares, 'he passed over on the other side.'[10]

4. How contrary to this is both the spirit and behaviour of even 10 people of the highest rank in a neighbouring nation! In Paris ladies of the first quality—yea, princesses of the blood, of the royal family—constantly visit the sick, particularly the patients in the Grand Hospital. And they not only take care to relieve their wants (if they need anything more than is provided for them) but 15 attend on their sick-beds, dress their sores, and perform the meanest offices for them. Here is a pattern for the English, poor or rich, mean or honourable! For many years we have abundantly copied after the follies of the French. Let us for once copy after their wisdom and virtue, worthy the imitation of the whole 20 Christian world. Let not the gentlewomen, or even the countesses in England, be ashamed to imitate those princesses of the blood! Here is a fashion that does honour to human nature. It began in France; but God forbid it should end there![11]

repeats this in a context similar to Wesley's (cf. Hall's *Select Works*, III.86); George Herbert has it also in *Jacula Prudentium*, p. 906.

[10] Cf. Luke 10:31, 32.

[11] Cf. Samuel Wesley, Jun., 'A Letter from a Guardian to a Young Lady', *Poems* (1736), p. 98:

> And thus, if we may credit Fame's Report,
> The best and fairest in the Gallick Court,
> An Hour sometimes in Hospitals employ,
> To give the dying Wretch a Glimpse of joy;
> T' attend the Crowds that hopeless Pangs endure,
> And sooth the Anguish which they cannot cure:
> To clothe the Bare and give the Empty Food,
> As bright as Guardian Angels and as good.
> Better import this Custom out of France,
> Than the last Top-knot, or the newest Dance.

See also Anthony Horneck, 'A Letter . . . Concerning the Lives of the Primitive Christians', which Wesley extracted and printed in the *Christian Lib.*, XXIX.120 ('the greatest ladies [nursed the sick] as if they were their meanest servants'), and William Cave, *Primitive Christianity* (also printed in the *Christian Lib.*, XXXI.229), Pt. II, ch. 1 (how the Empress Placilla visited hospitals and nursed the sick with her own hands); cf. also Pt. III, ch. 2 (*ibid.*, pp. 272-73).

5. And if your delicacy will not permit you to imitate those truly honourable ladies, by abasing yourselves in the manner which they do, by performing the lowest offices for the sick, you may, however, without humbling yourselves so far, supply them with whatever they want. And you may administer help of a more 5 excellent kind, by supplying their spiritual wants; instructing them (if they need such instruction) in the first principles of religion; endeavouring to show them the dangerous state they are in, under the wrath and curse of God through sin, and point them to the Lamb of God, who taketh away the sins of the world.[12] 10 Beside this general instruction, you might have abundant opportunities of comforting those that are in pain of body or distress of mind; you might find opportunities of strengthening the feeble-minded, quickening those that are faint and weary; and of building up those that have believed, and encouraging 15 them to 'go on to perfection'.[13] But these things you must do in your own person; you see, they cannot be done by proxy. Or suppose you could give the same relief to the sick by another, you could not reap the same advantage to yourself. You could not gain that increase in lowliness, in patience, in tenderness of spirit, in 20 sympathy with the afflicted, which you might have gained if you had assisted them in person. Neither would you receive the same recompense in the resurrection of the just, when 'every man shall receive his own reward, according to his own labour.'[14]

II.1. I proceed to inquire, in the second place, How are we to 25 visit them? In what manner may this labour of love be most effectually performed? How may we do this most to the glory of God, and the benefit of our neighbour? But before ever you enter upon the work you should be deeply convinced that you are by no means sufficient for it; you have neither sufficient grace, nor 30 sufficient understanding, to perform it in the most excellent manner. And this will convince you of the necessity of applying to the Strong for strength,[15] and of flying to the Father of lights, the Giver of every good gift,[16] for wisdom; ever remembering, 'there is a spirit in man that giveth wisdom, and the inspiration of the 35

---

[12] See John 1:29; and cf. the *Agnus Dei*, after Communion in BCP.
[13] Heb. 6:1.
[14] 1 Cor. 3:8.
[15] See No. 48, 'Self-denial', III.4 and n.
[16] See Jas. 1:17.

Holy One that giveth understanding.'[17] Whenever therefore you
are about to enter upon the work, seek his help by earnest prayer.
Cry to him for the whole spirit of humility, lest if pride steal into
your heart, if you ascribe anything to yourself, while you strive to
5 save others you destroy your own soul. Before and through the
work, from the beginning to the end, let your heart wait upon him
for a continual supply of meekness and gentleness, of patience
and long-suffering, that you may never be angry or discouraged,
at whatever treatment, rough or smooth, kind or unkind, you may
10 meet with. Be not moved with the deep ignorance of some, the
dullness, the amazing stupidity of others; marvel not at their
peevishness or stubbornness, at their non-improvement after all
the pains that you have taken; yea, at some of them turning back to
perdition, and being worse than they were before. Still your
15 record is with the Lord, and your reward with the Most High.

2. As to the particular method of treating the sick, you need not
tie yourself down to any; but may continually vary your manner of
proceeding as various circumstances may require. But it may not
be amiss usually to begin with inquiring into their outward
20 condition. You may ask whether they have the necessaries of life.
Whether they have sufficient food and raiment. If the weather be
cold, whether they have fuel. Whether they have needful
attendance. Whether they have proper advice with regard to their
bodily disorder; especially if it be of a dangerous kind. In several
25 of these respects you may be able to give them some assistance
yourself: and you may move those that are more able than you to
supply your lack of service. You might properly say in your own
case, 'To beg I am ashamed;'[18] but never be ashamed to beg for
the poor; yea, in this case, be an importunate beggar—do not
30 easily take a denial. Use all the address, all the understanding, all
the influence you have; at the same time trusting in him that has
the hearts of all men in his hands.

3. You will then easily discern whether there is any good office
which you can do for them with your own hands. Indeed most of
35 the things which are needful to be done, those about them can do
better than you. But in some you may have more skill or more
experience than them. And if you have, let not delicacy or honour
stand in your way. Remember his word, 'Inasmuch as ye have

[17] Cf. Job 32:8, and note Wesley's unusual translation of Shaddai here as 'the Holy One'.
[18] Luke 16:3.

done it unto the least of these, ye have done it unto me.'[19] And think nothing too mean to do for him! Rejoice to be abased for his sake!

4. These little labours of love will pave your way to things of greater importance. Having shown that you have a regard for their bodies you may proceed to inquire concerning their souls. And here you have a large field before you; you have scope for exercising all the talents which God has given you. May you not begin with asking, Have you ever considered that God governs the world? That his providence is over all? And over *you* in particular? Does anything then befall you without his knowledge? Or without his designing it for your good? He knows all you suffer; he knows all your pains; he sees all your wants. He sees, not only your affliction in general, but every particular circumstance of it. Is he not looking down from heaven, and disposing all these things for your profit? You may then inquire whether he is acquainted with the general principles of religion. And afterwards lovingly and gently examine whether his life has been agreeable thereto. Whether he has been an outward, barefaced sinner, or has had a form of religion. See next whether he knows anything of the power [of godliness];[20] of worshipping God 'in spirit and in truth'.[21] If he does not, endeavour to explain to him, 'Without holiness no man shall see the Lord;'[22] and 'Except a man be born again, he cannot see the kingdom of God.'[23] When he begins to understand the nature of holiness, and the necessity of the new birth, then you may press upon him 'repentance toward God, and faith in our Lord Jesus Christ'.[24]

5. When you find any of them begin to fear God, it will be proper to give them one after another some plain tracts, as the *Instructions for Christians*,[25] *Awake, thou that Sleepest*,[26] and *The*

---

[19] Matt. 25:40.
[20] An apparent lacuna here in both early texts, but the phrase, 'the form and the power of godliness', is an old cliché and supports this conjecture; cf. 2 Tim. 3:5.
[21] John 4:23, 24.   [22] Cf. Heb. 12:14.
[23] John 3:3.   [24] Cf. Acts 20:21.
[25] In 1745 Wesley had published a revised English 'extract' of Pierre Poieret (1646–1719), *Les Principes solides de la Religion et de la Vie Chrétienne, appliqués à l' éducation des enfans et applicables à toutes sortes de personnes* (1705), under the title, *Instructions for Children*. In his *Works*, Vol. XXIV (1773), it appears with the title *Instructions for Christians (Bibliog*, No. 101, and cf. No. 245). Poiret was a prominent French mystic, disciple and biographer of Antoinette Bourignon and author of the famous *Bibliotheca mysticorum selecta* (1708).
[26] See No. 3, *'Awake Thou That Sleepest'*.

Nature and Design of Christianity.[27] At the next visit you may
inquire what they have read; what they remember; and what they
understand. And then will be the time to enforce what they
understand, and if possible impress it on their hearts. Be sure to
5   conclude every meeting with prayer. If you cannot yet pray
without a form you may use some of those composed by Mr.
Spinckes,[28] or any other pious writer. But the sooner you break
through this backwardness the better. Ask of God, and he will
soon open your mouth.

10   6. Together with the more important lessons which you
endeavour to teach all the poor whom you visit, it would be a deed
of charity to teach them two things more, which they are generally
little acquainted with—industry and cleanliness. It was said by a
pious man, 'Cleanliness is next to godliness.'[29] Indeed the want of
15 it is a scandal to all religion; causing the way of truth to be evil
spoken of.[30] And without industry we are neither fit for this world
nor for the world to come. With regard to both, 'Whatsoever thy
hand findeth to do, do it with thy might.'[31]

III.1. The third point to be considered is, By whom is this duty
20 to be performed? The answer is ready—by all that desire to
'inherit the kingdom' of their Father, which was prepared for
them from the foundation of the world.[32] For thus saith the Lord:
'Come, ye blessed . . . , inherit the kingdom . . . . For I was sick
and ye visited me.'[33] And to those on the left hand: 'Depart, ye
25 cursed . . . . For I was sick, and ye visited me not.'[34] Does not this
plainly imply that as all who do this are 'blessed', and shall 'inherit
the kingdom'; so all who do it not are 'cursed', and shall 'depart
into everlasting fire'?

2. All therefore who desire to escape everlasting fire and to
30 inherit the everlasting kingdom are equally concerned, according
to their power, to practise this important duty. It is equally

[27] An abridged extract from Law's *Christian Perfection* which Wesley had published in
1740 under the title, *The Nature and Design of Christianity*, and frequently reprinted
thereafter (cf. *Bibliog*, No. 41).

[28] Nathaniel Spinckes (1653–1727), *The Sick Man Visited and Furnished With
Instructions, Meditations and Prayers* (1712). Spinckes's *The Church of England-man's
Companion in the Closet* was the main source of Wesley's *Collection of Forms of Prayer* (1733);
cf. *Bibliog*, No. 1.

[29] Rabbi Phinehas ben Yair; see No. 88, 'On Dress', §5 and n.

[30] See 2 Pet. 2:2.   [31] Eccles. 9:10.

[32] See Matt. 25:34.   [33] Cf. Matt. 25:34, 36.

[34] Cf. Matt. 25:41-43.

incumbent on young and old, rich and poor, men and women, according to their ability. None are so young, if they desire to save their own souls, as to be excused from assisting their neighbours. None are so poor (unless they want the necessaries of life) but they are called to do something, more or less, at whatever time   5
they can spare, for the relief and comfort of their afflicted fellow-creatures.

3. But those who 'are rich in this world',[35] who have more than the conveniences of life, are peculiarly called of God to this blessed work, and pointed out to it by his gracious providence. As   10
you are not under a necessity of working for your bread, you have your time at your own disposal! You may therefore allot some part of it every day for this labour of love. If it be practicable it is far [the] best to have a fixed hour (for 'any time', we say, 'is no time'[36]), and not to employ that time in any other business without   15
urgent necessity. You have likewise a peculiar advantage over many, by your station in life. Being superior in rank to them, you have the more influence on that very account. Your inferiors of course look up to you with a kind of reverence. And the condescension which you show in visiting them gives them a   20
prejudice[37] in your favour which inclines them to hear you with attention, and willingly receive what you say. Improve this prejudice to the uttermost for the benefit of their souls, as well as their bodies. While you are as eyes to the blind and feet to the lame,[38] a husband to the widow and a father to the fatherless, see   25
that you still keep a higher end in view, even the saving of souls from death, and that you labour to make all you say and do subservient to that great end.

4. 'But have *the poor* themselves any part or lot in this matter? Are they any way concerned in visiting the sick?' What can they   30
give to others who have hardly the conveniences, or perhaps necessaries, of life for themselves? If they have not, yet they need not be wholly excluded from the blessing which attends the practice of this duty. Even those may remember that excellent

---

[35] 1 Tim. 6:17.

[36] In W. Gurney Benham's *Book of Quotations* we find, 'Any time means no time;' in James Kelly, *Complete Collection of Scottish Proverbs* (1721), the point is made thus: 'What may be done at any time will be done at no time.'

[37] Terms that have come to have largely negative connotations; not so here, where they denote quite positive and reciprocal feelings.

[38] Job 29:15.

rule, 'Let our conveniences give way to our neighbour's necessities; and our necessities give way to our neighbour's extremities.'[39] And few are so poor as not to be able sometimes to give 'two mites';[40] but if they are not, if they have no money to give,

5 may they not give what is of more value? Yea, of more value than thousands of gold and silver? If you speak 'in the name of Jesus Christ of Nazareth',[41] may not the words you speak be health to the soul, and marrow to the bones?[42] Can you give them nothing? Nay, in administering to them the grace of God you give them

10 more than all this world is worth! Go on! Go on! Thou poor disciple of a poor Master! Do as he did in the days of his flesh! Whenever thou hast an opportunity, go about doing good, and healing all that are oppressed of the devil;[43] encouraging them to shake off his chains, and fly immediately to him

15
> Who sets the prisoners free, and breaks
> The iron bondage from their necks.[44]

Above all, give them your prayers. Pray with them; pray for them! And who knows but you may save their souls alive?[45]

5. You that are *old*, whose feet are ready to stumble upon the

20 dark mountains,[46] may not you do a little more good before you go hence and are no more seen! O remember,

> 'Tis time to live, if you grow old:
> Of little life the best to make,
> And manage wisely the last stake![47]

25 As you have lived many years, it may be hoped you have attained such knowledge as may be of use to others. You have certainly more knowledge of men, which is commonly learnt by dear-bought experience. With what strength you have left, employ the few moments you have to spare in ministering to those

30 who are weaker than yourselves. Your grey hairs will not fail to

---

[39] Cf. Robert South, as in No. 30, 'Sermon on the Mount, X', §26 and n.
[40] Mark 12:42.
[41] Acts 3:6; 4:10.
[42] Prov. 3:8.   [43] See Acts 10:38.
[44] Cf. Watts, Hymn 97 in *Hymns and Spiritual Songs* (*Works*, IV.180). This had been included in Wesley's first *Collection of Psalms and Hymns* (1737), pp. 35-36, and thereafter in the enlarged collection under the same title in 1741. Both texts read 'He' for 'Who'.
[45] See Ezek. 13:18-19.   [46] Jer. 13:16.
[47] Cf. Abraham Cowley, *Anacreontiques*, Ode V, 'Age', in *Works* (10th edn., 1707), I.51. See also *Anacreontis Teii Odae et Fragmenta* (1732), pp. 48-49.

give you authority, and add weight to what you speak. You may frequently urge, to increase their attention,

> Believe me, youth; for I am read in cares,
> And groan beneath the weight of more than threescore years.[48]

You have frequently been a sufferer yourself; perhaps you are so 5 still. So much the more give them all the assistance you can, both with regard to their souls and bodies, before they and you go to the place whence you will not return.[49]

6. On the other hand, you that are *young* have several advantages that are almost peculiar to yourselves. You have 10 generally a flow of spirits, and a liveliness of temper which, by the grace of God, make you willing to undertake, and capable of performing, many good works at which others would be discouraged. And you have your health and strength of body, whereby you are eminently qualified to assist the sick and those 15 that have no strength. You are able to take up and carry the crosses which may be expected to lie in the way. Employ then your whole vigour of body and mind in ministering to your afflicted brethren. And bless God that you have them to employ in so honourable a service; like those heavenly 'servants of his that do 20 his pleasure'[50] by continually ministering to the heirs of salvation.

7. 'But may not *women* as well as men bear a part in this

[48] A favourite quotation with the biographers of Susanna Wesley. The original appears in a letter from Susanna to John in 1727; it was then quoted by George J. Stevenson, *Memorials of the Wesley Family* (1876), p. 204, and in his memoir of her death. Adam Clarke has it in his *Memoirs of the Wesley Family* (1823), p. 273, as does Eliza Clarke, *Susanna Wesley* (1886), p. 158, 200. See also John Dove, *Biographical History* (1840), p. 168, and John Kirk, *Mother of the Wesleys* (1864), p. 271. It seems to be a paraphrase of Alexander Pope's 'January and May: Or, the Merchant's Tale from Chaucer', ll. 87-88, in *Works* (1764), I.211:

> Beneath the weight of threescore years I bend
> And, worn with cares, am hastening to my end.

The 'original' in Chaucer, *Works* (1687), p. 54, is as follows:

> With face sad, his tale hath he them told:
> He said, good friends, I am hore and old
> And almost (God wot) on the pits brinke,
> Upon my soule somewhat I must I thinke.

[49] See Job 10:21, and Shakespeare, *Hamlet*, III.i.79-80:

> The undiscovered country, from whose bourne
> No traveller returns.

[50] Ps. 103:21 (BCP).

honourable service?' Undoubtedly they may; nay, they ought—it is meet, right, and their bounden duty.[51] Herein there is no difference: 'there is neither male nor female in Christ Jesus.'[52] Indeed it has long passed for a maxim with many that 'women are

5 only to be seen, not heard.'[53] And accordingly many of them are brought up in such a manner as if they were only designed for agreeable playthings! But is this doing honour to the sex? Or is it a real kindness to them? No; it is the deepest unkindness; it is horrid cruelty; it is mere Turkish barbarity. And I know not how

10 any woman of sense and spirit can submit to it. Let all you that have it in your power assert the right which the God of nature has given you. Yield not to that vile bondage any longer. You, as well as men, are rational creatures. You, like them, were made in the image of God: you are equally candidates for immortality.[54] You

15 too are called of God, as you have time, to 'do good unto all men'.[55] Be 'not disobedient to the heavenly calling'.[56] Whenever you have opportunity, do all the good you can, particularly to your poor sick neighbour. And every one of *you* likewise 'shall receive your own reward according to your own labour'.[57]

20   8. It is well known that in the primitive church there were women particularly appointed for this work. Indeed there was one or more such in every Christian congregation under heaven. They were then termed 'deaconesses', that is, 'servants'—servants of the church and of its great Master. Such was Phebe

25 (mentioned by St. Paul), 'a deaconess of the Church at Cenchrea'.[c] It is true most of these were women in years, and well experienced in the work of God. But were the young wholly excluded from that service? No; neither need they be, provided they know in whom they have believed,[58] and show that they are

[c] Rom. 16:1 [Cf. *Notes*].

---

[51] BCP, Communion, Preface to the Sanctus.
[52] Gal. 3:28.
[53] Derived from Sophocles, *Ajax*, l. 293 ('. . . For women, silence appears as an ornament'). In the *Oxford Dictionary of English Proverbs* the form 'Silence is the best ornament of a woman' is cited from Taverner (1545), *et al.* See also under 'Children (maidens) should be seen, and not heard.'
[54] Is this an echo of Dryden's 'To the Memory of Mrs. Killigrew' ('. . . while yet a young probationer and candidate for heaven')? Cf. No. 100, 'On Pleasing All Men', II.5.
[55] Gal. 6:10.
[56] Cf. Acts. 26:19.
[57] Cf. 1 Cor. 3:8.
[58] See 2 Tim. 1:12.

holy of heart by being holy in all manner of conversation.[59] Such a deaconess, if she answered her picture, was Mr. Law's Miranda.[60] Would anyone object to her visiting and relieving the sick and poor because she was a woman? Nay, and a young one too? Do any of you that are young desire to tread in her steps? Have you a pleasing form? An agreeable address? So much the better, if you are wholly devoted to God. He will use these, if your eye be single,[61] to make your words strike the deeper. And while you minister to others, how many blessings may redound into your own bosom! Hereby your natural levity may be destroyed, your fondness for trifles cured, your wrong tempers corrected, your evil habits weakened, until they are rooted out. And you will be prepared to adorn the doctrine of God our Saviour[62] in every future scene of life. Only be very wary if you visit or converse with those of the other sex, lest your affections be entangled on one side or the other, and so you find a curse instead of a blessing.

9. Seeing then this is a duty to which we are called, rich and poor, young and old, male and female (and it would be well if parents would train up their children herein, as well as in saying their prayers and going to church), let the time past suffice that almost all of us have neglected it, as by general consent. O what need has every one of us to say, 'Lord, forgive me my sins of omission!'[63] Well, in the name of God let us now from this day set about it with general consent. And, I pray, let it never go out of your mind that this is a duty which you cannot perform by proxy; unless in one only case—unless you are disabled by your own pain or weakness. In that only case it suffices to send the relief which you would otherwise give. Begin, my dear brethren, begin now: else the impression which you now feel will wear off; and possibly it may never return! What then will be the consequence? Instead of hearing that word, 'Come, ye blessed . . . . For I was sick and ye visited me,' you must hear that awful sentence, 'Depart, ye cursed! . . . For I was sick, and ye visited me not!'[64]

Aberdeen, May 23, 1786[65]

---

[59] 1 Pet. 1:15.
[60] An idealized character in Law, *Serious Call*, chs. 8-9.
[61] See Matt. 6:22.
[62] Titus 2:10.
[63] The dying words of Archbishop Ussher; see No. 14, *The Repentance of Believers*, I.14 and n.
[64] Cf. Matt. 25:34, 36, 41, 43.   [65] Place and date as in *AM*.

A

SERMON,

Preached *November* 23, 1777,

I N

LEWISHAM CHURCH,

BEFORE

The HUMANE SOCIETY.

By *JOHN WESLEY*, M. A.

L O N D O N:
PRINTED BY J. FRY AND CO. AND SOLD
AT THE FOUNDERY, UPPER-MOORFIELDS.
M.DCC.LXXVII.

[Price TWO-PENCE.]

THE REWARD OF RIGHTEOUSNESS

AN INTRODUCTORY COMMENT

This is one of the later Wesley's rare sermons ad aulam, *preached in Lewisham on November 23, 1777, and published as a pamphlet before the year was out. There is a reference to it in the* Journal: *'Sun. 23. I preached in Lewisham church for the benefit of the Humane Society, instituted for the sake of those who seem to be drowned, strangled, or killed by any sudden stroke. It is a glorious design, in consequence of which many have been recovered that must otherwise have inevitably perished.'*

We know from the Society's official history that it 'was founded on the 18th April, 1774, at the Chapter Coffee House in St. Paul's Churchyard, London, by Dr. William Hawes (1736–1808) and Dr. Thomas Cogan (1736–1818) and their friends, . . . the Lord Mayor of London being the Society's first President. Very quickly the Society and its work ['in the life saving and restoring field'] caught the imagination of the general public, . . . and in 1783 King George III became its patron. Four years later the Society was granted the prefix "Royal" . . .' (Annual Report, 1970, p. 9). The Royal Humane Society still continues as an active voluntary lifesaving agency, with headquarters in Watergate House, York Buildings, Adelphi, London, W.C.2. Its motto, from the beginning, has been 'Lateat Scintilla Forsan' *('Perhaps a scintilla [of life] remains'), and its medals for heroic service are still inscribed* Societas Londinii in Resuscitationem Intermortuorum *('The London Society for the Recovery of Persons Still Hanging between Life and Death'). It is noteworthy that Wesley should have been invited to preach the Society's annual 'Benefit Sermon' so early in its history (or that he should have accepted such an invitation) in view of the fact that one of its founders, Dr. William Hawes, had recently published (in 1776)* An Examination of Mr. John Wesley's Primitive Physick, showing that a great number of the prescriptions therein contained are founded on ignorance of the medical art . . . ; and that it is a publication calculated to do essential injury to the health of those persons who may place confidence in it . . . .

400   *Sermon 99*   Intro.–§1

*It is unsurprising, therefore, that on such an occasion Wesley should
have elevated his rhetoric and that he should have extended his range of
classical and literary allusions. It is equally natural that he should have
focused on the question of 'good works'. Even as he carefully avoids any
attribution of saving merit, he still firmly rejects the classical Protestant
notion that heroic services of the sort here extolled may be nothing more
than 'splendid sins'.*

*The sermon had no further editions until Wesley decided to include it
in* SOSO, *VIII.89-111, with only a barebones title, 'Preached Before
the Humane Society'. In his edition of Wesley's* Works *in 1809 Joseph
Benson gave it a more descriptive title, 'The Reward of Righteousness'
(VII.155-63), and was followed in this by Thomas Jackson in 1825
and again in 1829 (*Works, *VII.127-38). On this point we have
thought it suitable to follow in their train.*

The Reward of Righteousness

Preached before the Humane Society

Matthew 25:34

*Come, ye blessed of my Father! Inherit the kingdom prepared for you
from the foundation of the world.*

1. Reason alone will convince every fair inquirer that God 'is a
rewarder of them that diligently seek him'.[1] This alone teaches
him to say, 'Doubtless there is a reward for the righteous; there is
a God that judgeth the earth.'[2] But how little information do we
10 receive from unassisted reason touching the particulars contained in this general truth! As eye hath not seen, or ear heard, so
neither could it naturally enter into our heart to conceive,[3] the
circumstances of that awful day wherein God will judge the
world. No information of this kind could be given but from the
15 great Judge himself. And what an amazing instance of
condescension it is that the Creator, the Governor, the Lord, the

---

[1] Heb. 11:6.
[2] Cf. Ps. 58:10 (BCP).
[3] See 1 Cor. 2:9.

Judge of all, should deign to give us so clear and particular an account of that solemn transaction! If the learned heathen acknowledged the sublimity of that account which Moses gives of the creation,[4] what would he have said if he had heard this account of the Son of man coming in his glory?[5] Here indeed is no laboured pomp of words, no ornaments of language. This would not have suited either the speaker or the occasion. But what inexpressible dignity of thought! See him 'coming in the clouds of heaven'![6] 'And all the angels with him'![7] See him 'sitting on the throne of his glory, and all the nations gathered before him'![8] And shall he separate them, placing the good on his right hand, and the wicked on his left?[9] 'Then shall the King say'—With what admirable propriety is the expression varied! *The Son of man* comes down to judge the children of men; *the King* distributes rewards and punishments to his obedient or rebellious subjects—'Then shall the King say to them on his right hand, Come, ye blessed of my Father! Inherit the kingdom prepared for you from the foundation of the world.'

2. 'Prepared for you from the foundation of the world'. But does this agree with the common supposition that God created man merely to supply the vacant thrones of the rebel angels?[10] Does it not rather seem to imply that he would have created man, though the angels had never fallen? Inasmuch as he then prepared the kingdom for his human children when he laid the foundation of the earth.

3. 'Inherit the kingdom'—as being 'heirs of God, and joint-heirs'[11] with his beloved Son. It is your right, seeing I have purchased 'eternal redemption for all them that obey me'.[12] And ye did obey me in the days of your flesh. Ye 'believed in the Father, and also in me'.[13] Ye loved the Lord your God; and that

---

[4] This would have been Plato. Wesley's most probable source was Eusebius, *Praeparatio Evangelii*, IX.6, X.2-8, VII.8, 27, with its echoes of the familiar patristic theme that Plato and other Greek philosophers had borrowed their best ideas from Moses and the Hebrew prophets; cf. Johannes Quasten, *Patrology*, III.329.

[5] See Matt. 25:31. [6] Cf. Matt. 24:30, etc.
[7] Cf. Matt. 25:31. [8] Cf. Matt. 25:31-32.
[9] See Matt. 25:33.

[10] Cf. Augustine, *Enchiridion*, ix.28-29. Here, as in the question of whether Christ would have come if man had not sinned, Wesley supposes that in the history of salvation, the Fall and its effects had not been *prevented* by God's sovereign grace but rather anticipated and transcended; see above, No. 59, 'God's Love to Fallen Man', I.1 and n.

[11] Rom. 8:17. [12] Cf. Heb. 5:9; 9:12.
[13] Cf. John 14:1.

love constrained you to love all mankind. Ye continued in the faith
that wrought by love.[14] Ye showed your faith by your works.[15] 'For
I was hungry, and ye gave me meat; I was thirsty, and ye gave me
drink; I was a stranger, and ye took me in; naked, and ye clothed
5 me; I was sick, and in prison, and ye came unto me.'[16]

4. But in what sense are we to understand the words that
follow? 'Lord, when saw we thee hungry, and gave thee meat? Or
thirsty, and gave thee drink?'[17] They cannot be literally
understood; they cannot answer in these very words; because it is
10 not possible they should be ignorant that God had really wrought
by them. Is it not then manifest that these words are to be taken in
a figurative sense?[18] And can they imply any more than that all
which they have done will appear as nothing to them, will as it
were vanish away, in view of what God their Saviour had done and
15 suffered for them!

5. But 'the King shall answer and say unto them, Verily I say
unto you, Inasmuch as ye have done it to one of the least of these
my brethren, ye did it unto me.'[19] What a declaration this! Worthy
to be had in everlasting remembrance![20] May the finger of the
20 living God write it upon all our hearts!

I would take occasion from hence, first, to make a few
reflections on good works in general; secondly, to consider in
particular that institution for the promotion of which we are now
assembled; and, in the third place, to make a short application.

25 I.1. And, first, I would make a few reflections upon good works
in general.

I am not insensible that many, even serious people, are jealous
of all that is spoken upon this subject; nay, and whenever the
necessity of good works is strongly insisted on, take it for granted
30 that he who speaks in this manner is but one remove from
popery.[21] But should we for fear of this, or of any other reproach,

---

[14] See Gal. 5:6.　　　　　　　　　　　　　　　　　[15] See Jas. 2:18.
[16] Matt. 25:35.　　　　　　　　　　　　　　[17] Matt. 25:37 *(Notes)*.
[18] A rare instance of allegory in Wesley (cf. also No. 48, 'Self-denial', I.7); it is, however,
consistent with his hermeneutical rule to prefer a literal interpretation unless it involves an
absurdity; see No. 21, 'Sermon on the Mount, I', §6 and n.
[19] Matt. 25:40.　　　　　　　　　　　　　　　　　[20] See Ps. 112:6.
[21] A remembrance of the charges against him of being a 'crypto-Catholic', 'papist', etc.,
by the Calvinists and antinomians; cf. JWJ, Aug. 27, 1739, and Dec. 20, 1768; and *An
Earnest Appeal*, §68(11:74 in this edn.). See also, e.g., Francis Blackburne, *Considerations
on the Present State of Controversy Between the Protestants and Papists of Great Britain and
Ireland* (London, 1768), p.199: 'The Popish party boast much of the increase of the

refrain from speaking 'the truth as it is in Jesus'?[22] Should we on any consideration 'shun to declare the whole counsel of God'?[23] Nay, if a false prophet could utter that solemn word, how much more may the ministers of Christ—'We cannot go beyond the word of the Lord', to speak 'either more or less'![24]   5

2. Is it not to be lamented that any who fear God should desire us to do otherwise? And that by speaking otherwise themselves they should occasion the way of truth to be evil spoken of?[25] I mean, in particular, the way of salvation by faith, which on this very account is despised, nay, had in abomination by many   10 sensible men. It is now about forty years since this grand scriptural doctrine, 'By grace ye are saved through faith,'[26] began to be openly declared by a few clergymen of the Church of England. And not long after some who heard, but did not understand, attempted to preach the same doctrine, but   15 miserably mangled it, wresting the Scripture, and 'making void the law through faith'.[27]

3. Some of these, in order to exalt the value of faith, have utterly depreciated good works. They speak of them as not only not necessary to salvation, but as greatly obstructive of it. They   20 represent them as abundantly more dangerous than evil ones to those who are seeking to save their souls. One cries aloud, 'More people go to hell by praying than by thieving.' Another screams out: 'Away with your works! Have done with your works, or you cannot come to Christ!' And this unscriptural, irrational,   25 heathenish declamation is called, 'preaching the gospel'![28]

4. But 'shall not the Judge of all the earth' speak as well as 'do right?'[29] Will not 'he be justified in his saying, and clear when he is judged'?[30] Assuredly he will. And upon his authority we must continue to declare that whenever you do good to any for his   30 sake—when you feed the hungry, give drink to the thirsty; when you assist the stranger, or clothe the naked; when you visit them

---

Methodists and talk of that sect with rapture. How far the Methodists and Papists stand connected in principles I know not; but I believe it is beyond a doubt that they are in constant correspondence with each other.'

[22] Cf. Eph. 4:22.   [23] Cf. Acts 20:27.
[24] Cf. Num. 22:18.   [25] See 2 Pet. 2:2.
[26] Cf. Eph. 2:8.
[27] Cf. Rom. 3:31. Wesley's time reference here points to 1738 as the beginning of the Revival.
[28] Cf. No. 35, 'The Law Established through Faith, I', I.12 and n.
[29] Gen. 18:25.   [30] Cf. Ps. 51:4.

that are sick, or in prison—these are not 'splendid sins',[31] as one marvellously calls them, but 'sacrifices wherewith God is well pleased'.[32]

5. Not that our Lord intended we should confine our
5 beneficence to the bodies of men. He undoubtedly designed that we should be equally abundant in works of spiritual mercy. He died to 'purify unto himself a peculiar people, zealous of' all 'good works';[33] zealous, above all, to 'save souls from death', and thereby 'hide a multitude of sins'.[34] And this is unquestionably
10 included in St. Paul's exhortation, 'As we have time, let us do good unto all men;'[35] good in every possible kind, as well as in every possible degree. But why does not our blessed Lord mention works of spiritual mercy? He could not do it with any propriety. It was not for him to say: 'I was in error, and ye

[31] The original of this phrase, *splendida peccata*, has long been attributed to Augustine, and something of the idea does appear in *De Civ. Dei*, xix. 25; see Pierre Jaccard, *'De S. Augustin à Pascal: histoire d'une maxime sur les vertus des philosophes'*, *Revue de Théologie et de Philosophie*, N.S., XXVIII (1940), 41-55. But the phrase itself is not there. Its first instance, as far as I know, is in Peter Martyr Vermigli, *Loci Communes . . . (1st edn., 1576, but see London edn. of 1583)*, *'Classis Tertiae'*, ch. XII, *'De Cruce et Affectionibus perferendis, ubi etiam de Fortitudine, Fuga et Exilio'*, §7, p. 649: '. . . *Fateor equidem . . . splendida peccata'*. This had been translated into English as, 'And their works, although they were excellent (if we consider them after a civil manner), yet before God they were nothing else but glorious and glistering sinnes' (*The Commonplaces of the Most Famous and Renowned Divine Doctor Peter Martyr . . . , 1583*, p. 177). An English source for Wesley would have been Richard Fiddes, *Practical Discourses*, II.15. Cf. also Matthew Mead, *The Almost Christian Discovered* (1662), p. 97 of 1797 edn.; 'A man may obey much and yet be in his old nature; and so then all his obedience in that estate is but *splendidum peccatum*, a painted sin;' John Norris, *Considerations upon the Nature of Sin; Accommodated to the Ends of Speculation and Practice*, sect. 7, in *A Collection of Miscellanies* (1723), p. 288: '. . . the great question concerning the good actions done by heathens [is] whether they were properly virtues or only a kind of well-favoured sins, *splendida peccata*, as some have thought fit to call them;' Patrick Middleton, *A Short View of the Evidences upon which the Christian Religion and the Divine Authority of the Holy Scriptures is Established* (1734), Appendix, 1:7: 'Some of the [Calvinists'] learned authors do frankly drop all thoughts of any regard in God to the salvation of those famous men ['the virtuous pagans'], accounting their brightest virtues as only glittering iniquity *(splendida peccata)* because they did not proceed from a principle of faith and had not the glory of God for their only end . . . .' See also the Homily on Good Works, First Part, *Homilies*, p. 43, quoting Chrysostom: 'they which glister and shine in good works without faith in God be like dead men;' this is from a work wrongly attributed to Chrysostom *(Sermone de Fide, Lege et Spiritu Sancto;* cf. Migne, *PG*, XLVIII.1081). See also the *Minutes*, Aug. 2, 1745, *Q*. 8: 'Were those works of [Cornelius] splendid sins?' *A*. 'No; nor were they done without the grace of Christ;' and *Predestination Calmly Considered*, §32. Cf. Nos. 5, 'Justification by Faith', III.5 and n.; and 130, 'On Living without God', §14.

[32] Cf. Heb. 13:16.

[33] Titus 2:14.

[34] Cf. Jas. 5:20.

[35] Cf. Gal. 6:10; cf. also No. 24, 'Sermon on the Mount, IV', IV.1 and n.

convinced me; I was in sin, and you brought me back to God.' And it needed not; for in mentioning *some* he included *all* works of mercy.

6. But may I not add one thing more (only he that heareth, let him understand):[36] good works are so far from being hindrances 5 of our salvation, they are so far from being insignificant, from being of no account in Christianity, that, supposing them to spring from a right principle, they are the perfection of religion. They are the highest part of that spiritual building whereof Jesus Christ is the foundation. To those who attentively consider the 10 thirteenth chapter of the first Epistle to the Corinthians it will be undeniably plain that what St. Paul there describes as the highest of all Christian graces is properly and directly the love of our neighbour.[37] And to him who attentively considers the whole tenor both of the Old and New Testament it will be equally plain 15 that works springing from this love are the highest part of the religion therein revealed. Of these our Lord himself says, 'Hereby is my Father glorified, that ye bring forth much fruit.'[38] Much fruit! Does not the very expression imply the excellency of what is so termed? Is not the tree itself for the sake of the fruit? By 20 bearing fruit, and by this alone, it attains the highest perfection it is capable of, and answers the end for which it was planted. Who, what is he, then, that is called a Christian, and can speak lightly of good works?

II. From these general reflections I proceed to consider that 25 institution in particular for the promotion of which we are now assembled. And in doing this I shall first observe the rise of this institution; secondly, the success; and thirdly, the excellency of it; after which you will give me leave to make a short application.

(I).[39] On the first head, the rise of this institution, I may be very 30 brief, as a great part of you know it already.

[36] See Mark 13:14.
[37] See No. 91, 'On Charity', I.2 and n.
[38] Cf. John 15:8.
[39] The original numbering of these subdivisions is confusing; the attempted reconstruction here is indicated by adding parentheses. The second series, which begins here, and deals with the Humane Society, has been renumbered '(I)'-'(III)' instead of 'I'-'III'. The third series consists of a listing of the Society's principles as a subdivision of II.(I).4, and has been left untouched. The final section has been renumbered 'III' instead of the original 'IV', because Wesley apparently intended it to continue the general considerations begun in 'I' and 'II' rather than particular aspects of the Humane Society itself dealt with in '(I)'-'(III)'.

1. One would wonder (as an ingenious writer observes) that such an institution as this, of so deep importance to mankind, should appear so late in the world. Have we anything wrote upon the subject earlier than the tract published at Rome in the year 5 1637?[40] And did not the proposal then sleep for many years? Were there any more than one or two attempts, and those not effectually pursued, till the year 1700? By what steps it has been since revived and carried into execution we are now to inquire.

2. I cannot give you a clearer view of this than by presenting you 10 with a short extract from the introduction to the 'Plan and Reports of the Society', published two years ago.[41]

Many and indubitable are the instances of the possibility of restoring to life persons apparently struck with sudden death, whether by an apoplexy, convulsive fits, noxious vapours, strangling, or drowning. Cases of this nature 15 have occurred in every country. But they were considered and *neglected* as extraordinary phenomena, from which no salutary consequence could be drawn.

3. At length a few benevolent gentlemen in Holland conjectured that some at least might have been saved had proper means been used in time; and formed 20 themselves into a Society in order to make a trial. Their attempts succeeded far beyond their expectations. Many were restored who must otherwise have perished. And they were at length enabled to extend their plan over the seven provinces.

Their success instigated other countries to follow their example. In the year 25 1768 the Magistrates of Health at Milan and Venice issued orders for the treatment of drowned persons. The city of Hamburg appointed a similar ordinance to be read in all the churches. In the year 1769 the Empress of Germany published an edict, extending its directions and encouragements to every case that afforded a possibility of relief. In the year 1771 the magistrates of 30 Paris founded an institution in favour of the drowned.

4. In the year 1773 Dr. Cogan[42] translated the *Memoirs of the Society at Amsterdam*, in order to inform our countrymen of the practicability of recovering persons apparently drowned. And Mr. Hawes[43] uniting with him, these

[40] Details of the tract and the name of the 'ingenious writer' are not known.

[41] Wesley's abridged and emended précis of 'The Introduction' from *The Plan and Reports of the Society for the Recovery of Persons Apparently Drowned. Instituted at London. MDCCLXXIV* (With an Appendix), 1775, pp. 3-19; Wesley has altered the original's phrasing here and there but not its factual statements.

[42] Thomas Cogan had begun as a Nonconformist minister who served congregations in Rotterdam, Southampton, and The Hague. He then took a medical degree at Leyden in 1767 and practiced medicine, chiefly in London, until 1780, when he retired to Holland to pursue his studies in moral philosophy. In 1767, he had joined a society in Amsterdam, 'In Favour of Drowned Persons', and translated their *Memoirs* into English in 1773. As co-founder of the Humane Society, he prepared the Society's first six 'Annual Reports'.

[43] A London physician who had already been giving personal rewards for heroic rescues of apparent drowning victims before he joined with Cogan and others to found the

gentlemen proposed a plan for a similar institution in these kingdoms. They were soon enabled to form a Society for this excellent purpose. The plan is this:

I. The Society will publish, in the most extensive manner possible, the proper methods of treating persons in such circumstances.

II. They will distribute a premium of two guineas among the first persons who 5 attempt to recover anyone taken out of the water as dead. And this reward will be given even if the attempt is unsuccessful, provided it has been pursued two hours, according to the method laid down by the Society.

III. They will distribute a premium of four guineas where the person is restored to life.   10

IV. They will give one guinea to any that admits the body into his house without delay, and furnishes the necessary accommodations.

V. A number of medical gentlemen, living near the places where these disasters commonly happen, will give their assistance gratis.

(II). Such was the *rise* of this admirable institution. With what 15 success it has been attended is the point which I purpose in the next place very briefly to consider.

And it must be allowed to be not only far greater than those who despised it had imagined, but greater than the most sanguine expectations of the gentlemen who were immediately engaged in 20 it.

In the short space from its first establishment in May 1774, to the end of December, eight persons seemingly dead were restored to life.

In the year 1775 forty-seven were restored to life; thirty-two of 25 them by the direct encouragement and assistance of the gentlemen of this Society, and the rest by medical gentlemen and others in consequence of their method of treatment being generally known.

In the year 1776 forty-one persons were restored to life by the 30 assistance of this Society. And eleven cases of those who had been restored elsewhere were communicated to them.

So the number of lives preserved and restored in two years and an half since their first institution amounts to one hundred and seven! Add to these those that have been since restored, and out 35 of two hundred and eighty-four persons who were dead to all appearance no less than an hundred and fifty-seven have been restored to life! Such is the *success* which has attended them in so short a time! Such a blessing has the gracious providence of God given to this infant undertaking![44]   40

Humane Society. He long served it as Registrar; cf. his *Address on Premature Death and Premature Interment*, 1777.

[44] Cf. *Report of the Society* (1776), p. vii.

(III).1. It remains only to show the *excellency* of it. And this may appear from one single consideration. This institution unites together in one all the various acts of mercy. The several works of charity mentioned above are all contained in this. It comprises all corporal (if I may so speak) and all spiritual benefits—all the instances of kindness which can be shown either to the bodies or souls of men. To show this beyond all contradiction there needs no studied eloquence, no rhetorical colouring, but simply and nakedly to relate the thing as it is.

2. The thing attempted, and not only attempted but actually performed (so has the goodness of God prospered the labours of these lovers of mankind!), is no less, in a qualified sense, than restoring life to the dead! Is it any wonder then that the generality of men should at first ridicule such an undertaking? That they should imagine the persons who aimed at any such thing must be utterly out of their senses? Indeed one of old said, 'Why should it be thought a thing incredible with you that God should raise the dead?'[45] Cannot he who bestowed life at first just as well bestow it again? But it may well be thought a thing incredible that *man* should raise the dead! For no human power can create life. And what human power can restore it? Accordingly, when our Lord (whom the Jews at that time supposed to be a mere man) came to the house of Jairus in order to raise his daughter from the dead, upon the first intimation of his design 'they laughed him to scorn'.[46] 'The maid', said he, 'is not dead, but sleepeth'[47]—'this is rather to be called sleep than death, seeing her life is not at an end; but I will quickly awaken her out of this sleep.'

3. However, it is certain she was really dead, and so beyond all power but that of the Almighty. But see what power God has now given to man![48] (To his name be all the praise!) See with what wisdom he has endued these sons of mercy! Teaching them to stop the parting soul, to arrest the spirit just quitting the breathless clay, and taking wing for eternity! Who hath seen such a thing? Who hath heard such things? Who hath read them in the annals of antiquity? Sons of men, 'can these dry bones live?'[49] Can

[45] Acts 26:8. Cf. No. 116, 'What is Man? Ps. 8:4', §12, on the point of body-soul dualism; see also No. 41, *Wandering Thoughts*, III.5 and n.
[46] Matt. 9:24.
[47] *Ibid.*
[48] See Matt. 9:8.
[49] Ezek. 37:3.

this motionless heart beat again? Can this clotted blood flow any more? Can these dry, stiff vessels open, to give it passage? Can this cold flesh resume its native warmth, or those eyes again see the sun? Surely these are such things (might one not almost say, such miracles?) as neither we of the present generation, nor our 5 fathers had known!

4. Consider, I entreat you, how many miracles of mercy (so to speak) are contained in one! That poor man, who was lately numbered with the dead, by the care and pains of these messengers of God again breathes the vital air, opens his eyes, 10 and stands upon his feet. He is restored to his rejoicing family, to his wife, to his (late) helpless children, that he may again by his honest labour provide them with all the necessaries of life. See now what ye have done, ye ministers of mercy! Behold the fruit of your labour of love! Ye have been an husband to the widow, a 15 father to the fatherless. And hereby ye have given meat to the hungry, drink to the thirsty, clothes to the naked. For hungry, thirsty, and naked these little ones must have been had not you restored him that prevents it. You have more than relieved; you have prevented that sickness which might naturally have arisen 20 from their want of sufficient food to eat, or raiment to put on. You have hindered those orphans from wandering up and down, not having a place where to lay their head. Nay, and very possibly you have prevented some of them from being lodged in a dreary, comfortless prison. 25

5. So great, so comprehensive is the mercy which you have shown to the bodies of your fellow-creatures! But why should their souls be left out of the account? How great are the benefits you have conferred on these also! The husband has now again an opportunity of assisting his wife in things of the greatest moment. 30 He may now again strengthen her hands in God, and help her to run with patience the race that is set before her.[50] He may again join with her in instructing their children, and training them up in the way wherein they should go;[51] who may live to be a comfort to their aged parents, and useful members of the community. 35

6. Nay, it may be you have snatched the poor man himself, not only from the jaws of death, but from sinking lower than the waters, from the jaws of everlasting destruction. It cannot be

[50] See Heb. 12:1.
[51] See Prov. 22:6.

doubted but some of those whose lives you have restored, although they had been before without God in the world, will remember themselves, and not only with their lips, but in their lives, show forth his praise.[52] It is highly probable some of these
5 (as 'one' out of the 'ten lepers') will 'return and give thanks to God',[53] real, lasting thanks, by devoting themselves to his honourable service.

7. It is remarkable that several of those whom you have brought back from the margin of the grave were intoxicated at the very
10 time when they dropped into the water. And at that very instant (which is frequently the case) they totally lost their senses. Here therefore was no place for, no possibility of, repentance. They had not time, they had not sense, so much as to cry out, 'Lord, have mercy!' So they were sinking through the mighty waters into
15 the pit of destruction![54] And these instruments of divine mercy plucked them at once out of the water and out of the fire! By the same act delivered them from temporal and from eternal death!

8. Nay, one poor sinner (let it never be forgotten!) was just coming down from the ship when (overtaken by the justice and
20 mercy of God) her foot slipped and she fell into the river. Instantly her senses were lost, so that she could not call upon God. Yet he had not forgotten her. He sent those who delivered her from death; at least, from the death of the body. And who knows but she may lay it to heart, and turn from the error of her
25 ways? Who knows but she may be saved from the second death,[55] and with her deliverers 'inherit the kingdom'?[56]

9. One point more deserves to be particularly remarked. Many of those who have been restored to life (no less than eleven out of the fourteen that were saved in a few months) were in the number
30 of those that are a reproach to our nation—wilful self-murderers. As many of the desperate men who attempt this horrid crime are men who have had a liberal education, 'tis pity but they would consider those fine words, not of a poor narrow-souled Christian, but of a generous heathen, nay a Roman! Let them calmly
35 consider that beautiful passage:

[52] See BCP, Thanksgivings, A General Thanksgiving: 'And, we beseech thee, give us that due sense of all thy mercies, that our hearts may be unfeignedly thankful, and that we show forth thy praise, not only with our lips, but in our lives . . . .'
[53] Cf. Luke 17:15, 16.
[54] See Ps. 55:23 (AV).
[55] See Rev. 2:11.
[56] Matt. 25:34, etc.

Proxima deinde tenent maesti loca, qui sibi letum
Insontes perperere manu, lucemque perosi
Projecere animas. Quam vellent aethere in alto
Nunc et pauperiem, et duros perferre labores!
Fata obstant, tristique palus innabilis unda   5
Alligat, et novies[57] *Styx interfusa coercet.*[a]

Fata obstant![58] But in favour of many we see God has overruled
fate. They are brought back over the unnavigable river.[59] They do
behold the upper skies. They see the light of the sun. O let them
see the light of thy countenance! And let them so live their few   10
remaining days on earth that they may live with thee for ever!

III.1. Permit me now to make a short application. But to whom
should I direct this? Are there any here who are unhappily
prejudiced against that revelation which breathes nothing but
benevolence? Which contains the richest display of God's love to   15
man that ever was made from the foundation of the world? Yet
even to *you* I would address a few words; for if you are not
Christians, you are men. You too are susceptible of kind
impressions; you have the feelings of humanity. Has not your
heart too glowed at that noble sentiment (worthy the heart and the 20
lips of the highest Christian)

Homo sum: humani nihil a me alienum puto![60]

Have not you also sympathized with the afflicted? How many
times have you been pained at human misery? When you have

---

[a]
> Then crowds succeed, who, prodigal of breath,
> Themselves anticipate the doom of death;
> Though free from guilt, they cast their lives away,
> And sad and sullen hate the golden day.
> O with what joy the wretches now would bear
> Pain, toil, and woe, to breathe the vital air!
> In vain! By fate for ever are they bound
> And Styx with nine wide channels roars around!
> Mr. Pitt's Virgil.

[Virgil, *Aeneid*, vi.435-40. The translation of the *Aeneid* by Christopher Pitt (1699–1748) was published in 1740. For the last two lines, cf. also *Georgics*, iv.479-80: '*Tardaque palus inamabilis unda alligat et noviens Styx interfusa coercet.*']

---

[57] Virgil has '*tristisque*', '*inamabilis*' ('revolting') and '*noviens*'. Wesley's '*innabilis unda*' ('the waters that cannot be swum in') is an interjection from Ovid, *Metamorphoses*, i.16.
[58] 'The Fates oppose.' See Virgil, *Aeneid*, vi.439, quoted above, and cf. iv.440.
[59] I.e., the Styx.
[60] Terence, *The Self-Tormentor*, 77 (I.i.25): 'I am a man: nothing that partakes of

beheld a scene of deep distress, has not your soul melted within
you?

> And now and then a sigh you stole,
> And tears began to flow.[61]

5 But is it easy for anyone to conceive a scene of deeper distress
than this? Suppose you are standing by just when the messenger
comes in, and the message is delivered: 'I am sorry to tell
you—but you must know it—your husband is no more. He was
making haste out of the vessel, and his foot slipped . . . . It is
10 true, after a time his body was found. But there it lies, without any
signs of life.' In what a condition are now both the mother and the
children? Perhaps for a while stupid, overwhelmed, silent; staring
at each other; then bursting out into loud and bitter lamentation!
Now is the time to help them; by assisting those who make it their
15 business so to do. Now let nothing hinder you from improving the
glorious opportunity. Restore the husband to his disconsolate
wife, the father to his weeping children! It is true you cannot do
this in person; you cannot be upon the spot. But you may do it in
an effectual manner by assisting those that are. You may now by
20 your generous contribution *send* them the help which you cannot
personally give. O shut not up your bowels of compassion towards
them.[62] Now open your hearts and your hands! If you have much,
give plenteously! If not, give a little, with a willing mind!
   2. To you who believe the Christian revelation I may speak in a
25 still stronger manner. You believe your blessed Master 'left you
an example, that you might tread in his steps'.[63] Now you know his
whole life was one labour of love. You know how he 'went about
doing good',[64] and that without intermission, declaring to all, 'My
Father worketh hitherto, and I work.'[65] Is not that then the
30 language of your heart:

humanity is a matter of indifference to me.' Wesley used this quotation as a motto for *A
Letter to a Friend Concerning Tea* (1748), and for the 8th (1759) and subsequent edns. of
Primitive Physick. Steele, *The Spectator*, No. 502, Oct. 6, 1712, wrote that Terence's play 'is
from beginning to the end a perfect picture of humane life.'
   [61] Cf. Dryden, 'Alexander's Feast', 87-88:

> And, now and then, a sigh he stole,
> And tears began to flow.

   [62] See 1 John 3:17.
   [63] Cf. 1 Pet. 2:21.
   [64] Acts 10:38.   [65] John 5:17.

Thy mind throughout my life be shown,
While listening to the wretch's cry,
The widow's and the orphan's groan,
On mercy's wings I swiftly fly,
The poor and helpless to relieve;   5
My life, my all, for them to give.[66]

Occasions of doing this can never be wanting; for 'the poor ye have always with you.'[67] But what a peculiar opportunity does the solemnity of this day furnish you with of 'treading in his steps', after a manner which you did not before conceive? Did he say to 10 the poor, afflicted parent (doubtless to the surprise of many) 'weep not'?[68] And did he surprise them still more when he stopped her flowing tears by restoring life to her dead son, and 'delivering him to his mother'?[69] Did he (notwithstanding all that 'laughed him to scorn')[70] restore to life the daughter of Jairus? How many 15 things of a nearly resembling sort,

If human we may liken to divine,[71]

have been done, and continue to be done daily by these lovers of mankind. Let everyone then be ambitious of having a share in this glorious work! Let everyone (in a stronger sense than Mr. 20 Herbert meant)

Join hands with God, to make a poor man live.[72]

By your generous assistance be ye partakers of their work, and partakers of their joy!

3. To you I need add but one word more. Remember (what was 25 spoken at first) the solemn declaration of him whose ye are, and whom ye serve, coming in the clouds of heaven![73] While you are

---

[66] Charles Wesley, *Scripture Hymns* (1762), II.380, on Jas.1:27 (*Poet. Wks.*, XIII.167); cf. No. 59, 'God's Love to Fallen Man', I.9 and n.
[67] Cf. Mark 14:7.
[68] Luke 7:13.
[69] Cf. Luke 7:15.
[70] Luke 8:53.
[71] Cf. Samuel Wesley, Jun., 'On the Death of Mr. Morgan of Christ Church, Oxford', *Poems* (1736), p. 109: 'For human may be liken'd to divine;' cf. also 'The Prisons Open'd', *ibid.*, p. 191: 'If human joys we liken to divine.'
[72] Cf. George Herbert, *The Temple*, 'The Church Porch', ver. 63, l.4:

Join hands with God to make a man to live.

See also *A Plain Account of the People called Methodists* (1749), XV.2.
[73] Matt. 24:30, etc.

promoting this comprehensive charity, which contains feeding the hungry, clothing the naked, lodging the stranger, indeed all good works in one, let those animating words be written on your hearts, and sounding in your ears, 'Inasmuch as ye have done it
5 unto one of the least of these, ye have done it unto me.'[74]

Nov. 21, 1777[75]

---

[74] Matt. 25:40.
[75] Date in *AM* only.

ON PLEASING ALL MEN

AN INTRODUCTORY COMMENT

In this sermon Wesley turns back to the issues of Christian discipline—in this case the crucial distinction in his mind between, on the one hand, 'pleasing all men' with a view to serving their advantage and, on the other hand, all the self-serving arts of flattery. He had long abhorred the universal practice of 'dissimulation',[1] and his antipathies toward what seemed to him the essential hypocrisy of courtly etiquette had grown through the years, reinforced by his own experiences of life among the 'honest poor'. He had come to regard Lord Chesterfield (Philip Dormer Stanhope) as the public impersonation of this spirit of calculated insincerity. His task here, then, is to provide his people with an alternative description of good manners appropriate to their Christian experience of grace.

Wesley's visit to Ireland in the spring and summer of 1787 was unusually extended—from April 5 through July 11. May 20-22 he was in Castlebar, and it was there that he finished this written sermon on Rom. 15:2 (a rare text for him, used five times between 1783 and 1787). As far as one can tell from the Journal *and diaries, there was no particular occasion at the time for such a sermon, and there is nothing about courtesy or dissimulation in his letters of this period. The sermon first appeared in the* Arminian Magazine *in September and October 1787 (X.453-58, 510-14), without a title but numbered as 'Sermon XLI'. It was then promptly included in* SOSO, VIII.113-29.

---

[1] See No. 138A, 'On Dissimulation'; see also No. 24, 'Sermon on the Mount, IV', IV.3 and n.

On Pleasing All Men

Romans 15:2

Let every man please his neighbour for his good to edification.

1. Undoubtedly the duty here prescribed is incumbent on all
5 mankind; at least on every one of those to whom are entrusted the
oracles of God.[1] For it is here enjoined to everyone without
exception that names the name of Christ.[2] And the person whom
everyone is commanded to please is 'his neighbour', that is, every
child of man.[3] Only we are to remember here what the same
10 Apostle speaks upon a similar occasion. 'If it be possible, as much
as lieth in you, live peaceably with all men.'[4] In like manner we are
to please all men, if it be possible, as much as lieth in us. But
strictly speaking it is not possible; it is what no man ever did, nor
ever will perform. But suppose we use our utmost diligence, be
15 the event as it may, we fulfil our duty.[5]

2. We may farther observe in how admirable a manner the
Apostle limits this direction; otherwise, were it pursued without
any limitation, it might produce the most mischievous consequences. We are directed to please them 'for their good'; not
20 barely for the sake of pleasing them, or pleasing ourselves; much
less of pleasing them to their hurt, which is so frequently
done—indeed continually done, by those who do not love their
neighbour as themselves. Nor is it only their temporal good which
we are to aim at in pleasing our neighbour; but what is of infinitely
25 greater consequence; we are to do it 'for their edification'—in
such a manner as may conduce to their spiritual and eternal good.
We are so to please them that the pleasure may not perish in the
using, but may redound to their lasting advantage; may make
them wiser and better, holier and happier, both in time and in
30 eternity.

---

[1] See Rom. 3:2.

[2] See 2 Tim. 2:19.

[3] This definition of neighbour is consistent throughout all of Wesley's writings; cf.
No. 7, 'The Way to the Kingdom', I.8 and n.

[4] Rom. 12:18.

[5] I.e., in the course of doing what 'is in us' as our moral potency (*in se est*).

3. Many are the treatises and discourses which have been published on this important subject. But all of them that I have either seen or heard were miserably defective. Hardly one of them proposed the right end: one and all had some lower design in pleasing men than to save their souls, to build them up in love 5 and holiness. Of consequence they were not likely to propose the right means for the attainment of that end. One celebrated tract of this kind, entitled *The Courtier*,[6] was published in Spain about two hundred years ago, and translated into various languages. But it has nothing to do with edification, and is therefore quite wide of 10 the mark. Another treatise, entitled *The Refined Courtier*,[7] was published in our own country, in the reign of King Charles II, and (as it seems) by a retainer to his court. In this there are several very sensible advices concerning our outward behaviour; and many little improprieties in word or action are observed whereby men 15 displease others without intending it. But this author likewise has no view at all to the spiritual or eternal good of his neighbour. Seventy or eighty years ago another book was printed in London, entitled *The Art of Pleasing*;[8] but as it was wrote in a languid manner and contained only common, trite observations, it was not 20 likely to be of use to men of understanding, and still less to men of piety.

4. But it may be asked, Has not the subject been since treated of by a writer of a very different character? Is it not exhausted by one who was himself a consummate master of the art of pleasing? 25 And who writing to one he tenderly loved, to a favourite son, gives him all the advices which his great understanding, improved by various learning, and the experience of many years, and much converse with all sorts of men, could suggest? I mean, the late

[6] Probably the famous essay in Italian, *Il Cortegiano* (1528), by Baldassar Castiglione (1478–1529). Its first English translation (1561) was by Thomas Hoby.

[7] In both early texts of the sermon the title of this book is given as *The Compleat Courtier*. Wesley, however, corrected it in his own copy to read *The Refined Courtier*. This was an adaptation in English by Nathaniel Walker (1663) from *Il Galatheo* (1559) by Giovanni della Casa (1503–56), Archbishop of Benevento. Wesley was also preparing to publish extracts from Walker in *AM* (1788), XI.27 *et seq.*, and (1789), XII.28 *et seq.*, with a commendatory foreword: 'I read this tract above fifty years ago, and took an extract from it. But I have now made a larger extract, which I recommend to all those that are lovers of common sense. J. W.' He seems not to have known of Richard Graves's complete translation, *Galateo: Or, a Treatise on Politeness and Delicacy of Manners* (1774).

[8] *The Art of Pleasing in Conversation* (1691, 1707), supposedly from the French of Cardinal Richelieu, but actually by one Pierre d'Ortique de Vaumorière; cf. Halkett and Laing, *Anonyma and Pseudonyma, loc. cit.*

Lord Chesterfield,[9] the general darling of all the Irish as well as the English nation.

5. The means of pleasing which this wise and indulgent parent continually and earnestly recommends to his darling child, and 5 on which he doubtless formed both his tempers and outward conduct,

Till death untimely stopped his tuneful tongue,[10]

were, first, *making love* (in the grossest sense) to all the married women whom he conveniently could. (Single women he advises 10 him to refrain from, for fear of disagreeable consequences.) Secondly, constant and careful *dissimulation*, always wearing a mask; trusting no man upon earth so as to let him know his real thoughts, but perpetually seeming to mean what he did not mean, and seeming to be what he was not. Thirdly, well devised *lying* to 15 all sorts of people, speaking what was farthest from his heart; and in particular *flattering* men, women, and children, as the infallible way of pleasing them.[11]

It needs no great art to show that this is not the way to please our neighbour 'for his good', or 'to edification'. I shall endeavour 20 to show that there is a better way of doing it; and indeed a way diametrically opposite to this. It consists,

I. In removing hindrances out of the way, and
II. In using the means that directly tend to this end.

I.1. I advise all that desire to 'please their neighbour for his 25 good to edification', first, to remove all hindrances out of the way; or in other words to avoid everything which tends to displease wise and good men, men of sound understanding and real piety. Now 'cruelty, malice, envy, hatred, and revenge'[12] are displeasing

---

[9] Philip Dormer Stanhope (1694–1773), fourth Earl of Chesterfield, famous Georgian courtier, politician, and wit. His widow published a collection of his *Letters . . . to His Son* in 1774 (2 vols.). Wesley borrowed and read one of the two volumes in 1775, and reacted sharply to Chesterfield's unabashed amorality (JWJ, Oct. 12, 1775); cf. No. 128, 'The Deceitfulness of the Human Heart', II.7. Johnson had an even harsher verdict on the *Letters:* 'They teach the morals of a whore and the manners of a dancing master;' cf. Boswell's *Life* (1957), p. 188.

[10] Pope, 'Epistle to Robert, Earl of Oxford', l.2.

[11] One need not defend Chesterfield's avowed worldliness in order to recognize here a rare instance of Wesley's stooping to an uncharitable caricature; cf. Sir Sidney Lee's memoir in *DNB, loc. cit.*, or better yet, see also the *Letters* themselves as a whole.

[12] Cf. Titus 3:3.

to all wise and good men, to all who are endued with sound understanding and genuine piety. There is likewise another temper, nearly related to these, only in a lower kind, and which is usually found in common life, wherewith men in general are not pleased. We commonly call it *ill nature*. With all possible care 5 avoid all these; nay, and whatever bears any resemblance to them—as sourness, sternness, sullenness, on the one hand; peevishness and fretfulness on the other—if ever you hope to 'please your neighbour for his good to edification'.

2. Next to cruelty, malice, and similar tempers, with the words 10 and actions that naturally spring therefrom, nothing is more disgustful, not only to persons of sense and religion, but even to the generality of men, than pride, haughtiness of spirit, and its genuine fruit, an assuming, arrogant, overbearing behaviour.[13] Even uncommon learning joined with shining talents will not 15 make amends for this; but a man of eminent endowments, if he be eminently haughty, will be despised by many, and disliked by all. Of this the famous Master of Trinity College in Cambridge was a remarkable instance. How few persons of his time had a stronger understanding or deeper learning than Dr. Bentley![14] And yet 20 how few were less beloved! Unless one who was little if at all inferior to him in sense or learning, and equally distant from humility—the author of *The Divine Legation of Moses*.[15] Whoever therefore desires to please his neighbour for his good must take

[13] See Jer. 48:29. Cf. below, II.2; and No. 14, *The Repentance of Believers*, I.3 and n.

[14] Richard Bentley (1662–1742), royal librarian (1696), Master of Trinity (1700), and leader in the restoration of classical learning in England. His popular fame came from a controversy with Charles Boyle (of Christ Church, Oxford) over the 'Letters of Phalaris' (Boyle contending for their authenticity; Bentley denouncing them as forgeries). The dispute ranged Oxford (Francis Atterbury, *et al.*) against Cambridge, and the literary lights (Alexander Pope, *et al.*) against the pedants. Bishop Warburton joined the fray against Bentley, but Bentley's superior scholarship carried the day. However, Bentley's arrogance had found still another outlet in the course of a protracted feud with the Fellows of his college; cf. *DNB* and also Leslie Stephen, *History of English Thought in the Eighteenth Century* (New York, Harcourt, Brace, and World, 1962), I.205.

[15] William Warburton (1698–1779), whose *Divine Legation*, a sprawling dissertation on the development of the belief in a future life in the Old Testament and antiquity, was left unfinished even after forty years (Vol. I was published in 1738). Warburton was also famous for his arrogance and pomp and was constantly embroiled in controversy, including one with Wesley. Cf. *A Letter to the Bishop of Gloucester* (1763), in Vol. 11 of this edn.; see also Nos. 79, 'On Dissipation', §18; and 107, 'On God's Vineyard', I.3, for other references to Warburton. Wesley took quiet satisfaction from Bishop Robert Lowth's masterful critique of Warburton ('A Letter to the . . . Author of "The Divine Legation" ' [1765]). Cf. JWJ, Jan. 9, 1766: 'If anything human could be a cure for pride, surely such a medicine as this would.'

care of splitting upon this rock; otherwise the same pride which impels him to seek the esteem of his neighbour will infallibly hinder his attaining it.

3. Almost as disgustful to the generality of men as *haughtiness*
5 itself is a *passionate* temper and behaviour. Men of a tender disposition are afraid even to converse with persons of this spirit. And others are not fond of their acquaintance, as frequently (perhaps when they expected nothing less) meeting with shocks, which if they bear for the present yet they do not willingly put
10 themselves in the way of meeting with again. Hence passionate men have seldom many friends; at least, not for any length of time. Crowds indeed may attend them for a season, especially when it may promote their interest. But they are usually disgusted one after another, and fall off like leaves in autumn. If therefore
15 you desire lastingly to please your neighbour for his good, by all possible means avoid violent passion.

4. Yea, and if you desire to please, even on this account, take that advice of the Apostle, 'Put away all lying.'[16] It is the remark of an ingenious author that of all vices, *lying* never yet found an
20 apologist, any that would openly plead in its favour, whatever his private sentiments might be. But it should be remembered Mr. Addison went to a better world before Lord Chesterfield's *Letters* were published.[17] Perhaps his apology for it was the best that ever was, or can be made for so bad a cause. But after all the labour he
25 has bestowed thereon, it has only 'semblance of worth, not substance'.[18] It has no solidity in it; it is nothing better than a shining phantom. And as lying can never be commendable or innocent, so neither can it be pleasing; at least when it is stripped of its disguise, and appears in its own shape. Consequently it
30 ought to be carefully avoided by all those who wish to please their neighbour for his good to edification.

5. But is not *flattery*, a man may say, one species of lying? And has not this been allowed in all ages to be the sure means of pleasing? Has not that observation been confirmed by number-
35 less experiments,

---

[16] Cf. Eph. 4:25.

[17] Addison died in 1719; Chesterfield's *Letters to His Son* were published in 1774; no such quotation has yet been found in Addison's prose or poetry, though Addison's disdain for lying is evident enough, as in *The Spectator*, Nos. 352, 357, 505. Cf. Wesley's early sermon, No. 138A, 'On Dissimulation', I.3: 'So very generally is dissimulation despised that it never yet has found a defender;' see also No. 111, *National Sins and Miseries*, II.2.

[18] Milton, *Paradise Lost*, i.529.

Obsequium amicos, veritas odium parit[19]—

'flattery creates friends, plain-dealing enemies'? Has not a late witty writer,[20] in his *Sentimental Journey*, related some striking instances of this? I answer, It is true. Flattery is pleasing for a while, and that not only to weak minds; as the desire of praise,[21] 5 whether deserved or undeserved, is planted in every child of man. But it is pleasing only for a while. As soon as the mask drops off, as soon as it appears that the speaker meant nothing by his soft words, we are pleased no longer. Every man's own experience teaches him this. And we all know that if a man continues to flatter 10 after his insincerity is discovered it is disgustful, not agreeable. Therefore even this fashionable species of lying is to be avoided by all that are desirous of pleasing their neighbour to his lasting advantage.

6. Nay, whoever desires to do this must remember that not only 15 *lying*, in every species of it, but even *dissimulation* (which is not the same with lying, though nearly related to it) is displeasing to men of understanding,[22] though they have not religion. Terence represents even an old heathen, when it was imputed to him, as answering with indignation,   20

---

[19] Terence, *The Lady of Andros*, 68.

[20] Laurence Sterne (1713–68), whose fame for whimsy and satire (*Tristram Shandy*, 1760) overshadowed the fact that he was also a rural parson (Sutton-in-the-Forest) and prebend of York Minster. His *Sentimental Journey Through France and Italy* (1768) was a glorification of a rather 'pedestrian episode of travel' (*DNB*). Wesley looked into it casually in 1772, deplored Sterne's usage of 'sentimental' and concluded: 'For oddity, uncouthness, and unlikeness to all the world beside, I suppose the writer is without a rival' (JWJ, Feb. 11, 1772). Actually, Sterne was very much in vogue, as one may see in *The Correspondence of Samuel Richardson*, ed., Anna Laetitia Barbauld (London, 1804), IV.282, where Lady Bradshaigh inquires of the novelist: 'What, in your opinion, is the meaning of the word "sentimental", so much in vogue among the polite? Everything clever and agreeable is comprehended in that word; but I am convinced a wrong interpretation is given, because it is impossible everything clever and agreeable can be as common as this word. I am frequently astonished to hear such a one is a "sentimental" man; we were a "sentimental" party; I have been taking a "sentimental" walk. And that I might be reckoned a little in the fashion, and, as I thought, show them the proper use of the word, about six weeks ago, I declared I had just received a "sentimental" letter.'

[21] Cf. No. 14, *The Repentance of Believers*, I.7 and n.

[22] Chesterfield had drawn a sharp distinction between *dis*simulation and simulation, as in his letter of May 22, 1749 (*Letters*, I.419): 'It may be objected that I am now recommending dissimulation to you; I both own and justify it. . . . I go still further and say that without some dissimulation no business can be carried on at all. It is *simulation* that is false, mean, and criminal. . . . As [Lord Bacon] says, dissimulation is only to hide our own cards, whereas simulation is put on in order to look into other people's.'

Simulare non est meum[23]—

dissimulation is no part of my character. Guile, subtlety, cunning, the whole art of deceiving, by whatever terms it is expressed, is not accounted an accomplishment by wise men; but is indeed an abomination to them. And even those who practise it most, who are the greatest artificers of fraud, are not pleased with it in other men, neither are fond of conversing with those that practise it on themselves. Yea, the greatest deceivers are greatly displeased at those that play their own arts upon them.

10   II. Now if cruelty, malice, envy, hatred, revenge, ill nature; if pride and haughtiness; if irrational anger; if lying and dissimulation, together with guile, subtlety, and cunning, are all and every one displeasing to all men, especially to wise and good men, we may easily gather from hence what is the sure way to please them for their good to edification. Only we are to remember that there are those in every time and place whom we must not expect to please. We must not therefore be surprised when we meet with men who are not to be pleased any way. It is now as it was of old when our Lord himself complained: 'Whereunto shall I liken the men of this generation? They are like unto children sitting in the market-place and saying to each other, We have piped unto you, but ye have not danced: we have mourned unto you, but ye have not wept.'[24] But leaving these froward ones to themselves, we may reasonably hope to please others by a careful and steady observation of the few directions following.

1. First, let *love* not visit you as a transient guest, but be the constant ruling temper of your soul. See that your heart be filled at all times and on all occasions with real, undissembled benevolence, not to those only that love *you*, but to every soul of man. Let it pant in your heart, let it sparkle in your eyes, let it shine on all your actions. Whenever you open your lips, let it be with love, and let there be in your tongue the law of kindness.[25]

---

[23] Cf. Terence, *The Self-Tormentor*, 783-84; Wesley here has conflated separate lines from both Chremes and Syrus:

> Syrus: *Non ego dicebam in perpetuam ut illam illi dares,*
> *verum ut simulares.*
> Chremes: *Non meast simulatio. . . .*

(Syrus: '. . . only that you pretend'. Chremes: 'I'm not given to pretending.')
[24] Cf. Luke 7:31-32.   [25] See Prov. 31:26.

Your word will then distil as the rain, and as the dew upon the tender herb.[26] Be not straitened or limited in your affection, but let it embrace every child of man. Everyone that is born of a woman has a claim to your goodwill. You owe this not to some, but to all. And let all men know that you desire both their temporal and eternal happiness as sincerely as you do your own.

2. Secondly, if you would please your neighbour for his good, study to be *lowly* in heart.[27] Be little and vile in your own eyes, in honour preferring others before yourself. Be deeply sensible of your own weaknesses, follies, and imperfections; as well as of the sin remaining in your heart, and cleaving to all your words and actions. And let this spirit appear in all you speak or do: 'be clothed with humility.'[28] Reject with horror that favourite maxim of the old heathen, sprung from the bottomless pit,[29]

Tanti eris aliis, quanti tibi fueris[30]—   15

'the more you value yourself, the more others will value you.' Not so. On the contrary, both God and man 'resist the proud': and as 'God giveth grace to the humble',[31] so humility, not pride, recommends us to the esteem and favour of men, especially those that fear God.   20

3. If you desire to please your neighbour for his good to edification you should, thirdly, labour and pray that you may be *meek*, as well as lowly in heart. Labour to be of a calm, dispassionate temper, *gentle* towards all men. And let the gentleness of your disposition appear in the whole tenor of your conversation.[32] Let all your words and all your actions be regulated thereby. Remember likewise that advice of St. Peter. As an addition to your gentleness, 'be merciful; be courteous; be pitiful;'[33] be tenderly compassionate to all that are in distress, to all that are under any affliction of mind, body, or estate. Let   30

---

[26] See Deut. 32:2.   [27] Matt. 11:29.   [28] 1 Pet. 5:5.
[29] Cf. Rev. 9:11; 20:1; cf. also No. 32, 'Sermon on the Mount, XII', I.7 and n.
[30] Attributed to Cicero by James Wood, *Dictionary of Quotations* (1899), without citation; cf. W. Gurney Benham's *Book of Quotations*, following Wood. The text, as here, does not appear in the Loeb texts of Cicero. Cf., however, *De Amicitia*, xvi.56: *'quanti quisque se ipse facit, tanti fiat ab amicis'* ('whatever value a man places upon himself, the same value should be placed upon him by his friends'). A Greek version appears in Musonius Rufus, *Strobaeus, Florilegium*, XXXI.6.
[31] Cf. Jas. 4:6; 1 Pet. 5:5.
[32] Cf. No. 10, 'The Witness of the Spirit, I', II.6 and n.
[33] Cf. 1 Pet. 3:8.

The various scenes of human woe
Excite your softest sympathy![34]

Weep with them that weep.[35] If you can do no more, at least mix
your tears with theirs; and give them healing words, such as may
5 calm their minds, and mitigate their sorrows. But if you can, if you
are able to give them actual assistance, let it not be wanting. Be as
eyes to the blind, as feet to the lame,[36] a husband to the widow,
and a father to the fatherless.[37] This will greatly tend to conciliate
the affection, and to give a profitable pleasure not only to those
10 who are immediate objects of your compassion but to others
likewise that 'see your good works, and glorify your Father which
is in heaven'.[38]

4. And while you are *pitiful* to the afflicted, see that you are
courteous toward all men. It matters not in this respect whether
15 they are high or low, rich or poor, superior or inferior to you. No,
nor even whether good or bad, whether they fear God or not.
Indeed the *mode* of showing your courtesy may vary, as Christian
prudence will direct. But the thing itself is due to all: the lowest
and worst have a claim to our courtesy. But what is courtesy? It
20 may either be inward or outward; either a temper or a mode of
behaviour. Such a mode of behaviour as naturally springs from
courtesy of heart. Is this the same with good breeding or
politeness (which seems to be only a high degree of good
breeding)? Nay, good breeding is chiefly the fruit of education;
25 but education cannot give courtesy of heart. Mr. Addison's
well-known definition of politeness seems rather to be a
definition of this, 'A constant desire of pleasing all men,
appearing through the whole conversation.'[39] Now this may
subsist, even in a high degree, where there has been no advantage
30 of education. I have seen as real courtesy in an Irish cabin as could
be found in St. James's or the Louvre.[40]

---

[34] Cf. Charles Wesley, *Hymns of Intercession for all Mankind,* Bristol (1758), p. 3 (*Poet. Wks.,* VI.111). In *SOSO,* VIII.126, 'your' is corrected to 'our' (as in Charles's orig. text).
[35] Rom. 12:15.
[36] See Job 29:15.
[37] See Ps. 68:5.
[38] Matt. 5:16.
[39] Cf. *The Spectator,* No. 386, May 23, 1712; however, Steele was the author of this number, not Addison. See No. 22, 'Sermon on the Mount, II', III.8 and n.
[40] The Louvre in Wesley's time was a royal palace (as St. James's was), not a museum; the contrast here, then, is between the Irish *cabin* and the English and French *courts.*

5. Shall we endeavour to go a little deeper, to search into the foundation of this matter? What is the source of that desire to please which we term courtesy? Let us look attentively into our heart, and we shall soon find the answer. The same Apostle that teaches us to 'be courteous' teaches us to 'honour all men'.[41] And his Master teaches me to love all men. Join these together, and what will be the effect? A poor wretch cries to me for an alms: I look and see him covered with dirt and rags. But through these I see one that has an immortal spirit, made to know and love and dwell with God to eternity: I honour him for his Creator's sake. I see through all these rags that he is purpled over with the blood of Christ.[42] I love him for the sake of his Redeemer. The courtesy therefore which I feel and show toward him is a mixture of the honour and love which I bear to the offspring of God, the purchase of his Son's blood, and the candidate for immortality.[43] This courtesy let us feel and show toward all men; and we shall please all men to their edification.

6. Once more. Take all proper opportunities of *declaring* to others the *affection* which you really feel for them. This may be done with such an air and in such a manner as is not liable to the imputation of flattery. And experience shows that honest men are pleased by this, full as much as knaves are by flattery. Those who are persuaded that your expressions of goodwill toward them are the language of your heart will be as well satisfied with them, as with the highest encomiums which you could pass upon them. You may judge them by yourselves, by what you feel in your own breast. You like to be honoured; but had you not rather be beloved?

7. Permit me to add one advice more. If you would please all men for their good, at all events *speak* to all men the very *truth* from your heart. When you speak, open the window of your breast:[44] let the words be the very picture of your heart. In all company and on all occasions be a man of *veracity*. Nay, be not content with bare veracity; but 'in simplicity and godly sincerity have all your conversation in the world',[45] as 'an Israelite indeed, in whom is no guile'.[46]

---

[41] 1 Pet. 3:8; 2:17.
[42] See Edmund Spenser, *Faerie Queene*, Bk. IV, Canto 7, st. 6, l. 6: 'Full dreadfully empurpled all with blood.'
[43] Cf. No. 98, 'On Visiting the Sick', III.7 and n.
[44] See No. 4, *Scriptural Christianity*, III.5 and n.
[45] Cf. 2 Cor. 1:12.   [46] John 1:47.

8. To sum up all in one word—if you would please men, please God! Let truth and love possess your whole soul. Let them be the springs of all your affections, passions, tempers; the rule of all your thoughts. Let them inspire all your discourse; continually 5 seasoned with that salt,[47] and meet to 'minister grace to the hearers'.[48] Let all your actions be wrought in love. Never 'let mercy or truth forsake thee: bind them about thy neck.' Let them be open and conspicuous to all; and 'write them on the table of thy heart. So shalt thou find favour and good understanding in the 10 sight of God and man.'[49]

Castlebar, May 22, 1787[50]

---

[47] See Col. 4:6.
[48] Eph. 4:29.
[49] Cf. Prov. 3:3-4.
[50] Place and date as in *AM*.

THE DUTY OF CONSTANT COMMUNION

AN INTRODUCTORY COMMENT

*The most celebrated Anglican liturgist of his time was the Nonjuror,
Robert Nelson (1656–1715), whose* Companion for the Festivals
and Fasts of the Church of England . . . *(1704) had promptly
become a classic, with ten thousand copies printed and sold in its first five
years and more than thirty editions within the century. In 1707 he had
published an enlargement (and revision) of his* Companion*'s chapter
on 'Vigils' under the title,* The Great Duty of Frequenting the
Christian Sacrifice.

*Wesley had found Nelson a most helpful mentor in many ways; in
1732 he had written out an extract of* The Great Duty . . . , *for use
with his own pupils at Lincoln College. This extract has survived and
may be seen in Volume 20 of the Colman Collection, now in the
Methodist Archives in the John Rylands Library of the University of
Manchester. In his extract Wesley actually rewrote a good deal of
Nelson's text. Fifty-five years later, he proceeded to abridge that extract
(and to revise it still further); he then presented the result as an 'original
sermon' in the* Arminian Magazine *for May and June 1787
(X.229-36, 290-95). It has no title but is numbered as 'Sermon
XXXIX'—and also has a heading 'To the Reader', claiming the text as
Wesley's own. This, however, raises a nice question, since there is too
much of Nelson here for it to be acknowledged as truly 'original' and too
much of Wesley for it to be labelled as wholly 'borrowed' (as in the case of
the sermons 'collected' from William Tilly, Benjamin Calamy, et al.; see
Appendix, Vol. 4). The shift of emphasis from Nelson's 'frequenting the
Christian sacrifice' to Wesley's 'constant communion' seems to have
been suggested by a tract of Arthur Bury's, the controversial rector of
neighbouring Exeter College, entitled* The Constant Communicant
*(1681); the Holy Club had studied this in January 1734. When Wesley
decided to include the* Magazine *revision of his earlier revision of
Nelson in* SOSO, *VIII.131-52, he gave it its present title and repeated
the earlier heading, 'To the Reader'.*

*What may be the most noteworthy thing about this sermon is that it
represents Wesley's fullest and most explicit statement of his eucharistic*

427

doctrine and praxis, and yet his untroubled reliance upon a classic expression of the 'catholic tradition' in current Anglican doctrine at that time.

The Duty of Constant Communion

To the Reader

The following discourse was written above five and fifty years ago, for the use of my pupils at Oxford. I have added very little, but retrenched much; as I then used more words than I do now. But I thank God I have not yet seen cause to alter my sentiments in any point which is therein delivered. J.W.

Luke 22:19

Do this in remembrance of me.

10   It is no wonder that men who have no fear of God should never think of doing this. But it is strange that it should be neglected by any that do fear God, and desire to save their souls. And yet nothing is more common. One reason why any neglect it is, they are so much afraid of 'eating and drinking unworthily'[1] that they
15   never think how much greater the danger is when they do not eat or drink it at all. That I may do what I can to bring these well-meaning men to a more just way of thinking, I shall,

First, show that it is the duty of every Christian to receive the Lord's Supper as often as he can; and secondly, answer some
20   objections.

I. I am to show that it is the duty of every Christian to receive the Lord's Supper as often as he can.

1. The first reason why it is the duty of every Christian so to do is because it is a plain command of Christ. That this is his
25   command appears from the words of the text, 'Do this in remembrance of me:' by which, as the Apostles were obliged to bless, break, and give the bread to all that joined with them in

---

[1] Cf. 1 Cor. 11:29.

those holy things, so were all Christians obliged to receive those signs of Christ's body and blood. Here therefore the bread and wine are commanded to be received, in remembrance of his death, to the end of the world. Observe, too, that this command was given by our Lord when he was just laying down his life for our sakes.[2] They are therefore, as it were, his dying words to all his followers.

2. A second reason why every Christian should do this as often as he can is because the benefits of doing it are so great to all that do it in obedience to him; namely, the forgiveness of our past sins and the present strengthening and refreshing of our souls. In this world we are never free from temptations. Whatever way of life we are in, whatever our condition be, whether we are sick or well, in trouble or at ease, the enemies of our souls are watching to lead us into sin. And too often they prevail over us. Now when we are convinced of having sinned against God, what surer way have we of procuring pardon from him than the 'showing forth the Lord's death',[3] and beseeching him, for the sake of his Son's sufferings, to blot out all our sins?

3. The grace of God given herein confirms to us the pardon of our sins by enabling[4] us to leave them. As our bodies are strengthened by bread and wine, so are our souls by these tokens of the body and blood of Christ. This is the food of our souls: this gives strength to perform our duty, and leads us on to perfection. If therefore we have any regard for the plain command of Christ,[5] if we desire the pardon of our sins, if we wish for strength to believe, to love and obey God, then we should neglect no opportunity of receiving the Lord's Supper. Then we must never turn our backs on the feast which our Lord has prepared for us. We must neglect no occasion which the good providence of God affords us for this purpose. This is the true rule—so often are we to receive as God gives us opportunity. Whoever therefore does not receive, but goes from the holy table when all things are prepared, either does not understand his duty or does not care for the dying command of his Saviour,[6] the forgiveness of his sins, the strengthening of his soul, and the refreshing it with the hope of glory.

---

[2] Nelson's phrase for 'our Lord' is 'our Best Friend'.   [3] Cf. 1 Cor. 11:26.
[4] *SOSO*, VIII.135, revised this to 'and enables us'.
[5] Nelson's phrase here is 'our Saviour'.
[6] Nelson's phrase, 'for the plain command of his dying Saviour'.

4. Let everyone therefore who has either any desire to please God, or any love of his own soul, obey God and consult the good of his own soul by communicating every time he can; like the first Christians, with whom the Christian sacrifice was a constant part
5　of the Lord's day's service. And for several centuries they received it almost every day. Four times a week always, and every saint's day beside. Accordingly those that joined in the prayers of the faithful never failed to partake of the blessed sacrament. What opinion they had of any who turned his back upon it we may learn
10　from that ancient canon, 'If any believer join in the prayers of the faithful, and go away without receiving the Lord's Supper, let him be excommunicated, as bringing confusion into the church of God.'[7]

5. In order to understand the nature of the Lord's Supper, it
15　would be useful carefully to read over those passages in the Gospel and in the first Epistle to the Corinthians which speak of the institution of it. Hence we learn that the design of this sacrament is the continual remembrance of the death of Christ, by eating bread and drinking wine, which are the outward signs of
20　the inward grace,[8] the body and blood of Christ.

6. It is highly expedient for those who purpose to receive this, whenever their time will permit, to prepare themselves for this solemn ordinance by self-examination and prayer. But this is not absolutely necessary. And when we have not time for it, we should
25　see that we have the habitual preparation which is absolutely necessary, and can never be dispensed with on any account or any occasion whatever. This is, first, a full *purpose* of heart to keep all the commandments of God. And secondly, a sincere *desire* to receive all his promises.

30　II. I am, in the second place, to answer the common objections against constantly receiving the Lord's Supper.

---

[7] Cf. Canon II of the Dedication Council of Antioch ('*in Encaeniis*', A.D. 341): 'All who enter the Church of God and hear the Holy Scriptures but do not communicate with the people in the prayers, or who turn away, by reason of some disorder, from partaking of the Holy Supper, are to be cast out of the Church . . . as those who bring confusion into the order of the Church.' This is a paraphrase of the eighth and ninth of the so-called 'Apostolic Canons'. Cf. Thomas MacNally, *The Apostolical Canons* . . . (1867); see also Henry R. Percival, *NPNF, II,* XIV. 103-9; and K. J. Hefele, tr. H. Leclercq, *Histoire des Conciles* . . . (1907), I, Pt. 2, pp. 702-15 (a full text of Canon II is on p. 715); see also No. 27, 'Sermon on the Mount, VII', III.7.

[8] See BCP, Catechism.

1. I say 'constantly' receiving. For as to the phrase of 'frequent communion',[9] it is absurd to the last degree. If it means anything less than constant it means more than can be proved to be the duty of any man. For if we are not obliged to communicate 'constantly', by what argument can it be proved that we are obliged to communicate 'frequently'? Yea, more than once a year, or once in seven years? Or once before we die? Every argument brought for this either proves that we ought to do it *constantly*, or proves nothing at all. Therefore that indeterminate, unmeaning way of speaking ought to be laid aside by all men of understanding.

2. In order to prove that it is our duty to communicate constantly we may observe that the Holy Communion is to be considered either, (1), as a command of God, or (2), as a mercy to man.

First, as a command of God. God, our Mediator and Governor, from whom we have received our life and all things, on whose will it depends whether we shall be perfectly happy or perfectly miserable from this moment to eternity, declares to us that all who obey his commands shall be eternally happy; all who do not shall be eternally miserable. Now one of these commands is, 'Do this in remembrance of me.' I ask then, 'Why do you not do this, when you can do it if you will? When you have an opportunity before you, why do not you obey the command of God?'

3. Perhaps you will say, 'God does not command me to do this *as often as I can;*' that is, the words 'as often as you can' are not added in this particular place. What then? Are we not to obey every command of God as often as we can? Are not all the promises of God made to those, and those only, who 'give all diligence';[10] that is, to those who do all they can to obey his commandments?[11] Our power is the one rule of our duty. Whatever we can do, that we ought. With respect either to this or any other command, he that when he may obey it if he will does not, will have no place in the kingdom of heaven.[12]

[9] A quibble reflecting a conflict between three eucharistic traditions. High-Churchmen such as Nelson (and Samuel Wesley, Sen.) favoured the phrase *'frequent communion'*; Latitudinarians were usually content with the canonical minimum prescribed in 1549 (thrice in a year); the Puritans also communed infrequently but made of it a very solemn occasion, prepared for by earnest self-examination; cf. Isaac Barrow's comments on this question in *Works* (1859), VII.524-27.

[10] Cf. 2 Pet. 1:5.

[11] Cf. No. 25, 'Sermon on the Mount, V', II.2 and n.

[12] The implication here (II.1-3) that Wesley is 'correcting' Nelson is misleading.

4. And this great truth, that we are obliged to keep every command as far as we can, is clearly proved from the absurdity of the contrary opinion; for were we to allow that we are not obliged to obey every commandment of God as often as we can, we have
5 no argument left to prove that any man is bound to obey any command at any time. For instance, should I ask a man why he does not obey one of the plainest commands of God—why, for instance, he does not help his parents —he might answer, 'I will not do it now, but I will at another time.' When that time comes,
10 put him in mind of God's command again and he will say, 'I will obey it some time or other.' Nor is it possible ever to prove that he ought to do it now, unless by proving that he ought to do it as often as he can: and therefore he ought to do it now, because he can if he will.

15   5. Consider the Lord's Supper, secondly, as a mercy from God to man. As God, whose mercy is over all his works,[13] and particularly over the children of men, knew there was but one way for man to be happy like himself, namely, by being like him in holiness; as he knew we could do nothing toward this of
20 ourselves, he has given us certain means of obtaining his help. One of these is the Lord's Supper, which of his infinite mercy he hath given for this very end: that through this means we may be assisted to attain those blessings which he hath prepared for us; that we may obtain holiness on earth and everlasting glory in
25 heaven.

I ask, then, why do you not accept of his mercy as often as ever you can? God now offers you his blessing: why do you refuse it? You have an opportunity of receiving his mercy: why do you not receive it? You are weak: why do not you seize upon every
30 opportunity of increasing your strength? In a word: considering this as a command of God, he that does not communicate as often as he can has no piety; considering it as a mercy, he that does not communicate as often as he can has no wisdom.

6. These two considerations will yield a full answer to all the
35 common objections which have been made against constant

Nelson's phrase (see 4th edn., 1711, pp. 26-36) was 'frequent communion' (rejected by Wesley as 'absurd to the last degree'). But Nelson's point (p. 34) is that Christians ought to receive the Communion as frequently as they have *any* opportunity to do so, and this equals Wesley's rule at the very least. Actually, Nelson had used the terms 'frequent' and 'constant' as interchangeable: '. . . we must *constantly* attend this holy ordinance . . .' (p. 34).
13 Ps. 145:9 (BCP).

communion; indeed to all that ever were or can be made. In truth nothing can be objected against it but upon supposition that at this particular time, either the communion would be no mercy, or I am not commanded to receive it. Nay, should we grant it would be no mercy, that is not enough; for still the other reason would 5 hold: whether it does you any good or none, you are to obey the command of God.

7. However, let us see the particular excuses which men commonly make for not obeying it. The most common is, 'I am *unworthy*; and "he that eateth and drinketh unworthily, eateth and 10 drinketh damnation to himself."[14] Therefore I dare not communicate, lest I should eat and drink my own damnation.'[15]

The case is this. God offers you one of the greatest mercies on this side heaven, and commands you to accept it. Why do not you accept this mercy in obedience to his command? You say, 'I am 15 unworthy to receive it.' And what then? You are unworthy to receive any mercy from God. But is that a reason for refusing all mercy? God offers you a pardon for all your sins. You are unworthy of it, 'tis sure, and he knows it: but since he is pleased to offer it nevertheless, will not you accept of it? He offers to deliver 20 your soul from death. You are unworthy to live. But will you therefore refuse life? He offers to endue your soul with new strength. Because you are unworthy of it, will you deny to take it? What can God himself do for us farther, if we refuse his mercy, even because we are unworthy of it? 25

8. But suppose this were no mercy to us (to suppose which is indeed giving God the lie; saying, that is not good for man which he purposely ordered for his good), still I ask, Why do not you obey God's command? He says, 'Do this.' Why do you not? You answer, 'I am unworthy to do it.' What! Unworthy to obey God? 30 Unworthy to do what God bids you do? Unworthy to obey God's command? What do you mean by this? That those who are unworthy to obey God ought not to obey him? Who told you so? If he were even 'an angel from heaven, let him be accursed'.[16] If you think God himself has told you so by St. Paul, let us hear his 35 words. They are these: 'He that eateth and drinketh unworthily, eateth and drinketh damnation to himself.'[17]

---

[14] 1 Cor. 11:29.
[15] In the BCP (1662), Holy Communion, this point is dwelt on both in the preparatory announcements and in the priest's direct exhortation to the people.
[16] Cf. Gal. 1:8.   [17] 1 Cor. 11:29.

Why, this is quite another thing. Here is not a word said of 'being unworthy' to eat and drink. Indeed he does speak of eating and drinking 'unworthily'; but that is quite a different thing—so he has told us himself. In this very chapter we are told that by
5 eating and drinking unworthily is meant taking the holy sacrament in such a rude and disorderly way that one was 'hungry and another drunken'.[18] But what is that to *you*? Is there any danger of *your* doing so? Of your eating and drinking *thus* 'unworthily'? However unworthy you are to communicate, there
10 is no fear of your communicating thus. Therefore, whatever the punishment is of doing it thus unworthily, it does not concern *you*. You have no more reason from this text to disobey God than if there was no such text in the Bible. If you speak of 'eating and drinking unworthily' in the sense St. Paul uses the words you may
15 as well say, 'I dare not communicate "for fear the church should fall" as for fear I should "eat and drink unworthily".'

9. If then you fear bringing *damnation* on yourself by this, you fear where no fear is. Fear it not for eating and drinking unworthily; for that, in St. Paul's sense, ye cannot do. But I will
20 tell you for what you shall fear damnation: for not eating and drinking at all; for not obeying your Maker and Redeemer; for disobeying his plain command; for thus setting at nought both his mercy and authority. Fear ye this; for hear what his Apostle saith: 'Whosoever shall keep the whole law, and yet offend in one point,
25 is guilty of all.'[a]

10. We see then how weak the objection is, 'I dare not receive,[b] because I am unworthy.' Nor is it any stronger, though the reason why you think yourself unworthy is that you have lately fallen into sin. It is true our Church forbids those 'who have done any
30 grievous crime' to receive without repentance.[19] But all that follows from this is that we should repent before we come; not that we should neglect to come at all.

To say, therefore, that 'a man may turn his back upon the altar because he has lately fallen into sin; that he may impose this
35 penance upon himself', is talking without any warrant from

[a] Jas. 2:10.
[b] The Lord's Supper [an added note in *AM* because this is the opening paragraph in the second instalment of the sermon; it is repeated in *SOSO*, VIII.143].

---

[18] Cf. 1 Cor. 11:21.
[19] Cf. Edmund Gibson, *Codex Juris Ecclesiastici Anglicani* (1713), Canons XXVI and CIX.

Scripture. For where does the Bible teach to atone for breaking one commandment of God by breaking another? What advice is this—'Commit a new act of disobedience, and God will more easily forgive the past'!

11. Others there are who to excuse their disobedience plead 5 that they are unworthy in another sense, that they 'cannot live up to it; they cannot pretend to lead so holy a life as constantly communicating would oblige them to do.' Put this into plain words. I ask: Why do not you accept the mercy which God commands you to accept? You answer, 'Because I cannot live up 10 to the profession I must make when I receive it.' Then it is plain you ought never to receive it at all. For it is no more lawful to promise once what you know you cannot perform than to promise it a thousand times. You know, too, that it is one and the same promise whether you make it every year or every day. You 15 promise to do just as much whether you promise ever so often or ever so seldom.

If therefore you cannot live up to the profession they make who communicate once a week, neither can you come up to the profession you make who communicate once a year. But cannot 20 you, indeed? Then it had been good for you that you had never been born.[20] For all that you profess at the Lord's table you must both profess and keep, or you cannot be saved. For you profess nothing there but this, that you will diligently keep his commandments. And cannot you keep up to this profession? 25 Then you cannot enter into life.

12. Think then what you say, before you say you cannot live up to what is required of constant communicants. This is no more than is required of any communicants, yea, of everyone that has a soul to be saved. So that to say you cannot live up to this is neither 30 better nor worse than renouncing Christianity. It is in effect renouncing your baptism, wherein you solemnly promised to keep all his commandments. You now fly from that profession. You wilfully break one of his commandments, and to excuse yourself say you cannot keep his commandments! Then you 35 cannot expect to receive the promises, which are made only to those that keep them.

13. What has been said on this pretence against constant communion is applicable to those who say the same thing in other

[20] See Mark 14:21.

words: 'We dare not do it, because it requires so perfect an
obedience afterwards as we cannot promise to perform.' Nay, it
requires neither more nor less perfect obedience than you
promised in your baptism. You then undertook to keep the
5 commandments of God by his help, and you promise no more
when you communicate.

But observe upon the whole, this is not so properly an objection
against constantly communicating as against communicating at
all. For if we are not to receive the Lord's Supper till we are
10 worthy of it, it is certain we ought never to receive it.[21]

14. A second objection which is often made against constant
communion is the having so much business as will not allow time
for such a preparation as is necessary thereto. I answer: all the
preparation that is absolutely necessary is contained in those
15 words, 'Repent you truly of your sins past; have faith in Christ our
Saviour'[22] (and observe, that word is not here taken in its highest
sense!); 'amend your lives, and be in charity with all men; so shall
ye be meet partakers of these holy mysteries.' All who are thus
prepared may draw near without fear, and receive the sacrament
20 to their comfort.[23] Now what business can hinder you from being
thus prepared? From repenting of your past sins? From believing
that Christ died to save sinners? From amending your lives, and
being in charity with all men? No business can hinder you from
this, unless it be such as hinders you from being in a state of
25 salvation. If you resolve and design to follow Christ you are fit to
approach the Lord's table. If you do not design this, you are only
fit for the table and company of devils.

15. No business therefore can hinder any man from having that
preparation which alone is necessary, unless it be such as
30 unprepares him for heaven, as puts him out of a state of salvation.
Indeed every prudent man will, when he has time, examine
himself before he receives the Lord's Supper: whether he repents
him truly of his former sins; whether he believes the promises of
God; whether he fully designs to walk in his ways, and be in
35 charity with all men. In this, and in private prayer, he will
doubtless spend all the time he conveniently can. But what is this

---

[21] This paragraph is in the original *AM* text; it was dropped from *SOSO*, VIII, and
subsequent edns. (perhaps as redundant).

[22] Cf. BCP, Communion, Exhortation III.

[23] A paraphrase from 'The Invitation': '. . . draw near with faith, and receive this holy
Sacrament to your comfort . . . .'

to *you* who have not time? What excuse is this for not obeying God? He commands you to come, and prepare yourself by prayer if you have time; if you have not, however, come. Make not reverence to God's command a pretence for breaking it. Do not rebel against him for fear of offending him. Whatever you do or 5 leave undone besides, be sure to do what God bids you do. Examining yourself, and using private prayer, especially before the Lord's Supper, is good. But behold! 'To obey is better than' self-examination, 'and to hearken'[24] than the prayer of an angel.

16. A third objection against constant communion is that it 10 abates our reverence for the sacrament. Suppose it did? What then! Will you thence conclude that you are not to receive it constantly? This does not follow. God commands you, 'Do this.' You may do it now, but will not; and to excuse yourself say, 'If I do it so often, it will abate the reverence with which I do it now.' 15 Suppose it did. Has God ever told you that when the obeying his command abates your reverence to it then you may disobey it? If he has, you are guiltless; if not, what you say is just nothing to the purpose. The law is clear. Either show that the lawgiver makes this exception, or you are guilty before him. 20

17. Reverence for the sacrament may be of two sorts: either such as is owing purely to the newness of the thing, such as men naturally have for anything they are not used to; or such as is owing to our faith, or to the love or fear of God. Now the former of these is not properly a religious reverence, but purely natural. 25 And this sort of reverence for the Lord's Supper the constantly receiving of it must lessen. But it will not lessen the true religious reverence, but rather confirm and increase it.

18. A fourth objection is, 'I have communicated constantly so long, but I have not found the benefit I expected.' This has been 30 the case with many well-meaning persons, and therefore deserves to be particularly considered. And consider this first: whatever God commands us to do we are to do because he commands, whether we feel any benefit thereby or no. Now God commands, 'Do this in remembrance of me.' This therefore we are to do, 35 because he commands, whether we find present benefit thereby or not. But undoubtedly we shall find benefit sooner or later, though perhaps insensibly. We shall be insensibly strengthened, made more fit for the service of God, and more constant in it. At

---

[24] Cf. 1 Sam. 15:22.

least we are kept from falling back, and preserved from many sins and temptations. And surely this should be enough to make us receive this food as often as we can; though we do not presently feel the happy effects of it, as some have done, and we ourselves
5 may when God sees best.

19. But suppose a man has often been at the sacrament, and yet received no benefit. Was it not his own fault? Either he was not rightly prepared, willing to obey all the commands, and to receive all the promises of God; or he did not receive it aright, trusting in
10 God. Only see that you are duly prepared for it, and the oftener you come to the Lord's table the greater benefit you will find there.

20. A fifth objection which some have made against constant communion is that 'the Church enjoins it only three times a year.'
15 The words of the Church are: 'Note, that every parishioner shall communicate at the least three times in the year.'[25] To this I answer, first: What if the Church had not enjoined it at all? Is it not enough that God enjoins it? We obey the Church only for God's sake. And shall we not obey God himself? If then you
20 receive three times a year because the Church commands it, receive every time you can because God commands it. Else your doing the one will be so far from excusing you for not doing the other that your own practice will prove your folly and sin, and leave you without excuse.

25 But, secondly, we cannot conclude from these words that the Church excuses him who receives only thrice a year. The plain sense of them is that he who does not receive thrice at least shall be cast out of the Church. But they do by no means excuse him who communicates no oftener. This never was the judgment of
30 our Church. On the contrary, she takes all possible care that the sacrament be duly administered, wherever the Common Prayer is read, every Sunday and holiday in the year.

The Church gives a particular direction with regard to those that are in Holy Orders. 'In all cathedral and collegiate churches
35 and colleges, where there are many priests and deacons, they shall all receive the communion with the priest, every Sunday at the least.'[26]

[25] Cf. the closing rubrics in BCP, Communion, where it is further stipulated, '. . . of which Easter [is] to be one [of those three times]'.

[26] BCP, Communion, Closing ('Red') Rubrics, ¶ 8. Note that Wesley quietly drops the concluding clause ('except they have a reasonable cause to the contrary') which Nelson had printed in full as a matter of course.

21. It has been shown, first, that if we consider the Lord's Supper as a command of Christ, no man can have any pretence to Christian piety who does not receive it (not once a month, but) as often as he can; secondly, that if we consider the institution of it as a mercy to ourselves, no man who does not receive it as often as he 5 can has any pretence to Christian prudence; thirdly, that none of the objections usually made can be any excuse for that man who does not at every opportunity obey his command and accept this mercy.

22. It has been particularly shown, first, that unworthiness is no 10 excuse, because, though in one sense we are all unworthy, yet none of us need be afraid of being unworthy in St. Paul's sense, of 'eating and drinking unworthily'; secondly, that the not having time enough for preparation can be no excuse, since the only preparation which is absolutely necessary is that which no 15 business can hinder; nor indeed anything on earth, unless so far as it hinders our being in a state of salvation; thirdly, that its abating our reverence is no excuse, since he who gave the command, 'Do this', nowhere adds, 'unless it abates your reverence;' fourthly, that our not profiting by it is no excuse, since 20 it is our own fault in neglecting that necessary preparation which is in our own power; lastly, that the judgment of our own Church is quite in favour of constant communion. If those who have hitherto neglected it on any of these pretences will lay these things to heart, they will, by the grace of God, come to a better mind, and 25 never more forsake their own mercies.

Oxon., Feb. 19, 1732[27]

---

[27] Place and date as in *AM*.

OF FORMER TIMES

AN INTRODUCTORY COMMENT

This sermon provides an interesting sample of Wesley as a 'theologian of culture', concerned with various correlations between the Christian world view and emergent current issues. One such issue had become popular and controversial by the 1780s: the idea of 'progress'. Traditional philosophies of history (orthodox, Puritan, 'primitivist', 'restorationist', etc.) had premised some sort of 'golden age of mankind', long since decayed—or, alternatively, a pristine 'apostolic age' of authentic Christian faith and praxis, long since corrupted. As sophisticated a theologian as Robert South, in preaching from Eccles. 7:10,[1] had argued that the 'former times' mentioned there were not really better than our own—which was to say that every age has its own characteristic defects. Much earlier, Jean Bodin, in his Methodus, ad facilem historiarum cognitionem *(1566) had expounded a sort of 'law of oscillations', thus rejecting both extremes of pessimism and optimism. Louis Le Roy had followed with a variation on the same theme in* De la Vicissitude ou variété des choses en l'univers.[2]

The emergence of 'the idea of progress' has been traced, credibly enough, by J. B. Bury in his essay under that title (1932), with typically scant interest in its theological aspects or development. But this was precisely where Wesley's view of the problem found its focus. For example, he knew George Hakewill's rambling but pioneering Apologie or Declaration of the Power and Providence of God in the Government of the World . . . *(1627, 1630, 1635), with its argument to the effect that Christianity had made a decisive contribution to human progress over pagan times (cf. Bury's grudging praise of Hakewill's interest in social progress, p. 92). Closer to Wesley's time there had been Bishop Thomas Sprat's vision in his* History of the Royal Society *(1667) of the foreseeable 'absolute perfection of the true philosophy [of nature]'. Wesley also knew Joseph Glanvill's short essay,* Plus Ultra, or the Progress and Advancement of Knowledge since

[1] *Sermons* (1823), No. XIV, Vol.V, pp. 233-49.
[2] 1st edn., 1576; Eng. trans. by Robert Ashley, 1594.

the Days of Aristotle *(1668), which had celebrated the unprecedented progress in useful knowledge generated by the new sciences. What interested Wesley most in Glanvill was the extension of the idea to the newly discovered 'Transatlantic World'; this had been one of his recurring visions, too.*

But the idea as a general conversation-piece had been popularized in France and England by two widely discussed works of Bernard Le Bovier de Fontenelle: Dialogues of the Dead,[3] *and* Conversations on the Plurality of Worlds.[4] *How closely Wesley had read Fontenelle can only be conjectured. What is clear is that by 1787 he was convinced that his people needed a written sermon to connect two points not always held together by the apostles of progress: (1) the actuality of 'progress' and (2) the radical dependence of all so-called 'progress' upon the design and scope of God's providence. Here, then, is a secular idea embraced and transformed by an evangelical theologian. It is one of the earlier essays in this vein that one can point to.*

The written sermon was produced in June 1787, in the midst of Wesley's long stay in Ireland that year; it is dated 'Dublin, June 27', which would have been the day following Thomas Coke's return from a missionary journey to America: 'We were agreeably surprised with the arrival of Dr. Coke, who came from Philadelphia in nine-and-twenty days, and gave us a pleasing account of the work of God in America.'[5] It was published in the Arminian Magazine *in the winter of that same year (November and December, X. 566-72, 620-25); it had no title, but was numbered as 'Sermon XLII'. It is interesting to note that Wesley had preached from Eccles. 7:10 only once before (in 1759). Even when the sermon appeared in the* Arminian Magazine, *Wesley must have been planning for its inclusion in* SOSO, VIII, *where it appears with its present neutral title, pp. 153-72.*

---

[3] 1st edn. in French, 1683; Eng. trans. by John Hughes, 1708.
[4] 1st edn. in French, 1686; Eng. trans. by Mrs. Aphra Behn; four edns. from 1688 to 1760.
[5] JWJ, June 26, 1787.

Of Former Times

Ecclesiastes 7:10

Say not thou, What is the cause that the former days were better than these? For thou dost not inquire wisely concerning this.

5   1. It is not easy to discern any connection between this text and the context, between these words and either those that go before or those that follow after. It seems to be a detached, independent sentence, like very many in the Proverbs of Solomon. And like them, it contains a weighty truth, which deserves a serious
10 consideration. Is not the purport of the question this? It is not wise to inquire into the cause of a supposition unless the supposition itself be not only true but clearly proved so to be. Therefore it is not wise to inquire into the cause of this supposition that 'the former days were better than these', because, common as it is, it
15 was never yet proved, nor indeed ever can be.

2. Perhaps there are few suppositions which have passed more currently in the world than this, that the former days were better than these; and that in several respects. It is generally supposed that we now live in the dregs of time,[1] when the world is as it were
20 grown old, and consequently that everything therein is in a declining state. It is supposed, in particular, that men were, some ages ago, of a far taller stature than now; that they likewise had far greater abilities, and enjoyed a deeper and stronger understanding, in consequence of which their writings of every kind are far
25 preferable to those of later times. Above all it is supposed that the former generations of men excelled the present in virtue; that mankind in every age and in every nation have degenerated more and more, so that at length they have fallen from the golden into the iron age, and now justice is fled from the earth.[2]

---

[1] Cf. No. 52, *The Reformation of Manners*, II.1 and n.

[2] In the following month Wesley would be reading 'Mr. [Francis] Dobbs's [*Summary of*] *Universal History*', and giving it a mixed appraisal. Dobbs, an Irish politician, was also an ardent millenarian and some parts of his *History* (4 vols., 1787–88) left Wesley sceptical: 'It gave me a clearer view of ancient times than ever I had before, but I still doubt of many famous incidents which have passed current for many ages. To instance in one: I cannot believe there was ever such a nation as the Amazons in the world. The whole affair of the Argonauts I judge to be equally fabulous. . . .' (JWJ, July 26, 1787).

3. Before we consider the truth of these suppositions, let us inquire into the rise of them. And as to the general supposition, that the world was once in a far more excellent state than it is, may we not easily believe that this arose (as did all the fabulous accounts of the golden age) from some confused traditions 5 concerning our first parents and their paradisiacal state? To this refer many of the fragments of ancient writings which men of learning have gleaned up. Therefore we may allow that there is some truth in the supposition; seeing it is certain, the days which Adam and Eve spent in paradise were far better than any which 10 have been spent by their descendants, or ever will be till Christ returns to reign upon earth.

4. But whence could that supposition arise that men were formerly of a larger stature than they are now? This has been a generally prevailing opinion, almost in all nations and in all ages. 15 Hence near two thousand years ago the well-known line of Virgil,

Qualia nunc hominum producit corpora tellus.[3]

Hence near a thousand years before him, Homer tells us of one of his heroes throwing a stone which hardly ten men could lift, οἷοι νῦν βροτοί—'such as men are now'.[4] We allow indeed there have 20 been giants in all ages, in various parts of the world.[5] Whether the antediluvians mentioned in Genesis were such or no (which many have questioned), we cannot doubt but Og the King of Bashan[6] was such, as well as Goliath of Gath.[7] Such also were many of the children (or descendants) of Anak.[8] But it does not appear that in 25 any age or nation men in general were larger than they are now. We are very sure they were not for many centuries past, by the tombs and coffins that have been discovered, which are exactly of the same size with those that are now in use. And in the

---

[3] Virgil, *Aeneid*, xii.900: the context is Turnus's discovery of a landmark stone that not even a dozen men could lift, 'men of such frames as earth produces now'.

[4] An exaggeration of the interval between Virgil and Homer; and notice that in the *Iliad*, v.304, the stone is such as 'not *two* men could bear, such as mortals are now'. See also Wesley's letter to his brother Charles, July 9, 1766.

[5] Cf. Chambers's *Cyclopaedia*, on 'giants', and his list of witnesses to them (Caesar, Tacitus, Florus, Saxo Grammaticus, *et al.*). Chambers's main point is that giants are, and always have been, rarities and marvels; 'antique examples' may be matched by 'modern examples' (e.g., 'porters and archers belonging to the emperor of China, fifteen foot high', etc.).

[6] Deut. 3:11.

[7] 1 Sam. 17:4.

[8] Deut. 9:2.

catacombs at Rome the niches for the dead bodies which were
hewn in the rock sixteen hundred years ago are none of them six
feet in length, and some a little under. Above all, the Pyramids of
Egypt (that of King Cheops in particular) have beyond all
5 reasonable doubt remained at least three thousand years; yet
none of the mummies (embalmed bodies) brought therefrom are
above five feet ten inches long.[9]

5. But how then came this supposition to prevail so long and so
generally in the world? I know not but it may be accounted[10] for
10 from hence. Great and little are relative terms, and all men judge
of greatness and littleness by comparing things with themselves.
Therefore it is not strange if we think men are larger now than
they were when we were children. I remember a remarkable
instance of this in my own case. After having left it seven years I
15 had a great desire to see the school where I was brought up.[11]
When I was there, I wondered that the boys were so much smaller
than they used to be when I was at school. 'Many of my
schoolfellows ten years ago were taller by the head than me. And
few of them that are at school now reach up to my shoulders.'
20 Very true; but what was the reason of this? Indeed a very plain
one: it was not because they were smaller, but because I was
bigger than I was ten years before. I verily believe this is the cause
why men in general suppose the human race to decrease in
stature. They remember the time when most of those round
25 about them were both taller and bigger than themselves. Yea, and
all men have done the same in their successive generations. Is it

---

[9] Cf. William Derham, *Physico-Theology* (1716), pp. 291-92, where the evidence of the
ancient pyramids, catacombs, monumental tombs, etc., is surveyed (from classical history
and modern travel stories) and the conclusion drawn that 'there is no decay in nature
(though the question is as old as Homer); men of this age are of the same stature as they
were near three thousand years ago . . . .' For example, the Emperor Augustus was five
feet, seven inches, whereas Queen Elizabeth was five feet, nine inches. See also Samuel
Clarke, *A Mirrour or Looking-Glasse* (1654), pp. 608-11 (a description of the Egyptian
pyramids), '. . . whereby it appears that men's bodies are now almost as big as they were
three thousand years ago'. In his *Survey*, I.100 ff., Wesley reviews the same evidence and
reasserts the same conclusion; e.g., p. 151: 'Five feet and an half may be thought the
ordinary height of man'—Wesley was five feet, three inches—and 'seventy years the
ordinary period of his life'—Wesley died at age eighty-seven. Cf. Joseph G. Wright,
'Notes on Some Portraits of John Wesley', WHS, III.189; see also No. 54, 'On Eternity',
§8 and n.
[10] Both 1787 and 1788 read 'recounted', surely an unnoticed error.
[11] Wesley had grown up with historic landmarks on every side; e.g., the Charterhouse
School in London was in sight of Smithfield and close to St. Andrew's, Holborn. He had
entered the school on Jan. 28, 1714 (aged ten) and left it in June 1720, just before his
seventeenth birthday.

any wonder then that all should have run into the same mistake? When it has been transmitted unawares from father to son, and probably will be to the end of time.

6. But there is likewise a general supposition that the understanding of man and all his mental abilities were of a larger 5 size in the ancient days than they are now; and that the ancient inhabitants of the earth had far greater talents than the present. Men of eminent learning have been of this mind, and have contended for it with the utmost vehemence. It is granted that many of the ancient writers, both philosophers, poets, and 10 historians, will not easily be excelled, if equalled, by those of later ages. We may instance in Homer and Virgil as poets, Thucydides and Livy as historians. But this meantime is to be remarked concerning most of these writers—that each of them spent his whole life in composing and polishing one book. What wonder 15 then if they were exquisitely finished, when so much labour was bestowed upon them! I doubt whether any man in Europe or in the world has taken so much pains in finishing any treatise. Otherwise it might possibly have equalled, if not excelled, any that went before.[12] 20

7. But that the generality of men were not one jot wiser in ancient times than they are at the present time we may easily gather from the most authentic records. One of the most ancient nations concerning whom we have any certain account is the Egyptian. And what conception can we have of their under- 25 standing and learning when we reflect upon the objects of their worship? These were not only the vilest of animals, as dogs and cats, but the leeks and onions[13] that grew in their own gardens.

[12] Cf. R. W. Harris, *Reason and Nature in Eighteenth Century Thought*, pp. 237-38, citing Edward Young ('the poet') as having posed the same question with regard to the ancients, with a similar conclusion. John Dunton, editor of *The Athenian Mercury*, complained of his brother-in-law, Samuel Wesley, Sen., that 'he usually wrote too fast to write well'; see Dunton's *Life and Errors* (Westminster, J. Nichols, Son, and Bentley, 1818), I.164.

[13] Cf. Isaac Hawkins Browne, 'Of the Immortality of the Soul', translated from the Latin by Richard Grey, in *English Poems*, IX.12 (London, 1754):

> Those [idols] their propitious deities they called;
> As those unlucky, which would do them harm.
> Nay, to such height at last the frenzy grew,
> That little ugly beasts, nay even leeks
> And onions, were by mad antiquity
> Held sacred—and, as deities, adored.

See also John Hutchinson, *Works*, IV ('G').262, for a reference to 'Egyptian religion'; cf. *Works*, I ('B').93-96.

Indeed I knew[14] a great man (whose manner was to treat with the
foulest abuse all that dared to differ from him: I do not mean Dr.
Johnson—he was a mere courtier compared to Mr. Hutchinson[15])
who scurrilously abused all those who are so void of common
5 sense as to believe any such thing concerning them. He
peremptorily affirms (but without condescending to give us any
proof) that the ancient inhabitants of Egypt had a deep hidden
meaning in all this. Let him believe it who can. I cannot believe it,
on any man's bare assertion. I believe they had no deeper
10 meaning in worshipping cats than our schoolboys have in baiting
them. And I apprehend the common Egyptians were just as wise
three thousand years ago as the common ploughmen in England
and Wales are at this day. I suppose their natural understanding,
like their stature, was on a level with ours, and their learning, their
15 acquired knowledge, many degrees inferior to that of persons of
the same rank either in France, Holland, or Germany.
    8. 'However, did not the people of former times greatly excel us
in virtue?' This is the point of greatest importance; the rest are but
trifles in comparison of it. Now is it not universally allowed that
20 every age grows worse and worse? Was it not observed by the old
heathen poet, almost two thousand years ago,

> *Aetas parentum, peior avis, tulit*
> *Nos nequiores, iam daturos*
> *Progeniem vitiosiorem.*[16]

25 That is, in plain prose: 'The age of our parents was more vicious
·than that of our grandfathers. Our age is more vicious than that of
our fathers. We are worse than our fathers were, and our children
will be worse than us.'
    9. It is certain, this has been the common cry from generation
30 to generation. And if it is not true, whence should it arise? How
can we account for it? Perhaps another remark of the same poet
may help us to an answer. May it not be extracted from the
general character which he gives of old men?

---

[14] Altered in *SOSO* to 'we lately had'; if Wesley was personally acquainted with
Hutchinson, he left no other record of this fact.
[15] Cf. Spearman and Bate, Editors' Preface to Hutchinson's *Works*, I.xi: '[Hutchinson]
. . . offended sometimes with his tongue, spoke sometimes with more warmth than is
strictly justifiable, and [often allowed] unguarded expressions to drop. . . .'
[16] Cf. Horace, *Odes*, III.vi.46-48, orig., '*mox daturos*'. Wesley's 'plain prose' is a very
free translation, less subtle than Horace's intended satire.

Difficilis, querulus, laudator temporis acti
Se puero, censor, castigatorque minorum.[17]

Is it not the common practice of old men to praise the past and
condemn the present time? And this may probably operate much
farther than one would at first imagine. When those that have   5
more experience than us—and therefore, we are apt to think,
more wisdom—are almost continually harping upon this, the
degeneracy of the world; [when] those who are accustomed from
their infancy to hear how much better the world was formerly
than it is now (and so it really seemed to them when they were   10
young, and just come into the world, and when the cheerfulness
of youth gave a pleasing air to all that was round about them), the
idea of the world's being worse and worse would naturally grow
up with them. And so it will be till we, in our turn,[18] grow peevish,
fretful, discontented, and full of melancholy complaints, 'How   15
wicked the world is grown!' How much better it was when we
were young, in the golden days that we can remember!

10. But let us endeavour, without prejudice or prepossession,
to take a view of the whole affair. And upon cool and impartial
consideration it will appear that the former days were not better   20
than these; yea, on the contrary, that these are, in many respects,
beyond comparison better than them. It will clearly appear that as
the stature of men was nearly the same from the beginning of the
world, so the understanding of men in similar circumstances has
been much the same from the time of God's bringing a flood   25
upon the earth unto the present hour. We have no reason to
believe that the uncivilized nations of Africa, America, or the
South Sea Islands, had ever a better understanding, or were in a
less barbarous state than they are now. Neither, on the other
hand, have we any sufficient proof that the natural understanding   30
of men in the most civilized countries, Babylon, Persia, Greece,
or Italy, were stronger or more improved than those of the
Germans, French, or English now alive. Nay, have we not reason
to believe that by means of better instruments we have attained
that knowledge of nature which few, if any, of the ancients ever   35

---

[17] Cf. Horace, *Art of Poetry*, ll. 173-74: 'Hard to please, querulous, praising the times
when they were boys, and censorious reprovers of those who are young *now*.'
[18] *AM* (1787), p. 571: 'And so it would be till we, in our turn, grew peevish.' In *SOSO*
'would' is changed to 'will', and although 'grew' remains, it seems clear that this should
have been changed to 'grow'.

attained? So that in this respect the advantage (and not a little one) is clearly on our side: and we ought to acknowledge, with deep thankfulness to the Giver of every good gift, that the former days were not to be compared to these wherein we live.

5   11. But the principal inquiry still remains. Were not 'the former days better than these' with regard to virtue? Or to speak more properly, religion? This deserves a full consideration.

By religion I mean the love of God and man, filling the heart[19] and governing the life. The sure effect of this is the uniform
10 practice of justice, mercy, and truth. This is the very essence of it, the height and depth of religion, detached from this or that opinion, and from all particular modes of worship. And I would calmly inquire, 'Which of the former times were better than these with regard to this, to the religion experienced and practised by
15 Archbishop Fénelon[20] in France, Bishop Ken[21] in England, and Bishop Bedell[22] in Ireland?'

12. We need not extend our inquiry beyond the period when life and immortality were brought to light by the gospel.[23] And it is allowed that the days immediately succeeding the pouring out of
20 the Holy Ghost on the day of Pentecost were better even in this respect, even with regard to religion, than any which have succeeded them.

But setting aside this short age of golden days, I must repeat the question: 'Which of the former days were better than the present
25 in every known part of the habitable world?'

[19] Cf. No. 25, 'Sermon on the Mount, V', IV.13 and n.

[20] Archbishop of Cambrai (1651–1715), a major figure in the development of mysticism in eighteenth-century France. Wesley had published some of his 'Letters' in the *Christian Lib.* (Vol. XXXVIII), and recommended his *Télémaque* for use in the Kingswood School. For other references to Fénelon, cf. Nos. 106, 'On Faith, Heb. 11:6', II.3; and 123, 'On Knowing Christ after the Flesh', §14; see also Wesley's letter to Ann Bolton, Sept. 27, 1777.

[21] Thomas Ken (1637–1711), teacher, hymn writer, Bishop of Bath and Wells, famed for his piety and Christian courage. He denied Nell Gwyn's access to Charles II, he defied James II's order to read the royal 'Declaration of Indulgence' (1687), but he also declined to take the oath of allegiance to William of Orange (1689). He carried his shroud with him on his travels and, like John Donne before him, put it on whenever he fell ill. His morning and evening hymns may be more familiar than his name (e.g., 'Praise God, from whom all blessings flow,' etc.). Wesley included some of these hymns in *A Collection of Psalms and Hymns* (1738), and abridged Ken's *Exposition on the Church Catechism* (1686) in the *Christian Lib.*, Vol XXV.

[22] William Bedell (1571–1642), a remarkable Bishop of Kilmore and Ardagh, revered even by the Irish. He was fortunate to have Gilbert Burnet for his biographer; his *Life* appeared in 1685, and Wesley had abridged it for Vol.XXVII of the *Christian Lib*. Later he used excerpts from the abridgement for *AM*, 1778–79.

[23] See 2 Tim. 1:10.

13. Was the former part of this century better either in these islands or any part of the continent? I know no reason at all to affirm this. I believe every part of Europe was full as void of religion in the reign of Queen Anne as it is at this day. It is true, luxury increases to a high degree in every part of Europe. And so does the scandal of England, profaneness, in every part of the kingdom. But it is also true that the most infernal of all vices, cruelty, does as swiftly decrease. And such instances of it as in times past continually occurred are now very seldom heard of. Even in war that savage barbarity which was everywhere practised has been discontinued for many years.

14. Was the last century more religious than this? In the former part of it there was much of the form of religion. And some undoubtedly experienced the power thereof.[24] But how soon did the fine gold become dim![25] How soon was it so mingled with worldly design, and with a total contempt both of truth, justice, and mercy, as brought that scandal upon all religion which is hardly removed to this day.[26] Was there more true religion in the preceding century, the age of the Reformation? There was doubtless in many countries a considerable reformation of religious opinions; yea, and modes of worship, which were much changed for the better, both in Germany and several other places. But it is well known that Luther himself complained, almost with his dying breath, 'The people that are called by my name (though I wish they were only called by the name of Christ) are reformed as to their opinions and modes of worship; but their tempers and lives are the same they were before.'[27] Even then both justice and mercy were so shamelessly trodden under foot that an eminent writer computes the number of those that were slaughtered during those religious contests to have been no less than forty millions, within the compass of forty years![28]

15. We may step back above a thousand years from this without finding any better time. No historian gives us the least intimation of any such till we come to the age of Constantine the Great. Of this period several writers have given us most magnificent

---

[24] See 2 Tim. 3:5.
[25] See Lam. 4:1.
[26] A reflection of Wesley's bitter criticism of the Erastian corruptions of religion in the Restoration and also during 'the Whig Supremacy' (1714–60).
[27] See No. 68, 'The Wisdom of God's Counsels', §10 and n.; see also No. 14, *The Repentance of Believers*, I.9 and n.
[28] Cf. Nos. 22, 'Sermon on the Mount, II', III.18 and n.; and 92, 'On Zeal', §1 and n.

accounts. Yea, one eminent author—no less a man than Dr. Newton,[29] the late Bishop of Bristol—has been at no small pains to show that the conversion of Constantine to Christianity, and the emoluments which he bestowed upon the church with an
5 unsparing hand, were the event which is signified in the Revelation by 'the new Jerusalem coming down from heaven'![30]

16. But I cannot in any wise subscribe to the bishop's opinion in this matter. So far from it that I have been long convinced from the whole tenor of ancient history that this very event—Con-
10 stantine's calling himself a Christian, and pouring in that flood of wealth and power on the Christian church, the clergy in particular—was productive of more evil to the church than all the ten persecutions put together. From the time that power, riches, and honour of all kinds were heaped upon the Christians, vice of
15 all kinds came in like a flood, both on the clergy and laity. From the time that the church and state, the kingdoms of Christ and of the world, were so strangely and unnaturally blended together, Christianity and heathenism were so thoroughly incorporated with each other that they will hardly ever be divided till Christ
20 comes to reign upon earth.[31] So that instead of fancying that the glory of the new Jerusalem covered the earth at that period, we have terrible proof that it was then, and has ever since been, covered with the smoke of the bottomless pit.[32]

17. 'However, were not the days antecedent to this, those of the
25 third century, better beyond all comparison than any that followed them?' This has been almost universally believed. Few doubt but in the age before Constantine the Christian church was in its glory, worshipping God in the beauty of holiness. But was it so indeed? What says St. Cyprian, who lived in the midst of that
30 century, a witness above all exception, and one that sealed the truth with his blood? What account does he give of what he saw with his own eyes, and heard with his own ears? Such a one as would almost make one imagine he was painting to the life, not the ancient church of Carthage, but the modern church of Rome.

---

[29] Thomas Newton (1704–82); cf. No. 61, 'The Mystery of Iniquity', §27 and n.

[30] Rev. 21:2. Cf. Eusebius's ecstatic account of the dinner given by the Emperor Constantine for the bishops at Nicea: 'One might have thought that a picture of Christ's kingdom was thus shadowed forth . . .'; *Life of Constantine*, III.15 (*NPNF, II*, I.524).

[31] Note Wesley's ambivalence toward this assumption that the church is a *corpus mixtum* (a mixed society) and will always continue to be; cf. No. 104, 'On Attending the Church Service', §13 and n.

[32] Cf. Rev. 9:11; 20:1; cf. also No. 32, 'Sermon on the Mount, XII', I.7 and n.

According to his account, such abominations even then prevailed over all orders of men that it was not strange God poured out his fury upon them in blood, by the grievous persecutions which followed.[33]

18. Yea, and before this, even in the first century, even in the 5 apostolic age, what account does St. John give of several of the churches which he himself had planted in Asia? How little were those congregations better than many in Europe at this day? Nay, forty or fifty years before that, within thirty years of the descent of the Holy Ghost, were there not such abominations in the church 10 of Corinth as were 'not even named among the heathen'?[34] So early did 'the mystery of iniquity'[35] begin to work in the Christian church! So little reason have we to appeal to the former days, as though they were 'better than these'!

19. To affirm this, therefore, as commonly as it is done, is not 15 only contrary to truth, but is an instance of black ingratitude[36] to God, and a grievous affront to his blessed Spirit. For whoever makes a fair and candid inquiry will easily perceive that true religion has in no wise decreased, but greatly increased, in the present century. To instance in one capital branch of religion, the 20 love of our neighbour. Is not persecution wellnigh vanished from the face of the earth? In what age did Christians of various denominations show such forbearance toward each other?[37] When before was such lenity shown by governors toward their respective subjects? Not only in Great Britain and Ireland, but in 25 France and Germany; yea, every part of Europe? Nothing like this has been seen since the time of Constantine; no, not since the time of the apostles.[38]

20. If it be said, 'Why, this is the fruit of the general infidelity,

---

[33] Cf. above, No. 61, 'The Mystery of Iniquity', §25 and n.

[34] Cf. 1 Cor. 5:1 (*Notes*).

[35] 2 Thess. 2:7.

[36] Cf. John Dryden's drama, *The Spanish Fryar; Or the Double Discovery*, Act I, sc. 1: 'You brand us all with black ingratitude.' Wesley read this in Sept. 1729.

[37] *SOSO*, 1788, 'of every denomination show such forbearance to each other?' Cf. *OED* for 'denomination' as a new term in the eighteenth century.

[38] An echo of the age-old history of religious persecutions and of the comparative triumph of toleration in late Georgian England; cf. Wilbur K. Jordan, *The Development of Religious Toleration in England; Attainment of the Theory and Accommodations in Thought and Institutions (1664–60)* (Cambridge, Harvard Univ. Press, 1940). Wesley ignores the fact, however, that the Test and Corporation Acts against Dissenters still had the force of law; he also seems to have repressed his memories of the 'Lord Gordon (anti-Catholic) riots' of 1778, and his complicity in them.

the Deism which has overspread all Europe,' I answer, Whatever
be the cause, we have reason greatly to rejoice in the effect. And if
the all-wise God has brought so great and universal a good out of
this dreadful evil, so much the more should we magnify his
5 astonishing power, wisdom, and goodness herein. Indeed, so far
as we can judge, this was the most direct way whereby *nominal*
Christians could be prepared, first, for tolerating, and,
afterwards, for receiving, *real* Christianity. While the governors
were themselves unacquainted with it, nothing but this could
10 induce them to suffer it. O the depth both of the wisdom and
knowledge of God![39] Causing a total disregard for all religion to
pave the way for the revival of the only religion which was worthy
of God! I am not assured whether this be the case or no in France
and Germany. But it is so beyond all contradiction in North
15 America: the total indifference of the government there whether
there be any religion or none leaves room for the propagation of
true scriptural religion without the least let or hindrance.[40]

21. But above all this, while luxury and profaneness have been
increasing on the one hand, on the other benevolence and
20 compassion toward all the forms of human woe have increased in
a manner not known before, from the earliest ages of the world. In
proof of this we see more hospitals, infirmaries, and other places
of public charity have been erected, at least in and near London,
within this century, than in five hundred years before.[41] And
25 suppose this has been owing in part to vanity, desire of praise; yet
have we cause to bless God that so much good has sprung even
from this imperfect motive.

22. I cannot forbear mentioning one instance more of the
goodness of God to us in the present age. He has lifted up a
30 standard in our islands both against luxury, profaneness, and vice
of every kind. He caused near fifty years ago as it were a grain of
mustard seed to be sown near London, and it has now grown and
put forth great branches, reaching from sea to sea. Two or three

[39] Rom. 11:33.

[40] An interesting recognition of the positive effects of the principle of the separation of church and state. Wesley connects it here with Deism; it was also a belated triumph of one of the central ecclesial principles of the 'Radical Reformation'; cf. G. H. Williams, *The Radical Reformation.*

[41] Cf. George Rudé, *Hanoverian London, 1714–1808*, pp. 84-86, for a list of hospitals and infirmaries that were newly built or extensively rebuilt in the eighteenth century. See also No. 99, *The Reward of Righteousness*, for Wesley's testimony to the sense of philanthropy in the latter half of the century.

poor people met together in order to help each other to be real Christians. They increased to hundreds, to thousands, to myriads, still pursuing their one point, real religion, the love of God and man ruling all their tempers, and words, and actions.[42] Now I will be bold to say such an event as this, considered in all its circumstances, has not been seen upon earth before, since the time that St. John went to Abraham's bosom.

23. Shall we now say, 'The former days were better than these'? God forbid we should be so unwise and so unthankful. Nay, rather let us praise him all the day long; for he hath dealt bountifully with us. No 'former time' since the apostles left the earth has been 'better than the present'. None has been comparable to it in several respects. We are not born out of due time,[43] but in the day of his power, a day of glorious salvation,[44] wherein he is hastening to renew the whole race of mankind in righteousness and true holiness.[45] How bright hath the Sun of righteousness already shone on various parts of the earth! And how many gracious showers has he already poured down upon his inheritance! How many precious souls has he already gathered into his garner, as ripe shocks of corn! May we be always ready to follow them, crying in our hearts, 'Come, Lord Jesus! Come quickly!'[46]

Dublin, June 27, 1787[47]

---

[42] Another instance of Wesley's effortless triumphalism with regard to the historic import of the Methodist Revival. Cf. Nos. 63, 'The General Spread of the Gospel', §18; 81, 'In What Sense we are to Leave the World', §19; 104, 'On Attending the Church Service', §17; 107, 'On God's Vineyard', I.5; 112, *On Laying the Foundation of the New Chapel*, §4, II.11; and 122, 'Causes of the Inefficacy of Christianity', §8. See also Wesley's letters to John Fletcher, Jan. 15, 1787; to Mrs. Woodhouse, July 30, 1773; to a clergyman, June 18, 1787; and to James Barry, Sept. 26, 1787; and 'A Plain Account of the Kingswood School', in *AM* (1781), IV.381-84, 432-35, 486-93; 'Thoughts Upon a Late Phenomenon', §§7-10, in *AM* (1789), XII.46-49; and *A Farther Appeal*, Pt. III, I.4, 7 (11:274-76 in this edn.). For Wesley's Anglican triumphalism, see Nos. 38, 'A Caution against Bigotry', II.4; and 33, 'Sermon on the Mount, XIII', III.1.
[43] 1 Cor. 15:8.
[44] See Ps. 110:3; 2 Cor. 6:2; Col. 1:11.
[45] Eph. 4:24.
[46] Cf. Rev. 22:20.
[47] Place and date as in *AM*.

WHAT IS MAN? PSALM 8:3-4

AN INTRODUCTORY COMMENT

Here is yet another essay on Wesley's theology of culture, in which he seeks to correlate man's relative insignificance in creation as a whole with God's special interest in his role and worth. In the following year he will write another sermon, on Ps. 8:4, in which his stress is on man's unique place in God's creation (see No. 116, 'What is Man? Ps. 8:4'). Neither of these sermons has a history in Wesley's oral preaching; no use of Ps. 8:3-4 has been reported. This first discourse is therefore more of an essay than a sermon; its ending lacks Wesley's usual stress on 'application', and there is no proper rhetorical climax.

But the problem of man's unique place in creation had fascinated Wesley since his youth; see Vol. 4, the early unpublished sermon (No. 141) on Gen. 1:27. In those early days he would have read Joseph Addison's beautiful essay in The Spectator, *No. 565 (July 9, 1714) on Psalm 8:3-4, and most of what Wesley has to say thereafter on this question echoes Addison (e.g., the references to Huygens and Pascal, to the great chain of being, space as the sensorium of the Deity, etc.). It is interesting, therefore, that 'the late Wesley' should have returned, in these two complementary discourses, to the issue of an adequate theological anthropology after having neglected it in his oral preaching during the years between.*

This present essay was finished in Manchester on Monday, July 23, 1787, shortly after Wesley's return from an extended visit to Ireland. He reports that on the previous Wednesday he had 'retired to a little house of Mr. Brocklehurst's, two miles beyond Manchester . . . ,' and had spent the rest of that week 'in writing'. On Monday he 'preached morning and afternoon' in Manchester and 'in the evening met the bands and admired their liveliness and simplicity' (cf. JWJ, loc. cit.). The diary for the day refers to a sermon but gives no other detail. The result did not appear in the Arminian Magazine *until May and June 1788, which means it was published twice in the same year, since Wesley had already decided to include it in* SOSO, *VIII (1788). In its* Magazine *version (XI.228-32, 285-89) it had no title but was numbered 'Sermon XLV'. In* SOSO, *VIII.173-88, it has been given its present title, drawn from the Psalmist's query in verse 4.*

What is Man?

Psalm 8:3-4

When I consider thy heavens, the work of thy fingers, the moon and [the] stars, which thou hast ordained: What is man?

How often has it been observed that the book of Psalms is a rich 5
treasury of devotion, which the wisdom of God has provided to
supply the wants of his children in all generations! In all ages the
Psalms have been of singular use to those that loved or feared
God: not only to the pious Israelites, but to the children of God in
all nations. And this book has been of sovereign use to the church 10
of God, not only while it was in its state of infancy (so beautifully
described by St. Paul in the former part of the fourth chapter to
the Galatians) but also since, in the fullness of time, 'life and
immortality were brought to light by the gospel'.[1] The Christians
in every age and nation have availed themselves of this divine 15
treasure, which has richly supplied the wants, not only of 'babes in
Christ'[2]—of those who were just setting out in the ways of
God—but of those also who had made good progress therein,
yea, of such as were swiftly advancing toward 'the measure of the
stature of the fullness of Christ'.[3] 20

The subject of this psalm is beautifully proposed in the
beginning of it: 'O Lord, our Governor, how excellent is thy name
in all the earth! who hast set thy glory above the heavens!'[4] It
celebrates the glorious wisdom and love of God as the Creator
and Governor of all things. It is not an improbable conjecture that 25
David wrote this psalm in a bright starlight night, while he
observed the moon also 'walking in her brightness';[5] that while he
surveyed

> This fair half-round, the ample azure sky,
> Terribly large, and beautifully bright, 30
> With stars unnumbered and unmeasured light,[6]

---

[1] Cf. 2 Tim. 1:10.   [2] 1 Cor. 3:1.   [3] Eph. 4:13.
[4] Cf. Ps. 8:1, and note Wesley's reversion here to the BCP after having announced his text from the AV Psalter.
[5] Cf. Job 31:26.
[6] Prior, *Solomon*, i.638-40; cf. No. 78, 'Spiritual Idolatry', I.7 and n.

he broke out from the fullness of his heart into that natural exultation, 'When I consider thy heavens, the work of thy fingers, the moon and the stars which thou hast ordained: What is man?' How is it possible that the Creator of these, the innumerable
5 armies of heaven and earth, should have any regard to this speck of creation[7] whose time 'passeth away like a shadow'![8]

> Thy frame but dust, thy stature but a span,
> A moment thy duration, foolish man![9]

'What is man?' I would consider this, first, with regard to his
10 magnitude, and secondly, with regard to his duration.

I.1. Consider we, first, What is man with regard to his magnitude? And in this respect, what is any one individual compared to all the inhabitants of Great Britain? He shrinks into nothing in the comparison. How inconceivably little is one
15 compared to eight or ten millions of people?[10] Is he not

> Lost like a drop in the unbounded main?[11]

2. But what are all the inhabitants of Great Britain compared to all the inhabitants of the earth? These have frequently been supposed to amount to about four hundred millions. But will this
20 computation be allowed to be just by those who maintain China alone to contain fifty-eight millions?[12] If it be true that this one empire contains little less than sixty millions, we may easily suppose that the inhabitants of the whole terraqueous globe[13] amount to four thousand millions of inhabitants, rather than four
25 hundred.[14] And what is any single individual in comparison of this number!

[7] See Young, *The Last Day*, ii.221; and see No. 54, 'On Eternity', §18 and n.

[8] Ps. 144:4 (BCP).

[9] Cf. Prior, *Solomon*, i.551-52; see also Wesley, *A Collection of Moral and Sacred Poems* (1744), I.113.

[10] Cf. JWJ, Sept. 9, 1776, where Wesley reports Dr. Richard Price's estimate that 'the people of England are between four and five million . . .'; cf. Price's *Observations on the Expectations of Lives, the Increase of Mankind . . .* (1769), and *An Essay on the Population of England* (1780).

[11] Cf. Young, *The Last Day*, ii.196; see also No. 15, *The Great Assize*, II.4 and n.

[12] Cf. Jean Baptiste Du Halde, *General History of China*, translated from the French by R. Brookes (1736); see also Robert Wallace, *A Dissertation on the Numbers of Mankind in Ancient and Modern Times* (1753), pp. 3-13. For another reference to China, cf. No. 113, *The Late Work of God in North America*, I.14.

[13] Cf. No. 15, *The Great Assize*, I.1 and n.

[14] *Ibid.*, I.4 and n.; cf. also Wallace, *op. cit.*, pp. 10-11.

3. But what is the magnitude of the earth itself compared to that of the solar system![15] Including, beside that vast body the sun, so immensely larger than the earth, the whole train of primary and secondary planets; several of which (I mean of the secondary planets—suppose the satellites or moons of Jupiter and Saturn) 5 are abundantly larger than the whole earth.

4. And yet what is the whole quantity of matter contained in the sun and all these primary and secondary planets, with all the spaces comprised in the solar system, in comparison of that which is pervaded by those amazing bodies, the comets? Who but the 10 Creator himself can 'tell the number of' these, and 'call them all by their names'?[16] Yet what is even the orbit of a comet, and the space contained therein, to the space which is occupied by the fixed stars,[17] which are at so immense a distance from the earth that they appear when they are viewed through the largest 15 telescope just as they do to the naked eye?

5. Whether the bounds of the creation do or do not extend beyond the region of the fixed stars who can tell? Only 'the morning stars' who 'sang together' when the foundations thereof were laid.[18] But that it is finite, that the bounds of it are fixed, we 20 have no reason to doubt. We cannot doubt but when the Son of God had finished all the work which he created and made, he said,

> These be thy bounds!
> This be thy just circumference, O world![19]   25

But what is man to this?

6. We may take one step, and only one step, farther still. What is the space of the whole creation, what is all finite space that is or can be conceived, in comparison of infinite?[20] What is it but a point, a cipher, compared to that which is filled by him that is all in 30 all! Think of this, and then ask, 'What is man?'

[15] See below, II.9-12; cf. also No. 55, *On the Trinity*, §7 and n.
[16] Cf. Ps. 147:4.
[17] Cf. No. 56, 'God's Approbation of His Works', I.10 and n.
[18] Job 38:4, 7.
[19] Cf. Milton, *Paradise Lost*, vii.230-31:

> Thus far thy bounds;
> This be thy just circumference, O world!

See No. 69, 'The Imperfection of Human Knowledge', I.5 and n.
[20] Cf. No. 67, 'On Divine Providence', §13 and n.

7. What is man, that the great God who filleth heaven and earth, 'the high and lofty one that inhabiteth eternity',[21] should stoop so inconceivably low as to be 'mindful of him'?[22] Would not reason suggest to us that so diminutive a creature would be
5 overlooked by him in the immensity of his works? Especially when we consider,

II. Secondly, What is man with regard to his duration?

1. 'The days of man', since the last reduction of human life, which seems to have taken place in the time of Moses (and not
10 improbably was revealed to the man of God at the time that he made this declaration) 'are threescore years and ten.'[23] This is the general standard which God hath now appointed. 'And if men be so strong', perhaps one in a hundred, 'that they come to fourscore years, yet then is their strength but labour and sorrow: so soon
15 passeth it away, and we are gone!'[24]

2. Now what a poor pittance of duration is this compared to the life of Methuselah! 'And Methuselah lived nine hundred and sixty and nine years.'[25] But what are these nine hundred and sixty-nine years to the duration of an angel, which began 'or ever
20 the mountains were brought forth', or the foundations of the earth were laid?[26] And what is the duration which has passed since the creation of angels to that which passed before they were created—to unbeginning eternity? to that half of eternity (if one may so speak) which had then elapsed! And what are threescore
25 years and ten to this!

3. Indeed what proportion can there possibly be between any finite and infinite duration? What proportion is there between a thousand or ten thousand years, or ten thousand times ten thousand ages, to eternity? I know not that the inexpressible
30 disproportion between any conceivable part of time and eternity can be illustrated in a more striking manner than it is in the well-known passage of St. Cyprian: 'Suppose there was a ball of sand as large as the globe of earth; and suppose one grain of this were to be annihilated in a thousand years; yet that whole space of
35 time wherein this ball would be annihilating, at the rate of one grain in a thousand years, would bear less, yea, unspeakably, infinitely less proportion to eternity than a single grain of sand

[21] Isa. 57:15.   [22] Ps. 8:4.
[23] Cf. Ps. 90:10.   [24] *Ibid.* (BCP).
[25] Cf. Gen. 5:25, 27.   [26] Cf. Ps. 90:2.

would bear to that whole mass.'[27] What then are the seventy years of human life in comparison of eternity? In what terms can the proportion between these be expressed? It is nothing, yea, inifinitely less than nothing!

4. If then we add to the littleness of man the inexpressible shortness of his duration, is it any wonder that a man of reflection should sometimes feel a kind of fear, lest the great, eternal, infinite Governor of the universe should disregard so diminutive a creature as man? A creature so every way inconsiderable when compared either with immensity or eternity! Did not both these reflections glance through, if not dwell upon, the mind of the royal psalmist? Thus, in contemplation of the former, he breaks out into the strong words of the text, 'When I consider the heavens, the work of thy fingers, the moon and the stars which thou hast ordained, What is man, that thou shouldst be mindful of him? Or the son of man, that thou shouldst regard him?' He is indeed (to use St. Augustine's words), *aliqua portio creaturae tuae*:[28] some portion of thy creation. But *quantula portio!* —how amazingly small a portion! How utterly beneath thy notice! It seems to be in contemplation of the latter that he cries out in the hundred and forty-fourth psalm, 'Lord, what is man, that thou hast such respect unto him; or the son of man, that thou shouldst so regard him? Man is like a thing of nought.' Why? 'His time passeth away like a shadow.'[29] In this (although in a very few places) the new translation of the Psalms—that bound up in our Bibles—is perhaps more proper than the old, that which we have in the Common Prayer Book. It runs thus: 'Lord, what is man, that thou takest knowledge of him? or the son of man, that thou makest account of him?'[30] According to the former translation David seems to be amazed that the eternal God, considering the littleness of man, should have so much respect unto him, and should so much regard him! But in the latter he seems to wonder, seeing the life of man 'passeth away like a shadow', that God should take any knowledge of him at all, or make any account of him!

5. And it is natural for us to make the same reflection, and to

[27] Cf. No. 54, 'On Eternity', §10 and n.
[28] The exact quotation of a twice-repeated phrase from *The Confessions*, I.1. *Quantula portio* (lit., 'so small a portion') is, however, an annotation of Wesley's.
[29] Cf. Ps. 144:3-4 (BCP).
[30] *Ibid.* (AV); cf. No. 54, 'On Eternity', §20 and n.

entertain the same fear. But how may we prevent this uneasy reflection, and effectually cure this fear? First, by considering what David does not appear to have taken at all into his account, namely, that the body is not the man; that man is not only a house of clay,³¹ but an immortal spirit; a spirit made in the image of God, an incorruptible picture of the God of glory; a spirit that is of infinitely more value than the whole earth; of more value than the sun, moon, and stars put together; yea, than the whole material creation. Consider, that the spirit of man is not only of a higher order, of a more excellent nature than any part of the visible world, but also more durable, not liable either to dissolution or decay. We know all 'the things which are seen are temporal', of a changing, transient nature; 'but the things which are not seen' (such as is the soul of man in particular) 'are eternal.'³² 'They shall perish,'³³ but the soul remaineth. 'They all shall wax old as a garment.'³⁴ But when heaven and earth shall pass away, the soul shall not pass away.

6. Consider, secondly, that declaration which the Father of spirits hath made to us by the prophet Hosea: 'I am God, and not man:'³⁵ 'therefore my compassions fail not.'³⁶ As if he had said, 'If I were only a man, or an angel, or any finite being, my knowledge might admit of bounds, and my mercy might be limited. But "my thoughts are not as your thoughts," and my mercy is not as your mercy. "As the heavens are higher than the earth, so are my thoughts higher than your thoughts", and my mercy, my compassion, my ways of showing it, "higher than your ways".'³⁷

7. That no shadow of fear might remain, no possibility of doubting; to show what manner of regard the great eternal God bears to little, short-lived man, but especially to his immortal part, God gave his Son, 'his only Son, to the end that whosoever believeth in him should not perish, but have everlasting life'.³⁸ See how God loved the world! The Son of God, that was God of God, Light of light, very God of very God,³⁹ in glory equal with the Father, in majesty co-eternal,⁴⁰ 'emptied himself, took upon him the form of a servant, and being found in fashion as a man, was

³¹ See Job 4:19; also No. 28, 'Sermon on the Mount, VIII', §21 and n.
³² 2 Cor. 4:18.   ³³ Heb. 1:11.
³⁴ Cf. *ibid.*   ³⁵ Hos. 11:9.
³⁶ Cf. Lam. 3:22.   ³⁷ Cf. Isa. 55:9.
³⁸ Cf. John 3:16.
³⁹ BCP, Communion, Nicene Creed.
⁴⁰ BCP, Athanasian Creed.

obedient unto death, even the death of the cross'.[41] And all this he suffered not for himself, but for us men and for our salvation.[42] 'He bore all our sins in his own body upon the tree, that by his stripes we might be healed.'[43] After this demonstration of his love is it possible to doubt any longer of God's tender regard for man, 5 even though he was 'dead in trespasses and sins'?[44] Even when he saw us in our sins and in our blood he said unto us, Live! Let us then fear no more! Let us doubt no more. 'He that spared not his own Son, but delivered him up for us all, shall he not with him freely give us all things?'[45] 10

8. 'Nay', says the philosopher, 'if God so loved the world, did he not love a thousand other worlds as well as he did this?[46] It is now allowed that there are thousands, if not millions of worlds, besides this in which we live. And can any reasonable man believe that the Creator of all these, many of which are probably as large, 15 yea, far larger than ours, would show such astonishingly greater regard to one than to all the rest?' I answer, Suppose there were millions of worlds, yet God may see, in the abyss of his infinite wisdom, reasons that do not appear to us why he saw good to show this mercy to ours in preference to thousands or millions of other 20 worlds.

9. I speak this even upon the common supposition of the plurality of worlds,[47] a very favourite notion with all those who deny the Christian revelation—and for this reason: because it affords them a foundation for so plausible an objection to it. But 25 the more I consider that supposition, the more I doubt of it.

---

[41] Cf. Phil. 2:7-8. [42] BCP, Communion, Nicene Creed.
[43] Cf. 1 Pet. 2:24. [44] Eph. 2:1.
[45] Rom. 8:32.

[46] An echo of an old problem (cf. Augustine, *De Civ. Dei*, xii. 18-19) and a current controversy (cf. the *London Magazine*, 1764–65). In his *Survey* (1763), II.143, Wesley had commented: 'It is now almost universally supposed that the moon is just like the earth. . . . And hence it is generally inferred that she is inhabited like the earth, and by parity of reason that all the other planets, as well as the earth and the moon, have their respective inhabitants.' He had then observed that Huygens (see n. to II.10) 'brings strong reasons why the moon is not and cannot be inhabited', adding, 'and so the whole ingenious hypothesis of innumerable suns and worlds moving round them vanishes into air.' A correspondent in the *London Magazine* for Nov. 1764 (pp. 570-73), had disputed this interpretation. In his reply, Jan. 1765 (pp. 26-29, reprinted in subsequent edns. of the *Survey*), Wesley holds the point that such hypotheses are no more than probable at best.

[47] Put forward by such men as Louis Dutens and Bernard Le Bovier de Fontenelle whose *Conversations on the Plurality of Worlds* turns up in the 3rd edn. of the *Survey* (1777), V.114. Wesley may have read *The Plurality of Worlds* in Jan. 1727 (there is a bare listing in the diary, 'Fontenelle'). Cf. Nos. 64, 'The New Creation', §8; and 102, 'Of Former Times', intro.

Insomuch that if it were allowed by all the philosophers in Europe, still I could not allow it without stronger proof than any I have met with yet.

10. 'Nay, but is not the argument of the great Huygens[48]
5 sufficient to put it beyond all doubt? When we view, says that able astronomer, the moon through a good telescope, we clearly discover

> Rivers and mountains on her spotty globe.[49]

Now where rivers are, there are doubtless plants and vegetables
10 of various kinds. And where vegetables are, there are undoubtedly animals, yea, rational ones as on earth. It follows then that the moon has its inhabitants, and probably near akin to ours. But if our moon is inhabited, we may easily suppose, so are all the secondary planets; and in particular all the satellites or
15 moons of Jupiter and Saturn. And if the secondary planets are inhabited, why not the primary? Why should we doubt it of Jupiter and Saturn themselves, as well as Mars, Venus, and Mercury.'

11. But do not you know that Mr. Huygens himself, before he died, doubted of this whole hypothesis? For upon farther
20 observation he found reason to believe that the moon has no atmosphere. He observed that in a total eclipse of the sun, on the removal of the shade from any part of the earth, the sun immediately shines bright upon it; whereas if the moon had an atmosphere the solar light, while it shone through that
25 atmosphere, would appear dim and dusky. Thus after an eclipse of the moon, first a dusky light appears on that part of it from which the shadow of the earth removes, while that light passes through the atmosphere of the earth. Hence it appears that the moon has no atmosphere. Consequently it has no clouds, no rain,
30 no springs, no rivers; and therefore no plants or animals. But there is no proof or probability that the moon is inhabited; neither have we any proof that the other planets are. Consequently, the foundation being removed, the whole fabric falls to the ground.

---

[48] Christiaan Huygens (1629–95); Wesley, in JWJ, Sept. 21, 1759, mentions having read his *Celestial Worlds Discovered, Or Conjectures on the Planetary Worlds* (Eng. trans. 1689, 1698, 1722, 1757): 'He surprised me. I think he clearly proves that the moon is not habitable. . . . Hence he very rationally infers that "neither are any of the secondary planets inhabited". And who can prove that the primary are? I know the earth is. Of the rest I know nothing.'

[49] Cf. Milton, *Paradise Lost*, i.291; see No. 69, 'The Imperfection of Human Knowledge', I.5 and n.

12. 'But', you will say, 'suppose this argument fails, we may infer the same conclusion, the plurality of worlds, from the unbounded wisdom, and power, and goodness of the Creator. It was full as easy to him to create thousands or millions of worlds as one. Can anyone then believe that he would exert all his power and wisdom in creating a single world? What proportion is there between this speck of creation and the great God that filleth heaven and earth! While

> We know the power of his Almighty hand
> Could form another world from every sand![50]

13. To this boasted proof, this *argumentum palmarium*[51] of the learned infidels, I answer, Do you expect to find any proportion between finite and infinite? Suppose God had created a thousand more worlds than there are grains of sand in the universe, what proportion would all these together bear to the infinite Creator? Still, in comparison of him, they would be, not a thousand times, but infinitely less than a mite compared to the universe. Have done then with this childish prattle about the proportion of creatures to their Creator; and leave it to the all-wise God to create what and when he pleases! For 'who', besides himself, 'hath known the mind of the Lord? Or who hath been his counsellor?'[52]

14. Suffice it then for us to know this plain and comfortable truth—that the almighty Creator hath shown that regard to these poor little creatures of a day which he hath not shown even to the inhabitants of heaven, 'who kept not their first estate'.[53] He hath given us his Son, his only Son, both to live and to die for us! O let us live unto him, that we may die unto him, and live with him for ever!

Manchester, July 23, 1787[54]

[50] Cf. William Broome (1689–1745), 'The Forty-third Chapter of Ecclesiasticus Paraphrased', the closing couplet:

> And yet the pow'r of thy almighty hand
> Can build another world from every sand.

See Wesley, *A Collection of Moral and Sacred Poems* (1744), II.99.

[51] A 'knockdown argument', supposedly unanswerable; *'palmarium'* means 'a masterpiece' or 'prizewinner', as in Terence, *The Eunuch*, V.iv.8. Wesley had used this same phrase in No. 90, 'An Israelite Indeed', II.7 (see n.), and again in a letter to his brother Charles, Nov. 3, 1775.

[52] Rom. 11:34.   [53] Cf. Jude 6.   [54] Place and date as in *AM*.

ON ATTENDING THE CHURCH SERVICE

AN INTRODUCTORY COMMENT

This sermon is dated from 'Bristol, Oct. 7, 1787', at the end of a three weeks' stay there during which time John Wesley had a last extended visit with his brother Charles. One may, indeed, read it as a response to the clash of two conflicting views. On the one hand, resistance had continued to mount against Wesley's 'original rule that every member of our society should attend the church and sacraments, unless he had been bred among Christians of any other denomination' (§4). This is what called forth Wesley's argument that God does 'bless the ministry of ungodly men'. On the other hand, Charles Wesley's dismay over what he clearly saw as the virtual separation of the Methodists from the Church of England continued unabated and also had to be taken into account. The result is an interesting late statement of John Wesley's 'churchmanship' on one of its more ambiguous levels. Charles Wesley died on March 29, 1788.

The sermon, with its present title, was included in SOSO, *VIII. 189-211 (1788), even before it appeared in the* Arminian Magazine *(July and August, 1788), XI.340-48, 397-403, untitled but numbered as 'Sermon XLVI'. There is no record of Wesley's having used 1 Sam. 2:17 as an earlier sermon text.*

On Attending the Church Service

1 Samuel 2:17

The sin of the young men was very great.

1. The corruption not only of the heathen world, but likewise of them that were called Christians, has been matter of sorrow and 5 lamentation to pious men almost from the time of the apostles. And hence, as early as the second century, within a hundred years of St. John's removal from the earth,[1] men who were afraid of being partakers of other men's sins thought it their duty to separate from them.[2] Hence in every age many have retired from 10 the world lest they should be stained with the pollutions of it. In the third century many carried this so far as to run into deserts and turn hermits.[3] But in the following age this took another turn. Instead of turning hermits they turned monks. Religious houses now began to be built in every Christian country. And religious 15 communities were established, both of men and women, who were entirely secluded from the rest of mankind, having no intercourse with their nearest relations, nor with any but such as were confined, generally for life, within the same walls.

2. This spirit of literally renouncing the world by retiring into 20 religious houses did not so generally prevail after the Reformation. Nay, in Protestant countries houses of this kind were totally suppressed. But still too many serious persons (chiefly incited thereto by those that are commonly called mystic writers) were eager to seclude themselves from the world and run into solitude; 25 supposing this to be the best, if not the only way, of escaping the pollution that is in the world.[4]

---

[1] Cf. No. 57, 'On the Fall of Man', II.3 and n.

[2] See 1 Tim. 5:22.

[3] Late in the century; cf. the Latin edn. of Palladius by M. de la Bigne (1654), and W. K. Lowther Clarke (trans.), *The Lausiac History of Palladius* (New York, Macmillan, 1918), i-iii. See also Athanasius, *Vita S. Antonii* (Migne, *PG*, XXVI.835-978), and Robert T. Meyer, *St. Athanasius: The Life of St. Anthony*, in *Ancient Christian Writers* (Westminster, Maryland, Newman Press, 1950).

[4] An example of this, in Wesley's own experience, would have been William Law's retirement to King's Cliffe; cf. A. Keith Walker, *William Law: His Life and Thought* (London, SPCK, 1973), pp. 168-75. See also the abridged account of an earlier and more

465

3. One thing which powerfully inclined them to separate from the several churches or religious societies to which they had belonged, even from their infancy, was the belief that no good was to be expected from the ministration of unholy men. 'What!' said
5 they, 'Can we think that a holy God will bless the ministry of wicked men? Can we imagine that they who are themselves strangers to the grace of God will manifest[5] that grace to others? Is it to be supposed that God ever did, or ever will work by the children of the devil? And if this cannot be supposed, ought we
10 not to "come out from among them and be separated"?'[6]

4. For more than twenty years this never entered into the thought of those that were called Methodists. But as more and more who had been brought up Dissenters joined with them, they brought in more and more prejudice against the Church. In
15 process of time various circumstances concurred to increase and confirm it. Many had forgotten that we were all at our first setting out determined members of the Established Church. Yea, it was one of our original rules that every member of our Society should attend the church and sacrament unless he had been bred among
20 Christians of any other denomination.[7]

5. In order therefore to prevent others from being puzzled and perplexed, as so many have been already, it is necessary in the highest degree to consider this matter thoroughly; calmly to inquire whether God ever did bless the ministry of ungodly men;
25 and whether he does so at this hour. Here is a plain matter of fact: if God never did bless it, we ought to separate from the Church, at least where we have reason to believe that the minister is an unholy man; if he ever did bless it, and does so still, then we ought to continue therein.

30 6. Nineteen years ago we considered this question in our public Conference at Leeds, 'whether the Methodists ought to separate from the Church?'[8] And after a long and candid inquiry it was

---

famous retirement (this one of the Ferrar family at 'Little Gidding in Huntingdonshire') in *AM* (1780), III.326 ff.; see also No. 81, 'In What Sense we are to Leave the World', *passim.*

[5] Both early texts here read 'manifest'. But Wesley's own copy of *AM* has a marginal correction to 'minister'. This is a plausible reading, and in some ways superior, but the correction is not in Wesley's own hand.

[6] 2 Cor. 6:17.

[7] Cf. No. 32, 'Sermon on the Mount, XII', I.7 and n.; see also No. 107, 'On God's Vineyard', II.8. For the notion that nonconformity was imported into what had been Anglican societies, cf. Wesley's letter to Henry Brooke, June 14, 1786.

[8] Wesley's own dating of this sermon, 'nineteen years ago' would take us back to 1766. But the Conference (at Leeds) in which the question of separation was first raised urgently

determined, *nemine contradicente*,[9] that it was not expedient for them to separate. The reasons were set down at large; and they stand equally good at this day.[10]

7. In order to put this matter beyond all possible dispute I have chosen to speak from these words, which give a fair occasion of observing what the dealings of God in his church have been even from so early a period; for it is generally allowed that Eli lived at least a thousand years before our Lord came into the world. In the verses preceding the text we read, 'Now the sons of Eli were sons of Belial; they knew not the Lord.'[a] They were wicked to an uncommon degree. Their profane violence with respect to the sacrifices is related with all its shocking circumstances in the following verses. But (what was a greater abomination still) 'They lay with the women that assembled at the door of the tabernacle of the congregation!'[b] On both these accounts 'the sin of the young men was very great, and men abhorred the offering of the Lord.'

8. May I be permitted to make a little digression in order to correct a mistranslation in the twenty-fifth verse? In our translation it runs thus, 'They hearkened not unto the voice of their father, because the Lord would slay them.' Ought it not rather to be rendered, '*Therefore* the Lord was about to slay them'? As if he had said, 'The Lord would not suffer their horrid and stubborn wickedness to escape unpunished; but because of that wickedness he slew them both in one day, by the hand of the Philistines.'[11] They did not sin (as might be imagined from the common translation) because God had determined to slay them:

[a] Ver. 12, etc.   [b] Ver. 22.

---

was May 6, 1755; cf. Baker, *John Wesley and the Church of England*, pp. 326-40. This was the occasion of Wesley's memorandum, 'Ought we to separate from the Church of England?', published as a pamphlet, *Reasons against a Separation from the Church of England*, in 1760 (cf. Vol. 9 of this edn.). Separation had also been a major issue for the 1766 Conference (also at Leeds). Wesley's point here is that the 1766 Conference had ratified the earlier decisions of 1755. Actually, once raised in 1755, the issue of separation was never thereafter downed; it was, rather, staved off year after year by Wesley's imposition of his personal authority, together with the general acceptance among the Methodists of the formula of 1755: 'separation may be *lawful* but is not *expedient;'* cf. JWJ, May 6, 1755; and Oct. 24, 1786; and his letter to Henry Brooke, *op. cit.*

[9] 'No one speaking in opposition', i.e., without dissent.

[10] Cf. n.8, above.

[11] Scarcely a *correction* of the Hebrew text of 1 Sam. 2:25; it is, rather, a reinterpretation aimed at avoiding the implied notion of a predestined retribution. The AV translation catches the literal sense of the original: '*because* the Lord would slay them.' Cf. S. Goldman, *Samuel: Hebrew Text and English Translation . . . Introduction and Commentary*

but God therefore determined to slay them, because they had thus sinned.

9. But to return. Their sin was the more inexcusable because they could not be ignorant of that dreadful consequence thereof, that, by reason of their enormous wickedness, 'men abhorred the offering of the Lord.'[12] Many of the people were so deeply offended that if they did not wholly refrain from the public worship, yet they attended it with pain; abhorring the priests, while they honoured the sacrifice.

10. And have we any proof that the priests who succeeded them were more holy than them, than Hophni and Phinehas, not only till God permitted ten of the tribes to be separated from their brethren and from the worship he had appointed, but even till Judah, as well as Israel, for the wickedness of the priests as well as the people, were carried into captivity?

11. What manner of men they were about the time of the Babylonish captivity we learn from various passages in the prophecy of Jeremiah. From which it manifestly appears that people and priests wallowed in all manner of vices. And how little they were amended after they were brought back into their own land we may gather from those terrible words in the prophecy of Malachi: 'And now, O ye priests, this commandment is for you. If ye will not hear, and if ye will not lay it to heart, to give glory unto my name, saith the Lord of hosts, I will send even a curse upon you, and I will curse your blessings. Yea, I have cursed them already, because ye would not lay it to heart. Behold, I will curse your seed, and I will spread dung upon their faces, even the dung of your solemn feasts; and men shall take you away with it.'[c]

12. Such were the priests of God in their several generations,

[c] Mal. 2:1-3.

(*The Soncino Bible*): 'because the Lord was pleased to slay them;' see also later translations and commentaries. Goldman cites Rabbi David Kimchi as having said that 'the sons of Eli were so confirmed in their sins that they were incapable of repentance and so beyond redemption; their punishment was therefore necessary as a warning to others.' Poole, *Annotations*, had followed the text and Kimchi here: '. . . i.e., *because* God had determined to destroy them for their many and great sins; and therefore would not, and did not, give them grace to hearken to Eli's counsel. . . .' H. P. Smith, *Samuel*, in the *International Critical Commentary*, translated, 'for Yahweh was minded to slay them;' and J. Mauchline in 1 and 2 Sam., *The New Century Bible* (1971), p. 53, comments that 'the second sentence of ver. 25 is expressed in a form which . . . is tantamount to saying that their sin was predetermined and inescapable . . . .' Wesley would have found none of this acceptable; cf. No.110, *Free Grace, passim*.

[12] 1 Sam. 2:17.

till he brought the great High Priest into the world! And what manner of men were they during the time that he ministered upon earth? A large and particular account of their character we have in the twenty-third chapter of St. Matthew; and a worse character it would be difficult to find in all the oracles of God. But may it not 5 be said, 'Our Lord does not there direct his discourse to the priests, but to the scribes and Pharisees'? He does; but this is the same thing. For the scribes were what we now term divines, the public teachers of the people.[13] And many if not most of the priests, especially all the strictest sort of them, were Pharisees; so 10 that in giving the character of the scribes and Pharisees he gives that of the priests also.

13. Soon after the pouring out of the Holy Ghost on the day of Pentecost, in the infancy of the Christian church, there was indeed a glorious change. 'Great grace was then upon them 15 all'[14]—ministers as well as people. 'The multitude of them that believed were of one heart and of one soul.'[15] But how short a time did this continue! How soon did 'the fine gold become dim'![16] Long before even the apostolic age expired, St. Paul himself had ground to complain that some of his fellow-labourers had 20 'forsaken' him, 'having loved the present world'.[17] And not long after St. John reproved divers of the angels—that is, the ministers of the churches in Asia—because even in that early period their 'works were not found perfect before God'.[18]

14. Thus did 'the mystery of iniquity'[19] begin to 'work' in the 25 ministers as well as the people, even before the end of the apostolic age. But how much more powerfully did it work as soon as those master-builders, the apostles, were taken out of the way![20] Both ministers and people were then farther and farther removed from the hope of the gospel. Insomuch that when St. 30 Cyprian, about an hundred and fifty years after the death of St. John, describes the spirit and behaviour both of the laity and

[13] For this usage of 'divine' as a public teacher of doctrine, cf. *OED*, usage 2: 'One who has officially to do with "divine things" . . . now, one skilled in divinity; a theologian' (1380, Wycliffe; 1450, Cuthbert [*Surtees*, 6706]; 1662, Gauden's edn. of Hooker's works); see also Johnson, *Dictionary*, 'divine', N.S., 2; cf. No. 25, 'Sermon on the Mount, V', IV.1.

[14] Acts 4:33. A variation on the theme of the church as a *corpus mixtum;* cf. Thomas Ken, *An Exposition on the Church Catechism* (1686), pp. 47-48 (one of Wesley's more important sources). Cf. also §15, below; as well as Nos. 61, 'The Mystery of Iniquity', §25; 66, 'Signs of the Times', II.7; and 102, 'Of Former Times', §16.

[15] Acts 4:32.   [16] Cf. Lam. 4:1.   [17] Cf. 2 Tim. 4:10.
[18] Cf. Rev. 3:2.   [19] Cf. 2 Thess. 2:7.   [20] *Ibid.*

clergy that were round about him, one would be ready to suppose he was giving us a description of the present clergy and laity of Europe.[21] But the corruption which had been creeping in drop by drop during the second and third century, in the beginning of the
5   fourth, when Constantine called himself a Christian, poured in upon the church with a full tide.[22] And whoever reads the history of the church from the time of Constantine to the Reformation, will easily observe that all the abominations of the heathen world, and in following ages of the Mahometans, overflowed every part
10 of it. And in every nation and city the clergy were not a whit more innocent than the laity.

15. 'But was there not a very considerable change in the body of the clergy, as well as the laity, at the time of the glorious Reformation from popery?' Undoubtedly there was. And they
15 were not only reformed from very many erroneous opinions, and from numberless superstitious and idolatrous modes of worship, till then prevailing over the western church; but they were also exceedingly reformed with respect to their lives and tempers. More of the ancient, scriptural Christianity was to be found,
20 almost in every part of Europe. Yet notwithstanding this all the works of the devil, all ungodliness and unrighteousness, sin of every kind, continued to prevail both over clergy and laity in all parts of Christendom. Even those clergymen who most warmly contended about the externals of religion were very little
25 concerned for the life and power of it, for piety, justice, mercy, and truth.[23]

16. However, it must be allowed that ever since the Reformation, and particularly in the present century, the behaviour of the clergy in general is greatly altered for the better.
30 And should it be granted that in many parts of the Romish Church they are nearly the same as they were before, it must be granted likewise that most of the Protestant clergy are far different from what they were. They have not only more learning of the most valuable kind, but abundantly much more religion.
35 Insomuch that the English and Irish clergy are generally allowed to be not inferior to any in Europe, for piety as well as for knowledge.[24]

---

[21] Cf. No. 61, 'The Mystery of Iniquity', §25 and n.
[22] *Ibid.*, §27 and n.   [23] See above, §13 and n.
[24] A rare but important concession that Wesley's harsh criticisms of the Anglican clergy did not apply to all—and here not even to the generality; cf. §18 below.

17. And all this being allowed, what lack they yet? Can anything be laid to their charge? I wish calmly and candidly to consider this point, in the fear and in the presence of God. I am far from desiring to aggravate the defects of my brethren, or to paint them in the strongest colours. Far be it from me to treat others as I have been treated myself; to return evil for evil, or railing for railing.[25] But to speak the naked truth[26]—not with anger or contempt, as too many have done—I acknowledge that many, if not most, of those that were appointed to minister in holy things with whom it has been my lot to converse, in almost every part of England or Ireland, for forty of fifty years last past, have not been eminent either for knowledge or piety. It has been loudly affirmed that most of those persons now in connexion with *me* who believe it their duty to call sinners to repentance, having been taken immediately from low trades, tailors, shoemakers, and the like, are a set of poor, stupid, illiterate men, that scarce know their right hand from their left; yet I cannot but say that I would sooner cut off my right hand than suffer one of them to speak a word in any of our chapels if I had not reasonable proof that he had more knowledge in the Holy Scriptures, more knowledge of himself, more knowledge of God and of the things of God, than nine in ten of the clergymen I have conversed with, either at the universities or elsewhere.[27]

18. In the meantime I gladly allow that this charge does not concern the whole body of the clergy. Undoubtedly there are many clergymen in these kingdoms that are not only free from outward sin,[28] but men of eminent learning, and what is infinitely more, deeply acquainted with God. But still I am constrained to confess that the far greater part of those ministers I have conversed with for above half a century have not been holy men, not devoted to God, not deeply acquainted either with God or themselves. It could not be said that they 'set' their 'affections on things above, not on things of the earth';[29] or that their desire and the business of their lives was to save their own souls and those that heard them.[30]

[25] 1 Pet. 3:9; cf. *General Rules*, I.4.
[26] Cf. No. 90, 'An Israelite Indeed', II.7 and n.
[27] For other comments on Methodist 'triumphalism', cf. No. 102, 'Of Former Times', §22 and n.
[28] Cf. No. 13, *On Sin in Believers*, intro., III.1-9, and n.
[29] Col. 3:2.
[30] See 1 Tim. 4:16.

19. I have taken this unpleasing view of a melancholy scene, of the character of those who have been appointed of God to be shepherds of souls for so many ages, in order to determine this question: 'Ought the children of God to refrain from his
5 ordinances because they that administer them are unholy men?'—a question with which many serious persons have been exceedingly perplexed. 'Ought we not', say they, 'to refrain from the ministrations of ungodly men? For is it possible that we should receive any good from the hands of those that know not God? Can
10 we suppose that the grace of God was ever conveyed to men by the servants of the devil?'

What saith the Scripture? Let us keep close to this, and we shall not be misled. We have seen there what manner of men most of these have been who have ministered in holy things for many
15 ages. Two or three thousand years ago, we read, 'The sons of Eli were sons of Belial; they knew not the Lord.'[31] But was this a sufficient reason for the Israelites to refrain from their administrations? It is true they 'abhorred the offerings of the Lord'[32] on their account. And yet they constantly attended them.
20 And do you suppose that Samuel, holy as he was, ever advised them to do otherwise? Were not the priests and public teachers equally strangers to God from this time to that of the Babylonish captivity? Undoubtedly they were. But did Isaiah or any of the prophets exhort them for that cause to forsake the ordinances of
25 God? Were they not equally ungodly from the time of the Babylonish captivity to the coming of Christ? How clearly does this appear, were there no other proof, from the prophecies of Jeremiah and Malachi! Yet did either Malachi or Jeremiah, or any other of the prophets, exhort the people to separate themselves
30 from these ungodly men?

20. But to bring the matter nearer to ourselves. Never were any priests or public teachers more corrupt, more totally estranged from God, than those in the days of our blessed Lord. Were they not mere whited walls?[33] Were not those that were the best of
35 them painted sepulchres?[34] Full of pride, lust, envy, covetousness? Of all ungodliness and unrighteousness?[35] Is not this the account

[31] 1 Sam. 2:12.
[32] 1 Sam. 2:17.
[33] Acts 23:3.
[34] See Matt. 23:27.
[35] Rom. 1:18.

which our Lord himself, who knew what was in man,[36] gives of them? But did he therefore refrain from that public service which was performed by these very men? Or did he direct his apostles so to do? Nay, just the contrary: in consequence of which, as he constantly attended them himself, so likewise did his disciples. 5

21. There is another circumstance in our Lord's conduct which is worthy of our peculiar consideration. 'He calls to him the twelve, and sends them forth, two by two,'[d] to preach the gospel. And as they did not go the warfare at their own cost,[37] the very 'devils were subject unto them'.[38] Now one of these was Judas 10 Iscariot. And did our Lord know that 'he had a devil'?[39] St. John expressly tells us he did. Yet he was coupled with another of the apostles, and joined with them all in the same communion. Neither have we any reason to doubt but God blessed the labour of all his twelve ambassadors. But why did our Lord send him 15 among them? Undoubtedly for our instruction. For a standing, unanswerable proof that he 'sendeth by whom he will send';[40] that he can and doth send salvation to men even by those who will not accept of it themselves.

22. Our Lord gives us farther instruction upon this head. In the 20 twenty-third chapter of Matthew (verses 1, 2, 3) we have those very remarkable words: 'Then Jesus spoke to the multitude and to his disciples, saying, The scribes and Pharisees sit in Moses' chair; all things therefore whatsoever they bid you observe, observe and do. But do not according to their works; for they say 25 and do not.' Of these very men he gives the blackest character in the following verses. Yet is he so far from forbidding either 'the multitude' or 'his own disciples' to attend their ministrations that he expressly commands them so to do, even in those words, 'All things whatsoever they bid you observe, observe and do.' These 30 words imply a command to hear them; for how could they 'observe and do what they bid them' if they did not hear it? I pray consider this, ye that say of the successors of these ungodly men, ' "They say and do not", therefore we ought not to hear them.' You see, your Master draws no such inference; nay, the direct 35

---

d Mark 6[:7].

---

36 See John 2:25.
37 See 1 Cor. 9:7.
38 Cf. Luke 10:17.   39 John 6:70.
40 Cf. Exod. 4:13; cf. also No. 4, *Scriptural Christianity*, IV.2 and n.

contrary. O be not wiser than your Master: follow his advice and do not reason against it.

23. But how shall we reconcile this with the direction given by St. Paul to the Corinthians? 'If any that is called a brother be a
5 fornicator, or covetous, or an idolater, or a railer, with such an one, no not to eat.'ᵉ How is it reconcilable with that direction in his Second Epistle, 'Come out from the midst of them, and be ye separate, saith the Lord, and touch not the unclean thing'?ᶠ I answer, the former passage has no relation at all to the present
10 question. It does not concern ministers good or bad. The plain meaning of it is: have no intimacy with any that is called a Christian, and lives in any open sin—a weighty exhortation which should be much attended to by all the children of God. As little does the other passage refer to ministers or teachers of any kind.
15 In this the Apostle is exhorting the children of God to break off all intercourse with the children of the devil. The words literally are, 'Go out from the midst of them, and be ye separate, and touch not the unclean thing'—intimating that they could not continue united with them without being more or less partakers of their
20 sins. We may therefore boldly affirm that neither St. Paul nor any other of the inspired writers ever advised holy men to separate from the church wherein they were because the ministers were unholy.

24. Nevertheless it is true that many pious Christians, as was
25 observed before, did separate themselves from the church, some even in the second, and many more in the third century. Some of these retired into the desert, and lived altogether alone; others built themselves houses, afterwards termed 'convents', and only secluded themselves from the rest of the world. But what was the
30 fruit of this separation? The same that might easily be foreseen. It increased and confirmed⁴¹ in an astonishing degree the total corruption of the church. The salt which was thus heaped up in a corner had effectually lost its savour. The light which was put under a bushel no longer shone before men.⁴² In consequence of
35 this, ungodliness and unrighteousness reigned without control. The world, being given up into the hands of the devil, wrought all

---

ᵉ 1 Cor. 5:11.   ᶠ Chap. 6, ver. 17.

---

⁴¹ Both early printed texts read 'increased and bestowed'—an obvious error. In Wesley's copy of *AM* he has corrected it as above.
⁴² See Matt. 5:13, 15-16.

his works with greediness. And gross darkness, joined with all manner of wickedness, covered the whole earth.[43]

25. 'But if all this wickedness was not a sufficient reason for separating from a corrupt church, why did Calvin and Luther[44] with their followers separate from the Church of Rome?' I answer, they did not properly separate from it, but were violently thrust out of it. They were not suffered to continue therein upon any other terms than subscribing to all the errors of that Church, and joining in all their superstition and idolatry. Therefore this separation lay [not] at *their* door. With [them][45] it was not a matter of choice, but of necessity. And if such necessity was now laid upon us, we ought to separate from any church under heaven.

26. There were not the same reasons why various bodies of men should afterwards separate from the Church of England. No sinful terms of communion were imposed upon them; neither are [they] at this day. Most of them separated either because of some *opinions* or some *modes of worship* which they did not approve of. Few of them assigned the unholiness either of the clergy or laity as the cause of their separation. And if any did so it did not appear that they themselves were a jot better than those they separated from.

27. But the grand reason which many give for separating from the Church, namely, that the ministers are unholy men, is founded on this assertion, that the ministration of evil men can do no good;[46] that we may call the sacraments 'means of grace'; but men who do not receive the grace of God themselves cannot convey that grace to others. So that we can never expect to receive the blessing of God through the servants of the devil.

This argument is extremely plausible, and is indeed the

---

[43] See Isa. 60:2.

[44] For Wesley's other references to Luther, cf. No. 14, *The Repentance of Believers*, I.9 and n.

[45] The early texts here pose an interesting problem. They both read: 'Therefore, this separation lay at *their* door [i.e., Luther's and Calvin's—a notion already denied two sentences earlier]. With *us* [i.e., the Methodists] it was not a matter of choice . . . [as if a separation from the Church of England had already been forced upon *them* after the analogy of Luther and Calvin]'. The editorial brackets are intended to allow for one of the sermon's main points to be understood more clearly.

[46] This, as Wesley was implying, would have been an outright denial of Art.XXVI, 'Of the Unworthiness of the Ministers, which hinders not the effect of the Sacraments.' But note that Wesley had already omitted this article from his abridgement of 'The Articles of Religion' in *The Sunday Service* (1784); see No. 32, 'Sermon on the Mount, XII', III.8 and n.

strongest that can be urged. Yet before you allow it to be conclusive you should consider a few things.

28. Consider, first, did the Jewish sacraments convey no saving grace to the hearers because they were administered by unholy
5 men? If so, none of the Israelites were saved from the time of Eli to the coming of Christ. For their priests were not a whit better than ours, if they were not much worse. But who will dare to affirm this? Which is no less, in effect, than to affirm that all the children of Israel went to hell for eleven or twelve hundred years
10 together.

29. Did the ordinances administered in the time of our blessed Lord convey no grace to those that attended them? Surely then the Holy Ghost would not have commended 'Zacharias and Elizabeth for walking in these ordinances'![47] If the ministrations
15 of wicked men did no good, would our Lord have commanded his followers (so far from forbidding them) to attend those of the scribes and Pharisees? Observe again the remarkable words: 'Then spake Jesus to the multitude, and to his disciples, saying, The scribes and Pharisees sit in Moses' seat,' are your appointed
20 teachers; 'all therefore whatsoever they bid you observe, that observe and do.'[g] Now what were these scribes and Pharisees? Were they not the vilest of men? Yet these very men he commands them to hear. This command is plainly implied in those words, 'Whatsoever they command you to observe, that observe and do.'
25 For unless they heard what they said, they could not do it.

30. Consider a little farther the dreadful consequences of affirming that wicked ministers do no good: that the ordinances administered by them do not convey saving grace to those that attend them. If it be so, then wellnigh all the Christians from the
30 time of the apostles to that of the Reformation are perished! For what manner of men were wellnigh all the clergy during all those centuries? Consult the history of the church in every age, and you will find more and more proofs of their corruption. It is true they have not been so openly abandoned since, but ever since that
35 happy period there has been a considerable change for the better, in the clergy as well as the laity. But still there is reason to fear that even those who now minister in holy things, who are outwardly devoted to God for that purpose (yea, and in Protestant as well as

g Matt. 23:1-3.

---

47 Cf. Luke 1:5-6.

Romish countries), are nevertheless far more devoted to the world, to riches, honour, or pleasure (a few comparatively excepted) than they are to God; so that in truth they are as far from Christian holiness as earth is from heaven. If then no grace is conveyed by the ministry of wicked men, in what a case is the Christian world! How hath God forgotten to be gracious![48] How hath he forsaken his own inheritance! O think not so! Rather say with our own Church (though in direct opposition to the Church of Rome, which maintains, 'If the priest does not minister with *a pure intention*, which no wicked man can do, then the sacrament is no sacrament at all'[49]), the unworthiness of the minister doth not hinder the efficacy of God's ordinance.[50] The reason is plain; because the efficacy is derived, not from him that administers, but from him that ordains it. He does not, will not, suffer his grace to be intercepted, though the messenger will not receive it himself.

31. Another consequence would follow from the supposition that no grace is conveyed by wicked ministers, namely, that a conscientious person cannot be a member of any national church in the world. For wherever he is, it is great odds whether a holy minister be stationed there; and if there be not, it is mere lost labour to worship in that congregation. But, blessed be God, this is not the case; we know by our own happy experience, and by the experience of thousands, that the word of the Lord is not bound, though uttered by an unholy minister; and the sacraments are not dry breasts,[51] whether he that administers be holy or unholy.

32. Consider one more consequence of this supposition, should it ever be generally received. Were all men to separate from those churches where the minister was an unholy man (as they ought to do, if the grace of God never did nor could attend his ministry) what confusion, what tumults, what commotions

[48] Ps. 77:9.

[49] An inference, drawn up as if it were a quotation, from Canon XI of Trent, Seventh Session, 'Of the Sacraments in General', and the *Catechism of the Council of Trent for Parish Priests* (1566), Pt. II, 'Unworthiness of the Minister and Validity.' The Tridentine doctrine stresses the administrant's intention to replicate the *church's* intention in a given sacrament. For Wesley's linking pure intention to holiness, cf. No. 26, 'Sermon on the Mount, VI', §1 and n.

[50] See Art.XXVI, 'Of the Unworthiness of the Ministers, which hinders not the effects of the Sacraments.'

[51] Cf. Henry Smith, *Sermons* (1657), p. 48: 'The Word and the Sacraments are the two breasts of the Church;' see also the frontispiece of Joseph Mede's *Works*, 1677 (i.e., the picture there of *Ecclesia's* flowing breasts). The closest biblical allusion would be Hos. 9:14.

would this occasion throughout Christendom! What evil surmisings, heart-burnings, jealousies, envyings, must everywhere arise! What censuring, tale-bearing, strife, contention! Neither would it stop here; but from evil words the contending
5 parties would soon proceed to evil deeds; and rivers of blood would soon be shed, to the utter scandal of Mahometans and heathens.

33. Let us not then trouble and embroil ourselves and our neighbours with unprofitable disputations, but all agree to
10 spread, to the uttermost of our power, the quiet and peaceable gospel of Christ. Let us make the best of whatever ministry the providence of God has assigned us. Near fifty years ago, a great and good man, Dr. Potter, then Archbishop of Canterbury,[52] gave me an advice for which I have ever since had occasion to bless
15 God: 'If you desire to be extensively useful, do not spend your time and strength in contending for or against such things as are of a disputable nature; but in testifying against open, notorious vice, and in promoting real, essential holiness.' Let us keep to this; leaving a thousand disputable points to those that have no
20 better business than to toss the ball of controversy to and fro, let us keep close to our point. Let us bear a faithful testimony, in our several stations, against all ungodliness and unrighteousness; and with all our might recommend that inward and outward holiness 'without which no man shall see the Lord'.[53]

25 Bristol, Oct. 7, 1787[54]

---

[52] John Potter (1674–1747) who, as Bishop of Oxford, had ordained Wesley as deacon in 1725 and as priest in 1728. For the occasion mentioned here, cf. CWJ, Feb. 21, 1739—the report of a visit by the brothers to the archiepiscopal palace in Lambeth: 'He [Archbishop Potter] showed us great affection; . . . cautioned us to give no more umbrage than was necessary for our own defence; to forebear exceptionable phrases; to keep to the doctrines of the church . . . ; avowed justification by faith . . . .' This visit is noted in Wesley's diary for the same date.
[53] Heb. 12:14.
[54] Place and date as in *AM*.

ON CONSCIENCE

AN INTRODUCTORY COMMENT

In his Journal *for March 3, 1788, Wesley reports that he 'went on to Bristol and, having two or three quiet days, finished [his] sermon on Conscience'. This was then published with that title in* SOSO, *VIII. 213-31 (there is no record of Wesley's previous use of 2 Cor. 1:12 as a preaching text).*

When the sermon appeared in the September and October issues of the Arminian Magazine, *1788 (XI.453-58, 508-13), numbered 'Sermon XLVII' (but without a title), it was dated 'Bristol,* April 8, 1788'. *According to the diary, however, Wesley was in* Stockport *on April 8 (Sermon XLVIII, which appeared in the November and December issues of the* Arminian Magazine, *is dated 'Stockport, April 9, 1788'). The diary confirms that Wesley did indeed arrive in Bristol on* March 3, *and worked on a sermon on* March 4, 5, 6, *and 8 (the date he probably finished transcribing it), and supports our dating it from the* Journal *rather than from the* Arminian Magazine.

What seems clear, in any case, is that Wesley was under pressure to complete the fourteen sermons that would make up the concluding volume of his Sermons on Several Occasions. *This present sermon, 'On Conscience', is a summing up of reflections on a theme that had fascinated Wesley all his life, as it had his Puritan forebears. Thus, the crucial point, that our* universal *'moral sense' is not 'natural' (as Francis Hutcheson had argued) but rather the effect of prevenient grace, had already been made in No. 85, 'On Working Out Our Own Salvation', and in many another text as well. And, Wesley's conscious link with the Puritans on this point is emphasized by his inclusion of an untypically extensive quotation from a century-old sermon by his maternal grandfather, Samuel Annesley. It was as if grandfather and grandson were able to speak with one voice on one of the basic presuppositions of Christian ethics.*

On Conscience

2 Corinthians 1:12

For our rejoicing is this, the testimony of our conscience.

1. How few words are there in the world more common than
5 this—'conscience'! It is almost in everyone's mouth. And one
would thence be apt to conclude that no word can be found which
is more generally understood. But it may be doubted whether this
is the case or no, although numberless treatises have been written
upon it. For it is certain a great part of those writers have rather
10 puzzled the cause than cleared it, that they have usually 'darkened
counsel by uttering words without knowledge'.[1]

2. The best treatise on the subject which I remember to have
seen is translated from the French of Mons. Placette,[2] which
describes in a clear and rational manner the nature and offices of
15 conscience. But though it was published near a hundred years
ago, it is in very few hands. And indeed a great part of those that
have read it complain of the length of it. An octavo volume[3] of
several hundred pages upon so plain a subject was likely to prove a
trial of patience to most persons of understanding. It seems
20 therefore there is still wanting a discourse upon the subject, short
as well as clear. This by the assistance of God I will endeavour to
supply, by showing, first, the nature of conscience; and then the
several sorts of it; after which I shall conclude with a few
important directions.

---

[1] Cf. Job 38:2.

[2] I.e., Jean La Placette (1639–1718), a Huguenot exile, whose *Divers traités sur des matières de conscience . . .* (1697) had been translated by Basil Kennett as *The Christian Casuist; or, A Treatise of Conscience* (1705). Wesley's complaint about the inadequacy of the 'numberless treatises [that] have been written upon [conscience]' is an echo of La Placette's preface but ignores his citation of Bishop Sanderson's 'uncompleted' but 'promising inquiry' which had 'induced [La Placette] to lend [his] hand to the service'. The complaint is puzzling in any case, since Wesley's views are not strikingly different from the 'numberless treatises' of Richard Baxter, Jeremy Taylor, Dean Swift, the Danish bishop J. R. Brochmand, Robert South, *et al.*, save on the particular point of conscience as a constant work of prevenience and, therefore, supernatural. And it may well be that it was this point that Wesley regarded as crucial. (The original 'Placatt' is altered to 'Placette' in notes added to Wesley's own copy of *AM*.)

[3] An indication that Wesley was using the Kennett translation, which is octavo; the original is duodecimo.

I.1. And, first, I am to show the nature of conscience. This a very pious man in the last century (in his sermon on *Universal Conscientiousness*[4]) describes in the following manner: 'This word, which literally signifies "knowing with another", excellently sets forth the scriptural notion of it. So Job 16:19, "My witness is in [5] heaven;"[5] and so the Apostle, Rom. 9:1, "I say the truth, my conscience also bearing me witness in the Holy Ghost." In both places it is as if he had said, God witnesseth with my conscience.[6] Conscience is placed in the middle—under God, and above man. It is a kind of silent reasoning of the mind, whereby those things [10] which are judged to be right are approved of with pleasure; but those which are judged evil are disapproved of with uneasiness.'[7] This is a tribunal in the breast of men to accuse sinners and excuse them that do well.

2. To view it in a somewhat different light, conscience, as well [15] as the Latin word from which it is taken, and the Greek word συνειδήσεως,[8] necessarily imply *the knowledge of two or more things together*—suppose the knowledge of our words and actions, and at the same time of their goodness or badness; if it be not rather the faculty whereby we know at once our actions and the [20] quality of them.

3. *Conscience*, then, is that faculty whereby we are at once conscious of our own thoughts, words, and actions, and of their merit or demerit, of their being good or bad, and consequently deserving either praise or censure. And some pleasure generally [25] attends the former sentence, some uneasiness the latter. But this varies exceedingly, according to education and a thousand other circumstances.

4. Can it be denied that something of this is found in every man born into the world? And does it not appear as soon as the [30]

---

[4] This was Samuel Annesley (1620–96), father of Susanna Wesley. His sermon (on Acts 24:16) was published in *The Morning-Exercise at Cripplegate*, a sermon collection which he had edited in 1661. Wesley had abridged and published it in the *Christian Lib.*, XXXVIII. 297-338, where it is mistakenly attributed to 'The Rev. Matthew Pool' (author of the *Annotations*). A long quotation from the same sermon, correctly attributed, appears below as Wesley's conclusion (I.19).

[5] Cf. Poole, *Annotations*, on Job 16:19: 'Besides the witness of men and of my own conscience, God is witness of my integrity.'

[6] Cf. Robert Sanderson, *De obligatione conscientiae . . .* (1660), I.17:23.

[7] Annesley's quotation (garbled) from the Danish Lutheran polemicist, J. R. Brochmand (1585–1652), *Universae Theologiae Systema* (1658), I.i.3:7.

[8] Cf. 2 Cor. 1:12; the nominative form is συνείδησις (variations of which occur twenty-five times in the New Testament).

understanding opens? as soon as reason begins to dawn? Does not everyone then begin to know that there is a difference between good and evil, how imperfect soever the various circumstances of this sense of good and evil may be? Does not every man, for
5   instance, know, unless blinded by the prejudice of education (like the inhabitants of the Cape of Good Hope[9]) that it is good to honour his parents? Do not all men, however uneducated or barbarous, allow it is right to do to others as we would have them do to us? And are not all who know this condemned in their own
10   mind when they do anything contrary thereto? As, on the other hand, when they act suitable thereto they have the approbation of their own conscience.

5. This faculty seems to be what is usually meant by those who speak of 'natural conscience', an expression frequently found in
15   some of our best authors, but yet not strictly just. For though in one sense it may be termed 'natural', because it is found in all men, yet properly speaking it is not *natural;* but a supernatural gift of God, above all his natural endowments.[10] No, it is not nature but the Son of God that is 'the true light, which enlighteneth
20   every man which cometh into the world'.[11] So that we may say to every human creature, 'He', not nature, 'hath shown thee, O man, what is good.'[12] And it is his Spirit who giveth thee an inward check, who causeth thee to feel uneasy, when thou walkest in any instance contrary to the light which he hath given thee.

25   6. It may give a peculiar force to that beautiful passage to consider by whom, and on what occasion, the words were uttered. The persons speaking are Balak the King of Moab, and Balaam, then under divine impressions (it seems, then, 'not far from the kingdom of God',[13] although afterward he so foully revolted).
30   Probably Balak too at that time experienced something of the same influence. This occasioned his 'consulting with', or asking counsel of, Balaam; his proposing the question to which Balaam gives so full an answer: 'O my people' (saith the prophet in the name of God), 'remember what Balak the King of Moab

[9] For Wesley's knowledge of the Cape of Good Hope and its inhabitants ('the Hottentots'), cf. Nos. 28, 'Sermon on the Mount, VIII', §9 and n.; and 69, 'The Imperfection of Human Knowledge', II.5 and n.
[10] Cf. Nos. 85, 'On Working Out Our Own Salvation', III.4; and 129, 'Heavenly Treasure in Earthen Vessels', I.1.
[11] Cf. John 1:9.
[12] Cf. Mic. 6:8.
[13] Mark 12:34.

consulted' (it seems in the fullness of his heart), 'and what Balaam the son of Beor answered him. Wherewith', said he, 'shall I come before the Lord, and bow myself before the high God? Shall I come before him with calves of a year old? Will the Lord be pleased with thousands of rams, or with ten thousand rivers of oil? Shall I give my first-born for my transgression? The fruit of my body for the sin of my soul?' (This the kings of Moab had actually done on occasions of deep distress; a remarkable account of which is recorded in the third chapter of the second book of Kings.) To this Balaam makes that noble reply (being doubtless then taught of God): 'He hath showed thee, O man, what is good. And what doth the Lord thy God require of thee but to do justly, to love mercy, and to walk humbly with thy God!'[a]

7. To take a more distinct view of conscience, it appears to have a threefold office. First, it is a *witness*, testifying what we have done, in thought, or word, or action. Secondly, it is a *judge*, passing sentence on what we have done, that it is good or evil. And thirdly, it in some sort *executes* the sentence, by occasioning a degree of complacency in him that does well, and a degree of uneasiness in him that does evil.[14]

8. Professor Hutcheson, late of Glasgow,[15] places conscience in a different light. In his *Essay on the Passions* he observes that we have several *senses*, or natural avenues of pleasure and pain, besides the five external senses. One of these he terms, 'the public sense', whereby we are naturally pained at the misery of a fellow-creature, and pleased at his deliverance from it. And every man, says he, has a 'moral sense', whereby he approves of benevolence and disapproves of cruelty. Yea, he is uneasy when

[a] Micah 6:5-8. [Note the anachronistic conflation here of Balaam and Micah.]

[14] Cf. the parallels between conscience and the judicial process, as in No. 15, *The Great Assize*, IV.4 and n.
[15] Both early texts have 'Hutchinson' here, but Wesley's own copy of *AM* has it correctly in the margin. The reference is to Francis Hutcheson (see No. 12, 'The Witness of Our Own Spirit', §5 and n.) and to his *Essay on the Nature and Conduct of the Passions and Affections with Illustrations Upon the Moral Sense* (1726), which was prescribed reading for the scholars at the Kingswood School (cf. *A Short Account of the School in Kingswood*, Supplement, 1768). Wesley, however, had decided that Hutcheson's ethical theory excluded the supernatural on principle and thereby denied the concept of prevenience on which he himself set such great store; cf. JWJ, Dec. 17, 1772, and Nov. 9, 1773; see also No. 90, 'An Israelite Indeed', proem. Hutcheson's analysis of the various moral senses is on pp. 4-6 of his *Essay*. Cf. his *System of Moral Philosophy* (1755), where he adds yet another 'sense': *viz.*, 'the sense of the admiration of excellence'.

he himself has done a cruel action, and pleased when he has done a generous one.

9. All this is in some sense undoubtedly true. But it is not true that either the 'public' or the 'moral sense' (both of which are included in the term conscience) is now *natural* to man. Whatever may have been the case at first, while man was in a state of innocence, both the one and the other is now a branch of that supernatural gift of God which we usually style 'preventing grace'. But the professor does not at all agree with this. He sets God wholly out of the question. God has nothing to do with his scheme of virtue from the beginning to the end. So that to say the truth, his scheme of virtue is atheism all over.[16] This is refinement indeed! Many have excluded God out of the world: he excludes him even out of religion!

10. But do we not mistake him? Do we take his meaning right? That it may be plain enough, that no man may mistake him, he proposes this question: 'What if a man in doing a virtuous, that is, a generous action, in helping a fellow-creature, has an eye to God, either as commanding or as promising to reward it? Then', says he, 'so far as he has an eye to God, the virtue of the action is lost. Whatever actions spring from an eye to the recompense of reward have no virtue, no moral goodness in them.'[17] Alas! Was this man called a Christian? How unjustly was he slandered with that appellation![18] Even Dr. Taylor, though he does not allow Christ to be God, yet does not scruple to term him, 'a person of consummate *virtue*'.[19] But the professor cannot allow him any virtue at all!

[16] That Wesley and Hutcheson stood poles apart in their theories of ethical motivation is obvious. But that Hutcheson's theory 'sets God wholly out of the question' is a misreading at the very least. 'As endowed by our Creator' is a phrase as pat in Hutcheson as 'moral sense' (the two are often linked). 'Good dispositions . . . must be originally implanted in our nature by its Great Author . . .'; cf. *An Inquiry into the Original of Our Ideas of Beauty and Virtue* (2nd edn., 1726), p. 270; see also xiv. 44, 46, 50, 93, 101, 166, 184, 211, etc.

[17] Hutcheson's point, throughout, is that virtue must be disinterested, devoid of any motive of reward, even from God. Cf. William T. Blackstone, *Francis Hutcheson and Contemporary Ethical Theory* (Athens, Georgia, Univ. of Georgia Press, 1965), pp. 11-40.

[18] The two early texts here read 'assertion'; 'appellation' appears as a marginal correction in Wesley's own copy of *AM*.

[19] Dr. John Taylor (1694–1761), Unitarian minister of Norwich, against whose *The Scripture-Doctrine of Original Sin: Proposed to Free and Candid Examination* (1740) Wesley published *The Doctrine of Original Sin* (1757). Cf. the 4th edn. of Taylor (1767), p. 75: 'The worthiness of Christ is his consummate virtue. It is virtue, obedience to the truth, or the divine will, and benevolence to his creatures that wins every prize, that carrieth every cause to heaven.' P. 74: 'What was it that gave this glorious personage, emblemized by the Lamb (Rev. 5) his superior WORTHINESS, his prevailing interest in God beyond all

11. But to return. What is conscience in the Christian sense? It is that faculty of the soul which, by the assistance of the grace of God, sees at one and the same time, (1), our own tempers and lives, the real nature and quality of our thoughts, words, and actions; (2), the rule whereby we are to be directed, and (3), the 5 agreement or disagreement therewith. To express this a little more largely: conscience implies, first, the faculty a man has of knowing himself, of discerning both in general and in particular his own tempers, thoughts, words, and actions. But this it is not possible for him to do without the assistance of the Spirit of God. 10 Otherwise self-love, and indeed every other irregular passion, would disguise and wholly conceal him from himself. It implies, secondly, a knowledge of the rule whereby he is to be directed in every particular, which is no other than the written Word of God. Conscience implies, thirdly, a knowledge that all his thoughts and 15 words and actions are or are not[20] conformable to that rule. In all the offices of conscience the 'unction of the Holy One'[21] is indispensably needful. Without this neither could we clearly discern our lives or tempers, nor could we judge of the rule whereby we are to walk, or of our conformity or disconformity to 20 it.

12. This is properly the account of a *good* conscience, which may be in other terms expressed thus: a divine consciousness of walking in all things according to the written Word of God. It seems, indeed, that there can be no conscience which has not a 25 regard to God. If you say, 'Yes: there certainly may be a consciousness of having done right or wrong without any reference to him.' I answer, This I cannot grant. I doubt whether the very words, 'right and wrong', according to the Christian system, do not imply, in the very idea of them, agreement and 30 disagreement to the will and word of God. If so, there is no such

---

others in heaven and earth? Evidently, it was his being slain, and having redeemed us unto God by his blood. This is to say, it was his obedience to God and goodwill to men—it was his *consummate virtue*.' Elsewhere (pp. 73, 65, 47, 45, etc.), Taylor speaks of Christ's perfect obedience, even unto death, as the ground and power of our redemption. This is, at best, an exemplarist theory of atonement; even so, Jesus Christ, for Taylor, was more than merely 'a man of consummate virtue'; cf. pp. 82-83. See also No. 123, 'On Knowing Christ after the Flesh', §4; and note that in No. 70, 'The Case of Reason Impartially Considered', II.6, Wesley had applied the term, 'consummate virtue', to Socrates.

[20] The phrase, 'or are not', stands as a marginal note in Wesley's copy of *AM*, though not in his own hand; clearly it improves the sense here.

[21] Cf. 1 John 2:20.

thing as conscience in a Christian if we leave God out of the question.

13. In order to the very existence of a good conscience, as well as to the continuance of it, the continued influence of the Spirit of God is absolutely needful. Accordingly the Apostle John declares to the believers of all ages: 'Ye have an unction from the Holy One; and ye know all things:'[22] all things that are needful to your having 'a conscience void of offence toward God and toward man'.[23] So he adds, 'Ye have no need that anyone should teach you,' otherwise 'than as that anointing teacheth you'.[24] That anointing clearly teacheth us those three things, first, the true meaning of God's Word; secondly, our own tempers and lives, bringing all our thoughts, words, and actions to remembrance; and thirdly, the agreement of all with the commandments of God.

14. Proceed we now to consider, in the second place, the several *sorts* of conscience.[25] A good conscience has been spoken of already. This St. Paul expresses various ways. In one place he simply terms it, a 'good conscience toward God';[26] in another, 'a conscience void of offence toward God and toward man'.[27] But he speaks still more largely in the text: 'Our rejoicing is this, the testimony of our conscience, that in simplicity'—with a single eye—'and godly sincerity, we have had our conversation in the world.'[28] Meantime he observes that this was done, 'not by fleshly wisdom', commonly called prudence (this never did, nor ever can produce such an effect), 'but by the grace of God',[29] which alone is sufficient to work this in any child of man.

15. Nearly allied to this (if it be not the same placed in another view, or a particular branch of it) is a *tender* conscience. One of a tender conscience is exact in observing any deviation from the Word of God, whether in thought, or word, or work, and immediately feels remorse and self-condemnation for it. And the constant cry of his soul is,

> O that my tender soul may fly
> The first abhorred approach of ill:
> Quick as the apple of an eye
> The slightest touch of sin to feel.[30]

[22] *Ibid.*   [23] Cf. Acts 24:16.   [24] Cf. 1 John 2:27.
[25] Cf., for the basic argument from here on, Dr. Annesley's sermon in *The Morning-Exercise at Cripplegate* (1661), pp. 7-13.
[26] Cf. Acts 23:1.   [27] Cf. Acts 24:16.   [28] 2 Cor. 1:12.   [29] *Ibid.*
[30] John and Charles Wesley, 'Watch in All Things', *Hymns and Sacred Poems* (1742), p. 218 (*Poet. Wks.*, II.273); see No. 12, 'The Witness of Our Own Spirit', §19 and n.

16. But sometimes this excellent quality, *tenderness* of conscience, is carried to an extreme. We find some who fear where no fear is, who are continually condemning themselves without cause; imagining some things to be sinful which the Scripture nowhere condemns; and supposing other things to be 5 their duty which the Scripture nowhere enjoins. This is properly termed a 'scrupulous' conscience, and is a sore evil. It is highly expedient to yield to it as little as possible; rather it is a matter of earnest prayer that you may be delivered from this sore evil, and may recover a sound mind: to which nothing would contribute 10 more than the converse of a pious and judicious friend.

17. But the extreme which is opposite to this is far more dangerous. A 'hardened' conscience is a thousand times more dangerous than a scrupulous one: that can violate a plain command of God without any self-condemnation, either doing 15 what he has expressly forbidden, or neglecting what he has expressly commanded, and yet without any remorse; yea, perhaps glorying in this very hardness of heart! Many instances of this deplorable stupidity we meet with at this day—and even among people that suppose themselves to have no small share of religion. 20 A person is doing something which the Scripture clearly forbids. You ask, 'How do you dare to do this?' and are answered with perfect unconcern, 'Oh, my heart does not condemn me.' I reply: 'So much the worse. I would to God it did. You would then be in a safer state than you are now. It is a dreadful thing to be 25 condemned by the Word of God, and yet not to be condemned by your own heart!' If we can break the least of the known commands of God without any self-condemnation, it is plain, the god of this world[31] hath hardened our hearts. If we do not soon recover from this we shall be 'past feeling',[32] and our consciences (as St. Paul 30 speaks) will be 'seared as with a hot iron'.[33]

18. I have now only to add a few important directions. The first great point is this: suppose we have a tender conscience, how shall we preserve it? I believe there is only one possible way of doing this, which is—to obey it. Every act of disobedience tends to blind 35 and deaden it, to put out its eyes, that it may not see the good and the acceptable will of God,[34] and to deaden the heart that it may

[31] 2 Cor. 4:4.
[32] Eph. 4:19.
[33] 1 Tim. 4:2 (*Notes*); see also No. 85, 'On Working Out Our Own Salvation', III.4.
[34] See Rom. 12:2.

not feel self-condemnation when we act in opposition to it. And, on the contrary, every act of obedience gives to the conscience a sharper and stronger sight, and a quicker feeling of whatever offends the glorious majesty of God. Therefore if you desire to
5 have your conscience always quick to discern and faithful to accuse or excuse you; if you would preserve it always sensible and tender, be sure to obey it at all events. Continually listen to its admonitions, and steadily follow them. Whatever it directs you to do according to the Word of God, do, however grievous to flesh
10 and blood. Whatever it forbids, if the prohibition be grounded on the Word of God, see you do it not, however pleasing it may be to flesh and blood. The one or the other may frequently be the case. What God forbids may be pleasing to our evil nature. There you are called to deny yourself, or you deny your Master. What he
15 enjoins may be painful to nature: there take up your cross. So true is our Lord's word, 'Except a man deny himself, and take up his cross daily',[35] 'he cannot be my disciple'.[36]

19. I cannot conclude this discourse better than with an extract from Dr. Annesley's sermon on *Universal Conscientiousness*.[b]

20 Be persuaded to practise the following directions, and your conscience will continue right.

(1). Take heed of every sin; count no sin small; and obey every command with your might. Watch against the first risings of sin, and beware of the borders of sin. Shun the very appearance of evil. Venture not upon temptations or
25 occasions of sin.

(2). Consider yourself as living under God's eye: live as in the sensible presence of the jealous God. Remember all things are naked and open before him! You cannot deceive him; for he is infinite wisdom. You cannot fly from him; for he is everywhere. You cannot bribe him; for he is righteousness itself!
30 Speak as knowing God hears you: walk as knowing God besets you on every side. The Lord is with you while you are with him; that is, you shall enjoy his favourable presence while you live in his awful presence.

(3). Be serious and frequent in the examination of your heart and life. There are some duties like those parts of the body, the want of which may be supplied
35 by other parts; but the want of these nothing can supply. Every evening review your carriage through the day: what you have done, or thought, that was unbecoming your character; whether your heart has been instant upon religion,

---

[b] Dr. Annesley (my mother's father), was rector of the parish of Cripplegate. [The quotation begins in Annesley on p. 21 and runs through p. 24. It is severely abridged and freely revised; all of Annesley's annotations are omitted.]

---

[35] Cf. Luke 9:23.
[36] Luke 14:26, 27, 33.

and indifferent to the world. Have a special care of two portions of your time, namely morning and evening: the morning to forethink what you have to do, and the evening to examine whether you have done what you ought.

(4). Let every action have reference to your whole life, and not to a part only. Let all your subordinate ends be suitable to the great end of your living. 5 'Exercise yourself unto godliness.'[37] Be as diligent in religion as thou wouldst have thy children that go to school be in learning. Let thy whole life be a preparation for heaven, like the preparation of wrestlers for the combat.

(5). Do not venture on sin because Christ hath purchased a pardon; that is a most horrible abuse of Christ. For this very reason there was no sacrifice under 10 the law for any wilful sin; lest people should think they knew the price of sins, as those do who deal in popish indulgences.

(6). Be nothing in your own eyes: for what is it, alas, that we have to be proud of? Our very conception was sinful, our birth painful, our life toilsome, our death we know not what! But all this is nothing to the state of our soul. If we 15 know this, what excuse have we for pride?

(7). Consult duty, not events. We have nothing to do but to mind our duty. All speculations that tend not to holiness are among your superfluities; but forebodings of what may befall you in doing your duty may be reckoned among your sins; and to venture upon sin to avoid danger is to sink the ship for fear of 20 pirates. O how quiet, as well as holy, would our lives be had we learned that single lesson, to be careful for nothing but to do our duty, and leave all consequences to God! What madness for silly dust to prescribe to Infinite Wisdom! To let go our work and meddle with God's! He hath managed the concerns of the world, and of every individual in it, without giving cause of 25 complaint to any, for above these five thousand years. And does he now need *your* counsel? Nay, it is *your* business to mind your own duty.

(8). What advice you would give another, take yourself: the worst of men are apt enough to lay burdens on others, which if they would take on themselves they would be rare Christians. 30

(9). Do nothing on which you cannot pray for a blessing. Every action of a Christian that is good is sanctified by the Word and prayer.[38] It becomes not a Christian to do anything so trivial that he cannot pray over it. And if he would but bestow a serious ejaculation on every occurrent action, such a prayer would cut off all things sinful and encourage all things lawful. 35

(10). Think, and speak, and do what you are persuaded Christ himself would do in your case were he on earth. It becomes a Christian rather to be an example than to follow one. But by imitating Christ you become an example to all, who was, and is, and ever will be, our absolute pattern. O Christians, how did Christ pray and redeem time for prayer? How did Christ preach, out of whose mouth 40 proceeded no other but gracious words? What time did Christ spend in impertinent discourse? How did Christ go up and down doing good to men, and what was pleasing to God? Beloved, I commend to you these four memorials: i, mind duty; ii, what is the duty of another in your case is your own; iii, do not meddle with anything if you cannot say, 'The blessing of the Lord be upon it'; iv, 45

---

[37] Cf. 1 Tim. 4:7.
[38] Cf. 1 Tim. 4:5.

above all, sooner forget your Christian name than forget to eye Christ! Whatever treatment you meet with from the world, remember him and follow his steps, 'who did no sin, neither was guile found in his mouth! Who, when he was reviled, reviled not again, but committed himself to him that judgeth
5   righteously.'[39]

Bristol, April 8, 1788[40]

---

[39] 1 Pet. 2:22-23.
[40] Place and date as in *AM;* but see above, No. 105, 'On Conscience', intro.

ON FAITH, HEBREWS 11:6

AN INTRODUCTORY COMMENT

This sermon was first published in SOSO, *VIII.233-48 (1788), with the title as given here but with no indication of place and date. In the* Arminian Magazine, *where it appeared in the November and December issues (without title but numbered as 'Sermon XLVIII'), it was dated as at 'Stockport, April 9, 1788'. Wesley was in Stockport on April 9, and probably put the finishing touches on a manuscript that he had already been writing in snatches before sending it back to London to be printed. It may be interesting that Wesley had not preached on Heb. 11:6 before. However, on June 8, 1790 (in Newcastle), he returned to it; moreover, in his last two years he wrote two more sermons about 'faith' (Nos. 117, 'On the Discoveries of Faith'; and 132, 'On Faith, Heb. 11:1') and another on 2 Cor. 5:7 (No. 119, 'Walking by Sight and Walking by Faith').*

This present sermon summarizes Wesley's gradual but decisive move away from his early, stark disjunctions between the conscious assurance *of God's favour and its total absence. Here, we find a sort of tacit retraction of his earlier harsh judgments against 'lower degrees of faith', as in* The Almost Christian *and* Scriptural Christianity. *It can be read, therefore, as a concluding comment on the whole idea of degrees of faith (each valid in its degree); indeed, it comes closer to an explicit statement of his vision of universal saving grace than anything else in the Wesley corpus.[1]*

---

[1] Cf. Michael Hurley, S.J., 'Salvation Today and Wesley Today', in *The Place of Wesley in the Christian Tradition*, ed. Kenneth E. Rowe, pp. 94-116; note that Fr. Hurley does not mention this sermon but recognizes its motif as characteristic in other writings of Wesley.

On Faith

Hebrews 11:6

Without faith it is impossible to please him.

1. But what is *faith?* It is a divine 'evidence, and conviction of
5 things not seen';[1] of things which are not seen now, whether they
are visible or invisible in their own nature. Particularly, it is a
divine evidence and conviction of God and of the things of God.
This is the most comprehensive definition of faith that ever was or
can be given, as including every species of faith, from the lowest to
10 the highest. And yet I do not remember any eminent writer that
has given a full and clear account of the several sorts of it, among
all the verbose and tedious treatises which have been published
upon the subject.
2. Something indeed of a similar kind has been written by that
15 great and good man, Mr. Fletcher, in his treatise on the various
dispensations of the grace of God.[2] Herein he observes that there
are four dispensations that are distinguished from each other by
the degree of light which God vouchsafes to them that are under
each. A small degree of light is given to those that are under the
20 *heathen* dispensation. These generally believed 'that there was a
God, and that he was a rewarder of them that diligently sought
him.'[3] But a far more considerable degree of light was vouchsafed
to the Jewish nation; inasmuch as to them *were entrusted* the grand
means of light, the oracles of God.[4] Hence many of these had
25 clear and exalted views of the nature and attributes of God; of
their duty to God and man; yea, and of the great promise, made to
our first parents and transmitted by them to their posterity, that
'the seed of the woman should bruise the serpent's head.'[5]
3. But above both the heathen and Jewish dispensation was that
30 of John the Baptist. To him a still clearer light was given: and he

---

[1] Cf. Heb. 11:1; see No. 3, *'Awake, Thou That Sleepest'*, I.11 and n.
[2] Cf. John W. Fletcher, *The Doctrines of Grace and Justice . . .* (1777), sect. I, pp. 1-13.
Fletcher's 'four capital dispensations' are 'I. Gentilism, which is frequently called "natural
religion";' 'II. Judaism, which is frequently called the Mosaic dispensation;' 'III. The
Gospel of John the Baptist;' and 'IV. The Perfect Gospel of Christ.'
[3] Cf. Heb. 11:6.   [4] See Rom. 3:2.
[5] Cf. Gen. 3:15.

was himself 'a burning and a shining light'.[6] To him it was given to 'behold the Lamb of God, that taketh away the sin of the world'.[7] Accordingly our Lord himself affirms that, 'of all which had been born of women', there had not till that time arisen 'a greater than John the Baptist'! But nevertheless, he informs us, 'He that is least in the kingdom of God', the Christian dispensation, 'is greater than he.'[8] By one that is under the Christian dispensation Mr. Fletcher means one that has received the Spirit of adoption, that has the Spirit of God witnessing 'with his spirit that he is a child of God'.[9]

In order to explain this still farther I will endeavour by the help of God, first, to point out the several sorts of faith, and, secondly, to draw some practical inferences.

I. In the first place I will endeavour to point out the several sorts of faith. It would be easy either to reduce these to a smaller number or to divide them into a greater. But it does not appear that this would answer any valuable purpose.

1. The lowest sort of faith, if it be any faith at all, is that of a *materialist*—a man who (like the late Lord Kames)[10] believes there is nothing but matter in the universe. I say, if it be any faith at all; for properly speaking, it is not. It is not 'an evidence or conviction of God',[11] for they do not believe there is any; neither is it a conviction of things not seen, for they deny the existence of such. Or if, for decency['s] sake, they allow there is a God, yet they suppose even him to be material. For one of their maxims is,

Jupiter est quodcumque vides—[12]
Whatever you see is God.

'Whatever you see'! A visible, tangible god! Excellent divinity! Exquisite nonsense!

---

[6] John 5:35.   [7] Cf. John 1:29.
[8] Cf. Luke 7:28.   [9] Cf. Rom. 8:15-16.
[10] Henry Home, Lord Kames (1696–1782), a Scottish jurist and philosopher (of Castle Kames, Berwickshire); Wesley consistently misspelled his title as 'Kaim'. A follower of David Hume, Kames had expounded his materialism in his *Essays on the Principles of Morality and Natural Religion* (1751) and *Sketches of the History of Man* (1774). Wesley had responded to the essay, 'On Liberty and Necessity', in his *Thoughts Upon Necessity* (1774), and in 1781 had denounced the *Sketches* as 'a masterpiece of infidelity' (cf. JWJ, May 24-25, 1774; July 6, 1781).
[11] Cf. Heb. 11:1 *(Notes)*.
[12] Cf. Lucan, *Civil War*, ix.580: '*Jupiter est quodcumque vides, quodcumque moveris*', 'God is whatever we see, wherever we move.'

2. The second sort of faith, if you allow a materialist to have any, is the faith of a *deist*. I mean, one who believes there is a God, distinct from matter, but does not believe the Bible. Of these we may observe two sorts: one sort are mere beasts in human shape,
5 wholly under the power of the basest passions, and having

A downright appetite to mix with mud.[13]

Other deists are, in most respects, rational creatures, though unhappily prejudiced against Christianity. Most of these believe the being and attributes of God; they believe that God made and
10 governs the world, and that the soul does not die with the body, but will remain for ever in a state of happiness or misery.

3. The next sort of faith is the faith of *heathens*,[14] with which I join that of Mahometans. I cannot but prefer this before the faith of the deists; because, though it embraces nearly the same
15 objects, yet they are rather to be pitied than blamed for the narrowness of their faith. And their not believing the whole truth is not owing to want of sincerity, but merely to want of light. When one asked Chicali, an old Indian chief, 'Why do not you *red* men know as much as us *white* men?' he readily answered, 'Because
20 you have *the Great Word*, and we have not.'[15]

4. It cannot be doubted but this plea will avail for millions of modern 'heathens'. Inasmuch as to them little is given, of them little will be required.[16] As to the ancient heathens, millions of them likewise were savages. No more, therefore, will be expected
25 of them than the living up to the light they had.[17] But many of them, especially in the civilized nations, we have great reason to hope, although they lived among heathens, yet were quite of another spirit; being taught of God, by his inward voice, all the essentials of true religion. Yea, and so was that Mahometan, an
30 Arabian, who a century ago wrote the life of Hai Ebn Yokton.[18]

[13] π; Source unidentified.

[14] See No. 1, *Salvation by Faith*, I.2 and n.

[15] A blurred memory of Wesley's conversation with Chicali in Savannah on July 3, 1736 (cf. JWJ, July 1).

[16] See Luke 12:48.

[17] For Wesley's other references to the salvability of the heathen, see No. 91, 'On Charity', I.3 and n.

[18] Cf. *The Improvement of Human Reason, exhibited in the Life of Hai Ebn Yokdhan, written above five hundred years ago, by Abu Jaafar Ebn Tuphail, translated from the original Arabic by Simon Ockley [1678–1728], with an appendix, in which the possibility of man's attaining the true knowledge of God, and things necessary to salvation without instruction, is briefly considered*

The story seems to be feigned; but it contains all the principles of pure religion and undefiled.[19]

5. But in general we may surely place the faith of a Jew above that of a heathen or Mahometan. By *Jewish* faith I mean the faith of those who lived between the giving of the law and the coming of Christ. These—that is, those that were serious and sincere among them—believed all that is written in the Old Testament. In particular they believed that in the fullness of time the Messiah would appear 'to finish the transgression, to make an end of sin, and bring in everlasting righteousness'.[20]

6. It is not so easy to pass any judgment concerning the faith of our modern Jews. It is plain, 'The veil is still upon their hearts, when Moses and the prophets are read.'[21] The god of this world still hardens their hearts, and still blinds their eyes, 'lest at any time the light of the glorious gospel'[22] should break in upon them. So that we may say of this people, as the Holy Ghost said to their forefathers, 'The heart of this people is waxed gross, and their ears are dull of hearing, and their eyes have they closed; lest they should see with their eyes, and hear with their ears, and understand with their hearts, and should be converted, and I should heal them.'[a] Yet it is not our part to pass sentence upon them, but to leave them to their own Master.

7. I need not dwell upon the faith of *John the Baptist*, any more than the dispensation which he was under, because these, as Mr. Fletcher well describes them, were peculiar to himself. Setting him aside, the faith of *Roman Catholics* in general seems to be

[a] Acts 28:27.

(1708). This went through two other editions in the eighteenth century (1711 and 1731) and has been more recently 'revised and edited with an introduction' by A. S. Fulton (1929). The work of Abu Bakr Ibn Al-Tufail was introduced to the Western world by Edward Pocock (1671) in a Latin translation from the Arabic *(Philosophus Autodidactus)*. Wesley read it in 1734, in a version entitled, *The Life of Ebenezer Yokton, An Exact Entire Mystic;* cf. Green, *Wesley*, p. 319. See also Robert Barclay's *Apology*, Props. V-VI, 'The Universal Saving Light'. The gist of the story in all these versions is the growth to maturity of a solitary child on a desert isle who, without benefit of schools or mosques, acquired the principles of 'true religion, pure and undefiled' (as well as the elements of science and philosophy)—hence Pocock's *Autodidactus*. Abu Bakr has a similar story of 'Don Antonio Trezzanio, who was self-educated and lived forty-five years in an uninhabited island in the East Indies'. Pope tells another version of the story in *The Guardian*, No. 61, May 21, 1713; its author is cited as 'Telliamed'. Cf. No. 44, *Original Sin*, II.4.

[19] See Jas. 1:27.   [20] Dan. 9:24.
[21] Cf. 2 Cor. 3:15.
[22] Cf. 2 Cor. 4:4.

above that of the ancient Jews. If most of these are volunteers in faith,[23] believing more than God has revealed, it cannot be denied that they believe all which God has revealed as necessary to salvation. In this we rejoice on their behalf: we are glad that none of those new articles which were[24] added at the Council of Trent to 'the faith once delivered to the saints',[25] does so materially contradict any of the ancient articles as to render them of no effect.

8. The faith of the *Protestants*, in general, embraces only those truths as necessary to salvation which are clearly revealed in the oracles of God.[26] Whatever is plainly declared in the Old and New Testament is the object of their faith. They believe neither more nor less than what is manifestly contained in, and provable by, the Holy Scriptures. The Word of God is 'a lantern to their feet, and a light in all their paths'.[27] They dare not on any pretence go from it to the right hand or the left. The written Word is the whole and sole rule of their faith, as well as practice. They believe whatsoever God has declared, and profess to do whatsoever he hath commanded. This is the proper faith of Protestants:[28] by this they will abide and no other.

9. Hitherto faith has been considered chiefly as an evidence and conviction of such or such truths. And this is the sense wherein it is taken at this day in every part of the Christian world. But in the meantime let it be carefully observed (for eternity depends upon it) that neither the faith of a Roman Catholic nor that of a Protestant, if it contains no more than this, no more than the embracing such and such truths, will avail any more before God than the faith of a Mahometan or a heathen, yea of a deist or

<hr/>

[23] I.e., credulous, not to say gullible. Wesley could have found this phrase in Shaftesbury's 'Letter Concerning Enthusiasm' (1708): 'If a reverend Christian prelate may be so great a volunteer in faith, as beyond the ordinary prescription of the Catholic church, to believe in fairies, why may not a heathen poet, in the ordinary way of his religion, be allowed to believe in muses?'; cf. Anthony Ashley Cooper, third Earl of Shaftesbury, *Characteristicks of Men, Manners, Opinions and Times* (5th edn.; 1773), I.6. Wesley found the phrase (and idea) useful for polemical purposes, as in *An Earnest Appeal*, §14 (11:49 in this edn.); in JWJ, June 2, 1755; in *Serious Thoughts Occasioned by the Late Earthquake at Lisbon*, 1755; and in his letter to the *London Magazine*, Jan. 1, 1765.
[24] Orig., 'they' changed to 'were' in the MS errata in Wesley's copy of the *Sermons*.
[25] Jude 3.
[26] Cf. No. 5, 'Justification by Faith', §2 and n.
[27] Cf. Ps. 119:105 (BCP).
[28] An echo of William Chillingworth's famous slogan, 'The Scripture is the only rule to judge all controversies by,' in *The Religion of Protestants* (4th edn., 1674), p. 87; cf. the whole of Pt. I, ch. ii.

materialist. For 'can' this 'faith save him?'[29] Can it save any man either from sin or from hell? No more than it could save Judas Iscariot; no more than it could save the devil and his angels—all of whom are convinced that every title of Holy Scripture is true.

10. But what is the faith which is properly saving? Which brings 5 eternal salvation to all those that keep it to the end? It is such a divine conviction of God and of the things of God as even in its infant state enables everyone that possesses it to 'fear God and work righteousness'.[30] And whosoever in every nation believes thus far the Apostle declares is 'accepted of him'.[31] He actually is 10 at that very moment in a state of acceptance. But he is at present only a *servant* of God, not properly a *son*.[32] Meantime let it be well observed that 'the wrath of God' no longer 'abideth on him'.[33]

11. Indeed nearly fifty years ago, when the preachers commonly called Methodists began to preach that grand 15 scriptural doctrine, salvation by faith, they were not sufficiently apprised of the difference between a servant and a child of God. They did not clearly understand that even one 'who feared God, and worketh righteousness, is accepted of him'. In consequence of this they were apt to make sad the hearts of those whom God 20 had not made sad. For they frequently asked those who feared God, 'Do you know that your sins are forgiven?' And upon their answering, 'No', immediately replied, 'Then you are a child of the devil.' No; that does not follow. It might have been said (and it is all that can be said with propriety) 'Hitherto you are only a *servant;* 25 you are not a *child* of God.[34] You have already great reason to praise God that he has called you to his honourable service. Fear not. Continue crying unto him: "and you shall see greater things than these".'[35]

12. And, indeed, unless the servants of God halt by the way, 30 they will receive the adoption of sons.[36] They will receive the *faith* of the children of God by his *revealing* his only-begotten Son in their hearts.[37] Thus the faith of a child is properly and directly a

---

[29] Jas. 2:14.   [30] Cf. Acts 10:35.   [31] *Ibid.*
[32] See No. 117, 'On the Discoveries of Faith', §§13-14; No. 119, 'Walking by Sight and Walking by Faith', §1; and Wesley's letters to Ann Bolton, Apr. 7, 1768, and Nov. 16, 1770; and to Alexander Knox, Aug. 29, 1777. Cf. also No. 9, 'The Spirit of Bondage and of Adoption', §2 and n.
[33] John 3:36.
[34] Cf. No. 3, *'Awake, Thou That Sleepest'*, III.6 and n.
[35] Cf. John 1:50.
[36] Gal. 4:5.   [37] See Gal. 1:16.

divine conviction whereby every child of God is enabled to testify, 'The life that I now live, I live by faith in the Son of God, who loved me, and gave himself for me.'[38] And whosoever hath this, 'the Spirit of God witnesseth with his spirit that he is a child of God.'[39] So the Apostle writes to the Galatians, 'Ye are the sons of God by faith.'[40] 'And because ye are sons, God hath sent forth the Spirit of his Son into your hearts, crying, Abba, Father;'[41] that is, giving you a childlike confidence in him, together with a kind affection toward him. This then it is that (if St. Paul was taught of God, and wrote as he was moved by the Holy Ghost) properly constitutes the difference between a servant of God and a child of God. 'He that believeth', as a child of God, 'hath the witness in himself.'[42] This the servant hath not. Yet let no man discourage him; rather, lovingly exhort him to expect it every moment!

13. It is easy to observe that all the sorts of faith which we can conceive are reducible to one or other of the preceding. But let us covet the best gifts, and follow the most excellent way.[43] There is no reason why you should be satisfied with the faith of a materialist, a heathen, or a deist; nor indeed with that of a servant: I do not know that God requires it at your hands. Indeed if you have received this you ought not to cast it away; you ought not in any wise to undervalue it, but to be truly thankful for it. Yet, in the meantime, beware how you rest here: press on till you receive the Spirit of adoption. Rest not till that Spirit clearly witnesses with your spirit that you are a child of God.[44]

II. I proceed, in the second place, to draw a few inferences from the preceding observations.

1. And I would, first, infer in how dreadful a state, if there be a God, is a materialist—one who denies not only 'the Lord that bought him',[45] but also the Lord that made him! 'Without faith it is impossible to please God.'[46] But it is impossible he should have any faith at all, any conviction of any invisible world—for he

[38] Cf. Gal. 2:20.
[39] Cf. Rom. 8:16; see No. 5, 'Justification by Faith', IV.2 and n.
[40] Cf. Gal. 3:26 *(Notes)*.
[41] Gal. 4:6.
[42] Cf. 1 John 5:10.
[43] See 1 Cor. 12:31.
[44] Rom. 8:15-16; the Pauline version of the doctrine of assurance.
[45] Cf. 2 Pet. 2:1.
[46] Cf. Heb. 11:6.

believes there is no such thing; any conviction of the being of a God—for a *material* God is no god at all. For you cannot possibly suppose the sun or skies to be God, any more than you can suppose a god of wood or stone. And farther, whosoever believes all things to be mere matter must of course believe that all things 5 are governed by dire necessity! Necessity, that is as inexorable as the winds, as ruthless as the rocks, as merciless as the waves that dash upon them, or the poor shipwrecked mariners! Who then shall help thee, thou poor desolate wretch, when thou art most in need of help? Winds, and seas, and rocks, and storms! Such are 10 the best helpers which the materialists can hope for!

2. Almost equally desperate is the case of the poor *deist*, how learned, yea, how moral soever he be. For you likewise, though you may not advert to it, are really 'without God in the world'.[47] See your religion, 'the religion of nature delineated' by the 15 ingenious Mr. Wollaston[48] (whom I remember to have seen when I was at school, attending the public service at the Charterhouse chapel). Does he found his religion upon God? Nothing less. He founds it on truth—abstract truth. But does he not by that expression mean God? No; he sets him out of the question, and 20 builds a beautiful castle in the air, without being beholden either to him or his word. See your smooth-tongued orator of Glasgow,[49] one of the most pleasing writers of the age. Has he any more to do with God on his system than Mr. Wollaston? Does he deduce his 'Idea of Virtue'[50] from him? As the Father of lights, the 25 Source of all good? Just the contrary. He not only plans his whole theory without taking the least notice of God, but toward the close of it proposes that question, 'Does the having an eye to God in an action enhance the virtue of it?' He answers, 'No! it is so far from this that if, in doing a virtuous, that is, a benevolent action, a man 30 mingles a desire to please God, the more there is of this desire, the less virtue there is in that action.'[51] Never before did I meet with either Jew, Turk, or heathen, who so flatly renounced God as this Christian professor!

[47] Eph. 2:12.
[48] William Wollaston; cf. No. 90, 'An Israelite Indeed', §4 and n.
[49] Francis Hutcheson; cf. No. 12, 'The Witness of Our Own Spirit', §5 and n. Samuel Wesley, Jun., *Poems*, p. 104, had referred to Thomas Hobbes as 'a sweet-tongued orator'.
[50] Wesley's own inscribed copy of the third edn. of Hutcheson's *Inquiry into the Original of Our Ideas of Beauty and Virtue* (1729) is still in the library of the Kingswood School.
[51] Cf. No. 105, 'On Conscience', I.8-10 and n.; it is interesting to note Wesley's return to this emphatic misrepresentation of Hutcheson's text and intention.

3. But with heathens, Mahometans, and Jews, we have at present nothing to do; only we may wish that their lives did not shame many of us that are called Christians. We have not much more to do with the members of the Church of Rome. But we cannot doubt that many of them, like the excellent Archbishop of Cambrai,[52] still retain (notwithstanding many mistakes) that faith that worketh by love.[53] And how many of the Protestants enjoy this, whether members of the Church of England,[54] or of other congregations? We have reason to believe a considerable number, both of one and the other (and, blessed be God! an increasing number) in every part of the land.

4. Once more. I exhort you that fear God and work righteousness, you that are servants of God, first, flee from all sin as from the face of a serpent,[55] being

> Quick as the apple of an eye,
> The slightest touch of sin to feel;[56]

and to work righteousness, to the utmost of the power you now have; to abound in works both of piety and mercy.[57] And, secondly, continually to cry to God that he would reveal his Son in your hearts, to the intent you may be no more servants, but sons;[58] having his love shed abroad in your hearts,[59] and walking in 'the glorious liberty of the children of God'.[60]

5. I exhort you, lastly, who already feel the Spirit of God witnessing with your spirit that you are the children of God,[61] follow the advice of the Apostle, 'Walk in all the *good works* whereunto ye are created in Christ Jesus.'[62] And then, 'leaving the principles of the doctrine of Christ, and not laying again the

---

[52] François de Salignac de la Mothe-Fénelon; cf. No. 102, 'Of Former Times', §11 and n.

[53] Gal. 5:6; cf. No. 2, *The Almost Christian*, II.6 and n.

[54] The early texts read 'of the church'. A marginal annotation in Wesley's copy of *AM* (not in Wesley's hand) adds 'of England'.

[55] See Rev. 12:14.

[56] John and Charles Wesley, 'Watch in All Things', *Hymns and Sacred Poems* (1742), p. 218 (*Poet. Wks.*, II.273). For other quotations from this hymn, see No. 12, 'The Witness of Our Own Spirit', §19 and n.

[57] Cf. No. 14, *The Repentance of Believers*, I.13 and n.

[58] See Gal. 4:7.

[59] See Rom. 5:5.

[60] Rom. 8:21.

[61] See Rom. 8:16.

[62] Cf. Eph. 2:10.

foundation of repentance from dead works, and of faith toward God', go on to perfection.[63] Yea, and when ye have attained a measure of perfect love, when God has 'circumcised your hearts',[64] and enabled you to love him with all your heart and with all your soul, think not of resting there. That is impossible. You 5 cannot stand still; you must either rise or fall—rise higher or fall lower. Therefore the voice of God to the children of Israel, to the children of God is, 'Go forward.'[65] 'Forgetting the things that are behind, and reaching forward unto those that are before, press on to the mark, for the prize of your high calling of God in Christ 10 Jesus!'[66]

Stockport, April 9, 1788[67]

---

[63] Cf. Heb. 6:1.
[64] Cf. Deut. 30:6.
[65] Exod. 14:15.
[66] Cf. Phil. 3:13-14.
[67] Place and date as in *AM;* but see above, p. 491, and cf. p. 479.

ON GOD'S VINEYARD

AN INTRODUCTORY COMMENT

Isa. 5:4 was something of a favourite of Wesley's; there are fourteen notices of its use in his oral preaching from 1748 to 1788. He knew William Tilly's reference to it in his university sermon, 'On Grieving the Holy Spirit'; cf. Sermon XI *in his* Sixteen Sermons (1712), *p. 320. Wesley's abridgement of this, copied out in 1733, was found among his papers after his death and published as a Wesley original by Thomas Jackson in 1825. Wesley also knew Jeremiah Seed's sermon on the same text; cf.* Sermon III *in Seed's* Posthumous Works *(1750), I. 69-94 (for Wesley's admiring reference to him as a preacher, see the* Preface *to* SOSO, *V-VIII, §5, II.355-57).*

What is wholly original in this present sermon, however, is Wesley's direct identification of 'God's Vineyard' with his own Methodist movement, together with the special pathos of his estimate of God's special blessings to the Methodist people and of their failures to fulfil their original promise and prospects. I.8-9 is a capsule history of Methodism; V.1-7 is a candid summary of its leader's discontents. Clearly, this was a sermon chiefly for Methodists, which raises the interesting question as to how widely Wesley expected the sermons in SOSO, *VIII, to be read.*

At any rate, this sermon was written at Witney (near Oxford), on October 17, 1787 (see JWJ for October 16 and diary for October 17) and was first published in SOSO, *VIII. 249-72 (1788), with its present title. In the January and February issues of the* Arminian Magazine *(1789), XII.6-14, 62-68, it was reprinted without a title and numbered 'Sermon XLVIII' (on p. 6) and 'Sermon XLIX' (on p. 62)—the latter number is the correct one. The present text here is based on* SOSO, *VIII, which is very nearly identical with the* Magazine *reprint.*

On God's Vineyard

Isaiah 5:4

What could have been done more to my vineyard, that I have not done in it? Wherefore, when I looked that it should bring forth grapes, brought it forth wild grapes?

The 'vineyard of the Lord', taking the word in its widest sense, may include the whole world. All the inhabitants of the earth may in some sense be called 'the vineyard of the Lord', who 'hath made all nations of men to dwell on all the face of the earth, that they might seek the Lord, if haply they may feel after him, and 10 find him'.[1] But in a narrower sense the vineyard of the Lord may mean the Christian world; that is, all that name the name of Christ[2] and profess to obey his word. In a still narrower sense it may be understood of what is termed the reformed part of the Christian church. In the narrowest of all one may by that phrase, 15 'the vineyard of the Lord', mean the body of people commonly called Methodists.[3] In this sense I understand it now, meaning thereby that Society only, which began at Oxford in the year 1729, and remain united at this day. Understanding the word in this sense I repeat the question which God proposes to[4] the 20 Prophet: 'What could have been done more to my vineyard that I have not done in it? Wherefore, when I looked that it should bring forth grapes, brought it forth wild grapes?'

What could God have done more in this his vineyard (suppose he had designed it should put forth great branches, and spread 25 over the earth) which he hath not done in it?

First, with regard to doctrine;

Secondly, with regard to scriptural helps;

Thirdly, with regard to discipline; and

Fourthly, with regard to outward protection. 30

These things being considered, I would then briefly inquire,

[1] Cf. Acts 17:26-27 *(Notes);* Isa. 5:7.
[2] Cf. 2 Tim. 2:19.
[3] An echo of Thomas Crane's metaphor about the concentric circles of Providence; see No. 67, 'On Divine Providence', §16 and n.
[4] *AM,* 'by'.

'Wherefore, when he looked [that] it should bring forth grapes, brought it forth wild grapes?'

I.1. First, what could have been done in this his vineyard which God hath not done in it? What could have been done more with
5 regard to *doctrine?* From the very beginning, from the time that four young men united together, each of them was *homo unius libri*—a man of one book.[5] God taught them all to make his 'Word a lantern unto their feet, and a light in all their paths'.[6] They had one, and only one rule of judgment with regard to all their
10 tempers, words, and actions, namely, the oracles of God. They were one and all determined to be *Bible-Christians.* They were continually reproached for this very thing; some terming them in derision *Bible-bigots;* others *Bible-moths*—feeding, they said, upon the Bible as moths do upon cloth. And indeed unto this day it is
15 their constant endeavour to think and speak as the oracles of God.

2. It is true a learned man, Dr. Trapp,[7] soon after their setting out, gave a very different account of them. 'When I saw', said the Doctor, 'these two books, *The Treatise on Christian Perfection,* and the *Serious Call to a Holy Life,*[8] I thought, these books will certainly
20 do mischief. And so it proved; for presently after up sprung the Methodists. So he (Mr. Law) was their parent.'[9] Although this was not entirely true, yet there was some truth in it. All the Methodists carefully read these books, and were greatly profited thereby. Yet they did by no means spring from them, but from the
25 Holy Scriptures; 'being born again', as St. Peter speaks, 'by the word of God, which liveth and abideth for ever'.[10]

---

[5] See above, 'Preface' (1746), §5 and n. (1:104-5 in this edn.). For Wesley's dating the Revival from 1729, cf. No. 63, 'The General Spread of the Gospel', §16 and n.; see also below, I.3.

[6] Cf. Ps. 119:105 (BCP).

[7] Joseph Trapp (1679–1747), ally of Henry Sacheverell and first professor of poetry at Oxford, whose four sermons on *The Nature, Folly, Sin, and Danger of Being Righteous Overmuch* (1739), aimed mostly at Law and Whitefield, gained him more fame among the Methodists than he enjoyed elsewhere.

[8] Law, *A Practical Treatise Upon Christian Perfection* (1726), and *A Serious Call to a Devout and Holy Life* (1729).

[9] Cf. Trapp, *A Reply to Mr. Law's Earnest and Serious Answer (as it is called) to Dr. Trapp's Discourse of the Folly, Sin, and Danger of Being Righteous Overmuch* (London, Gilliver, 1741), pp. 6-7. Wesley paraphrases Trapp, whose references are mainly to Law's *Christian Perfection.* Cf. Moore, *Wesley,* I.171, for Samuel Wesley, Sen.'s claim that if 'my son John has the honour of being styled the "Father of the Holy Club", I must be the grandfather of it . . .'.

[10] Cf. 1 Pet. 1:23.

3. Another learned man, the late Bishop Warburton, roundly affirms that 'they were the offspring of Mr. Law and Count Zinzendorf together.'[11] But this was a greater mistake still. For they had met together several years before they had the least acquaintance with Count Zinzendorf, or even knew there was 5 such a person in the world.[12] And when they did know him, although they esteemed him very highly in love, yet they did not dare to follow him one step farther than they were warranted by the Scripture.

4. The book which, next to the Holy Scripture, was of the 10 greatest use to them in settling their judgment as to the grand point of justification by faith was the *Book of Homilies*.[13] They were never clearly convinced that we are justified by faith alone till they carefully consulted these, and compared them with the Sacred Writings, particularly St. Paul's Epistle to the Romans.[14] And no 15 minister of the Church can with any decency oppose these, seeing at his ordination he subscribed to them in subscribing the Thirty-sixth Article of the Church.[15]

5. It has been frequently observed that very few were clear in their judgment both with regard to justification and sanctifica- 20 tion. Many who have spoken and written admirably well concerning justification had no clear conception, nay, were totally ignorant, of the doctrine of sanctification. Who has wrote more ably than Martin Luther on justification by faith alone? And who was more ignorant of the doctrine of sanctification, or more 25 confused in his conceptions of it? In order to be thoroughly convinced of this, of his total ignorance with regard to sanctification, there needs no more than to read over, without prejudice, his celebrated comment on the Epistle to the Galatians.[16] On the other hand, how many writers of the Romish 30

---

[11] William Warburton (1698–1779), Bishop of Gloucester. In his *Doctrine of Grace* (1762), p. 152 (cf. *Works*, VII.342-43), he had asserted that 'Mr. Law begot Methodism and Count Zinzendorf rocked the cradle.' See No. 100, 'On Pleasing All Men', I.2 and n. For other references to Zinzendorf, cf. No. 13, *On Sin in Believers*, I.5 and n.

[12] Another pointer to the origins of Methodism in the Holy Club in 1729. See above I.1; and No. 63, 'The General Spread of the Gospel', §16 and n.

[13] Cf. Wesley's abridgement of the first Edwardian *Homilies* in his little tract, *The Doctrine of Salvation, Faith, and Good Works, Extracted from the Homilies of the Church of England* (1739). Cf. LPT *Wesley*, pp. 121-33; see *Bibliog*, No. 11, and Vol. 12 of this edn.

[14] See JWJ, Nov. 11, 1738.

[15] Actually, it was the thirty-fifth 'Article': 'Of the Homilies'.

[16] Cf. JWJ, June 15, 1741, for Wesley's disparaging evaluation of Luther's *Commentary on Galatians;* see also No. 14, *The Repentance of Believers*, I.9 and n.

Church (as Francis Sales[17] and Juan de Castaniza[18] in particular) have wrote strongly and scripturally on sanctification; who nevertheless were entirely unacquainted with the nature of justification. Insomuch that the whole body of their divines at the

5 Council of Trent in their *Catechismus ad Parochos*ª totally confound sanctification and justification together. But it has pleased God to give the Methodists a full and clear knowledge of each, and the wide difference between them.[19]

6. They know, indeed, that at the same time a man is justified

10 sanctification properly begins. For when he is justified he is 'born again',[20] 'born from above',[21] 'born of the Spirit';[22] which, although it is not (as some suppose) the whole process of sanctification, [it] is doubtless the gate of it. Of this likewise God has given them a full view. They know the new birth implies as

15 great a change in the soul, in him that is 'born of the Spirit', as was wrought in his body when he was born of a woman; not an outward change only, as from drunkenness to sobriety, from robbery or theft to honesty (this is the poor, dry, miserable conceit of those that know nothing of real religion); but an inward change,

20 from all unholy to all holy tempers, from pride to humility, from passionateness to meekness, from peevishness and discontent to patience and resignation—in a word, from an earthly, sensual, devilish[23] mind to the mind that was in Christ Jesus.[24]

ª Catechism which every parish priest is to teach his people. [Wesley had read this Catechism in Oct. 1732. Cf. *The Catechism of the Council of Trent for Parish Priests* (1566), translated into English, with notes, by T. A. Buckley, 1852.]

---

[17] Francis de Sales (1567–1622), Bishop of Geneva and author of two classics of devotional literature: *An Introduction to the Devout Life* (1609), and *A Treatise on the Love of God* (1616). Wesley had read the former in 1733.

[18] Juan de Castañiza (*c.* 1536–99), a Spanish Benedictine, credited in the eighteenth century as author of *Pugna Spiritualis; tractatus vere aureus de perfectione vitae christianae* (1599). Susanna Wesley owned a copy of its English translation (by Richard Lucas in 1698) and used it in the family devotions in the Epworth rectory. Since then, it has been more often attributed to Lorenzo Scupoli, a Spanish Theatine. Cf. M. Alamo in *Dictionnaire d'histoire et de géographie ecclésiastiques*, XI. 1414-15; see also No. 3, '*Awake, Thou That Sleepest*', II.9 and n.

[19] For other comments on Methodist 'triumphalism', cf. No. 102, 'Of Former Times', §22 and n.

[20] John 3:3, 7.

[21] John 3:3, where ἄνωθεν literally means 'from above'. Cf. No. 45, 'The New Birth', II.3; and below, I.9.

[22] John 3:6, 8.

[23] Jas. 3:15.

[24] Phil. 2:5.

7. It is true a late very eminent author, in his strange treatise on regeneration,[25] proceeds entirely on the supposition that it is the whole, gradual progress of sanctification. No; it is only the threshold of sanctification—the first entrance upon it. And as in the natural birth a man is born at once, and then grows larger and stronger by degrees, so in the spiritual birth a man is born at once, and then gradually increases in spiritual stature and strength. The new birth, therefore, is the first point of sanctification, which may increase more and more unto the perfect day.[26]

8. It is then a great blessing given to this people that, as they do not think or speak of justification so as to supersede sanctification, so neither do they think or speak of sanctification so as to supersede justification. They take care to keep each in its own place, laying equal stress on one and the other. They know God has joined these together, and it is not for man to put them asunder.[27] Therefore they maintain with equal zeal and diligence the doctrine of free, full, present justification on the one hand, and of entire sanctification both of heart and life on the other—being as tenacious of inward holiness as any mystic, and of outward as any Pharisee.

9. Who then is a Christian, according to the light which God hath vouchsafed to this people? He that, being justified by faith, hath peace with God through our Lord Jesus Christ;[28] and at the same time is 'born again', 'born from above', 'born of the Spirit';[29] inwardly changed from the image of the devil to that 'image of God wherein he was created'.[30] He that finds the love of God shed abroad in his heart by the Holy Ghost which is given unto him;[31] and whom this love sweetly constrains to 'love his neighbour', every man, 'as himself'.[32] He that has learned of his Lord to be meek and lowly in heart,[33] and in every state to be content.[34] He in

---

[25] William Law, whose *The Grounds and Reasons of Christian Regeneration* (1739) had been read straightway by Charles Wesley to the Methodist Society in London in 1739. Cf. Moore, *Wesley*, I.300, and see Law's *Works* (1762), V.180, 170. Echoed in No. 45, 'The New Birth', IV.3. The most famous eighteenth-century essay on this theme, however, was Daniel Waterland's *Regeneration Stated and Explained* (1740), which Wesley had also read.

[26] Prov. 4:18.   [27] See Matt. 19:6.

[28] See Rom. 5:1.   [29] See above, I.6.

[30] Cf. Col. 3:10.   [31] See Rom. 5:5.

[32] Cf. Mark 12:33 and Matt. 22:38-40; see also No. 7, 'The Way to the Kingdom', I.8 and n. For Wesley's definition of inward and outward holiness (love of God and love of neighbour), cf. *ibid.*, I.10 and n.

[33] Matt. 11:29.   [34] See Phil. 4:11.

whom is that whole mind, all those tempers, which were also in Christ Jesus.[35] He that abstains from all appearance of evil[36] in his actions, and that 'offends not' with 'his tongue'.[37] He that walks in all the commandments of God, and in all his ordinances,
5 blameless.[38] He that in all his intercourse with men does to others as he would they should do to him;[39] and in his whole life and conversation, whether he eats or drinks, or whatsoever he doth, doth all to the glory of God.[40]

Now what could God have done more for this his vineyard
10 which he hath not done in it, with regard to *doctrine?*

II. We are to inquire, secondly, what could have been done which he hath not done in it, with regard to *spiritual helps.*

1. Let us consider this matter from the very beginning. Two young clergymen, not very remarkable any way, of middle age,
15 having a tolerable measure of health, though rather weak than strong, began about fifty years ago to call sinners to repentance. This they did, for a time, in many of the churches in and about London. But two difficulties arose: first, the churches were so crowded that many of the parishioners could not get in; secondly,
20 they preached new doctrines—that we are saved by faith, and, that 'without holiness no man could see the Lord'.[41] For one or other of these reasons they were not long suffered to preach in the churches. They then preached in Moorfields, in Kennington Common, and in many other public places.[42] The fruit of their
25 preaching quickly appeared. Many sinners were changed both in heart and life. But it seemed this could not continue long; for everyone clearly saw these preachers would quickly wear

---

[35] See Phil. 2:5.   [36] See 1 Thess. 5:22.   [37] Cf. Ps. 39:1 (BCP).
[38] See Luke 1:6.   [39] See Matt. 7:12.   [40] See 1 Cor. 10:31.
[41] Cf. Heb. 12:14. A recollection of the first critical reactions to 'Methodism'; the most popular charge was 'enthusiasm', the most serious was doctrinal inconsistency. Cf. Josiah Tucker's letter, June 14, 1739, in the *Gent's Mag.* (1739), IX.292-97 ('. . . this *new* set of principles', etc.). But see also Tucker's longer critique of the 'medley of [Wesley's] principles' in his *Brief History of the Principles of Methodism; Wherein the Rise and Progress . . . and Present Inconsistencies of this Sect Are . . . Traced Out and Accounted For* (1742), p. 32. Tucker's main thesis (pp. 32-39) is that Wesley was trying to reconcile William Law, John Calvin, and James Arminius, a venture that was patently absurd.
[42] Wesley records having first preached in Moorfields on June 17, 1739. This was the large open tract outside the City of London, north of Moorgate. The Foundery was there, and later it became Wesley's headquarters and home. Also on June 17, he preached on Kennington Common, another open space south of the Thames, across London Bridge and just east of the pleasure gardens of Vauxhall. Note that this account ignores the fact that he had already begun his field preaching near Bristol Apr. 2, 1739.

themselves out, and no clergyman dared to assist them. But soon one and another, though not ordained, offered to assist them. God gave a signal blessing to their word. Many sinners were thoroughly convinced of sin, and many truly converted to God. Their assistants increased both in number and in the success of 5 their labours. Some of them were learned, some unlearned. Most of them were young, a few middle-aged. Some of them were [of] weak, some, on the contrary, of remarkably strong understanding. But it pleased God to own them all, so that more and more brands were plucked out of the burning.[43] 10

2. It may be observed that these clergymen, all this time, had no plan at all. They only went hither and thither, wherever they had a prospect of saving souls from death. But when more and more asked, 'What must I do to be saved?'[44] they were desired to meet all together. Twelve came the first Thursday night;[45] forty, the 15 next; soon after, a hundred. And they continued to increase, till three or four and twenty years ago the London Society amounted to about 2,800.[46]

3. But how should this multitude of people be kept together? And how should it be known whether they walked worthy of their 20 profession? They were providentially led, when they were thinking on another thing (namely, paying the public debt),[47] to divide all the people into little companies, or classes, according to their places of abode, and appoint one person in each class to see all the rest weekly. By this means it was quickly discovered if any 25 of them lived in any known sin. If they did, they were first admonished; and, when judged incorrigible, excluded from the Society.

4. This division of the people, and exclusion of those that walked disorderly, without any respect of persons, were helps 30 which few other communities had. To these, as the societies increased, was soon added another. The stewards of the societies

[43] See Amos 4:11; Zech. 3:2; cf. No. 4, *Scriptural Christianity*, II.2 and n.
[44] Acts 16:30.
[45] Would Wesley's choice of Thursday night have been influenced by his memories that it was the special evening of the week that his mother had 'formerly bestowed upon [him]' for study and counselling? Cf. his letter to her from Oxford, Feb. 28, 1732; and see Susanna's letter to her husband, dated Feb. 6, 1712, which Wesley included in his *Journal* account of her death and burial, Aug. 1, 1742.
[46] The first official record of membership in the Society at London is in the *Minutes*, Aug. 18, 1767, §8: '2250'.
[47] Debts owed to lenders outside the Methodist Societies.

in each district were desired to meet the preachers once a quarter, in some central place, to give an account of the spiritual and temporal state of their several societies. The use of these Quarterly Meetings was soon found to be exceeding great; in
5 consideration of which they were gradually spread to all the societies in the kingdom.

5. In order to increase the union between the preachers (as well as that of the people) they were desired to meet all together in London, and, some time after, a select number of them.[48]
10 Afterwards, for more convenience, they met at London, Bristol, and Leeds, alternately. They spent a few days together in this general Conference in considering what might most conduce to the general good. The result was immediately signified to all their brethren.[49] And they soon found that what St. Paul observes of the
15 whole church may be in a measure applied to every part of it: 'The whole body being fitly framed together, and compacted by that which every joint supplieth, maketh increase of the body, to the edifying of itself in love.'[b]

6. That this may be the more effectually done, they have
20 another excellent help in the constant change of preachers;[50] it being their rule that no preacher shall remain in the same circuit more than two years together, and few of them more than one year. Some indeed have imagined that this was a hindrance to the work of God. But long experience in every part of the kingdom
25 proves the contrary. This has always shown that the people profit less by any one person than by a variety of preachers; while they

[b] Eph. 4:16.

---

[48] This annual 'Conference of Preachers in Connexion with Mr. Wesley' was a unique feature of Methodist polity from 1744 onwards. Cf. Wesley's description of it in the *Minutes*, Aug. 12, 1766, §§4-5, and his insistence that it was a consultative body only, without any legislative function or authority. For a summary of the history and role of the conference in Methodist polity, see also his 'Thoughts Upon Some Late Occurrences', dated Mar. 3, 1785, and published in *AM* (1785), VIII.267-69.

[49] In 'Minutes of Several Conversations Between the Rev. Mr. John and Charles Wesley and Others.' There are such records for 1744-47, and also 'brief notices' of the fifteen Conferences between 1749 and 1765; then a continuous run of *Minutes* from 1765 onwards (see Vol. 10 of this edn.).

[50] Wesley set especial store by this idea of itinerancy, making it a distinctive feature of Methodist polity which has continued, in one form or another in Methodism until modern times. Cf. his letters to Joseph Benson, Dec. 11, 1772; to Samuel Walker, Sept. 3, 1756; to Mrs. Ward, July 16, 1788; see also, Baker, *John Wesley and the Church of England*, pp. 114, 172, 226, 320.

Used the gifts on each bestowed,
Tempered by the art of God.[51]

7. Together with these helps which are peculiar to their own
Society, they have all those which are enjoyed in common by the
other members of the Church of England. Indeed they have been 5
long pressed to separate from it, to which they have had
temptations of every kind. But they cannot, they dare not, they
will not separate from it, while they can remain therein with a
clear conscience. It is true, if any sinful terms of communion were
imposed upon them, then they would be constrained to separate; 10
but as this is not the case at present we rejoice to continue therein.

8. What then could God have done more for this his vineyard
which he hath not done in it, with regard to spiritual helps? He has
hardly dealt so with any other people in the Christian world! If it
be said, He could have made them a separate people like the 15
Moravian Brethren, I answer, This would have been a direct
contradiction to his whole design in raising them up; namely, to
spread scriptural religion throughout the land, among people of
every denomination,[52] leaving everyone to hold his own opinions
and to follow his own mode of worship. This could only be done 20
effectually by leaving these things as they were, and endeavouring
to leaven the whole nation with that 'faith that worketh by love'.[53]

III.1. Such are the *spiritual helps* which God has bestowed on
this his vineyard, with no sparing hand. *Discipline* might be
inserted among these; but we may as well speak of it under a 25
separate head. It is certain that in this respect the Methodists are
a highly favoured people. Nothing can be more simple, nothing
more rational, than the Methodist discipline: it is entirely
founded on common sense, particularly applying the general
rules of Scripture. Any person determined to save his soul may be 30
united (this is the only condition required) with them. But this
desire must be evidenced by three marks: avoiding all known sin,
doing good after his power, and attending all the ordinances of
God.[54] He is then placed in such a class as is convenient for him,

---

[51] Cf. John and Charles Wesley, *Hymns and Sacred Poems* (1740), p. 195 (*Poet. Wks.*,
I.362; see also No. 504 in *Collection*, 7:693-94 of this edn.). For quotations of other lines
from this hymn, see Nos. 13, *On Sin in Believers*, IV.6; and 132, 'On Faith, Heb. 11:1', §6.

[52] A relatively new usage for this term; cf. No. 104, 'On Attending the Church Service',
§4 and n.

[53] Cf. Gal. 5:6; see also No. 2, *The Almost Christian*, II.6 and n.

[54] A summary of the *General Rules;* cf. Vol. 9 of this edn.

where he spends about an hour in a week. And the next quarter, if nothing is objected to him, he is admitted into the Society. And therein he may continue as long as he continues to meet his brethren and walks according to his profession.

5   2. Their public service is at five in the morning and six or seven in the evening, that their temporal business may not be hindered. Only on Sunday it begins between nine and ten, and concludes with the Lord's Supper. On Sunday evening the Society meets; but care is taken to dismiss them early, that all the heads of
10 families may have time to instruct their several households. Once a quarter the principal preacher in every circuit examines every member of the societies therein. By this means, if the behaviour of anyone is blameable, which is frequently to be expected in so numerous a body of people, it is easily discovered, and either the
15 offence or the offender removed in time.

    3. Whenever it is needful to exclude any disorderly member out of the Society, it is done in the most quiet and inoffensive manner—only by not renewing his ticket[55] at the quarterly visitation. But in some cases, where the offence is great, and there
20 is danger of public scandal, it is judged necessary to declare when all the members are present, 'A. B. is no longer a member of our Society.' Now what can be more rational or more scriptural than this simple discipline—attended from the beginning to the end with no trouble, expense, or delay?

25   IV.1. But was it possible that all these things should be done without a flood of opposition? The prince of this world was not dead, nor asleep: and would he not fight that his kingdom might not be delivered up? If the word of the Apostle be found true, in all ages and nations 'all they that will live godly in Christ Jesus
30 shall suffer persecution.'[56] If this be true with regard to every individual Christian, how much more with regard to bodies of men visibly united together with the avowed design to overthrow his kingdom! And what could withstand the persecution he would not fail to stir up against a poor, defenceless, despised people,
35 without any visible help, without money, without power, without friends?

---

[55] These tokens of membership in good standing, personally subscribed by Wesley or one of his Assistants, were required for admission to class meetings and to Holy Communion.
[56] Cf. 2 Tim. 3:12.

2. In truth the god of this world was not asleep. Neither was he idle. He *did* fight, and that with all his power, that his kingdom might not be delivered up. He 'brought forth all his hosts to war'.[57] First, he stirred up the beasts of the people.[58] They roared like lions: they encompassed the little and defenceless flock on every 5 side.[59] And the storm rose higher and higher till deliverance came, in a way that none expected. God stirred up the heart of our late gracious Sovereign[60] to give such orders to his magistrates as, being put in execution, effectually quelled the madness of the people. It was about the same time that a great man applied 10 personally to his Majesty, begging that he would please to 'take a course to stop these run-about preachers'. His Majesty, looking sternly upon him, answered without ceremony, like a king, 'I tell you, while I sit on the throne, no man shall be persecuted for conscience' sake.'[61]   15

3. But in defiance of this, several who bore his Majesty's commission have persecuted them from time to time, and that under colour of law, availing themselves of what is called the Conventicle Act—one in particular, in Kent, who some years since took upon him to fine one of the preachers and several of his 20 hearers. But they thought it their duty to appeal to his Majesty's Court of King's Bench. The cause was given for the plaintiffs,

---

[57] Cf. Charles Wesley, 'Christ the Friend of Sinners', 'And call forth all his hosts to war', in *Hymns and Sacred Poems* (1739), p. 102. This hymn was also published in *A Collection of Hymns* (1780), No. 29, omitting st. 6. This is probably the hymn which Charles Wesley wrote on his conversion; cf. CWJ, May 23, 1738. For a more complete history of the hymn, cf. Baker, *Representative Verse of Charles Wesley* (London, Epworth Press, 1962), pp. 3-4.

[58] Ps. 68:30 (BCP). Cf. No. 52, *The Reformation of Manners*, I.5 and n.

[59] 'Flock' is inserted in ink in Wesley's own copies of the *Sermons* and *AM*, though not in his hand.

[60] George II (1683–1760); cf. Wesley's comment upon the king's death ('When will England have a better Prince?'), JWJ, Oct. 25, 1760. See also Leslie Stephen's account in *DNB* of Samuel Chandler's funeral sermon (Nov. 9, 1760) in which he compared George II to David ('a man after God's own heart'). In the Appendix to Chandler's *History of Persecution from the Patriarchal Age to the Reign of George II; A New Edition* (Hull, 1813), p. 416, the late king is quoted as having declared in open court that 'no man should be persecuted for conscience' sake in his dominions'. Cf. also Wesley's *Thoughts upon Liberty*, §19, and No. 127, 'On the Wedding Garment', §14. For other comments on George II, cf. No. 15, *The Great Assize*, §1.

[61] On Nov. 1, 1762, Howell Harris recorded bits of gossip he picked up in Bath, including the statement: 'Archbishop Secker offered to Mr. Onslow, late Speaker, a scheme against the Methodists, and he [the elder Pitt, Leader of the House of Commons] said he did not like persecution;' cf. Tom Beynon, ed., *Howell Harris, Reformer and Soldier* (Caernarvon, Calvinistic Methodist Bookroom, 1958), p. 139. See also Baker, *John Wesley and the Church of England*, pp. 180, 376.

who have ever since been permitted to worship God according to their own conscience.[62]

4. I believe this is a thing wholly without precedent. I find no other instance of it in any age of the church, from the day of Pentecost to this day. Every opinion, right and wrong, has been tolerated, almost in every age and nation. Every mode of worship has been tolerated, however superstitious or absurd. But I do not know that true, vital, scriptural religion was ever tolerated before. For this the people called Methodists have abundant reason to praise God. In their favour he hath wrought a new thing in the earth: he hath stilled the enemy and the avenger.[63] This then they must ascribe unto him, the author of their outward as well as inward peace.

V.1. What indeed could God have done more for this his vineyard which he hath not done in it? This having been largely showed, we may now proceed to that strong and tender expostulation: 'After all that I had done, might I not have looked for the most excellent grapes? Wherefore then brought it forth wild grapes? Might I not have expected a general increase of faith and love, of righteousness and true holiness? Yea, and of the fruit of the Spirit—love, joy, peace, long-suffering, meekness, gentleness, fidelity, goodness, temperance?'[64] Was it not reasonable to expect that these fruits would have overspread his whole church? Truly, when I saw what God had done among his people between forty and fifty years ago, when I saw them, warm in their first love, magnifying the Lord and rejoicing in God their Saviour,[65] I could expect nothing less than that all these would have lived like angels here below; that they would have walked as continually seeing him that is invisible,[66] having constant communion with the Father and the Son, living in eternity and

---

[62] For this case in Rolvenden, Kent, in 1760, see WHS, XVIII.113-20; cf. John Wesley's letter to his brother Charles, June 24, 1760. There are other references to the Methodists appealing to His Majesty's Court of King's Bench. The Canterbury rioters (Kent) are mentioned in JWJ, Nov. 11, 1751: 'We had not any disturbance from first to last, the Court of King's Bench having broke the spirit of the rioters.' See also entries for Aug. 30, 1766; Apr. 20, 1752; July 29, 1786; and Wesley's letter to Richard Bailey, Aug. 15, 1751.

[63] See Ps. 8:2.

[64] Cf. Gal. 5:22-23 *(Notes);* note Wesley's rearrangement of the order of these Christian virtues.

[65] See Luke 1:46-47.

[66] Heb. 11:27.

walking in eternity. I looked to see 'a chosen generation, a royal priesthood, a holy nation, a peculiar people', in the whole tenor of their conversation 'showing forth his praise who had called them into his marvellous light'.[67]

2. But instead of this it brought forth wild grapes, fruit of a quite contrary nature. It brought forth error in ten thousand shapes, turning many of the simple out of the way. It brought forth enthusiasm, imaginary inspiration, ascribing to the all-wise God all the wild, absurd, self-inconsistent dreams of an heated imagination. It brought forth pride, robbing the Giver of every good gift of the honour due to his name. It brought forth prejudice, evil surmising, censoriousness, judging, and condemning one another—all totally subversive of that brotherly love which is the very badge of the Christian profession; without which, whosoever liveth is counted dead before God. It brought forth anger, hatred, malice, revenge, and every evil word and work—all direful fruits, not of the Holy Spirit, but of the bottomless pit.

3. It brought forth likewise in many—particularly those that are increased in goods—that grand poison of souls, the love of the world, and that in all branches: 'the desire of the flesh', that is, the seeking happiness in the pleasures of sense; 'the desire of the eyes', that is, seeking happiness in dress, or any of the pleasures of imagination;[68] and 'the pride of life',[69] that is, seeking happiness in the praise of men;[70] or in that which ministers to all these, laying up treasures on earth. It brought forth self-indulgence of every kind, delicacy, effeminacy, softness; but not softness of the right kind, that melts at human woe. It brought [forth] such base, grovelling affections, such deep earthly-mindedness as that of the poor heathens, which occasioned the lamentation of their own poet over them,

O curvae in terras animae et caelestium inanes![71]—
O souls bowed down to earth, and void of God!

[67] Cf. 1 Pet. 2:9.   [68] Cf. No. 44, *Original Sin*, II.10 and n.
[69] Cf. 1 John 2:16; and No. 7, 'The Way to the Kingdom', II.2 and n.
[70] Cf. No. 14, *The Repentance of Believers*, I.7 and n.
[71] Cf. Persius, *Satires*, ii.61. Wesley had already used this tag in his letter to Colonel Oglethorpe, Apr. 20, 1736, and would use it again in No. 125, 'On a Single Eye', III.8. He could have read it in Lactantius, *Divinarum Institutionum*, II.ii; and in Jeremy Taylor, 'The House of Feasting' (Sermon XVI), *Works*, I.701, where it appears in both Greek and Latin.

4. O ye that have riches in possession,[72] once more hear the word of the Lord! Ye that are rich in this world,[73] that have food to eat, and raiment to put on, and something over, are you clear of the curse of loving the world? Are you sensible of your danger? Do
5 you feel, 'How hardly will they that have riches enter into the kingdom of heaven?'[74] Do you continue unburnt in the midst of the fire? Are you untouched with the love of the world? Are you clear from the desire of the flesh, the desire of the eyes, and the pride of life? Do you 'put a knife to your throat'[75] when you sit
10 down to meat, lest your 'table' should 'be a snare to you'?[76] Is not your belly your god? Is not eating and drinking, or any other pleasure of sense, the greatest pleasure you enjoy? Do not you seek happiness in dress, furniture, pictures, gardens; or anything else that pleases the eye? Do not you grow soft and delicate?
15 Unable to bear cold, heat, the wind, or the rain, as you did when you were poor? Are you not increasing in goods, laying up treasures on earth;[77] instead of restoring to God in the poor, not so much, or so much, but all that you can spare? Surely 'it is easier for a camel to go through the eye of a needle than for a rich man to
20 enter into the kingdom of heaven'![78]

5. But why will ye still bring forth wild grapes? What excuse can ye make? Hath God been wanting on *his* part? Have you not been warned over and over? Have ye not been fed with the sincere milk of the word?[79] Hath not the whole word of God been delivered to
25 you, and without any mixture of error? Were not the fundamental doctrines both of free, full, present justification delivered to you, as well as sanctification, both gradual and instantaneous? Was not every branch both of inward and outward holiness clearly opened and earnestly applied? And that by preachers of every kind, young
30 and old, learned and unlearned? But it is well if some of you did not despise the helps which God had prepared for you. Perhaps you would hear none but clergymen; or at least, none but men of learning. Will you not then give God leave to choose his own messengers? To send by whom he *will* send?[80] It is well if this bad
35 wisdom was not one cause of your 'bringing forth wild grapes'!

[72] Ps. 73:12 (BCP).
[73] 1 Tim. 6:17.
[74] Cf. Mark 10:23.   [75] Cf. Prov. 23:2.
[76] Cf. Ps. 69:22 (AV); Rom. 11:9.   [77] See Matt. 6:19.
[78] Cf. Matt. 19:24.   [79] 1 Pet. 2:2.
[80] See Exod. 4:13; cf. No. 4, *Scriptural Christianity*, IV.2 and n.

6. Was not another cause of it your despising that excellent help, union with a Christian society? Have you not read, 'How can one be warm alone?'[81] And, 'Woe be unto him that is alone when he falleth'?[82] 'But you have companions enough.' Perhaps more than enough; more than are helpful to your soul. But have you 5 enough that are athirst for God? And that labour to make *you* so? Have you companions enough that watch over your soul as they that must give account?[83] And that freely and faithfully warn you if you take any false step, or are in danger of doing so? I fear you have few of these companions, or else you would bring forth 10 better fruit.

7. If you are a member of the Society, do you make a full use of your privilege? Do you never fail to meet your class? And that, not as matter of form, but expecting that when you are met together in his name your Lord will be in the midst of you? Are you truly 15 thankful for the amazing liberty of conscience which is vouchsafed to you and your brethren? Such as never was enjoyed before by persons in your circumstances?[84] And are you thankful to the Giver of every good gift for the general spread of true religion? Surely you can never praise God enough for all these 20 blessings, so plentifully showered down upon you, till you praise him with angels and archangels, and all the company of heaven.[85]

Witney, October 17, 1787[86]

---

[81] Eccles. 4:11.
[82] Cf. Eccles. 4:10.
[83] See Heb. 13:17.
[84] The Methodists profited from the growing spirit of religious toleration even more than the Nonconformists or the Roman Catholics; cf. John H. Overton and Frederic Relton, *The English Church from the Accession of George I to the End of the Eighteenth Century (1714–1800)*, Vol. VII in *A History of the English Church*, W. R. W. Stephens and William Hunt, eds. (London, Macmillan and Co., Ltd., 1924), pp. 226-29.
[85] See BCP, Communion, Preface to the Sanctus. For Wesley's use of ascriptions, cf. No. 1, *Salvation by Faith*, III.9 and n.
[86] Place and date as in *AM*.

ON RICHES

AN INTRODUCTORY COMMENT

The last sermon in SOSO, *IV (1760), had been on 'The Use of Money'. Now, the last sermon in* SOSO, *VIII (1788), is 'On Riches'—and the parallels between the two sermons (and their placement) are noteworthy. In the three-decade interim, however, many Methodists by their diligence and thrift and the general prosperity of the times had become affluent (comparatively, at least), and Wesley had found it quite in vain to try to persuade them to follow his third rule: 'Give all you can.' The tone of 'The Use of Money' had been admonitory (what a Christian should do with riches,* in case; *for as he says below, II.10, not a single Methodist was rich 'when they first joined together'). Now he is in an earnest pastoral conflict with people whose actual 'riches' were, as he believed fervently, a mortal danger to their souls, a hindrance to their 'entering the kingdom of heaven'. It was, therefore, fitting that his last word to them in his collected sermons should be a warning and an exhortation.*

Along with its two predecessors, 'On Riches' was finished within the fortnight between April 8 and 23, in the midst of an arduous preaching mission in Lancashire, which suggests that he was working under the pressure of a deadline to complete the quota of fourteen sermons designed for his concluding volume of collected sermons; it was published in the ensuing summer. Indeed, it is a reasonable guess that he wrote out these last three sermons expressly for this volume.

At any rate, 'On Riches' first appeared in SOSO, *VIII.273-91, and this is the primary text for this edition. That text was then reprinted, with negligible alterations, in the* March *and* April *issues of the* Arminian Magazine *(1789), XII.117-22, 174-80, without title but numbered as 'Sermon L'. There is, however, a problem with the postscripted place and date as given in the* Arminian Magazine: *'Rochdale, April 22, 1788'. Both* Journal *and diary agree that he did not arrive in Rochdale until the afternoon of April 23—which means that since Rochdale was almost certainly the right place, then April 23 was almost certainly the right date.*

On Riches

Matthew 19:24

It is easier for a camel to go through the eye of a needle than for a rich man to enter into the kingdom of God.

1. In the preceding verses we have an account of 'a young man' who 'came running' to our Lord, 'and kneeling down', not in hypocrisy, but in deep earnestness of soul, and said unto him, 'Good Master, what good thing shall I do, that I may have eternal life?' 'All the commandments', saith he, 'I have kept from my youth: what lack I yet?'[1] Probably he had kept them in the literal sense; yet he still loved the world. And he who knew what was in man[2] knew that in this particular case (for this is by no means a general rule) he could not be healed of that desperate disease but by a desperate remedy. Therefore he answered, 'Go and sell all that thou hast, and give it to the poor, and come and follow me. But when he heard this, he went away sorrowful; for he had great possessions.'[3] So all the fair blossoms withered away! For he would not lay up treasure in heaven at so high a price! 'Jesus', observing this, 'looked round about and said unto his disciples, How hardly shall they that have riches enter into the kingdom of God! It is easier for a camel to go through the eye of a needle, than for a rich man to enter into the kingdom of God. And they were astonished out of measure, and said among themselves, Who then can be saved?'[a]—if it be so difficult for rich men to be saved, who have so many and so great advantages, who are free from the cares of this world, and a thousand difficulties to which the poor are continually exposed!

2. It has indeed been supposed, he partly retracts what he had said concerning the difficulty of rich men's being saved by what is added in the tenth chapter of St. Mark. For after he had said,

---

[a] Mark 10:23, etc.

---

[1] Matt. 19:16, 20; cf. Mark 10:17.
[2] John 2:25.
[3] Cf. Matt. 19:21-22.

'How hardly shall they that have riches enter into the kingdom of God,'[b] when 'the disciples were astonished at his words', Jesus answered again, and said unto them, 'How hard is it *for them that trust in riches* to enter into the kingdom of God!'[c] But observe, (1),
5 our Lord did not mean hereby to retract what he had said before. So far from it that he immediately confirms it by that awful declaration, 'It is easier for a camel to go through the eye of a needle than for a rich man to enter into the kingdom of God.' Observe, (2), both one of these sentences and the other assert the
10 very same thing. For it is easier for a camel to go through the eye of a needle than for those that *have riches* not to *trust* in them.

3. Perceiving their astonishment at this hard saying, 'Jesus looked upon them' (undoubtedly with an air of inexpressible tenderness, to prevent their thinking the case of the rich
15 desperate), [and said,] 'With men it is impossible, but not with God: for with God all things are possible.'[4]

4. I apprehend by a rich man here is meant, not only a man that has immense treasures, one that has heaped up gold as dust, and silver as the sand of the sea,[5] but anyone that possesses more than
20 the necessaries and conveniences of life.[6] One that has food and raiment sufficient for himself and his family, and something over, is rich. By the kingdom of God, or of heaven (exactly equivalent terms) I believe is meant (not the kingdom of glory, although that will without question follow, but) the kingdom of heaven, that is,
25 true religion upon earth. The meaning, then, of our Lord's assertion is this: that it is absolutely impossible, unless by that power to which all things are possible, that a rich man should be a Christian—to have the mind that was in Christ,[7] and to walk as Christ walked.[8] Such are the hindrances to holiness, as well as the
30 temptations to sin, which surround him on every side.

I. First, such are the hindrances to holiness which surround him on every side. To enumerate all these would require a large volume: I would only touch upon a few of them.

[b] Ver. 23.   [c] Ver. 24.

---

[4] Mark 10:27.
[5] See Job 22:24; 27:16; Zech. 9:3; Ps. 78:28 (BCP).
[6] Cf. No. 30, 'Sermon on the Mount, X', §26 and n.; see also No. 50, 'The Use of Money', intro.
[7] See Phil. 2:5.   [8] See 1 John 2:6.

1. The root of all religion is *faith,* without which it is impossible to please God.[9] Now if[10] you take this in its general acceptation, for an 'evidence of things not seen',[11] of the invisible and the eternal world, of God and the things of God—how natural a tendency have riches to darken this evidence, to prevent your attention to God and the things of God, and to things invisible and eternal! And if you take it in another sense, for a confidence in God,[12] what a tendency have riches to destroy this! To make you trust, either for happiness or defence, in them, not 'in the living God'![13] Or if you take faith in the proper Christian sense, as a divine confidence in a pardoning God, what a deadly, what an almost insuperable, hindrance to this faith are riches! What? Can a wealthy, and consequently an honourable man, come to God as having nothing to pay? Can he lay all his greatness by and come as a sinner, a mere sinner, the vilest of sinners? As on a level with those that feed the dogs of his flock? With that 'beggar' who 'lies at his gate full of sores'?[14] Impossible, unless by the same power that made the heavens and the earth. Yet without doing this he cannot in any sense 'enter into the kingdom of God'.

2. What a hindrance are riches to the very first fruit of faith, namely, the love of God! 'If any man love the world', says the Apostle, 'the love of the Father is not in him.'[15] But how is it possible for a man not to love the world, who is surrounded with all its allurements? How can it be that he should then hear the still small voice[16] which says, 'My son, give me thy heart'?[17] What power less than almighty can send the rich man an answer to that prayer,

> Keep me dead to all below,
> Only Christ resolved to know:
> Firm, and disengaged and free,
> Seeking all my bliss in Thee![18]

---

[9] Cf. Heb. 11:6; cf. also No. 3, *'Awake, Thou That Sleepest',* I.11 and n.

[10] Both early texts here read 'whether'; in Wesley's copy of *AM* this is corrected to 'if', though not in Wesley's hand.

[11] Heb. 11:1.

[12] 'in God': Wesley's marginal annotation in *SOSO,* VIII (1788).

[13] 1 Tim. 4:10.   [14] Cf. Luke 16:20.

[15] 1 John 2:15.   [16] 1 Kgs. 19:12.

[17] Cf. Prov. 23:26.

[18] John and Charles Wesley, *Hymns and Sacred Poems* (1739), p. 220. See also Wesley's letters to Lady Rawdon, Mar. 18, 1760; to Philothea Briggs, June 20, 1772; and to Ann Bolton, Jan. 5, 1783. See also 'A Thought Upon Marriage', §7, in *AM* (1785), VIII.535.

3. Riches are equally a hindrance to the loving our neighbour as ourselves, that is, to the loving all mankind as Christ loved us. A rich man may indeed love them that are of his own party, or his own opinion. He may love them that love him: 'do not even
5 heathens', baptized or unbaptized, 'the same'?[19] But he cannot have pure, disinterested goodwill to every child of man. This can only spring from the love of God, which his great possessions expelled from his soul.

4. From the love of God, and from no other fountain, true
10 humility likewise flows. Therefore so far as they hinder the love of God riches must hinder humility likewise. They hinder this also in the rich by cutting them off from that freedom of conversation whereby they might be made sensible of their defects, and come to a true knowledge of themselves. But how seldom do they meet
15 with a faithful friend, with one that can and will deal plainly with them! And without this we are likely to grow grey in our faults; yea, to die

> With all our imperfections on our head.[20]

5. Neither can meekness subsist without humility; for 'of pride'
20 naturally 'cometh contention.'[21] Our Lord accordingly directs us to learn of him at the same time to be 'meek and lowly in heart'.[22] Riches therefore are as great a hindrance to meekness as they are to humility. In preventing lowliness of mind[23] they of consequence prevent meekness, which increases in the same
25 proportion as we sink in our own esteem; and on the contrary necessarily decreases as we think more highly of ourselves.

6. There is another Christian temper which is nearly allied to meekness and humility.[24] But it has hardly a name. St. Paul terms it, ἐπιείκεια.[25] Perhaps till we find a better name in English[26] we

---

[19] Cf. Luke 6:33.   [20] Cf. Shakespeare, *Hamlet*, I.v.76-79:

> Cut off even in the blossoms of my sin,
> Unhousel'd, disappointed, unaneled,
> No reckoning made, but sent to my account
> With all my imperfections on my head.

[21] Cf. Prov. 13:10.   [22] Matt. 11:29.   [23] Phil. 2:3.
[24] See No. 21, 'Sermon on the Mount, I', I.7 and n.
[25] As in 2 Cor. 10:1 (cf. Greek of Acts 24:4). See *Notes;* and Nos. 97, 'On Obedience to Pastors', III.13 and n.; and 10, 'The Witness of the Spirit, I', II.6 and n.
[26] In Wesley's own copy of *AM* by a hand other than Wesley's, 'in English' is a marginal addition.

may call it 'yieldingness'—a readiness to submit to others, to give up our own will. This seems to be the quality which St. James ascribes to 'the wisdom from above', when he styles it εὐπειθής,[27] which we render 'easy to be entreated'; *easy to be convinced* of what is true; *easy to be persuaded.* But how rarely is this amiable temper to be found in a wealthy man! I do not know that I have found such a prodigy ten times in above threescore and ten years.

7. And how uncommon a thing is it to find patience in those that have large possessions! Unless when there is a counterbalance of long and severe affliction with which God is frequently pleased to visit those he loves, as an antidote to their riches. This is not uncommon: he often sends pain and sickness, and great crosses, to them that have great possessions. By these means 'patience has its perfect work, till they are perfect and entire, lacking nothing'.[28]

II. Such are some of the hindrances to holiness which surround the rich on every side! We may now observe, on the other side, what a temptation riches are to all unholy tempers.

1. And, first, how great is the temptation to *atheism,*[29] which naturally flows from riches; even to an entire forgetfulness of God,[30] as if there was no such Being in the universe! This is at present usually termed 'dissipation'[31]—a pretty name affixed by the great vulgar[32] to an utter disregard for God, and indeed for the whole invisible world. And how is the rich man surrounded with all manner of temptations to continual dissipation! Yes, how is the art of dissipation studied among the rich and great! As Prior keenly says,

> Cards are dealt and dice are brought, . . .
> Happy effects of human wit,
> That Alma may herself forget.[33]

Say rather,

> That mortals may their God forget!

[27] Jas. 3:17. Cf. No. 97, 'On Obedience to Pastors', III.2 and n.; also No. 10, 'The Witness of the Spirit, I', II.6 and n.

[28] Cf. Jas. 1:4; see No. 83, 'On Patience', §5 and n.

[29] See No. 23, 'Sermon on the Mount, III', I.11 and n.

[30] For 'dissipation' as an 'uncentring from God', see No. 79, 'On Dissipation', §6 and n.

[31] A 'cant word' of the day used in the sense of relaxation, diversion, distraction; see No. 79, 'On Dissipation', §1 and n.

[32] See No. 31, 'Sermon on the Mount, XI', I.6 and n.

[33] A paraphrase of Matthew Prior's 'Alma', III.488-91.

That they may keep him utterly out of their thoughts, who, though he sitteth on the circle of the heavens,[34] yet is 'about their bed, and about their path, and spieth out all their ways'.[35] Call this wit, if you please; but is it wisdom? O no! It is far, very far from it! 5 Thou fool, dost thou imagine because thou dost not see God that God doth not see thee? Laugh on! Play on! Sing on! Dance on! But 'for all these things God will bring thee to judgment!'[36]

2. From atheism there is an easy transition to *idolatry*—from the worship of no God to the worship of false gods. And, in fact, 10 he that does not love God (which is his proper and his only proper worship) will surely love some of the works of his hands; will love the creature if not the Creator. But to how many species of idolatry is every rich man exposed! What continual and almost insuperable temptations is he under to 'love the world'![37] And that 15 in all its branches—'the desire of the flesh, the desire of the eyes, and the pride of life'.[38] What innumerable temptations will he find to gratify 'the desire of the flesh'! Understand this right. It does not refer to one only, but to all the outward senses. It is equal idolatry to seek our happiness in gratifying any or all of these. But 20 there is the greatest danger lest men should seek it in gratifying their taste; in a moderate sensuality; in a regular kind of epicurism. Not in gluttony or drunkenness—far be that from them! They do not disorder the body; they only keep the soul dead—dead to God and all true religion.

25 3. The rich are equally surrounded with temptations from 'the desire of the eyes'; that is, the seeking happiness in gratifying the imagination; [to] the pleasures of which the eyes chiefly minister. The objects that give pleasure to the imagination[39] are grand, or beautiful, or new. Indeed all rich men have not a taste for grand 30 objects; but they have for new and beautiful things; especially for new, the desire of novelty being as natural to men as the desire of meat and drink. Now how numerous are the temptations to this kind of idolatry which naturally spring from riches! How strongly and continually are they solicited to seek happiness (if not in 35 grand, yet) in beautiful houses, in elegant furniture, in curious pictures, in delightful gardens![40] Perhaps in that trifle of all trifles,

---

[34] See Isa. 40:22.   [35] Cf. Ps. 139:2 (BCP).
[36] Cf. Eccles. 11:9.   [37] 1 John 2:15.
[38] 1 John 2:16 *(Notes);* cf. No. 7, 'The Way to the Kingdom', II.2 and n.
[39] Cf. No. 44, *Original Sin*, II.10 and n.
[40] An echo from William Law; cf. No. 28, 'Sermon on the Mount, VIII', §§23-24 and n.

rich or gay apparel! Yea, in every new thing, little or great, which fashion, the mistress of fools,[41] recommends? How are rich men of a more elevated turn of mind tempted to seek happiness, as their various tastes lead, in poetry, history, music, philosophy, or curious arts and sciences! Now, although it is certain all these have their use, and therefore may innocently be pursued, yet the seeking happiness in any of them instead of God is manifest idolatry. And therefore were it only on this account—that riches furnish him with the means of indulging all these desires—it might well be asked, 'Is not the life of a *rich* man' (above all others) 'a temptation upon earth?'[42]

4. What temptation likewise must every rich man have to seek happiness in 'the pride of life'! I do not conceive the Apostle to mean thereby pomp, or state, or equipage, so much as 'the honour that cometh of men',[43] whether it be deserved or not. A rich man is sure to meet with this: it is a snare he cannot escape. The whole city of London uses the words 'rich' and 'good' as equivalent terms. 'Yes', say they, 'He is a good man: he is worth a hundred thousand pounds.'[44] And indeed everywhere if 'thou dost well unto thyself', if thou increasest in goods, 'men will speak well of thee.'[45] All the world is agreed,

> A thousand pound supplies
> The want of twenty thousand qualities.[46]

And who can bear general applause without being puffed up—without being insensibly induced 'to think of himself more highly than he ought to think'?[47]

5. How is it possible that a rich man should escape pride, were it only on this account, that his situation necessarily occasions praise to flow in upon him from every quarter. For praise is generally poison to the soul; and the more pleasing, the more fatal—particularly when it is undeserved. So that well might our poet say:

> Parent of evil, bane of honest deeds,
> Pernicious flattery! Thy destructive seeds

---

[41] Cf. No. 25, 'Sermon on the Mount, V', IV.3 and n.
[42] Cf. 1 Tim. 6:9.   [43] Cf. John 5:41.
[44] I.e., a 'plum'; cf. No. 131, 'The Danger of Increasing Riches', I.6 and n. For Wesley's use of 'a good sort of man', cf. No. 80, 'On Friendship with the World', §21 and n.
[45] Cf. Ps. 49:18 (BCP).
[46] π; Cf. No. 113, *The Late Work of God in North America*, I.12.   [47] Rom. 12:3.

In an ill hour, and by a fatal hand
Sadly diffused o'er virtue's gleby land,
With rising pride amid the corn appear,
And check the hope and promise of the year![48]

5   And not only praise, whether deserved or undeserved, but everything about him tends to inspire and increase pride. His noble house, his elegant furniture, his well-chosen pictures, his fine horses, his equipage, his very dress, yea, even 'the embroidery plaistered on his tail':[49] all these will be matter of
10 commendation to some or other of his guests, and so have an almost irresistible tendency to make him think himself a better man than those who have not these advantages.

6. How naturally likewise do riches feed and increase the *self-will* which is born in every child of man! As not only his
15 domestic servants and immediate dependants are governed implicitly by his will, finding their account therein, but also most of his neighbours and acquaintance study to oblige him in all things; so his will, being continually indulged, will of course be continually strengthened, till at length he will be ill able to submit
20 to the will either of God or men.

7. Such a tendency have riches to beget and nourish every temper that is contrary to the love of God. And they have equal tendency to feed every passion and temper that is contrary to the love of our neighbour. *Contempt*, for instance, particularly of
25 inferiors, than which nothing is more contrary to love: *resentment* of any real or supposed offence; perhaps even *revenge*, although God claims this as his own peculiar prerogative;[50] at least *anger*, for it immediately rises in the mind of a rich man: 'What! to use *me* thus! Nay, but he shall soon know better: I am now able to do
30 myself justice.'

8. Nearly related to anger, if not rather a species of it, are *fretfulness* and *peevishness*. But are the rich more assaulted by these than the poor? All experience shows that they are. One remarkable instance I was a witness of many years ago. A
35 gentleman of large fortune,[51] while we were seriously conversing, ordered a servant to throw some coals on the fire. A puff of smoke

---

[48] Cf. Prior, *Solomon*, i.693-98.
[49] Cf. Pope, *Moral Essays*, Epistle III, 'To Lord Bathurst', 90:
         With all th' embroid'ry plaister'd at thy tail.
[50] See Rom. 12:19.
[51] Sir John Phillipps (*c*. 1701–64); see No. 87, 'The Danger of Riches', II.16 and n.

came out. He threw himself back in his chair and cried out, 'O Mr. Wesley, these are the crosses which I meet with every day!' I could not help asking, 'Pray, Sir John, are these the heaviest crosses you meet with?' Surely these crosses would not have fretted him so much if he had had fifty instead of five thousand 5 pounds a year!

9. But it would not be strange if rich men were in general void of all good dispositions, and an easy prey to all evil ones, since so few of them pay any regard to that solemn declaration of our Lord, without observing which we cannot be his disciples: 'And 10 he said unto them all'—the whole multitude, not unto his apostles only—'If any man will come after me', will be a real Christian, 'let him deny himself, and take up his cross daily, and follow me.'d O how hard a saying is this to those that are at ease 'in the midst of their possessions'![52] Yet the Scripture cannot be broken. 15 Therefore unless a man do 'deny himself' every pleasure which does not prepare him for taking pleasure in God, 'and take up his cross daily'—obey every command of God, however grievous to flesh and blood—he cannot be a disciple of Christ, he cannot 'enter into the kingdom of God'.   20

10. Touching this important point of 'denying ourselves, and taking up our cross daily', let us appeal to matter of fact; let us appeal to every man's conscience in the sight of God. How many rich men are there among the Methodists[53] (observe, there was not one when they were first joined together!) who actually do 25 'deny themselves, and take up their cross daily'? Who resolutely abstain from every pleasure, either of sense or imagination, unless they know by experience that it prepares them for taking pleasure in God? Who declines no cross, no labour or pain, which lies in the way of his duty? Who of you that are now rich deny 30 yourselves just as you did when you were poor? Who as willingly endure labour or pain now as you did when you were not worth five pounds? Come to particulars. Do you fast now as often as you did then? Do you rise as early in the morning? Do you endure cold or heat, wind or rain, as cheerfully as ever? See one reason among 35

d Luke 9:23.

---

[52] Cf. Ecclus. 41:1.
[53] From 1776 until his death Wesley's complaints against Methodists who have not '*given* all they can' multiply and gain in stridency. He was, in effect, trying to counteract the surge of capitalistic ideas given impetus by Adam Smith's *Wealth of Nations* (1776).

many why so few increase in goods without decreasing in grace—because they no longer deny themselves and take up their daily cross! They no longer, alas! endure hardship, as good soldiers of Jesus Christ![54]

5   11. 'Go to now, ye rich men! Weep and howl for the miseries that are coming upon you!'[55] That must come upon you in a few days, unless prevented by a deep and entire change! 'The canker of your gold and silver will be a testimony against you, and will eat your flesh as fire.'[56] O how pitiable is your condition! And who is
10 able to help you? You need more plain dealing than any men in the world. And you meet with less. For how few dare speak as plain to *you* as they would do to one of your servants? No man living that either hopes to gain anything by your favour, or fears to lose anything by your displeasure. O that God would give me
15 acceptable words, and cause them to sink deep into your hearts! Many of you have known me long, wellnigh from your infancy! You have frequently helped me when I stood in need. May I not say you loved me? But now the time of our parting is at hand: my feet are just stumbling upon the dark mountains.[57] I would leave
20 one word with you before I go hence; and you may remember it when I am no more seen.[58]

12. O let your heart be whole with God! Seek your happiness in him and him alone. Beware that you cleave not to the dust![59] 'This *earth* is not your place.'[60] See that you use this world as not
25 abusing[61] it: *use* the world, and *enjoy* God.[62] Sit as loose to all things here below[63] as if you was a poor beggar. Be a good steward of the manifold gifts of God,[64] that when you are called to give an account of your stewardship[65] he may say, 'Well done, good and faithful servant: enter thou into the joy of thy Lord'![66]

30 Rochdale, April 23, 1788[67]

[54] See 2 Tim. 2:3.   [55] Cf. Jas. 5:1.   [56] Cf. Jas. 5:3.
[57] An echo of Jer. 13:16.   [58] See Ps. 39:15 (BCP).   [59] See Ps. 119:25.
[60] Charles Wesley; see No. 3, '*Awake, Thou That Sleepest*', II.5 and n.
[61] Cf. No. 20, *The Lord Our Righteousness*, II.20 and n.
[62] Cf. Pascal, *Pensées*, ed., H. F. Stewart (London, Routledge and Kegan Paul, 1950), pp. 304-5; see also No. 30, 'Sermon on the Mount, X', §7 and n.
[63] See No. 44, *Original Sin*, II.9 and n.
[64] See 1 Pet. 4:10; cf. No. 51, *The Good Steward*.
[65] See Luke 16:2.   [66] Matt. 25:21.
[67] The place and date were added in *AM* as 'Rochdale, April 22, 1788'—'22' apparently a printer's error for '23'; see JWJ, and his diary for the latter date: '3.15 Rochdale, sermon, prayed, tea; 6'.

A
MISCELLANY
OF
PUBLISHED SERMONS
NOT INCLUDED IN ANY OF
WESLEY'S
COLLECTIONS OF
SERMONS ON SEVERAL OCCASIONS

IN THEIR
CHRONOLOGICAL SEQUENCE

A
SERMON

PREACHED AT

St. *Mary*'s in *OXFORD*,

On Sunday, *September* 21, 1735.

By JOHN WESLEY, M. A.
Fellow of *Lincoln* College, Oxon.

Publifh'd at the Requeft of feveral of the Hearers.

LONDON:

Printed for C. Rivington, at the *Bible*
and *Crown*, in St. *Paul's Church-Yard*;
and J. Roberts in *Warwick-Lane*, 1735.

THE TROUBLE AND REST OF GOOD MEN

AN INTRODUCTORY COMMENT

Wesley embarked for Georgia on October 14, 1735. The decision for that surprising venture had been only recently taken, and the seven weeks since August 28 (when the invitation was first tendered by Dr. John Burton) had been filled with distractions—an array of family problems complicating his preparations for his voyage into the unknown. In the midst of all this, however, he had kept a previous appointment to preach to the university, in Oxford, on Sunday, September 21. There is no mention of this in any of Wesley's records, and there is no evidence about its provenance other than its title page. Even so, it stands as Wesley's first published sermon, and it is from the same text as his very first sermon ten years before (see No. 133, 'Death and Deliverance'). That he intended for it to be published, 'at the request of several of the hearers', is suggested by the fact that he left it with the same publisher who had just brought out his new translation of Thomas à Kempis, The Imitation of Christ *(viz.,* The Christian's Pattern: Or, a Treatise of the Imitation of Christ, *London, C. Rivington, 1735). The sermon was published during Wesley's absence from England, and never reprinted in his lifetime. Its title was,* A Sermon Preached at St. Mary's in Oxford, on Sunday, September 21, 1735. *The present title was supplied by Thomas Jackson in his edition of Wesley's* Sermons *in 1825. For fuller details of its history, see Bibliog, No. 6.*

Its significance for us lies in its lucid mirroring of Wesley's mind—at a critical stage in his theological development—of an idea already adumbrated in the funeral sermon for Robin Griffith, January 11, 1727 (see No. 136, 'On Mourning for the Dead'). It is yet another comment in the famed ars moriendi *tradition, with special stress on the notion that while death is the* effect *of sin, it has also been appointed by God as the* cure *of sin. Thomas Jackson found himself moved to warn all readers against this 'unevangelical' idea and to 'observe that while the sermon displays great seriousness and zeal, it exhibits a very inadequate view of real Christianity' (see his editorial note in* Works, *1829, VII.365-66).*

Clearly, Jackson was indifferent to the fact, if indeed he knew it, that the sermon's point about death as deliverance from our mortal ills and sin would have been familiar to an Oxford audience as an oversimplification of the old tradition of 'the art of dying' which had flourished in England since at least the fifteenth century; see Nancy Lee Beaty, 'The Ars Moriendi: *Wellspring of the Tradition', ch. 1, in* The Craft of Dying: A Study in the Literary Tradition of the Ars Moriendi in England *(New Haven, Yale University Press, 1970); see also Mary Catherine O'Connor,* The Art of Dying Well *(New York, Columbia University Press, 1942). Wesley knew this tradition best from Jeremy Taylor, although he seems to ignore Taylor's crucial distinction between death as deliverance from the* bodily *agent of sin and death as deliverance from the* guilt *of sin. Many of his hearers would also have recognized in it a variation on the well-known Lutheran doctrine of invincible concupiscence and its implication that 'the* sense *of sin [though not its guilt, reatus] is removed in death and the* matter *of sin in the dissolution of the body,' as in J. A. Quenstedt,* Theologia Didactico-Polemica *(1685), II.62; cf. Heinrich Schmid,* Doctrinal Theology of the Evangelical Lutheran Church *(1889), pp. 238, 250, 624.*

'Unevangelical' or not, Wesley's doctrine here represents two established traditions and reflects a stage of Wesley's theological development that deserves careful notice in special relationship to the earlier university sermons on 'The Image of God' (No. 141), and 'The Circumcision of the Heart' (No. 17). For when he later changed his basic understanding of 'sin in believers', he quite pointedly left this sermon in limbo, where it has remained ever since, as far as any attention paid to it in Wesley studies is concerned. This means that it might be ready for reconsideration in the light of the whole question of his theological development and in connection with his doctrine of perfection in love in this life.

The Trouble and Rest of Good Men

Job 3:17

There the wicked cease from troubling, and there the weary be at rest.

When God at first surveyed all the works he had made, behold, they were very good.[1] All were perfect in beauty, and man, the 5 lord of all, was perfect in holiness. And as his holiness was, so was his happiness; knowing no sin, he knew no pain. But when sin was conceived, it soon brought forth pain; the whole scene was changed in a moment. He now groaned under the weight of a mortal body and—what was far worse—a corrupted soul. That 10 'spirit' which could have borne all his other 'infirmities' was itself 'wounded'[2] and sick unto death. Thus 'in the day wherein he sinned he' began to 'die';[3] and thus, 'in the midst of life we are in death;'[4] yea, 'the whole creation groaneth together',[5] 'being in bondage to sin',[6] and therefore to misery. 15

The whole world is indeed, in its present state, only one great infirmary:[7] all that are therein are sick of sin, and their one business there is to be healed. And for this very end the great Physician of souls is continually present with them, marking all the diseases of every soul, and 'giving medicines to heal its 20 sickness'.[8] These medicines are often painful, too. Not that God willingly afflicts his creatures, but he allots them just as much pain as is necessary to their health; and for that reason—because it is so.

The pain of cure must then be endured by every man, as well as 25 the pain of sickness.[9] And herein is manifest the infinite wisdom

---

[1] See Gen. 1:31.   [2] Cf. Prov. 18:14.   [3] Cf. Ezek. 18:4, 20; 33:12.
[4] BCP, Burial.   [5] Cf. Rom. 8:22.   [6] Cf. Rom. 8:21.
[7] Cf. Sir Thomas Browne, *Religio Medici* (1642), II.11 ('For the world I count not an inn but an hospital . . .'); see also Jeremy Taylor, *The Rule and Exercises of Holy Dying* (1651), ch. I, sect. IV, 3 (*Works*, I.530): 'an hospital . . . is indeed a map of the whole world, where you see the effects of Adam's sin and the ruins of human nature;' and Taylor's *Great Exemplar* (1649), Pt. I, sect. IX, Discourse V, §10 (*Works*, I.105): 'Those are the persons of Christ's infirmary whose restitution and reduction to a state of life and health was his great design.'
[8] Cf. Ps. 147:3 (BCP).
[9] See No. 73, 'Of Hell', I.1 and n., for a later comment on a distinction that Wesley would have learned in Oxford between *poena sensus* and *poena damni*.

of him who careth for us, that the very sickness of those with whom he converses may be a great means of every man's cure. The very wickedness of others is, in a thousand ways, conducive to a good man's holiness. They trouble him, 'tis true, but even
5 that trouble is 'health to his soul, and marrow to his bones'.[10] He suffers many things from them; but it is to this end, that he may be 'made perfect through' those 'sufferings'.[11]

But as perfect holiness is not found on earth, so neither is perfect happiness: some remains of our disease will ever be felt,
10 and some physic be necessary to heal it.[12] Therefore we must be more or less subject to the pain of cure, as well as the pain of sickness. And, accordingly, neither do 'the wicked' here 'cease from troubling', nor can 'the weary be at rest.'

'Who then will deliver us from the body of this death?'[13] Death
15 will deliver us. Death shall set those free in one moment who were 'all their lifetime subject to bondage'.[14] Death shall destroy at once the whole body of sin,[15] and therewith of its companion, pain. And therefore, 'there the wicked cease from troubling, and there the weary be at rest.'

20 The Scriptures give us no account of the place where the souls of the just remain from death to the resurrection.[16] But we have an account of their state in these words; in explaining which I shall consider,

I. How the 'wicked' do here 'trouble' good men. And,
25 II. How the 'weary are there at rest'.

[I.] Let us consider, first, how the 'wicked' here 'trouble' good men. And this is a spacious field. Look round the world, take a view of all the troubles therein—how few are there whereof the wicked are not the occasion! 'From whence come wars and
30 fightings among you?'[17] Whence all the ills that embitter society? That often turn that highest of blessings into a curse, and make it

---

[10] Cf. Prov. 3:8.

[11] Cf. Heb. 2:10.

[12] An explicit assertion of the Puritan doctrine that perfection is reserved for 'the state of glory only' *(in statu gloriae)*. Wesley will reverse himself on this point completely. Cf. Nos. 40, *Christian Perfection;* and 76, 'On Perfection'; see also, below, II.3.

[13] Cf. Rom. 7:24; see also No.136, 'On Mourning for the Dead', ¶¶6-7.

[14] Heb. 2:15.

[15] An echo from *The Apology of the Augsburg Confession* (1531), sections 151-54, and of 'The Second Part of the Sermon Against the Fear of Death' in the Edwardian *Homilies*, IX. Contrast this with No. 13, *On Sin in Believers*, I.4 and n.

[16] See below, I.3 and n.   [17] Jas. 4:1.

'good for man to be alone'?[18] 'Come they not hence',[19] from
self-will, pride, inordinate affection—in one word, from
wickedness? And can it be otherwise, so long as it remains upon
earth? As well may 'the Ethiopian change his skin'[20] as a wicked
man cease to trouble both himself and his neighbour, but   5
especially good men; inasmuch as while he is wicked he is
continually injuring either them, or himself, or God.

1. First, wicked men trouble those who serve God by the
injuries they do them. As at first 'he that was born after the flesh
persecuted him that was born after the Spirit, even so it is now.'[21]   10
And so it must be till all things are fulfilled; till 'heaven and earth
pass away',[22] 'all that will live godly in Christ Jesus shall suffer
persecution.'[23] For there is an irreconcilable enmity between the
Spirit of Christ and the spirit of the world. If the followers of
Christ 'were of the world, the world would love its own; but,   15
because they are not of the world, therefore the world hateth
them'.[24] And this hatred they will not fail to show by their words:
'they will say all manner of evil against them falsely;'[25] 'they will
find out many inventions'[26] whereby even 'the good that is in them
may be evil spoken of',[27] and in a thousand instances 'lay to their   20
charge' the ill 'that they know not'.[28] From words in due time they
proceed to deeds; treating the servants as their forefathers did
their Master, wronging and despitefully using them in as many
ways as fraud can invent and force accomplish.

[2.] 'Tis true these troubles sit heaviest upon those who are yet   25
weak in the faith; and the more of the Spirit of Christ any man
gains the lighter do they appear to him; so that to him who is truly
renewed therein, who is full of the knowledge and love of God, all
the wrongs of wicked men are not only no evils, but are matter of
real and solid joy. But still, though he rejoices for his own sake, he   30
cannot but grieve for theirs. 'He hath great heaviness and
continual sorrow in his heart' for his 'brethren according to the
flesh',[29] who are thus 'treasuring up to themselves wrath against
the day of wrath, and revelation of the righteous judgment of
God'.[30] 'His eyes weep for them in secret places;'[31] he is 'horribly   35

---

[18] A curious inversion of Gen. 2:18; wickedness confounds God's judgment that 'it is
not good that man should be alone.'

[19] Jas. 4:1.   [20] Jer. 13:23.   [21] Gal. 4:29.
[22] Matt. 24:35, etc.   [23] 2 Tim. 3:12.   [24] Cf. John 15:19.
[25] Cf. Matt. 5:11.   [26] Cf. Eccles. 7:29.   [27] Cf. Rom. 14:16.
[28] Cf. Ps. 35:11.   [29] Cf. Rom. 9:2-3.
[30] Cf. Rom. 2:5.   [31] Cf. Jer. 13:17.

afraid'[32] for them; yea, 'he could even wish to be accursed himself,'[33] so they might inherit a blessing. And thus it is that they who can not only slight but rejoice in the greatest injury done to them, yet are troubled at that which wicked men do to themselves,
5 and the grievous misery that attends them.

[3.] How much more are they troubled at the injuries wicked men are continually offering to God! This was the circumstance which made the contradiction of sinners[34] so severe a trial to our Lord himself: 'He that despiseth me, despiseth him that sent
10 me.'[35] And how are these despisers now multiplied upon earth! Who fear not the Son, neither the Father. How are we surrounded with those who blaspheme the Lord and his Anointed, either reviling the whole of his glorious gospel, or making him a liar as to some of the blessed truths which he hath
15 graciously revealed therein! How many of those who profess to believe the whole, yet in effect preach another gospel; so disguising the most essential doctrines thereof by their new interpretations as to retain the words only, but nothing of the faith once delivered to the saints![36] How many who have not yet made
20 shipwreck of the faith[37] are strangers to the fruits of it! It hath not purified their hearts; it hath not overcome the world; they are yet 'in the gall of bitterness, and in the bond of iniquity'.[38] They are still 'lovers of themselves',[39] 'lovers of the world',[40] 'lovers of pleasure', and not 'lovers of God'.[41] Lovers of God? No. 'He is not
25 in all their thoughts!'[42] They delight not in him, they thirst not after him; they do not rejoice in doing his will, neither make their boast of his praise! O faith working by love,[43] whither art thou fled? Surely the Son of man did once plant thee upon earth. Where then art thou now? Among the wealthy? No. The
30 'deceitfulness of riches' there 'chokes the word, and it becometh unfruitful'.[44] Among the poor? No. 'The cares of the world'[45] are there, 'so that it bringeth forth no fruit to perfection.'[46] However, there is nothing to prevent its growth among those who have neither poverty nor riches.—Yes, the desire of other things. And

[32] Ezek. 32:10. [33] Cf. Rom. 9:3.
[34] See Heb. 12:3. [35] Luke 10:16.
[36] Jude 3. [37] 1 Tim. 1:19.
[38] Acts 8:23. [39] 2 Tim. 3:2.
[40] Cf. 1 John 2:15. [41] 2 Tim. 3:4.
[42] Cf. Ps. 10:4.
[43] See Gal. 5:6; cf. No. 2, *The Almost Christian*, II.6 and n.
[44] Cf. Mark 4:19. [45] *Ibid.* [46] Cf. Luke 8:14.

experience shows, by a thousand melancholy examples, that the allowed desire of anything, great or small, otherwise than as a means to the one thing needful,[47] will by degrees banish the care of that out of the soul, and unfit it for every good word or work.[48]

Such is the trouble, not to descend to particulars which are 5 endless, that wicked men continually occasion to the good. Such is the state of all good men while on earth. But it is not so with their souls in paradise. In the moment wherein they are loosed from the body they know pain no more. Though they are not yet possessed of the fullness of joy, yet all grief is done away.[49] For 10 'there the wicked cease from troubling; and there the weary be at rest.'

II.[1.] 'There the weary are at rest'—which was the second thing to be considered—not only from those evils which prudence might have prevented or piety removed even in this life, 15 but from those which were inseparable therefrom, which were their unavoidable portion on earth. They are now at rest whom wicked men would not suffer to rest before; for into the seat of the spirits of just men, none but the spirits of the just can enter.[50] They are at length hid from the scourge of the tongue:[51] their 20 name is not here cast out as evil.[52] Abraham, Isaac, and Jacob, and the prophets do not revile or separate them from their company.[53] They are no longer despitefully used and persecuted;[54] neither do they groan under the hand of the oppressor.[55] No injustice, no malice, no fraud is there; they are all 'Israelites indeed, in whom is 25 no guile'.[56] There are no sinners against their own souls;[57] therefore there is no painful pity, no fear for them. There are no blasphemers of God or of his Word, no profaners of his name or of his sabbaths; no denier of the Lord that bought him;[58] none that tramples upon the blood of his everlasting covenant:[59] in a word, 30

---

[47] See Luke 10:42. Cf. Jeremy Taylor's *Unum Necessarium* (1655). Charles Wesley frequently reported having preached on 'the one thing needful' in CWJ; cf., e.g., Sept. 27, 1736; Oct. 30, 1737; Oct. 15, 22, 1738. John preached from this text from 1734 to the end of his ministry (seven times recorded in 1790); see No. 146, 'The One Thing Needful', the text of which Charles copied from John's manuscript.

[48] See 2 Thess. 2:17.

[49] Cf. proem, above, and No. 115, 'Dives and Lazarus', I.3 and n.

[50] See Heb. 12:23.   [51] Job 5:21.

[52] See Luke 6:22.   [53] *Ibid.*

[54] See Matt. 5:44.   [55] Jer. 21:12; 22:3.

[56] Cf. John 1:47.   [57] Num. 16:38.

[58] See 2 Pet. 2:1.   [59] See Heb. 13:20.

no earthly or sensual, no devilish spirit;[60] none who do not love the Lord their God with all their heart.[61]

2. There, therefore, 'the weary are at rest' from all the troubles which the wicked occasioned; and, indeed, from all the other evils
5 which are necessary in this world, either as the consequence of sin or for the cure of it. They are at rest, in the first place, from bodily pain. In order to judge of the greatness of this deliverance, let but those who have not felt it take a view of one who lies on a sick- or death-bed.[62] Is this he that was made a little lower than
10 the angels?[63] How is the glory departed from him! His eye is dim and heavy, his cheek pale and wan, his tongue falters, his hand trembles, his breast heaves and pants, his whole body is now distorted and writhed[64] to and fro, now moist and cold and motionless, like the earth to which it is going. And yet all this
15 which you see is but the shadow of what he feels. You see not the pain that tears his heart, that shoots through all his veins, and chases the flying soul through every part of her once loved habitation. Could we see this, too, how earnestly should we cry out: 'O sin, what hast thou done? To what hast thou brought the
20 noblest part of the visible creation? Was it for this the good God made man?' O no! Neither will he suffer it long. Yet a little while, and all the storms of life shall be over! And thou shalt be gathered into the storehouse of the dead! And there 'the weary are at rest.'

3. 'They are at rest,' from all these infirmities and follies which
25 they could not escape in this life.[65] They are no longer exposed to the delusions of sense, or the dreams of imagination. They are not hindered from seeing the noblest truths, by inadvertence, nor do they ever lose the sight they have once gained, by inattention. They are not entangled with prejudice, nor ever misled by hasty
30 or partial views of the object. And consequently, no error is there. O blessed place, where truth alone can enter! Truth unmixed, undisguised, enlightening every man who cometh into the world.[66] Where there is no difference of opinions, but all think

---

[60] See Jas. 3:15.   [61] See Matt. 22:37, etc.
[62] An echo here of Wesley's memories of his own father's prolonged illness and painful death just five months earlier (Apr. 25). Cf. John's letter to 'John Smith', Mar. 22, 1748 (§6); and Charles's letter to their brother Samuel Wesley, Jun., in Tyerman, *Samuel Wesley*, pp. 445-46.
[63] Ps. 8:5.
[64] I.e., 'twisted'; for this past participle of 'writhe', cf. *OED*, and JWJ, Jan. 13, 1743.
[65] Cf. proem, above, and No. 76, 'On Perfection', II.7 and n.
[66] See John 1:9.

alike, all are of one heart and of one mind.[67] Where that offspring of hell, controversy,[68] which turneth this world upside down, can never come. Where those who have been sawn asunder thereby, and often cried out in the bitterness of their soul,[69] 'Peace, peace,'[70] shall find what they then sought in vain, even a peace   5
which none taketh from them.[71]

4. And yet all this, inconceivably great as it is, is the least part of their deliverance. For in the moment wherein they shake off the flesh they are delivered, not only from the troubling of the wicked, not only from pain and sickness, from folly and infirmity, but also   10
from sin. A deliverance this in sight of which all the rest vanish away. This is the triumphal song which everyone heareth when he entereth the gates of paradise: 'Thou, being dead, sinnest no more. Sin hath no more dominion over thee. For in that thou diedst, thou diedst unto sin once, but in that thou livest, thou   15
livest unto God.'[72]

5. 'There' then 'the weary be at rest.' The blood of the Lamb hath healed all their sickness,[73] 'hath washed them throughly from their wickedness, and cleansed them from their sin'.[74] The disease of their nature is cured; they are at length made whole;   20
they are restored to perfect soundness. They no longer mourn the 'flesh lusting against the Spirit';[75] 'the law in their members' is now at an end, and no longer 'wars against the law of their mind, and brings them into captivity to the law of sin.'[76] There is no root of bitterness[77] left, no remains even of that sin which did so easily   25
beset them;[78] no forgetfulness of 'him in whom they live, move, and have their being';[79] no ingratitude to their gracious

---

[67] See Acts 4:32. Cf. Wesley's later claim of such a unity among the early Methodists in JWJ, Nov. 9, 1740. The phrase recurs in his *Short Method of Converting All the Roman Catholics in the Kingdom of Ireland* (1752), §2, and in Charles Wesley's 'Primitive Christianity', first published appended to *An Earnest Appeal*, §101 (11:91 in this edn.):

> They all are of one heart and soul,
> And only love informs the whole.

See also Nos. 63, 'The General Spread of the Gospel', §20 and n.; and 68, 'The Wisdom of God's Counsels', §7.

[68] Cf. No. 52, *The Reformation of Manners*, IV.4, where Wesley defines dissimulation (what the world calls 'prudence') as 'the offspring of hell'.

[69] Cf. Job 10:1, etc.   [70] Jer. 6:14; 8:11.   [71] Cf. John 16:22.

[72] Cf. Rom. 6:7, 9-14; see also Rom. 14:7-9, 11-12.

[73] See Rev. 7:14.   [74] Cf. Ps. 51:2 (BCP).

[75] Cf. Gal. 5:17.   [76] Cf. Rom. 7:23.

[77] Heb. 12:15.   [78] See Heb. 12:1.

[79] Cf. Acts 17:28.

Redeemer, who poured out his soul unto the death for them;[80] no unfaithfulness to that blessed Spirit who so long bore with their infirmities. In a word, no pride, no self-will is there; so that they who are thus delivered from the bondage of corruption[81] may
5 indeed say one to another, and that in an emphatical sense, 'Beloved, now we are the children of God; and it doth not yet appear what we shall be; but we shall be like him; for we shall see him as he is.'[82]

6. Let us view a little more nearly the state of a Christian at his
10 entrance into the other world. Suppose 'the silver cord' of life just 'loosed', and 'the wheel broken at the cistern';[83] the heart can now beat no more; the blood ceases to move; the last breath flies off from the quivering lips, and the soul springs forth into eternity. What are the thoughts of such a soul, that has just subdued her
15 last enemy, death?[84] That sees the body of sin lying beneath her, and is new born into the world of spirits? How does she sing: 'O death, where is thy sting? O grave, where is thy victory? Thanks be unto God, who hath given me the victory, through our Lord Jesus Christ!'[85] O happy day, wherein I begin to live, wherein I taste my
20 native freedom! When I was 'born of a woman', I had 'but a short time to live', and that time was 'full of misery';[86] that corruptible body pressed me down,[87] and enslaved me to sin and pain. But 'the snare is broken, and I am delivered.'[88] 'Henceforth I know them no more.'[89] That head is no more an aching head; those eyes
25 shall no more run down with tears;[90] that heart shall no more pant with anguish or fear, or be weighed down with sorrow or care; those limbs shall no more be racked with pain; yea, 'sin hath no more dominion over me.'[91] At length I have parted from thee, O my enemy, and I shall see thy face no more. I shall never more be
30 unfaithful to my Lord, or offend the eyes of his glory![92] I am no longer that wavering, fickle, self-inconsistent creature, sinning and repenting, and sinning again. No. I shall never cease, day or night to love and praise the Lord my God, with all my heart, and

---

[80] Isa. 53:12.
[81] Rom. 8:21.
[82] Cf. 1 John 3:2 *(Notes)*.
[83] Cf. Eccles. 12:6.
[84] See 1 Cor. 15:26.
[85] Cf. 1 Cor. 15:55, 57.
[86] BCP, Burial, At the grave (cf. Job 14:1-2).
[87] Cf. Wisd. 9:15; see also No. 41, *Wandering Thoughts*, II.3 and n.
[88] Cf. Ps. 124:6 (BCP).
[89] Cf. 2 Cor. 5:16.
[90] See Jer. 9:18.
[91] Cf. Rom. 6:14; see also No. 13, *On Sin in Believers*, I.4 and n.
[92] Isa. 3:8.

with all my strength. But what are ye? 'Are all these ministering spirits sent forth to minister' unto one 'heir of salvation?'[93] Then, dust and ashes, farewell. I hear a voice from heaven saying, Come away, and rest from thy labours; 'thy warfare is accomplished, thy sin is pardoned,'[94] 'and the days of thy mourning are ended.'[95] 5

7. Brethren, these truths need little application. Believe ye that these things are so?[96] What then hath each of you to do but to 'lay aside every weight, and run with patience the race set before him'?[97] 'To count all things else but dung and dross'?[98]—especially those grand idols, learning and reputation, if they are 10 pursued in any other measure, or with any other view, than as they conduce to the knowledge and love of God. To have this one thing 'continually in thine heart',[99] 'when thou sittest in thine house, and when thou walkest by the way, and when thou liest down, and when thou risest up';[100] to have thy 'loins' ever 'girt', 15 and 'thy light burning';[101] to serve the Lord thy God with all thy might;[102] if by any means, when he requireth thy soul of thee,[103] perhaps in an hour when thou lookest not for him,[104] thou mayst enter 'where the wicked cease from troubling, and where the weary be at rest'. 20

---

[93] Cf. Heb. 1:14.
[94] Cf. Isa. 40:2.
[95] Cf. Isa. 60:20.
[96] See Acts 7:1.
[97] Cf. Heb. 12:1.
[98] Cf. Phil. 3:8.
[99] Cf. Prov. 6:21.
[100] Deut. 6:7; 11:19.
[101] Cf. Luke 12:35.
[102] See Deut. 6:5.
[103] See Luke 12:20.
[104] See Luke 12:46.

FREE GRACE

AN INTRODUCTORY COMMENT

This sermon is noteworthy as the signal of a major schism in the ranks of English evangelicals, the consequences of which have outlasted the lives of the antagonists. It marks a personal breach between John Wesley and George Whitefield which was never more than partially healed (see No. 53, On the Death of George Whitefield). *What we have here, however, is a total rejection of predestination in any and all its Calvinist versions, with the predictable result that terms for further doctrinal dialogue between the 'Calvinists' and 'Arminians' were sharply constricted. That Wesley was content that this should be is plain enough in his curt response to Whitefield's anguished protests (as in his letter of August 9, 1740) that their private differences should not be aired in public.*

Whitefield and Wesley had been active allies for a brief span in 1734–35, and later it was Whitefield who had opened Wesley's way into the Revival in 1739. He was Wesley's junior by ten years, but already he was a bold, exciting preacher, who took for granted that the doctrine of justification by faith stood or fell with some sort of presupposition of irresistible grace. Wesley's brusque reaction to this position suggests something of the still toplofty don's disdain for the erstwhile Oxford servitor. He had preached against predestination within weeks of the launching of the Revival, asking for divine signs—and believing that he received them—that this kind of preaching was a necessary corollary of preaching universal redemption by faith. On April 26, 1739, he again sought divine guidance by drawing lots about restricting his attack on predestination to preaching, but received the lot, 'preach and print'. Forthwith, at Bristol, he published this sermon, Free Grace *(see* Letters, 25:639-40). *As a separate sermon it went through ten or eleven editions during his lifetime, but he did not include it in his collected* Sermons, *and in reprinting it in his* Works *it was inserted among his controversial writings. For a stemma illustrating its publishing history and a list of substantive variants, see Appendix, Vol. 4 (for fuller details on its publishing history, see* Bibliog, No. 14). *One of the neglected problems in Wesley interpretation is a critical analysis of his inability to recognize his aggressive role in this controversy (here, or in* Predestination Calmly Considered, *1752, or in his provocative 'Minute' of 1770, etc.). This was matched by an interesting insensitivity to the outrage of the Calvinists over what they regarded as a deliberate distortion of both the letter and the spirit of their teachings. For even though he would mellow in later years on this and other points, he would never accept any responsibility for the heat and bitterness of the conflict. In 1765, for example, he would freely grant to John Newton (then newly ordained, and curate at Olney) that 'holding particular election and final perseverance is compatible with . . . a love to Christ and a work of grace,' and reaffirm that on the point of justification, he never has differed 'from [Mr. Calvin] an hair's breadth' (letter of May 14, 1765). It would seem that he had forgotten, the charges levied here in* Free Grace *that those who hold and teach predestination are blasphemers (§§23, 25-27). If Wesley had forgotten, the Calvinists never did. If Wesley came later to share and commend a truly 'catholic spirit',* Free Grace *is a useful illustration of Wesley's temper and methods as a polemicist.*

For Whitefield's side of this story, and his detailed refutation of Wesley's sermon, see George Whitefield's Journals *(Banner of Truth Trust, 1960), pp. 242-43, 260-61, 289, and 'Appendix', pp. 564-68, but especially 'A Letter to the Rev. Mr. John Wesley in Answer to his Sermon entitled* Free Grace' *(December 24, 1740), pp. 571-88.*

Free Grace

To the Reader

Nothing but the strongest conviction, not only that what is here
5 advanced is 'the truth as it is in Jesus',[1] but also that I am
indispensably obliged to declare this truth to all the world, could
have induced me openly to oppose the sentiments of those whom
I highly esteem for their works' sake: at whose feet may I be found
in the day of the Lord Jesus![2]
10   Should any believe it his duty to reply hereto I have only one
request to make: let whatsoever you do be done in charity, in love,
and in the spirit of meekness.[3] Let your very disputing show that
you have 'put on, as the elect of God, bowels of mercies,
gentleness, long-suffering':[4] that even according to this time it
15 may be said, 'See how these Christians love one another.'[5]

Romans 8:32

*He that spared not his own Son, but delivered him up for us all, how
shall he not with him also freely give us all things?*

1. How freely does God love the world! While we were yet
20 sinners,[6] 'Christ died for the ungodly.'[7] While we were 'dead in
sin',[8] God 'spared not his own Son, but delivered him up for us
all.' And how 'freely with him' does he 'give us all things'! Verily,
free grace is all in all!
2. The grace or love of God, whence cometh our salvation, is
25 free in all, and free for all.

---

[1] Cf. Eph. 4:21.

[2] 2 Cor. 1:14.

[3] 1 Cor. 4:21.

[4] Cf. Col. 3:12.

[5] Cf. Tertullian, *Apology*, 39; see No. 22, 'Sermon on the Mount, II', III.8 and n. In the 1740 edn. (only) Wesley added a peremptory 'Advertisement' here: 'Whereas a pamphlet entitled *Free Grace Indeed* has been published against this sermon, this is to inform the publisher that I cannot answer his tract till he appears to be more *in earnest*. For I dare not speak of the deep things of God in the spirit of a prize-fighter or a stage-player.' *Free Grace Indeed*, an anonymous counterblast published in London in 1740 and subsequently reprinted in Philadelphia and Boston in 1741, illustrates from the other side how unbridgeable the chasm between the two doctrines and their partisans really was—and would continue to be.

[6] Rom. 5:8.

[7] Rom. 5:6.

[8] Cf. Eph. 2:5.

3. First, it is free in all to whom it is given. It does not depend on any power or merit in man; no, not in any degree, neither in whole, nor in part. It does not in any wise depend either on the good works or righteousness of the receiver; not on anything he has done, or anything he is. It does not depend on his endeavours. It does not depend on his good tempers, or good desires, or good purposes and intentions; for all these flow from the free grace of God. They are the streams only, not the fountain. They are the fruits of free grace, and not the root. They are not the cause, but the effects of it. Whatsoever good is in man, or is done by man, God is the author and doer of it. Thus is his grace free in all, that is, no way depending on any power or merit in man, but on God alone, who freely gave us his own Son, and 'with him freely giveth us all things'.[9]

4. But is it free for all, as well as in all? To this some have answered: 'No: it is free only for those whom God hath ordained to life, and they are but a little flock. The greater part of mankind God hath ordained to death; and it is not free for them. Them God hateth; and therefore before they were born decreed they should die eternally. And this he absolutely decreed; because so was his good pleasure, because it was his sovereign will. Accordingly, they are born for this: to be destroyed body and soul in hell. And they grow up under the irrevocable curse of God, without any possibility of redemption. For what grace God gives he gives only for this: to increase, not prevent, their damnation.'[10]

5. This is that decree of predestination. But methinks I hear one say: 'This is not the predestination which I hold. I hold only "the election of grace".[11] What I believe is no more than this, that God, before the foundation of the world, did elect a certain number of men to be justified, sanctified, and glorified. Now all these will be saved, and none else. For the rest of mankind God leaves to themselves: so they follow the imaginations of their own

---

[9] Cf. Rom. 8:32.

[10] Wesley's sources for this caricature of the High Calvinist doctrine of reprobation would have included Elisha Coles, *Practical Discourse of God's Sovereignty* (1673); it was this essay that had convinced Whitefield (so Josiah Tucker, *Brief History of the Principles of Methodism*, p. 14). Wesley might also have known the anonymous pamphlet, *A Vindication of the Doctrine of Predestination* (1709), ascribed to Richard Jenks in the Dr. Williams's Library copy. He also knew the nine quasi-official theses of The Lambeth Articles (1595) and the more complete exposition of the position in William Perkins's *Golden Chaine* (1591). It is doubtful if he had read Calvin's polemic against Pighius and Georgius, *The Eternal Predestination of God* (1552); cf. *Predestination Calmly Considered* (1752), §§8-15.

[11] Rom. 11:5.

hearts, which are only evil continually,[12] and, waxing worse and worse, are at length justly punished with everlasting destruction.'

6. Is this all the predestination which you hold? Consider; perhaps this is not all. Do not you believe 'God ordained them to this very thing'? If so, you believe the whole decree; you hold predestination in the full sense, which has been above described. But it may be you think you do not. Do not you then believe God hardens the hearts of them that perish? Do not you believe he (literally) hardened Pharaoh's heart,[13] and that for this end he raised him up (or created him)? Why, this amounts to just the same thing. If you believe Pharaoh, or any one man upon the earth, was created for this end—to be damned—you hold all that has been said of predestination. And there is no need you should add that God seconds his decree, which is supposed unchangeable and irresistible, by hardening the hearts of those vessels of wrath whom that decree had before fitted for destruction.[14]

7. Well, but it may be you do not believe even this. You do not hold any decree of reprobation. You do not think God decrees any man to be damned, nor hardens, irresistibly fits him for damnation. You only say, 'God eternally decreed that, all being dead in sin, he would say to some of the dry bones, "Live",[15] and to others he would not; that consequently these should be made alive, and those abide in death[16]—these should glorify God by their salvation, and those by their destruction.'[17]

8. Is not this what you mean by 'the election of grace'? If it be, I would ask one or two questions. Are any who are not thus elected, saved? Or were any, from the foundation of the world? Is it possible any man should be saved unless he be thus elected? If you say 'No', you are but where you was. You are not got one

[12] See Jer. 23:17; Luke 1:51; Gen. 6:5.

[13] Exod. 7:13; cf. Calvin's candid comment on this verse in his *Commentaries on the Four Last Books of Moses, Arranged in the Form of a Harmony* (Eng. tr. by C. W. Bingham, 1852): '. . . if God . . . inflicts deserved punishment upon the reprobate, he not only permits them to do what they themselves please, but actually executes a judgment which he knows to be just. Whence it follows that he not only withdraws the grace of his Spirit, but delivers over to Satan those whom he knows to be deserving of blindness of mind and obstinacy of heart.' However, they are 'foul calumniators who . . . pretend that God is made the author of sin. . . . The hardness of heart is the sin of man, but the hardening of the heart is the judgment of God.'

[14] Rom. 9:22; cf. Poole, *Annotations*, on this whole passage.

[15] Cf. Ezek. 37:2-6.   [16] 1 John 3:14.

[17] Cf. the quoted summaries of major reformed theologians on this point of reprobation and preterition in Heinrich Heppe, *Reformed Dogmatics*, ch. viii, §§22-32, pp.178-89.

hair's breadth further. You still believe that in consequence of an unchangeable, irresistible decree of God the greater part of mankind abide in death, without any possibility of redemption: inasmuch as none *can* save them but God; and he *will not* save them. You believe *he hath absolutely decreed not to save them;* and what is this but decreeing to damn them? It is, in effect, neither more nor less; it comes to the same thing. For if you are dead, and altogether unable to make yourself alive; then if God has absolutely decreed he will make others only alive, and not you, he hath absolutely decreed your everlasting death—you are absolutely consigned to damnation. So then, though you use softer words than some, you mean the selfsame thing. And God's decree concerning the election of grace, according to your own account of it, amounts to neither more nor less than what others call, 'God's decree of reprobation'.

9. Call it therefore by whatever name you please—'election', 'preterition', 'predestination', or 'reprobation'—it comes in the end to the same thing. The sense of all is plainly this: 'By virtue of an eternal, unchangeable, irresistible decree of God, one part of mankind are infallibly saved, and the rest infallibly damned; it being impossible that any of the former should be damned, or that any of the latter should be saved.'[18]

10. But if this be so, then is all preaching vain. It is needless to them that are elected. For they, whether with preaching or without, will infallibly be saved. Therefore the end of preaching, 'to save souls',[19] is void with regard to them. And it is useless to them that are not elected. For they cannot possibly be saved. They, whether with preaching or without, will infallibly be damned. The end of preaching is therefore void with regard to

[18] Cf. the pamphlet, *Free Grace Indeed,* p. 4, and Wesley's footnote to the 1740, 1741, and 1754 edns. of this sermon: 'That this is the true state of the question the anonymous author of a pamphlet lately published acknowledges (p. 4) in the following words: "You have been at some pains, sections 4, 5, 6, 7, and 8, to put the Calvinistical notion of election in a clear light." You might have said all in less bounds, viz., "They hold an eternal, absolute, personal election of a certain number of Adam's seed to salvation, without an antecedent respect to any qualification in them, and they leave you to conjecture how God shall deal with the rest." '

[19] Cf. Jas. 5:19-20. See also Wesley's letter to Christopher Hopper, Oct. 8, 1755: 'You have one business on earth—to save souls.' Also his letter to his brother Charles, Mar. 25, 1772: 'Oh what a thing it is to have *curam animarum* ["the care of souls"]. You and I are called to this; to save souls from death, to watch over them as those that must give account.' Also another letter to Charles, Apr. 26, 1772: 'Your business as well as mine is to save souls. When we took priests' orders, we undertook to make it our *one* business.' See No. 142, 'The Wisdom of Winning Souls', II.

them likewise. So that in either case, our preaching is vain,[20] as your hearing is also vain.

11. This then is a plain proof that the doctrine of pre-destination is not a doctrine of God, because it makes void the ordinance of God; and God is not divided against himself. A second is that it directly tends to destroy that holiness which is the end of all the ordinances of God. I do not say, 'None who hold it are holy' (for God is of tender mercy to those who are unavoidably entangled in errors of any kind), but that the doctrine itself—that every man is either elected or not elected from eternity, and that the one must inevitably be saved, and the other inevitably damned—has a manifest tendency to destroy holiness in general, for it wholly takes away those first motives to follow after it, so frequently proposed in Scripture: the hope of future reward and fear of punishment, the hope of heaven and fear of hell. That 'these shall go away into everlasting punishment, and those into life eternal'[21] is no motive to him to struggle for life who believes his lot is cast already: it is not reasonable for him so to do if he thinks he is unalterably adjudged either to life or death. You will say, 'But he knows not whether it is life or death.' What then? This helps not the matter. For if a sick man knows that he must unavoidably die or unavoidably recover, though he knows not which, it is not reasonable for him to take any physic at all. He might justly say (and so I have heard some speak, both in bodily sickness and in spiritual), 'If I am ordained to life, I shall live; if to death, I shall die. So I need not trouble myself about it.' So directly does this doctrine tend to shut the very gate of holiness in general, to hinder unholy men from ever approaching thereto, or striving to enter in thereat.

12. As directly does this doctrine tend to destroy several particular branches of holiness. Such are meekness and love: love, I mean, of our enemies, of the evil and unthankful. I say not that none who hold it have meekness and love (for as is the power of God, so is his mercy), but that it naturally tends to inspire or increase a sharpness or eagerness of temper which is quite contrary to the meekness of Christ[22]—as then especially appears, when they are opposed on this head. And it as naturally inspires contempt or coldness toward those whom we suppose outcasts

---

[20] See 1 Cor. 15:14.
[21] Cf. Matt. 25:46.
[22] 2 Cor. 10:1.

from God. 'Oh, (but you say) I suppose no particular man a reprobate.' You mean, you would not, if you could help it. You can't help sometimes applying your general doctrine to particular persons. The enemy of souls will apply it for you. You know how often he has done so. But you 'rejected the thought with 5 abhorrence'. True; as soon as you could. But how did it sour and sharpen your spirit in the meantime! You well know it was not the spirit of love which you then felt towards that poor sinner, whom you supposed or suspected, whether you would or no, to have been hated of God from eternity. 10

13. Thirdly, this doctrine tends to destroy the comfort of religion, the happiness of Christianity. This is evident as to all those who believe themselves to be reprobated, or who only suspect or fear it. All the great and precious promises are lost to them. They afford them no ray of comfort. 'For they are not the 15 elect of God; therefore they have neither lot nor portion in them.' This is an effectual bar to their finding any comfort or happiness, even in that religion whose 'ways' were designed to be 'ways of pleasantness, and all her paths peace'.[23]

14. And as to you who believe yourselves the elect of God, what 20 is your happiness? I hope, not a notion, a speculative belief, a bare opinion of any kind; but a feeling possession of God in your heart, wrought in you by the Holy Ghost; or, 'the witness of God's Spirit with your spirit, that you are a child of God'.[24] This, otherwise termed 'the full assurance of faith',[25] is the true ground of a 25 Christian's happiness. And it does indeed imply a full assurance that all your past sins are forgiven, and that you are *now* a child of God. But it does not necessarily imply a full assurance of our future perseverance. I do not say, 'This is never joined to it,' but that it is not necessarily implied therein; for many have the one 30 who have not the other.

15. Now, this witness of the Spirit experience shows to be much obstructed by this doctrine; and not only in those who, believing themselves reprobated, by this belief thrust it far from them, but even in them that have 'tasted of that good gift',[26] who 35

---

[23] Prov. 3:17.

[24] Cf. Rom. 8:16, and Wesley's later sermons on this text: Nos. 10, 'The Witness of the Spirit, I' (1746); and 11, *The Witness of the Spirit*, II (Apr. 4, 1767).

[25] Heb. 10:22; cf. also Nos. 117, 'On the Discoveries of Faith', §15 and n.; and 3, *'Awake, Thou That Sleepest'*, III.6 and n.

[26] Cf. Heb. 6:4, 5.

yet have soon lost it again, and fallen back into doubts, and fears, and darkness—'horrible darkness that might be felt'.[27] And I appeal to any of you who hold this doctrine to say, between God and your own hearts, whether you have not often a return of
5 doubts and fears concerning your election or perseverance? If you ask, 'Who has not?' I answer, 'Very few of those that hold this doctrine.' But many, very many of those that hold it not, in all parts of the earth; many of those who know and feel they are in Christ today, and 'take no thought for the morrow';[28] who 'abide
10 in him'[29] by faith from hour to hour, or rather from moment to moment. Many of these have enjoyed the uninterrupted witness of his Spirit, the continual light of his countenance,[30] from the moment wherein they first believed, for many months or years to this day.

15   16. That assurance of faith which these enjoy excludes all doubt and fear. It excludes all kind of doubt and fear concerning their future perseverance; though it is not properly (as was said before) an assurance of what is future, but only of what *now* is. And this needs not for its support a speculative belief that
20 whoever is once ordained to live, must live. For it is wrought from hour to hour by the mighty power of God, 'by the Holy Ghost which is given unto them'.[31] And therefore that doctrine is not of God, because it tends to obstruct, if not destroy, this great work of the Holy Ghost, whence flows the chief comfort of religion, the
25 happiness of Christianity.

    17. Again, how uncomfortable a thought is this, that thousands and millions of men, without any preceding offence or fault of theirs, were unchangeably doomed to everlasting burnings![32] How peculiarly uncomfortable must it be to those who have put
30 on Christ![33] To those who being filled with 'bowels of mercy, tenderness, and compassion',[34] could even 'wish themselves accursed for their brethren's sake'.[35]

    18. Fourthly, this uncomfortable doctrine directly tends to destroy our zeal for good works. And this it does, first, as it

[27] Cf. Exod. 10:21.
[28] Matt. 6:34.
[29] 1 John 2:27, 28.
[30] See Ps. 4:6.
[31] Rom. 5:5.
[32] Isa. 33:14.
[33] Gal. 3:27.
[34] Cf. Col. 3:12.   [35] Cf. Rom. 9:3.

naturally tends (according to what was observed before) to destroy our love to the greater part of mankind, namely, the evil and unthankful. For whatever lessens our love must so far lessen our desire to do them good. This it does, secondly, as it cuts off one of the strongest motives to all acts of bodily mercy, such as 5 feeding the hungry, clothing the naked, and the like, viz., the hope of saving their souls from death. For what avails it to relieve their temporal wants who are just dropping into eternal fire?[36] 'Well; but run and snatch them as brands out of the fire.'[37] Nay, this you suppose impossible. They were appointed thereunto, you say, 10 from eternity, before they had done either good or evil. You believe it is the will of God they should die. And 'who hath resisted his will?'[38] But you say you 'do not know whether these are elected or not.' What then? If you know they are one or the other, that they are either elected or not elected, all your labour is 15 void and vain. In either case your advice, reproof, or exhortation, is as needless and useless as our preaching. It is needless to them that are elected; for they will infallibly be saved without it. It is useless to them that are not elected; for with or without it they will infallibly be damned. Therefore you cannot, consistently with 20 your principles, take any pains about their salvation. Consequently those principles directly tend to destroy your zeal for good works—for all good works, but particularly for the greatest of all, the saving of souls from death.[39]

19. But, fifthly, this doctrine not only tends to destroy Christian 25 holiness, happiness, and good works, but hath also a direct and manifest tendency to overthrow the whole Christian revelation. The point which the wisest of the modern unbelievers most industriously labour to prove is that the Christian revelation is not necessary. They well know, could they once show this, the 30 conclusion would be too plain to be denied. 'If it be not necessary, it is not true.' Now this fundamental point you give up. For supposing that eternal, unchangeable decree, one part of mankind must be saved, though the Christian revelation were not in being, and the other part of mankind must be damned, 35 notwithstanding that revelation. And what would an infidel desire more? You allow him all he asks. In making the gospel thus unnecessary to all sorts of men you give up the whole Christian

[36] Jude 7.
[37] See Zech. 3:2; cf. No. 4, *Scriptural Christianity*, II.2 and n.
[38] Rom. 9:19. [39] See Jas. 5:20.

cause. 'O tell it not in Gath! Publish it not in the streets of Askelon! Lest the daughters of the uncircumcised rejoice, lest the sons of unbelief triumph!'[40]

20. And as this doctrine manifestly and directly tends to overthrow the whole Christian revelation, so it does the same thing, by plain consequence, in making that revelation contradict itself. For it is grounded on such an interpretation of some texts (more or fewer it matters not) as flatly contradicts all the other texts, and indeed the whole scope and tenor of Scripture. For instance: the asserters of this doctrine interpret that text of Scripture, 'Jacob have I loved, but Esau have I hated,'[41] as implying that God in a literal sense hated Esau and all the reprobated from eternity. Now what can possibly be a more flat contradiction than this, not only to the whole scope and tenor of Scripture, but also to all those particular texts which expressly declare, 'God is love'?[42] Again, they infer from that text, 'I will have mercy on whom I will have mercy,'[a] that God is love only to some men, viz., the elect, and that he hath mercy for those only: flatly contrary to which is the whole tenor of Scripture, as is that express declaration in particular, 'The Lord is loving unto *every* man, and his mercy is over *all* his works.'[b] Again, they infer from that and the like texts, 'It is not of him that willeth, neither of him that runneth, but of God that showeth mercy,'[43] that he showeth mercy only to those to whom he had respect from all eternity. 'Nay, but who replieth against God' now?[44] You now contradict the whole oracles of God, which declare throughout, 'God is no respecter of persons;'[c] 'There is no respect of persons with him.'[d] Again, from that text, 'The children being not yet born, neither

[a] Rom. 9:15.
[b] Ps. 145:9 [(BCP); note the implied hermeneutical rule here which contrasts with Wesley's typical emphasis upon literal interpretation; see No. 21, 'Sermon on the Mount, I', §6 and n.].
[c] Acts 10:34.
[d] Rom. 2:11.

---

[40] Cf. 2 Sam. 1:20.
[41] Rom. 9:13. One might, therefore, expect such an interpretation in Luther's *Lectures on Romans*, Calvin's *Commentary*, Poole's *Annotations* (or even Karl Barth); nothing of the sort appears in any of them. Matthew Henry, himself a moderate Calvinist, knows of those who interpret this text as meaning God's love to Jacob and hatred of Esau, 'from eternity'. But, says he, 'the Apostle speaks of Jacob and Esau not in their own persons but as *ancestors* . . .' (see his *Exposition*).
[42] 1 John 4:16.   [43] Cf. Rom. 9:16.   [44] Cf. Rom. 9:20.

having done good or evil, that the purpose of God according to election might stand, not of works, but of him that calleth, it was said unto her (unto Rebecca), The elder shall serve the younger'[45]—you infer that our being predestinated or elect no way depends on the foreknowledge of God. Flatly contrary to this are all the Scriptures; and those in particular, 'elect according to the foreknowledge of God',[e] [and] 'Whom he did foreknow, he also did predestinate.'[f]

21. And, 'The same Lord over all is rich in mercy to all that call upon him.'[g] But you say, 'No: he is such only to those for whom Christ died. And those are not all, but only a few, "whom God hath chosen out of the world";[46] for he died not for all, but only for those who were "chosen in him before the foundation of the world".'[h] Flatly contrary to your interpretation of these Scriptures also is the whole tenor of the New Testament; as are in particular those texts: 'Destroy not him with thy meat for whom Christ died'[i]—a clear proof that Christ died, not only for those that are saved, but also for them that perish; He is 'the Saviour of the world';[j] He is 'the Lamb of God, that taketh away the sins of the world';[k] 'He is the propitiation, not for our sins only, but also for the sins of the whole world;'[l] 'He (the living God) is the Saviour of all men;'[m] 'He gave himself a ransom for all;'[n] 'He tasted death for every man.'[o]

22. If you ask, 'Why then are not all men saved?' the whole law and the testimony answer: first, not because of any decree of God, not because it is his pleasure they should die. For, 'as I live, saith the Lord God, I have no pleasure in the death of him that dieth.'[p] Whatever be the cause of their perishing it cannot be his will, if the oracles of God are true; for they declare, 'He is not willing that any should perish, but that all should come to repentance.'[q] He 'willeth that all men should be saved'.[47] And they, secondly, declare what is the cause why all men are not saved: namely, that they will not be saved. So our Lord expressly: 'They will not come

---

[e] 1 Pet. 1:2. [f] Rom. 8:29.
[g] Rom. 10:12. [h] Eph. 1:4.
[i] Rom. 14:15. [j] John 4:42.
[k] John 1:29. [l] 1 John 2:2.
[m] 1 Tim. 4:10. [n] 1 Tim. 2:6.
[o] Heb. 2:9. [p] Ezek. 18:32. [q] 2 Pet. 3:9.

---

[45] Rom. 9:11-12. [46] Cf. John 15:19.
[47] Cf. 1 Tim. 2:4.

unto me that they may have life;'ʳ 'The power of the Lord is present to heal them,'⁴⁸ but they will not be healed. They 'reject the counsel', the merciful counsel 'of God against themselves',⁴⁹ as did their stiff-necked forefathers. And therefore are they
5 without excuse, because God would save them, but they will not be saved. This is the condemnation, 'How often would I have gathered you together, and ye would not.'ˢ

23. Thus manifestly does this doctrine tend to overthrow the whole Christian revelation, by making it contradict itself; by
10 giving such an interpretation of some texts as flatly contradicts all the other texts, and indeed the whole scope and tenor of Scripture—an abundant proof that it is not of God. But neither is this all. For, seventhly, it is a doctrine full of blasphemy; of such blasphemy as I should dread to mention but that the honour of
15 our gracious God and the cause of his truth will not suffer me to be silent. In the cause of God, then, and from a sincere concern for the glory of his great name, I will mention a few of the horrible blasphemies contained in this horrible doctrine. But first, I must warn every one of you that hears, as ye will answer it at the great
20 day, not to charge me (as some have done) with blaspheming because I mention the blasphemy of others.⁵⁰ And the more you are grieved with them that do thus blaspheme, see that ye 'confirm your love towards them'⁵¹ the more, and that your heart's desire and continual prayer to God be, 'Father, forgive them; for
25 they know not what they do.'⁵²

24. This premised, let it be observed that this doctrine represents our Blessed Lord—'Jesus Christ the righteous',⁵³ 'the only-begotten Son of the Father, full of grace and truth'⁵⁴—as an hypocrite, a deceiver of the people, a man void of common
30 sincerity. For it cannot be denied that he everywhere speaks *as if*

ʳ John 5:40.
ˢ Matt. 23:37.

---

⁴⁸ Cf. Luke 5:17.   ⁴⁹ Cf. Luke 7:30.
⁵⁰ Cf. Wesley's bland disclaimer in *A Farther Appeal*, Pt. I, V. 29 (11:172-73 in this edn.), that he had never 'anathematized' Mr. Whitefield, but rather reverenced him 'both as a child of God and a true minister of Jesus Christ . . .'. See also his claim to Bishop Lavington (letter of Dec. 1751, §32), that he had 'opposed the doctrine of predestination, . . . but without any degree either of rancour or fierceness'.
⁵¹ Cf. 2 Cor. 2:8.   ⁵² Luke 23:34.
⁵³ 1 John 2:1.
⁵⁴ John 1:14.

he was willing that all men should be saved. Therefore, to say *he was not* willing that all men should be saved is to represent him as a mere hypocrite and dissembler. It can't be denied that the gracious words which came out of his mouth are full of invitations to all sinners. To say, then, he did not *intend* to save all sinners is 5 to represent him as a gross deceiver of the people. You cannot deny that he says, 'Come unto me, all ye that are weary and heavy laden.'[55] If then you say he calls those that cannot come, those whom he knows to be unable to come, those whom he can make able to come but will not, how is it possible to describe greater 10 insincerity? You represent him as mocking his helpless creatures by offering what he never intends to give. You describe him as saying one thing and meaning another; as pretending the love which he had not. Him 'in whose mouth was no guile'[56] you make full of deceit, void of common sincerity. Then especially, when, 15 drawing nigh the city, 'he wept over it',[57] and said, 'O Jerusalem, Jerusalem, thou that killest the prophets, and stonest them that are sent unto thee, how often *would* I have gathered thy children together . . . and *ye would not.*'[58] ($\dot{\eta}\theta\dot{\epsilon}\lambda\eta\sigma\alpha$ . . . $\kappa\alpha\dot{\iota}$ $o\dot{\upsilon}\kappa$ $\dot{\eta}\theta\epsilon\lambda\dot{\eta}\sigma\alpha\tau\epsilon$). Now if you say, 'They would', but 'he would not,' 20 you represent him (which who could hear?) as weeping crocodile's tears, weeping over the prey which himself had doomed to destruction.[59]

25. Such blasphemy this, as one would think might make the ears of a Christian tingle. But there is yet more behind; for just as 25 it honours the Son, so doth this doctrine honour the Father.[60] It destroys all his attributes at once. It overturns both his justice, mercy, and truth. Yea, it represents the most Holy God as worse than the devil; as both more false, more cruel, and more unjust. More false; because the devil, liar as he is, hath never said he 30 'willeth all men to be saved'. More unjust; because the devil cannot, if he would, be guilty of such injustice as you ascribe to God when you say that God condemned millions of souls to everlasting fire prepared for the devil and his angels[61] for continuing in sin, which for want of that grace *he will not* give 35 them, they cannot avoid. And more cruel; because that unhappy

---

[55] Cf. Matt. 11:28.   [56] Cf. 1 Pet. 2:22.
[57] Luke 19:41.   [58] Matt. 23:37.
[59] Cf. Shakespeare, *Henry VI, Part II*, iii.1; and Robert Burton, *Anatomy of Melancholy* (1621), Pt. III.2, §4; see also Brewer's *Dictionary of Phrase and Fable* ('Crocodile').
[60] See John 5:23.   [61] Matt. 25:41.

spirit 'seeketh rest and findeth none';[62] so that his own restless misery is a kind of temptation to him to tempt others. But God 'resteth in his high and holy place';[63] so that to suppose him of his own mere motion, of his pure will and pleasure, happy as he is, to
5 doom his creatures, whether they will or no, to endless misery, is to impute such cruelty to him as we cannot impute even to the great enemy of God and man. It is to represent the most high God (he that hath ears to hear, let him hear!)[64] as more cruel, false, and unjust than the devil.

10 26. This is the blasphemy clearly contained in 'the horrible decree'[65] of predestination. And here I fix my foot. On this I join issue with every asserter of it. You represent God as worse than the devil—more false, more cruel, more unjust. But you say you will 'prove it by Scripture'. Hold! What will you prove by
15 Scripture? That God is worse than the devil? It cannot be. Whatever that Scripture proves, it never can prove this. Whatever its true meaning be, this cannot be its true meaning. Do you ask, 'What is its true meaning, then?' If I say, 'I know not,' you have gained nothing. For there are many Scriptures the true sense
20 whereof neither you nor I shall know till death is swallowed up in victory.[66] But this I know, better it were to say it had no sense at all than to say it had such a sense as this. It cannot mean, whatever it mean besides, that the God of truth is a liar. Let it mean what it will, it cannot mean that the Judge of all the world is unjust. No
25 Scripture can mean that God is not love, or that his mercy is not over all his works.[67] That is, whatever it prove beside, no Scripture can prove predestination.

27. This is the blasphemy for which (however I love the persons who assert it) I abhor the doctrine of predestination: a
30 doctrine upon the supposition of which, if one could possibly

[62] Matt. 12:43.
[63] Cf. Isa. 57:15.
[64] Matt. 11:15.
[65] Cf. Calvin, *Institutes*, III.xxiii. 7: *Decretum quidem horribile fateor:* 'That this decree is dreadful, I admit.' 'But no one can deny that God foreknew what end man was to have. . . . And if anyone inveighs against God's foreknowledge . . . he stumbles rashly and heedlessly. . . .' (§8). 'And let us not be ashamed to submit our understandings to God's boundless wisdom. . . . For of those things which it is not given [us] . . . to know . . . the craving to know is a kind of madness.' Calvin and Wesley are here poles apart and, for once, Wesley scorns any 'third alternative'. Thereafter, all efforts at transcending these misunderstandings would have had the look of compromise.
[66] 1 Cor. 15:54.
[67] Ps. 145:9 (BCP).

suppose it for a moment (call it election, reprobation, or what you please, for all comes to the same thing) one might say to our adversary the devil:[68] 'Thou fool, why dost thou roar about any longer? Thy lying in wait for souls is as needless and useless as our preaching. Hearest thou not that God hath taken thy work out of thy hands? And that he doth it much more effectually? Thou, with all thy principalities and powers,[69] canst only so assault that we may resist thee; but he can irresistibly destroy both body and soul in hell![70] Thou canst only entice; but his unchangeable decree to leave thousands of souls in death compels them to continue in sin till they drop into everlasting burnings. Thou temptest; he forceth us to be damned; for we cannot resist his will. Thou fool, why goest thou about any longer seeking whom thou mayest devour?[71] Hearest thou not that God is the devouring lion, the destroyer of souls, the murderer of men? Moloch caused only children to pass through the fire;[72] and that fire was soon quenched; or, the corruptible body being consumed, its torment was at an end. But God, thou art told, by his eternal decree, fixed before they had done good or evil, causes not only "children of a span long"[73] but the parents also to pass through the fire of hell—that "fire which never shall be quenched";[74] and the body which is cast thereinto, being now incorruptible and immortal, will be ever consuming, and never consumed, but "the smoke of their torment", because it is God's good pleasure, "ascendeth up for ever and ever".'[75]

28. O how would the enemy of God and man rejoice to hear these things were so! How would he cry aloud and spare not! How would he lift up his voice and say: 'To your tents, O Israel!'[76] Flee from the face[77] of this God, or ye shall utterly perish.[78] But whither will ye flee? Into heaven? He is there. Down to hell? He is there also.[79] Ye cannot flee from an omnipresent, almighty tyrant. And whether ye flee or stay, I call heaven his throne, and earth his footstool[80] to witness against you, ye shall perish, ye shall die eternally. Sing, O hell, and rejoice ye that are under the earth! For God, even the mighty God, hath spoken, and devoted to death

[68] 1 Pet. 5:8.
[69] Col. 2:15, etc.
[70] Matt. 10:28.
[71] See 1 Pet. 5:8.
[72] See Lev. 18:21; Jer. 32:35.
[73] Lam. 2:20.
[74] Cf. Mark 9:43.
[75] Rev. 14:11.
[76] 1 Kgs. 12:16.
[77] See Gen. 16:8; Exod. 14:25.
[78] See Deut. 4:26.
[79] See Ps. 139:7-8 (AV).
[80] See Isa. 66:1.

thousands of souls, from the rising up of the sun unto the going
down thereof.[81] Here, O death, is thy sting![82] They shall not,
cannot escape; for the mouth of the Lord hath spoken it.[83] Here,
O grave, is thy victory![84] Nations yet unborn, or ever they have
5 done good or evil, are doomed never to see the light of life, but
thou shalt gnaw upon them for ever and ever. Let all those
morning stars sing together[85] who fell with Lucifer, son of the
morning.[86] Let all the sons of hell shout for joy! For the decree is
past, and who shall disannul it?'
10   29. Yea, the decree is past. And so it was before the foundation
of the world.[87] But what decree? Even this: ' "I will set before" the
sons of men "life and death, blessing and cursing";[88] and the soul
that chooseth life shall live, as the soul that chooseth death shall
die.' This decree, whereby 'whom God did foreknow, he did
15 predestinate,'[89] was indeed from everlasting. This, whereby all
who suffer Christ to make them alive are 'elect, according to the
foreknowledge of God',[90] now 'standeth fast, even as the moon,
and as the faithful witness in heaven'.[91] And when heaven and
earth shall pass away, yet this shall not pass away;[92] for it is as
20 unchangeable and eternal as is the being of God that gave it. This
decree yields the strongest encouragement to abound in all good
works, and in all holiness; and it is a well-spring of joy, of
happiness also, to our great and endless comfort. This is worthy
of God. It is every way consistent with all the perfections of his
25 nature. It gives us the noblest view both of his justice, mercy, and
truth. To this agrees the whole scope of the Christian revelation,
as well as all the parts thereof. To this Moses and all the prophets
bear witness, and our blessed Lord and all his apostles. Thus
Moses, in the name of his Lord: 'I call heaven and earth to record
30 against you this day, that I have set before you life and death,
blessing and cursing; therefore choose life, that thou and thy seed
may live.'[93] Thus Ezekiel (to cite one prophet for all): 'The soul
that sinneth, it shall die. The son shall not bear (eternally) the

---

[81] Ps. 113:3.
[82] See 1 Cor. 15:55.   [83] Isa. 1:20, etc.
[84] See 1 Cor. 15:55.   [85] See Job 38:7.
[86] Isa. 14:12. Cf. Milton, *Paradise Lost*, x.410-30; see also Tertullian, *Adv. Marc.*,
V.xi.17; and No. 72, 'Of Evil Angels', I.3.
[87] Cf. John 17:24.   [88] Cf. Deut. 30:19.
[89] Cf. Rom. 8:29.   [90] 1 Pet. 1:2.
[91] Cf. Ps. 89:36 (BCP).   [92] See Matt. 24:35, etc.
[93] Cf. Deut. 30:19.

iniquity of the father. The righteousness of the righteous shall be upon him, and the wickedness of the wicked shall be upon him.'[t] Thus our blessed Lord: 'If any man thirst, let him come to me and drink.'[u] Thus his great Apostle, St. Paul: 'God commandeth all men everywhere to repent.'[v] 'All men, everywhere'—every man in every place, without any exception, either of place or person. Thus St. James: 'If any of you lack wisdom, let him ask of God, who giveth to all men liberally and upbraideth not, and it shall be given him.'[w] Thus St. Peter: 'The Lord is . . . not willing that any should perish, but that all should come to repentance.'[x] And thus St. John: 'If any man sin, we have an advocate with the Father, . . . and he is the propitiation for our sins; and not for ours only, but for the sins of the whole world.'[y]

30. O hear ye this, ye that forget God! Ye cannot charge your death upon him. 'Have I any pleasure at all that the wicked should die, saith the Lord God? Repent, and turn from all your transgressions; so iniquity shall not be your ruin. Cast away from you all your transgressions, whereby ye have transgressed; . . . for why will ye die, O house of Israel? For I have no pleasure in the death of him that dieth, saith the Lord God. Wherefore turn yourselves, and live ye.'[z] 'As I live, saith the Lord God, I have no pleasure in the death of the wicked, . . . Turn ye, turn ye from your evil ways; for why will ye die, O house of Israel?'[aa]

Universal Redemption[94]

Hear, holy, holy, holy, Lord,
    Father of all mankind,
Spirit of love, eternal Word,
    In mystic union join'd.

Hear, and inspire my stammering tongue,
    Exalt my abject thought,
Speak from my mouth a sacred song,
    Who spak'st the world from nought.

[t] [Ezek.] 18:20.   [u] John 7:37.   [v] Acts 17:30.
[w] Jas. 1:5.   [x] 2 Pet. 3:9.   [y] 1 John 2:1-2.
[z] Ezek. 18:23, etc. [i.e., 30-32].   [aa] Ezek. 33:11.

[94] This hymn (one of several on 'Universal Redemption'), after its appearance appended to *Free Grace*, was then published in *Hymns and Sacred Poems* (1740), pp. 136-42, and in *AM* (May 1778), I.235-40, in each case with minor revisions. Some have conjectured that it was written by John Wesley himself, but its style and language make this doubtful (e.g., the 'darling' in 1.9). A larger consensus of partisans on both sides attributed its authorship to Charles; see No. 54, 'On Eternity', §14 and n.

Thy darling attribute I praise
    Which all alike may prove,
The glory of thy boundless grace,
    Thy universal love.

5   Mercy I sing, transporting sound,
    The joy of earth and heaven!
Mercy, by every sinner found,
    Who takes what God hath given.

Mercy for all thy hands have made,
10   Immense, and unconfin'd,
Throughout thy every work display'd,
    Embracing all mankind.

Thine eye survey'd the fallen race
    When sunk in sin they lay,
15   Their misery called for all thy grace,
    But justice stopped the way.

Mercy the fatal bar removed,
    Thy only Son it gave—
To save a world so dearly loved,
20   A sinful world to save.

For every man he tasted death,
    He suffered once for all,
He calls as many souls as breathe,
    And all may hear the call.

25   A power to choose, a will to obey,
    Freely his grace restores;
We all may find the Living Way,
    And call the Saviour ours.

Whom his eternal mind foreknew,
30   That they the power would use,
Ascribe to God the glory due,
    And not his grace refuse;

Them, only them, his will decreed,
    Them did he choose alone,
35   Ordained in Jesus' steps to tread,
    And to be like his Son.

Them, the elect, consenting few,
    Who yield to proffered love,
Justified here he forms anew,
40   And glorifies above.

For as in Adam all have died,
    So all in Christ may live,
May (for the world is justified)
    His righteousness receive.

Who'er to God for pardon fly,   5
    In Christ may be forgiven,
He speaks to all, 'Why will ye die,
    And not accept my heaven?'

No! in the death of him that dies
    (God by his life hath sworn)   10
He is not pleased; but ever cries,
    Turn, O ye sinners, turn.

He would that all his truths should own,
    His gospel all embrace,
Be justified by faith alone,   15
    And freely saved by grace.

And shall I, Lord, confine thy love,
    As not to others free?
And may not every sinner prove,
    The grace that found out me?   20

Doubtless through one eternal now
    Thou ever art the same,
The universal Saviour thou,
    And Jesus is thy name.

Ho! every one that thirsteth, come!   25
    Choose life; obey the Word;
Open your hearts to make him room,
    And banquet with your Lord.

When God invites, shall man repel?
    Shall man th'exception make?   30
'Come, freely come, *whoever will,*
    And living water take!'

Thou bidd'st; and would'st thou bid us choose,
    When purposed not to save?
Command us all a power to use,   35
    Thy mercy never gave?

Thou can'st not mock the sons of men,
    Invite us to draw nigh,
Offer thy grace to all, and then
    Thy grace to most deny!   40

Horror to think that God is hate!
    Fury in God can dwell,
God could an helpless world create,
    To thrust them into hell!

5   Doom them an endless death to die,
    From which they could not flee—
No, Lord! thine inmost bowels cry
    Against the dire decree!

Believe who will that human pain,
10   Pleasing to God can prove:
Let Moloch feast him with the slain,
    Our God, we know, is love.

Lord, if indeed, without a bound,
    Infinite love Thou art,
15   The *horrible decree* confound,
    Enlarge thy people's heart!

Ah! Who is as thy servants blind;
    So to misjudge their God!
Scatter the darkness of their mind,
20   And shed thy love abroad.

Give them conceptions worthy thee,
    Give them, in Jesu's face,
Thy merciful design to see,
    Thy all-redeeming grace.

25   Stir up thy strength, and help us, Lord,
    The preachers multiply;
Send forth thy light, and give the word,
    And let the shadows fly.

Oh! if thy Spirit send forth me,
30   The meanest of the throng,
I'll sing thy grace divinely free,
    And teach mankind the song.

Grace will I sing, through Jesu's name,
    On all mankind bestowed;
35   The everlasting truth proclaim,
    And seal that truth with blood.

Come then, thou all-embracing love,
    Our frozen bosom warm;
Dilating fire, within us move,
40   With truth and meekness arm.

Let us triumphantly ride on,
    And more than conquerors prove.
With meekness bear th'opposers down,
    And bind with cords of love.

Shine in our hearts, Father of light;   5
    Jesu, thy beams impart;
Spirit of truth, our minds unite,
    And make us one in heart.

Then, only then, our eyes shall see
    Thy promised kingdom come;   10
And every heart by grace set free,
    Shall make the Saviour room.

Thee every tongue shall then confess,
    And every knee shall bow.
Come quickly, Lord, we wait thy grace,   15
    We long to meet thee now.

NATIONAL SINS AND MISERIES

AN INTRODUCTORY COMMENT

Wesley had been bred up as a Tory and remained one all his life. He could even define the term (in 1785) in much the same sense as his father and elder brother before him: 'one who believes God, not the people, to be the origin of all civil power'.[1] From this 'divine right' premise, it followed that he recoiled as vigorously from John Wilkes's populism as from his radical secularism.[2] And it also followed equally that he had deplored the rising clamour among the American colonists for what he could only regard as a false 'liberty'. Suiting deeds to thought, he issued a whole series of adverse judgments upon the American Revolution, including a paraphrase of Samuel Johnson's Taxation No Tyranny *(1775) that gained a wider audience for Johnson's views than the original.[3] That these pamphlets had stirred a storm of controversy goes withot saying but, by the same token, it may also be taken for granted that Wesley went on unmoved; see* Some Observations on Liberty *(1776),* A Calm Address to the Inhabitants of England *(1777),* A Serious Address to the People of England *(1778), etc.*

The opening battles of the new revolution had come in April 1775—at Lexington, Concord, Bunker Hill—and had resulted in an unexpectedly large number of English casualties. Almost as if by reflex, such events had rekindled Wesley's dread and horror of yet another 'civil war', Briton against Briton.[4] Thus, when an invitation came to him to deliver a 'charity sermon' at St. Matthew's Church (Bethnal Green) on November 12, 1775, for the benefit of the widows and orphans of these early victims of the war, he was glad to respond. But, quite contrary to his custom, he wrote out a manuscript in full (dated November 7), organizing his political sentiments around his providential view of

---

[1] See his letter to *Gent's Mag.*, Dec. 24, 1785; see also his *Thoughts concerning the Origin of Power* (1772).

[2] See Wesley, *Free Thoughts on the Present State of Public Affairs* (1770); for an account of the Wilkes affair by a historian who was also interested in Wesley and Methodism, see W. E. H. Lecky, *A History of England in the Eighteenth Century* (1892), III.242-345.

[3] See Wesley, *A Calm Address to our American Colonies*, 1775 (*Bibliog*, No. 354, Vol. 15 of this edn.).

[4] Cf. Robertson, *England under the Hanoverians*, pp. 251-68.

history: viz., *a nation's 'miseries' are the bitter fruit of a nation's 'sins'. His mood at this time is reflected in the* Journal *entry for Saturday, November 11:*

I made some additions to the Calm Address to Our American Colonies. *Need anyone ask from what motive this was wrote? Let him look round: England is in a flame—a flame of malice and rage against the King and almost all that are in authority under him. I labour to put out this flame. Ought not every true patriot do the same? If hireling writers on either side judge of me by themselves, that I cannot help.*[5]

The sermon's actual occasion is then recorded as follows:

Sunday, 12. I was desired to preach, in Bethnal Green Church, a charity sermon. . . . Knowing how many would seek offence, I wrote down my sermon. I dined with Sir John Hawkins and three other gentlemen that are in commission for the peace;[6] *and was agreeably surprised at a very serious conversation, kept up during the whole time I stayed.*

The sermon was promptly printed, as A Sermon preached at St. Matthew's, Bethnal Green, on Sunday, Nov. 12, 1775. *It was reissued in a second edition nine years later (1784). Its present title was supplied by Thomas Jackson in 1825. For further bibliographical details, see* Bibliog, No. 356.

---

[5] Wesley had been accused of currying favour with the king: '. . . one hand stretched out to the King, the other raised up to God'; see *Gent's Mag.*, 1775, p. 561.

[6] I.e., local Justices of the Peace.

National Sins and Miseries

2 Samuel 24:17

Lo, I have sinned, and I have done wickedly: but these sheep, what have they done?

5   1. The chapter begins, 'And again the anger of the Lord was kindled against Israel, and he moved David against them to say, Go, number Israel and Judah.'[1] 'Again'—it had been kindled against them but a few years before; in consequence of which 'there had been a famine in the land three years', year after year,
10 till 'David inquired of the Lord', and was taught the way of appeasing it.[a] We are not informed in what particular manner Israel had now offended God, by what particular cause his anger was kindled, but barely with the effect. 'He moved David against them to say, Go, number Israel and Judah.' 'He'—not God!
15 Beware how you impute this to the fountain of love and holiness! It was not God, but Satan, who thus moved David.[2] So the parallel Scripture expressly declares: 'And Satan stood up against Israel, and provoked David to number Israel.'[b] 'Satan stood' before God to accuse David and Israel, and to beg God's permission to tempt
20 David.[3] *Standing* is properly the accuser's posture before the tribunals of men. And therefore the Scripture, which uses to speak of the things of God after the manner of men, represents Satan as appearing in this posture before the tribunal of God. 'And David said to Joab, and to the rulers of the people, Go,
25 number Israel from Beersheba even to Dan; and bring the number of them to me, that I may know it.'[c]

---

[a] Chap. 21:1.
[c] Ver. 2.

[b] 1 Chr. 21:1.

---

[1] 2 Sam. 24:1.
[2] An exegesis determined by a theological bias: the bare text of 2 Sam. 24:1 leaves the translator no option with respect to the antecedent of 'he'; it is God. But Wesley knew the difficulties here and implies that 1 Chr. 21:1 establishes the *sense* of 2 Sam. 24:1. He also knew the juggling act attempted by Poole, *Annotations*, on 2 Sam. 24:1, and Henry's conclusion in his *Exposition* that despite what the text might seem to say, still 'God is not the author of sin; he tempts no man.'
[3] An echo of Job 1:6-12.

2. It does not clearly appear wherein the sin of thus numbering the people consisted. There is no express prohibition of it in any of the Scriptures which were then extant. Yet we read, 'The king's word was abominable to Joab,'[d] who was not a man of the tenderest conscience, so that he expostulated with David before he obeyed. 'Joab answered, Why doth my lord require this thing? Why will he be a cause of trespass'—of punishment or calamity—'to Israel?'[4] God frequently punishes a people for the sins of their rulers, because they are generally partakers of their sins in one kind or other. And the righteous Judge takes this occasion of punishing them for all their sins. In this Joab was right; for after they were numbered it is said, 'And God was displeased with this thing.'[5] Yea, 'David's heart smote him, and he said unto the Lord, I have sinned greatly in that I have done: and now, I beseech thee, O Lord, take away the iniquity of thy servant.'[e] Did not the sin lie in the motive on which the thing was done? Did he not do it in the pride of his heart?[6] Probably out of a principle of vanity and ostentation, glorying not in God, but in the number of his people.

3. In the sequel we find that even Joab was for once a true prophet: David was 'a cause of trespass', of punishment, 'to Israel'. His sin, added to all the sins of the people, filled up the measure of their iniquities. So 'the Lord sent a pestilence upon Israel, from the morning'—wherein Gad the prophet gave David his choice of war, famine, or pestilence[7]—'unto the evening of the third day.' 'And there died of the people from Dan unto Beersheba seventy thousand men.'[f] 'And when David saw the angel that smote the people', who appeared in the form of a man with a drawn sword in his hand,[8] to convince him the more fully that this plague was immediately from God, 'he said, Lo, I have sinned, I have done wickedly: but these sheep, what have they done?'

4. Is there not in several respects a remarkable resemblance between the case of Israel and our own? General wickedness then

---

[d] Ver. 6.   [e] 2 Sam. 24:10.
[f] Ver. 15.

---

[4] 1 Chr. 21:3.   [5] 1 Chr. 21:7.
[6] See No. 14, *The Repentance of Believers*, I.3 and n.
[7] See 2 Sam. 24:13.
[8] See Josh. 5:13; this particular detail is not in the 2 Sam. story.

occasioned a general visitation; and does not the same cause now produce the same effect? We likewise have sinned, and we are punished; and perhaps these are only the beginning of sorrows.[9] Perhaps 'the angel' is now 'stretching out his hand over' England
5 to destroy it. O that the Lord would at length say to him that destroyeth, 'It is enough; stay now thine hand!'[10]

     5. That vice is the parent of misery, few deny; it is confirmed by the general suffrage of all ages. But we seldom bring this home to ourselves: when we speak of sin as the cause of misery we usually
10 mean the sin of other people, and suppose *we* suffer because *they* sin. But need we go so far? Are not our own vices sufficient to account for all our sufferings? Let us fairly and impartially consider this: let us examine our own hearts and lives. We all suffer: and we have *all* sinned. But will it not be most profitable
15 for us to consider every one his own sins as bringing sufferings both on himself and others? To say, 'Lo, I have sinned, I have done wickedly: but these sheep, what have they done?'

     I. 1. Let us inquire, first, what they suffer. And afterwards,
20 what is the cause of these sufferings. That the people suffer none can deny, that they are afflicted in a more than ordinary manner. Thousands and tens of thousands are at this day deeply afflicted through want of business. It is true that this want is in some measure removed in some large and opulent towns. But it is also
25 true that this is far, very far, from being the general case of the kingdom. Nothing is more sure than that thousands of people in the west of England—throughout Cornwall in particular—in the north, and even in the midland counties, are totally unemployed. Hence those who formerly wanted nothing are now in want of all
30 things. They are so far from the plenty they once enjoyed that they are in the most deplorable distress, deprived not only of the conveniences, but most of the necessaries of life. I have seen not a few of these wretched creatures, within little more than an hundred miles of London, standing in the streets with pale looks,
35 hollow eyes, and meagre limbs; or creeping up and down like walking shadows. I have known families who a few years ago lived in an easy, genteel manner, reduced to just as much raiment as they had on, and as much food as they could gather in the field.

---

[9] See Matt. 24:8.
[10] Cf. 2 Sam. 24:16.

To this one or other of them repaired once a day, to pick up the turnips which the cattle had left; which they boiled, if they could get a few sticks, or otherwise ate them raw. Such is the want of food to which many of our countrymen are at this day reduced by want of business.[11]　　　　　　　　　　　　　　　　　　　　5

2. Grievous enough is this calamity, which multitudes every day suffer. But I do not know whether many more do not labour under a still more grievous calamity. It is a great affliction to be deprived of bread; but it is a still greater to be deprived of our senses. And this is the case with thousands upon thousands of our　10 countrymen at this day. Widespread poverty (though not in so high a degree) I have seen several years ago. But so widespread a lunacy I never saw, nor I believe the oldest man alive. Thousands of plain, honest people throughout the land are driven utterly out of their senses by means of the poison which is so diligently　15 spread through every city and town in the kingdom. They are screaming out for liberty while they have it in their hands,[12] while they actually possess it; and to so great an extent that the like is not known in any other nation under heaven; whether we mean civil liberty, a liberty of enjoying all our legal property, or religious　20 liberty, a liberty of worshipping God according to the dictates of our own conscience. Therefore all those who are either passionately or dolefully crying out, 'Bondage! Slavery!' while there is no more danger of any such thing than there is of the sky falling upon their head, are utterly distracted; their reason is　25 gone; their intellects are quite confounded. Indeed many of these have lately recovered their senses; yet are there multitudes

[11] Wesley knew as much of rural England at first hand as any other man of his time, and his observations of the adverse economic (and human) effects of the Industrial Revolution are scattered through his *Journal* and *Letters* during the 1770s; cf., e.g., JWJ, Oct. 27, 1772; Dec. 21, 1772; Jan. 7, 1773; and his letters to Mrs. Barton, Jan. 21, 1773; and to Lord North, June 14, 1775; see also *Thoughts on the Present Scarcity of Provisions*, Jan. 20, 1773 (*Bibliog*, No. 344, Vol. 15 of this edn.). Something of the same picture appears in William Cobbett, *Rural Rides* (1830); William Marshall, *A General Survey . . . of the Rural Economy of England* (1787–98); F. M. Eden, *The State of the Poor* (1797), which forms the background for T. R. Malthus's gloomy *Essay on the Principle of Population* (1798). Cf. Samuel Johnson's comments that support Wesley's observations reported in Boswell's *Life of Johnson* (Oct. 20, 1769; Apr. 6, 1772; and Mar. 30, 1778). See also George Rudé, *Hanoverian London, 1714–1808*, pp. 191 ff.

[12] An echo of Wesley's favourable comments on the character and government of George III; in addition to the citations already given, see *A Word to a Freeholder* (*Bibliog*, No. 139, Vol. 14 of this edn.); and 'How Far is it the Duty of a Christian Minister to Preach Politics?' in *AM* (1782), V.151-52.

still remaining who are in this respect as perfectly mad as any of the inhabitants of Bedlam.[13]

3. Let not anyone think this is but a small calamity which is fallen upon our land. If you saw, as I have seen, in every county, city, town, men who were once of a calm, mild, friendly temper, mad with party zeal,[14] foaming with rage against their quiet neighbours, ready to tear out one another's throats, and to plunge their swords into each other's bowels; if you had heard men who once feared God and honoured the king[15] now breathing out the bitterest invectives against him, and just ripe, should any occasion offer, for treason and rebellion; you would not then judge this to be a little evil, a matter of small moment, but one of the heaviest judgments which God can permit to fall upon a guilty land.

4. Such is the condition of Englishmen at home. And is it any better abroad? I fear not. From those who are now upon the spot I learn that in our colonies,[16] also, many are causing the people to drink largely of the same deadly wine; thousands of whom are thereby inflamed more and more, till their heads are utterly turned, and they are mad to all intents and purposes. Reason is lost in rage; its small still voice is drowned by popular clamour. Wisdom is fallen in the streets.[17] And where is the place of understanding?[18] It is hardly to be found in these provinces. Here is *slavery*, real slavery indeed, most properly so called. For the regular, legal, constitutional form of government is no more. Here is real, not imaginary, bondage; not the shadow of English liberty is left. Not only no *liberty of the press* is allowed—none dare print a page or a line unless it be exactly conformable to the sentiments of our lords, the people—but no *liberty of speech*. Their 'tongue' is not 'their own'.[19] None must dare to utter one word

---

[13] The Hospital of St. Mary of Bethlehem (London), used since the sixteenth century as an asylum for the mentally deranged; hence by extension 'a lunatic asylum'. The original Bedlam was situated near London Wall, not far from Wesley's headquarters in Upper Moorfields.

[14] Cf. James Thomson, *The Seasons*, 'Spring', l.929: 'And honest zeal, unwarped by party-rage'.

[15] See 1 Pet. 2:17.

[16] In the early stages of resistance to British rule in America Wesley had commented favourably on American demands for civil liberties; see his letter to the Earl of Dartmouth, June 14, 1775: 'I cannot avoid thinking (if I think at all) that an oppressed people asked for nothing more than their legal rights, and that in the most modest and inoffensive manner which the nature of the thing would allow;' see also his letter to Lord North, June 15, 1775. But when the colonists raised the cry of independence, Wesley turned against them.

[17] See Isa. 59:14.   [18] Job 28:12, 20.   [19] Cf. Acts 2:8.

either in favour of King George, or in disfavour of the idol they have set up—the new, illegal, unconstitutional government, utterly unknown to us and to our forefathers. Here is no *religious liberty;* no liberty of conscience for them that 'honour the King', and whom consequently a sense of duty prompts them to defend from the vile calumnies continually vented against him. Here is no *civil liberty;* no enjoying the fruit of their labour any further than the populace pleases. A man has no security for his trade, his house, his property, unless he will swim with the stream. Nay, he has no security for his life if his popular neighbour has a mind to cut his throat. For there is no law, and no legal magistrate to take cognizance of offences. There is the gulf of tyranny—of arbitrary power on one hand, and of anarchy on the other.[20] And, as if all this were not misery enough, see likewise the fell monster, war![21] But who can describe the complicated misery which is contained in this? Hark! The cannons roar! A pitchy cloud covers the face of the sky. Noise, confusion, terror, reign over all! Dying groans are on every side. The bodies of men are pierced, torn, hewed in pieces; their blood is poured on the earth like water! Their souls take their flight into the eternal world; perhaps into everlasting misery. The ministers of grace turn away from the horrid scene; the ministers of vengeance triumph. Such already has been the face of things in that once happy land where peace and plenty, even while banished from great part of Europe, smiled for near an hundred years.

5. And what is it which drags on these poor victims into the field of blood? It is a great phantom which stalks before them, which they are taught to call, 'liberty'! It is this which breathes

> . . . into their hearts stern love of war,
> And thirst of vengeance, and contempt of death.[22]

---

[20] An echo of Horace Walpole's dictum that 'the name of the opposition is *anarchy*', cited in Robertson, *England Under the Hanoverians*, p. 265.

[21] See No. 128, 'The Deceitfulness of the Human Heart', II.4, where Wesley, quoting from Nicholas Rowe's *Tamerlane*, Act I, sc. 1, ll. 96-100, speaks of 'that foul monster, war'. For his other comments on war, see No. 22, 'Sermon on the Mount, II', III.18 and n.

[22] Cf. Samuel Wesley, Jun., 'The Battle of the Sexes', vi. 6-8 (*Poems*, 1736, p. 24):

> Male banners wave, while sounding trumpets' breath
> Kindles in martial breasts stern love of war,
> Delib'rate valour, and contempt of death.

See also John Wesley, *A Collection of Moral and Sacred Poems* (1744), III.21.

Real liberty, meantime, is trampled underfoot, and is lost in anarchy and confusion.

6. But which of these warriors all the while considered the wife of his youth, that is now left a disconsolate widow—perhaps with none that careth for her; perhaps deprived of her only comfort and support, and not having where to lay her head? Who considered his helpless children, now desolate orphans; it may be, crying for bread, while their mother has nothing left to give them but her sorrows and her tears?

II. 1. And yet 'these sheep, what have they done', although all this is come upon them? 'Suppose ye that' they are 'sinners above other men, because they suffer such things? I tell you, Nay; but except ye repent, ye shall all likewise perish.'[23] It therefore behoves us to consider our own sins—the cause of all our sufferings. It behoves each of us to say, 'Lo, I have sinned; I have done wickedly.'[24]

2. The time would fail should I attempt to enumerate all the ways wherein we have sinned; but in general, this is certain:

> The rich, the poor, the high, the low,
> Have wandered from his mild command;
> The floods of wickedness o'erflow,
> And deluge all the guilty land:
> People and priest lie drowned in sin,
> And Tophet yawns to take them in.[25]

How innumerable are the violations of justice among us! Who does not adopt the old maxim,

> *Si possis, recte; si non, quocunque modo rem:* [26]
> If you can get money honestly, do; but, however, get money.

Where is mercy to be found, if it would stand in opposition to interest? How few will scruple, for a valuable consideration, to oppress the widow or fatherless?[27] And where shall we find truth? Deceit and fraud go not out of our streets. Who is it that speaks

---

[23] Cf. Luke 13:2-3.
[24] 2 Sam. 24:17.
[25] See John and Charles Wesley, *Hymns for Times of Persecution* (London, 1744), p. 4 (*Poet. Wks.*, IV.4).
[26] Horace, *Epistles*, I.i.65-66; cf. No. 95, 'On the Education of Children', §19 and n.
[27] See Zech. 7:10.

the truth from his heart? Whose words are the picture of his thoughts? Where is he that has 'put away all lying',[28] that never speaks what he does not mean? Who is ashamed of this? Indeed it was once said, and even by a statesman, 'All other vices have had their patrons; but lying is so base, so abominable a vice, that never 5 was anyone found yet who dared openly to plead for it.'[29] Would one imagine this writer lived in a court? Yea, and that in the present century? Did not he himself, then, as well as all his brother statesmen, plead for a trade of deliberate lying? Did he not plead for the innocence, yea, and the necessity, of employing 10 *spies?* The vilest race of liars under the sun? Yet who ever scrupled using them, but Lord Clarendon?[30]

3. O truth, whither art thou fled? How few have any acquaintance with thee? Do not we continually tell lies for the nonce, without gaining thereby either profit or pleasure? Is not 15 even our common language replete with falsehood? Above an hundred years ago the poet complained,

> It never was good day
> Since lowly fawning was called compliment.[31]

What would he have said had he lived a century later, when that 20 art was brought to perfection?

4. Perhaps there is one palpable evidence of this which is not usually attended to. If you blame a man in many other respects, he is not much affronted. But if you say he is a liar, he will not bear it; he takes fire at once. Why is this? Because a man can bear to be 25 blamed when he is conscious of his own innocence. But if you say

---

[28] Cf. Eph. 4:25.

[29] Cf. No. 100, 'On Pleasing All Men', I.4, where Wesley identifies Addison.

[30] Edward Hyde, first Earl of Clarendon (1604–74), whose *History of the Rebellion* (1702–4) Wesley had read in 1726 and had often recommended (cf. his letter to Samuel Furly, Mar. 7, 1758; and JWJ, Oct. 18, 1774). On this point of spies and spying (and an explanation of how spies had come to be called 'lions'), cf. Addison's essay in *The Guardian*, No. 17, June 2, 1713; see also his remarks about the Earl of Clarendon in *The Spectator*, No. 439, July 24, 1712. Actually, of course, Clarendon's scruples were not strong enough to prevent his making use of them; see T. H. Lister, *Life and Administration of Edward, first Earl of Clarendon* (1838), Vol. 2.

[31] Cf. Shakespeare, *Twelfth Night*, III.i.109–10:

> 'Twas never merry world
> Since lowly *feigning* was called compliment.

In this context 'fawning' is clearly the wrong word; it may have been a printer's misreading; but see No. 90, 'An Israelite Indeed', II.8 and n.

he is a liar you touch a sore spot; he is guilty, and therefore cannot bear it.

5. Is there a character more despicable than even that of a liar? Perhaps there is; even that of an epicure. And are we not a
5 generation of epicures? Is not our 'belly' our 'god'?[32] Are not eating and drinking our chief delight, our highest happiness? Is it not the main study (I fear, the only study) of many honourable men to enlarge the pleasure of tasting?[33] When was luxury (not in food only, but in dress, furniture, equipage) carried to such an
10 height in Great Britain, ever since it was a nation? We have lately extended the British empire almost over the globe. We have carried our laurels into Africa, into Asia, into the burning and the frozen climes of America. And what have we brought thence? All the elegance of vice which either the eastern or western world
15 could afford.

6. Luxury is constantly the parent of sloth.[34] Every glutton will in due time be a drone. The more of meat and drink he devours, the less taste will he have for labour. This degeneracy of the Britons from their temperate, active forefathers, was taken notice
20 of in the last century. But if Mr. Herbert then said,

O England, full of sin, but most of sloth,[35]

what would he have said now? Observe the difference between the last and the present century, only in a single instance. In the last, the Parliament used to meet *hora quinta ante meridiem!*[36]—at
25 five in the morning. Could these Britons look out of their graves, what would they think of the present generation?

7. Permit me to touch on one article more wherein indeed we excel all the nations upon earth. Not one nation under the canopy of heaven can vie with the English in profaneness. Such a total

---

[32] Cf. Phil. 3:19.

[33] See No. 50, 'The Use of Money', II.2 and n.

[34] Cf. Plato, *Republic*, IV.422: 'Wealth is the parent of luxury and sloth. . . .' But see also the proverb in Nicholas Ling, *Politeuphuia, Wits Common-wealth* (1699): 'Sloth is the mother of poverty.' In No. 89, 'The More Excellent Way', III.1, Wesley had said that sloth is inconsistent with religion; see also No. 113, *The Late Work of God in North America*, I.14.

[35] George Herbert, *The Temple*, 'The Church Porch', ver. 16, l. 1.

[36] π; There is another reference to this alleged custom in Wesley's *Estimate of the Manners of the Present Times*, §1: 'With regard to sloth, it was the constant custom of our ancestors to rise at four in the morning. This was the stated hour, summer and winter, for all that were in health. The two Houses of Parliament met "at five"; *hora quinta antemeridiana*, says their Journal.' A proper citation for this is lacking.

neglect, such an utter contempt of God, is nowhere else to be found. In no other streets, except in Ireland, can you hear on every side,

> . . . the horrid oath, the direful curse,
> That latest weapon of the wretch's war,   5
> And blasphemy, sad comrade of despair![37]

8. Now let each of us lay his hand upon his heart and say, 'Lord, is it I?'[38] Have I added to this flood of unrighteousness and ungodliness, and thereby to the misery of my countrymen? Am not I guilty in any of the preceding respects? And do not *they* suffer because I have sinned?' If we have any tenderness of heart, any bowels of mercies,[39] any sympathy with the afflicted, let us pursue this thought till we are deeply sensible of *our* sins as one great cause of *their* sufferings.

9. But now the plague is begun, and has already made such ravages both in England and America, what can *we* do in order that it may be stayed? How shall we stand between the living and the dead? Is there any better way to turn aside the anger of God than that prescribed by St. James, 'Purge your hands, ye sinners, and purify your hearts, ye double-minded'?[40] First, 'Purge your hands'. Immediately put away the evil of your doings. Instantly flee from sin, from every evil word and work, as from the face of a serpent.[41] 'Let no corrupt communication proceed out of your mouth,'[42] no uncharitable, no unprofitable conversation. Let no guile be found in your mouth:[43] speak to every man the truth from your heart. Renounce every way of acting, however gainful, which is contrary either to justice or mercy. Do to everyone as, in parallel circumstances, you would wish he should do unto you.[44] Be sober, temperate, active; and in every word and work labour to have a conscience void of offence toward God and toward man.[45] Next, through the almighty grace of him that loved you and gave himself for you,[46] 'purify your hearts by faith.'[47] Be no longer

---

[37] Cf. Prior, 'Henry and Emma', ll. 464-66, beginning, 'Must hear the frequent oath, the direful curse.' See also, *A Serious Address to the People of England*, §9 (*Bibliog*. No. 386, Vol. 15 of this edn.).

[38] Matt. 26:22.   [39] Col. 3:12.

[40] Cf. Jas. 4:8.   [41] Rev. 12:14.

[42] Eph. 4:29.   [43] See 1 Pet. 2:22.

[44] See Matt. 7:12.   [45] See Acts 24:16.

[46] See Gal. 2:20.

[47] Cf. Acts 15:9.

double-minded, halting between earth and heaven, striving to serve God and mammon.[48] Purify your hearts from pride, humbling yourselves under the mighty hand of God;[49] from all party zeal, anger, resentment, bitterness, which now especially
5 will easily beset you; from all prejudice, bigotry, narrowness of spirit; from impetuosity, and impatience of contradiction; from love of dispute, and from every degree of an unmerciful or implacable temper. Instead of this 'earthly, devilish wisdom' let 'the wisdom from above' sink deep into your hearts; that 'wisdom'
10 which 'is first pure', then 'peaceable, easy to be entreated', convinced, persuaded, or appeased, 'full of mercy and good fruits; without partiality', embracing all men; 'without hypocrisy',[50] genuine and unfeigned. Now, if ever, 'putting away with all malice, all clamour'—railing—'and evil-speaking; be ye kind one
15 to another', to all your brethren and countrymen; 'tenderhearted' to all that are in distress, 'forgiving one another, even as God for Christ's sake hath forgiven you.'[51]

10. And now 'let my counsel be acceptable to you', to every one of you present before God. 'Break off thy sins by repentance, and
20 thy iniquities by showing mercy to the poor, if it may be a lengthening of thy tranquility'[52]—of what degree of it still remains among us. Show mercy more especially to the poor widows, to the helpless orphans of your countrymen who are now numbered among the dead, who fell among the slain in a distant land. Who
25 knoweth but the Lord will yet be entreated, will calm the madness of the people, will quench the flames of contention, and breathe into all the spirit of love, unity, and concord. Then brother shall not lift up sword against brother, neither shall they know war any more.[53] Then shall plenty and peace flourish in our land, and all
30 the inhabitants of it be thankful for the innumerable blessings which they enjoy, and shall 'fear God, and honour the king'.[54]

London, Nov. 7, 1775

[48] See Matt. 6:24.
[49] See 1 Pet. 5:6.
[50] Jas. 3:15, 17.
[51] Cf. Eph. 4:31-32.
[52] Cf. Dan. 4:27.
[53] See Isa. 2:4; Mic. 4:3.
[54] Cf. 1 Pet. 2:17.

ON LAYING THE FOUNDATION OF THE NEW CHAPEL

AN INTRODUCTORY COMMENT

Wesley's home and headquarters for the first four decades after 'the rise of the United [Methodist] Society' had been in 'The Foundery', a renovated cannon factory on the northern edge of Upper Moorfields, London. Wesley had leased and refurbished it at a total cost of some £800 (£115 for the lease, £685 for repairs and furnishings). This improvisation and its various uses reflected much of the ethos of Methodism in its first generation. But as the Revival flourished and as he looked toward the expiring of his lease, Wesley began to envisage a 'New Foundery', that might serve Methodism's future as well as the old one had done in its day. He broached the idea to his brother in a letter of October 7, 1775, and reported its development some five months later in the Journal *for March 1, 1776: 'As we cannot depend on having the Foundery long, we met to consult about building a new chapel. Our petition to the City for a piece of ground lies before the Committee.' In due course a lease was granted the Methodists for a piece of land 'near the City Road' (across from Bunhill Fields) and a building campaign was begun. Wesley's circular letter to Methodists throughout the country (October 18, 1776) reflects his presuppositions as to the connexional character of Methodism:*

The Society at London have given assistance to their brethren in various parts of England. They have done this for upwards of thirty years; they have done it cheerfully and liberally. . . . They now stand in need of assistance themselves. They are under a necessity of building, as the Foundery, with all the adjoining houses, is shortly to be pulled down. And the City of London has granted ground to build on, but on condition of covering it [i.e., screening it from the City Road] with large houses in front, which, together with the New Chapel, will, at a very moderate computation, cost upward of six thousand pounds. I must therefore beg the assistance of all our brethren.

By the following April, the project was ready for the laying of a 'foundation stone' and for the construction to be turned over to a newly affluent Methodist builder, Samuel Tooth of 'Messrs. Tooth and Co. of Worship Street, Upper Moorfields'.

This move represented a deliberate upward step toward 'respectabili-

ty' for the Methodists, as is confirmed by the ringing triumphalist tone of the whole occasion in Wesley's Journal:

> *Monday the 21st was the day appointed for the laying the foundation of the New Chapel. The rain befriended us much by keeping away thousands who purposed to be there. But there were still such multitudes that it was with great difficulty I got through them to lay the first stone. Upon this was a plate of brass . . . on which was engraved: 'This was laid by Mr. John Wesley on April 21, 1777.' Probably this will be seen no more by any human eye, but will remain there till the earth and the works thereof are burned up.*

This, of course, was in the full knowledge that his lease had been granted for only fifty-nine years.[1] A Sermon on Numbers xxiii.23, preached Monday, April 21, 1777, on Laying the Foundation of the New Chapel, near the City Road, London, *provides us with an interesting retrospective on the Revival, together with a few intriguing historical revisions. For example, in his review of Methodist origins Wesley has blotted out all memory of the early influences of the Moravians; moreover, he omits all mention of the Methodist beginnings at Bristol and Kingswood. His special concern, however, was to stress the unique relationship between Methodism and the Church of England;* viz., *the symbiosis of a connexion of religious* societies *within a national* church. *That this particular vision was not as heartily shared by the Methodists generally as by Wesley is suggested by the fact that the sermon had only two editions, both in 1777, and then was not published again until 1809, when it appeared, with its present title, in Joseph Benson's edition of the* Works, *VI.106-15. The text here is based on the first edition, with minor corrections taken from the second. For fuller details, see* Bibliog, *No. 366.*

The Calvinists were quick to recognize that the New Chapel signified a new stage in the development of what they had come to regard as a rival movement. Rowland Hill promptly denounced the sermon as 'a false and libellous harangue', in Imposture Detected and the Dead *[i.e., George Whitefield]* Vindicated. . . *(1777). He then went on to identify Wesley as 'this grey-headed enemy to all righteousness'—and charged him with brazen duplicity in his 'building dissenting meeting-houses the kingdom over', even while continuing to protest that these 'houses' were only adjuncts to the national church. Professor Frank Baker has pointed out the kernel of truth in Hill's otherwise unedifying invective:*

---

[1] See George J. Stevenson, *City Road Chapel* (1872), pp. 67-68; see also John Telford, *Wesley's Chapel and Wesley's House* (1926).

Wesley's New Chapel was not simply another preaching-house. It was seen by him as a special symbol of connexional unity, meriting universal Methodist support. . . . This new Methodist headquarters was separatist even in its architecture. . . . [It] was from the outset a centre for sacramental worship as well as for preaching and fellowship and social service. . . . These premises, in fact, functioned very much like those of a very active Anglican parish church, though without recognizing any allegiance to diocesan or parochial authorities.[2]

On Laying the Foundation of the New Chapel

Numbers 23:23

According to this time it shall be said, What hath God wrought!

1. We need not now inquire in what sense this was applicable to the children of Israel. It may be of more use to consider in what sense the words are applicable to ourselves; how far the people of England have reason to say, 'According to this time, what hath God wrought!'

2. A great man, indeed, who I trust is now in a better world, Dr. Gibson, late Lord Bishop of London, in one of his charges to his clergy flatly denies that God has wrought any 'extraordinary work' in our nation; nay, affirms that to imagine any such thing is no better than downright enthusiasm.[1] It is so if his lordship's supposition is true, if God has not wrought any extraordinary work. But if he really has, then we may believe and assert it without incurring any such imputation.

3. Yet a still greater man of a neighbouring nation, a burning and a shining light,[2] equally eminent in piety and in learning, partly confirmed the bishop's supposition. For Bengelius,[3] being asked why he placed the grand revival of religion so late as the year 1836, replied: 'I acknowledge all the prophecies would

[2] Baker, *John Wesley and the Church of England*, pp. 213-14.

---

[1] Edmund Gibson; see No. 66, 'The Signs of the Times', II.2 and n.
[2] John 5:35.
[3] J. A. Bengel (1687–1752). Bengel's prophecy of a revival appeared in his *Ordo temporum a principio per periedos oeconomiae divinae* (1741).

incline me to place it a century sooner. But an insurmountable difficulty lies in the way: I cannot reconcile this to matter of fact. For I do not know of any remarkable work of God which has been wrought upon earth between the years 1730 and 1740.' This is really surprising. It is strange that sensible men should know so little of what is done at so small a distance. How could so great a man be ignorant of what was transacted no farther off than England? Especially considering the accounts then published in Germany, some of which were tolerably impartial; nay, considering the particular account which I had sent as early as the year 1742 to one well known through all the empire, Pastor (afterwards Superintendent) Steinmetz.[4]

4. 'But has there indeed been any extraordinary work of God wrought in England during this century?' This is an important question; it is certainly worthy of our serious consideration. And it is capable of being answered to the full satisfaction of every fair inquirer. He may easily be informed what work it is, and in what manner it has been wrought. It is true I am in one respect an improper person to give this information, as it will oblige me frequently to speak of myself, which may have the appearance of ostentation. But with regard to this I can only cast myself upon the candour of my hearers, being persuaded they will put the most favourable construction upon what is not a matter of choice, but of necessity. For there is no other person, if I decline the task, who can supply my place, who has a perfect knowledge of the work in question from the beginning of it to this day.[5]

We may consider, first, the rise and progress of this work; secondly, the nature of it.

I.1. As to the rise of it. In the year 1725 a young student at Oxford was much affected by reading Kempis's *Christian Pattern*, and Bishop Taylor's *Rules of Holy Living and Dying*.[6] He found an

[4] Johann Adam Steinmetz (1689–1762), pietistic Lutheran, pastor of Teschen (Silesia), General Superintendent of the duchy of Magdeburg from 1732. Wesley had first heard of him, during his visit to Herrnhut, from Christian David; cf. JWJ, Aug. 10, 1738. In his early career Steinmetz had been on friendly terms with Count von Zinzendorf and the Herrnhuters, but afterwards broke with them. Wesley's 'particular account' of the Revival sent to Steinmetz seems not to have survived; its substance may be seen in *Letters*, II, 26:49-51 in this edn. There is no evidence of any reaction from Steinmetz or of Steinmetz's connections with Bengel, if any.

[5] For other instances of Methodist triumphalism, see below, II.11; and No. 102, 'Of Former Times', §22 and n.

[6] Cf. Wesley's preface to JWJ, §1.

earnest desire to live according to those rules, and to flee from the wrath to come.[7] He sought for some that would be his companions in the way, but could find none; so that for several years he was constrained to travel alone, having no man either to guide or to help him. But in the year 1729 he found one who had 5 the same desire. They then endeavoured to help each other, and in the close of the year were joined by two more. They soon agreed to spend two or three hours together every Sunday evening. Afterwards they sat two evenings together, and in a while six evenings in the week; spending that time in reading the 10 Scriptures, and provoking one another to love and to good works.[8]

2. The regularity of their behaviour gave occasion to a young gentleman of the college to say, 'I think we have got a new set of *Methodists*'—alluding to a set of physicians who began to flourish at Rome about the time of Nero, and continued for several ages.[9] 15 The name was new and quaint; it clave to them immediately. And from that time both those four young gentlemen, and all that had any religious connection with them, were distinguished by the name of 'Methodists'.

3. In the four or five years following another and another were 20 added to the number, till in the year 1735 there were fourteen of them who constantly met together. Three of these were tutors in their several colleges; the rest, Bachelors of Arts, or undergraduates.[10] They were all precisely of one judgment as well as of one

---

[7] Matt. 3:7.

[8] See Heb. 10:24.

[9] Wesley has more than one explanation of the term 'Methodist'; see his open letter to Dr. Warburton, Nov. 26, 1762 (11:481-82 in this edn.); the Preface to *The Character of a Methodist;* and his letter to Richard Morgan, Oct. 18, 1732. See also Fred C. Wright, 'On the Origin of the Name Methodist', WHS, III.10-13, and T. E. Brigden, 'Notes and Queries', in *ibid.*, III.112. The first citation in the *OED* is from 1593; later usages include 'a class of Roman Catholic apologists (1686)'. Dr. Johnson refers to 'a physician who practises by theory' and yet also to 'one of a new kind of puritans lately arisen, so called from their profession to live by rules and in constant method'. This latter would correspond to the usage in *A War Among the Angels of the Churches Wherein is Shewed the Principles of the New Methodists in the Great Point of Justification* (1693), 'By a Country Professor of Jesus Christ.' There 'the New Methodists' are associated with John Goodwin and accused of 'tending to set man's personal inherent righteousness as an element of our justifying righteousness . . .' (p. 7), and of designing 'to promote holiness and . . . self-righteousness'. There is no record of Wesley having read the *War Among the Angels*, but the association of 'Methodists' with ideas of 'personal inherent righteousness' and of 'holy living' must already have been familiar.

[10] This account of the Oxford Methodists as of 1735 should be compared with 'A Short History of the People called Methodists' (dated Nov. 16, 1781), §§2-3, where Wesley says they were 'fourteen or fifteen in number' (*Bibliog*, No. 420); his letter to Henry Brooke,

soul. All tenacious of order to the last degree, and observant, for conscience' sake, of every rule of the church, and every statute both of the university and of their respective colleges.[11] They were all orthodox in every point; firmly believing not only the three
5   creeds, but whatsoever they judged to be the doctrine of the Church of England, as contained in her Articles and Homilies. As to that practice of the apostolic church (which continued till the time of Tertullian,[12] at least in many churches) the 'having all things in common',[13] they had no rule, nor any formed design
10 concerning it. But it was so, in effect, and it could not be otherwise; for none could want anything that another could spare. This was the infancy of the work. They had no conception of anything that would follow. Indeed they took 'no thought for the morrow',[14] desiring only to live *today*.
15   4. Many imagined, that little society would be dispersed, and Methodism (so called) come to an end, when in October 1735 my brother, Mr. Ingham,[15] and I, were induced by a strange chain of providences to go over to the new colony in Georgia. Our design was to preach to the Indian nations bordering upon that province.
20 But we were detained at Savannah and Frederica by the importunity of the people, who, having no other ministers, earnestly requested that we would not leave them. After a time I desired the most serious of them to meet me once or twice a week at my house. Here were the rudiments of a Methodist Society;[16]

June 14, 1786, where he says the number was sixteen; and his 'Thoughts upon Methodism' (dated Aug. 4, 1786), §3, where he says the number was fifteen (see *AM*, 1787, X.101); see also *A Short History of Methodism*, §4. It is almost impossible to arrive at an exact membership list of the Oxford Methodists, since several groups met at several levels in the early 1730s, and membership in each fluctuated widely. Cf. Richard P. Heitzenrater, 'The Oxford Diaries and the First Rise of Methodism', *A.M.E Zion Quarterly Review/Methodist History* (July 1974), pp. 111-35, espec. pp. 126-28. See also No. 53, *On the Death of George Whitefield*, III.2 and n.; and II.15, below.
   [11] See No. 150, 'Hypocrisy in Oxford', II.9-10.
   [12] Cf. Tertullian, *Apology*, espec. ch. 39.
   [13] Cf. Acts 2:44; 4:32.   [14] Matt. 6:34.
   [15] Benjamin Ingham (1712-72), an Oxford Methodist from at least the autumn of 1733 (see Heitzenrater, above, n. 10). He was ordained by Bishop Potter in June 1735. After thirteen months in Georgia, he returned to become an Anglican evangelist in Yorkshire and the Midlands. He married Lady Margaret Hastings, sister-in-law to the Countess of Huntingdon, and eventually formed a cluster of religious societies under his own direction. It is odd that Wesley should have omitted the name of a third companion on the voyage, Charles Delamotte, whose service in Georgia outlasted all the others and who continued as a friend long after the Wesleys and Ingham had gone their separate ways; cf. JWJ, May 16, 1782.
   [16] Cf. JWJ, Apr. 1736.

but notwithstanding this, both my brother and I were as vehemently attached to the church as ever, and to every rubric of it: insomuch that I would never admit a Dissenter to the Lord's Supper unless he would be rebaptized. Nay, when the Lutheran minister of the Saltzburgers at Ebenezer, being at Savannah, desired to receive it, I told him I did not dare to administer it to him, because I looked upon him as unbaptized, as I judged baptism by laymen to be invalid; and such I counted all that were not episcopally ordained.[17]

5. Full of these sentiments, of this zeal for the Church (from which I bless God he has now delivered me), I returned to England in the beginning of February 1738. I was now in haste to retire to Oxford, and bury myself in my beloved obscurity.[18] But I was detained in London week after week by the Trustees for the Colony of Georgia.[19] In the meantime I was continually importuned to preach in one and another church, and that not only morning, afternoon, and night, on Sunday, but on weekdays also. As I was lately come from a far country, vast multitudes flocked together. But in a short time, partly because of those unwieldy crowds, partly because of my unfashionable doctrine, I

[17] This was Johann Martin Bolzius (cf. JWJ, July 17, 1737). But see also JWJ, Sept. 30, 1749, for Wesley's belated apology to Bolzius. Cf. Martin Schmidt, *John Wesley: A Theological Biography*, I.169-78, for the important differences between the more moralistic ('Halle-type') pietism of Bolzius and the Salzburgers and the more mystical pietism of the Moravians.

[18] Public figure that he was, Wesley had a strong, lifelong bent to seclusion. Cf. his letter to Prof. John Liden (Lund, Sweden), Nov. 30, 1769 ('having from my infancy loved silence and obscurity'). See the letter to his brother Charles, Dec. 15, 1772, and Editor's Intro. (1:1-2 in this edn.). Despite his constant involvements, he arranged for as much privacy as possible for prayer, meditation, and study; cf. his letter to Miss March, Dec. 10, 1777, where he says: 'It is true I travel four or five thousand miles in a year. But I generally travel alone in my carriage, and consequently am as retired ten hours in a day as if I was in a wilderness.' This taste for solitude, however personal, was also in accord with the monastic tradition as Wesley had found it in Kempis, *Imitation*, I.xix, xx ('On the Love of Solitude and Silence'), or in Richard Lucas, *Enquiry After Happiness* (1717), I.228-29, or even in John Hughes's drama, *The Siege of Damascus*, Act V, sc. 1, 'Let me wear out my small remains of life, /Obscure, content with humble poverty.'

[19] He had left Georgia under a cloud of grand jury indictments and his employment by the Georgia Trustees had not yet been formally terminated. It was not until Apr. 26 (nearly three months after his return to England) that the matter was settled. Cf. the *Diary of Viscount Percival, Afterwards First Earl of Egmont* (London, Historical Manuscript Commission, 1920-23), II.481: 'Mr. John Wesley, our minister at Savannah, left with us his license for performing ecclesiastical service at Savannah, which we took for a resignation, and therefore resolved to revoke his commission. In truth the Board did it with great pleasure, he appearing to us to be a very odd mixture of a man, an enthusiast and at the same time a hypocrite. . . .' Egmont was one of the Trustees; cf. some of his other references to Wesley in II.349-50, 370, 449-51, 466-67.

was excluded from one and another church, and at length shut out of all. Not daring to be silent, after a short struggle between honour and conscience I made a virtue of necessity, and preached in the middle of Moorfields.[20] Here were thousands upon 5 thousands, abundantly more than any church could contain; and numbers among them who never went to any church or place of public worship at all. More and more of them were cut to the heart, and came to me all in tears, inquiring with the utmost eagerness what they must do to be saved.[21] I said, 'If all of you will 10 meet on Thursday evening, I will advise you as well as I can.' The first evening about twelve persons came; the next week, thirty or forty. When they were increased to about an hundred, I took down their names and places of abode, intending, as often as it was convenient, to call upon them at their own houses. Thus, 15 without any previous plan or design, began the Methodist Society in England—a company of people associating together to help each other to work out their own salvation.

6. The next spring we were invited to Bristol and Kingswood, where likewise Societies were quickly formed.[22] The year 20 following we went to Newcastle upon Tyne, and preached to all the colliers and keelmen round it. In 1744 we went through Cornwall, as far as Sennen,[23] near the Land's End; and in the compass of two or three years more to almost every part of England. Some time after we were desired to go over to Ireland,[24] 25 and in process of time to every county therein. Last of all we were invited to Musselburgh, Glasgow, and several other parts of Scotland.[25] But it was in Edinburgh, Glasgow, Dundee,

---

[20] But cf. JWJ, Sunday, June 17, 1739: 'I preached at seven in Upper Moorfields [i.e., very close by the site of this present sermon] to (I believe) six or seven thousand people on "Ho! everyone that thirsteth, come ye to the waters." ' This quietly ignores that his initial venture in field preaching had been near Bristol ten weeks earlier; see JWJ, Apr. 2: 'At four in the afternoon I submitted to be more vile, and proclaimed in the highways the glad tidings of salvation, speaking from a little eminence in the ground adjoining to the city [St. Philip's Plain] to about three thousand people.'

[21] See Acts 16:30. Cf. the opening sections to the *General Rules* for an official summary of this telescoped history of Methodist origins.

[22] An inversion of the order of events; it was, in fact, the spring just past (cf. JWJ, Mar. 10 to Apr. 4, 1739).

[23] Wesley's spelling, 'Sennan'; see also JWJ, Sept. 10, 1743.

[24] John Wesley's first visit to Dublin was Aug. 8-20, 1747. In Sept. Charles Wesley followed for a lengthy visit.

[25] In Apr. 1751, by Captain Bartholomew Gallatin, a Methodist whose regiment had been transferred to Musselburgh from Manchester.

Arbroath, and Aberdeen, that we saw the greatest fruit of our labour.

II.1. Such was the rise, and such has been the progress of Methodism from the beginning to the present time. But you will naturally ask, What is Methodism? What does this new word 5 mean? Is it not a new religion? This is a very common, nay, almost an universal supposition. But nothing can be more remote from the truth. It is a mistake all over. Methodism, so called, is the old religion, the religion of the Bible, the religion of the primitive church, the religion of the Church of England. This 'old religion' 10 (as I observed in the *Earnest Appeal to Men of Reason and Religion*) is

no other than love: the love of God and of all mankind; the loving God with all our heart, and soul, and strength, as having first loved *us*, as the fountain of all the good we have received, and of all we ever hope to enjoy; and the loving every soul which God hath made, every man on earth, as our own soul.[26] This love is 15 the great medicine of life, the never-failing remedy for all the evils of a disordered world, for all the miseries and vices of men. Wherever this is, there are virtue and happiness, going hand in hand. There is humbleness of mind, gentleness, long-suffering, the whole image of God, and at the same time a peace that passeth all understanding, with joy unspeakable, and full of glory. 20 This religion of love, and joy, and peace, has its seat in the inmost soul, but is ever showing itself by its fruits, continually springing up, not only in all innocence—for love worketh no ill to his neighbour—but likewise in every kind of beneficence, spreading virtue and happiness all around it.[27]

2. This is the *religion of the Bible*, as no one can deny who reads 25 it with any attention. It is the religion which is continually inculcated therein, which runs through both the Old and New Testament. Moses and the prophets, our Blessed Lord and his apostles, proclaim with one voice, 'Thou shalt love the Lord thy God with all thy soul, and thy neighbour as thyself.'[28] The Bible 30 declares, 'Love is the fulfilling of the Law,'[29] 'the end of the commandment',[30] of all the commandments which are contained in the oracles of God. The inward and outward fruits of this love are also largely described by the inspired writers. So that whoever

[26] Cf. No. 7, 'The Way to the Kingdom', I.8 and n. For the love of God being the substance of inward holiness and the love of neighbour the substance of outward holiness, cf. *ibid.*, I.10 and n.

[27] Cf. *An Earnest Appeal*, §§2-4 (11:45-46 in this edn.), and note Wesley's revisions here of that published text.

[28] Cf. Deut. 6:5; Lev. 19:18; Matt. 22:37, 39, etc.

[29] Rom. 13:10.   [30] 1 Tim. 1:5.

allows the Scripture to be the Word of God must allow this to be true religion.

3. This is the *religion of the primitive church,* of the whole church in the purest ages. It is clearly expressed even in the small remains
5 of Clemens Romanus, Ignatius, and Polycarp. It is seen more at large in the writings of Tertullian, Origen, Clemens Alexandrinus, and Cyprian. And even in the fourth century it was found in the works of Chrysostom, Basil, Ephrem Syrus, and Macarius.[31] It would be easy to produce a cloud of witnesses
10 testifying the same thing, were not this a point which no one will contest who has the least acquaintance with Christian antiquity.

4. And this is the *religion of the Church of England,* as appears from all her authentic records, from the uniform tenor of her liturgy, and from numberless passages in her Homilies. The
15 scriptural primitive religion of love, which is now reviving throughout the three kingdoms, is to be found in her morning and evening service, and in her daily as well as occasional prayers; and the whole of it is beautifully summed up in that one, comprehensive petition, 'Cleanse the thoughts of our hearts by
20 the inspiration of thy Holy Spirit, that we may perfectly love thee, and worthily magnify thy holy name.'[32]

5. Permit me to give a little fuller account, both of the progress and nature of this religion, by an extract from a treatise which was published many years ago.[a]

25   Just at the time when we wanted little of 'filling up the measure of our iniquities', two or three clergymen of the Church of England began vehemently to 'call sinners to repentance'. Many thousands gathered together to hear them; and in every place where they came many began to show such concern for religion as they never had done before. Many were in a short time deeply
30 convinced of the number and heinousness of their sins, of their evil tempers, of their inability to help themselves, and of the insignificancy of their *outside religion.* And from this repentance sprung 'fruits meet for repentance': the whole form of their life was changed. They 'ceased to do evil, and learned to do well'. Neither was this all; but over and above this outward change they began to
35 experience *inward religion.* 'The love of God was shed abroad in their hearts,'

---

[a] *Farther Appeal,* Part III [I.4-5, 11:274-75 in this edn. which see for scriptural citations].

---

[31] Note the omission here of Irenaeus; otherwise, this is Wesley's standard roster of 'the fathers of the church' who represented, for him, the primitive Christian tradition; it is typical of Anglican patrology in general. See No. 43, *The Scripture Way of Salvation,* I.7 and n.; also LPT *Wesley,* p. 9, n. 26.

[32] BCP, Communion, Collect for Purity.

which they enjoy to this day. They 'love him, because he first loved us'; and this love constrains them to love all mankind, and inspires them with every holy and heavenly temper, with the mind which was in Christ. Hence it is that they are now uniform in their behaviour, unblameable in all manner of conversation, and in whatsoever state they are, they have learned therewith to be content. Thus 5
they calmly travel on through life, never repining, or murmuring, or dissatisfied, till the hour comes that they shall drop this covering of earth,[33] and return to the Father of spirits.[34]

6. This revival of religion has spread to 'such a degree as neither we nor our fathers had known'. How *extensive* has it been! 10
There is scarce a considerable town in the kingdom where some have not been made witnesses of it. It has spread to every age and sex, to most orders and degrees of men; and even to abundance of those who in time past were accounted monsters of wickedness.

Consider the *swiftness* as well as extent of it. In what age has such a number of 15
sinners been recovered in so short a time from the error of their ways? When has true religion—I will not say since the Reformation, but since the time of Constantine the Great—made so large a progress in any nation within so small a space? I believe, hardly can either ancient or modern history afford a parallel instance. 20

7. We may likewise observe the *depth* of the work so extensively and swiftly wrought. Multitudes have been throughly 'convinced of sin'; and shortly after, so filled with joy and love that whether they were in the body, or out of the body, they could hardly tell. And in the power of this love they have trampled underfoot whatever the world accounts either terrible or desirable, having 25
evidenced in the severest trials an invariable and tender goodwill to mankind, and all the fruits of holiness. Now so deep a repentance, so strong a faith, so fervent love, and so unblemished holiness, wrought in so many persons in so short a time, the world has not seen for many ages.

8. No less remarkable is the *purity* of the religion which has extended itself so 30
deeply and swiftly. I speak particularly as to the doctrines held by those who are the subjects of it. Those of the Church of England at least must acknowledge this. For where is there a body of people who, number for number, so closely adhere to the doctrines of the Church?

Nor is their religion more pure from *heresy* than it is from *superstition*. In 35
former times, wherever any unusual religious concern has appeared, there has sprung up with it a *zeal* for things that were no part of religion. But it has not been so in the present case. No stress has been laid on anything as though it was necessary to salvation but what is plainly contained in the Word of God. And of the things contained therein the stress laid on each has been in proportion to the 40
nearness of its relation to what is there laid down as the sum of all—the love of

---

[33] Cf. No. 28, 'Sermon on the Mount, VIII', §21 and n.
[34] An abridgement and further revision of *A Farther Appeal*, Pt. III, I.4-5 (11:274-75 in this edn.), continued in sects. 6-11 by revised extracts from I.7-11, 13-14 (11:276-80). (Again it should be noted that in the normal course quotations and allusions within even lengthy passages quoted from some other source are not cited.)

God and our neighbour. So pure both from superstition and error is the religion which has lately spread in this nation.

9. It is likewise *rational.* It is as pure from *enthusiasm* as from superstition. It is true the contrary has been continually affirmed. But to affirm is one thing; to
5 prove is another. Who will prove that it is *enthusiasm* to love God? Yea, to love him with all our heart? Who is able to make good this charge against the love of all mankind? (I do but just touch on the general heads.) But if you cannot make it good, own this religion to be sober, manly, rational, divine.

10. It is also pure from *bigotry.* Those who hold it are not bigoted to *opinions.*
10 They would hold right opinions; but they are peculiarly cautious not to rest the weight of Christianity there. They have no such overgrown fondness for any opinions as to think those alone will make them Christians, or to confine their affection or esteem to those that agree with them therein. Nor are they bigoted to any particular branch, even of practical religion. They are not attached to one
15 point more than another; they aim at uniform, universal obedience. They contend for nothing circumstantial as if it were essential to religion, but for everything in its own order.

11. They dread that *bitter zeal,* that spirit of *persecution,* which has so often accompanied the spirit of reformation. They do not approve of using any kind of
20 violence, on any pretence, in matters of religion. They allow no method of bringing any to the knowledge of the truth, except the methods of reason and persuasion. And their practice is consistent with their profession. They do not in fact hinder their dependents from worshipping God, in every respect, according to their own conscience.

25 But if these things are so, may we not well say, 'What hath God wrought!'[35] For such a work, if we consider the *extensiveness* of it, the *swiftness* with which it has spread, the *depth* of the religion so swiftly diffused, and its *purity* from all corrupt mixtures, we must acknowledge, cannot easily be paralleled in all these concurrent
30 circumstances by anything that is found in the English annals since Christianity was first planted in this island.[36]

12. It may throw considerable light upon the nature of this work to mention one circumstance more attending the present revival of religion, which I apprehend is quite peculiar to it. I do
35 not remember to have either seen, heard, or read of anything parallel. It cannot be denied that there have been several considerable revivals of religion in England since the Reformation. But the generality of the English nation were little profited thereby; because they that were the subjects of those revivals,
40 preachers as well as people, soon separated from the Established Church, and formed themselves into a distinct sect. So did the

[35] See JWJ, Aug. 8, 1779, for Wesley's account of his last night spent in the Foundery; note his repetition of this text from Num. 23:23.
[36] See §4, above, and n.

Presbyterians first, afterwards the Independents, the Anabaptists, and the Quakers. And after this was done they did scarce any good, except to their own little body. As they chose to separate from the Church, so the people remaining therein separated from them, and generally contracted a prejudice against them. But these were immensely the greatest number; so that by that unhappy separation the hope of a general, national reformation was totally cut off.

13. But it is not so in the present revival of religion. The Methodists (so termed) know their calling. They weighed the matter at first, and upon mature deliberation determined to continue in the Church. Since that time they have not wanted temptations of every kind to alter their resolution. They have heard abundance said upon the subject, perhaps all that can be said. They have read the writings of the most eminent pleaders for separation, both in the last and present century. They have spent several days in a general conference upon this very question, 'Is it *expedient* (supposing, not granting, that it is *lawful*) to separate from the established Church?'[37] But still they could see no sufficient cause to depart from their first resolution. So that their fixed purpose is—let the clergy or laity use them well or ill—by the grace of God to endure all things, to hold on their even course, and to continue in the Church, maugre[38] men or devils, unless God permits them to be thrust out.

14. Near twenty years ago, immediately after their solemn consultation on the subject, a clergyman who had heard the whole said with great earnestness: 'In the name of God, let nothing move you to recede from this resolution. God is with you of a truth; and so he will be, while you continue in the Church. But whenever the Methodists leave the Church, God will leave them.'[39] Lord, what is man! In a few months after, Mr. Ingham

---

[37] Agitation among the Methodists for a separation from the Church of England had begun early but never reached crisis proportions until the Conference at Leeds in 1755. Wesley anticipated this crisis with a MS tract (still extant) entitled, 'Ought We to Separate from the Church of England?'; it may actually have been read at the Conference. Shortly thereafter, he revised it for publication as item No. 13 in the collection entitled *A Preservative against Unsettled Notions in Religion*, 1758.

[38] I.e., 'despite' or 'notwithstanding'; cf. *OED*.

[39] I.e., Benjamin Ingham, whose separation followed closely on the heels of this warning; the Conference session was in May 1755, and in Leeds rather than London (as scheduled) mainly for the convenience of William Grimshaw of Haworth, Wesley's chief clerical ally in the north; cf. Baker, *William Grimshaw*, pp. 234-38. The Inghamite separation began in Dec., but the movement failed to flourish.

himself left the Church, and turned all the societies under his care into congregations of Independents. And what was the event? The same that he had foretold. They swiftly mouldered into nothing.

5   Some years after a person of honour told me: 'This is the peculiar glory of the Methodists. However convenient it might be, they will not on any account or pretence whatever form a distinct sect or party. Let no one rob you of this glorying.'[40] I trust none will as long as I live. But the giver of this advice entirely
10 forgot it in a very short time, and has almost ever since been labouring to form Independent congregations.

15. This has occasioned many to ask, 'Why do you say the Methodists form no distinct party? That they do not leave the Church? Are there not thousands of Methodists who have in fact
15 left the Church? Who never attend the Church service? Never receive the Lord's Supper there? Nay, who speak against the Church, even with bitterness, both in public and private? Yea, who appoint and frequent meetings for divine service at the same hour? How then can you affirm that the Methodists do not leave
20 the Church?'

I am glad of so public an opportunity of explaining this; in order to which it will be necessary to look back some years. The Methodists at Oxford were all one body,[41] and as it were one soul, zealous for the religion of the Bible, of the primitive church, and
25 in consequence of the Church of England; as they believed it to come nearer the scriptural and primitive plan than any other national church upon earth.

When my brother and I returned from Georgia we were in the same sentiments. And at that time we and our friends were the
30 only persons to whom that innocent name was affixed. Thus far, therefore, all the Methodists were firm to the Church of England.

16. But a good man who met with us when we were at Oxford, while he was absent from us, conversed much with Dissenters, and contracted strong prejudices against the Church. I mean Mr.

[40] Cf. 'Thoughts upon a Late Phenomenon', *AM* (Jan. 1789), XII.47-48: 'This is a new thing in the world: this is the peculiar glory of the people called Methodists. In spite of all manner of temptations, they will not separate from the Church.' The 'person of honour' mentioned here may have been Henry Venn; cf. Curnock's note in JWJ, V.279 (Venn's connection with the founding of the Highfield Independent Chapel in Huddersfield), and Wesley's letter to Thomas Adam, July 19, 1768.
[41] See above, I.2; also No. 53, *On the Death of George Whitefield*, III.2 and n.

Whitefield. And not long after he totally separated from *us*.[42] In some years William Cudworth[43] and several others separated from him, and turned Independents; as did Mr. Maxfield[44] and a few more after separating from us. Lastly, a school was set up near Trevecka in Wales; and almost all who were educated there 5 (except those that were ordained, and some of them too), as they disclaimed all connection with the Methodists, so they disclaimed the Church also.[45] Nay, they spoke of it upon all occasions with exquisite bitterness and contempt.

Now let every impartial person judge whether we are 10 accountable for any of these! None of these have any manner of connection with the original Methodists. They are branches broken off from the tree: if they break from the Church also, we are not accountable for it.

These therefore cannot make our glorying void,[46] that we do 15 not, will not, form any separate sect, but from principle remain what we always have been, true members of the Church of England.

17. Brethren, I presume the greater part of you also are members of the Church of England. So at least you are called; but 20 you are not so indeed unless you are witnesses of the religion above described. And are you really such? Judge not one another;

[42] Cf. *A Short History of Methodism* (1765), §11. Whitefield contradicts this charge of initiating the schism. His version is that Wesley's publication of *Free Grace* (see No. 110) caused the open break that was never really healed thereafter. Cf. *George Whitefield's Journals* (The Banner of Truth Trust, 1960), Appendix II, pp. 561-88; see also Seymour, *Countess of Huntingdon*, I.87-88, 118, 474.

[43] With James Relly, William Cudworth led the antinomian wing of the Revival; they turned Wesley's doctrine of perfection-in-process into one of *guiltless* perfection (cf. intro. on the triple essay on Law and Grace, Nos. 34–36). They are the targets of Wesley's two *Dialogues between an Antinomian and his Friend* and also his *Blow at the Root; Or, Christ Stabbed in the House of his Friends*, 1762. See also *A Short History of Methodism*, §12.

[44] Thomas Maxfield, the first lay preacher accepted by Wesley as an assistant. His first endorsement in this office came to Wesley from the Countess of Huntingdon (cf. Seymour, I.32-35), but it was Susanna Wesley's direct intervention on Maxfield's behalf that decided the issue in her son's mind (cf. Moore, *Wesley*, I.505-6). Maxfield was later ordained by Dr. William Bernard, Bishop of Derry, and in 1763 (with George Bell) he separated from Wesley in a bitter schism. He died in 1784. See JWJ, Jan. 23–Feb. 7, 1763, for Wesley's account of the Maxfield schism; cf. *A Short History of Methodism*, §14; and Charles Atmore, *The Methodist Memorial*, pp. 266-69.

[45] For a more sympathetic account of the 'history of the college at Trevecka' in South Wales, cf. Seymour, II.78-86. It was 'founded by the Countess of Huntingdon for the instruction of candidates for the Christian ministry', and its first principal was John William Fletcher. Its alumni 'might enter into the ministry either in the Established Church of England or among Protestants of any other denomination'.

[46] See 1 Cor. 9:15.

but every man look into his own bosom. How stands the matter in your own breast? Examine your conscience before God. Are *you* an happy partaker of this scriptural, this truly primitive religion? Are you a witness of the religion of love? Are you a lover of God
5 and all mankind? Does your heart glow with gratitude to the Giver of every good and perfect gift?[47] The Father of the spirits of all flesh, who giveth you life, and breath, and all things?[48] Who hath given you his Son, his only Son, that you 'might not perish, but have everlasting life'?[49] Is your soul warm with benevolence to all
10 mankind? Do you long to have all men virtuous and happy? And does the constant tenor of your life and conversation bear witness of this? Do you 'love, not in word only, but in deed and in truth'?[50] Do you persevere in the 'work of faith, and the labour of love'?[51] Do you 'walk in love, as Christ also loved us, and gave himself for
15 us'?[52] Do you, as you have time, 'do good unto all men'?[53] And in as high a degree as you are able? 'Whosoever' thus 'doeth the will of my Father which is in heaven, the same is my brother, and sister, and mother.'[54] Whosoever thou art whose heart is herein as my
20 heart, give me thine hand.[55] Come and let us magnify the Lord together,[56] and labour to promote his kingdom upon earth. Let us join hearts and hands in this blessed work, in striving to bring glory to God in the highest, by establishing peace and goodwill among men[57] to the uttermost of our power. First let our hearts be
25 joined herein; let us unite our wishes and prayers; let our whole soul pant after a general revival of pure religion and undefiled,[58] of the restoration of the image of God, pure love, in every child of man. Then let us endeavour to promote in our several stations this scriptural, primitive religion; let us with all diligence diffuse
30 the religion of love among all we have any intercourse with; let us provoke all men, not to enmity and contention, but to love and to good works;[59] always remembering those deep words (God engrave them on all our hearts!), 'God is love; and he that dwelleth in love, dwelleth in God, and God in him.'[60]

---

[47] See Jas. 1:17.
[48] See Acts 17:25.
[49] Cf. John 3:16.
[50] Cf. 1 John 3:18.
[51] 1 Thess. 1:3.
[52] Cf. Eph. 5:2.
[53] Gal. 6:10.
[54] Matt. 12:50.
[55] See 2 Kgs. 10:15.
[56] See Ps. 34:3.
[57] See Luke 2:14.
[58] Jas. 1:27.
[59] See Heb. 10:24.
[60] 1 John 4:16.

SOME

ACCOUNT

OF

THE LATE WORK OF GOD

IN

North-America,

IN A

SER.MON

ON

EZEKIEL i. 16.

By JOHN WESLEY, M.A.

LONDON: Printed by R. HAWES,

And sold at the Foundery in *Moorfields*, and at the
Rev. Mr. *Wesley's* Preaching-Houses, in Town
and Country. 1778. [*Price* Two-Pence.]

THE LATE WORK OF GOD IN NORTH AMERICA

AN INTRODUCTORY COMMENT

This sermon was still another of Wesley's tracts in opposition to the American Revolution—here viewed as a temporary hindrance to 'the work of God' that had been flourishing in the New World up until the outbreak of the revolt. It was written after all the preachers he had sent to the colonies had fled them, with the exception of Francis Asbury, who was waiting out the war in Maryland. Even though its date falls after the revolution's turning point (i.e., Burgoyne's surrender at Saratoga and the interventions of the French and Spanish), the possibility that the revolution might actually succeed seems not yet to have dawned on Wesley. In the sermon, then, he seeks to review the background of the war and to look beyond it to the providential end in which God would still make the wrath of men to praise him.

*It should, of course, be remembered that in the early stages of the American protests against their alleged ill usage at the hands of the British government Wesley had expressed at least some sympathy with what he believed to be the legitimate grievances of the Americans. His point was that they deserved to be treated as all other subjects of the British Crown and under the same law. He had written letters to this effect to both the Earl of Dartmouth, Secretary of State to the Colonies (June 14, 1775), and to Lord North, King George's 'prime minister' without that title (June 15, 1775). If John Hampson's account is to be credited, Wesley's preaching had been openly critical—'at that period he was decidedly adverse to the war.' But when the clamour for 'Independence' increased, Wesley changed his mind. Hampson speaks of his 'conversion' on this point as 'instantaneous . . . , absolute, and complete' (*Memoirs, III.135*).*

The sermon itself is a reflection upon the doctrine of providence in history; Ezekiel's image of concentric wheels serves as a metaphor for the situation in America and of its prospects. Wesley's explanation of the American revolt is in terms of a concurrence of a spirit of arrogance born of affluence and self-indulgence and of the false spirit of 'independency'. The pending defeat of the Americans will illustrate 'the adorable providence of God' (II.13) and will prove to be 'the remedy' for their 'disease'. His closing vision is of 'a happy land' freed from its present 'curse' of the spirit of 'independency' and thus richly blessed with the recovery of 'real, legal liberty, . . . true British liberty'.

The text here is based on the first edition of 1778; there were two further editions in the same year. There is no record that Wesley ever preached this sermon or any other from Ezek. 1:16. For a brief publishing history and a list of substantive variant readings, see Appendix, Vol. 4, and Bibliog, *No. 398. Its full title was presumably supplied by Wesley:* Some Account of the Late Work of God in North America, in a Sermon on Ezekiel 1:16. *In Wesley's catalogues, however, from its first appearance in 1781 until Wesley's death, it was entitled 'A Wheel within a Wheel'* (Bibliog, *Nos. 767-74).*

The Late Work of God in North America

Ezekiel 1:16

The appearance was as it were a wheel in the middle of a wheel.

1. Whatever may be the primary meaning of this mysterious passage of Scripture, many serious Christians in all ages have 5 applied it in a secondary sense, to the manner wherein the adorable providence of God usually works in governing the world.[1] They have judged this expression manifestly to allude to the complicated wheels of his providence, adapting one event to another, and working one thing by means of another. In the whole 10 process of this, there is an endless variety of wheels within wheels. But they are frequently so disposed and complicated that we cannot understand them at first sight. Nay, we can seldom fully comprehend them till they are explained by the event.

2. Perhaps no age ever afforded a more striking instance of this 15 kind than the present does, in the dispensations of divine providence with respect to our colonies in North America. In order to see this clearly, let us endeavour, according to the measure of our weak understanding,

---

[1] Cf. Edmund Burke, *Philosophical Inquiry into the Origins of Our Ideas of the Sublime and the Beautiful* (1756), I.228: 'the adorable wisdom of God in his works'.

First, to trace each wheel apart; and,
Secondly, to consider both as they relate to and answer each other.

I. And, first, we are to trace each wheel apart.

5   It is by no means my design to give a particular detail of the late transactions in America; but barely to give a simple and naked deduction of a few well-known facts.

I know this is a very delicate subject, and that it is difficult, if not impossible, to treat it in such a manner as not to offend any;
10 particularly those who are warmly attached to either party. But I would not willingly offend; and shall therefore studiously avoid all keen and reproachful language, and use the softest terms I can without either betraying or disguising the truth.

1. In the year 1736 it pleased God to begin a work of grace in
15 the newly planted colony of Georgia, then the southernmost of our settlements on the continent of America. To those English who had settled there the year before were then added a body of Moravians, so called; and a larger body who had been expelled from Germany by the Archbishop of Salzburg. These were men
20 truly fearing God and working righteousness. At the same time there began an awakening among the English, both at Savannah and Frederica; many inquiring what they must do to be saved,[2] and 'bringing forth fruits meet for repentance'.[3]

2. In the same year there broke out a wonderful work of God in
25 several parts of New England.[4] It began in Northampton, and in a little time appeared in the adjoining towns. A particular and beautiful account of this was published by Mr. Edwards, minister of Northampton.[5] Many sinners were deeply convinced of sin, and many truly converted to God. I suppose there had been no
30 instance in America of so swift and deep a work of grace for an hundred years before; nay, or perhaps since the English settled there.

---

[2] See Acts 16:30.   [3] Cf. Matt. 3:8.

[4] Actually, this had begun in 1733 and had been in full swing for two years before the Wesleys arrived in Georgia. Wesley would not have known of the even earlier 'awakenings' in 'the middle colonies' (1720s) led by the Tennents (father and son) and Theodorus Freylinghuysen; cf. Robert T. Handy, *A History of the Churches in the U.S. and Canada* (New York, Oxford Univ. Press, 1977), ch. III.

[5] Jonathan Edwards (1703–58). See his *Faithful Narrative of the Surprizing Work of God in the Conversion of Many Hundred Souls in Northhampton . . . in a letter to Dr. [Benjamin] Colman* (n.p., n.d.; reprinted in London, 1736). For its crucial impact on Wesley, cf. JWJ, Oct. 9, 1738; see also his abridged edn., 1744 (*Bibliog*, No. 85).

3. The following year the work of God spread by degrees from New England towards the south. At the same time it advanced by slow degrees from Georgia towards the north. In a few souls it deepened likewise; and some of them witnessed a good confession, both in life and in death.

4. In the year 1738 Mr. Whitefield came over to Georgia with a design to assist me in preaching, either to the English or the Indians.[6] But as I was embarked for England before he arrived, he preached to the English altogether, first in Georgia, to which his chief service was due, then in South and North Carolina, and afterwards in the intermediate provinces, till he came to New England. And all men owned that God was with him, wheresoever he went; giving a general call, to high and low, rich and poor, to 'repent, and believe the gospel'.[7] Many were not disobedient to the heavenly calling;[8] they did repent and believe the gospel. And by his ministry a line of communication was formed, quite from Georgia to New England.

5. Within a few years he made several more voyages to America, and took several more journeys through the provinces. And in every journey he found fresh reason to bless God, who still prospered the work of his hands, there being more and more in all the provinces who found his word to be 'the power of God unto salvation'.[9]

6. But the last journey he made he acknowledged to some of his friends that he had much sorrow and heaviness in his heart on account of multitudes who for a time ran well, but afterwards 'drew back unto perdition'.[10] Indeed in a few years the far greater part of those who had once 'received the word with joy',[11] yea, had 'escaped the corruption that is in the world',[12] were 'entangled again, and overcome'.[13] Some were like those who 'received the

---

[6] Cf. JWJ, Jan. 29, 1738, for a slightly different account of this sequence: 'Toward evening was a calm; but in the night a strong north wind brought us safe into the Downs [i.e., near Deal and Gravesend, England]. The day before, Mr. Whitefield had sailed out [for Georgia], neither of us knowing anything of the other.' Cf. *A Letter to the Rev. Mr. John Wesley* (*George Whitefield's Journals*, pp. 572-73) for an actual correspondence between the two at this time and Wesley's order (by divine lot) that Whitefield should return to England forthwith.

[7] Mark 1:15.   [8] See Acts 26:19.
[9] Rom. 1:16.
[10] Cf. Heb. 10:39.
[11] Cf. Luke 8:13.
[12] 2 Pet. 1:4.
[13] Cf. 2 Pet. 2:20.

seed on stony ground',[14] which 'in time of temptation withered away'.[15] Others were like those who 'received it among thorns':[16] the thorns soon 'sprang up and choked it';[17] insomuch that he found exceeding few who 'brought forth fruit to perfection'.[18] A
5 vast majority had entirely 'turned back from the holy command-ment once delivered to them'.[19]

7. And what wonder! For it was a true saying, which was common in the ancient church, 'The soul and the body make a man, and the spirit and discipline make a Christian.'[20] But those
10 who were more or less affected by Mr. Whitefield's preaching had no discipline at all. They had no shadow of discipline; nothing of the kind. They were formed into no societies. They had no Christian connection with each other, nor were ever taught to watch over each others' souls. So that if any fell into
15 lukewarmness, or even into sin, he had none to lift him up; he might fall lower and lower, yea, into hell, if he would, for who regarded it?

8. Things were in this state when about eleven years ago I received several letters from America giving a melancholy
20 account of the state of religion in most of the colonies, and earnestly entreating that some of our preachers would 'come over and help them'.[21] It was believed they might confirm many that were weak or wavering, and lift up many that were fallen; nay, and that they would see more fruit of their labours in America than
25 they had done either in England or Ireland.

9. This was considered at large in our yearly Conference at Bristol, in the year 1767.[22] And two of our preachers willingly offered themselves, viz., Richard Boardman[23] and Joseph

---

[14] Cf. Matt. 13:20.   [15] Cf. Matt. 13:6.   [16] Cf. Matt. 13:22.
[17] Cf. Luke 8:7.   [18] Cf. Luke 8:14.   [19] Cf. 2 Pet. 2:21.

[20] π; But see No. 122, 'Causes of the Inefficacy of Christianity', §7; and cf. JWJ, Aug. 17, 1750; and letters to William Church, Oct. 13, 1778; and to Adam Clarke, Jan. 3, 1787.

[21] Cf. Acts 16:9. Wesley had received letters from Whitefield, Samuel Davies (among others), but most important of all, from Thomas Taylor (Apr. 11, 1768), a late arrival from England, converted on shipboard and newly associated with the Methodists at John Street, New York. For the text and its history, see Baker, 'Early American Methodism: A Key Document', *Methodist History*, Vol. III, No. 2 (Jan. 1965), pp. 3-15; and *From Wesley to Asbury*, pp. 70-83.

[22] Actually, in 1768. After due consideration, the question was deferred for a year (during which time Taylor's letter, now printed, was circulated among the preachers) and then brought up again at the Leeds Conference of 1769. The result was the appointment of the two Yorkshiremen, Boardman and Pilmore.

[23] An itinerant in the Connexion since 1763; he served in America for less than five years, returned to England in 1774, and died in 1782.

Pilmore.[24] They were men well reported of by all, and (we believed) fully qualified for the work. Accordingly, after a few days spent in London, they cheerfully went over. They laboured first in Philadelphia and New York, afterwards in many other places. And everywhere God was eminently with them, and gave 5 them to see much fruit of their labour. What was wanting before was now supplied. Those who were desirous to save their souls were no longer a rope of sand,[25] but clave to one another, and began to watch over each other in love. Societies were formed, and Christian discipline introduced in all its branches. Within a 10 few years after, several more of the preachers were willing to go and assist them.[26] And God raised up many natives of the country who were glad to act in connexion with them, till there were two and twenty Travelling Preachers in America, who kept their circuits as regularly as those in England.[27]   15

10. The work of God then not only spread wider, particularly in North Carolina, Maryland, Virginia, Pennsylvania, and the Jerseys, but sunk abundantly deeper than ever it had done before. So that at the beginning of the late troubles there were three thousand souls connected together in religious societies, and a 20 great number of these witnessed that the Son of God hath power on earth to forgive sin.[28]

[24] Recalled to England in 1774, but later returned to America, was ordained as priest in the newly formed Protestant Episcopal Church (1785), and served in the Philadelphia area until his death in 1825.

[25] A proverb used in the sense of undertaking an impossible task. Cf. Aristeides 2.309-10, τὸ ἐκ τῆς ψάμμου σχοινίον πλέκειν; also Lucius Junius Moderatus Columella (fl. A.D. 50), *Rei Rusticae (On Agriculture)*, Bk. X, pref. §4: '. . . although there are many branches of the subject, so to speak, about which we can find something to say, they are, nevertheless, as unimportant as the imperceptible grains of sand of which, according to the Greek saying, it is impossible to make a rope' (Loeb, 408:5). Cf. also Irenaeus, *Against Heresies*, I.viii.1, (*ANF* I.326); Francis Bacon, *Fromus*, 778; George Herbert, *The Temple*, 'The Collar', l. 22; Samuel Butler, *Hudibras*, Pt. I, Canto I, l. 158. The *OED* cites Gataker, *Transubst.* 152 (1624), and Clarendon, *Contempl.* Ps. Tracts (1727), 583. Wesley frequently used the phrase to describe polities other than his own; cf. *A Farther Appeal*, Pt. III, III.16 (11:301 in this edn.); *A Plain Account of the People called Methodists*, I.11; his letter to Mr. T. H., Dec. 12, 1760; and to the Travelling Preachers, Aug. 4, 1769.

[26] Note the absence, here and elsewhere, of any reference to Francis Asbury, who had volunteered for America in 1771.

[27] The 'travelling preachers' listed in the *Minutes* were: seventeen in 1774, twenty in 1775, twenty-four in 1776. But there are discrepancies in the sources from which these lists were compiled, and some of the men (e.g., Joseph Yearbry, William Glendenning, Robert Strawbridge) were not 'in connexion with Mr. Wesley'.

[28] See Matt. 9:6. The Conference at Philadelphia (May 17, 1775) reported a total membership of 3,148.

11. But now it was that a bar appeared in the way, a grand hindrance to the progress of religion. The immense trade of America, greater in proportion than even that of the mother country, brought in an immense flow of wealth; which was also
5   continually increasing. Hence both merchants and tradesmen of various kinds accumulated money without end; and rose from indigence to opulent fortunes quicker than any could do in Europe. Riches poured in upon them as a flood, and treasures were heaped up as the sand of the sea. And hence naturally arose
10 unbounded *plenty*, of all the necessaries, conveniencies, yea, and superfluities of life.[29]
      12. One general consequence of this was *pride*. The more riches they acquired, the more they were regarded by their neighbours as men of weight and importance. And they would
15 naturally see themselves in at least as fair a light as their neighbours saw them. And accordingly, as they rose in the world, they rose in their opinion of themselves. As it is generally allowed,

> A thousand pound supplies
> The want of twenty thousand qualities.[30]

20 So the richer they grew, the more admiration they gained, and the more applause they received. Wealth then bringing in more applause, of course brought in more pride, till they really thought themselves as much wiser as they were wealthier than their neighbours.
25   13. Another natural consequence of wealth was *luxury*, particularly in food. We are apt to imagine nothing can exceed the luxurious living which now prevails in Great Britain and Ireland. But alas! what is this to that which lately prevailed in Philadelphia, and other parts of North America? A merchant or middling
30 tradesman there kept a table equal to that of a nobleman in England; entertaining his guests with ten, twelve, yea, sometimes twenty dishes of meat at a meal! And this was so far from being blamed by anyone that it was applauded as generosity and hospitality.
35   14. And is not *idleness* naturally joined with 'fullness of bread'?[31] Doth not *sloth* easily spring from luxury?[32] It did so here in an

---

[29] An obvious hyperbole in support of the thesis in I.12; see also No. 30, 'Sermon on the Mount, X', §26 and n.
[30] π; See also No. 108, 'On Riches', II.4.   [31] Ezek. 16:49.
[32] Cf. No. 111, *National Sins and Miseries*, II.6 and n.

eminent degree; such sloth as is scarce named in England. Persons in the bloom of youth, and in perfect health, could hardly bear to put on their own clothes. The *slave* must be called to do this, and that, and everything: it is too great labour for the master or mistress! It is a wonder they would be at the pains of putting 5 meat into their own mouths! Why did they not imitate the lordly lubbers in China,[33] who are fed by a slave standing on each side?

15. Who can wonder if *sloth* alone beget *wantonness?* Has it not always had this effect? Was it not said near two thousand years ago,   10

> *Quaeritur, Aegysthus quare sit factus adulter?*
> *In promptu causa est; desidiosus erat.*[34]

And when sloth and luxury are joined together, will they not produce an abundant offspring? This they certainly have done in these parts. I was surprised a few years ago at a letter I received 15 from Philadelphia, wherein were (nearly) these words: 'You think the women in England (many of them, I mean) do not abound in chastity. But yet the generality of your women, if compared with ours, might almost pass for vestal virgins.' Now this complication of pride, luxury, sloth, and wantonness, naturally arising from 20 vast wealth and plenty, was the grand hindrance to the spreading of true religion through the cities of North America.

II. Let us now see the other wheel of divine providence.

1. It may reasonably be supposed that the colonies in New England had from their very beginning an hankering after 25 independency. It could not be expected to be otherwise, considering their families, their education, their relations, and the connections they had formed before they left their native country. They were farther inclined to it by the severe and unjust treatment which many of them had met with in England. This 30 might well create in them a fear lest they should meet with the like again, a jealousy of their governors, and a desire of shaking off that dependence to which they were never thoroughly reconciled.

---

[33] A stereotype derived from Jean Baptiste DuHalde's popular *General History of China, containing a geographical . . . and physical description of the Empire of China, Chinese Tartary, Corea and Thibet . . .* , translated from the French by R. Brookes (1736), in 4 vols, frequently cited in the literature of the times. See Samuel Johnson's extract in *Gent's Mag.* (1742), 320-23, 353-57, 484-86; see also No. 103, 'What is Man? Ps. 8:3-4', I.2.

[34] 'If it be asked why Aegisthus came to be an adulterer, the answer is easy: he was a sluggard' (i.e., slothful); cf. Ovid, *Remedia Amoris (The Remedies of Love)*, ll. 161-62.

The same spirit they communicated to their children, from whom it descended to the present generation. Nor could it be effaced by all the favours and benefits which they continually received from the English government.

5   2. This spirit generally prevailed, especially in Boston, as early as the year 1737. In that year my brother, being detained there some time,[35] was greatly surprised to hear almost in every company, whether of ministers, gentlemen, merchants, or common people, where anything of the kind was mentioned: 'We
10 must be independent; we will be independent. We will bear the English yoke no longer. We will be our own governors.' This appeared to be even then the general desire of the people; although it is not probable that there was at that time any formed design. No; they could not be so vain as to think they were able to
15 stand alone against the power of Great Britain.

    3. A gentleman who was there in the following year observed the same spirit in every corner of the town: 'Why should these English blockheads rule over *us!*' was then the common language. And as one encouraged another herein, the spirit of independen-
20 cy rose higher and higher, till it began to spread into the other colonies bordering upon New England. Nevertheless the fear of their troublesome neighbours, then in possession of Canada, kept them within bounds, and for a time prevented the flame from breaking out. But when the English had removed that fear from
25 them, when Canada was ceded to the King of Great Britain, the desire then ripened into a formed design.[36] Only a convenient opportunity was wanting.

    4. It was not long before that opportunity appeared. The Stamp Act was passed and sent over to America.[37] The malcontents saw
30 and pressed their advantage. They represented it as a common

[35] Charles Wesley spent a month in Boston en route from Charleston to London; cf. CWJ, Sept. 24–Oct. 25, 1736.

[36] In the debate over a peace treaty with France to conclude 'The Seven Years' War', it was argued against Pitt that 'the American colonists, once the French danger on their border was removed, might become too independent and even secede.' But Pitt prevailed, and the Treaty of Paris was signed Feb. 10, 1763; cf. Williams, *The Whig Supremacy, 1714–1760*, pp. 345-49.

[37] A controversial tax, designed by Lord North to raise revenue from the sale of stamps to be affixed to legal documents, imposed by Parliament Mar. 22, 1765; it was withdrawn in Mar. 1766, in the face of a public clamour that revived an old independent slogan, 'No taxation without representation;' cf. C. G. Robertson, *England Under the Hanoverians*, pp. 233-38; see also Samuel Eliot Morison, *The Oxford History of the American People* (New York, Oxford Univ. Press, 1965), pp. 185-88.

cause; and by proper emissaries spread their own spirit through another and another colony. By inflammatory papers of every kind they stirred up the minds of the people. They vilified first the English Ministry, representing them one and all as the veriest wretches alive, void of all honesty, honour, and humanity. By the 5 same methods they next inflamed the people in general against the British Parliament, representing them as the most infamous villains upon earth, as a company of base, unprincipled hirelings. But still they affected to reverence the King, and spoke very honourably of him. Not long; a few months after they treated *him* 10 in the same manner they had done his ministers and his Parliament.

5. Matters being now, it was judged, in sufficient forwardness, an association was formed between the northern and southern colonies; both took up arms, and constituted a supreme power 15 which they termed 'The Congress'.[38] But still they affirmed their whole design was to secure their liberty; and even to insinuate that they aimed at anything more was said to be quite cruel and unjust. But in a little time they threw off the mask, and boldly asserted their own independence. Accordingly, Dr. Withers- 20 poon,[39] President of the College in New Jersey, in his address to the Congress (added to a Fast Sermon published by him, August 3, 1776) uses the following words: 'It appears now, in the clearest manner, that till very lately those who seemed to take the part of America in the British Parliament never did it on American 25 principles. They either did not understand, or were not willing to admit, *the extent of our claim.* Even the great Lord Chatham's Bill for reconciliation would not have been accepted here, and *did not materially differ from what the Ministry would have consented* to.'[40]

[38] The Stamp Act Congress—the first spontaneous movement toward colonial union that came from the Americans themselves—met in New York City, Oct. 7, 1765; cf. Morison, *op. cit.*, p. 187.

[39] John Witherspoon (1723–94), a Scottish Presbyterian minister who emigrated from Paisley to Princeton in 1768 to become president of The College of New Jersey (later, Princeton University). He was a delegate to the First Continental Congress in Philadelphia (Sept. 5, 1774), a signer of the Declaration of Independence and an influential statesman through the Revolution and in the formative years of the new nation.

[40] Cf. *The Dominion of Providence over the Passions of Men. A Sermon Preached at Princeton on the 17th of May, 1776. Being the General Fast appointed by the Congress through the United Colonies. To which is added, An Address to the Natives of Scotland residing in America* (Philadelphia, Aitken, 1776), p. 63. Cf. William B. Sprague, *Annals of the American Pulpit* (New York, Robert Carter and Brothers, 1859), III.293. That Witherspoon's words bespeak his politics (and those of the Congress) is clear enough; what is not clear is whether he addressed them directly to the Congress itself.

Here it is avowed that their claim was *independency;* and that they would accept of nothing less.

6. By this open and avowed defection from, and defiance of, their mother country (whether it was defensible or not is another question) at least nine parts in ten of their immense trade to Europe, Asia, Africa, and other parts of America were cut off at one stroke. In lieu of this they gained at first perhaps an hundred thousand pounds a year by their numerous privateers. But even then, this was upon the whole no gain at all, for they lost as many ships as they took. Afterwards they took fewer and fewer; and in the meantime they lost four or five millions yearly (perhaps six or seven) which their trade brought them in. What was the necessary consequence of this? Why, that as the fountain of their wealth was dammed up, the streams of it must run lower and lower, till they were wholly exhausted. So that at present these provinces are no richer than the poorest parts either of Scotland or Ireland.

7. Plenty declined in the same proportion as wealth, till universal scarcity took place. In a short time there was everywhere felt a deep want, not only of the superfluities, not only of the common conveniencies, but even of the necessaries of life. Wholesome food was not to be procured but at a very advanced price. Decent apparel was not to be had, not even in the large towns. Not only velvets and silks, and fashionable ornaments (which might well be spared), but even linen and woollen clothes were not to be purchased at any price whatsoever.

8. Thus have we observed each of these wheels apart: on the one hand, trade, wealth, pride,[41] luxury, sloth, and wantonness spreading far and wide through the American provinces; on the other, the spirit of independency diffusing itself from north to south. Let us now observe how each of these wheels relates to, and answers the other; how the wise and gracious providence of God uses one to check the course of the other, and even employs (if so strong an expression may be allowed) Satan to cast out Satan! Probably that subtle spirit hoped, by adding to all those other vices the spirit of independency, to have overturned the whole work of God, as well as the British Government, in North America. But he that sitteth in heaven laughed him to scorn,[42] and took the wise in his own craftiness.[43] By means of this very spirit,

---

[41] Cf. No. 14, *The Repentance of Believers,* I.3 and n.
[42] See Ps. 2:4.   [43] See Job 5:13.

there is reason to believe, God will overturn every hindrance of that work.

9. We have seen how by the breaking out of this spirit, in open defiance of the British Government, an effectual check was given to the trade of those colonies. They themselves, by a wonderful 5 stroke of policy, threw up the whole trade of their mother country and all its dependencies! Made an Act that no British ship should enter into any of their harbours![44] Nay, they fitted out numberless privateers which seized upon all the British ships they could find. The King's ships seized an equal number of theirs. So their 10 foreign trade too was brought almost to nothing. Their riches died away with their trade, especially as they had no internal resources; the flower of their youth, before employed in husbandry, being now drawn off into their armies, so that the most fruitful lands were of no use, none being left to till the 15 ground. And when wealth fled away (as was before observed) so did plenty too; abundance of all things being succeeded by scarcity of all things.

10. The wheel now began to move within the wheel. The trade and wealth of the Americans failing, the grand incentives of pride 20 failed also; for few admire or flatter the poor. And being deserted by most of their admirers, they did not altogether so much admire themselves; especially when they found, upon the trial, that they had grievously miscalculated their own strength, which they had made no doubt would be sufficient to carry all before it. It is true 25 many of them still exalted themselves; but others were truly and deeply humbled.

11. Poverty, and scarcity consequent upon it, struck still more directly at the root of their *luxury*. There was no place now for that immoderate superfluity either of food or apparel. They sought no 30 more, and could seldom obtain, so much as plain food, sufficient to sustain nature. And they were content if they could procure coarse apparel to keep them clean and warm. Thus they were reduced to the same condition their forefathers were in when the providence of God brought them into this country. They were 35

---

[44] On Oct. 20, 1774, the Continental Congress, in reaction to laws passed by the British Parliament following the Boston Tea Party (the so-called Coercive or Intolerable Acts), adopted a 'non-importation, non-exportation, non-consumption agreement, virtually cutting off imports from Britain after Dec. 1, 1774, and exports to Britain after Sept. 10, 1775, if by that time the Coercive Acts had not been repealed'; cf. Morison, *Oxford History of the American People*, p. 208.

nearly in the same outward circumstances. Happy, if they were likewise in the same spirit!

12. Poverty and want struck at the root of *sloth* also. It was now no time to say, 'A little more sleep, a little more slumber, a little more folding of the hands to rest.'[45] If a man would not work now, it was plain he could not eat.[46] All the pains he could take were little enough to procure the bare necessaries of life: seeing, on the one hand, so few of them remained—their own armies having swept away all before them—and, on the other, what remained bore so high a price that exceeding few were able to purchase them.

13. Thus by the adorable providence of God the main hindrances of his work are removed. And in how wonderful a manner! Such as it never could have entered into the heart of man to conceive. Those hindrances had been growing up and continually increasing for many years. What God foresaw would prove the remedy grew up with the disease; and when the disease was come to its height, then only began to operate. Immense trade, wealth, and plenty begot and nourished proportionable pride, and luxury, and sloth, and wantonness. Meantime the same trade, wealth, and plenty begot or nourished the spirit of independency. Who would have imagined that this evil disease would lay a foundation for the cure of all the rest? And yet so it was. For this spirit, now come to maturity, and disdaining all restraint, is now swiftly destroying the trade, and wealth, and plenty whereby it was nourished, and thereby makes way for the happy return of humility, temperance, industry, and chastity. Such unspeakable good does the all-wise God bring out of all this evil! So does 'the fierceness of man', of the Americans, 'turn to his praise',[47] in a very different sense from what Dr. Witherspoon supposes.

14. May we not observe how exactly in this grand scene of providence one wheel answers to the other? The spirit of *independency*, which our poet so justly terms

The glorious fault of angels and of God;[48]

---

[45] Cf. Prov. 6:10; 24:33; see also No. 12, 'The Witness of Our Own Spirit', §18.
[46] See 2 Thess. 3:10. [47] Cf. Ps. 76:10 (BCP).
[48] Cf. Pope, 'Elegy to the Memory of an Unfortunate Lady', l. 13: 'The glorious fault of angels and of gods.'

(that is, in plain terms, of devils) the same which so many call *liberty*, is overruled by the justice and mercy of God, first to punish those crying sins, and afterwards to heal them. He punishes them by poverty, coming as an armed man, and overrunning the land; by such scarcity as has hardly been known 5 there for an hundred years past; by want of every kind, even of necessary clothing, even of bread to eat. But with what intent does he do this? Surely that mercy may rejoice over judgment.[49] He punishes that he may amend; that he may first make them sensible of their sins, which anyone that has eyes to see may read 10 in their punishment; and then bring them back to the spirit of their forefathers, the spirit of humility, temperance, industry, chastity; yea, and a general willingness to hear and receive the word which is able to save their souls. 'O the depth, both of the wisdom and knowledge of God! How unsearchable are his 15 judgments! And his ways past finding out!'[50] Unless so far as they are revealed in his Word and explained by his providence!

15. From these we learn that the spiritual blessings arc what God principally intends in all these severe dispensations. He intends they should all work together for the destruction of 20 Satan's kingdom, and the promotion of the kingdom of his dear Son; that they should all minister to the general spread of righteousness, and peace, and joy in the Holy Ghost.[51] But after the inhabitants of these provinces are brought again to 'seek the kingdom of God and his righteousness', there can be no doubt 25 but 'all' other 'things', all temporal blessings, 'will be added unto'[52] them. He will send through all the happy land, with all the necessaries and conveniencies of life, not *independency* (which would be no blessing, but an heavy curse, both to them and their children) but *liberty*—real, legal liberty, which is an unspeakable 30 blessing. He will superadd to Christian liberty, liberty from sin, true civil liberty; a liberty from oppression of every kind; from illegal violence; a liberty to enjoy their lives, their persons and their property—in a word, a liberty to be governed in all things by the laws of their country. They will again enjoy true British 35 liberty, such as they enjoyed before these commotions. Neither less nor more than they have enjoyed from their first settlement in

[49] See Jas. 2:13.
[50] Rom. 11:33.
[51] Rom. 14:17.
[52] Cf. Matt. 6:33.

America. Neither less nor more than is now enjoyed by the inhabitants of their mother country. If their mother country had ever designed to deprive them of this, she might have done it long ago. And that this was never done is a demonstration that it was 5 never intended. But God permitted this strange dread of imaginary evils to spread over all the people that he might have mercy upon all, that he might do good to all, by saving them from the bondage of sin, and bringing them into the glorious liberty of the children of God.[53]

---

[53] See Rom. 8:21.

A

SERMON

P R E A C H E D

On Occafion of the D E A T H of the

Rev. Mr. JOHN FLETCHER,

VICAR OF MADELEY, SHROPSHIRE.

By J O H N W E S L E Y, M. A.

L O N D O N:

Printed by J. PARAMORE, at the Foundry, 1785,

[PRICE SIX-PENCE.]

ON THE DEATH OF JOHN FLETCHER

AN INTRODUCTORY COMMENT

This funeral sermon stands in the Puritan tradition. In this tradition one begins with an idealized summary of the Christian life, proceeds to a mixed biography and eulogy of the deceased, and ends with a brief application to the attendant congregation. William Bates, whom Wesley had read and would recommend in his second 'Preface' to SOSO, V-VIII *(1788), had preached two famous sermons in this vein, on the deaths of Richard Baxter (published 1692) and of Thomas Manton (1678).*

Wesley's subject here was the man who, he had hoped, might have succeeded him as leader of the Methodist movement. (See his letter to Fletcher, January 15, 1773; see also what is still the best biography of Fletcher to date: Luke Tyerman, Wesley's Designated Successor *[1882], especially ch. XIII.) This sermon was for Wesley a solemn obligation and a labour of love. He had not only admired Fletcher more unreservedly than any other of his associates; he stood deeply in his debt. Fletcher had been the ablest apologist for Wesley's views in their protracted struggle with the Calvinists; of all the technically competent theologians in the eighteenth century (with the possible exception of Alexander Knox), Fletcher had understood Wesley's vision of the Christian life most clearly and taken him most seriously as a theologian. Moreover, he himself was an eminent exemplar of that vision, a man 'holy in heart and life . . . [whose] equal I have not known'. Thus, Wesley's sermon is a down payment on his debt. Another instalment would be paid in the following year with* A Short Account of [Fletcher's] Life and Death *(1786).*

Wesley's sources in the sermon are chiefly his own acquaintance, over the span of thirty years, and at least two long letters from Mrs. Fletcher—herself a devoted and eminent Methodist of long standing—written to Wesley and to her brother-in-law in Switzerland shortly after her husband's death. These letters are noted below. Fletcher died in Madeley on August 14, 1785, just before his fifty-sixth birthday. Wesley wrote this sermon during a visit to Norwich, October 22-24, and then delivered it in London on November 6.[1]

---

[1] See his letter to Mrs. Fletcher, Oct. 22; and JWJ, Nov. 6, 1785.

It was promptly published, as A Sermon preached on occasion of the Death of the Rev. Mr. John Fletcher, Vicar of Madeley, Shropshire, *and thereafter went through five more editions in Wesley's lifetime. For a brief publishing history and a list of substantive variant readings, see Appendix, Vol. 4; see also* Bibliog, *Nos. 441, for the* Sermon, *and 442, for the* Life.

On the Death of John Fletcher

To the Reader[1]

It was a consciousness of my own inability to describe in a manner worthy of the subject such a person as Mr. Fletcher which was one great reason of my not writing this sooner.[2] I judged only an Apelles was proper to paint an Alexander.[3] But I at length submitted to importunity, and hastily put together some memorials of this great man; intending, if God permit, when I have more leisure and more materials, to write a fuller account of his life.[4]

John Wesley

London, Nov. 9, 1785

Psalm 37:37

Mark the perfect man, and behold the upright!
For the end of that man is peace.

In the preceding verses, taken together with this, there is a beautiful contrast between the death of a wicked and that of a good man. 'I myself', says the Psalmist, 'have seen the ungodly in great power, and flourishing like a green bay tree. I went by and

---

[1] This foreword was tipped-in after the title-page of the 1st edn., and does not appear in all copies. It was omitted from the 1791 edn.

[2] Fletcher had died on Sunday, Aug. 14, 1785, and had been buried in the Madeley churchyard on the following Wednesday. Mrs. Fletcher recalls that 'the service was performed by the Rev. Mr. Hatton, Rector of [nearby] Waters Upton, whom the Lord moved, in a pathetic manner, to speak to the weeping flock.' Wesley began to compose this sermon on Oct. 22 and finished it on Oct. 24.

[3] Apelles of Colophon (4th century B.C.), commonly regarded as the greatest painter of antiquity; one of his masterpieces was a picture of Alexander holding a thunderbolt.

[4] This appeared as *A Short Account of the Life and Death of the Rev. John Fletcher* in 1786.

lo, he was gone: I sought him, but his place could nowhere be found.'[5] Dost thou desire to be found happy, both in life and in death? Then 'keep innocency, and take heed unto the thing that is right; for that shall bring a man peace at the last.'[6] The words are rendered in the new translation,[7] with far more force and elegance: 'Mark the perfect man, and behold the upright! For the end of that man is peace.' It is not improbable that David, while he uttered these words, had a particular instance before his eyes. Such an instance was that of the great and good man whom God has not long ago taken to himself.

In discoursing on these words I purpose, first, briefly to inquire who is the person that is here spoken of, 'the perfect, the upright man'. I will endeavour, secondly, to explain the promise, 'that shall bring a man peace at the last'; or as it is expressed in the other version, 'the end of that man is peace.' I will then, with the divine assistance, show a little more at large in how glorious a manner it was fulfilled in the end of that 'perfect and upright man' who has been lately removed from us.

I.1. I am, first, briefly to inquire who is the person that is here spoken of, 'the upright and perfect man'. In speaking on this head I shall not endeavour to describe the character of an upright Jew, such as David himself was, or any of those holy men that lived under the Mosaic dispensation. It more nearly imports us to consider such an upright man as are those that live under the Christian dispensation, such as have lived and died since 'life and immortality' have been 'brought to light by the gospel'.[8]

2. In this sense, he is a perfect and upright man who believes in the name of the Son of God; he is one in whom it has pleased the Father to reveal the Son of his love, and who consequently is able to declare, 'The life that I now live, I live by faith in the Son of God, who loved me and gave himself for me.'[9] He is one that finds 'the Spirit of God witnessing with his spirit, that he is a child of God';[10] and unto whom 'Jesus Christ is made of God, wisdom, and righteousness, and sanctification, and redemption.'[11]

3. This faith will undoubtedly 'work by love'.[12] Accordingly every Christian believer has 'the love of God shed abroad in his

---

[5] Ps. 37:36-37 (BCP).   [6] Ps. 37:38 (BCP).   [7] AV (1611).
[8] Cf. 2 Tim. 1:10.   [9] Gal. 2:20.
[10] Cf. Rom. 8:16.   [11] Cf. 1 Cor. 1:30.
[12] Cf. Gal. 5:6; see also No. 2, *The Almost Christian*, II.6 and n.

heart, by the Holy Ghost which is given unto him'.[13] And, loving God, he loves his brother also; his goodwill extends to every child of man.[14] By this, as well as by the fruits of love—lowliness, meekness, and resignation—he shows that there is the same 'mind in him which was in Christ Jesus'.[15]   5

4. As to his outward behaviour, the upright Christian believer is blameless and unreprovable.[16] He is holy, as Christ that has called him is holy, in all manner of conversation;[17] ever labouring to 'have a conscience void of offence toward God and toward man'.[18] He not only avoids all outward sin, but 'abstains from all   10 appearance of evil'.[19] He steadily walks in all the public and private ordinances of the Lord blameless.[20] He is zealous of good works;[21] as he hath time doing good, in every kind and degree, to all men.[22] And in the whole course of his life he pursues one invariable rule, 'whether he eats or drinks, or whatever he does, to 15 do all to the glory of God'.[23]

II. And surely 'the end of this man is peace'—the meaning of which words we are now, in the second place, to consider.

I do not conceive this immediately to refer to that glorious peace which is prepared for him in the presence of God to all   20 eternity, but rather to that which he will enjoy in the present world, before his spirit returns to God that gave it.[24] Neither does it seem directly to refer to outward peace, or deliverance from outward trouble. Although it is true many good men, who have been long buffeted by adversity, and troubled on every side, have 25 experienced an entire deliverance from it, and enjoyed a remarkable calm before they went hence. But this seems chiefly to refer to inward peace, even that 'peace of God which passeth all understanding'.[25] Therefore it is no wonder that it cannot be fully and adequately expressed in human language. We can only say it 30 is an unspeakable calmness and serenity of spirit, a tranquillity in the blood of Christ, which keeps the souls of believers, in their latest hour, even as a garrison keeps a city; which keeps not only their hearts, all their passions and affections, but also their minds, all the motions of their understanding and imagination, and all 35

---

[13] Cf. Rom. 5:5.   [14] Cf. No. 7, 'The Way to the Kingdom', I.8 and n.
[15] Cf. Phil. 2:5.   [16] See Col. 1:22. The 1791 edn. reads 'unreproachable'.
[17] See 1 Pet. 1:15.   [18] Cf. Acts 24:16.   [19] Cf. 1 Thess. 5:22.
[20] See Luke 1:6.   [21] See Titus 2:14.   [22] See the second 'General Rule'.
[23] Cf. 1 Cor. 10:31.   [24] See Eccles. 12:7.   [25] Phil. 4:7.

the workings of their reason, in Christ Jesus. This peace they experienced in a higher or lower degree (suppose they continued in the faith) from the time they first found redemption in the blood of Jesus, even the forgiveness of sins.[26] But when they have
5 nearly finished their course it generally flows as a river, even in such a degree as it had not before entered into their hearts to conceive.[27] A remarkable instance of this, out of a thousand, occurred many years ago. Enoch Williams,[28] one of the first of our preachers that was stationed at Cork (who had received this peace
10 when he was eleven years old, and never lost it for an hour), after he had rejoiced in God with joy unspeakable during the whole course of his illness, was too much exhausted to speak many words, but just said 'Peace! Peace!' and died.

III. So was the Scripture fulfilled. But it was far more
15 gloriously fulfilled in that late eminent servant of God; as will clearly appear if we consider a few circumstances, first, of his life, and secondly, of his triumphant death.

1. Indeed we have as yet but a very imperfect knowledge of his life. We know little more of his early years than that he was from
20 his infancy so remarkably regardless[29] of food that he would scarce take enough to sustain life; and that he had always much of the fear of God, and a real sense of religion. He was born September 12, in the year 1729, at Nyon, in Switzerland, of a very reputable family. He went through the usual course of academical
25 studies in the University of Geneva.[30] One of his uncles, who was at that time a General Officer in the Imperial service, then invited him into the same service, promising to procure him a commission. But just as he came into Germany the war was at an end.[31]

[26] See Col. 1:14.   [27] See Isa. 66:12; 1 Cor. 2:9.
[28] Cf. William Myles, *A Chronological History of the People called Methodists* (1803), p. 298, which notes that Williams was ordained, that he joined Wesley's movement in 1742, and died in service in 1744. See also Atmore, *The Methodist Memorial*, p. 508: 'He [Williams] was among the first instruments which the "Great Shepherd" and "Bishop of Souls" was pleased to make use of in the revival . . . but the hardships he was called to endure proved too much for his constitution and soon brought him to "the house appointed for all living". . . .'
[29] I.e., 'heedless'; cf. *OED*.
[30] What became the University of Geneva was then an academy. It is recorded that Fletcher was matriculated there, but never graduated; this has been confirmed by the personal researches of my friends, Dr. Frank Northam (of Geneva) and Professor Jacques Courvoisier (of the University).
[31] The so-called 'War of the Austrian Succession', concluded by the Treaty of Aix-la-Chapelle, Oct. 18, 1748.

Being so far on his way, he was then invited into Holland by another uncle, who had a little before been desired by a correspondent in England to procure a tutor for a gentleman's sons. He asked Mr. Fletcher whether he was willing to go into England and undertake this office. He consented, and accord- 5 ingly went over to England and undertook the care of Mr. Hill's two sons, at Tern, in Shropshire, and he continued in that office till the young gentlemen went to the university.[32]

2. When Mr. Hill went up to London to attend the Parliament he took his lady and Mr. Fletcher with him. While they were 10 dining at St. Alban's he walked out into the town, but did not return till the coach was set out for London. However, a saddle-horse being left, he came after, and overtook them on the same evening. Mrs. Hill asking him why he stayed behind, he said, 'I was walking through the market-place, and I heard a poor 15 old woman talk so sweetly of Jesus Christ that I knew not how the time past away.' 'I will be hanged', said Mrs. Hill, 'if our tutor does not turn Methodist by and by!' 'Methodist, Madam', said he, 'pray what is that?' She replied, 'Why, the Methodists are a people that do nothing but pray. They are praying all day and all 20 night.' 'Are they?' said he, 'Then with the help of God I will find them out, if they be above ground.' He did, not long after, find them out, and had his desire, being admitted into the society. While he was in town he met in Mr. Richard Edwards's class, and lost no opportunity of meeting. And he retained a peculiar regard 25 for Mr. Edwards to the day of his death.

3. It was not long before he was pressed in spirit to call sinners to repentance. Seeing the world all around him lying in wickedness, he found an earnest desire

> To pluck poor brands out of the fire, 30
> To snatch them from the verge of hell.[33]

---

[32] Thomas Hill (c. 1693–1782), Member of Parliament for Shrewsbury (1749–68); cf. Raymond F. Skinner, *Nonconformity in Shropshire, 1662–1816* (Shrewsbury, Wilding and Son, 1964), p. 58. 'But Hill dismissed Fletcher as tutor and gave him the living of Madeley' (ten miles from Tern Hall), pp. 59-60.

[33] Cf. Charles Wesley, Hymn 12, 'Hymns for a Preacher of the Gospel', in *Hymns and Sacred Poems* (1749), I.301 (*Poet. Wks.*, V. 105):

> I want an even strong desire,
> I want a calmly fervent zeal,
> To save poor souls out of the fire,
> To snatch them from the verge of hell.

And though he was yet far from being perfect in the English tongue, particularly with regard to the pronunciation of it, yet the earnestness with which he spake, seldom to be seen in England, and the unspeakably tender affection to poor, lost sinners which
5   breathed in every word and gesture, made so deep an impression on all that heard that very few went empty away.

4. About the year 1753 (being now of a sufficient age), he was ordained deacon and priest, and soon after presented to the little living of Madeley in Shropshire.[34] This, he had frequently said, was
10   the only living which he ever desired to have. He was ordained at Whitehall, and the same day, being informed that I had no one to assist me at West Street Chapel, he came away as soon as ever the ordination was over, and assisted me in the administration of the Lord's Supper. And he was now doubly diligent in preaching, not
15   only in the chapels of West Street and Spitalfields,[35] but wherever the providence of God opened a door to proclaim the everlasting gospel. This he did frequently in French (as well as in English), of which all judges allowed him to be a complete master.

5. Hence he removed into the vicarage house at Madeley. Here
20   he was fully employed among his parishioners, both in the town and in Madeley Wood, a mile or two from it—a place much resembling Kingswood, almost wholly inhabited by poor colliers and their numerous families. These forlorn ones (little wiser than the beasts that perish)[36] he took great pains to reform and instruct.
25   And they are now as judicious and as well-behaved a people as most of their station in the three kingdoms.

6. But after some time he was prevailed upon by the Countess of Huntingdon to leave his beloved retreat and remove into Wales, in order to superintend her school at Trevecka.[37] This he

---

[34] A printer's error for 1757? Fletcher was ordained deacon on Sunday, Mar. 6, and priest Mar. 13, 1757, and presented to the living of Madeley in Oct. 1760; cf. Joseph Benson, *The Life of the Rev. John Wm. De La Fléchère* (1817), p. 31. Cf. JWJ, Mar. 13, 1757: 'Mr. Fletcher came, who had just then been ordained priest [at Whitehall], on purpose to assist, as he supposed me to be alone.' The West Street Chapel, near Seven Dials, was a former Huguenot church and was episcopally consecrated. Wesley used it as a centre for preaching and the sacraments.

[35] Another former Huguenot chapel, in Grey Eagle Street, which had been taken over by Wesley in 1750. It was here, in 1755, that he held the first Methodist 'Covenant Service'.

[36] Ps. 49:12, 20.

[37] See No. 112, *On Laying the Foundation of the New Chapel*, II.16. Fletcher did not resign his living at Madeley; this work at Trevecka was added to that of his parish; cf. Tyerman, *Wesley's Designated Successor*, pp. 134-44, 175-86; see also Seymour, II.78-86.

did with all his power, instructing the young men both in learning and philosophy, till he received a letter from the Countess, together with the circular letter signed by Mr. Shirley, summoning all that feared God in England to meet together at Bristol at the time of the Methodist Conference, 'in order to bear 5 testimony against the *dreadful heresy* contained in the *Minutes* of the preceding Conference'.[38] Her Ladyship declared that all who did not absolutely renounce those eight propositions which were contained in the *Minutes* of that Conference must immediately 10 leave her house. Mr. Fletcher was exceedingly surprised at this peremptory declaration. He spent the next day in fasting and prayer, and in the evening wrote to her Ladyship that he not only could not utterly renounce, but must entirely approve of, all those eight propositions, and therefore had obeyed her order by leaving 15 her house and returning to his own at Madeley.[39]

7. That circular letter was the happy occasion of his writing those excellent *Checks to Antinomianism,* in which one knows not which to admire most, the purity of the language (such as a foreigner scarce ever wrote before), the strength and clearness of 20 the argument, or the mildness and sweetness of the spirit which breathes throughout the whole. Insomuch that I nothing wonder at a clergyman that was resolved never to part with his dear Decrees, who, being pressed to read them, replied, 'No, I will never read Mr. Fletcher's writings; for if I did, I should be of his 25 mind.' He now likewise wrote several other valuable tracts.[40]

[38] An open letter authorized by the Countess of Huntingdon, written by Walter Shirley: 'Whereas Mr. Wesley's conference is to be held at Bristol on Tuesday, the 6th of August next, it is proposed by Lady Huntingdon . . . to have a meeting at Bristol at the same time of such principal persons . . . who disapprove the underwritten minutes [§6 of the *Minutes* of 1770] . . . to insist upon a formal recantation of the said minutes . . . in opposition to such a *dreadful heresy;*' cf. Tyerman *(JW),* III.93-94. This was the formal declaration of a protracted war that overshadowed the last two decades of Wesley's career. (See also Benson's *Life of Fletcher,* pp. 149-50.)

[39] A full text is given in Tyerman, *Wesley's Designated Successor,* pp. 180-86; it is an incisive summary of Fletcher's unavailing efforts as mediator between high-spirited partisans, even while his sympathies lay more largely with Wesley.

[40] Cf. *An Appeal to Matter of Fact and Common Sense* (1772); *The First Part of An Equal Check to Pharisaism and Antinomianism* (1774); *Remarks on Mr. Toplady's Scheme of Christian and Philosophical Necessity* (1777); *An Answer to Mr. Toplady's 'Vindication of the Decrees'* (1776); *American Patriotism Farther Confronted with Reason, Scripture, and the Constitution* (1776); *Bible Arminianism Bible Calvinism* (1777); *The Doctrines of Grace and Justice Equally Essential to the Pure Gospel* (1777). Fletcher published some thirty works large and small, in English and in French, some of which passed through many editions. A few were edited and published by Wesley, who kept most of them on sale in the Methodist

Meantime he was more abundant in his ministerial labours, both in public and private, visiting his whole parish, early and late, in all weathers, regarding neither heat nor cold, rain nor snow, whether he was on horseback or on foot. But this insensibly weakened his

5 constitution, and sapped the foundation of his health; which was still more effectually done by his intense and uninterrupted studies, at which he frequently continued with scarce any intermission, fourteen, fifteen, or sixteen hours a day. Meantime he did not allow himself necessary food: he seldom took any

10 regular meals unless he had company; but twice or thrice in four and twenty hours ate some bread and cheese, or fruit; instead of which he sometimes took a draught of milk, and then wrote on again. When one reproved him for this, for not allowing himself a sufficiency of necessary food, he replied with surprise, 'Not allow

15 myself food? Why, our food seldom costs my housekeeper and me less than two shillings a week.'

8. Being informed that his health was greatly impaired, I judged nothing was so likely to restore it as a long journey. So I proposed his taking a journey with me into Scotland, to which he

20 willingly consented. We set out in spring, and after travelling eleven or twelve hundred miles, returned to London in autumn.[41] I verily believe had he travelled with me a few months longer he would have quite recovered his health. But being stopped by his friends, he quickly relapsed, and fell into a true pulmonary

25 consumption.

9. But this sickness was not unto death. It was only sent that the glory of the Lord might appear.[42] During the whole course of it he remained at Newington,[43] and was visited by persons of all ranks. And they all marvelled at the grace of God that was in him. In all

30 his pain no complaint came out of his mouth, but his every breath was spent either in praising God or exhorting and comforting his neighbour.

10. When nothing else availed he was advised to take a journey

---

Book-room (see *Bibliog*, Nos. 518-39). In 1808 his collected *Works* reached a total of nine volumes, which were several times reprinted.

[41] This is repeated in *A Short Account of the Life and Death of John Fletcher*, V.10, but there is no mention of it in JWJ. Indeed, a very different account is given in JWJ, Aug. 11 and Sept. 22, 1776, where we are told that Fletcher declined, on physician's orders, to join Wesley in his travels to Cornwall, Somerset, etc.

[42] See John 11:4.

[43] I.e., Stoke Newington, at the home of Charles Greenwood; cf. *A Short Account . . . ,* V.10-21.

by sea and by land into his own country. He did this in company with Mr. Ireland,[44] a well-tried and faithful friend, who loved him as a brother, and thought no pains ill bestowed if he could preserve so valuable a life. He resided in his own country about a year, and was a blessing to all that were round about him. Being much recovered, he spent some months in France, and then returned in perfect health to Madeley.

11. In the year 1781, with the full approbation of all his friends, he married Miss Bosanquet:[45] of whom, as she is still alive, I say no more at present than that she was the only person in England whom I judged to be worthy of Mr. Fletcher. By her tender and judicious care his health was confirmed more and more. And I am firmly convinced that had he used this health in travelling all over the kingdom five or six or seven months every year (for which never was man more eminently qualified; no, not Mr. Whitefield himself) he would have done more good than any other man in England. I cannot doubt but this would have been the more excellent way.[46] However, though he did not accept of this honour, he did abundance of good in that narrower sphere of action which he chose, and was a pattern well worthy the imitation of all the parochial ministers in the kingdom.

12. His manner of life during the time that he and his wife lived together it may be most satisfactory to give in her own words:[47]

It is no little grief to me that my dearly beloved husband has left no account of himself in writing. And I am not able to give many particulars of a life the most angelical I have ever known.

He was born at Nyon in the Canton of Berne in Switzerland. In his infancy he discovered a lively genius, and great tenderness of heart. One day, having

---

[44] An extended visit with James Ireland of Brislington, near Bristol; Fletcher did not return to England until Apr. 1781; cf. Tyerman, *Wesley's Designated Successor*, pp. 407-47.

[45] Mary Bosanquet (1739–1815), the daughter of a wealthy London merchant and mistress of a manor in Leytonstone, Essex. She had been converted as a child and, much later, had maintained her home as an orphanage. In 1768 she moved to Cross Hall, near Leeds; she and Fletcher were married there, Nov. 12, 1781; cf. Tyerman, *Wesley's Designated Successor*, pp. 473-98.

[46] See 1 Cor. 12:31.

[47] A conflation of several manuscripts that were written by Mrs. Fletcher after her husband's death. One was printed by J. Edmunds of Madeley: *A Letter to the Rev. Mr. Wesley on the Death of the Rev. Mr. Fletcher, Vicar of Madeley;* it is dated Aug. 18, 1785. Another, to Mr. Fletcher's brother, was not published until the following year: *A Letter to Mons. H. L. de la Fléchère . . . on the death of his brother, the Reverend John William de la Fléchère, twenty-five years vicar of Madeley, Shropshire.* Wesley here depends chiefly on her letter to him but has added material from her other manuscripts, abridging them severely and freely revising them while preserving their substance and spirit.

offended his father, who threatened to correct him, he kept himself at a distance in the garden, till seeing his father approach, and fearing his anger would be renewed by the sight of him, he ran away. But he was presently struck with a deep remorse, thinking, 'What! Do I run away from my father? What a wicked
5 wretch! Maybe I may live to grow up and have a son that will run away from *me*!' And it was some years before the impression of sorrow then made upon him wore off.

When he was about seven years old he was reproved by his nursemaid saying, 'You are a naughty boy, and the devil takes all such.' After he was in bed he
10 began to reflect on her words, his heart smote him, and he said, 'I am a naughty boy, and perhaps God will let the devil fetch me away.' He got up on the bed and for a considerable time wrestled with God in prayer, till he felt such a sense of the love of God as made him quite easy.

(Part of the next paragraph I omit, being nearly the same with
15 **what I inserted before.)**

When he entered Mr. Hill's family he did not know Christ in his heart. One Sunday evening, as he was writing some music, the servant came in to make up the fire, and looking at him said, 'Sir, I am very sorry to see you so employed on the Lord's day.' He immediately put away his music, and from that hour became
20 a strict observer of that holy day.

Not long after he met with a person who asked him to go with her and hear the Methodists. He readily consented. The more he heard, the more uneasy he grew. And doubling his diligence, he hoped by *doing much* to render himself acceptable to God; till one day hearing Mr. Green[48] he was convinced he did not
25 know what true faith was. This occasioned many reflections in his mind. 'Is it possible (said he) that I who have made divinity my study, and have received "the premium of piety" (so called)[49] from the university for my writings on divine subjects; that I should still be so ignorant as not to know what faith is?' But the more he examined, the more he was convinced: then sin revived, and hope
30 died away. He now sought by the most rigorous austerities to conquer an evil nature, and bring heaven-born peace into his soul. But the more he struggled, the more he was convinced that all his fallen soul was sin, and that nothing but a revelation of the love of Jesus could make him a Christian.[50] For this he groaned with unwearied assiduity; till one day, after much wrestling with God, lying
35 prostrate on his face before the throne, he felt the application of the blood of Jesus. Now his bonds were broken, and his free soul began to breathe a pure air. Sin was beneath his feet, and he could triumph in the Lord, the God of his salvation.

From this time he walked valiantly in the ways of God; and thinking he had
40 not leisure enough in the day he made it a constant rule to sit up two nights in a week for reading, prayer, and meditation, in order to sink deeper[51] into that

[48] Just possibly William Green, later of Rotherham, a free-lance Methodist preacher, reputed author of *A Dialogue Between the Pulpit and Reading Desk;* see JWJ, June 16, 1777.
[49] There is no official record of any such award.
[50] Orig., 'a true believer'.
[51] Orig., 'to enter more deeply'.

communion with God which was become his soul's delight. Meantime he took only vegetable food, and for above six months lived wholly on bread, with milk and water.

Notwithstanding the nights he sat up, he made it a rule never to sleep as long as he could possibly keep awake. For this purpose he always took a candle and book to bed with him. But one night, being overcome of sleep before he had put out the candle, he dreamed his curtains, pillow, and cap were on fire, without doing him any harm. And so it was. In the morning part of his curtains, pillow, and cap were burnt. But not an hair of his head was singed. So did God give his angels charge over him!

Some time after he was favoured with a particular manifestation of the love of God; so powerful that it appeared to him as if body and soul would be separated. Now all his desires centred in one, that of devoting himself to the service of his precious Master. This he thought he could do best by entering into Orders.[52] God made his way plain, and he soon after settled in Madeley. He received this parish as from the immediate hand of God, and unweariedly laboured therein, and in the adjacent places, till he had spent himself in his Master's service, and was ripening fast for glory.[53] Much opposition he met with for many years, and often his life was in danger. Sometimes he was inwardly constrained to warn obstinate sinners that if they did not repent the hand of God would cut them off. And the event proved the truth of the prediction. But notwithstanding all their opposition, many were the seals of his ministry.

He had an earnest desire that the pure gospel should remain among his people after he was taken away. For this purpose he surmounted great difficulties in building the house in Madeley Wood. He not only saved for it the last farthing he had, but when he was abroad proposed to let the vicarage house (designing at his return to live in a little cottage near it) and appropriating the rent of it for clearing that house.

Since the time I had the honour and happiness of living with him, every day made me more sensible of the mighty work of the Spirit upon him. The fruits of this were manifest in all his life and conversation, but in nothing more than in his meekness and humility. It was a meekness which no affront could move—an humility which loved to be unknown, forgotten, and despised.[a] How hard is it to find an eminent person who loves an equal! But his delight was in preferring others to himself. It appeared so natural in him that it seemed as his meat to set everyone before himself. He spake not of the fault of an absent person but when necessary; and then with the utmost caution. He made no account of his own labours, and perhaps carried to an extreme his dislike of hearing them mentioned.

Patience is the daughter of humility.[54] In him it discovered itself in a manner which I wish I could either describe or imitate. It produced in him a ready mind

---

[a] I think this was going to an extreme. [Mrs. Fletcher's original manuscript runs on for two full pages expanding on Fletcher's self-effacement; Wesley, with his aversion to overwriting, cut this short.]

---

[52] Orig., 'holy Orders'.
[53] Cf. 'ripening for heaven' in John Flavell, *Husbandry Spiritualized, or, the Heavenly Use of Earthly Things,* in *Works* (1740), p. 272; see also No. 132, 'On Faith, Heb. 11:1', §5.
[54] See No. 83, 'On Patience', §5 and n.

to embrace every cross with alacrity and pleasure. And for the good of his neighbour (the poor in particular) nothing seemed hard, nothing wearisome. When I have been grieved to call him out of his study, from his closet-work, two or three times in an hour, he would answer, 'O my dear, never think of that; it
5 matters not what we do, so we are always ready to meet the will of God: 'tis only conformity to this which makes any employment excellent.'

He had a singular love for the lambs of the flock, the children, and applied himself with the greatest diligence to their instruction, for which he had a peculiar gift: and this populous parish found him full exercise for it. The poorest
10 met with the same attention from him as the rich. For their sakes he almost grudged himself necessaries, and often expressed a pain in using them while any of his parish wanted them.

But while I mention his meekness and love, let me not forget the peculiar favour of his Master in giving him the most firm and resolute *courage*. In
15 reproving sin and daring sinners he was a 'son of thunder', and regarded neither fear nor favour when he had a message from God to deliver.

With respect to his communion with God, 'tis much to be lamented that we have no account of it from his own pen. But thus far I can say, it was his constant care to keep an uninterrupted sense of the divine presence. In order to this he
20 was slow of speech, and had the exactest government of his words. To this he was so inwardly attentive as sometimes to appear stupid to those who knew him not; though few conversed in a more lively manner when he judged it would be for the glory of God. It was his continual endeavour to draw up his own and every other spirit to an immediate intercourse with God. And all his intercourse
25 with me was so mingled with prayer and praise that every employment and every meal was, as it were, perfumed therewith. He often said, ''Tis a very little thing so to hang upon God by faith as to feel no departure from him. But I want to be filled with the fullness of his Spirit.' 'I feel', said he, 'sometimes such gleams of light, as it were wafts of heavenly air, as seem ready to take my soul with them to
30 glory.' A little before his last illness, when the fever began to rage among us, he preached a sermon on the duty of visiting the sick, wherein he said: 'What do you fear? Are you afraid of catching the distemper and dying! O fear it no more! What an honour to die in your Master's work! If permitted to me, I should account it a singular favour.' In his former illness he wrote thus: 'I calmly wait, in
35 unshaken resignation, for the full salvation of God; ready to venture on his faithful love, and on the sure mercies of David. His time is best, and is my time. Death has lost its sting. And I bless God I know not what hurry of spirits is, or unbelieving fears.'

For his last months he scarce ever lay down or rose up without these words in
40 his mouth:

> I nothing have, I nothing am;
> My treasure's in the bleeding Lamb
> Both now and evermore.[55]

---

[55] π; But see Charles Wesley's hymn on Mic. 6:6, st. 8, l. 2, in *Poet. Wks.*, I.277 (beginning, 'Wherewith, O God, shall I draw near'):

> What have I then wherein to trust?
> I nothing have, I nothing am:
> Excluded is my every boast,
> My glory swallow'd up in shame.

In one of the letters which he wrote some time since to his dear people of Madeley, some of his words are: 'I leave this blessed island for awhile; but I trust I shall never leave the kingdom of God—the shadow of Christ's cross, the clefts of the Rock, smitten and pierced for us. There I meet you in spirit; thence, I trust, I shall joyfully leap into the ocean of eternity, to go and join those ministering spirits who wait on the heirs of salvation. And if I am no more allowed to minister to you on earth, I rejoice at the thought that I shall perhaps be allowed to accompany the angels, who (if you abide in the faith) will be commissioned to carry you into Abraham's bosom.'

The thought enlivens my faith! Lord give me to walk in his steps! Then shall I see him again, and my heart shall rejoice, and we shall eternally behold the Lamb together. Faith brings near the welcome moment! And now he beckons me away! And Jesus bids me come!

I know not that anything can or need be added to this but Mrs. Fletcher's account of his death, which follows also in her own words:

For some time before his late illness he was particularly penetrated with the nearness of eternity. There was scarce an hour in which he was not calling upon us to drop every thought and every care, that we might attend to nothing but drinking deeper into God. We spent much time in wrestling with God, and were led in a peculiar manner to abandon our whole selves into the hands of God, to do or suffer whatever was pleasing to him.

On Thursday, August 4, he was employed in the work of God from three in the afternoon till nine at night. When he came home he said, 'I have taken cold.' On Friday and Saturday he was not well, but seemed uncommonly drawn out in prayer. On Saturday night his fever appeared very strong. I begged him not to go to church in the morning; but he told me it was the will of the Lord, in which case I never dared to persuade. In reading prayers he almost fainted away. I got through the crowd and entreated him to come out of the desk. But he let me and others know, in his sweet manner, that we were not to interrupt the order of God. I then retired to my pew, where all around me were in tears. When he was a little refreshed by the windows being opened, he went on; and then preached with a strength and recollection that surprised us all.

After sermon he went up to the communion table with these words, 'I am going to throw myself under the wings of the cherubim, before the mercy-seat.' The service held till near two. Sometimes he could scarce stand, and was often obliged to stop. The people were deeply affected; weeping was on every side. Gracious Lord! how was it my soul was kept so calm in the midst of the most tender feelings? Notwithstanding his extreme weakness he gave out several verses of hymns and lively sentences of exhortation. When service was over we hurried him to bed, where he immediately fainted away. He afterward dropped into a sleep for some time, and on waking cried out with a pleasant smile: 'Now, my dear, thou seest I am no worse for doing the Lord's work: he never fails me when I trust in him.' Having got a little dinner, he dozed most of the evening, now and then waking full of the praises of God. At night his fever returned, though not violent; but his strength decreased amazingly. On Monday and Tuesday we had a little paradise together: he lay on a couch in the study, and

though often changing posture, was sweetly pleasant, and frequently slept a good while. When awake he delighted in hearing me read hymns and tracts on faith and love. His words were all animating, and his patience beyond expression. When he had any nauseous medicines to take he seemed to enjoy
5 the cross, according to a word he used often to repeat—that we are to seek a perfect conformity to the will of God, and leave him to give us what comfort he saw good. I asked him whether he had any advice to leave me, if he should be taken from me. He replied: 'I have nothing particular to say. The Lord will open all before thee.' I said, 'Have you any conviction that God is about to take you?'
10 He said, 'No, not in particular; only I always see death so inexpressibly near that we both seem to stand on the very verge of eternity.' While he slept a little I besought the Lord, if it was his good pleasure, to spare him to me a little longer. But my prayer seemed to have no wings, and I could not help mingling continually therewith, 'Lord, give me perfect resignation.' This uncertainty
15 made me tremble, lest God was going to put into my hand the bitter cup which he lately threatened my husband. Some weeks before I myself was ill of the fever. My husband then felt the whole parting scene, and struggled for perfect resignation. He said: 'O Polly, shall I ever see the day when thou must be carried out to bury? How will the little things which thy tender care has prepared for me
20 in every part of the house, how will they wound and distress me! How is it? I think I feel jealousy! I am jealous of the worms. I seem to shrink at giving my dear Polly to the worms!'

Now all these reflections returned upon my heart with the weight of a millstone. I cried to the Lord, and those words were deeply impressed on my
25 spirit, 'Where I am, there shall my servants be, that they may behold my glory.' This promise was full of comfort to my soul. I saw that in Christ's immediate presence was our home, and that we should find our reunion in being deeply centred in him. I received it as a fresh marriage for eternity. As such, I trust for ever to hold it. All that day, whenever I thought of that expression, 'to behold my
30 glory', it seemed to wipe away every tear, and was as the ring whereby we were joined anew.

Awaking some time after he said: 'Polly, I have been thinking it was Israel's fault that they asked for *signs*. We will not do so, but abandoning our whole selves into the hands of God will lie patiently before him, assured that he will do
35 all things well.'

'My dear love', said I, 'if ever I have done or said anything to grieve thee, how will the remembrance wound my heart, shouldst thou be taken from me!'

He entreated and charged me, with inexpressible tenderness, not to allow the thought; declaring his thankfulness for our union, in a variety of words written
40 on my heart as with the adamantine pen of friendship deeply dipped in blood.

On Wednesday, after groaning all day under the weight of the power of God, he told me he had received such a manifestation of the full meaning of those words, 'God is love,' as he could never be able to tell. 'It fills me', said he, 'every moment. O Polly, my dear Polly, God is love. Shout, shout aloud! I want a gust
45 of praise to go to the ends of the earth. But it seems as if I could not speak much longer. Let us fix on a sign between ourselves: (tapping me twice with his fingers) now I mean, "God is love". And we will draw each other into God. Observe! By this we will draw each other into God.'

Sally coming in, he cried out: 'O Sally, God is love. Shout, both of you. I want to hear you shout his praise.' All this time the medical friend who diligently attended him hoped he was in no danger; as he had no bad headache, much sleep, without the least delirium, and an almost regular pulse. So was the disease, though commissioned to take his life, restrained by the power of God.

On Thursday his speech began to fail. While he was able he spoke to all that 5 came in his way. Hearing a stranger was in the house, he ordered her to be called up, though uttering two sentences almost made him faint. To his friendly doctor he would not be silent while he had any power of speech, saying,[56] 'O Sir, you take much thought for my body; give me leave to take thought for your soul.' When I could scarce understand anything he said, I spoke these words, 'God is 10 love.' Instantly, as if all his powers were awakened, he broke out in a rapture: 'God is love! Love! Love! O for that gust of praise I want to sound!' Here his voice again failed. He suffered many ways; but with such patience as none but those then present can conceive. If I named his sufferings he would smile and make the sign.   15

On Friday, finding his body covered with spots, I felt a sword pierce through my soul.[57] As I was kneeling by his side with my hand in his, entreating the Lord to be with us in this tremendous hour, he strove to say many things, but could not; pressing my hand, and often repeating the sign. At last he breathed out, 'Head of the church, be Head to my wife!' When for a few moments I was forced 20 to leave him, Sally said to him, 'My dear master, do you know me?' He replied, 'Sally, God will put his right hand under you.' She added, 'O my dear master, should you be taken away, what a disconsolate creature will my poor dear mistress be!' He replied, 'God will be her all in all.' He had always delighted much in these words,   25

> Jesu's blood through earth and skies,
> Mercy, free, boundless mercy cries.[58]

Whenever I repeated them to him he would answer, 'Boundless! Boundless! Boundless!' He now added, though with great difficulty,

> Mercy's full power I *soon* shall prove,   30
> Loved with an everlasting love.[59]

On Saturday afternoon his fever seemed quite off, and a few friends standing near the bed, he reached his hand to each, and looking on a minister, said, 'Are you ready to assist tomorrow?' His recollection surprised us, as the day of the week had not been named in his room. Many believed he would recover; and 35 one said, 'Do you think the Lord will raise you up?' He strove to answer, saying, 'Raise me in the resurr . . . ,' meaning, 'in the resurrection.' To another, asking the same question, he said, 'I leave it all to God.'

In the evening the fever returned with violence, and the mucus falling on his throat almost strangled him. It was supposed the same painful emotion would 40 grow more and more violent to the last. As I felt this exquisitely,[60] I cried to the Lord to remove it; and, glory be to his name, he did. From that time it returned

---

[56] Orig., 'often saying'.

[57] Orig., '. . . finding his dear body covered with spots, I so far understood them as to feel a sword . . .'.

[58] John Wesley, 'Redemption Found' (from the German), in *Hymns and Sacred Poems* (1740), p. 92.

[59] *Ibid.*   [60] Orig., 'exquisitively'.

no more. As night drew on I perceived him dying very fast. His fingers could hardly make the sign (which he scarce ever forgot), and his speech seemed quite gone. I said, 'My dear creature, I ask not for myself—*I know thy soul!*—but for the sake of others: if Jesus is very present with thee, lift thy right hand.' He did.
5 'If the prospect of glory sweetly opens before thee, repeat the sign.' He immediately raised it again; and in half a minute, a second time: he then threw it up, as if he would reach the top of the bed. After this, his dear hands moved no more; but on my saying, 'Art thou in much pain?' he answered, 'No.' From this time he lay in a kind of sleep, though with his eyes open and fixed. For the most
10 part he sat upright against pillows, with his head a little inclining to one side. And so remarkably composed and triumphant was his countenance that the least trace of death was scarce discernible in it.

Twenty-four hours[61] he was in this situation, breathing like a person in common sleep. About thirty-five minutes past ten on Sunday night, August
15 14th, his precious soul entered into the joy of his Lord, without one struggle or groan, in the fifty-sixth year of his age.

And here I break off my mournful story: but on my bleeding heart the fair picture of his heavenly excellence will be for ever drawn. When I call to mind his ardent zeal, his laborious endeavours to seek and save the lost, his diligence in
20 the employment of his time, his Christlike condescension toward me, and his uninterrupted converse with heaven—I may well be allowed to add, my loss—is beyond the power of words to paint. I have gone 'through deep waters'; but all my afflictions were nothing compared to this. Well: I want no pleasant prospect, but upwards; nor anything whereon to fix my hope, but immortality.
25 On the 17th his dear remains were deposited in Madeley churchyard, amid the tears and lamentations of thousands. The service was performed by the Rev. Mr. Hatton, Rector of Waters Upton, whom God enabled to speak in a pathetic manner to his weeping flock. In the conclusion, at my request, he read the following paper:

30 As it was the desire of my beloved husband to be buried in this plain manner, so out of tenderness he begged that I might not be present. And in all things I would obey him.

Permit me then, by the mouth of a friend, to bear my open testimony, to the glory of God, that I who have known him in the most perfect manner, am
35 constrained to declare that I never knew anyone walk so closely in the ways of God as he did. The Lord gave him a conscience tender as the apple of an eye. He literally preferred the interest of everyone to his own.

He was rigidly just, but perfectly loose from all attachment to the world. He shared *his all* with the poor, who lay so close to his heart that at the approach of
40 death, when he could not speak without difficulty, he cried out: 'O my poor! What will become of my poor?' He was blessed with so great a degree of humility as is scarce to be found. I am witness how often he has rejoiced in being treated with contempt. Indeed, it seemed the very food of his soul to be little and unknown. When he desired me to write a line to his brother if he died, I replying,
45 'I will write him all the Lord's dealings with thee;' 'No, no', said he, 'write nothing about me. I only desire to be forgotten. *God is all!*'

---

[61] In the orig., this is crossed out and corrected to 'eighteen' in the margin.

His zeal for souls I need not tell *you*. Let the labours of twenty-five years, and a martyr's death in the conclusion, imprint it on your hearts. His diligent visitation of the sick occasioned the fever which, by God's commission, tore him from you and me. And his vehement desire to take his last leave of you, with dying lips and hands, gave, it is supposed, the finishing stroke, by preparing his 5 blood for putrefaction. Thus has he lived and died your servant. And will any of you refuse to meet him at God's right hand in that day?

He walked with death always in sight. About two months ago he came to me and said, 'My dear love, I know not how it is, but I have a strange impression death is very near us, as if it would be some sudden stroke upon one of us. And it 10 draws out all my soul in prayer, that we may be ready.' He then broke out: 'Lord, prepare the soul thou wilt call. And Oh, stand by the poor disconsolate one that shall be left behind!'

A few days before his departure he was filled with love in an uncommon manner, saying to me: 'I have had such a discovery of the depth of that word, 15 "God is love". I cannot tell thee half. O shout his praise.' The same he testified as long as he had a voice, and continued to testify to the end, by a most lamb-like patience, in which he smiled over death, and set his last seal to the glorious truths he had so long preached among you.

Three years, nine months, and two days, I have possessed my heavenly- 20 minded husband. But now the sun of my earthly joy is set for ever, and my soul filled with an anguish which only finds its consolation in a total resignation to the will of God. When I was asking the Lord if he pleased to spare him to me a little longer, the following promise was impressed on my mind with great power (in the accomplishment of which *I look for our reunion*), 'Where I am, there shall my 25 servants be, that they may behold my glory.' Lord, hasten the hour.[62]

There is little need of adding any farther character of this man of God to the foregoing account, given by one who wrote out of the fullness of her heart. I would only observe that for many years I despaired of finding any inhabitant of Great Britain that could 30 stand in any degree of comparison with Gregory Lopez[63] or Monsieur de Renty.[64] But let any impartial person judge if Mr. Fletcher was at all inferior to them! Did he not experience as deep communion with God, and as high a measure of inward holiness, as was experienced either by one or the other of those burning 35 and shining lights?[65] And it is certain his outward holiness shone before men with full as bright a lustre as theirs. But if any should attempt to draw a parallel between them there are two circumstances that deserve consideration. One is, we are not assured that the writers of *their* lives did not extenuate, if not 40

---

[62] This personal testimony of Mrs. Fletcher has scarcely been abridged or revised at all.
[63] See No. 55, *On the Trinity*, §1 and n.
[64] See No. 14, *The Repentance of Believers*, I.15 and n.
[65] See John 5:35.

suppress, what was amiss in them. And some things amiss we are assured there were, namely, many touches of superstition, and some of idolatry, in worshipping saints—the Virgin Mary in particular. But I have not suppressed or extenuated anything in
5 Mr. Fletcher's character. For indeed I knew nothing that was amiss, nothing that needed to be extenuated, much less suppressed. A second circumstance is that the writers of *their* lives could not have so full a knowledge of them as both Mrs. Fletcher and I had of Mr. Fletcher's, being eye- and
10 ear-witnesses of his whole conduct. Consequently we know that his life was not sullied with any mixture of either idolatry or superstition. I was intimately acquainted with him for above thirty years. I conversed with him morning, noon, and night, without the least reserve, during a journey of many hundred miles. And in
15 all that time I never heard him speak one improper word nor saw him do an improper action. To conclude. Many exemplary men have I known, holy in heart and life, within fourscore years. But one equal to him I have not known—one so inwardly and outwardly devoted to God. So unblameable a character in every
20 respect I have not found either in Europe or America. Nor do I expect to find another such on this side of eternity.

As it is possible we all may be such as he was, let us endeavour to follow him as he followed Christ![66]

Norwich, October 24, 1785

25   His Epitaph:

                            Here lies the Body of
                    The Rev. John William de la Fléchère,
                            Vicar of Madeley,
                    Who was born at Nyon, in Switzerland,
30   September the 12th, 1729,
              And finished his course, August the 14th, 1785,
                            In this Village;
                    Where his unexampled Labours
                        Will never be forgotten.
35   He exercised his Ministry for the space of
                            Twenty-five Years
                            In this Parish,

---

[66] Thomas Jackson (1825), presumably on the basis of a later annotation in Wesley's hand, revised this conditional form to a declarative: 'But it is possible we may all be such as he was. Let us then endeavour. . . .' However, the subjunctive seems wholly consonant with the 'logic' of Wesley's argument.

With uncommon Zeal and Ability.
But though many believed his report,
Yet he might with justice have adopted
The Lamentation of the Prophet,
All the Day long have I stretched out my Hands   5
Unto a disobedient and gainsaying People:[67]
Yet surely my Judgment is with the Lord,
And my Work with my God.[68]

---

[67] See Isa. 65:2.

[68] Cf. Isa. 49:4. The variations between this version of the epitaph and those in Wesley's *Short Account,* Atmore's *Methodist Memorial,* p. 142, Tyerman's *Wesley's Designated Successor,* p. 573, and Benson's *Life,* p. 376, may be explained by the fact that Mrs. Fletcher composed it and later amended the text herself. Wesley's version transcribes the original.

APPENDIX A

The Sermons as Ordered in this Edition

(Included is the location of the text as it is to be found in Jackson's edition of Wesley's *Works* (1829-31), Vols. V-VII, which has been popularly reproduced during this generation from the 1872 edition.)

[This edition, Vol. 1]

Sermons on Several Occasions (1771), I-IV

Jackson
(1872)

Preface (1746)..V. 1-6

1. Salvation by Faith..V. 7-16
   Eph. 2:8
2. The Almost Christian..V. 17-25
   Acts 26:28
3. 'Awake, Thou That Sleepest'....................................V. 25-36
   Eph. 5:14
4. Scriptural Christianity...V. 37-52
   Acts 4:31
5. Justification by Faith...V. 53-64
   Rom. 4:5
6. The Righteousness of Faith.......................................V. 65-76
   Rom. 10:5-8
7. The Way to the Kingdom...V. 76-86
   Mark 1:15
8. The First-fruits of the Spirit....................................V. 87-97
   Rom. 8:1
9. The Spirit of Bondage and of Adoption....................V. 98-111
   Rom. 8:15
10. The Witness of the Spirit, Discourse I....................V. 111-23
    Rom. 8:16
11. The Witness of the Spirit, Discourse II..................V. 123-34
    Rom. 8:16
12. The Witness of Our Own Spirit..............................V. 134-44
    2 Cor. 1:12
13. On Sin in Believers..V. 144-56
    2 Cor. 5:17
14. The Repentance of Believers...................................V. 156-70
    Mark 1:15

15. The Great Assize.. V. 171-85
    Rom. 14:10
16. The Means of Grace.. V. 185-201
    Mal. 3:7
17. The Circumcision of the Heart...........................V. 202-12
    Rom. 2:29
18. The Marks of the New Birth............................. V. 212-23
    John 3:8
19. The Great Privilege of those that are Born of God......... V. 223-33
    1 John 3:9
20. The Lord Our Righteousness...............................V. 234-46
    Jer. 23:6
21. Upon our Lord's Sermon on the Mount, I.......................V. 247-61
    Matt. 5:1-4
22. Upon our Lord's Sermon on the Mount, II.....................V. 262-77
    Matt. 5:5-7
23. Upon our Lord's Sermon on the Mount, III................... V. 278-94
    Matt. 5:8-12
24. Upon our Lord's Sermon on the Mount, IV.....................V. 294-310
    Matt. 5:13-16
25. Upon our Lord's Sermon on the Mount, V.......................V. 310-27
    Matt. 5:17-20
26. Upon our Lord's Sermon on the Mount, VI.....................V. 327-43
    Matt. 6:1-15
27. Upon our Lord's Sermon on the Mount, VII................... V. 344-60
    Matt. 6:16-18
28. Upon our Lord's Sermon on the Mount, VIII................ V. 361-77
    Matt. 6:19-23
29. Upon our Lord's Sermon on the Mount, IX.................... V. 378-93
    Matt. 6:24-34
30. Upon our Lord's Sermon on the Mount, X.....................V. 393-404
    Matt. 7:1-12
31. Upon our Lord's Sermon on the Mount, XI................... V. 405-13
    Matt. 7:13-14
32. Upon our Lord's Sermon on the Mount, XII...................V. 413-22
    Matt. 7:15-20
33. Upon our Lord's Sermon on the Mount, XIII................ V. 423-33
    Matt. 7:21-27

[This edition, Vol. 2]

34. The Original, Nature, Properties, and Use of the Law....V. 433-46
    Rom. 7:12
35. The Law Established through Faith, Discourse I............. V. 447-57
    Rom. 3:31
36. The Law Established through Faith, Discourse II............V. 458-66
    Rom. 3:31
37. The Nature of Enthusiasm... V. 467-78
    Acts 26:24

38. A Caution against Bigotry...V. 479-92
    Mark 9:38-39
39. Catholic Spirit...V. 492-504
    2 Kgs. 10:15
40. Christian Perfection...VI. 1-22
    Phil. 3:12
41. Wandering Thoughts...VI. 23-32
    2 Cor. 10:5
42. Satan's Devices...VI. 32-43
    2 Cor. 2:11
43. The Scripture Way of Salvation.....................................VI. 43-54
    Eph. 2:8
44. Original Sin.. VI. 54-65
    Gen. 6:5
45. The New Birth..VI. 65-77
    John 3:7
46. The Wilderness State...VI. 77-91
    John 16:22
47. Heaviness through Manifold Temptations....................... VI. 91-103
    1 Pet. 1:6
48. Self-denial..VI. 103-14
    Luke 9:23
49. The Cure of Evil-speaking... VI. 114-24
    Matt. 18:15-17
50. The Use of Money... VI. 124-36
    Luke 16:9
51. The Good Steward... VI. 136-49
    Luke 16:2
52. The Reformation of Manners...VI. 149-67
    Ps. 94:16
53. On the Death of George Whitefield................................ VI. 167-82
    Num. 23:10

Sermons on Several Occasions (1788), V-VIII

Preface (1788)...VI. 185-87

54. On Eternity... VI. 189-98
    Ps. 90:2
55. On the Trinity... VI. 199-206
    1 John 5:7
56. God's Approbation of His Works...................................VI. 206-15
    Gen. 1:31
57. On the Fall of Man.. VI. 215-24
    Gen. 3:19
58. On Predestination..VI. 225-30
    Rom. 8:29-30
59. God's Love to Fallen Man.. VI. 231-40
    Rom. 5:15

60. The General Deliverance..VI. 241-52
    Rom. 8:19-22
61. The Mystery of Iniquity..VI. 253-67
    2 Thess. 2:7
62. The End of Christ's Coming...VI. 267-77
    1 John 3:8
63. The General Spread of the Gospel................................. VI. 277-88
    Isa. 11:9
64. The New Creation.. VI. 288-96
    Rev. 21:5
65. The Duty of Reproving our Neighbour.............................VI. 296-304
    Lev. 19:17
66. The Signs of the Times.. VI. 304-13
    Matt. 16:3
67. On Divine Providence..VI. 313-25
    Luke 12:7
68. The Wisdom of God's Counsels.......................................VI. 325-37
    Rom. 11:33
69. The Imperfection of Human Knowledge...........................VI. 337-50
    1 Cor. 13:9
70. The Case of Reason Impartially Considered.....................VI. 350-60
    1 Cor. 14:20

[This edition, Vol. 3]

71. Of Good Angels... VI. 361-70
    Heb. 1:14
72. Of Evil Angels.. VI. 370-80
    Eph. 6:12
73. Of Hell..VI. 381-91
    Mark 9:48
74. Of the Church... VI. 392-401
    Eph. 4:1-6
75. On Schism.. VI. 401-10
    1 Cor. 12:25
76. On Perfection.. VI. 411-24
    Heb. 6:1
77. Spiritual Worship...VI. 424-35
    1 John 5:20
78. Spiritual Idolatry..VI. 435-44
    1 John 5:21
79. On Dissipation..VI. 444-52
    1 Cor. 7:35
80. On Friendship with the World...VI. 452-63
    Jas. 4:4
81. In What Sense we are to Leave the World........................VI. 464-75
    2 Cor. 6:17-18
82. On Temptation...VI. 475-84
    1 Cor. 10:13

83. On Patience.. VI. 484-92
    Jas. 1:4
84. The Important Question................................ VI. 493-505
    Matt. 16:26
85. On Working Out Our Own Salvation............... VI. 506-13
    Phil. 2:12-13
86. A Call to Backsliders................................ VI. 514-27
    Ps. 77:7-8
87. The Danger of Riches............................... VII. 1-15
    1 Tim. 6:9
88. On Dress.. VII. 15-26
    1 Pet. 3:3-4
89. The More Excellent Way............................ VII. 26-37
    1 Cor. 12:31
90. An Israelite Indeed................................. VII. 37-45
    John 1:47
91. On Charity... VII. 45-57
    1 Cor. 13:1-3
92. On Zeal.. VII. 57-67
    Gal. 4:18
93. On Redeeming the Time............................. VII. 67-75
    Eph. 5:16
94. On Family Religion.................................. VII. 76-86
    Josh. 24:15
95. On the Education of Children....................... VII. 86-98
    Prov. 22:6
96. On Obedience to Parents............................ VII. 98-108
    Col. 3:20
97. On Obedience to Pastors............................ VII. 108-16
    Heb. 13:17
98. On Visiting the Sick................................ VII. 117-27
    Matt. 25:36
99. The Reward of Righteousness........................ VII. 127-38
    Matt. 25:34
100. On Pleasing All Men................................ VII. 139-46
     Rom. 15:2
101. The Duty of Constant Communion................... VII. 147-57
     Luke 22:19
102. Of Former Times.................................... VII. 157-66
     Eccles. 7:10
103. What is Man?....................................... VII. 167-74
     Ps. 8:3-4
104. On Attending the Church Service................... VII. 174-85
     1 Sam. 2:17
105. On Conscience...................................... VII. 186-94
     2 Cor. 1:12
106. On Faith... VII. 195-202
     Heb. 11:6
107. On God's Vineyard.................................. VII. 202-13
     Isa. 5:4

108. On Riches...VII. 214-22
        Matt. 19:24

A Miscellany of Published Sermons
(Sermons not included in any of Wesley's collections
of *Sermons on Several Occasions*)

109. The Trouble and Rest of Good Men...............................VII. 365-72
        Job 3:17
110. Free Grace..VII. 373-86
        Rom. 8:32
111. National Sins and Miseries...VII. 400-408
        2 Sam. 24:17
112. On Laying the Foundation of the New Chapel................VII. 419-30
        Num. 23:23
113. The Late Work of God in North America.......................VII. 409-19
        Ezek. 1:16
114. On the Death of John Fletcher.......................................VII. 431-49
        Ps. 37:37

[This edition, Vol. 4]

Sermons published in The Arminian Magazine
Vols. XII-XV, 1789-92

115. Dives and Lazarus...VII. 244-55
        Luke 16:31
116. What is Man?...VII. 225-30
        Ps. 8:4
117. On the Discoveries of Faith...VII. 231-38
        Heb. 11:1
118. On the Omnipresence of God...VII. 238-44
        Jer. 23:24
119. Walking by Sight and Walking by Faith...........................VII. 256-64
        2 Cor. 5:7
120. The Unity of the Divine Being..VII. 264-73
        Mark 12:32
121. Prophets and Priests...VII. 273-81
        Heb. 5:4
122. Causes of the Inefficacy of Christianity...........................VII. 281-90
        Jer. 8:22
123. On Knowing Christ after the Flesh..................................VII. 291-96
        2 Cor. 5:16
124. Human Life a Dream..VII. 318-25
        Ps. 73:20
125. On a Single Eye...VII. 297-305
        Matt. 6:22-23
126. On Worldly Folly...VII. 305-11
        Luke 12:20

127. On the Wedding Garment...VII. 311-17
    Matt. 22:12
128. The Deceitfulness of the Human Heart...........................VII. 335-43
    Jer. 17:9
129. Heavenly Treasure in Earthen Vessels............................VII. 344-48
    2 Cor. 4:7
130. On Living without God.. VII. 349-54
    Eph. 2:12
131. The Danger of Increasing Riches................................... VII. 355-62
    Ps. 62:10
132. On Faith... VII. 326-35
    Heb. 11:1

Manuscript Sermons

133. Death and Deliverance..[not present]
    Job 3:17
134. Seek First the Kingdom...[not present]
    Matt. 6:33
135. On Guardian Angels.. [not present]
    Ps. 91:11
136. On Mourning for the Dead...VII. 463-68
    2 Sam. 12:23
137. On Corrupting the Word of God......................................VII. 468-73
    2 Cor. 2:17
138A. On Dissimulation.. [not present]
    John 1:47
138B-C. Two Fragments on Dissimulation............................. [not present]
139. On the Sabbath.. [not present]
    Exod. 20:8
140. The Promise of Understanding....................................... [not present]
    John 13:7
141. The Image of God.. [not present]
    Gen. 1:27
142. The Wisdom of Winning Souls.......................................[not present]
    Prov. 11:30
143. Public Diversions Denounced...VII. 500-508
    Amos 3:6
144. The Love of God..[not present]
    Mark 12:30
145. In Earth as in Heaven, a fragment..................................[not present]
    Matt. 6:10
146. The One Thing Needful... [not present]
    Luke 10:42
147. Wiser than the Children of Light................................... [not present]
    Luke 16:8
148. A Single Intention... [not present]
    Matt. 6:22-23
149. On Love..VII. 492-99
    1 Cor. 13:3

150. Hypocrisy in Oxford, English text.................................... VII. 452-62
        Isa. 1:21
151. Hypocrisy in Oxford, Latin text.. [not present]
        Isa. 1:21

*Sermons not by John Wesley, but included
in Jackson's edition (see Appendices B and C, Vol. 4)*

The Cause and Cure of Earthquakes (Charles Wesley)............ VII. 386-99
On the Resurrection of the Dead (Benjamin Calamy)............... VII. 474-85
On Grieving the Holy Spirit (William Tilly).............................. VII. 485-92
On the Holy Spirit (John Gambold)... VII. 508-20

Appendix A
(Wesley's text: editions, transmission, presentation, and variant readings)

Appendix B
(Sermons ascribed to Wesley on inconclusive grounds)

Appendix C
(Manuscript sermons abridged from other authors)

Appendix D
(Samples of Wesley's sermon registers)

Bibliography

Indexes

APPENDIX B

The Sermons
in Chronological Sequence

(Number in this edition)   (Date of composition, if known; otherwise, date preached or published)

133. Death and Deliverance...................................... Oct. 1, 1725
    Job 3:17
134. Seek First the Kingdom................................... Nov. 21, 1725
    Matt. 6:33
135. On Guardian Angels... Sept. 29, 1726
    Ps. 91:11
136. On Mourning for the Dead............................... Jan. 11, 1727
    2 Sam. 12:23
137. On Corrupting the Word of God...................... Oct. 6, 1727
    2 Cor. 2:17
138A. On Dissimulation.. Jan. 17, 1728
    John 1:47
138B-C Two Fragments on Dissimulation...................... ?
139. On the Sabbath... July 4, 1730
    Exod. 20:8
140. The Promise of Understanding......................... Oct. 13, 1730
    John 13:7
141. The Image of God... Nov. 1, 1730
    Gen. 1:27
142. The Wisdom of Winning Souls......................... July 12, 1731
    Prov. 11:30
143. Public Diversions Denounced............................ Sept. 3, 1732
    Amos 3:6
17. The Circumcision of the Heart......................... Jan. 1, 1733
    Rom. 2:29
144. The Love of God... Sept. 15, 1733
    Mark 12:30
145. In Earth as in Heaven....................................... Apr. 20, 1734
    Matt. 6:10
146. The One Thing Needful.................................... May 1734
    Luke 10:42
147. Wiser than the Children of Light..................... 1735 (?)
    Luke 16:8
109. The Trouble and Rest of Good Men............... Sept. 21, 1735
    Job 3:17

148. A Single Intention.. Feb. 3, 1736
    Matt. 6:22-23
149. On Love... Feb. 20, 1737
    1 Cor. 13:3
  1. Salvation by Faith... June 11, 1738
    Eph. 2:8
110. Free Grace... Apr. 29, 1739
    Rom. 8:32
150. Hypocrisy in Oxford, English text..................... June 24, 1741
    Isa. 1:21
151. Hypocrisy in Oxford, Latin text......................... June 27, 1741
    Isa. 1:21
  2. The Almost Christian.. July 25, 1741
    Acts 26:28
 40. Christian Perfection... 1741
    Phil. 3:12
  3. 'Awake, Thou That Sleepest'............................ Apr. 4, 1742
    Eph. 5:14
  4. Scriptural Christianity....................................... Aug. 24, 1744
    Acts 4:31
  5. Justification by Faith... 1746
    Rom. 4:5
  6. The Righteousness of Faith............................... 1746
    Rom. 10:5-8
  7. The Way to the Kingdom.................................. 1746
    Mark 1:15
  8. The First-fruits of the Spirit............................. 1746
    Rom. 8:1
  9. The Spirit of Bondage and of Adoption........... 1746
    Rom. 8:15
 10. The Witness of the Spirit, Discourse I.............. 1746
    Rom. 8:16
 12. The Witness of Our Own Spirit....................... 1746
    2 Cor. 1:12
 16. The Means of Grace.. 1746
    Mal. 3:7
 18. The Marks of the New Birth............................ 1748
    John 3:8
 19. The Great Privilege of those that are Born
    of God... 1748
    1 John 3:9
 21. Upon our Lord's Sermon on the Mount, I...... 1748
    Matt. 5:1-4
 22. Upon our Lord's Sermon on the Mount, II..... 1748
    Matt. 5:5-7
 23. Upon our Lord's Sermon on the Mount, III... 1748
    Matt. 5:8-12
 24. Upon our Lord's Sermon on the Mount, IV.... 1748
    Matt. 5:13-16

25. Upon our Lord's Sermon on the Mount, V..... 1748
   Matt. 5:17-20
26. Upon our Lord's Sermon on the Mount, VI.... 1748
   Matt. 6:1-15
27. Upon our Lord's Sermon on the Mount, VII.. 1748
   Matt. 6:16-18
28. Upon our Lord's Sermon on the Mount, VIII. 1748
   Matt. 6:19-23
29. Upon our Lord's Sermon on the Mount, IX... 1748
   Matt. 6:24-34
30. Upon our Lord's Sermon on the Mount, X..... 1750
   Matt. 7:1-12
31. Upon our Lord's Sermon on the Mount, XI... 1750
   Matt. 7:13-14
32. Upon our Lord's Sermon on the Mount, XII.. 1750
   Matt. 7:15-20
33. Upon our Lord's Sermon on the Mount, XIII... 1750
   Matt. 7:21-27
34. The Original, Nature, Properties, and Use of
   the Law.. 1750
   Rom. 7:12
35. The Law Established through Faith, I.............. 1750
   Rom. 3:31
36. The Law Established through Faith, II............ 1750
   Rom. 3:31
37. The Nature of Enthusiasm................................ 1750
   Acts 26:24
38. A Caution against Bigotry................................ 1750
   Mark 9:38-39
39. Catholic Spirit.. 1750
   2 Kgs. 10:15
42. Satan's Devices... 1750
   2 Cor. 2:11
15. The Great Assize.. Mar. 10, 1758
   Rom. 14:10
44. Original Sin.. 1759
   Gen. 6:5
45. The New Birth.. 1760
   John 3:7
46. The Wilderness State.. 1760
   John 16:22
47. Heaviness through Manifold Temptations........ 1760
   1 Pet. 1:6
48. Self-denial... 1760
   Luke 9:23
49. The Cure of Evil-speaking................................ 1760
   Matt. 18:15-17
50. The Use of Money.. 1760
   Luke 16:9

41. Wandering Thoughts.............................. 1762
    2 Cor. 10:5
52. The Reformation of Manners...................... Jan. 30, 1763
    Ps. 94:16
13. On Sin in Believers............................. Mar. 28, 1763
    2 Cor. 5:17
43. The Scripture Way of Salvation................. 1765
    Eph. 2:8
20. The Lord our Righteousness..................... Nov. 24, 1765
    Jer. 23:6
11. The Witness of the Spirit, Discourse II.......... Apr. 4, 1767
    Rom. 8:16
14. The Repentance of Believers.................... Apr. 24, 1767
    Mark 1:15
51. The Good Steward............................... May 14, 1768
    Luke 16:2
53. On the Death of George Whitefield.............. Nov. 18, 1770
    Num. 23:10
58. On Predestination.............................. June 5, 1773
    Rom. 8:29-30
55. On the Trinity................................. May 7, 1775
    1 John 5:7
84. The Important Question......................... Sept. 11, 1775
    Matt. 16:26
111. National Sins and Miseries.................... Nov. 7, 1775
    2 Sam. 24:17
112. On Laying the Foundation of the New Chapel... Apr. 21, 1777
    Num. 23:23
99. The Reward of Righteousness................... Nov. 23, 1777
    Matt. 25:34
86. A Call to Backsliders......................... May 20, 1778
    Ps. 77:7-8
113. The Late Work of God in North America....... 1778
    Ezek. 1:16
77. Spiritual Worship............................. Dec. 22, 1780
    1 John 5:20
78. Spiritual Idolatry............................ Jan. 5, 1781
    1 John 5:21
62. The End of Christ's Coming.................... Jan. 20, 1781
    1 John 3:8
87. The Danger of Riches.......................... Jan.—Feb. 1781
    1 Tim. 6:9
92. On Zeal....................................... May 6, 1781
    Gal. 4:18
70. The Case of Reason Impartially Considered... July 6, 1781
    1 Cor. 14:20
60. The General Deliverance....................... Nov. 30, 1781
    Rom. 8:19-22

93. On Redeeming the Time.................................. Jan. 20, 1782
    Eph. 5:16
57. On the Fall of Man.. Mar. 13, 1782
    Gen. 3:19
59. God's Love to Fallen Man.............................. July 9, 1782
    Rom. 5:15
56. God's Approbation of His Works..................... July—Aug. 1782
    Gen. 1:31
73. Of Hell.. Oct. 10, 1782
    Mark 9:48
72. Of Evil Angels.. Jan. 7, 1783
    Eph. 6:12
71. Of Good Angels.. Jan.—Feb. 1783
    Heb. 1:14
63. The General Spread of the Gospel.................. Apr. 22, 1783
    Isa. 11:9
94. On Family Religion.. May 26, 1783
    Josh. 24:15
61. The Mystery of Iniquity.................................... May—June 1783
    2 Thess. 2:7
95. On the Education of Children.......................... July 12, 1783
    Prov. 22:6
79. On Dissipation... Jan.—Feb. 1784
    1 Cor. 7:35
69. The Imperfection of Human Knowledge.......... Mar. 5, 1784
    1 Cor. 13:9
83. On Patience.. Mar.—Apr. 1784
    Jas. 1:4
68. The Wisdom of God's Counsels...................... Apr. 28, 1784
    Rom. 11:33
81. In What Sense we are to Leave the World...... July 17, 1784
    2 Cor. 6:17-18
96. On Obedience to Parents................................. Sept.—Oct. 1784
    Col. 3:20
91. On Charity... Oct. 15, 1784
    1 Cor. 13:1-3
76. On Perfection.. Dec. 6, 1784
    Heb. 6:1
97. On Obedience to Pastors................................. Mar. 18, 1785
    Heb. 13:17
90. An Israelite Indeed.. July—Aug. 1785
    John 1:47
74. Of the Church... Sept. 28, 1785
    Eph. 4:1-6
85. On Working Out Our Own Salvation.............. Sept.—Oct. 1785
    Phil. 2:12-13
114. On the Death of John Fletcher....................... Oct. 24, 1785
    Ps. 37:37

64. The New Creation.. Nov.—Dec. 1785
      Rev. 21:5
67. On Divine Providence...................................... Mar. 3, 1786
      Luke 12:7
75. On Schism.. Mar. 30, 1786
      1 Cor. 12:25
80. On Friendship with the World......................... May 1, 1786
      Jas. 4:4
98. On Visiting the Sick.................................... May 23, 1786
      Matt. 25:36
54. On Eternity.. June 28, 1786
      Ps. 90:2
82. On Temptation... Oct. 7, 1786
      1 Cor. 10:13
88. On Dress.. Dec. 30, 1786
      1 Pet. 3:3-4
100. On Pleasing All Men..................................... May 22, 1787
      Rom. 15:2
101. The Duty of Constant Communion.................. (1787)
      Luke 22:19
102. Of Former Times... June 27, 1787
      Eccles. 7:10
103. What is Man?.. July 23, 1787
      Ps. 8:3-4
65. The Duty of Reproving our Neighbour............ July 28, 1787
      Lev. 19:17
89. The More Excellent Way................................ July—Aug. 1787
      1 Cor. 12:31
66. The Signs of the Times................................. Aug. 27, 1787
      Matt. 16:3
104. On Attending the Church Service..................... Oct. 7, 1787
      1 Sam. 2:17
107. On God's Vineyard....................................... Oct. 17, 1787
      Isa. 5:4
115. Dives and Lazarus....................................... Mar. 25, 1788
      Luke 16:31
105. On Conscience... Apr. 8, 1788
      2 Cor. 1:12
106. On Faith.. Apr. 9, 1788
      Heb. 11:6
108. On Riches.. Apr. 22, 1788
      Matt. 19:24
116. What is Man?.. May 2, 1788
      Ps. 8:4
117. On the Discoveries of Faith........................... June 11, 1788
      Heb. 11:1
118. On the Omnipresence of God.......................... Aug. 12, 1788
      Jer. 23:24

119. Walking by Sight and Walking by Faith........... Dec. 30, 1788
     2 Cor. 5:7
120. The Unity of the Divine Being......................... Apr. 9, 1789
     Mark 12:32-33
121. Prophets and Priests.. May 4, 1789
     Heb. 5:4
122. Causes of the Inefficacy of Christianity........... July 2, 1789
     Jer. 8:22
123. On Knowing Christ after the Flesh.................. Aug. 15, 1789
     2 Cor. 5:16
124. Human Life a Dream....................................... Aug. 1789
     Ps. 73:20
125. On a Single Eye.. Sept. 25, 1789
     Matt. 6:22-23
126. On Worldly Folly... Feb. 19, 1790
     Luke 12:20
127. On the Wedding Garment............................... Mar. 26, 1790
     Matt. 22:12
128. The Deceitfulness of the Human Heart........... Apr. 21, 1790
     Jer. 17:9
129. Heavenly Treasure in Earthen Vessels.............. June 17, 1790
     2 Cor. 4:7
130. On Living without God..................................... July 6, 1790
     Eph. 2:12
131. The Danger of Increasing Riches.................... Sept. 21, 1790
     Ps. 62:10
132. On Faith.. Jan. 17, 1791
     Heb. 11:1

APPENDIX C

The Sermons
in Alphabetical Order

(N.B. Where a title is italicized, the sermon was published as a separate item before being issued in a collection. Some of the titles thus italicized here, however, abridge the titles under which Wesley originally published them; others (Nos. 3, 55, 58, 99, 109, 111) are quite different. For detailed descriptions of all Wesley's contemporary editions of each sermon see the Bibliography in this edition, here noted as 'B.50', etc. Titles supplied by the editor, whether to sermons separately published or to those first appearing in collected editions, or from manuscript sources, are given in this listing only within parentheses. These parentheses, however, are dropped from other listings, as from running titles and footnotes. Frequently the titles come from a lengthy tradition, which is noted, along with all the original titles used, in the introductory comment to the appropriate sermon. In alphabetizing the words 'a', 'an', 'of', 'on', 'the' are ignored. F.B.)

The Distribution of the Sermons in this Edition

Vol. 1, Nos. 1–33
Vol. 2, Nos. 34–70
Vol. 3, Nos. 71–114
Vol. 4, Nos. 115–51

Number	Title	Date
2.	*The Almost Christian* (B. 50)............................ Acts 26:28	1741, July 25
[App.	The Apostolic Ministry (Ben. Calamy)........... Mark 6:12	1732, Apr. 1-2]
104.	On Attending the Church Service.................. 1 Sam. 2:17	1787, Oct. 7
3.	('*Awake, Thou That Sleepest*') (CW) (B.59,...... *A Sermon preached on Sunday, April 4, 1742, before the University of Oxford*) Eph. 5:14	1742, Apr. 4
86.	*A Call to Backsliders* (B. 388)........................... Ps. 77:7-8	1778, May 20
70.	The Case of Reason Impartially Considered. 1 Cor. 14:20	1781, July 6
39.	Catholic Spirit.. 2 Kgs. 10:15	(1750)
122.	(Causes of the Inefficacy of Christianity)....... Jer. 8:22	1789, July 2

646

Number	*Title*	*Date*

38. A Caution against Bigotry.............................. (1750)
Mark 9:38-39

91. On Charity... 1784, Oct. 15
1 Cor. 13:1-3

[App. *(Christ Crucified) (B.624, A Sermon, preached...* 1774, Apr. 28]
at the Opening of the New Meeting-House, at
Wakefield. . .)
1 Cor. 1:23

40. *Christian Perfection (B. 53)*.............................. 1741
Phil. 3:12

74. Of the Church....................................... 1785, Sept. 28
Eph. 4:1-6

17. The Circumcision of the Heart..................... 1733, Jan. 1
Rom. 2:29

105. On Conscience..................................... 1788, Apr. 8
2 Cor. 1:12

137. (On Corrupting the Word of God)................. 1727, Oct. 6
2 Cor. 2:17

49. The Cure of Evil-speaking............................ 1760
Matt. 18:15-17

131. (The Danger of Increasing Riches)................ 1790, Sept. 21
Ps. 62:10

87. The Danger of Riches................................... 1781, Jan.—Feb.
1 Tim. 6:9

133. (Death and Deliverance)................................. 1725, Oct. 1
Job 3:17

53. *On the Death of George Whitefield (B. 324,......* 1770, Nov. 18
A Sermon on the Death of the Rev.
Mr. George Whitefield . . .)
Num. 23:10

114. *On the Death of John Fletcher (B. 442,............* 1785, Oct. 24
A Sermon preached on occasion of the Death of
the Rev. Mr. John Fletcher, Vicar of Madeley,
Shropshire)
Ps. 37:37

[App. The Death of the Righteous (Ben. Calamy).. 1732, Mar.
Num. 23:10   11-12]

128. (The Deceitfulness of the Human Heart)...... 1790, Apr. 21
Jer. 17:9
[*A Discourse on Sin in Believers*—see *Sin in*
. . .]
[*Discourses* on the Sermon on the Mount—see
'Upon Our Lord's Sermon on the Mount]

117. (On the Discoveries of Faith)........................ 1788, June 11
Heb. 11:1

138A. (On Dissimulation).. 1728, Jan. 17
John 1:47

138B-C. (Dissimulation, two fragments on)................. ?

Number	Title	Date
79.	On Dissipation.................................. 1 Cor. 7:35	1784, Jan.—Feb.
115.	(Dives and Lazarus)........................ Luke 16:31	1788, Mar. 25
67.	On Divine Providence.................... Luke 12:7	1786, Mar. 3
88.	On Dress.. 1 Pet. 3:3-4	1786, Dec. 30
101.	The Duty of Constant Communion............... Luke 22:19	(1787)
65.	The Duty of Reproving our Neighbour......... Lev. 19:17	1787, July 28
145.	(In Earth as in Heaven) (a fragment)............ Matt. 6:10	1734, Apr. 20
95.	On the Education of Children.................... Prov. 22:6	1783, July 12
62.	The End of Christ's Coming................... 1 John 3:8	1781, Jan. 20
54.	On Eternity.................................... Ps. 90:2	1786, June 28
	[The Eternity of Hell Torments—see Of Hell]	
72.	Of Evil Angels............................... Eph. 6:12	1783, Jan. 7
106.	(On Faith, Heb. 11:6)....................... Heb. 11:6	1788, Apr. 9
132.	(On Faith, Heb. 11:1)....................... Heb. 11:1	1791, Jan. 17
57.	On the Fall of Man........................... Gen. 3:19	1782, Mar. 13
94.	On Family Religion........................... Josh. 24:15	1783, May 26
8.	The First-fruits of the Spirit.................... Rom. 8:1	(1746)
102.	Of Former Times.............................. Eccles. 7:10	1787, June 27
110.	*Free Grace* (*B*. 14)............................. Rom. 8:32	1739, Apr. 29
80.	On Friendship with the World.................. Jas. 4:4	1786, May 1
60.	The General Deliverance...................... Rom. 8:19-22	1781, Nov. 30
63.	The General Spread of the Gospel............. Isa. 11:9	1783, Apr. 22
56.	God's Approbation of His Works............... Gen. 1:31	1782, July—Aug.
59.	God's Love to Fallen Man..................... Rom. 5:15	1782, July 9

Number	Title	Date
107.	On God's Vineyard	1787, Oct. 17
	Isa. 5:4	
71.	Of Good Angels	1783, Jan.—Feb.
	Heb. 1:14	
51.	*The Good Steward* (B. 311)	1768, May 14
	Luke 16:2	
15.	*The Great Assize* (B. 224)	1758, Mar. 10
	Rom. 14:10	
19.	The Great Privilege of those that are	(1748)
	Born of God	
	1 John 3:9	
[App.	On Grieving the Holy Spirit (Wm. Tilly)	1732, Oct. 28]
	Eph. 4:30	
135.	On Guardian Angels	1726, Sept. 29
	Ps. 91:11	
129.	(Heavenly Treasure in Earthen Vessels)	1790, June 17
	2 Cor. 4:7	
47.	Heaviness through Manifold Temptations	(1760)
	1 Pet. 1:6	
73.	Of Hell	1782, Oct. 10
	Mark 9:48	
[App.	On the Holy Spirit (John Gambold)	1736, June 13]
	2 Cor. 3:17	
124.	(Human Life a Dream)	1789, Aug.
	Ps. 73:20	
150.	(Hypocrisy in Oxford) [Eng.]	1741, June 24
	Isa. 1:21	
151.	(Hypocrisy in Oxford) [Lat.]	1741, June 27
	Isa. 1:21	
[App.	If Any Man Thinketh (Wm. Tilly)	1732, Nov. 17-18]
	1 Cor. 8:2	
141.	(The Image of God)	1730, Nov. 1
	Gen. 1:27	
69.	The Imperfection of Human Knowledge	1784, Mar. 5
	1 Cor. 13:9	
84.	*The Important Question* (B. 355)	1775, Sept. 11
	Matt. 16:26	
81.	In What Sense we are to Leave the World	1784, July 17
	2 Cor. 6:17-18	
90.	An Israelite Indeed	1785, July—Aug.
	John 1:47	
5.	Justification by Faith	(1746)
	Rom. 4:5	
123.	(On Knowing Christ after the Flesh)	1789, Aug. 15
	2 Cor. 5:16	
113.	*The Late Work of God in North America* (B. 398,...	1778
	Some Account of the Late Work of God . . .)	
	Ezek. 1:16	

Number	Title	Date
35.	The Law Established through Faith, I .... Rom. 3:31	(1750)
36.	The Law Established through Faith, II .... Rom. 3:31	(1750)
112.	*On Laying the Foundation of the New Chapel...* (*B. 366, A Sermon on Numbers XXIII.23 . . .*) Num. 23:23	1777, Apr. 21
130.	(On Living without God) .... Eph. 2:12	1790, July 6
20.	*The Lord Our Righteousness* (*B. 295*) .... Jer. 23:6	1765, Nov. 24
149.	(On Love) .... 1 Cor. 13:3	1737, Feb. 20
144.	The Love of God .... Mark 12:30	1733, Sept. 15
18.	The Marks of the New Birth .... John 3:8	(1748)
16.	The Means of Grace .... Mal. 3:7	(1746)
	[The Ministerial Office—see Prophets and Priests]	
89.	The More Excellent Way .... 1 Cor. 12:31	1787, July—Aug.
136.	(On Mourning for the Dead) .... 2 Sam. 12:23	1727, Jan. 11
61.	The Mystery of Iniquity .... 2 Thess. 2:7	1783, May—June
111.	(*National Sins and Miseries*) .... (*B. 356, A Sermon preached at St. Matthew's, Bethnal Green*) 2 Sam. 24:17	1775, Nov. 7
37.	The Nature of Enthusiasm .... Acts 26:24	(1750)
45.	The New Birth .... John 3:7	(1760)
64.	The New Creation .... Rev. 21:5	1785, Nov.—Dec.
96.	On Obedience to Parents .... Col. 3:20	1784, Sept.—Oct.
97.	On Obedience to Pastors .... Heb. 13:17	1785, Mar. 18
118.	(On the Omnipresence of God) .... Jer. 23:24	1788, Aug. 12
146.	The One Thing Needful .... Luke 10:42	1734, May
34.	The Original, Nature, Properties, and .... Use of the Law Rom. 7:12	(1750)

Number	Title	Date
44.	*Original Sin (B. 235, A Sermon on* *Original Sin)* Gen. 6:5	1759
83.	On Patience Jas. 1:4	1784, Mar.—Apr.
76.	On Perfection Heb. 6:1	1784, Dec. 6
100.	On Pleasing All Men Rom. 15:2	1787, May 22
58.	*(On Predestination) (B. 362, A Sermon on Romans viii. 29, 30)* Rom. 8:29-30	1773, June 5
140.	(The Promise of Understanding) John 13:7	1730, Oct. 13
121.	(Prophets and Priests) Heb. 5:4	1789, May 4
143.	(Public Diversions Denounced) Amos 3:6	1732, Sept. 3
93.	On Redeeming the Time Eph. 5:16	1782, Jan. 20
52.	*The Reformation of Manners (B. 254, A Sermon preached before the Society for the Reformation of Manners)* Ps. 94:16	1763, Jan. 30
14.	*The Repentance of Believers (B. 305)* Mark 1:15	1767, Apr. 24
[App.	A Rest for the People of God Heb. 4:9 [Rest for the Weary—see Death and Deliverance]	1758, June 15]
[App.	On the Resurrection of the Dead (Ben. Calamy) 1 Cor. 15:25	1732, June 7]
99.	*(The Reward of Righteousness) (B. 370, A Sermon preached November 23, 1777, in Lewisham Church, before the Humane Society)* Matt. 25:34	1777, Nov. 23
108.	On Riches Matt. 19:24	1788, Apr. 22
6.	The Righteousness of Faith Rom. 10:5-8	(1746)
139.	On the Sabbath Exod. 20:8	1730, July 4
1.	*Salvation by Faith (B. 10, A Sermon on Salvation by Faith)* Eph. 2:8	1738, June 11
42.	Satan's Devices 2 Cor. 2:11	(1750)

Number	Title	Date
75.	On Schism..	1786, Mar. 30
	1 Cor. 12:25	
4.	*Scriptural Christianity (B. 92)*............................	1744, Aug. 24
	Acts 4:31	
43.	*The Scripture Way of Salvation (B. 265)*............	1765
	Eph. 2:8	
134.	(Seek First the Kingdom).................................	1725, Nov. 21
	Matt. 6:33	
48.	Self-denial...	(1760)
	Luke 9:23	

[*A Sermon on 1st John 5:7*—see *On the Trinity*]
[*A Sermon on Numbers XXIII. 23*—see *On Laying the Foundation of the New Chapel*]
[*A Sermon on Original Sin*—see *Original Sin*]
[*A Sermon on Romans viii. 29, 30*—see *On Predestination*]
[*A Sermon on Salvation by Faith*—see *Salvation by Faith*]
[*A Sermon on the Death of the Rev. Mr. George Whitefield*—see *On the Death of George Whitefield*]
[Sermon on the Mount—see 'Upon our Lord's Sermon on the Mount']
[*A Sermon preached at St. Mary's, Oxford, on Sunday, September 21, 1735*—see *The Trouble and Rest of Good Men*]
[*A Sermon preached at St. Matthew's, Bethnal Green*—see *National Sins and Miseries*]
[*A Sermon preached at the opening of the New Meeting-House, Wakefield*—see *Christ Crucified*]
[*A Sermon preached before the Society for the Reformation of Manners*—see *The Reformation of Manners*]
[*A Sermon preached November 23, 1777, in Lewisham Church, before the Humane Society*—see *The Reward of Righteousness*]
[*A Sermon preached on occasion of the Death of the Rev. Mr. John Fletcher* . . . see *On the Death of John Fletcher*]
[*A Sermon preached on Sunday, April 4, 1742, before the University of Oxford*—see 'Awake, Thou That Sleepest']

66.	The Signs of the Times.................................	1787, Aug. 27
	Matt. 16:3	
13.	*On Sin in Believers (B. 257,*...........................	1763, Mar. 28
	A Discourse on Sin in Believers)	
	2 Cor. 5:17	
125.	(On a Single Eye)..	1789, Sept. 25
	Matt. 6:22-23	
148.	(A Single Intention).....................................	1736, Feb. 3
	Matt. 6:22-23	
113.	[*Some Account of the Late Work of God in North America*—see *The Late Work of God* . . .]	
9.	The Spirit of Bondage and of Adoption.......	(1746)
	Rom. 8:15	

Number	Title	Date
78.	Spiritual Idolatry.. 1 John 5:21	1781, Jan. 5
77.	Spiritual Worship.. 1 John 5:20	1780, Dec. 22
82.	On Temptation.. 1 Cor. 10:13	1786, Oct. 7
55.	*(On the Trinity)* (B. 353, *A Sermon* on 1st John 5:7) 1 John 5:7	1775, May 7
109.	*(The Trouble and Rest of Good Men)* (B. 6, *A Sermon preached at St. Mary's, Oxford . . .)* Job 3:17	1735, Sept. 21
120.	(The Unity of the Divine Being) Mark 12:32	1789, Apr. 9
21.	Upon our Lord's Sermon on the Mount, I... Matt. 5:1-4	(1748)
22.	Upon our Lord's Sermon on the Mount, II.. Matt. 5:5-7	(1748)
23.	Upon our Lord's Sermon on the Mount, III Matt. 5:8-12	(1748)
24.	Upon our Lord's Sermon on the Mount, IV Matt. 5:13-16	(1748)
25.	Upon our Lord's Sermon on the Mount, V.. Matt. 5:17-20	(1748)
26.	Upon our Lord's Sermon on the Mount, VI Matt. 6:1-15	(1748)
27.	Upon our Lord's Sermon on the Mount, VII Matt. 6:16-18	(1748)
28.	Upon our Lord's Sermon on the Mount, VIII Matt. 6:19-23	(1748)
29.	Upon our Lord's Sermon on the Mount, IX Matt. 6:24-34	(1748)
30.	Upon our Lord's Sermon on the Mount, X.. Matt. 7:1-12	(1750)
31.	Upon our Lord's Sermon on the Mount, XI... Matt. 7:13-14	(1750)
32.	Upon our Lord's Sermon on the Mount, XII Matt. 7:15-20	(1750)

Number	Title	Date
33.	Upon our Lord's Sermon on the Mount,...... XIII Matt. 7:21-27	(1750)
50.	The Use of Money... Luke 16:9	(1760)
98.	On Visiting the Sick..................................... Matt. 25:36	1786, May 23
119.	(Walking by Sight and Walking by Faith)...... 2 Cor. 5:7	1788, Dec. 30
41.	*Wandering Thoughts* (B. 251)............................ 2 Cor. 10:5	(1762)
7.	The Way to the Kingdom............................... Mark 1:15	(1746)
127.	(On the Wedding Garment)............................ Matt. 22:12	1790, Mar. 26
103.	What is Man? Ps. 8:3-4................................ Ps. 8:3-4	1787, July 23
116.	What is Man? Ps. 8:4.................................... Ps. 8:4	1788, May 2
[App.	Who Went About Doing Good....................... (Ben. Calamy) Acts 10:38	1732, June 2-5]
46.	The Wilderness State..................................... John 16:22	(1760)
68.	The Wisdom of God's Counsels.................... Rom. 11:33	1784, Apr. 28
142.	(The Wisdom of Winning Souls).................... Prov. 11:30	1731, July 12
147.	Wiser than the Children of Light................... Luke 16:8	(1735?)
12.	The Witness of Our Own Spirit..................... 2 Cor. 1:12	(1746)
10.	The Witness of the Spirit, I........................... Rom. 8:16	(1746)
11.	*The Witness of the Spirit*, II (B. 303)............... Rom. 8:16	1767, Apr. 4
[App.	Work Out Your Own Salvation, I................... Phil. 2:12-13	1732, Aug. 12-14]
[App.	Work Out Your Own Salvation, II................. Phil. 2:12-13	1732, Sept. 29-Oct. 1]
85.	On Working Out Our Own Salvation............ Phil. 2:12-13	1785, Sept.—Oct.
126.	(On Worldly Folly).. Luke 12:20	1790, Feb. 19
92.	On Zeal.. Gal. 4:18	1781, May 6